Lecture Notes in Economics and Mathematical Systems 399

Founding Editors:

M. Beckmann
H. P. Künzi

Editorial Board:

H. Albach, M. Beckmann, P. Dhrymes, G. Feichtinger, W. Hildenbrand
W. Krelle, H. P. Künzi, K. Ritter, U. Schittko, P. Schönfeld, R. Selten

Managing Editors:

Prof. Dr. G. Fandel
Fachbereich Wirtschaftswissenschaften
Fernuniversität Hagen
Feithstr. 140/AVZ II, W-5800 Hagen 1, FRG

Prof. Dr. W. Trockel
Institut für Mathematische Wirtschaftsforschung (IMW)
Universität Bielefeld
Universitätsstr. 25, W-4800 Bielefeld 1, FRG

AF829369

F. Gori L. Geronazzo M. Galeotti (Eds.)

Nonlinear Dynamics in Economics and Social Sciences

Proceedings of the Second Informal Workshop
Held at the Certosa di Pontignano, Siena, Italy
May 27-30, 1991

Springer-Verlag
Berlin Heidelberg New York
London Paris Tokyo
Hong Kong Barcelona
Budapest

Editors

Prof. Dr. Franco Gori
Dipartimento di Matematica per le Decisioni
Economiche, Finanziarie, Attuariali e Sociali
Università di Firenze
Via Lombroso 6/17, I-50134 Firenze, Italia

Prof. Dr. Lucio Geronazzo
Dipartimento di Economia Politica
Università di Siena
Piazza San Francesco 1, I-53100 Siena, Italia

Prof. Dr. Marcello Galeotti
Istituto di Matematica e Statistica
Università di Ancona
Via Pizzecolli 37, I-60121 Ancona, Italia

ISBN 3-540-56704-6Springer-Verlag Berlin Heidelberg New York
ISBN 0-387-56704-6Springer-Verlag New York Berlin Heidelberg

This work is subject to copyright. All rights are reserved, whether the whole or part of the material is concerned, specifically the rights of translation, reprinting, re-use of illustrations, recitation, broadcasting, reproduction on microfilms or in any other way, and storage in data banks. Duplication of this publication or parts thereof is permitted only under the provisions of the German Copyright Law of September 9, 1965, in its current version, and permission for use must always be obtained from Springer-Verlag. Violations are liable for prosecution under the German Copyright Law.

© Springer-Verlag Berlin Heidelberg 1993
Printed in Germany

Typesetting: Camera ready by author
42/3140-543210 - Printed on acid-free paper

Foreword

This volume constitutes the Proceedings of the "Nonlinear Dynamics in Economics and Social Sciences" Meeting held at the Certosa di Pontignano, Siena, on May 27-30, 1991.

The Meeting was organized by the National Group "Modelli Nonlineari in Economia e Dinamiche Complesse" of the Italian Ministery of University and Scientific Research, M.U.R.S.T.

The aim of the Conference, which followed a previous analogous initiative taking place in the very same Certosa, on January 1988*, was the one of offering a come together opportunity to economists interested in a new mathematical approach to the modelling of economical processes, through the use of more advanced analytical techniques, and mathematicians acting in the field of global dynamical systems theory and applications.

A basic underlying idea drove the organizers: the necessity of focusing on the use that recent methods and results, as those commonly referred to the overpopularized label of "Chaotic Dynamics", did find in the social sciences domain; and thus to check their actual relevance in the research program of modelling economic phenomena, in order to individuate and stress promising perspectives, as well as to curb excessive hopes and criticize not infrequent cases where research reduces to mechanical, ad hoc, applications of "à la mode" techniques.

In a word we felt the need of looking about the state of the arts in non-linear systems theory applications to economics and social processes: hence the title of the workshop and the volume.

The Meeting lasted four days. Mornings were devoted entirely to four minicourses given by R. Abraham, Economics and the Environment: Global Erodynamic Models; R.H. Day, Chaotic Dynamics in Micro and Macro Economic Processes; H.-W. Lorenz, Complextity in Deterministic, Nonlinear Business-Cycle Models; C. Mira, Toward a Knowledge of the Two-Dimensional Diffeormophism. Afternoons were taken by invited lectures and contributed papers.

About one hundred participants came from Europe and the Americas and more than 30 articles were presented.

Materials in the present volume are organized following the meeting structure.

The first section contains the notes of the minicourses given by R. Abraham, H.-W. Lorenz, within the text of one of the lectures given by C. Mira.

Lessons by R.H. Day related essentially to his joint paper with G.Pianigiani "Statistical Dynamics and Economics", (J. of Economic Behaviour and Organization, volume 16, July 1991, pp.37-84), to which we refer the interested reader.

In the second part the texts of three invited lectures, by W. Böhm, R. Goodwin and A.G. Malliaris, are published. Even if these articles were prepared on the occasion of the meeting, only the first has been formally presented there.

Finally, the third section is devoted to thirteen contributed papers presented in Pontignano, which the authors submitted for publication and were positively refereed.

It is our feeling that the meeting was really successfull in attaining its intended goals and we would like to express our gratitude to the invited speakers for the quality of the lectures they delivered in Pontignano, and to all the participants for their highly interesting contributions, the lively discussions and the stimulating and friendly atmosphere they were able to create.

We would also like to express our thanks to the many referees for their important help in selecting the papers to be included in this volume.

The University of Florence and the University of Siena jointly sponsored the meeting and we gratefully acknowledge their scientific and financial support, as well as the contributions which the Organizing Committee received from the Monte dei Paschi di Siena Bank.

A final particular thank goes to Mrss. Marcella Dragoni and Bianca Maria Fabrini, whose secretary work during the Meeting and the editing process has been invaluable.

Franco Gori
Lucio Geronazzo
Marcello Galeotti

* M. Galeotti, L. Geronazzo, F. Gori, *Non Linear Dynamics in Economics and Social Sciences*, Pitagora Editrice, Bologna, 1990.

TABLE OF CONTENTS

MINICOURSES

ECONOMICS AND THE ENVIRONMENT: GLOBAL ERODYNAMIC MODELS

Ralph Abraham

Mathematics Department, University of California, Santa Cruz, CA 95064

1. Introduction

Simple dynamical systems theory evolved from celestial mechanics in the work of Poincaré a century ago. Complex dynamical systems theory (also known as systems dynamics) began during World War II, with the work of Von Bertalanffy on general systems theory and Wiener on cybernetics. Cellular dynamical systems theory developed in the early days of biological morphogenesis in the work of Rashevsky and Turing. Since the advent of massively parallel computation, these modeling strategies have been increasingly used to simulate highly complex natural systems. The challenge to understand our global problems — combining physical systems of the atmosphere and ocean (Chaos) with biological systems of the biosphere (Gaia) and the social systems of human and other species (Eros) — will test and extend our mathematical and scientific capabilities. The name *erodynamics* has been coined to describe this application of dynamical systems theory to the complex global system of our human civilization and environment. In this minicourse we develop the basic concepts of erodynamics in the frame of economics and the environment.

2. Types of dynamical systems

In mathematics, there are three categories of dynamical systems: flows, cascades, and semi-cascades. A *flow* is a continuous dynamical system, generated by a *vectorfield,* in which the trajectories are curves, parameterized by real numbers. A *cascade* is a discrete dynamical system, generated by a *diffeomorphism* (smooth invertible map with a smooth inverse), in which the trajectories are discrete point sets, parameterized by integers (positive and negative). A *semi-cascade* is a discrete dynamical system, generated by an *endomorphism* (smooth map, not neccesarily invertible) in which the trajectories are discrete point sets, parameterized by natural numbers (non-negative). In any case, the dynamics occurs on a smooth manifold called the *state space,* which may have dimension one or more. In Fig. 1, the three categories and the state space dimensions are used to spread out the family of all dynamical systems in a tableau. In this tableau, a three-dimensional flow may sometimes be sectioned, in a procedure invented by Poincaré, to a two-dimensional cascade. This, in turn, might be projected into a one-dimensional semi-cascade, in a procedure introduced by Lorenz. Each of these constructions is reversible. Thus, these three boxes, shaded in Fig. 1, are closely related, and have similar behavior. For example, each is the lowest-dimensional box in which chaotic behavior is observed. Thus, we call it *the stairway to chaos.* All of the parallel stairways are interrelated by similar constructions.

Let F, C, and S denote the rows, and 1, 2, 3, $\cdots$, denote the columns of the tableau. Thus, S1, C2, and F3 denote the stairway to chaos, and S2, C3, and F4 the adjacent stairway, and so on. The most familiar dynamical systems are distributed as follows:

Pendulum, Van der Pol: F2
Forced pendulum, forced Van der Pol, Rössler, Lorenz: F3
Hénon: C2
Logistic: S1

The exemplary dynamic models of mathematical economics are described in (Goodwin, 1990), the

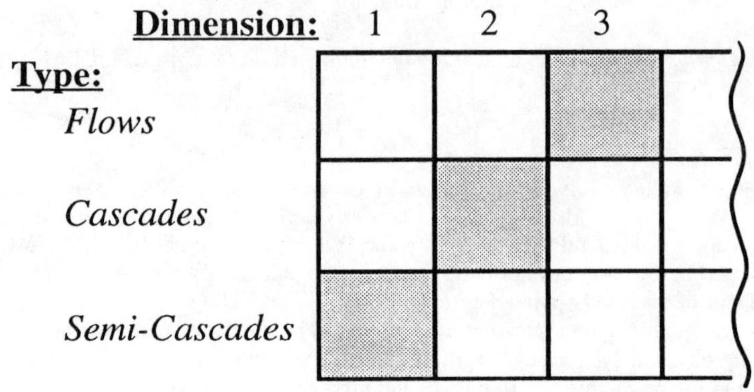

Figure 1. The dynamical system tableau.

chapters of which are distributed over the tableau as follows:

Róssler: F3 — Ch.1, 4, 5, 6, 7, 8, 9
Forced Van der Pol: F3 — Ch. 10
Forced Róssler: F4 — Ch.10
Logistic: S1 — Ch. 1, 2
Von Neumann: S2 — Ch. 3

The latter (Ch. 3) belongs to the frontier of current research on discrete dynamical systems.

In this outline of dynamical systems theory and modeling practice, we will concentrate on the top row of the tableau, flows, keeping in mind that the discussions apply without significant modification to the other two rows, cascades and semi-cascades. In any case, a dynamical system may be visualized by its *portrait*, in which the state space is decomposed into *basins*, with one *attractor* in each.

3. Simple dynamical schemes

We begin with the basic building block of complex dynamics, the simple scheme. This is a dynamical system depending on control parameters. Just as the portrait of attractors and basins is the visual representative of a dynamical system, the response diagram is the visual representative of a scheme.

Definitions. Recall that a *manifold* is a smooth geometrical space. (Abraham, 1988) Let C be a manifold modeling the control parameters of a system, and S another manifold, representing its instantaneous states. Then a *simple dynamical scheme* is a smooth function assigning a smooth vectorfield on S to every point of C. Alternatively, we may think of this function as a smooth vectorfield on the product manifold, $C x S$, which is tangent to the state fibers, $\{c\} x S$. For each control point, $c \in C$, let $X(c)$ be the vectorfield assigned by the scheme. We think of this as a dynamical system on S, or system of first order ordinary differential equations.

Attractors and basins. In each vectorfield of a scheme, $X(c)$, the main features are the *attractors*. These are asymptotic limit sets, under the flow, for a significant set of initial conditions in S. These initial states, tending to a given attractor asymptotically as time goes to plus infinity, comprise the *basins* of $X(c)$. Every point of S which is not in a basin belongs to the *separator* of $X(c)$. The decomposition of S into basins, each containing a single attractor, is the *phase portrait* of $X(c)$. Attractors occur in three types: *static* (an attractive limit point), *periodic* (an attractive limit cycle, or oscillation), and *chaotic* (meaning any other attractive limit set). The phase portrait is the primary representation of the qualitative behavior of the simple dynamical system, and provides a qualitative model for a natural system in a fixed (or laboratory) setting. Its chief features are the basins and attractors. The attractors provide qualitative models for the observed states of dynamical equilibrium of the target system, while the basins model the initial states, which move rapidly to the observed states as startup transients die away.

Response Diagrams. For each point c of the control manifold, the portrait of $X(c)$ may be visualized in the corresponding state fiber, $\{c\}xS$, of the product manifold, CxS. The union of the attractors of $X(c)$, for all control points $c \in C$, is the *attractrix* or *locus of attraction* of the scheme. These sets, visualized in the product manifold, comprise the *response diagram* of the scheme. The response diagram is the primary representation of the qualitative behavior of the dynamical scheme, and provides a qualitative model for a natural system in a setting with control variables. Its chief features are the loci of the attractors as they move under the influence of the control variables, and the *bifurcations* at which the locus af attraction undergoes substantial change. The response diagram provides the qualitative model for the dynamical equilibria of the target system, and their transformations, as control parameters are changed. A typical response diagram, for a model with a single control parameter (the stirred fluid system of Couette and Taylor). For a discussion of this diagram, and many others, see the pictorial *Bifurcation Behavior. (Abraham, 1992)*

Catastrophes and Subtle Bifurcations. For most control points, $c \in C$, the portrait of $X(c)$ is structurally stable. That is, perturbation of the control parameters from c to another nearby point cause a change in the phase portrait of $X(c)$ which is small, and qualitatively insignificant. In exceptional cases, called *bifurcation control points,* the phase portrait of $X(c)$ significantly changes as control parameters are passed through the exceptional point. Many cases, generic in a precise mathematical sense, are known, and the list is growing. These *bifurcation events* all fall into three categories. A bifurcation is *subtle* if only one attractor is involved, and its significant qualitative change is small in magnitude. For example, in a *Hopf bifurcation,* a static attractor becomes a very small periodic attractor, which then slowly grows in amplitude. Other bifurcations are *catastrophic*. In some of these, called blue-sky catastrophes, an attractor appears from, or disappears into, the blue (that is, from a separator). In those of the third category, called *explosions,* a small attractor suddenly explodes into a much larger one. All of these events are very common in the simplest dynamical schemes, such as forced oscillators. The bifurcations are clearly visualized in the response diagram of a scheme, which is sometimes called the bifurcation diagram. The theory up to this point is adequately described in the literature (see the picture books, and references therein). (Abraham, 1992)

4. Complex dynamical systems

A complex dynamical system is a network, or directed graph, of nodes and directed edges. The nodes are simple dynamical schemes or dynamical systems depending on control parameters. The directed edges are static schemes, or output/input functions depending on control parameters. These provide the serial coupling from the instantaneous states at one node into the control parameters of another.

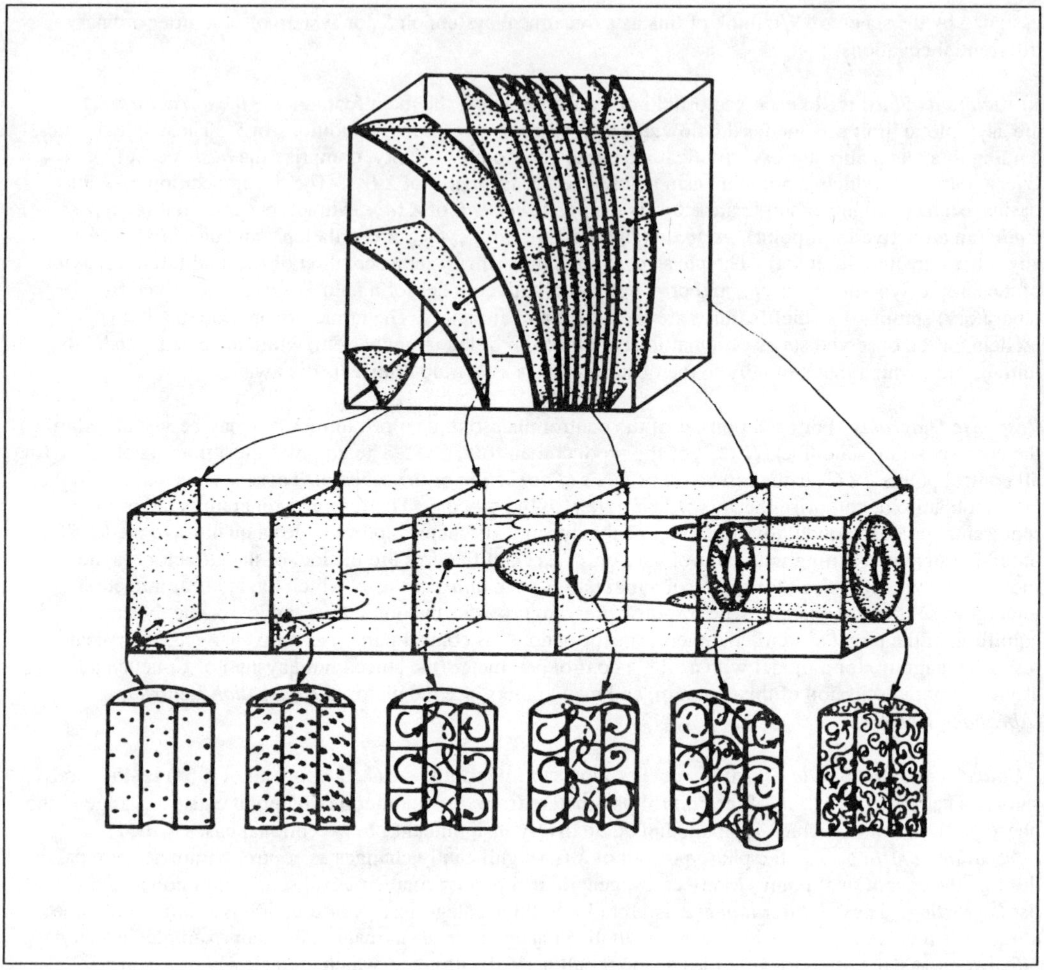

Figure 2. A typical response diagram

Static Coupling Schemes. Consider two simple dynamical schemes, X on CxS and Y on DxT. The two schemes may be serially coupled by a function which, depending on the instantaneous state of the first (a point in S), sets the controls of the second (a point in D). A static coupling scheme is just such a function, but may also depend on control parameters of its own. Thus, let E be another control manifold, and $g : E \times S \to D$. Then the serial coupling of X and Y by the static coupling scheme g is a dynamical scheme with control manifold CxE, and state space SxT, defined by

$$Z((c,e)(s,t))=(X(c,s), Y(g(e,s),t))$$

This is the simplest example of a complex dynamical scheme, symbolized in the literature by schematic diagrams such as those shown in Fig. 3 or equivalently in Fig. 4. In Fig. 3, the bullet icons represent dynamical schemes, with the state spaces, S or T, vertical, and the control spaces, C or D, horizontal. The

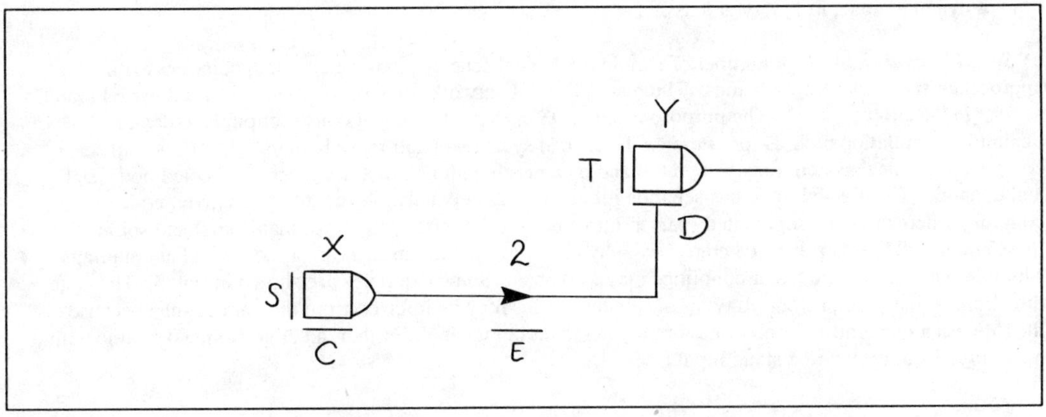

Figure 3. Static coupling of two simple schemes, pictorial

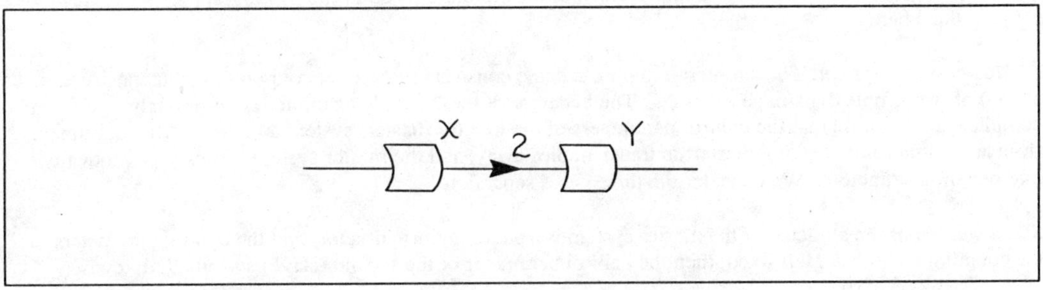

Figure 4. Static coupling of two simple schemes, schematic

total spaces of the dynamical schemes are cartesian product manifolds. For example, $C \times S$. The solid triangle represents a static coupling scheme, g, with its control space, E, horizontal. That is, g is a mapping, $g\colon\ S \times E \to D$. In Fig. 4, the symbols are further abstracted.

* *Other coupling schemes*

Coupling by static functions is the most common device found in applications, but there are others. The most frequent variation is a *delay function*. Thus, the coupling device must remember inputs for a given time (usually fixed), the *lag*, and at a present time, must deliver a function calculated from past inputs. This uses up memory in the simulation machine, but otherwise is straightforward and familiar. In many applications, delays are unavoidable. One unfortunate aspect of this neccessity is the fact that the completed CDS model is then a dynamical-delay scheme (system of differential-delay equations depending on control parameters), rather than a standard dynamical scheme.

Another coupling variation sometimes encountered in complex systems is an *integral function*. In this case, the coupling device must accumulate inputs over a fixed time, but need not remember the incremental values. This kind of static node can be replaced by a dynamical node, in which the integration of inputs becomes the solution of an equivalent differential equation. Thus, a static node may be regarded as a trivial type of dynamic node, in theory at least.

* *Serial Networks*. A large number of simple dynamical schemes may be coupled, pairwise, with appropriate static coupling schemes. The result, a serial network, may be symbolized by a directed graph, at least in the simpler cases. The purpose of the CDS, as a mathematical construction, is to create qualitative simulation models for complex dynamical systems in nature. (Abraham, 1988) The full scale complex dynamical system may be symbolized by a graph with two distinct types of directed node, static and dynamic. (A directed node has separate input and output panels.) As controls at a given node or coupling scheme may be segmented (parsed into a product of different control manifolds) and some of these connected to other directed edges, we may have multiple inputs arriving at nodes and at couplings. Multiple outputs from nodes or couplings may also occur. Some examples are shown in Fig. 5. The edge directions of these graphs of two types of directed nodes may be inferred from the connections because of the rule: each edge must connect an output panel to an input panel. Further, an edge from a dynamic output may only be connected to a static input.

5. Exemplary complex systems

Several pedagogic examples have been presented in the literature listed in the Bibliography. We review some of them here.

* *Master-Slave Systems* The simplest complex scheme consists of the serial coupling (as illustrated above) of two simple dynamical schemes. The behavior of these simple examples is notoriously complicated. Suppose that the control parameters of the first (or master) system are fixed. After startup, from an arbitrary initial state, the startup transient dies away, and the master system settles asymptotically into one of its attractors. We consider the three cases separately.

Static master. If the attractor of the master system is a static (point) attractor, and the control parameters of the coupling scheme are left fixed, then the control parameter of the second (slave) system are likewise

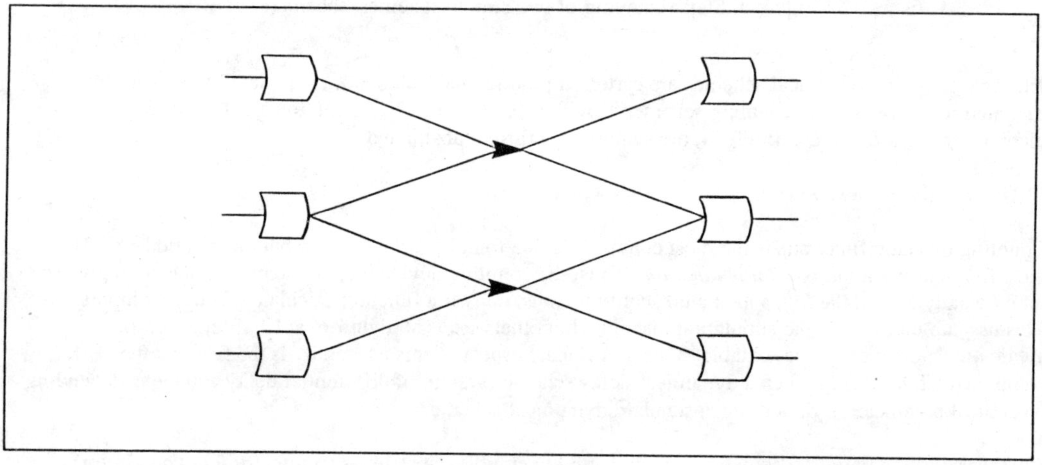

Figure 5. Multiple couplings.

fixed. Typically, this static control point of the slave system will be a typical (nonbifurcation) point, and the slave system will be observed in one of its attractors (static, periodic, or chaotic).

Periodic master. With fixed controls of the master and the coupling function, a periodic master attractor will drive the slave controls in a periodic cycle. This is the situation in the classical theory of forced oscillation. Experimental study of these systems began a century or so ago, and continues today. Here are the two classic examples.

1. Duffing systems. If the slave system is a soft spring or pendulum, the coupled system is the classic one introduced by Rayleigh in 1882, in which Duffing found hysteresis and catastrophes in 1918. (Abraham, 1992) The bifurcation diagram is very rich, full of harmonic periodic attractors and chaos. (Ueda, 1980)

2. *Van der Pol systems.* If the slave system is a self-sustained oscillator, the coupled system is another classic one introduced by Rayleigh, in which Van der Pol found subtle bifurcations of harmonics and Cartwright and Littlewood apparently found chaos. Both of these classical systems have been central to experimental dynamics, and research continues today.

Chaotic master. This situation, chaotic forcing, has received little attention so far. Many experiments suggest themselves, in analogy with forced oscillations. One situation which has been extensively studied is the perturbation of a conventional dynamical system by noise.

* *Chains of Dynamical Schemes.* If three schemes are connected in a serial chain by two static coupling schemes (Fig. 6) a complex system with a very complicated bifurcation diagram may result. If the first pair comprises a periodic master forcing a simple pendulum, as described above, the terminal slave may be either a periodically or chaotically forced system. Of course, if all three systems are pendulum-like (one basin, static attractor) the serial chain is also pendulum-like. But a periodic attractor in either the first or second dynamical scheme is adequate to produce rich dynamics in the coupled chain.

* *Cycles of Dynamical Schemes.* If the directed graph of a complex scheme contains a cycle (closed loop) then complicated dynamics may occur, no matter how simple the component schemes. The minimal example is the serially bicoupled pair (Fig. 7). Even if the two dynamical schemes are pendulum-like, the complex system may have a periodic attractor. For example, Smale finds a periodic attractor (and a Hopf bifurcation) in exactly this situation, in a discrete reaction-diffusion model for two biological cells. (Smale, 1976) A cycle of three pendulum-like nodes is discussed next, as we turn now to more complex examples.

* *Intermittency in an Endocrine System Model.* Models for physiological and biochemical systems have a natural complex structure. A recent model for the reproductive system of mammals (hypothalamus, pituitary, gonads) is a very simple network (Fig. 8). (Abraham, 1985) Although the simple dynamical scheme at each node is a point attractor in a one-dimensional state space, the complex system may have two periodic basins, each containing a periodic attractor. This phenomenon, sometimes called

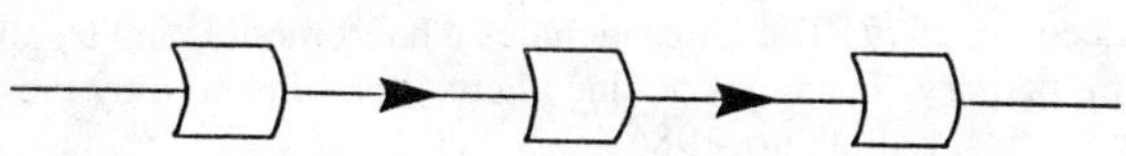

Figure 6. A chain

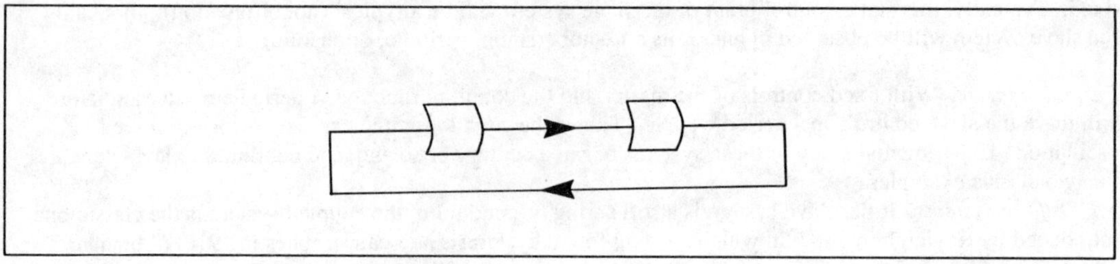

Figure 7. Bicoupled pair.

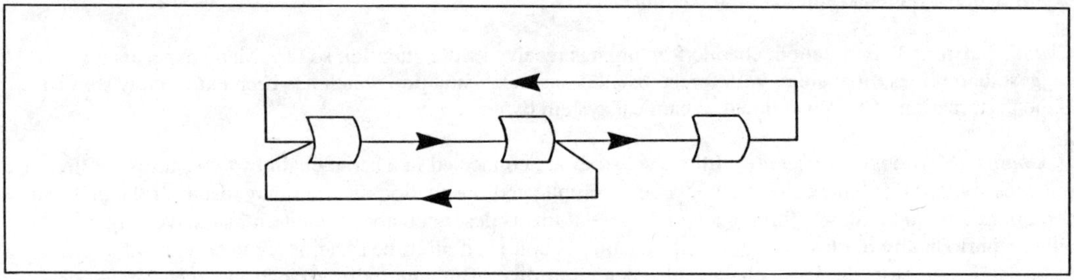

Figure 8. An endocrine system model

birhythmicity, has also been found in a biochemical model. (Decroly, 1982) Small changes in the control parameters of the coupling functions cause intermittent jumps between the two distinct oscillatory states.

6. Cellular dynamical systems

Here we introduce *cellular dynamical systems theory,* a mathematical strategy for creating dynamical models for the computer simulation of biological organs and membranes, and other systems exhibiting natural intelligence. Reaction/diffusion equations were introduced by the pioneers of biological morphogenesis: Fisher (in 1930), (Fisher, 1930/1958) Kolmogorov-Petrovsky-Piscounov (in 1937), (Kolmogorov, 1937) Rashevsky (in 1938), (Rashevsky, 1938) Southwell (around 1940), (Southwell, 1940) and Turing (in 1952). (Turing, 1952) Rashevsky introduced spatial discretization corresponding to biological cells. These discretized reaction/diffusion systems are examples of cellular dynamical systems, probably the first in the literature. Further developments were made by Thom (1966-1972) (Thom, 1975) and Zeeman (1972-1977). (Zeeman, 1977) The latter includes a heart model, and a simple brain model exhibiting short and long-term memory. The ideas outlined here are all inspired by these pioneers. The strategy is based upon CDS concepts. (Abraham, 1986)

* *Definitions.* By *cellular dynamical system* we mean a complex dynamical system in which the nodes are all identical copies of a single dynamical scheme, the *standard cell,* and are associated with specific locations in a supplementary space, the *physical substrate,* or *location space.* Exemplary systems have been developed for reaction/diffusion systems by discretization of the spatial variables. In these examples, pattern formation occurs by Turing bifurcation. One of the most-studied examples of this class is the *Brussellator* of Lefever and Prigogine. Other important examples of this construction are the heart and

brain models of Zeeman. These models have something in common with the *cellular automata* of Von Neumann, yet possess more structure. We might call them *cellular dynomata.*

The behavior of a cellular dynamical system may be visualized by Zeeman's *projection method:* an image of the location space (physical substrate) is projected into the response diagram of the standard cell, where it moves about, clinging to the attractrix, or locus of attraction. Alternatively, the behavior may be vizualized by the *graph method:* attaching a separate copy of the standard response diagram to each cell of the location space. Within this product space, the instantaneous state of the model may be represented by a graph, showing the attractor occupied by each cell, within its own response diagram. In either case, the behavior of the complete cellular system may be tracked, as the controls of each cell are separately manipulated, through an understanding of the standard response diagram provided by *dynamical systems theory:* attractors, basins, separators, and their bifurcations.

7. Exemplary cellular systems

Cellular dynamical systems began in the context of reaction-diffusion equations.

* *Reaction-Diffusion Systems.* An unusual example of serial coupling is provided by the reaction-diffusion model for biological morphogenesis, introduced by Fischer in 1930 (see Section 5 for more history). Given a spatial domain or substrate, D, and a biochemical state space, B, the state space is an infinite-dimensional manifold, F, of functions from D to B. The reaction-diffusion equation may be regarded as a simple dynamical scheme of vectorfields on F, depending on a control space, C. Meanwhile, the spatial substrate is actually composed of biological cells, considered identical in structure. As the reaction-diffusion scheme, the master in this context, determines instantaneous states of biochemical (morphogen, or control metabolite) concentrations in the substrate, $f : D \rightarrow B$, the cell at a fixed position in the domain will extract the values of this function at its location, $f(d)$. This is a point of B, which may be regarded as the control space for another simple dynamical scheme, modeling the dynamics within the standard cell. Let $g_d(f) = f(d)$. Then g_d is the static coupling function from master to slave. But there are many slaves, each distinguished by its own location, hence coupling function. The directed graph is thus a radial spray, or star, of slaves of a common master, as shown in Fig. 9. If in addition each cell may be a source or sink of biochemical (metabolite) controls, then each connection is a bicoupling.

* *Neural Nets.* Neural nets may be regarded as a special case of CDS network. The dynamical nodes are all identical schemes, in which a simple scheme with one dimensional control and state spaces has a single basin of attraction (with a static attractor). The control value adjusts the location of the attractor, and there are no bifurcations. The planar response diagram has an inclined line as attractrix. The coupling schemes are all identical as well, and are simple amplifiers, $g(e,s)=es$. All nodes interconnected, as shown (Fig. 10). The intelligence of a neural net depends on the matrix of controls, $E=(e_{ij})$. This strategy, called *connectionism,* may be extended directly to any CDS.

* *Biological organ example.* Organs typically contain many different types of cells. In the unusual case that there were only one type of cell, one could imagine a model for the organ consisting of a single cellular dynamical system. This is the case with Zeeman's heart model. An explicit cellular dynamical model for the organ will require an explicit model for the standard cell, which (with luck) may be found in the specialized literature devoted to that cell.

However, if there are two distinct cells, then each will give rise to a distinct cellular dynamical model. The model for the organ will then consist of a coupled system of *two cellular dynamical systems,* one for each cell type. More generally, the organ model will consist of a *complex dynamical system,* comprising a network of distinct cellular dynamical models, one for each of the distinct cell types, visualized (intermixed) in a common physical substrate.

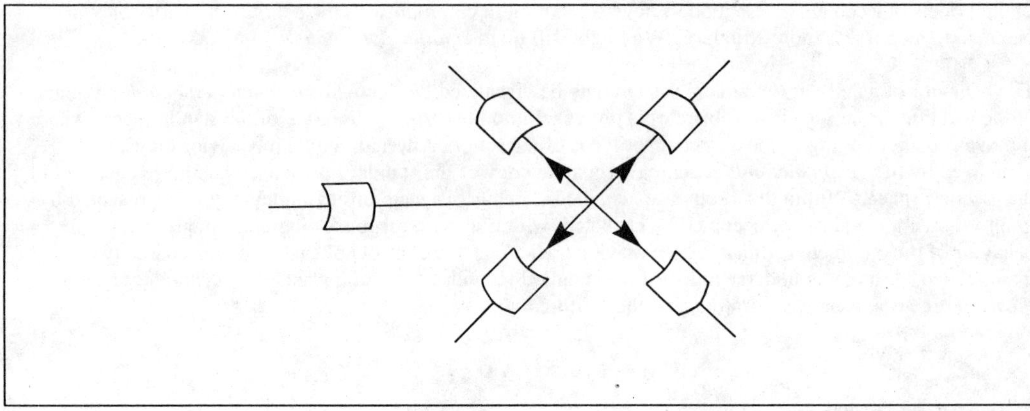

Figure 9. A star complex

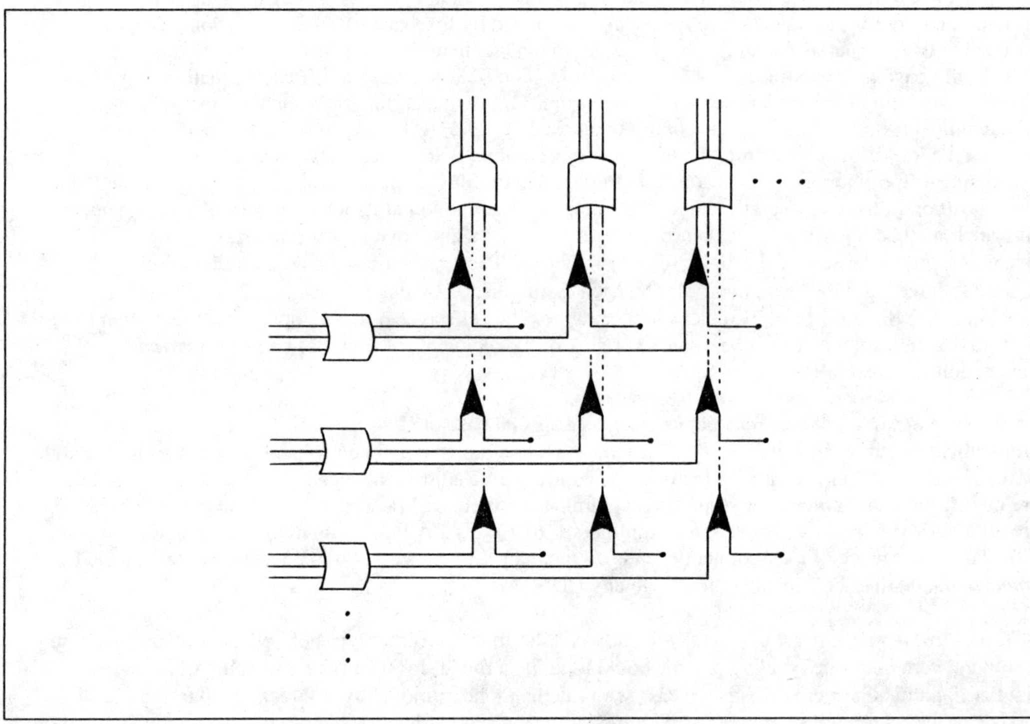

Figure 10. Neural Net

Moreover, even if there is only a single cell type in the organ (for example, a liver cell) a network of cellular models may nevertheless be required. For there are usually at least two important compartments in the organ: the intracellular space, and the extracellular space. The concentration of control metabolites or humoral substances (such as the pacemaker substance in Zeeman's heart model) in the extracellular space contributes a second cellular dynamical system to the model. This second system arises through the discretization of the nonlinear Fickian diffusion equation for the perfusion of metabolites through the organ. Even if the substance in the two compartments is the same (for example, cortisol in the adrenal cortex), there will be two distinct cellular systems in the organ model. The dynamics of the extracellular substance will be modeled by a (discretized) reaction/diffusion system, while the intracellular dynamics may be modeled by reaction kinetics alone.

8. Simulation methods

After the strategies of complex dynamical systems have been used in an application, the resulting model is simply a large dynamical scheme. That is, a system of coupled ordinary differential equations with free control parameters, or partial differential equations of evolution type (parabolic or hyperbolic) must be explored experimentally. The goal of the exploration is to obtain the response diagram, which is the useful outcome of the qualitative modeling activity. As the exploration of the response diagram is an unfamiliar goal for simulation, we review here some of the strategies used.

* *Orbit Methods*. When the dynamical scheme consists of a modest number of ordinary differential equations of first order, simulation by the standard digital algorithms (Euler, Runge-Kutta and so on) or analog techniques provide curve tracing in the bifurcation diagram. A large number of curves, for various values of control parameters and initial conditions, may reveal the principal features of the diagram. Monte Carlo techniques are sometimes used to select the control parameters and/or initial states.

* *Relaxation Methods*. When partial differential equations (reaction-diffusion, hydrodynamic, plasma, liquid crystal, solid state, elastodynamic, and so on) are part of the model, they may be treated most naturally as dynamical systems by discretization of the spatial variables. Thus, the infinite-dimensional state spaces are projected into finite-dimensional approximations. Finally, these may be treated by orbit methods, to obtain a bifurcation diagram with loci of attraction and separation. This is essentially the relaxation technique of Southwell (method-of-lines).

* *Dynasim Methods*. Whether small or large, ordinary or partial, the exploration of a bifurcation diagram by analog, digital, or hybrid simulation is extremely time intensive. A considerable gain in speed may be obtained with dynasim methods. (Abraham, 1979) Here, special purpose hardware traces a large number of orbits in parallel. Having thus found all the most probable attractors at once, time is reversed and the basin of each is filled with its own color. This process is repeated (perhaps in parallel) for different values of the control parameters. When dimensions are large, new techniques of visualization may be needed. (Inselberg, 1985)

* *Distributed processing*. For the simulation of a complex dynamical model, the static coupling schemes may be implemented by look-up tables, or fast arithmetic. It is the dynamical schemes which are FLOP intensive. It makes sense, if distributed processors are available, to devote one to each dynamical node. Thus, the architecture of the simulation device is identical to that of the complex dynamical model, and similar to that of the target natural system. Message passing traffic may be decreased by the following trick, if the model is loosely coupled. This means that although an output may be changing rapidly, the node it controls is only slowly sensitive to the rapid changes. Thus, occasional updates of control may be transmitted in place of rapid ones. Further, if all current states are broadcast on a schedule to the static nodes and controls of the rapid integration routines running in each processor, the node processors may (if they can afford the time) make predictions of the next broadcast. A cheap predictor, such as Euler

integration, may be used to change the local controls linearly with each local time step, in ignorance of the real values at the neighboring nodes.

* *Numerical methods for cellular systems.* The destiny of a cellular dynamical model is a computer program for qualitative simulation. Although we may expect someday a theory of these models, it may not replace simulation as the dominant method of science, but only supplement it. Thus, we need a technology of numerical methods adapted to these large-scale simulations. Beyond brute-force integration of thousands of identical copies of the standard dynamical scheme with differing (and slowly changing) values of the control parameters, lookup-table methods might be employed for acceleration or economy. In any case, massively parallel hardware and software will be needed, along with new methods of monitoring large numbers of state variables. Color graphics is the method of choice at the moment, and we may imagine a color movie projected upon a model of the physical substrate of the organ as the monitoring scheme.

The current state of the art seems to be simple experiments with standard cells culled from the literature of the physical sciences, such as the Duffing pendulum, the cusp catastrophe, and so on. From these experiments, we may try to recognize some functions of natural intelligence, such as memory, perception, decision, learning, and the like, as in neural net theory.

9. Global modeling

Now we discuss the adaptation of the techniques of complex dynamical systems theory to the modeling of large-scale economic systems in contact with environmental factors. Recent developments in the mathematical theory of complex and cellular dynamical (CD) systems and their simulation give new promise to the social sciences, especially, economics. Some proposals for CD economic system simulations (see, for example, Abraham, 1990A; and Abraham, 1990B) are based on this technology.

Biospherics is the synthesis of the biological and earth sciences (biogeography, atmospheric science, climatology, oceanography, geology and the like) into a unified understanding of planetary ecology and physiology (see Snyder, 1985; and, Lovelock, 1990). It is increasingly important to study biospherics, and CD models are promising here as well. The adoption of a common modeling strategy for biospherics and for economics enables their combination into a single massive model, in which environmental factors are coupled to the economy. In this section, we apply the techniques of cellular erodynamics to the problem of building a spatially distributed model coupling biospherics and economics.

* *Spatial economic models.* Spatial economics denotes a theory of spatially extended economic systems, in which transportation times and other geographic factors may be considered (see Puu.) We consider now a global model, in which the entire globe is covered by more-or-less uniform plaques, of a size such that even the smallest country has several plaques within its borders. We chose an economic model for the dynamics of a regional economic system, as for example in Chapter 3 of (Goodwin, 1991). By appropriate choice of parameters, adapt a copy of the model to each plaque. Finally, couple each local regional model to each of the other regions, with appropriate coupling functions. The result is a cellular dynamical model for the global economy: a spatial economic model. Simulation of the model will be most natural on a massively parallel supercomputer.

* *Biospheric models.* Spatially distributed models for various aspects of the biosphere currently exist in various laboratories. In particular, those aspects intervening in the climate --- such as atmospheric dynamics and chemistry (including the greenhouse effect and the ozone hole), solar radiation, ocean currents --- have been extensively modeled. Other aspects, such as those of the hydrologic cycle --- forest transpiration, ground water, top soil --- and others, such as toxic wastes, have models in development, either in laboratories or in consumer-level computer games such as SimEarth (Maxus Software, Santa

Clara, CA). The synthesis of these distinct CD models into a complex CD model for the biopshere is a relatively simple matter, as they are devised in the common modeling environment of complex dynamical systems theory.

* *Erodynamic models.* Consider now two CD models, one for the global economy, the other for the biosphere. Suppose that both are made of cells for the same regions. All that is neccesary now is to couple the two CD models into a single system. This could be done most simply by coupling, in each region, the economic cell and the biospheric cell. This coupling is the subject of current research in the new field of environmental economics. More general coupling would allow the influence of the biospherics of all regions upon the economics of each region, and vice versa. Such coupling, in the style of connectionist neural nets, might be created by an evolving and learning system. In any case, the result is a monolithic CD model for the spatially distributed economic biosphere, a cellular erodynamic model.

10. Conclusion

While this simple prescription for a world model could be made immediately, perhaps little could be learned from it. This is because the associated mathematics, the theory of massive CD systems, is still in its infancy. Along with the advances in massively parallel computers and the arts of scientific visualization, this theory may be crucial to our future.

Acknowledgments. A recent book by Richard Goodwin has been very stimulating for this approach. It is a pleasure to thank Richard Goodwin, K. Velupillai, Graciela Chichilnisky, and Goeffrey Heal for helpful discussions of these ideas.

REFERENCES

References

Abraham, 1979.
Ralph H. Abraham, ''Dynasim: Exploratory research in bifurcations using interactive computer graphics,'' *Annals N. Y. Acad. Sciences* **316** pp. 676-684 (1979).

Abraham, 1985.
Ralph H. Abraham, Huseyin Kocak, and William R. Smith, ''Chaos and intermittency in an endocrine system,'' pp. 33-70 in *Chaos, Fractals, and Dynamics*, ed. William R. Smith and Pal Fischer,Plenum, New York (1985).

Abraham, 1986.
Ralph H. Abraham, ''Cellular dynamical systems,'' pp. 7-8 in *Mathematics and Computers in Biomedical Applications, Proc. IMACS World Congress, Oslo, 1985*, ed. J. Eisenfeld and C. DeLisi,North-Holland, Amsterdam (1986).

Abraham, 1988.
Ralph H. Abraham, Jerrold E. Marsden, and Tudor Ratiu, *Manifolds, Tensor Analysis, and Applications, 2nd ed.*, Springer-Verlag, Berlin (1988).

Abraham, 1988.
Ralph H. Abraham and Christopher D. Shaw, ''Dynamics, a visual introduction,'' pp. 543-597 in *Self-Organization*, ed. F. Eugene Yates,Plenum, New York (1988).

Abraham, 1992.
Ralph H. Abraham and Christopher D. Shaw, *Dynamics, the Geometry of Behavior, Second Edition*, Addison-Wesley, Reading, MA (1992).

Decroly, 1982.
Olivier Decroly and Albert Goldbeter, ''Birhythmicity, chaos and other patterns of temporal self-organization in a multiply regulated biochemical system.,'' *Proc. Natl. Acad. Sci. USA* **79** pp. 6917-6921 (1982).

Fisher, 1930/1958.
Ronald A. Fisher, *The Genetical Theory of Natural Selection*, Dover, New York (1930/1958).

Inselberg, 1985.
Alfred Inselberg, ''The plane with parallel coordinates,'' *The Visual Computer* **1** pp. 69-91 (1985).

Kolmogorov, 1937.
A. Kolmogorov, I. Petrovski, and N. Piskunov, ''Etude de l'equation de la diffusion avec croissance de la quantite de matiee et son application a une probleme biologique,'' *Bull. de l'Universite d'Etat a Moscou, Ser. International* **1(6)** pp. 1-25 (1937).

Rashevsky, 1938.
Nicolas Rashevsky, *Mathematical Biophysics*, University of Chicago Press, Chicago, IL (1938).

Smale, 1976.
Steve Smale, ''A mathematical model of two cells via Turing's equation,'' in *The Hopf Bifurcation and its Applications*, ed. J. E. Marsden and M. McCracken,Springer, New York (1976).

Southwell, 1940.
Richard V. Southwell, *Relaxation Methods in Engineering Science*, Oxford University Press, London (1940).

Thom, 1975.
René Thom and David Fowler, tr., *Structural Stability and Morphogenesis*, Addison-Wesley, Reading, MA (1975).

Turing, 1952.
Alan Turing, ''A chemical basis for biological morphogenesis,'' *Phil. Trans. Roy. Soc. (London), Ser. B* **237** p. 37 (1952).

Ueda, 1980.
Yoshisuke Ueda, ''Explosion of strange attractors exhibited by Duffing's equation,'' *Ann. N.Y. Acad. Sci.* **357** pp. 422-434 (1980).

Zeeman, 1977.
E. Christopher Zeeman, *Catastrophe Theory*, Addison-Wesley, Reading, MA (1977).

Complexity in Deterministic, Nonlinear Business-Cycle Models – Foundations, Empirical Evidence, and Predictability

HANS-WALTER LORENZ

Department of Economics, Georg-August-Universität Göttingen
Platz der Göttinger Sieben 3, D-W-3400 Göttingen

1. Introduction

Business-cycle theory represents one of the oldest fields in economics. While it was treated as a nearly esoteric field in specialized graduate texts during the late 1960s and early 1970s, the last fifteen years saw it resurrecting even as a synonym for dynamic macroeconomics. The Rational Expectations literature of the late 1970s and early 1980s and the development of sophisticated econometric tools in investigations of an economy's fluctuations occasionally seemed to encourage the believe that business-cycle theory was an invention of the so-called New Classical economics. However, it is a fact that the observed cycling of an economy constituted the major impetus for many a classical and neoclassical economist in the 19th and early 20th century to engage in economic theorizing at all. HABERLER's (1937) seminal text on the history of business-cycle theory demonstrates in an enlightening fashion that the ups and downs in economic activity were central not only in – to name just a few – HAWTREY's (1913), HAYEK's (1933), MARX's (1867), PIGOU's (1929), or SISMONDI's (1837) work but that numerous, usually forgotten writers concentrated on oscillations in particular markets or the entire economy.

Traditional business-cycle theory (roughly until the interwar era of this century) can be characterized by two properties:

- The explanations of business cycles were typically *monocausal.* Theories of *underconsumption* and *overproduction* or exotica like JEVON's (1884) sunspot theory (which should not be confused with recent sunspot models) considered a single factor, phenomenon, or event responsible for the initiation of cyclic motion in the economy.
- From a modern standpoint, traditional business-cycle models can be called non-mathematical and informal. The explanation of turning points by means of verbal arguments was the central intention of most inquiries; logical inconsistencies could not always be avoided.

Things changed drastically with the increasing use of mathematics in economic theory. The formalization of CLARK's (1917) acceleration principle and the Keynesian multiplier analysis initiated the well-known business-cycle models in the HICKS (1950) and SAMUELSON (1939) tradition which dominated texts on business-cycle theory for nearly 30 years. The cycling of macroeconomic variables was considered a mathematical phenomenon in a particular dynamical system. Thus, the formal properties of a system's trajectory (like dampened or explosive oscillations) were emphasized instead of providing the economic reasoning behind turning points: occasionally it is difficult to decide which economic elements of a formal model are actually responsible for these turning points.

Most mathematical models of the business cycle in the postwar era generate smooth, regular trajectories of the system variables. The frequency of the oscillations in linear multiplier-accelerator models and in the few nonlinear models is constant and depends on the system parameters; the amplitude (also depending on the constant parameters) is constant or increases/ decreases in a monotonic fashion. This is the scenario known from introductory science texts dealing with the dampened or undamped pendulum. It is not astonishing that many economic textbooks present a sinusoidal curve as an abstract idealization of business cycles.

Obviously, empirical time series do not reveal the regularity known from these postwar business-cycle models. Traditional, non-mathematical business-cycle theorists had no severe problems with changing frequencies and seemingly irregular changes in the trajectory's amplitudes because they typically concentrated on explanations of turning points (prediction was not really a subject of early writings in business-cycle theory). On the contrary, models of the multiplier-accelerator type had found their way into large econometric models in the 1950s and 1960s, whose major *raison d'être* was the prediction of the future development of an economy. While pure business-cycle *theory* still concentrated on the generation of a stylized motion, econometricians had enriched the theory by a common statistical practice: the world is conceived as a system with infinitely many degrees of freedom; as a statistical procedure can take only a finite number of endogenous variables into account, the remaining infinite number of degrees of freedom are considered random variables. Econometric models with multiplier-accelerator elements and superimposed stochastic variables did not feature the regularity property of purely endogenous theoretic models, and in many cases the trajectories generated by these models resembled actual time series in a more than satisfactory manner.

This econometric practice had an important (possibly originally unintended) consequence for the modelling of classical business-cycle models in the 1970s and 1980s. Suppose the business-cycle model represents a two-dimensional, discrete-time, linear dynamical system (like most traditional business-cycle models):

$$\begin{aligned} \Delta x_{1,t} &= a_1 + a_2 x_{1,t-1} + a_3 x_{2,t-1} \\ \Delta x_{2,t} &= b_1 + b_2 x_{1,t-1} + b_3 x_{2,t-1}, \end{aligned} \tag{1}$$

and assume parameter values which imply a dampened oscillation (*e.g.*, the continuous line in Figure 1). It had been known for a long time (cf. SAMUELSON (1947)) that the superposition of random variables in the form

$$\begin{aligned} \Delta x_{1,t} &= a_1 + a_2 x_{1,t-1} + a_3 x_{2,t-1} + u_{1,t} \\ \Delta x_{2,t} &= b_1 + b_2 x_{1,t-1} + b_3 x_{2,t-1} + u_{2,t}, \end{aligned} \tag{2}$$

with $u_{i,t}$ as random variables (and usually $E(u_{it}) = 0$), does not only change the continuous nature of the trajectory but that it also influences its convergence properties. Linear stochastic models like (2) with parameter values that imply a dampened oscillation in (1) generate persistent irregular oscillations (cf. the irregular trajectory in Figure 1).

Business-cycle models in the New Classical fashion make extensive use of higher-dimensional analogs of dynamical systems of the form (2). The endogenous economic part of the model (the *kernel* in the form of systems like (1)) is deterministic and characterized by dampened oscillations. Thus, the economy is endogenously stable (in the sense of a stable fixed point). Oscillations emerge only because exogenous, possibly non-economic forces prevent an economy from converging toward its stationary values. It cannot be denied that the irregular trajectory in Figure 1 at least resembles actual detrended time series of income or employment rates. However, SLUTZKY (1937) made the important observation that, by choice of appropriate random distributions, filters, etc., actual time series can be reconstructed to a nearly arbitrary precision with the help of systems like (2). The often heard justification for the use of New Classical models, namely that they *fit the data* very well,[1] should be evaluated in the light of the dynamic properties of (2): it seems as if the economic content which influences the parameters in the kernel (1) is of secondary matter when the shape (*i.e.*, the changing frequency and amplitude) of a trajectory is dominated by the stochastic, exogenous disturbances.

[1] It was demonstrated by BLATT (1978, 1980, 1983) that a linear econometric model like (2) might not be able to reject the hypothesis of a linear structure even when the economy is in fact nonlinear.

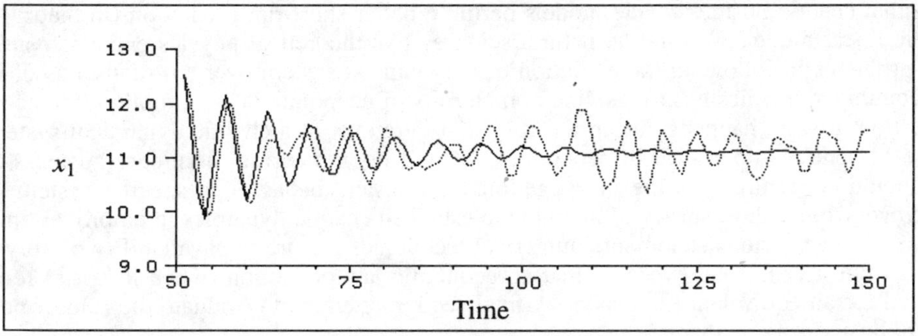

Figure 1: Persistent Oscillations in a Stochastic Linear Dynamical System

The New Classical business-cycle theory can therefore be characterized as a non-economic explanation and description of persistent cycles.[2] It is even difficult to consider the economic kernel a propagation mechanism of an exogenous shock when new shocks occur in each period. Business-cycle models that can be reduced to dynamical systems of the form (2) with possibly higher dimensions (like multiplier-accelerator models, real-business-cycle models, or various other models in the New Classical fashion) are unsuited to explain the driving forces behind *persistent* oscillations in an endogenous manner. An endogenous economic explanation of cycles thus requires different analytical tools, and it is well-known that nonlinear business-cycle theory is nearly as old as its linear counterpart. The models developed by GOODWIN (1951), HICKS (1950), or KALDOR (1940) represent dynamical systems in which persistent oscillations (after initial displacements form their fixed points) emerge solely because of their functional structure. Analytical treatments of these nonlinear dynamical systems are somewhat more complicated than solving simple linear systems. This may explain why nonlinear business-cycle models never gained the popularity of linear models of the multiplier-accelerator type. Besides, nonlinear business-cycle theory searched for regular cycles for a long time, *i.e.,* cycles whose shapes are indeed very similar to those generated by linear, non-stochastic systems with constant amplitude. The differences between both approaches seemed to be important only for economists interested in methods for stabilizing a fluctuating economy: oscillations in nonlinear models might be suppressed by changing a system's parameters while the effects of exogenous disturbances usually cannot be controlled by policy measures.

The event of the discovery of chaotic dynamics in nonlinear dynamical systems has changed the relative importance of nonlinear business-cycle theory in a fundamental way. It has become obvious that the observable irregularities in actual time series do not *necessarily* require the modelling of stochastic dynamical systems: irregular time series can be the outcome of a purely deterministic nonlinear dynamical system, and the mathematical research on chaotic systems during the last 15 years has provided several criteria for the occurrence of complicated dynamics in appropriate nonlinear models. While most original nonlinear business-cycle models are unable to generate complex motion, they inhibit several ingredients necessary for the emergence of chaotic or otherwise complex dynamics. In many cases, minor variations in the original versions of the models or adoptions of essential functional forms in different scenarios are sufficient for the generation of irregular time series.

In the following, a few topics regarding this complex motion in nonlinear business-cycle theory will be discussed. After a short survey of existing approaches (with an emphasis on continuous-time models), the possibility of prediction in chaotic systems is investigated. It will

[2] Note the ideological component in this statement: an economist convinced of the blessing of a free-market economy will not feel uncomfortable with the idea that an economy isolated from external interruptions converges to a fixed point.

turn out that chaotic business-cycle models permit a better short-run prediction (in theory) than stochastic linear models. While the natural sciences like theoretical physics encounter no conceptual problems in following the evolution of a dynamical system over ten-thousands of iterations, economic dynamics has to take the non-eternity of economic laws of motion into account. The question of what happens during the very first iterations of a chaotic dynamical systems is therefore of central importance in economics. It will be argued that nonlinear business-cycle theory should concentrate on the investigations of transient behavior in specific system. The lesson drawn from a short survey of attempts to establish chaotic dynamics in empirical time series confirms the previous statement: numerical techniques require the availability of very long time series but it cannot be expected that an economic law of motion (when it exists) remains unchanged for an equivalent time span. A final section attempts to evaluate the role of nonlinearities in business-cycle theory.

2. Complex Motion in Nonlinear Business-Cycle Theory – A Brief Overview of Existing Approaches

There exist several definitions of chaotic motion. For the purpose of this brief and rather informal survey it suffices to say that a deterministic dynamical system is chaotic if[3]

- the time series generated by the system is bounded and aperiodic,
- the system displays a *sensitive dependence on initial conditions*, *i.e.*, two time series starting at two different initial points (which may be arbitrarily close together) eventually diverge and imply completely different frequencies, amplitudes, and locations of turning points.

The theory of chaotic dynamical systems has provided a multitude of results and insights but is far from being as completed as, *e.g.*, the theory of two-dimensional ordinary differential equations. Whatsoever, while it is difficult (or impossible) to describe the minimal requirements the functional forms of a dynamical system must fulfill, a rough classification of known low-dimensional, chaotic dynamical systems is possible. Table 1 mentions some possibly chaotic systems in discrete and continuous time.

The large number of economic applications of chaotic dynamics makes it impossible to provide a short survey of the existing literature.[4] Thus, the following pages only intend to recall a few basic models, the dynamic structure of which seems to be representative for a larger number of different scenarios in other specific applications. The author's personal preferences suggest a concentration on continuous-time approaches to business cycles.

2.1. Discrete-Time Approaches

Most economic examples of chaotic dynamics have exploited the properties of unimodal one-dimensional maps topologically equivalent to the logistic map. A major reason for the concentration on these maps can certainly be found in the relative ease with which chaos can be detected in these systems. In addition, existing models occasionally requested only minor modifications (often called *ad-hoc* variations) in order to transform them into a logistic system.

---

[3] Other definitions emphasize the simultaneous presence of period and aperiodic time series, or do not include the sensitive dependence on initial conditions. In investigations of empirical time series measures like the largest Lyapunov exponent (cf. Section 5 below) are used for establishing chaotic motion.

[4] Surveys of the existing economic literature on chaotic dynamical systems can be found in, *e.g.*, LORENZ (1989), ROSSER (1991), and ZHANG (1990b).

Dimension	Discrete Time	Continuous Time
$n = 1$	endomorphisms (noninvertible maps)	impossible
$n = 2$	diffeomorphisms (invertible maps) endomorphisms	impossible
$n = 3$	ditto	forced oscillators Shil'nikov scenario (homoclinic orbits)
$n > 3$	ditto	coupled oscillators ($n = 6$)

Table 1: Examples of Families of Chaotic Dynamical Systems

Many pioneering papers on chaotic dynamics in economics deal with macroeconomic issues but it is problematic to interpret these models as business-cycle models when the systems represent 1D maps. One-dimensional maps typically display a sawtooth pattern, but business-cycles – when measured in monthly, quarterly or annual time units – are characterized by longer upswing and downswing phases with troughs occasionally lasting for several (usually too many) periods. It is, of course, possible to assume longer time periods such that a business-cycle model explains only the succession of peaks and troughs. This is particularly evident in overlapping-generations models with a typical period length of 20-30 years. However, in such a framework the non-eternity of economic laws of motion (to be discussed in greater detail in Section 4) enters the picture. It therefore seems as if one-dimensional maps represent more promising analytical tools in the investigation of long-term phenomena like urban economics, migration, and other socio-demographic phenomena than in short-run business-cycle theory. The upper part of Table 2 lists a sample of one-dimensional, discrete-time models that emphasize macroeconomic issues.

When short-run business-cycle models should be able to generate monotonic up- and downswings that last for several periods, the minimum dimension in discrete-time models is $n = 2$. However, a search for such 2D models in traditional nonlinear business-cycle theory will not be very fruitful: the majority of these models were formulated in continuous-time because the theory of two-dimensional ordinary differential equations was much more developed already in the 1940s and 1950s than the theory of 2D maps.

If one concentrates on two-dimensional maps in order to model business cycles in discrete time there exist two different approaches:

1. A new nonlinear business-cycle model in two dimensions is designed from scratch.
2. An established continuous-time model is transformed into a discrete-time model.

The present paper deals with some fundamental conceptual problems in business-cycle theory and it seems preferable to concentrate on well-established models in the literature. However, the transformation of a given continuous-time model into a discrete map raises a multitude of problems, many of which have never been extensively discussed in economic dynamics.[5] A common

[5] Cf., *e.g.*, SPARROW (1980), MEDIO (1991a), and INVERNIZZI/MEDIO (1991) for proper transformations of continuous-time systems into 1D maps. A short description of Poincaré-section techniques can be found in LORENZ (1989).

Dimension	Economic Application
$n = 1$	Neoclassical Growth, DAY (1982, 1983); Growth Cycles, POHJOLA (1981), STUTZER (1980); Keynesian Macromodel, DAY/SHAFER (1986); Multiplier-Accelerator Model, NUSSE/HOMMES (1990); Optimal Growth, BOLDRIN (1989), BOLDRIN/MONTRUCCHIO (1986, 1988), DENECKERE/PELIKAN (1986); Overlapping Generations, GRANDMONT (1985, 1986); Financial Intermediation, WOODFORD (1989); Exchange-Rate Dynamics, CHIARELLA (1992); Very Long-Run Growth, DAY/WALTERS (1989).
$n = 2$	Kaldor's Business-Cycle Model, DANA/MALGRANGE (1984), HERRMANN (1986); Hicks' Business-Cycle Model, HOMMES/NUSSE (1990); Non-Walrasian Macromodel, HOMMES (1989); Keynesian Growth Theory, JARSULIC (1991a,b); Corporate Debt, DELLI GATTI/GARDINI (1991); Dynamic Input-Output Model, FRANKE/WEGHORST (1988).

Table 2: Macroeconomic Examples of Chaotic Motion in Discrete-Time Models

practice in transforming systems with different time concepts consists in applying the following method. Consider a given continuous-time system, replace the differential operators by finite differences, and (seldomly performed, actually) adjust the dimension of the variables and the adjustment speeds in order to take the length of the assumed period into account.[6] From a formal point of view the resulting discrete-time system represents a completely different dynamical system than the original continuous-time system, and it can be suspected that the dynamic patterns generated by both systems will also be very different. Whatsoever, as the emphasis will not be put on the dynamics of the original continuous-time system, this method will nevertheless be used in the following (keeping in mind the inappropriateness of the method for transforming dynamical systems).

The business-cycle model studied by KALDOR (1940) is one of the simplest nonlinear dynamical systems in economic dynamics. It is also one of the few business-cycle models which has been under constant attack since its introduction. The investment function $I(Y, K)$ with its characteristic sigmoid shape in the (I, Y)-space (and/or the savings-function counterpart $S(Y, K)$ with a mirror-imaged shape) has been called unrealistic, it was criticized because of its lack of microfoundation, etc. All these economic objections will be ignored for the purpose of this paper, and the Kaldor model will be used in several sections because of its formal simplicity and easy handling. The results of all following sections could have been obtained with other, economically more convincing models as well. [7]

[6] Cf. GANDOLFO/MARTINENGO/PADOAN (1981) for a summary of several arguments against the superstition that the discrete nature of available data requires a discrete time concept in the modelling of an economy.

[7] Several other examples of chaotic 2D maps deal with microeconomic issues, *e.g.*, GAERTNER (1986, 1987) in models of interdependent consumer behavior or LORENZ (1992b) in a price-quantity-adjustment model.

KALDOR's original model (which he himself never studied as a formal dynamical system) can be formulated as:[8]

$$\begin{aligned}\dot{Y} &= \alpha\big(I(Y, K) - S(Y, K)\big) \\ \dot{K} &= I(Y, K) - \delta K,\end{aligned} \qquad \alpha > 0, \tag{3}$$

with Y as net income, K as the capital stock, and $\delta > 0$ as the constant depreciation rate. Substituting the differential operator by finite differences, *i.e.*, considering

$$\Delta x_{t+1} = x_{t+1} - x_t = f(x_t) \quad \text{instead of} \quad \dot{x}(t) = f\big(x(t)\big).$$

yields

$$\begin{aligned}\Delta Y_{t+1} &= \alpha\big(I(Y_t, K_t) - S(Y_t, K_t)\big) \\ \Delta K_{t+1} &= I(Y_t, K_t) - \delta K_t.\end{aligned} \tag{4}$$

System (4) has been intensively studied in the literature. For various specifications of the functional forms of $I(Y, K)$ and $S(Y, K)$ it has been demonstrated that a *ceteris paribus* increase in the adjustment coefficient α implies that a formerly stable fixed point becomes unstable and a stable closed orbit emerges. For high values of α the closed orbit can become unstable and chaotic motion cannot be excluded (cf. the simulations performed by DANA/MALGRANGE (1984)).

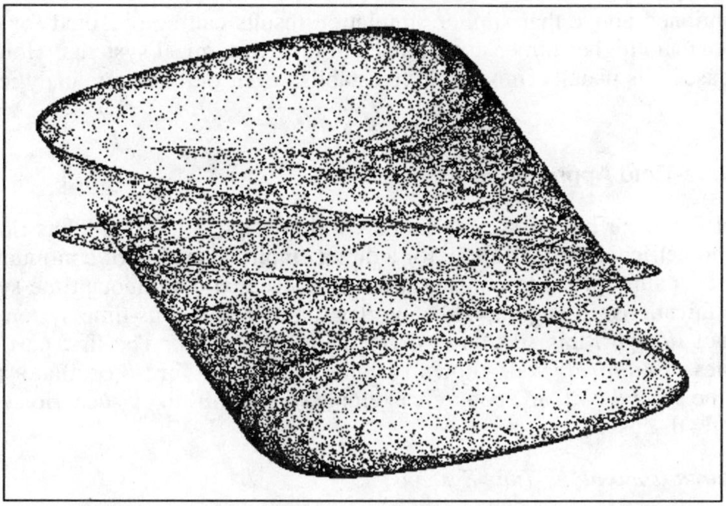

Figure 2: Chaos in a Discrete-Time Kaldor Model; $\alpha = 25.0$, $k = 2.0$, $\beta = 0.1$

The following simulation is based on a specific version of the Kaldor model studied by HERRMANN (1986). He studied the model

$$\begin{aligned}\Delta Y_{t+1} &= \alpha\big(\beta(K_t^d - K_t) + \delta K_t + C(Y_t) - Y_t\big) \\ \Delta K_{t+1} &= \beta(K_t^d - K_t)\end{aligned} \tag{5}$$

with $I(Y_t, K_t) = \beta(K_t^d - K_t) + \delta K_t$, $\beta > 0$, and $K_t^d = kY_t$, $k > 0$, *i.e.*, a gradual adjustment between the desired and actual capital stock. HERRMANN (1986) used a sigmoid consumption

[8] Cf., *e.g.*, GABISCH/LORENZ (1989), pp. 122ff., for a more detailed description.

function instead of the Kaldorian sigmoid investment function.[9] Chaotic motion can be established in this model with the help of MAROTTO's (1978) notion of a *snap-back repeller.*[10] In order to provide an idea of the complexity of the dynamic pattern in this model for high values of α, the result of a single simulation of (5) is depicted in Figure 2. The cloud of points is a *strange attractor* with a positive largest Lyapunov exponent (cf. Section 5 for details). The sensitive dependence on initial conditions is evident from Figure 3: two nearby initial points imply completely different time series after a few iterations.

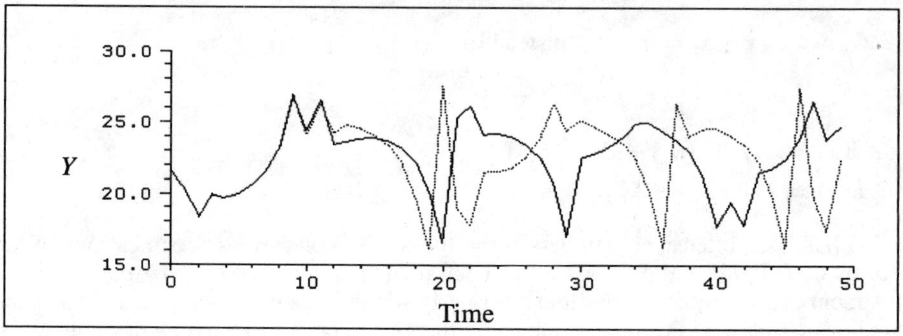

Figure 3: Two Time Series With Slightly Different Initial Values

It was mentioned above that similar simulation results can be obtained for other nonlinear, two-dimensional and higher-dimensional, discrete-time dynamical systems. However, in higher-dimensional cases it is usually impossible to establish even rudimentary analytical results.[11]

2.2. Continuous-Time Approaches

Many original nonlinear business-cycle models were designed in continuous time, and recently emerging econometric techniques allow for a direct empirical testing of continuous-time models. It therefore seems appropriate to concentrate on the original continuous-time systems and their necessary modifications. As a general categorization of continuous-time systems with complex dynamics is not in sight, this section is divided into two parts. The first part deals with economic examples of *relatively* well-known systems such as the forced oscillator and the coupled oscillator. In the second part, an economic example of the Shil'nikov scenario as a more esoteric system is briefly discussed.

Simply-Structured Continuous-Time Systems

Chaotic motion in continuous-time dynamical systems requires an at least three-dimensional state space. However, there does not exist a common structural form of all known dynamical systems with chaotic properties. In addition to the simply-structured dynamical systems to be discussed in the following, a variety of prototype equations (like the Lorenz eqs. or the diverse Rössler eqs.) exist whose potential irregular behavior cannot always be immediately suspected.[12]

---

9 The assumed consumption function is $C(Y_t) = c_0 + \frac{2}{\pi} c_1 \arctan\left(\frac{\pi c_2}{2c_1}(Y_t - Y^*)\right)$ with $c_0, c_1, c_2 > 0$ and Y^* as the equilibrium level of income.

10 Cf. LORENZ (1989) for a short description.

11 Cf. MIRA (1987) for a mathematical survey of existing analytical tools to establish chaos in 2D systems.

12 Extensive lists of established, chaotic, dynamical systems can be found in GARRIDO/SIMÓ (1983) and the multivolume book by ABRAHAM/SHAW (1983) with many graphical illustrations.

Two simple families of dynamical systems deserve particular attention because they emerge in several economic models. *Coupled oscillators* and *forced oscillators* constitute variations of the basic notion of an oscillator: a dynamical system

$$\dot{\mathbf{x}} = \mathbf{f}(\mathbf{x}, \mu), \quad \mathbf{x} \in \mathbb{R}^n, \quad n \geq 2, \quad \mu \in \mathbb{R}, \tag{6}$$

with μ as a parameter is called an oscillator if the specific form of $\mathbf{f}$ allows for endogenous fluctuations in the vector of state variables.[13] Equation (6) can be written as a second-order differential equation when $n = 2$:

$$\ddot{x} + g_1(x)\dot{x} + g_2(x) = 0, \quad x \in \mathbb{R}. \tag{7}$$

Assume that there exists a fixed point x^* with $\dot{x} = 0$ at the origin. The equation constitutes an oscillator when the expressions $g_1(x)$ and $g_2(x)$ fulfill certain requirements. For example, when $g_1(x)$ is a parabolic expression with $g_1(0) < 0$ and $g_1'(0) = 0$, and when $g_2(x)$ is an odd function with $g_2'(x) > 0 \, \forall \, x$, then every trajectory approaches a unique limit cycle.[14]

The first family of simply-structured dynamical systems in which chaotic motion can be observed is represented by *coupled oscillator systems*. Two dynamical systems (6) are coupled when the evolution of the vector of endogenous variables $\mathbf{x}_i$, $i = 1, 2$, in system i is not only determined by the magnitude of the variables in i but when it is also influenced by the motion of the variables in the second system $j \neq i$, *i.e.*,

$$\begin{aligned} \dot{\mathbf{x}}_1 &= \mathbf{f}_1(\mathbf{x}_1, \mathbf{x}_2), \quad \mathbf{x}_1 \in \mathbb{R}^n, \quad n \geq 2, \\ \dot{\mathbf{x}}_2 &= \mathbf{f}_2(\mathbf{x}_1, \mathbf{x}_2), \quad \mathbf{x}_2 \in \mathbb{R}^m, \quad m \geq 2. \end{aligned} \tag{8}$$

When at least three two-dimensional oscillators are coupled, it follows from a theorem of NEWHOUSE/RUELLE/TAKENS (1978)[15] that the motion can be chaotic.

Equation (7) can be interpreted as a special form of the more general non-autonomous equation

$$\ddot{x} + g_1(x)\dot{x} + g_2(x) = h(t), \quad x \in \mathbb{R}, \quad t \in \mathbb{R}, \tag{9}$$

where $h(t)$ is a function of time. When $h(t)$ is periodic, equation (9) is called a *forced oscillator*. When the (exogenous) forcing is strong as compared with the amplitude of the endogenous variable x, the dynamic behavior of (9) can be chaotic.[16]

The emergence of both families of dynamical systems in economics will be illustrated with the help of an extremely simple example from international trade theory.[17] Assume that the dynamic behavior of n economies is precisely described by the set of two-dimensional differential equation systems:

$$\begin{aligned} \dot{Y}_i &= \alpha_i\big(I_i(Y_i, K_i) - S_i(Y_i) + EX_i(Y_j) - IM_i(Y_i)\big) \\ \dot{K}_i &= I_i(Y_i, K_i) - \delta_i K_i \end{aligned} \qquad i = 1, \ldots, n \quad i \neq j, \tag{10}$$

[13] The Poincaré-Bendixson theorem or the Hopf bifurcation theorem can be appropriate tools for establishing the emergence of endogenous fluctuations in these systems. Cf. LORENZ (1989) for a survey.

[14] Cf. LEVINSON/SMITH (1942) or GALEOTTI/GORI (1990) for details.

[15] Cf. LORENZ (1989), pp. 147f.

[16] Cf. GUCKENHEIMER/HOLMES (1983), pp. 67ff. for details.

[17] Cf. PUU (1987) for a similar example. Other examples can easily be constructed, cf. LORENZ (1987b) for a model of a multisector economy. The pioneering paper is GOODWIN (1947) who investigated spill-over effects between markets.

with the usual meaning of the symbols. Consider first the autarkic case without any international trade activities, *i.e.*, $EX_i(\cdot) = IM_i(\cdot) = 0 \, \forall \, i$. Assume that all n autarkic economies are endogenously oscillating due to nonlinearities in the investment functions $I_i(\cdot)$ and/or the savings functions $S_i(\cdot)$. The entire dynamical system consisting of n economies represents a system of n uncoupled two-dimensional oscillators. The introduction of international trade in the way of equations (10) represents a dynamic coupling of the n economies. When $n \geq 3$, international trade can result in chaotic motion of $(Y_i, K_i) \, \forall \, i$.

The international trade example can also be used as a demonstration of the emergence of a forced oscillator.[18] Let $n = 2$ in (10) and assume that the trade flow is unidirectional in the sense that country 1 is exporting goods to country 2 but does not import goods from that country. In that case, the entire dynamical system consists of the four equations

$$\begin{aligned} \dot{Y}_1 &= \alpha_1\big(I_1(Y_1, K_1) - S_1(Y_1) + EX_1(Y_2)\big) \\ \dot{K}_1 &= I_1(Y_1, K_1) - \delta_1 K_1 \\ \dot{Y}_2 &= \alpha_2\big(I_2(Y_2, K_2) - S_2(Y_2) - IM_2(Y_2)\big) \\ \dot{K}_2 &= I_2(Y_2, K_2) - \delta_2 K_2, \end{aligned} \tag{11}$$

i.e., the change in the variables Y_2 and K_2 in country 2 depends only on internal variables.

It may be possible to solve the differential equation system of country 2 explicitly. Suppose that such a solution is available, *i.e.*,

$$\begin{aligned} Y_2(t) &= Y\big(Y_2(0), K_2(0), t\big) \\ K_2(t) &= K\big(Y_2(0), K_2(0), t\big), \end{aligned} \tag{12}$$

and that $Y_2(t)$ and $K_2(t)$ are both oscillating with a constant amplitude.[19]

With an oscillating income in country 2, the export of country 1 will be oscillating as well. The motion of Y_1 and K_1 in country 1 is described by

$$\begin{aligned} \dot{Y}_1 &= \alpha_1\big[I_1(Y_1, K_1) - S_1(Y_1) + EX_1\big(Y_2(t)\big)\big] \\ \dot{K}_1 &= I_1(Y_1, K_1) - \delta_1 K_1 \end{aligned} \tag{13}$$

or, written as a second-order differential equation,

$$\ddot{Y}_1 + f(Y_1)\dot{Y}_1 + g(Y_1) = \alpha_1 EX_1\big(Y_2(t)\big) = h(t). \tag{14}$$

Depending on the structural forms of the terms $f(Y_1)$ and $g(Y_1)$ and the magnitude of the forcing term, equation (14) may constitute a forced oscillator such that chaotic motion prevails in the first country.

Other economic examples of strongly forced oscillators can be found in a variety of business cycle models like a version of GOODWIN's (1951) nonlinear accelerator model (HAXHOLDT ET AL. (1991), LORENZ (1987d)), models of long waves (BRØNS/STURIS (1991), LARSEN ET AL. (1988)), system dynamics approaches to macroeconomics (MOSEKILDE ET AL. (1992)), and a Keynesian stabilization model (LORENZ (1989)). One of the first investigations of exogenous, periodic forcing can be found in GOODWIN (1946) in a study of Schumpeterian innovation swarms. All these

[18] The following example is inspired by PUU (1987).

[19] Note that this is a strong assumption. A dynamical system can be solved only in very particular cases, *e.g.*, when only linearities are involved. In addition, a specific parameter constellation is required for permanent oscillations in the linear case.

Dimension	Economic Application
$n \leq 2$	Impossible
$n = 3$	International Trade, PUU (1987); Urban Economics, DENDRINOS (1985); Business-Cycle Theory, HAXHOLDT ET AL. (1991), LORENZ (1987c,d), MOSEKILDE ET AL. (1992).
$n > 3$	Long Waves, LARSEN ET AL. (1988), RASMUSSEN ET AL. (1985), BRØNS/STURIS (1991); Multi-Sector Models, LORENZ (1987b); International Trade, PUU (1987), LORENZ (1987a).

Table 3: Economic Examples of Chaotic Motion in Continuous Time

models are characterized by the assumption that exogenous influences which are usually considered constant are themselves periodic.

The above mentioned dynamical systems, for which economic examples exist, are summarized in Table 3. These systems constitute only a part of the spectrum of dynamical systems with chaotic properties. The majority of those systems which have intensively been investigated in the mathematical literature do not seem to possess much relevance to economics. It is, for example, possible to construct examples of the emergence of the well-known Lorenz attractor in models of urban evolution (*e.g.*, DENDRINOS (1985)), but the models are highly structurally unstable and the results depend crucially on the numerical specification of the models. A family of dynamical systems that allow for a broader spectrum of possible applications will be outlined in the following section together with an economic example from standard business-cycle theory.

The Shil'nikov scenario and spiral-type chaotic attractors

It has been observed that almost all chaotic dynamical systems in higher-dimensional state spaces possess so-called *homoclinic orbits*. A homoclinic orbit or a *saddle loop* is a trajectory that leaves a saddle point on the unstable manifold and returns to it on the stable manifold. One of the few theorems that refer to the existence of such homoclinic orbits in establishing chaotic motion is due to SHIL'NIKOV (1965).[20] The Shil'nikov theorem deals with a specific homoclinic orbit which is depicted in Figure 4. The homoclinic orbit approaches the fixed point in a spiraling fashion on the stable manifold.

It is difficult to apply the Shil'nikov theorem directly to a specific dynamical system[21] but it was demonstrated by ARNEODO/COULLET/TRESSER (1981, 1982) that the third-order differential equation

$$\dddot{x} + a\ddot{x} + \dot{x} = f_\mu(x), \qquad a > 0, \tag{15}$$

---

[20] Compare, *e.g.*, GUCKENHEIMER/HOLMES (1983) for a discussion of a particular version of the theorem that makes use of the notion of SMALE's (1967) horseshoes (cf. GRANDMONT (1988) for the construction of these maps).

[21] The main difficulty consists in proofing the existence of a homoclinic orbit. Cf. BEYN (1990) for an algorithm.

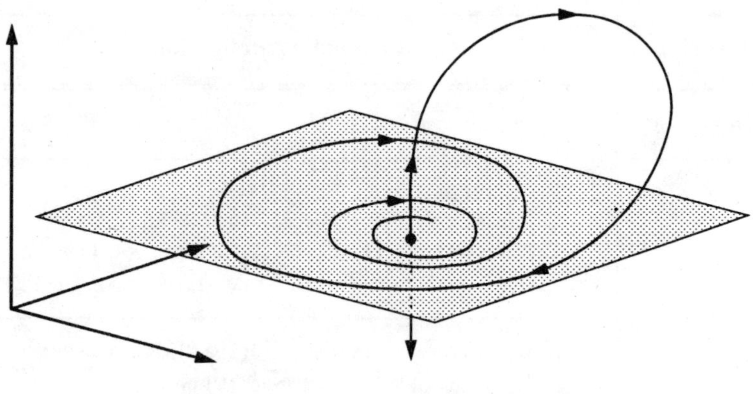

Figure 4: A Shil'nikov-Type Homoclinic Orbit

is compatible with the Shil'nikov theorem for several members of the one-parameter family of functions $f_\mu(x)$, including

$$f_\mu(x) = \begin{cases} 1 + bx & \text{if} \quad x < 0 \\ 1 - \mu x & \text{if} \quad x \geq 0, \end{cases} \qquad \text{and} \qquad f_\mu = \mu x(1 - x),$$

i.e., a linear tent function, and the logistic function, respectively, for appropriate values of the parameter μ. The essential property of the function $f_\mu(x)$ is that an interval $J \subset \mathbb{R}$ is mapped to itself and that the function is unimodal. In contrast to unimodal chaotic maps in one-dimensional, discrete-time systems, rather flat shapes of the function are sufficient to encounter chaotic motion in (15) in many cases.

As a simple pedagogical economic example of the emergence of equation (15) a continuous-time version of METZLER's (1941) business-cycle model with inventories will be considered in the following.[22]

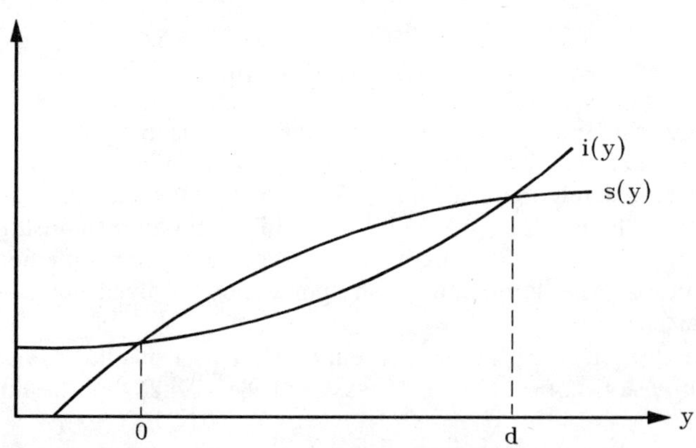

Figure 5: Savings and Investment in a Modified Metzler Model

[22] A more detailed discussion of the following model can be found in LORENZ (1992a) and MEDIO (1991b). The original Metzler model is formulated in discrete time. The continuous-time version is due to GANDOLFO (1983) and is better suited for modelling stocks and flows. Another economic example of the Shil'nikov scenario can be found in LORENZ (1992a) in a reconsideration of PHILLIPS' (1954) multiplier-accelerator model.

The Metzler model describes the changes in the output of a firm as a function of the difference between desired and actual inventory stocks. The actual stock changes when demand is greater or smaller than supply in the market. The desired inventory stock depends linearly on expected output. Expected output is determined according to a modified extrapolative expectation hypothesis: Expected output does not only depend on the rate of change of current output but also on the *changes* in this rate. The model can be reduced to the third-order differential equation

$$\dddot{Y} + A_1\ddot{Y} + A_2\dot{Y} = A_3\big(S(Y) - I(Y)\big) \tag{16}$$

with A_1, A_2, and A_3 constant. In terms of deviations from the stationary equilibrium, (16) can be written as

$$\dddot{y} + A_1\ddot{y} + A_2\dot{y} = A_3\big(s(y) - i(y)\big). \tag{17}$$

GANDOLFO (1983) demonstrated that (17) is globally unstable when savings $s(y)$ is a linear function of output, when investment $i(y)$ is constant, and when $A_1 < 0$, $A_2 > 0$, and $A_3 > 0$. Suppose on the contrary that $s(y)$ and $i(y)$ are nonlinear but monotonic functions of output, and assume that the difference $s(y) - i(y)$ is a unimodal function of y with a critical value $y_c > 0$ (cf. Figure 5). The steepness of the the expression on the r.h.s. of (17) can be controlled by the parameter A_3. When $A_1 > 0$ and A_2 close to 1, equation (17) is qualitatively identical with equation (15) with a logistic form of $f_\mu(\cdot)$. Figure 6 shows a plot of a numerically calculated trajectory of (17).[23] The largest Lyapunov exponent for the chosen parameter constellation is slightly positive, the sum of all exponents is negative. The set of points in the figure is therefore characterized by a sensitive dependence on initial conditions.

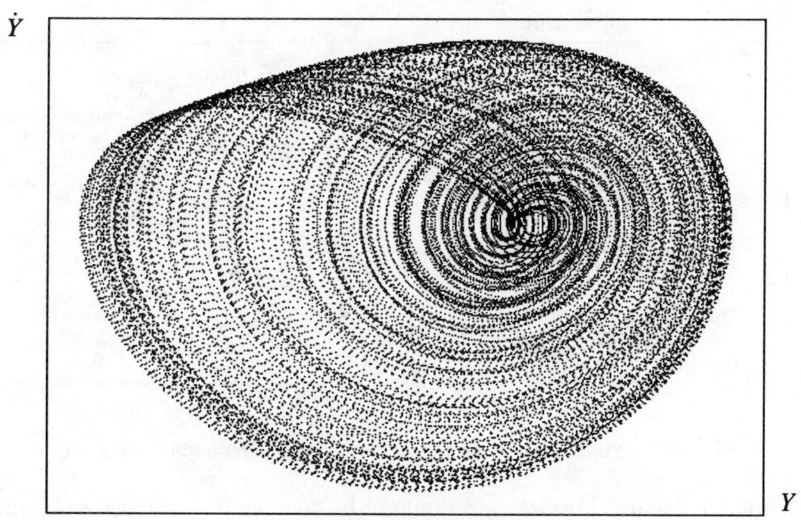

Figure 6: The Spiral-Type Attractor of (17); Y versus $\dot{Y}$

The example presented above is not very robust with respect to structural changes. In fact, when the hypothesis of extrapolative expectations is modified by assuming higher-order time derivatives of actual output in the determination of expectations it cannot be guaranteed anymore that the dynamic behavior is still characterized by objects like the one in Figure 6. However, small variations in the parameters or replacing the constant coefficients by slightly nonlinear functions do not immediately destroy the chaotic behavior in these systems.

[23] The simulated equation is $\dddot{Y} + 0.4\ddot{Y} + 0.95\dot{Y} = 0.6Y(1.3 - Y)$

It is unclear whether the object in Figure 6 represents a strange attractor or just a complicated and long-lasting transient motion. The mathematical background of the Shil'nikov scenario involves horseshoe maps which have been used by SMALE (1967) for demonstrating the emergence of Cantor sets. Trajectories starting in the vicinity of such a set display a complicated motion for a while and eventually converge toward a regular attractor. Whatsoever, for practical purposes, the possibly long-lasting transient motion is qualitatively identical with a true chaotic motion on a strange attractor (cf. Section 4 for a longer discussion).

3. Predictability in the Face of Complex Motion – Order in Chaos

At first glance, the presence of deterministic chaos seems to imply rather destructive effects on the predictability of an actual time series or the trajectories in a theoretical economic model: if a model has sensitive dependence on initial conditions, arbitrarily (but finitely) precise digital computers are conceptually unable to calculate the future evolution of the system. When prediction is impossible, economics looses a major justification for its mere existence.

Statements like the one above contrast chaotic dynamical systems with models constructed in the classic deterministic tradition. Compared with the regular behavior in linear or many nonlinear dynamical systems, chaotic systems display a wild and irregular behavior, a superficial inspection of which suggests that it does not seem to possess structure at all. When standard prediction techniques are applied to purely deterministic approaches, it is easy to claim a general failure of forecasting procedures in the face of chaotic systems.

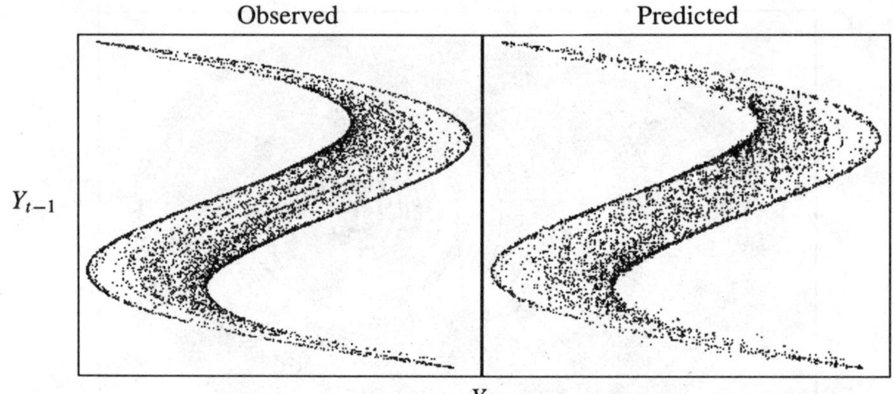

Figure 7: Actual and Predicted Phase Spaces, Prediction: 1 Period

However, chaotic dynamical systems should not be compared with regular deterministic systems but with purely random systems or deterministic linear systems on which stochastic influences are superimposed. The foregoing presentation of theoretical results on chaotic dynamics has shown that the presence of structure is the essential property of chaotic dynamical systems as compared with random series (see also Section 5). If structure prevails, it is possible (at least to some degree) to predict the evolution of the system. If a system is purely deterministic and chaotic, trajectories in a higher-dimensional system diverge exponentially (cf. the two time series in Fig. 1), but for sufficiently small time horizons it is possible to predict the system's evolution with an acceptable preciseness. FARMER /SIDOROWICH (1987) proposed local prediction techniques for chaotic time series which seem to be promising for short-term economic forecasting. The approach relies on the reconstruction of an attractor from a time series with the

Takens method[24] and the search for the nearest neighbor of a given point on the attractor. The simplest method for predicting the next realized value consists in assigning this neighbor to the predicted value. Applications of this technique to different prototype equations show surprisingly low prediction errors for short prediction intervals.

Figure 7 shows the results of applying the nearest-neighbor technique to the data obtained from simulating the two-dimensional, discrete-time Kaldor model of Section 2.1. The figure contains the phase spaces Y_t vs. Y_{t-1} and Y_t^P vs. Y_{t-1}^P of the original system and the predicted evolution. The two phase spaces were obtained in the following way.[25] The time evolution of Y and K in the discrete-time Kaldor model was calculated in the standard fashion for $n = 10000$ iterations. A transient motion of 1000 iteration has been excluded from the consideration. The sequence $\{(Y_t, K_t)\}_{t=1}^{t_{\max}}$ represents the true motion of the system. Suppose that the observer considers only income as the relevant variable. The observer's (predictor's) task consists in deriving information on income's future evolution from an available data set. Assume that the predictor has access to n_0 past values of income. The number n_0 of past values is called the number of *atlas points*. For the purpose of demonstrating the potential power of the prediction technique the economically rather unrealistic number of 2000 initial atlas points has been assumed. When the observer predicts the time evolution of income based on the available information, the true system continues to evolve according to the underlying deterministic laws of motion. In the phase space in the left part of Figure 7 the pairs (Y_t, Y_{t-1}) are shown for the iterations $t = 2001$ to $t = 10000$.

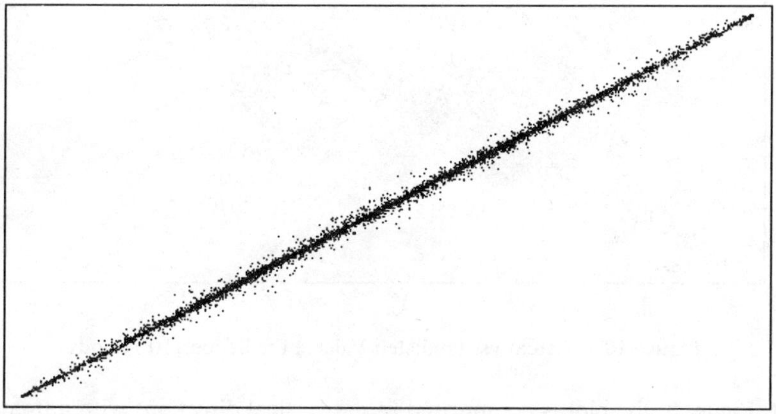

Figure 8: Actual vs. Predicted Values, Prediction: 1 Period

At $t_0 = 2000$, the observer analyses the available data with the nearest-neighbor technique. Suppose he attempts predictions only for one iteration (time step), *i.e.*, he calculates $Y_{t_0+1}^P$. At the end of $t_0 + 1$, it will be obvious whether he was wrong or right. At least, he will know another actual (true) value of income, namely Y_{t_0+1}. Based on the knowledge of $n_0 + 1$ true values of income, he will predict the next income value etc. The phase space in the right part of Figure 7 shows the lagged pairs (Y_t^P, Y_{t-1}^P) of predicted values. Aside from a neglectable fuzziness, the two objects in the phase spaces are astonishingly similar. Indeed, a statistical regression of the actual versus the predicted time series uncovers a nearly one-to-one relation between the

[24] Cf. Takens (1980) and Section 5 below. For illustrations, compare Bergé et al. (1986) or Lorenz (1989).

[25] The calculations were performed with the NLF program of Dynamical Software.

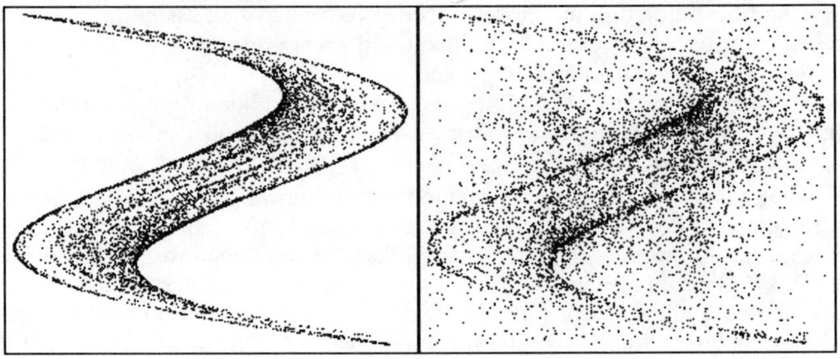

Figure 9: Actual and Predicted Phase Spaces, Prediction: 10 Periods

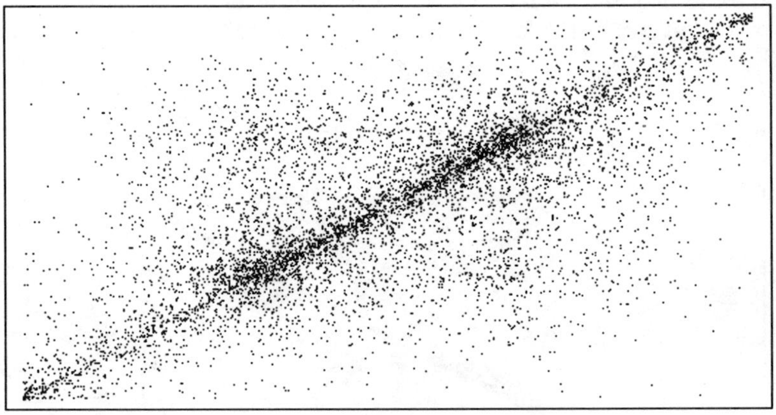

Figure 10: Actual vs. Predicted Values, Prediction: 10 Periods

variables (cf. Figure 8, the plot is compressed in the vertical direction) with a tremendous $r^2 = 0.9984$.

Trajectories starting at nearby points stay together for some time even in systems with chaotic dynamics. Thus, the coincidence of actual and predicted values in Figures 7 and 8 is not really surprising. The more relevant question concerns the longer-run predictability of chaotic systems. For this purpose the nearest-neighbor technique has been applied to the above income time-series with longer prediction intervals. The phase spaces in Figure 9 show the evolution of the true values of income (left part) and the lagged pairs (Y_t^P, Y_{t-1}^P) of the evolution of the series of predicted values Y_{t+10}^P predicted in t (right part). While the structure of the phase space of the true system can still be recognized in the right part, the fuzziness has considerably grown. In fact, the regression in Figure 10 yields an r^2 of only 0.44 which is obviously not suited to support the hypothesis of a strong correlation between the observed and predicted values. When even longer prediction intervals are assumed, the correlation between the actual and observed values becomes negligible.

Although research in predicting chaotic time series is still in its infancy, the following conclusion can already be drawn: if a time series is chaotic it may be possible to predict the short-run evolution with a sufficient accuracy. The presence of deterministic chaos encourages short-term predictions; the desperate view that complex motion does not permit predictions is inappropriate.

The possibility of predicting a chaotic time series does not mean that standard econometric procedures constitute worse forecasting techniques *per se*. In addition to the fact that linear or completely random systems can best be treated with these techniques, it may even be possible to approximate the short-term evolution of a chaotic time series fairly well. However, when chaos prevails, the development of forecasting techniques which explicitly take the uncovered structure into account is desirable.

4. The Long-Run and the Short-Run – The Importance of Transients

The complicated objects in Figure 2 and 6 have nice geometric shapes which become apparent when the underlying dynamical systems are iterated several ten-thousand times. As the systems represent economic models, the question naturally arises whether such a large number of iterations still makes sense. Economic "laws of motions" do not belong to the class of eternal laws known from the physical sciences. The structure of economies is more or less permanently changing, and it can be expected that (even if the functional form of the dynamical system is constant) parameters change in the course of this structural change. As chaos often becomes (geometrically and statistically) visible only after a considerable time span, it may be argued that chaotic dynamics bear no relevance at all for economic dynamics.

Astonishingly, a particular property of nonlinear dynamical systems (which has been known in the dynamical systems literature for a rather long time) has not been widely used in economic dynamics. The transient behavior of a dynamical system in its initial phase can be as complicated as the motion on a strange attractor itself. Furthermore, transients can be complicated even when the attractor of a given system is regular, *e.g.*, when it displays periodic behavior.

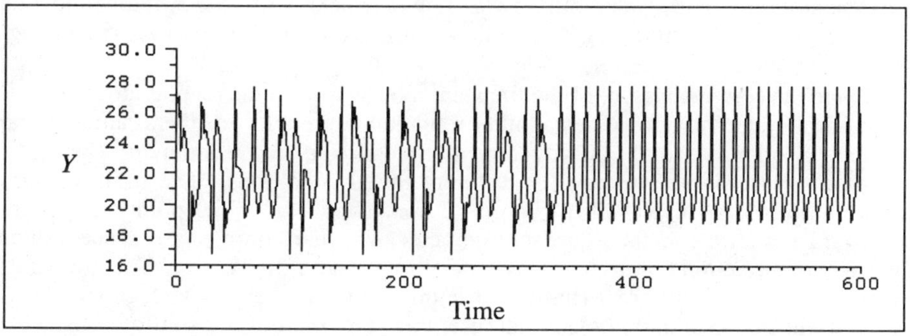

Figure 11: The Transient Motion in a Kaldorian Model; $\alpha = 21.0$

Complicated transient behavior can be shown to exist in the popular logistic map and other higher-dimensional dynamical systems. In the following, the Kaldor model, used above in different contexts, will again serve as a didactical example.

The attractor in Figure 2 was generated for a relatively high value of the adjustment coefficient $\alpha = 25.$ and 50000 time periods. Figure 11 shows the time series of Y generated by (5) with a smaller value of α. For this value, no strange attractor could have been detected. Figure 11 shows only the first 600 iterations. During the first 350 periods the motion is apparently irregular; after this transient phase the trajectory jumps to a regular periodic motion (it is actually converging to a periodic orbit in a smooth manner, reaching the orbit after approximately 2500 periods).

Figure 12 shows the (Y, K) space with the trajectory generated by (5) for the first 5000 iterates. The shape of the object in Figure 12 resembles the boundary of the chaotic attractor in

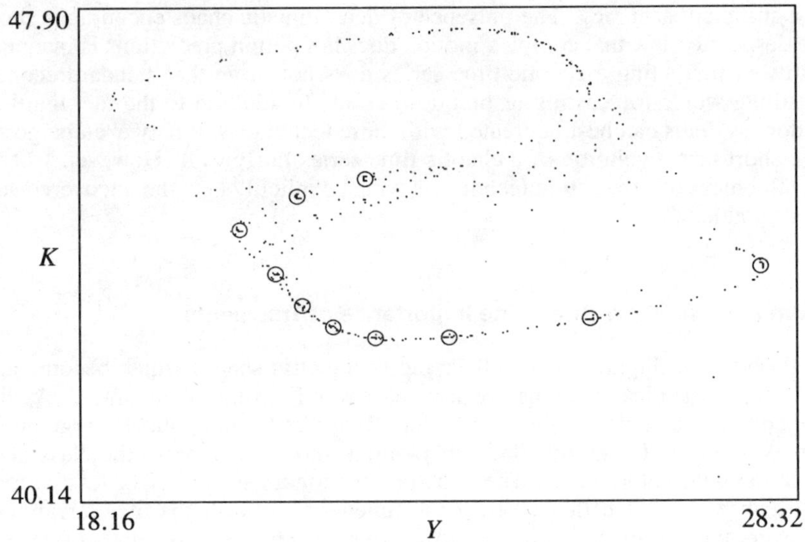

Figure 12: Motion in a Kaldorian Model, $\alpha = 21.0$; T=1-5000. The circles indicate the location of the pieces of a period-80 attractor.

Figure 2 but most points in the phase space represent points on the transient. The circles in Figure 12 enclose the points on the attractor of (5) for the assumed value of α. The attractor is a period-80 orbit, geometrically organized in 10 groups, each of which includes 8 points. The largest Lyapunov exponent of the attractor in Figure 12 is strictly negative ($T > 2500$). When only the transient motion is considered the Lyapunov exponent is $\lambda^L = 0.5$, indicating a chaotic motion. The exponent is getting negative only when more than 2000 periods (including transients) are considered.

In addition to the complex nature of the transient motion toward the regular attractor in Figure 12, the dynamical system (5) possesses another remarkable property for the assumed parameter values which is also known from other dynamical systems like the Henon map. The system (5) possesses more than a single attractor for different initial conditions. The basin of attraction $B(A_1)$ of the attractor A_1 displayed in Figure 12, *i.e.,* the set of initial points that eventually converge toward the attractor, thus does not coincide with the entire phase space. Figure 13 shows the basin of attraction (white region) of the attractor described above. The grey and black regions represent basins of different (finite and infinite) attractors A_n, $n \geq 2$, of (5). The basin $B(A_1)$ is a complicated geometric object that resembles the basin of the well-established Henon map. The outer parts of the basin with the thin, discontinuous strips suggest a fractal nature of the basin boundary.

The simulation results of this Kaldorian model (5) allow to draw the following conclusions:

- For parameter values lower than the critical value for which a strange attractor emerges the model can possess n-period orbits organized in disconnected groups of periodic points. The basin of attraction is a complicated object in phase space. The study of initial points located in particular parts of the basin boundary requires a precise knowledge of the numerical starting values.
- The iterates of an initial point located in the basin of attraction of a particular attractor can be characterized as a long and complicated transient motion, a collapse of the complicated transient, and a final smooth convergence toward an n-period orbit. The complicated transient is characterized as chaotic in the sense of a positive largest Lyapunov exponent.

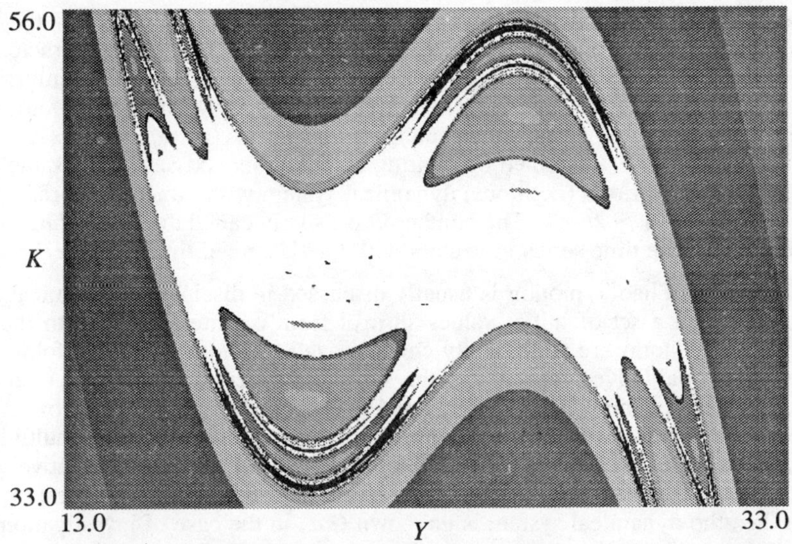

Figure 13: The basin of attraction of the attractor in Figure 12 (white regions). Grey-shaded areas represent basins of attraction of different (finite and/or infinite) attractors with different divergence speeds. The attractor itself is contained in the white area and shown by the 10 black spots.

Similar results on the nature of the basin of attraction can be found in simulations of different, two-dimensional, discrete-time dynamical systems in economic dynamics. For example, a partial model of the simultaneous adjustment of prices and quantities in a single market[26] yields basins of attraction for n-piece attractors which possess a form very similar to the basin in Figure 13.

5. Empirical Evidence – Are Economic Time Series Chaotic?

Chaotic motion and complex transients have been discussed in the framework of economic *models* in the preceding sections. A model is usually understood as an abstract, reduced-form picture of reality, and it is trivial to say that we do not know whether these models represent satisfactory approaches to real phenomena. It follows that the entire discussion of chaotic dynamics in economics would be meaningless if

- the models turn out to be inappropriate descriptions of real life (particularly when human behavior cannot be described by deterministic laws of motion), or if
- actual time series do not posses the chaos property.

The first item tackles basic problems of scientific modelling, and cannot be discussed further at this place. The second item, however, has an immediate consequence. When it turns out that chaotic motion cannot be observed in actual time series the investigation of complex motion in theoretic models is at least questionable.[27] Thus, statistical investigations of actual time series for the presence of nonlinearities and chaotic motion are desirable.

Three statistical measures are suited to provide evidence of particular aspects of nonlinearities and complex dynamic behavior. All of these measures rely on the existence of an attractor

[26] Cf. Lorenz (1992b) for a description of the model.

[27] The mere fact that chaotic models generate *irregular* time series cannot serve as the only justification for a concentration on these systems.

and thus on the existence of a generating dynamical system. As we do not know the underlying dynamical system, its fictitious existence must be assumed. However, the attractor, *i.e.*, an n-dimensional object (with n probably large), is not available when a typically univariate time series should be investigated. Fortunately, TAKENS (1980) has shown that the re-arrangement of a univariate time series $\{x_t\}_1^T$ in m-dimensional vectors $\mathbf{x}_j = (x_j, x_{j-1}, \ldots, x_{j-m+1})$, $j = m, \ldots, T$ implies that the object obtained by plotting all vectors $\mathbf{x}_j$ possesses the same topological properties as the attractor of a (fictitious) dynamical system with dimension n that generates the time series $\{x_t\}_1^T$ when $m \geq 2n+1$. The number m is usually called the *embedding dimension* of embedding the univariate time series in vectors with the described time-delay technique.

- *Lyapunov exponents*. Chaotic motion is usually discussed in dissipative dynamical systems, *i.e.*, systems in which a set of initial values shrinks from one iteration step to the other.[28] Chaotic dynamical systems are additionally characterized by a stretching and folding of this shrinking set. The qualitative properties of the shrinking process can be expressed with the help of Lyapunov exponents. An n-dimensional system possesses n Lyapunov exponents. The exponents are calculated from the eigenvalues of a matrix obtained by multiplying the Jacobian matrices evaluated along a system's trajectory. The system is dissipative when the sum of all exponents is negative; the system can be called chaotic when the largest exponent is positive.[29] When the dynamical system is unknown (*i.e.*, in the case of investigations of empirical time series), only the largest exponent is usually calculated via particular algorithms.
- *Fractal dimensions*. Most chaotic dynamical systems possess complicated geometric forms of its attractors. The Hausdorff dimension (calculated by counting the number of squares, cubes, etc. with side length ε necessary to cover a geometric object) is identical with the common Euclidian dimension in the case of regular geometric objects but yields a non-integer (fractal) value in most chaotic systems. The upper value of the Hausdorff dimension is bounded by the dimension of the system itself; most prototype systems have fractal dimensions in the range $(n-1, n)$ with n as the number of state variables. Practical calculations of fractal dimensions make use of approximations via the correlation integral, *i.e.*, a measure obtained by counting the number of neighboring points of all points on the trajectory on a re-constructed attractor. The fractal dimension should converge to a finite, typically low value when the embedding in the reconstruction process of the attractor is increased.
- *Entropies*. In non-chaotic, dissipative systems two nearby points in a particular basin of attraction approach even further under the action of the system. It follows that it may be impossible to determine from which initial value a point very close to the attractor originated. Chaotic dynamical systems are, however, characterized by the stretching and folding of the shrinking set mentioned above. Thus, two nearby points eventually diverge, and it is possible to identify two trajectories as originating in two different initial points. In this sense, a chaotic dynamical system produces information (about the initial points); the particular measure of this information gain is therefore called the (Kolmogorov) entropy and defined in probabilistic terms. Practical applications of this concept employ approximations based on the notion of the correlation integral mentioned above. A time series can be called chaotic when the entropy converges to a positive, finite value for increasing values of the embedding dimension in the reconstruction process of the attractor.

Technically, all three measures are defined for infinitely large data sets. In practical applications of the measures, "infinity" is often identified with a "large" number of entries in the time series. Thus, when the statistical tools described above are applied to economic time series, a serious problem arises. In contrast to signal measurement in laboratory experiments where several tens

---

[28] For example, in systems with stable fixed points the set of initial points in a neighborhood of a fixed point shrinks to that point.

[29] There is some room for an interpretation whether a calculated exponent is significantly different from zero. Most prototype chaotic systems display positive exponents between 0.5 and 3.0.

of thousands of data points can easily be obtained in a reasonable time span in many cases, the shortest time unit of measurement in economics is usually a single day. Remembering that the majority of economic time series consists of annual, quarterly, or monthly data (with some weekly or daily data in well-organized surroundings like financial markets) and that the history of reliable empirical research encompasses a period of at best 80-100 years, the length of a standard time series is shorter than the maximal value of approximately 10,000 observations, and will typically consist of a few hundred (or less) data points. The reliability of the calculated indices is therefore obviously limited.

Subjects	**Authors**
Social Products	BROCK (1986), BROCK/SAYERS (1988), FRANK/STENGOS (1988a, 1988c), SCHEINKMAN/LEBARON (1989)
Unemployment	Frank/Sayers/Stengos (1989), SAYERS (1988a, 1988b)
Gold/Silver-Returns	FRANK/STENGOS (1987)
Stock-Market Returns	SCHEINKMAN/LEBARON (1988) PETERS (1991)
Exchange-Rate Dynamics	HSIEH (1989), BAJO-RUBIO ET AL. (1992)
Monetary Aggregates	BARNETT/CHEN (1988a, 1988b), BARNETT/CHOI (1989), RAMSEY/SAYERS/ROTHMAN (1988)
Price-Quantity-Adjustments (Industrial Data)	SCHMIDT/STAHLECKER (1989)
Experimental Behavior	STERMAN (1988), STERMAN/MOSEKILDE/LARSEN (1988)

Table 4: A Sample of Empirical Investigations of Chaotic Time Series

In the face of this ambiguity additional tests are desirable. BROCK's (1986) *residual diagnostic* represents an attempt to support or to reject the results of the standard procedures. BROCK has shown that the correlation dimension and the largest Lyapunov exponent of a chaotic time series and of the residuals of a linear fitting of that series should coincide. Another additional procedure was proposed by SCHEINKMAN/LEBARON (1989) in the form of the *shuffle diagnostics.* In contrast to a stochastic process, the (re)-constructed attractor of a nonlinear dynamical system via m-histories of observed values possesses a geometrically ordered form if the motion is regular or chaotic. Suppose now that the same data points are observed, but that the time indexes are changed. This leads to different m-histories and therefore a different form of the attractor in phase space. If the interchange of the time indexes is arbitrary, it can be expected that the attractor will no longer display an ordered form, and, consequently, the correlation dimension will increase. This shuffling of the data can thus be used as a test for deterministic nonlinear dynamics versus stochastic processes: after shuffling the data, a nonlinear system will have a (probably substantially) higher correlation dimension, while a stochastic process will almost always imply the same high dimension before and after the shuffling.[30]

The numerical tools presented above have been applied to a variety of economic data. Table 4 lists a few examples of this ongoing empirical work. More extensive surveys can be found in FRANK/STENGOS (1988b), BROCK (1987b) and BROCK/HSIEH/LEBARON (1991). An example of the direct application of correlation dimensions and Lyapunov exponents to macroeconomic data with a small sample size is reported in BROCK (1986) in a test for deterministic chaos in detrended quarterly US real GNP data from 1947-1985. The correlation dimension is calculated as $D^C \approx 3.0$ to 4.0 for an embedding dimension of $m = 20$, and the largest Lyapunov exponent is slightly larger than zero. With some precaution it could therefore be concluded that chaotic motion in the GNP data cannot be excluded. The residual test has been applied to the same detrended U.S. GNP data. An autoregressive AR(2) model fits the data very well, and BROCK's residual test implies that, *e.g.*, the correlation dimension of the residuals $\{u_t\}$ must equal the formerly calculated value for $\{x_t\}$. However, the dimension nearly doubles for alternate values of the length of the involved ε-cubes. It follows that the presence of chaos in the US GNP data should be excluded.

While BROCK's results on GNP data already suggest to reject the hypothesis of chaotic dynamics for US data, FRANK/STENGOS' investigations of Canadian (FRANK/STENGOS (1988a)) and international (FRANK/GENCAY/STENGOS (1988)) GNP data support the above findings. For detrended Canadian data the authors calculate a correlation dimension of ≈ 2.4 to 4.0 for varying embedding dimensions up to $m = 20$. However, the residual test nearly doubles the dimension. Shuffling does not lead to higher dimensions, as would be the case in the presence of chaos. Instead, the dimensions of the shuffled residuals even decrease. The average dimension of German, Italian, and U.K. data is between 6.0 and 7.0; and the residuals do not possess significantly higher dimensions. However, shuffling the residuals alters the dimensions only slightly. Japanese data have a lower dimension, which is tripled by shuffling. In all countries, the largest Lyapunov exponents are slightly negative. Summarizing, international GNP data do not seem to be chaotic, though there is evidence of low-dimensional nonlinearities. SAYERS (1988a,b) studied possible nonlinearities in the unemployment rates indirectly via man-days idle to work-stoppages. Calculations of the correlation dimension and the Lyapunov exponents and application of the residual diagnostics to the detrended data suggested to deny the presence of deterministic chaos but it seemed as if nonlinear structure prevails in the series.

One of the very few studies that unambiguously established low-order deterministic chaos in an economic time series is due to BARNETT/CHEN (1988a) (cf. also BARNETT/CHOI (1988). The authors examined several monetary aggregates with sample sizes of > 800 observations for the presence of chaos. For example, the correlation dimensions of the Divisa analogs of the monetary aggregates M2 and M3 lie between 1.0 and 2.0 for embedding dimensions up to $m = 6$. The largest Lyapunov exponents are reported to be slightly positive. Other indices like a simple sum index of M2 or supply-side analogs of the Divisa-M2 index display more noise. No evidence for low-dimensional chaos can be found in the simple sum and Divisa aggregates of M1. An alternative result was reported by RAMSEY/SAYERS/ROTHMAN (1988) who demonstrated that the same original data set used by BARNETT/CHEN (1988a) does not show evidence of chaos when the data is transformed to a stationary time series.

It might be argued that one reason for the relatively weak results reported in the previous studies consists in the small data sets. Much larger data sets are available for financial data. At first glimpse, financial data like foreign exchange rates, stock exchange rates, etc. indeed appear to be potentially good candidates for chaotic time series. SCHEINKMAN/LEBARON (1988) studied time series based on a set of more than 5000 daily stock return rates. The correlation dimension

[30] Cf. BROCK/DECHERT/SCHEINKMAN (1987) and SCHEINKMAN/LEBARON (1988) for additional procedures.

was found to be $\approx$ 5.0 to 6.0 for $m = 14$. The dimension of the residuals are reported to be the same as those of the original series. Shuffling the data significantly increases the dimension, implying that chaos should not be rejected. FRANK/STENGOS (1987) studied gold and silver rates of return based on London daily prices. The correlation dimension of the daily data lies between 6.0 and 7.0 for $m = 25$. Shuffling yields higher dimensions for all series. The K_2 entropies of the series are in the range of $0.15 < K_2 < 0.24$, and thus indicate the presence of deterministic chaos. Recent papers by HSIEH (1989) and BAJO-RUBIO ET AL. (1992) also indicate the possible presence of chaos in exchange-rate time series.

Summarizing this recent empirical work on deterministic chaos in economic time series, the following conclusions can be drawn:

- Actual economic time series differ from their analogs in the natural sciences almost always with respect to the relatively small sample size. As the small sample size does not lead to reliable results, supplementary tests are necessary in empirical economics. These additional tests can reject the chaos hypothesis in those cases in which the standard procedures indicate the presence of deterministic chaos.
- Chaotic motion cannot be excluded in several micro- and macroeconomic time series but the chaos hypothesis can be supported only occasionally. Quarterly or annual GNP data do not seem to display chaotic dynamics.
- Even when the presence of chaotic motion cannot be established, evidence of low-dimensional nonlinearities exists in many economic time series.
- It does not seem that microeconomic data like, *e.g.*, financial-markets data, are *per se* better candidates for the presence of chaos. The presence of noise in official data, the generation of structure in constructing particular indexes, or statistical preliminaries like detrending can play essential roles in the findings. Whatsoever, microeconomic time series with large sample sizes tend to display more evidence of nonlinearities and deterministic chaos than macroeconomic data.
- Large data sets on the macroeconomic level can usually be collected only over long time spans. As all mathematically defined measures refer to the presence of an attractor and its underlying dynamical system, the calculation of, *e.g.*, a largest Lyapunov exponent for GNP data of the last one hundred years implies the assumption of an unchanged dynamical system. Even if this system is not known it can savely be assumed that the system (if it exists) has changed its structural form. On the other hand, it can be doubted whether a dynamical system always exists for those available large data sets that cover only a relatively short time span. Exchange-rate markets and financial markets are probably extremely vulnerably to exogenous shocks. Speculation might be independent of the fundamentals of an economy, the evolution of which might be described by a deterministic law of motion. It follows that the positive results on chaotic motion in these markets and in long-run macroeconomic data should be regarded with some care.

6. Chaos in Business-Cycle Theory – What is it Good For?

All examples of nonlinear, endogenous cycle models mentioned above are extremely simple models with respect to their economic content. No single model can claim to explain more than one or two items in the list of so-called stylized facts. Nonlinear business-cycle theory thus has to be confronted with the common linear approach. It has often been argued that linear business-cycle theory in the form of real business-cycle models or other models in the New Classical fashion represent more adequate approaches to an explanation of observable fluctuations in empirical time series because considerably more stylized facts can be modeled with this approach. At least three objections can be made at this point.

- Whether or not a phenomenon is called a stylized fact depends to some degree on the dominating paradigm. An example is the discussion on the symmetry or asymmetry of up- and downswings over a cycle. Only rarely can this (empirically actually ambiguous) phenomenon be found in the list of stylized facts in the rational expectations literature, while nonlinear time series analysts usually consider this phenomenon as their starting point.
- How many stylized facts can be explained by a model depends mainly on the dimension of the model. It cannot be expected that a simple nonlinear model whose dynamic behavior is determined by a two-dimensional or three-dimensional difference or differential equation system can generate motions in its variables that are completely satisfactory from an empirical point of view. The advantage of the linear approach consists in the fact that higher-dimensional systems of linear difference equations can be handled more easily. The model economy can then be more sophisticated than a nonlinear version.
- Linear business-cycle models represent only a subset of all possible structural forms of dynamical systems in economics. Nevertheless, when exogenous, stochastic terms are superimposed on these models, they can fit empirical time series amazingly well. However, from a theoretical point of view it is rather unsatisfactory when noneconomic forces are finally responsible for the persistence of economic cycles. On the other hand, recent work in nonlinear time series analysis has (tentatively) demonstrated that nonlinearities probably play a dominant role in the generation of empirical time series. Linear stochastic models can be very good statistical approximations of nonlinear time series, but they might not reflect the true dynamical structure of the economy.

The dynamic complexity of nonlinear dynamical systems does not provide much hope that large-scale nonlinear economic models can be investigated by purely analytical methods. In most cases numerical simulations will constitute the only way to derive information on the dynamical behavior of a model economy. It should be noted that numerical simulations are also required in the linear case when permanent exogenous shocks are superimposed on the endogenous system dynamics, *i.e.,* when irregularities are to be modeled. The analytical advantage of linear models therefore vanishes in the really interesting case. However, in addition to the standard arguments against the use of simulation experiments, another objection emerges when the dynamical system is nonlinear. While a simulation can nicely demonstrate the dynamical behavior of a system when, *e.g.,* parameters are changed, the origin of a particular type of motion usually cannot be determined anymore. The interaction of the elements of a dynamical system which are actually responsible for the onset of, *e.g.,* chaotic motion, can be hidden for an experimenter although he may know precise parameter values for the onset of turbulence.

In the dynamical systems literature, oscillating behavior in a dynamical system is synonymous with the presence of nonlinearities. Whatsoever, nonlinear models represent an alternative to the linear approach only when these models generate endogenous and persistent fluctuations. The nonlinearities which have to be assumed in the existing, low-dimensional models in order to generate limit cycles or complex motion often initiate basic objection against the usefulness of the nonlinear approach. However, the short discussion of the Metzlerian model in Section 2 has (hopefully) uncovered that in higher-dimensional systems the strong nonlinearity assumptions can often be relaxed. When more examples of oscillating behavior in higher-dimensional systems can be constructed, nonlinear dynamics might contribute to a paradigmatic shift. In linear approaches the concept of a stable economy is identified with the existence of a stable fixed point. In a nonlinear model an unstable fixed point does not necessarily imply the global instability of the economy. For example, when a nonlinear system possesses an attracting closed orbit, the notion of fixed-point stability simply has to be replaced by the notion of orbital stability. When a model economy has an attracting set in the form of a fixed-point attractor, a limit cycle, or a strange attractor, the motion is bounded in a neighborhood of this set, and the paradigm of a stable economy is actually not violated.

When a nonlinear dynamical system allows for endogenous oscillations, the onset of chaotic motion can be expected in a variety of models with a sufficiently high dimension. If the task of business-cycle theory consists in providing theoretical descriptions of those economic forces which imply an irregular oscillating behavior of an economy, nonlinearities should be natural ingredients in cycle models. The analytical problems mentioned above will prevent the construction of large-scale models, and (existing) nonlinear business-cycle models can serve only as pedagogical examples of the onset of complex cyclical motion.

This pedagogical character also follows from another consideration. Chaotic dynamical systems emerge in completely deterministic environments. The assumption of deterministic relations, *i.e.,* fixed one-to-one laws of motion, is an unrealistic hypothesis that can be dated back to early neoclassical economists who were inspired by the mechanistic world view. The best that can be done in many if not most descriptions of actual behavior is to provide upper and lower bounds to the change in a variable. Modelling stochastic dynamical systems or differential inclusions might be considered the only satisfactory way to depict the evolution of actual economies.[31] However, an analytical treatment of chaotic dynamical systems with stochastic components involves severe mathematical difficulties, implying that numerical simulations will once again be necessary for an illustration of the system dynamics.[32]

Summarizing, the following conclusions might be drawn for economic dynamics and business-cycle theory.

- Business-cycle theory deals with analytical explanations of observable irregular fluctuations. Economic theory should therefore disregard exogenous influences when they are mainly responsible for the onset and persistence of cycles. It follows that business-cycle models should be nonlinear models that allow for chaotic motion. The main result of the recent empirical work on chaotic dynamics has uncovered that the presence of nonlinearities in the time series usually cannot be denied. However, the real challenge for empirical economics is the rejection of the hypothesis of the functional relations itself. Only when nonlinearities like, *e.g.,* sigmoid investment or savings functions, cannot be observed in reality, the empirical foundation for the nonlinear approach to business cycles definitely ceases.
- Existing nonlinear business-cycle models are typically low-dimensional dynamical systems because higher-dimensional analogues usually cannot be treated analytically. It follows that these systems cannot explain such a large number of stylized facts as is known from standard linear business-cycle models. Higher-dimensional models require the use of numerical simulation techniques, to which the standard objections apply. As there is not much hope to gain a lot of economic insight into the working of the models in such numerically simulated high-dimensional systems (*i.e.,* into the economic reason for the existence of turning points, for example), it is worthwhile to concentrate on low-dimensional models instead. The study of low-dimensional models can contribute to a better understanding of the dynamic effects of nonlinearities.
- When low-dimensional systems are the appropriate objects in studying nonlinear economic systems, traditional business-cycle models like the ones presented above should be revived. The linear character of most models can usually be overcome by assuming economically plausible nonlinearities. Most elements of modern business cycle models which are responsible for the onset of oscillations like accelerators, production lags, inventory holdings, expectations, etc. can be found in traditional models.
- Further developments of nonlinear business-cycle theory should take stochastic elements in economic relations into account. It is not required that such stochastic elements dominate

[31] This uncertainty can be incorporated into nonlinear dynamic economic models in the same qualitative way as in stochastic linear models, but it is not required that stochastic elements have a dominating influence.

[32] An introduction to the mathematical aspects of such systems can be found in Kapitaniak (1990).

the dynamic output of a model (as is the case in linear models) but a purely deterministic model can hardly claim to deliver a satisfactory picture of real life phenomena when it ignores certainly existing degrees of freedom. Without stochastic elements, most existing models have a classroom character.

7. Bibliography on Nonlinear Economic Dynamics

The literature on nonlinear dynamical systems is rapidly growing, and it seems to be impossible to keep track of all publications in the field. The following collection should be understood as a more or less arbitrary selection of those publications the author considers to be particularly relevant for the scientific progress in the field or enlightening from a didactical standpoint.

7.1. Nonlinear Economic Dynamics

I. MONOGRAPHS AND SURVEY ARTICLES ON NONLINEAR ECONOMIC DYNAMICS

BAUMOL, W.J./BENHABIB, J. (1989): "Chaos: Significance, Mechanism, and Economic Applications". *Journal of Economic Perspective 3*, pp. 77-105.

BLATT, J.M. (1983): *Dynamic Economic Systems - A Post-Keynesian Approach.* Armonk: M. E. Sharpe.

BOLDRIN, M./WOODFORD, M. (1990): "Equilibrium Models Displaying Endogenous Fluctuations and Chaos. A Survey". *Journal of Monetary Economics 25*, pp. 189-222.

BOYD, I./BLATT, J.M. (1988): *Investment Confidence and Business Cycles.* Berlin-Heidelberg-New York: Springer-Verlag.

BROCK, W.A./HSIEH, D.A./LEBARON, B. (1991): *Nonlinear Dynamics, Chaos, and Instability: Statistical Theory and Economic Evidence.* Cambridge-London: The MIT Press.

BROCK, W.A./MALLIARIS, A.G. (1989): *Differential Equations, Stability and Chaos in Dynamic Economics.* Amsterdam: North-Holland.

CHIARELLA, C. (1990): *The Elements of a Nonlinear Theory of Economic Dynamics.* Berlin-Heidelberg-New York: Springer-Verlag.

GOODWIN, R.M. (1990): *Chaotic Economic Dynamics.* Oxford: Claredon Press.

GUESNERIE, R./WOODFORD, M. (1991): "Endogenous Fluctuations". DELTA research paper # 91-10.

HOMMES, C.H. (1991): *Chaotic Dynamics in Economic Models.* Groningen: Wolters-Noordhoff.

LORENZ, H.-W. (1989): *Nonlinear Dynamical Economics and Chaotic Motion.* Berlin-Heidelberg-New York: Springer-Verlag.

KELSEY, D. (1988): "The Economics of Chaos or the Chaos of Economics". *Oxford Economic Papers 40*, pp. 1-31.

MEDIO, A./GALLO, G. (1992): *Chaotic Dynamics.* Forthcoming. Cambridge University Press.

MIROWSKI, P. (1990): "From Mandelbrot to Chaos in Economic Theory". *Southern Economic Journal 57*, pp. 289-307.

PETERS, E.E. (1991): *Chaos and Order in the Capital Markets.* New York–Chichester: John Wiley & Sons.

PUU, T. (1989): *Nonlinear Economic Dynamics.* Berlin-Heidelberg-New York: Springer-Verlag.

ROSSER, J.B. (1991): *From Catastrophe to Chaos: A General Theory of Economic Discontinuities.* Boston-Dordrecht-London: Kluwer Academic Publishers.

SCHEINKMAN, J.A. (1990): "Nonlinearities in Economic Dynamics". *Economic Journal 100, Supplement*, pp. 33-48.

VARIAN, H.R. (1981): "Dynamical Systems with Application to Economics". In: ARROW, K.J./INTRILIGATOR, M.D. (eds.): *Handbook of Mathematical Economics*, Vol. I, pp. 93-110. Amsterdam: North Holland.

ZHANG, W-B. (1990a): *Economic Dynamics. Growth and Development.* Berlin-Heidelberg-New York: Springer-Verlag

ZHANG, W-B. (1990b): *Synergetic Economics.* Berlin–Heidelberg–New York: Springer–Verlag.

II. Specialized Papers on Nonlinear Economic Dynamics

Bajo-Rubio, O./Fernández-Rodríguez, F./Sosvilla-Rivero, S. (1992): "Chaotic Behaviour in Exchange-Rate Series: First Results for the Peseta–U.S. Dollar Case". *Economics Letters 39*, pp. 199-211.

Barnett, W.A./Chen, P. (1986): "Economic Theory as a Generator of Measurable Attractors". *Extrait de Mondes en Développement 54-55*, pp. 209-224.

Barnett, W.A./Chen, P. (1988a): "The Aggregation-Theoretic Monetary Aggregates are Chaotic and have Strange Attractors: An Econometric Application of Mathematical Chaos". In: Barnett, W.A./Berndt, E.R./White, H. (eds.): *Dynamic Econometric Modeling*. Cambridge: Cambridge University Press.

Barnett, W.A./Chen, P. (1988b): "Deterministic Chaos and Fractal Attractors as Tools for Nonparametric Dynamical Inferences". *Mathematical Computing and Modelling 10*, pp. 275-296.

Barnett, W.A./Choi, S. (1989): "A Comparison Between the Conventional Econometric Approach to Structural Inference and the Nonparametric Chaotic Attractor Approach". In: Barnett, W.A./Geweke, J./Shell, K. (eds.): *Economic Complexity: Chaos, Sunspots, Bubbles, and Nonlinearity*, pp. 141-212. Cambridge: Cambridge University Press.

Barnett, W.A./Hinich, M.J./Weber, W.E (1986): "The Regulatory Wedge between the Demand-Side and Supply-Side Aggregation Theoretic Monetary Aggregates". *Journal of Econometrics 33*, pp. 165-185.

Baumol, W.J. (1987): "The Chaos Phenomenon: A Nightmare for Forecasters". *LSE Quarterly 1*, pp. 99-114.

Benassy, J.P. (1984): "A Non-Walrasian Model of the Business Cycle". *Journal of Economic Behavior and Organization 5*, pp. 77-89.

Benhabib, J./Day, R.H. (1980): "Erratic Accumulation". *Economics Letters 6*, pp. 113-117.

Benhabib, J./Day, R.H. (1981): "Rational Choice and Erratic Behaviour". *Review of Economic Studies 48*, pp. 459-471.

Benhabib, J./Day, R.H. (1982): "A Characterization of Erratic Dynamics in the Overlapping Generations Model". *Journal of Economic Dynamics and Control 4*, pp. 37-55.

Benhabib, J./Miyao, T. (1981): "Some New Results on the Dynamics of the Generalized Tobin Model". *International Economic Review 22*, pp. 589-596.

Benhabib, J./Nishimura, K. (1979): "The Hopf Bifurcation and the Existence of Closed Orbits in Multisector Models of Optimal Economic Growth". *Journal of Economic Theory 21*, pp. 421-444.

Benhabib, J./Nishimura, K. (1985): "Competitive Equilibrium Cycles". *Journal of Economic Theory 35*, pp. 284-306.

Blatt, J.M. (1978): "On the Econometric Approach to Business Cycle Analysis". *Oxford Economic Papers 30*, pp. 292-300.

Blatt, J.M. (1980): "On the Frisch Model of Business Cycles". *Oxford Economic Papers 32*, pp. 467-479.

Boldrin, M. (1984): "Applying Bifurcation Theory: Some Simple Results on Keynesian Business Cycles". DP 8403 University of Venice.

Boldrin, M. (1989): "Paths of Optimal Accumulation in Two-Sector Models". In: Barnett, W.A./Geweke, J./Shell, K. (eds.): *Economic Complexity: Chaos, Sunspots, Bubbles, and Nonlinearity*, pp. 231-252. Cambridge: Cambridge University Press.

Boldrin, M./Montrucchio, L. (1986): "On the Indeterminacy of Capital Accumulation Paths". *Journal of Economic Theory 40*, pp. 26-39.

Boldrin, M./Montrucchio, L. (1988): "Acyclicity and Stability for Intertermporal Optimization Models". *International Economic Review 29*, pp. 137-146.

Brock, W.A. (1986): "Distinguishing Random and Deterministic Systems: Abridged Version". *Journal of Economic Theory 40*, pp. 168-195.

Brock, W.A. (1987a): "Nonlinearity in Finance and Economics". Mimeo. University of Wisconsin.

Brock, W.A. (1987b): "Introduction to Chaos and Other Aspects of Nonlinearity". Mimeo. University of Wisconsin.

Brock, W.A. (1988): "Nonlinearity and Complex Dynamics in Economics and Finance". In: Anderson, P./Arrow, K./Pines, D. (eds.): *The Economy as an Evolving Complex System*. Redwood City: Addison-Wesley.

BROCK, W.A. (1990): "Chaos and Complexity in Economic and Financial Science". In: v. FURSTENBERG, G.M. (ed.): *Acting Under Uncertainty: Multidisciplinary Conceptions*, pp. 423-450. Boston: Kluwer.

BROCK, W.A. (1988b): "Hicksian Nonlinearity". Mimeo. University of Wisconson.

BROCK, W.A./DECHERT, W.D. (1988): "Theorems on Distinguishing Deterministic from Random Systems". In: BARNETT, W.A./BERNDT, E.R./WHITE, H. (eds.): *Dynamic Econometric Modeling*, pp. 247-265. Cambridge: Cambridge University Press.

BROCK, W.A./DECHERT, W.D./SCHEINKMAN, J.A. (1987): "A Test for Independance based on the Correlation Dimension". Mimeo. University of Wisconsin.

BROCK, W.A./SAYERS, C.L. (1988): "Is the Business Cycle Characterized by Deterministic Chaos?" *Journal of Monetary Economics 22*, pp. 71-90.

BRØNS, M./STURIS, J. (1991): "Local and Global bifurcations in a Model of the Economic Long Wave". *System Dynamics Review 7*, pp. 41-60.

CHEN, P. (1988a): "Empirical and Theoretical Evidence of Economic Chaos". *System Dynamics Review 4*, pp. 81-108.

CHEN, P. (1988b): "Multiperiodicity and Irregularity in Growth Cycles: A Continuous Model of Monetary Attractors". *Mathematical Computing and Modelling 10*, pp. 647-660.

CHIARELLA, C. (1992): " The Dynamics of Speculative Dynamics". *Annals of Operations Research 37*, pp. 101-124.

CUGNO, F./MONTRUCCHIO, L. (1982): "Stability and Instability in a Two Dimensional Dynamical System: a Mathematical Approach to Kaldor's Theory of the Trade Cycle". In: SZEGŒ, G.P. (ed.): *New Quantitative Techniques for Economic Analysis*, New York: Academic Press, pp. 265-278.

CUGNO, F./MONTRUCCHIO, L. (1984): "Some New Techniques for Modelling Non-Linear Economic Fluctuations: A Brief Survey". In: GOODWIN, R.M./KRÜGER, M./VERCELLI, A. (eds.): *Nonlinear Models of Fluctuating Growth*, pp. 146-165. Berlin-Heidelberg-New York: Springer-Verlag.

DANA, R.A./MALGRANGE, P. (1984): "The Dynamics of a Discrete Version of a Growth Cycle Model". In: ANCOT, J.P. (ed.): *Analysing the Structure of Economic Models*. The Hague: Martinus Nijhoff, pp. 205 -222.

DAY, R.H. (1982): "Irregular Growth Cycles". *American Economic Review 72*, pp. 406-414.

DAY, R.H. (1983): "The Emergence of Chaos from Classical Economic Growth". *Quarterly Journal of Economics 98*, pp. 201-213.

DAY, R.H. (1984): "Disequilibrium Economic Dynamics". *Journal of Economic Behaviour and Organisation 5*, pp. 57-76.

DAY, R.H . (1986a): "Unscrambling the Concept of Chaos Through Thick and Thin: Reply". Quarterly Journal of Economics, 101, pp. 425-426.

DAY, R.H . (1986b): "On Endogenous Preferences and Adaptive Economizing". In: DAY, R.H./ELIASSON, G. (eds.): *The Dynamics of a Market Economy*, pp. 153-170. Amsterdam: North-Holland.

DAY, R.H./KIM, K.-H. (1987): "A Note on Non-Periodic Demoeconomic Fluctuations with Positive Measure". *Economics Letters 23*, pp. 251-256.

DAY, R.H./PIANIGIANI, G. (1991): "Statistical Dynamics and Economics". *Journal of Economic Behavior and Organization 16*, pp. 37-83.

DAY, R.H./SHAFER, W. (1986): "Keynesian Chaos". *Journal of Macroeconomics 7*, pp. 277-95.

DAY, R.H./WALTER, J.-L. (1989): "Economic Growth in the Very Long Run: On the Multiple-Phase Interaction of Population, Technology, and Social Infrastructure". In: BARNETT, W.A./GEWEKE, J./SHELL, K. (eds.): *Economic Complexity: Chaos, Sunspots, Bubbles, and Nonlinearity*, pp. 253-289. Cambridge: Cambridge University Press.

DEBREU, G. (1986): "Theoretic Models: Mathematical Form and Economic Content". *Econometrica 54*, pp. 1259-1270.

DELLI GATTI, D./GALLEGATI, M./GARDINI, L. (1991): "Investment Confidence, Corporate Debt, and Income Fluctuations". Mimeo Urbino.

DENDRINOS, D.S. (1985): "Turbulence and Fundamental Urban/Regional Dynamics". Task Force on Dynamic Analysis of Spatial Development. IIASA, Laxenburg.

DENDRINOS, D.S. (1986): "On the Incongruous Spatial Employment Dynamics". In: NIJKAMP, P. (ed.) *Technological Change, Employment and Spatial Dynamics*. Berlin-Heidelberg-New York: Springer-Verlag.

DENECKERE, R./PELIKAN, S. (1986): "Competititve Chaos". *Journal of Economic Theory 40*, pp. 13-25.

FLASCHEL, P. (1989): "Stability – Independent of Economic Structure? A Prototype Analysis". Mimeo. University of Bielefeld.

FOLEY, D.K. (1986): "Stabilization Policy in a Nonlinear Business Cycle Model". In: SEMMLER, W. (ed.): *Competition, Instability, and Nonlinear Cycles*, pp. 200-211. Berlin-Heidelberg-New York: Springer-Verlag.

FRANK, M.Z./GENCAY, R./STENGOS, T. (1988): "International Chaos?" *European Economic Review 32*, pp. 1569-1584.

FRANK, M.Z./STENGOS, T. (1987): "Measuring the Strangeness of Gold and Silver Rates of Return". Mimeo. University of Guelph.

FRANK, M.Z./STENGOS, T. (1988a): "The Stability of Canadian Macroeconomic Data as Measured by the Largest Lyapunov Exponent". *Economics Letters 27*, pp. 11-14.

FRANK, M.Z./STENGOS, T. (1988b): "Chaotic Dynamics in Economic Time Series". *Journal of Economic Surveys*, pp. 423-438.

FRANK, M.Z./STENGOS, T. (1988c): "Some Evidence Concerning Macroeconomic Chaos". *Journal of Monetary Economics 22*, pp. 423-438.

FRANKE, R./WEGHORST, W. (1988): "Complex Dynamics in a Simple Input-Output Model without the Full Capacity Utilization Hypothesis". *Metroeconomica 39*, pp. 1-29.

FRISCH, R. (1933): "Propagation Problems and Impulse Problems in Dynamic Economics". In: *Economic Essays in Honor of Gustav Cassel*. London: Allen & Unwin.

GABISCH, G. (1987): "Nonlinearities in Dynamic Economic Systems". *Atlantic Economic Journal 15*, pp. 22-31.

GAERTNER, W. (1986): "Zyklische Konsummuster". *Jahrbücher für Nationalökonomie und Statistik 201*, pp. 54-65. W.

GAERTNER, W. (1987): "Periodic and Aperiodic Consumer Behavior". *Applied Mathematics and Computation 22*, pp. 233-254. W.

GALEOTTI, M./GORI, F. (1990): "Uniqueness of Periodic Orbits in Lienard-Type Business-Cycle Models". *Metroeconomica 40*, pp. 135-146.

GOODWIN, R.M. (1946): "Innovations and the Irregularity of Economic Cycles". *Review of Economic Statistics 28*, pp. 95-102.

GOODWIN, R.M. (1947): "Dynamical Coupling with Especial Reference to Markets Having Production Lags". *Econometrica 15*, pp. 181-204.

GOODWIN, R.M. (1951): "The Nonlinear Accelerator and the Persistence of Business Cycles". *Econometrica 19*, pp. 1-17.

GOODWIN, R.M. (1953): "Static and Dynamic General Equilibrium Models". Reprinted in: GOODWIN, R.M. (1983): *Essays in Linear Economic Structures*. London: Macmillan.

GOODWIN, R.M. (1967): "A Growth Cycle". In: FEINSTEIN, C.H. (ed.): *Socialism, Capitalism and Economic Growth*. Cambridge: Cambridge University Press. Revised version in: HUNT, E.K./SCHWARZ, J.G. (eds.) (1969): *A Critique of Economic Theory*, pp. 442-449, Harmondsworth: Penguin.

GOODWIN, R.M. (1970): *Elementary Economics from the Higher Standpoint*. Cambridge: Cambridge University Press.

GOODWIN, R.M. (1986): "The Economy as an Evolutionary Pulsator". *Journal of Economic Behavior and Organization 7*, pp. 341-349.

GRANDMONT, J.-M. (1985): "On Endogenous Competitive Business Cycles". *Econometrica 53*, pp. 995-1045.

GRANDMONT, J.-M. (1986): "Stabilizing Competitive Business Cycles". *Journal of Economic Theory 40*, pp. 57-76.

GRANDMONT, J.-M./MALGRANGE, P. (1986): "Nonlinear Economic Dynamics: Introduction". *Journal of Economic Theory 40*, pp. 3-12.

HAHN, F.H. (1984): "Stability". In: ARROW, K.J./INTRILIGATOR, M.D. (eds.) (1984): *Handbook of Mathematical Economics*, Vol. II, pp. 745-793. Amsterdam: North-Holland.

HAXHOLDT, C./LARSEN, E./TVEDE, M./MOSEKILDE, E. (1991): "Comovements in Economic Models". Mimeo: Copenhagen Business School.

HERRMANN, R. (1985): "Stability and Chaos in a Kaldor-Type Model". DP 22, Department of Economics, University of Göttingen.

HOMMES, C. (1989): "Periodic, Quasi-Periodic and Chaotic Dynamics in a Simple Piecewise Linear Non-Walrasian Macromodel". Mimeo: University of Groningen.

HOMMES, C./NUSSE, H.E./SIMONOVITS, A. (1990): "Hicksian Cycles and Chaos in a Socialist Economy". Mimeo. University of Groningen.

HSIEH, D. (1989): "Testing for Nonlinear Dependence in Foreign Exchange Rates". *Journal of Business 62*, pp. 339-368.

ICHIMURA, S. (1955): "Towards a General Non-Linear Macrodynamic Theory of Economic Fluctuations". In: KURIHARA, K.K. (ed.): *Post-Keynesian Economics*, pp. 192-226. New Brunswick: Rutgers University Press.

INVERNIZZI, S./MEDIO, A. (1991): "On Lags and Chaos in Economic Dynamic Models". *Journal of Mathematical Economics 20*, pp. 521-550.

JARSULIC, M. (1991a): "Growth Cycles in a Discrete, Nonlinear Model". Mimeo. Department of Economics. Notre Dame.

JARSULIC, M. (1991b): "Complex Dynamics in a Keynesian Growth Model". Mimeo. Department of Economics. Notre Dame.

KALDOR, N. (1940): "A Model of the Trade Cycle". *Economic Journal 50*, pp. 78-92.

LARSEN, E.R./MOSEKILDE, E./RASMUSSEN, S./STERMAN, J. (1988): "Entrainment Between the Economic Long Wave and Other Macroeconomic Cycles". Mimeo. The Technical University of Denmark.

LORENZ, H.-W. (1987a): "International Trade and the Possible Occurrence of Chaos". *Economics Letters 23*, pp. 135-138.

LORENZ, H.-W. (1987b): "Strange Attractors in a Multisector Business Cycle Model". *Journal of Economic Behavior and Organization 8*, pp. 397-411.

LORENZ, H.-W. (1987c): "Can Keynesian Income Policy Imply Chaos?" DP 33, University of Göttingen, Department of Economics.

LORENZ, H.-W. (1987d): "Goodwin's Nonlinear Accelerator and Chaotic Motion". *Zeitschrift für Nationalökonomie - Journal of Economics 47*, pp. 413-418.

LORENZ, H.-W. (1988): "Optimal Economic Control and Chaotic Dynamics". In: FEICHTINGER, G. (ed.): *Optimal Control Theory and Economic Analysis*, Vol. III, pp. 59-71, Amsterdam: North-Holland.

LORENZ, H.-W. (1989a): "Strange Attractors in Dynamical Economics". In: AMES, W.F./BREZINSKI, C. (eds.): *IMACS Transactions on Scientific Computing, Vol. 1*, pp. 282-286. Basel: J.C. Baltzer.

LORENZ, H.-W. (1989b): "Forced Oscillator Systems and Chaotic Motion in Dynamical Economics". In: GALEOTTI, M./GERONAZZO, L./GORI, F. (eds.): *Non-Linear Dynamics in Economics and Social Sciences*, pp. 125-141. Bologna: Pitagora Editrice.

LORENZ, H.-W. (1992a): "Spiral-Type Attractors in Low-Dimensional Continuous-Time Dynamical Systems". *System Dynamics Review*. Forthcoming.

LORENZ, H.-W. (1992b): "On the Complexity of Simultaneous Price-Quantity Adjustment Processes". *Annals of Operations Research 37*, pp. 51-71.

MEDIO, A. (1984a): "Synergetics and Dynamic Economic Models". In: GOODWIN, R.M./KRÜGER, M./VERCELLI, A. (eds.): *Nonlinear Models of Fluctuating Growth*, pp. 166 - 191. Berlin-Heidelberg-New York: Springer-Verlag.

MEDIO, A. (1984b): "A Generalized Multiplier-Accelerator Model, via Ljapunov Vector Functions and Hopf Bifurcation". University of Venice, Department of Economics, Working Paper 8404.

MEDIO, A. (1987): "Oscillations in Optimal Growth Models". *Journal of Economic Behavior and Organization 8*, pp. 413-427.

MEDIO, A. (1991a): "Discrete and Continuous Models of Chaotic Dynamics". *Structural Change and Economic Dynamics 2*, pp. 99-118.

MEDIO, A. (1991b): "Continuous–time Models of Chaos in Economics". *Journal of Economic Behavior and Organization 16*, pp. 115-151.

MELESE, F./TRANSUE, W. (1986): "Unscrambling Chaos Through Thick and Thin". *Quarterly Journal of Economics 101*, pp. 419-423.

MONTRUCCHIO, L. (1988): "The Occurrence of Erratic Fluctuations in Models of Optimization over Infinite Horizon". In: RICCI, G./VELUPILLAI, K. (eds.): *Growth Cycles and Multisectoral Economics: the Goodwin Tradition*, pp. 83-92. Berlin-Heidelberg-New York: Springer-Verlag.

MOSEKILDE, E./LARSEN, E.R./STERMAN, J.D./THOMSEN, J.S. (1992): "Nonlinear Mode-Interaction in the Macroeconomy". *Annals of Operations Research 37*, pp. 185-216.

NIJKAMP, P. (1987): "Long-Term Economic Fluctuations: A Spatial View". *Socio-Economic Planning 21*, pp. 189-197.

NUSSE, H.E./HOMMES, C. (1990): "Resolution of Chaos with Application to a Modified Samuelson Model". *Journal of Economic Dynamics and Control 14*, pp. 1-19.

PLOEG, F. VAN DER (1986): "Rational Expectations, Risk and Chaos in Financial Markets". *Economic Journal 96, Suppl.*, pp. 151-162.

POHJOLA, M.J. (1981): "Stable and Chaotic Growth: the Dynamics of a Discrete Version of Goodwin's Growth Cycle Model". *Zeitschrift für Nationalökonomie 41*, pp. 27-38.

PUU, T. (1987): "Complex Dynamics in Continuous Models of the Business Cycle". In: BATTEN,D./CASTI, J./JOHANSSON, B. (eds.): *Economic Evolution and Structural Change*. Berlin-Heidelberg-New York: Springer-Verlag.

PUU, T. (1992): "Order and Disorder in Business Cycles". *Annals of Operations Research 37*, pp. 169-184.

RAMSEY, J.B./SAYERS, C.L./ROTHMAN, P. (1988): "The Statistical Properties of Dimension Calculations Using Small Data Sets: Some Economic Applications". *International Economic Review 31*, pp. 991-1020.

SAMUELSON, P.A. (1990): "Deterministic Chaos in Economics: An Occurrence in Axiomatric Utility Theory". In: VELUPILLAI, K. (ed.): *Nonlinear and Multisectoral Macrodynamics*, pp. 42-63. Cambridge: Cambridge University Press.

SAYERS, C.L. (1988a): "Diagnostic Tests for Nonlinearity in Time Series Data: An Application to the Work Stoppages Series". Mimeo. University of North Carolina.

SAYERS, C.L. (1988b): "Work Stoppages: Exploring the Nonlinear Dynamics". Mimeo. University of Houston.

SAYERS, C.L. (1991): "Statistical Inference Based upon Nonlinear Science". *European Economic Review 35*, pp. 306-312.

SCHEINKMAN, J.A./LEBARON, B. (1988): "Nonlinear Dynamics and Stock Returns". *Journal of Business 62*, pp. 311-337.

SCHEINKMAN, J.A./LEBARON, B. (1989): "Nonlinear Dynamics and GNP Data". In: BARNETT, W.A./ GEWEKE, J./SHELL, K. (eds.): *Economic Complexity: Chaos, Sunspots, Bubbles, and Nonlinearity*, pp. 213-227. Cambridge: Cambridge University Press.

STERMAN, J.D. (1988): "Deterministic Chaos in Models of Human Behavior: Methodological Issues and Experimental Results". *System Dynamics Review 4*, pp. 148-178.

STERMAN, J.D. (1989): "Deterministic Chaos in an Experimental Economic System". *Journal of Economic Behavior and Organization*, forthcoming.

STERMAN, J.D./MOSEKILDE, E./LARSEN, E. (1988): "Experimental Evidence of Deterministic Chaos in Human Decision Making Behavior". WP 2002-88, Sloan School of Management, MIT.

STUTZER, M. (1980): "Chaotic Dynamics and Bifurcation in a Macro-Model". *Journal of Economic Dynamics and Control 2*, pp. 253-276.

VARIAN, H.R. (1979): "Catastrophe Theory and the Business Cycle". *Economic Inquiry 17*, pp. 14-28.

VELUPILLAI, K./RICCI, G. (1988): "Introduction". In: RICCI, G./VELUPILLAI, K. (eds.): *Growth Cycles and Multisectoral Economics: the Goodwin Tradition*. Berlin-Heidelberg-New York: Springer-Verlag.

VERCELLI, A. (1989): "Structural Stability and the Epistemology of Change: A Critical Appraisal". In: GALEOTTI, M./GERONAZZO, L./GORI, F. (Hg.): *Non-Linear Dynamics in Economics and Social Sciences*, pp. 317-360. Bologna: Pitagora Editrice.

WHITE, R.W. (1985): "Transitions to Chaos with Increasing System Complexity: The Case of Regional Industrial Systems". *Environment and Planning A 17*, pp. 387-396.

WOODFORD, M. (1987): "Equilibrium Models of Endogenous Fluctuations". Mimeo. University of Chicago.

WOODFORD, M. (1989): "Imperfect Financial Intermediation and Complex Dynamics". In: BARNETT, W.A./ GEWEKE, J./SHELL, K. (eds.): *Economic Complexity: Chaos, Sunspots, Bubbles, and Nonlinearity*, pp. 309-334. Cambridge: Cambridge University Press.

WOODFORD, M. (1990): "Learning to Believe in Sunspots". *Econometrica 58*, pp. 277-307.

7.2. Mathematical Foundations

I. MONOGRAPHS AND SURVEY ARTICLES

ABRAHAM, R.H./SCOTT, K.A. (1985): "Chaostrophes of Forced Van der Pol Systems". In: FISCHER, P./ SMITH, W.R. (eds.): *Chaos, Fractals, and Dynamics*. New York-Basel: Marcel Dekker Inc.

ABRAHAM, R.H./SHAW, C.D. (1983): *Dynamics, the Geometry of Behavior*. Part I and II. Santa Cruz: Aerial.

ARROWSMITH, D.K./PLACE, C.M. (1982): *Ordinary Differential Equations*. London-New York: Chapman and Hall.

ARROWSMITH, D.K./PLACE, C.M. (1990): *An Introduction to Dynamical Systems*. Cambridge: Cambridge University Press.

BERGÉ, P./POMEAU, Y./VIDAL, C. (1986): *Order within Chaos*. New York: Wiley.

BOYCE, W.E./DIPRIMA, R.L. (1977): *Elementary Differential Equations and Boundary Value Problems*. 3rd ed., New York: Wiley.

COLLET, P./ECKMANN, J.-P. (1980): *Iterated Maps on the Interval as Dynamical Systems*. Basel-Boston: Birkhaeuser.

DEVANEY, R.L. (1986): *An Introduction to Chaotic Dynamical Systems*. Menlo Park: Benjamin/Cummings.

FALCONER, K. (1990): *Fractal Geometry. Mathematical Foundations and Applications*. Chichester-New York: John Wiley & Sons.

GRANDMONT, J.-M. (1988): "Nonlinear Difference Equations, Bifurcations, and Chaos". CEPREMAP # 8811. Forthcoming in: *Market Psychology and Business Cycles*.

GUCKENHEIMER, J./HOLMES, P. (1983): *Nonlinear Oscillations, Dynamical Systems, and Bifurcations of Vector Fields*. New York-Berlin-Heidelberg: Springer-Verlag.

HAKEN, H. (1983a): *Synergetics. An Introduction*. 3rd ed., Berlin-Heidelberg-New York: Springer-Verlag.

HAKEN, H. (1983b): *Advanced Synergetics*. Berlin-Heidelberg-New York : Springer-Verlag.

HIRSCH, M.W./SMALE, S. (1974): *Differential Equations, Dynamical Systems, and Linear Algebra*. New York: Academic Press.

IOOSS, G. (1979): *Bifurcations of Maps and Applications*. Amsterdam: North Holland.

IOOSS, G./JOSEPH, D.D. (1980): *Elementary Stability and Bifurcation Theory*. New York-Heidelberg-Berlin: Springer-Verlag.

KAPITANIAK, T. (1990): *Chaos in Systems with Noise*. 2nd ed. Singapore: World Scientific.

MEES, A.I. (1981): *Dynamics of Feedback Systems*. New York: Wiley.

MIRA, C. (1987): *Chaotic Dynamics – From the One–Dimensional Endomorphism to the Two-Dimensional Diffeomorphism*. Singapore: World Scientific.

NICOLIS, G./PRIGOGINE, I. (1989): *Exploring Complexity*. New York: W.H. Freeman.

PARKER, T.S./CHUA, L.O. (1989): *Practical Numerical Algorithms for Chaotic Systems*. New York-Berlin-Heidelberg: Springer-Verlag.

PRESTON, C. (1983): *Iterates of Maps on an Interval*. Berlin-Heidelberg-New York: Springer-Verlag.

RUELLE, D. (1989): *Elements of Differentiable Dynamics and Bifurcation Theory*. Boston-San Diego-New York: Academic Press.

RUELLE, D. (1990): *Chaotic Evolution and Strange Attractors*. Cambridge: Cambridge University Press.

RUELLE, D. (1991): *Chance and Chaos*. Princeton: Princeton University Press.

SCHUSTER, H.G. (1984): *Deterministic Chaos – An Introduction*. Weinheim: Physik-Verlag.

SPARROW, C. (1982): *The Lorenz Equations*. New York-Heidelberg-Berlin: Springer-Verlag.

THOMPSON, J.M.T./STEWART, H.B. (1986): *Nonlinear Dynamics and Chaos.* Chichester-New York: John Wiley.

WEST, B.J. (1985): *An Essay on the Importance of Being Nonlinear.* Berlin-Heidelberg-New York: Springer-Verlag.

WIGGINS, S. (1988): *Global Bifurcations and Chaos. Analytical Methods.* New York-Berlin-Heidelberg: Springer-Verlag.

WIGGINS, S. (1990): *Introduction to Applied Nonlinear Dynamical Systems and Chaos.* New York-Berlin-Heidelberg: Springer-Verlag.

II. SPECIALIZED PAPERS ON MATHEMATICAL TOPICS

ALEXANDER, J.C./YORKE, J.A. (1978): "Global Bifurcation of Periodic Orbits". *American Journal of Mathematics 100*, pp. 263-292.

ARNEODO, A./COULLET, P./TRESSER, C. (1981): "Possible New Strange Attractors with Spiral Structure". *Communications in Mathematical Physics 79*, pp. 573-579.

ARNEODO, A./COULLET, P./TRESSER, C. (1982): "Oscillations with Chaotic Behavior: An Illustration of a Theorem by Shil'nikov". *Journal of Statistical Physics 27*, pp. 171-182.

BENETTIN, G./GALGANI, L./STRELCYN, J.M. (1980): "Lyapunov Characteristic Exponents for Smooth Dynamical Systems and for Hamiltonian Systems: A Method for Computing all of Them". *Meccanica 15*, pp. 9-30.

BEYN, W.-J. (1990): "The Numerical Computation of Connecting Orbits in Dynamical Systems". *IMA Journal of Numerical Analysis 9*, pp. 379-405.

COULLET, P./TRESSER, C./ARNEODO, A. (1979): "Transition to Stochasticity for a Class of Forced Oscillators". *Physics Letters 72A*, pp. 268-270.

CRUTCHFIELD, J.P./FARMER, J.D./PACKARD, N.H./SHAW, R.S. (1986): "Chaos". *Scientific American*, Vol. 255, 6, pp. 46-57.

DIAMOND, P. (1976): "Chaotic Behaviour of Systems of Difference Equations". *International Journal of Systems Science 7*, pp. 953-956.

ECKMANN, J.-P. (1981): "Roads to Turbulence in Dissipative Dynamical Systems". *Reviews of Modern Physics 53*, pp. 643-654.

ECKMANN, J.-P./RUELLE, D. (1985): "Ergodic Theory of Chaos and Strange Attractors". *Reviews of Modern Physics 57*, pp. 617-656.

FARMER, J.D. (1982a): "Chaotic Attractors of an Infinite-Dimensional Dynamical System". *Physica 4D*, pp. 366-393.

FARMER, J.D. (1982b): "Dimension, Fractal Measures, and Chaotic Dynamics". In: HAKEN, H. (ed.): *Evolution of Order and Chaos in Physics, Chemistry and Biology*, pp. 228-246. Berlin-Heidelberg-New York: Springer-Verlag.

FARMER, J.D./OTT, E./YORKE, J.A. (1983): "The Dimension of Chaotic Attractors". *Physica 7D*, pp. 153-180.

FARMER, J.D./SIDOROWICH, J.J. (1987): "Predicting Chaotic Time Series". *Physical Reviews Letters 59*, pp. 845-848.

FEIGENBAUM, M. (1978): "Quantitative Universality for a Class of Non-Linear Transformations". *Journal of Statistical Physics 19*, pp. 25-52, and *21*, pp. 669-706.

GARRIDO, L./SIMÓ, C. (1983): "Prolog: Some Ideas About Strange Attractors". In: GARRIDO, L. (ed.): *Dynamical Systems and Chaos.* Berlin-Heidelberg-New York: Springer-Verlag.

GLENDINNING, P./SPARROW, C. (1984): "Local and Global Behavior near Homoclinic Orbits". *Journal of Statistical Physics 35*, pp. 645-696.

GREBOGI, C./OTT, E./PELIKAN, S./YORKE, J.A. (1984): "Strange Attractors that are not Chaotic". *Physica 13D*, pp. 261-268.

GREBOGI, C./OTT, E./YORKE, J.A. (1987): "Chaos, Strange Attractors, and Fractal Basin Boundaries in Nonlinear Dynamics". *Science 238*, pp. 632-638.

GRASSBERGER, P. (1986): "Estimating the Fractal Dimension and Entropies of Strange Attractors". In: HOLDEN, A.V. (ed.): *Chaos*, pp. 291-311. Manchester University Press.

GRASSBERGER, P./PROCACCIA, I. (1983a): "Measuring the Strangeness of Strange Attractors". *Physica 9D*, pp. 189-208.

GRASSBERGER, P./PROCACCIA, I. (1983b): "Estimation of the Kolmogorov Entropy from a Chaotic Signal". *Physical Review A 28*, pp. 2591-2593.

GUCKENHEIMER, J. (1973): "Bifurcation and Catastrophe". In: PEIXOTO, M.M. (ed.): *Dynamical Systems* pp. 95-109. New York-London: Academic Press.

GUCKENHEIMER, J. (1979): "Sensitive Dependence to Initial Conditions for One-Dimensional Maps". *Communications in Mathematical Physics 70*, pp. 133-160.

GUCKENHEIMER, J./OSTER, G./IPAKTCHI, A. (1977): "The Dynamics of Density Dependent Population Models". *Journal of Mathematical Biology 4*, pp. 101-147.

HAKEN, H. (1982): "Introduction". In: HAKEN, H. (ed.): *Evolution of Order and Chaos in Physics, Chemistry and Biology*, pp. 2-4. Berlin-Heidelberg-New York: Springer-Verlag.

HIRSCH, M.W. (1984): "The Dynamical Systems Approach to Differential Equations". *Bulletin of the American Mathematical Society 11*, pp. 1-64.

HIRSCH, M.W. (1985): "The Chaos of Dynamical Systems". In: FISCHER, P./SMITH, W.R. (eds.): *Chaos, Fractals, and Dynamics*. New York-Basel: Marcel Dekker Inc.

JACOBSON, M.V. (1981): "Absolutely Continuous Invariant Measures for One-Parameter Families of One-Dimensional Maps". *Communications in Mathematical Physics 81*, pp. 39-88.

LANFORD, O.E. (1983): "Introduction to the Mathematical Theory of Dynamical Systems". In: IOOSS, G./ HELLEMAN, R./STORA, R. (eds.): *Chaotic Behavior of Deterministic Systems*. Amsterdam-New York: North-Holland.

LAUWERIER, H.A. (1986): "One-Dimensional Iterative Maps". In: HOLDEN, A.V. (ed.): *Chaos*, pp. 39-57. Manchester University Press.

LEVI, M. (1981): "Qualitative Analysis of the Periodically Forced Relaxation Oscillation". *Memoirs of the American Mathematical Society 32-244*, pp. 1-147.

LEVINSON, N./SMITH, O.K. (1942): "A General Equation for Relaxation Oscillations". *Duke Mathematical Journal 9*, pp. 382-403.

LI, T.Y./MISIUREWICZ, M./PIANIGIANI, G./YORKE, J.A. (1982): "Odd Chaos". *Physics Letters 87A*, pp. 271-273.

LI, T.Y./YORKE, J.A. (1975): "Period Three Implies Chaos". *American Mathematical Monthly 82*, pp. 985-992.

LORENZ, E.N. (1963): "Deterministic Non-Period Flows". *Journal of Atmospheric Sciences 20*, pp. 130-141.

MAROTTO, F.R. (1978): "Snap-Back Repellers Imply Chaos in R^n". *Journal of Mathematical Analysis and Applications 72*, pp. 199-223.

MAY, R.M. (1976): "Simple Mathematical Models With Very Complicated Dynamics". *Nature 261*, pp. 459-467.

NEWHOUSE, S./RUELLE, D./TAKENS, F. (1978): "Occurrence of Strange Axiom A Attractors near Quasi-Periodic Flows on T^m, $m > 3$". *Communications in Mathematical Physics 64*, pp. 35-40.

NUSSE, H.E. (1986): "Persistence of Order and Structure in Chaos". *Physica 20D*, pp. 374-386.

NUSSE, H.E. (1987): "Asymptotically Periodic Behavior in the Dynamics of Chaotic Mappings". *SIAM Journal of Applied Mathematics 47*, pp. 498-515.

OTT, E. (1981): "Strange Attractors and Chaotic Motions of Dynamical Systems". *Review of Modern Physics 53*, pp. 655-671.

RAND, R.H./HOLMES, P.J. (1980): "Bifurcation of Periodic Motion in Two Weakly Coupled Van Der Pol Oscillators". *International Journal of Non-Linear Mechanics 15*, pp. 387-399.

RÖSSLER, O.E. (1977): "Continuous Chaos". In: HAKEN, H. (ed.): *Synergetics. A Workshop*. Berlin-Heidelberg-New York: Springer-Verlag.

RUELLE, D. (1979): "Strange Attractors". *Mathematical Intelligencer 2*, pp. 126-137.

RUELLE, D. (1981): "Small Random Perturbations of Dynamical Systems and the Definition of Attractors". *Communications in Mathematical Physics 82*, pp. 137-151.

RUELLE, D./TAKENS, F. (1971): "On the Nature of Turbulence". *Communications in Mathematical Physics 20*, pp. 167 - 192.

SINGER, D. (1978): "Stable Orbits and Bifurcation of Maps of the Interval". *SIAM Journal of Applied Mathematics 35*, pp. 260-267.

SHIL'NIKOV, L.P. (1965): "A Case of the Existence of a Countable Number of Periodic Motions". *Sov. Math. Dokl. 6*, pp. 163-166.

SMALE, S. (1967): "Differentiable Dynamical Systems". In: SMALE, S. (1980): *The Mathematics of Time*. New York-Heidelberg-Berlin: Springer-Verlag.

SPARROW, C. (1980): "Bifurcation and Chaotic Behaviour in Simple Feedback Systems". *Journal of Theoretical Biology 83*, pp. 93-105.

SWINNEY, H.L. (1983): "Observations of Order and Chaos in Nonlinear Systems". *Physica 7D*, pp. 3-15.

TAKENS, F. (1981): "Detecting Strange Attractors in Turbulence". In: RAND, D./YOUNG, L. (eds.): *Dynamical Systems and Turbulence*. Berlin-Heidelberg-New York: Springer-Verlag.

TOMITA, K. (1986): "Periodically Forced Nonlinear Oscillators". In: HOLDEN, A.V. (ed.): *Chaos*, pp. 211-236. Manchester: Manchester University Press.

TRESSER, C. (1982): "About some Theorems by L.P. Šil'nikov". *Annales de l'Institut Henri Poincaré 40*, pp. 441-461.

ULAM, S.M./v.NEUMANN, J. (1947): "On Combination of Stochastic and Deterministic Processes". *Bulletin of the American Mathematical Society 53*, p. 1120.

VASTANO, J.A./KOSTELICH, E.J. (1986): "Comparison of Algorithms for Determining Lyapunov Exponents from Experimental Data". In: MAYER-KRESS, G. (ed.): *Dimensions and Entropies in Chaotic Systems*, pp. 100-107. Berlin-Heidelberg-New York: Springer-Verlag.

WHITLEY, D. (1983): "Discrete Dynamical Systems in Dimensions One and Two". *Bulletin of the London Mathematical Society 15*, pp. 177-217.

WOLF, A. (1986): "Quantifying Chaos with Lyapunov Exponents". In: HOLDEN, A.V. (ed.): *Chaos*, pp. 273-290. Manchester University Press.

WOLF, A./SWIFT, J.B./SWINNEY, H.L./VASTANO, J.A. (1985): "Determining Lyapunov Exponents From a Time Series". *Physica 16 D*, pp. 285-317.

WOLF, A./VASTANO, J.A. (1986): "Intermediate Length Scale Effects in Lyapunov Exponent Estimation". In: MAYER-KRESS, G. (ed.): *Dimensions and Entropies in Chaotic Systems*, pp. 94-99. Berlin-Heidelberg-New York: Springer-Verlag.

7.3. Additional Publications Quoted in the Survey

BEGG, D.K.H. (1982): *The Rational Expectations Revolution in Macroeconomics*. Baltimore: John Hopkins Press.

BEGG, D.K.H. (1983): "Rational Expectations and Bond Pricing: Modelling the Term Structure with and without Certainty Equivalence". *Economic Journal 94*, Suppl., pp. 45-58.

CLARK, J.M. (1917): "Business Acceleration and the Law of Demand: A Technical Factor in Economic Cycles". *Journal of Political Economy 25*, pp. 217-235.

GANDOLFO, G. (1983): *Economic Dynamics: Methods and Models*. 2nd ed., Amsterdam: North-Holland.

GANDOLFO, G./MARTINENGO, G./PADOAN, P.C. (1981): *Qualitative Analysis and Econometric Estimation of Continuous Time Dynamic Models*. Amsterdam: North-Holland.

HABERLER, G. (1937): *Prosperity and Depression*. London: George Allen & Unwin.

HAWTREY, R.G. (1913): *Good and Bad Trade*. London: Constable.

HAYEK, F.A. (1933): *Monetary Theory and the Trade Cycle*. London: Jonathan Cape.

HICKS, J.R. (1950): *A Contribution to the Theory of the Trade Cycle*. Oxford: Oxford University Press. 2nd ed. (1965), Oxford: Claredon Press.

JEVONS, W.S. (1884): "Commercial Crises and Sunspots". In: FOXWELL, H.S. (ed.): *Investigations in Currency and Finance*. London: MacMillan.

KALECKI, M. (1937): "A Theory of the Business Cycle". *Review of Economic Studies 4*, pp. 77-97.

LUCAS, R.E. (1975): An Equilibrium Model of the Business Cycle. In: LUCAS, R.E. (1981): Studies in Business-Cycle Theory, pp. 179-214. Cambridge: The MIT Press.

MARX, K. (1867): *Das Kapital. Kritik der politischen Oekonomie*. Hamburg: Otto Meissner.

METZLER, L.A. (1941): "The Nature and Stability of Inventory Cycles". *Review of Economic Studies 23*, pp. 113-129.

PHILLIPS, A.W. (1954): Stabilisation Policy in a Closed Economy. Economic Journal, 64, pp. 290-323.

PIGOU, A.C. (1929): *Industrial Fluctuations*, 2nd edition. London: MacMillan.

SAMUELSON, P.A. (1939): "Interactions Between the Multiplier Analysis and Principle of Acceleration". *Review of Economic Statistics 21*, pp. 75-78.

SAMUELSON, P.A. (1947): *Foundations of Economic Analysis*. Cambridge: Harvard University Press.

SISMONDI, J.-C.-L. S. DE (1837): *Études sur l' économie politique*. Paris: Treuttel & Würtz.

SLUTZKY, E. (1937): "The Summation of Random Causes as the Source of Cyclic Processes". *Econometrica 5*, pp. 105-146.

FRACTAL "BOX-WITHIN-A-BOX" BIFURCATION STRUCTURE

Christian MIRA

G.E.S.N.L.A. - L.E.S.I.A.
Institut National des Sciences Appliquées
Complexe Scientifique de Rangueil
31077 TOULOUSE CEDEX - France

1. Introduction.

The *"box-within-a-box" (or "embedded boxes")* bifurcation structure is a typical *fractal* arrangement of a set of bifurcation points located in the *parameter space* of a given dynamic system. It is recalled that a *bifurcation* is a qualitative change of this system under the effect of variation of its parameters.

Such a fractal structure is widely encountered, when the behaviour of the considered dynamic system in the *phase space* is *chaotic,* i.e the behaviour is so complex that it may seem at first sight stochastic, whereas it is generated by a *deterministic* mechanism. Here this chaos may be *stable (strange attractor)*, or *unstable (chaotic transient, fuzzy basin boundary)* [1]. From another point of view, the "box-within-a-box" structure corresponds to an ordering of the Myrberg' spectra 1963 [2] (often called in the contemporary literature Feigenbaum's cascades (1978) of bifurcations by *period doubling*). This is made by using a "descriptive" symbolism.

After a section devoted to definitions, this paper presents the simplest situation, that of a one-dimensional quadratic map, which makes appear such a fractal situation. This map is non invertible and belong to the class of one-dimensional endomorphisms. The last section deals with some generalizations.

The essential results are given in an "abstract" form, but the book [1] (cf. chapters 2.4) gives the details of this matter.

2. Définitions.

Let T : $R^m \to R^m$ be a real smooth map, $X \to F(X, \Lambda)$, smooth also in the parameter vector Λ.

A *cycle of order k* (or periodic point of period *k*) is a set of k consequent points (iterates, or images) satisfying :

$$X = T^k X \qquad X \neq T^r X \quad r < k$$

So a *fixed point* is a cycle of order k = 1. The *multipliers* S of a cycle are the *m* eigenvalues of the Jacobian matrix of T^k in one of the cycle points.

For the one-dimensional map considered here $m = 1$. A cycle is *attractive* (or asymptotically stable) if all the $|S_i| < 1$, $i = 1, 2, \dots m$. It is *repulsive* if one of the multipliers is such that $|S| > 1$.

In the recurrence form the map is written :

$$X_{n+1} = T\, X_n \qquad , \qquad X_{n+k} = T^k\, X_n$$

X_{n+k} is the rank *k consequent* of X_n, X_n is the rank *k antecedent* of X_{n+k}.

3. The quadratic endomorphism.

3.1. Fundamental bifurcations.

Let T be now the following one-dimensional endomorphism :

(1) $x_{n+1} = f(x_n, \lambda)$,

where f is a smooth real function of x, λ, having only one extremum. For T, when λ varies two following "local" bifurcations :

(A) $\phi \to$ attr. cycle k + rep. cycle k, k = 1, 3, 4, ...
(B) attr. cycle $k2^i \to$ rep. cycle $k2^i$ + attr. cycle $k2^{i+1}$, i = 0, 1, 2, ...

play a fundamental role. Here ϕ indicates the absence of cycle, "attr." (resp. "rep.") corresponds to "attractive" (resp. "repulsive"), k, $k2^i$ are orders of cycles. For (A), called "*fold bifurcation*", the attractive cycle merges into the repulsive one, when S = 1 for these cycles. For (B), called "*flip bifurcation*", the bifurcation occurs when the multiplier S = - 1.

The bifurcations structure of T is fractal of "*box-within-a-box*" type [1] [3] [4] (or "*embedded boxes*"), and is related to the presence of chaotic behaviours (strange attractor, chaotic transient, fuzzy boundary). In the simplest case this structure appears for the quadratic case :

(2) $x_{n+1} = x_n^2 - \lambda$

So for k = 1, (A) takes place for $\lambda = \lambda_{(1)0} = -1/4$ (double root for the equation of fixed points ; fig. 1). When $\lambda < -1/4$, (2) has two real fixed points q_1, q_2 :

$$x(q_1) = 1/2 + (1/4 + \lambda)^{1/2}, \quad x(q_2) = 1/2 - (1/4 + \lambda)^{1/2},$$

with a multiplier $S = 2x(q_i)$, i = 1, 2. Then q_1 is always repulsive of type 1 with $S > 1$, and its multiplier increases when λ increases. The fixed point q_2 ($S < 1$) is attractive of type 1 ($0 < S < 1$) for $-1/4 < \lambda < 0$, attractive of type 2 ($-1 < S < 0$) for $0 < \lambda < 3/4$, repulsive of type 2 ($S < -1$) for $\lambda > 3/4$. Its multiplier decreases when λ is increasing.

For q_2 the bifurcation (B) (k = 1, i = 0) occurs when $\lambda = \lambda_b^0 = 3/4$, giving rise to a cycle of order two. When λ increases a sequence of bifurcations (B) (Myrberg's cascade, or Myrberg spectrum) takes place for k = 1, i = 1, 2, ..., when $\lambda = \lambda_b^i$. If $i \to \infty$, these bifurcation values have an accumulation point :

$$\lim_{i \to \infty} \lambda_b^i = \lambda_{(1)s} = 1.401155189...$$

This result obtained by Myrberg in 1963 [2], is wrongly attributed to Feigenbaum (1978) .

The value $\lambda_{(1)s}$ corresponds to a *non classical bifurcation.* For $\lambda < \lambda_{(1)s}$ the number of repulsive cycles is finite. They have the order 2^i, and have been created after crossing through each λ_b^{i+1} value. For $\lambda > \lambda_{(1)s}$, infinitely many repulsive cycles exist.

Another non classical bifurcation occurs when the critical point C_1 (rank two consequent of the minimum x = 0 of f(x, λ)) merges into the repulsive fixed point q_1 (fig. 2). Let $\lambda = \lambda_1^*$ be the parameter value such that $C_1 \equiv q_1$. For (2), $\lambda_1^* = 2$. Then if $\lambda \geq \lambda_1^*$, all the roots of $x = T^k x$, $k = 1, 2, 3, \ldots$ become real. So all the possible cycles have been created and they are repulsive. These cycles, their limit points when $k \to \infty$, and their antecedent of any rank, are located on the segment $q_1 q_1^{-1}$, q_1^{-1} being the first rank antecedent of q_1, which is not q_1 itself. When $\lambda > \lambda_1^*$ ($x(q_1) < x(c_1)$ fig. 3), all the corresponding repulsive points constitute a *strange repulsor,* no one attractor exists at finite distance. When $\lambda < \lambda_1^*$ ($x(q_1) > x(c_1)$ fig. 4), the quadratic map has at most one attractor (fixed point, cycle, or more complex set), located on the segment CC_1 (absorbing segment), C being the first rank consequent of the minimum x = 0.

For $\lambda \geq \lambda_1^*$, the maximum number N_k of cycles, having the same order k, is rapidly increasing with k. It is the same for the number $N_\lambda(k)$ of bifurcations (A) or (B) giving rise to such cycles, as indicated in the following table [1] [3] :

k...	2	3	4	5	6	7	8	9	10	11	12	13	14	15	16	...	20
N_k...	1	2	3	6	9	18	30	56	99	186	335	630	1161	2182	4080	...	52377
$N_\lambda(k)$	1	1	2	3	5	9	16	28	51	93	170	315	585	1091	2048	...	26214

For k = 30, $N_k = 35790267$, $N_\lambda(k) = 17895679$

When $\lambda = \lambda_1^*$, the segment $[q_1, q_1^{-1}] \equiv [C, C_1]$ is called a *chaotic segment.* An initial condition x_0 on this segment gives a bounded iterated sequence on $[C, C_1]$ which is very sensitive to very small changes of x_0.

Cycles having the same order k are differentiated by the permutation of their k points, by k successive applications of T. This permutation is characterized by a *Myrberg rotation sequence*. Such sequences verify the *Myrberg's ordering law* [2] (1963), the more recent notions of "invariant coordinate" and "kneading invariant" being variants of this law which permits to assign a running number j to each cycle. So a cycle will be identified by the symbolism (k ; j).

Two cycles given from the bifurcation (A) have the same index j. They are designated by (k ; j), and are called *basic cycles*. The bifurcation value is designated by $\lambda^{j}_{(k)_0}$ (S = + 1), and the curve T^k in the (x_n, x_{n+1}) plane has k tangential points with $x_n = x_{n+1}$ (fig. 5 for k = 3). Such a situation is equivalent, for T^k, to that obtained for T when $\lambda = \lambda_{(1)0}$. The limit of the cascade flip bifurcations, for the cycle (k ; j) with S < 1, is noted $\lambda^{j}_{(k)_S}$.

For a value $\lambda = \lambda^{*j}_{k}$, the repulsive cycle (k ; j) with S > 1, is in an equivalent situation to that of the fixed point when $\lambda = \lambda^{*}_{1}$ (fig. 6 for k = 3), the cycle points being also critical points of a defined rank. Then one has k cyclic chaotic segments with a permutation defined by j.

3.2. Succinct description of the "box-within-a-box" bifurcations stucture.

Consider the Myrberg's cascade(B)obtained from a basic cycle (k ; j) with S < 1. On the parameter axis λ, it takes place in the interval :

$$\omega^{j}_{k} \equiv \left[\lambda^{j}_{(k)_0}, \lambda^{j}_{(k)_S}\right]$$

The following symbolism

$$\Omega_1 \equiv \left[\lambda_{(1)_0}, \lambda^{*}_{1}\right], \ \Delta_1 \equiv \left]\lambda_{(1)_S}, \lambda^{*}_{1}\right]$$

and more generally :

$$\Omega^{j}_{k} \equiv \left[\lambda^{j}_{(k)_0}, \lambda^{*j}_{k}\right], \ \Delta^{j}_{k} \equiv \left]\lambda^{j}_{(k)_S}, \lambda^{*j}_{k}\right], \ \Omega^{j}_{k} \subset \Delta_1$$

is used. Ω^{j}_{k} is called the *box* (k ; j), ω^{j}_{k} is the *spectrum* (k ; j). Then a box (k ; j) reproduces all the bifurcations contained in the box Ω_1, in the same order (self similarity property), for a set of cycles having orders multiple of k (the basic cycles of Ω^{j}_{k} are (k ; j), those of Ω_1 are the fixed points q_1, q_2 (k = 1 ; j = 1)). So if k is a prime number, there are $N_\lambda(k)$ boxes $(k\ ;\ j),\ j = 1, 2, \ldots, N_\lambda(k)$.

Making $k = k_1$, $j = j_1$, and starting from T^{k_1}, one considers $\left(T^{k_1}\right)^{k_2}$ via a process equivalent to the one which leads to T^{k_1} from T. For each of the k_1 parabolic shaped segments of T^{k_1}, which gives rise to the definition of $\lambda^{j_1}_{(k_1)_0}$, $\lambda^{*j_1}_{k_1}$, the cycles(having an order multiple of the product k_1 k_2) undergo in the same order the bifurcations of the box Ω_1. From this process results the existence of boxes :

$$\Omega_{k_1 . k_2}^{j_1 . j_2} \equiv \left[\lambda_{(k_1 . k_2)_0}^{j_1 . j_2}, \lambda_{k_1 . k_2}^{*\, j_1 . j_2} \right] \quad , \qquad \Omega_{k_1 . k_2}^{j_1 . j_2} \equiv \Delta_{k_1 . k_2}^{j_1 . j_2} \cup \omega_{k_1 . k_2}^{j_1 . j_2} \subset \Delta_{k_1}^{j_1}$$

More generally boxes :

$$\Omega_{k_1 \dots k_a}^{j_1 \dots j_a} \equiv \left[\lambda_{(k_1 \dots k_a)_0}^{j_1 \dots j_a}, \lambda_{k_1 \dots k_a}^{*\, j_1 \dots j_a} \right] \subset \Delta_{k_1 \dots k_{a-1}}^{j_1 \dots j_{a-1}}$$

are defined. A box $(k_1, \dots, k_a \,;\, j_1, \dots, j_a)$ is embedded into a box $(k_1, \dots, k_{a-1} \,;\, j_1, \dots, j_{a-1})$.

All these boxes, for which the value λ^* is defined from the repulsive basic cycle with S > 1, are called *boxes of first kind.*

Values λ^* can be defined from a repulsive cycle with S < - 1, born from the bifurcation (B). So critical points of certain ranks merge into a cycle of order $k\ 2^{i-1}$, $i = 1, 2, \dots, k = 1, 3, 4, \dots,$, when $\lambda = \lambda_{k\,2^i}^{*\,j}$. Figs 7, 8 illustrate this situation for $k = 1, i = 1, 2$. A box of second kind has this value as one of the two boundary points, the other being the bifurcation value $\lambda_{(k 2^i)_0}^{j}$ giving an attractive cycle of order $k\ 2^i$ from (B) (by replacing i by i = i - 1). When $i \to \infty$, the two boundaries tend toward $\lambda_{k_s}^{j}$. The crossing of $\lambda_{2^1}^{*}$ is sometimes called "*snap back repeller bifurcation*".

Figs 9 and 10 represent the "*box-within-a-box*" (or *embedded boxes*) bifurcations structures. It is *fractal* because the boxes are self similar, or the organization of this set (Ω_1) is similar to that of its parts (the above defined boxes), even if these parts are infinitesimal.

More details on this questions (in particular the limit points of the boxes when $k \to \infty$) are given in [1].

4. Conclusion (generalizations).

The generalizations of the above notions are given in [1] [3]. They concern the following cases :

- (a) $y_{n+1} = a y_n^2 + 2\, b y_n + c$, which has the same behaviour as T with $f(x, \lambda) = x^2 - \lambda$. Indeed a linear change of variable, $y = \alpha\, x + b$, gives this map with $\lambda = b^2 - ac - b$, $\alpha\, a = 1$, $a\, \beta = -\, b$.

- (b) f(x, λ) is a continuous and differentiable function in x with only one extremum in one of the two situations : f(x, λ) has a negative Schwarzian derivative (T has only one attractor at finite distance), f(x, λ) has not this property (T can have more than one attractor at finite distance).

- (c) f(x, λ) has two extrema (cf. also [3]).

- (d) f(x, λ) is a continuous piecewise linear function with only one extremum [1] [3] [5].

- (e) $f(x, \lambda)$ is embedded into a two-dimensional diffeomorphism (differentiable, invertible map) such as :

$$x \to f(x, \lambda) + y \quad , \quad y \to bx$$

Now the "box-within-a-box" bifurcation structure occurs in a foliated parameter plane (λ, b), i.e this plane must be considered as made up of sheets, each one being associated to a given cycle (cf. chapter 5 of [1]).

- (f) The map mentioned can be considered as the result of a Poincaré Section of the phase space associated with an ordinary differential equation. It results that the "embedded boxes" structure is encountered in such equations.

References

[1] MIRA C. "Chaotic Dynamics. From the one-dimensional endomorphism to the two-dimensional diffeomorphism" World Scientific, 1987 (450 pages).

[2] MYRBERG P.J. "Iteration der reellen Polynome zweiten Grades" Ann. Acad. Sci. Fenn. ser. A, 336 (1963), 1 - 10.

[3] GUMOWSKI I. & MIRA C. "Dynamique Chaotique. Transition ordre-désordre" Cépaduès (Toulouse), 1980, (480 pages).

[4] GUMOWSKI I. & MIRA C. "Accumulations de bifurcations dans une récurrence" C.R. Acad. Sc. Paris, série A, 281 (1975), 45 - 48.

[5] MIRA C. "Dynamique complexe engendrée par une récurrence continue, linéaire par morceaux, du premier ordre" C.R. Acad. Sc. Paris, série A, 285 (1977), 731 - 734.

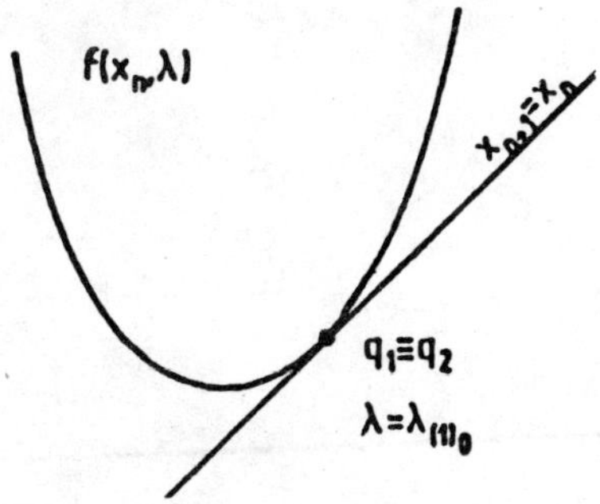

Fig. 1 $\lambda = \lambda_{(1)_0}$

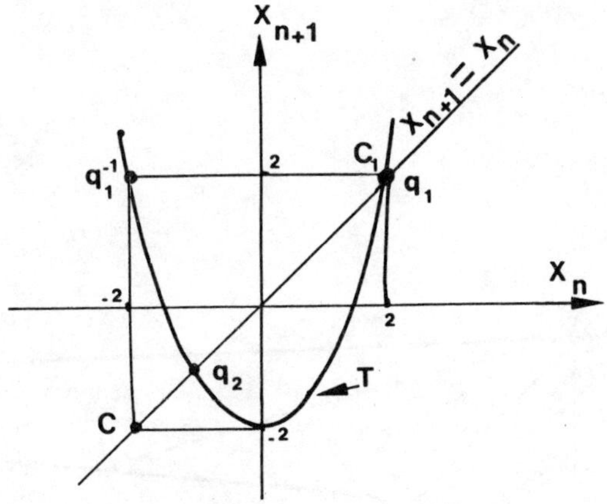

Fig. 2 $\lambda = \lambda_1^*$

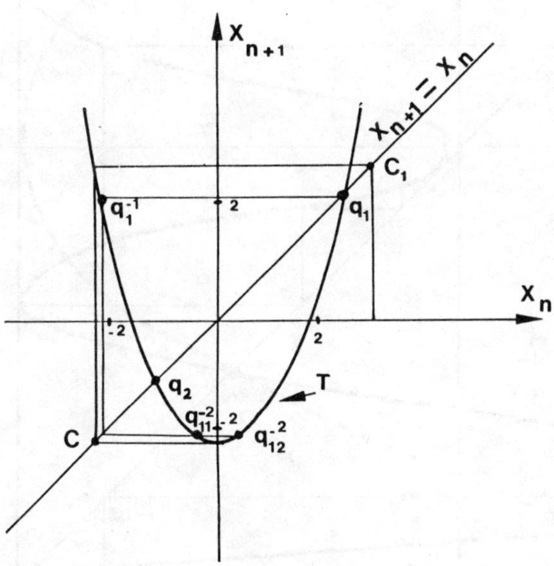

Fig. 3 $\lambda > \lambda_1^*$

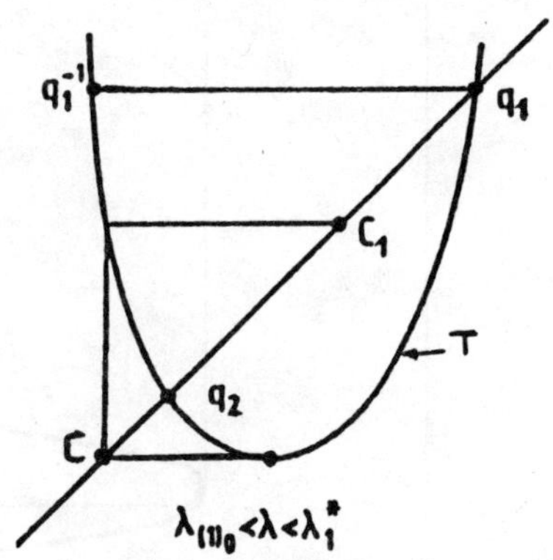

Fig. 4 $\lambda_{(1)_0} < \lambda < \lambda_1^*$

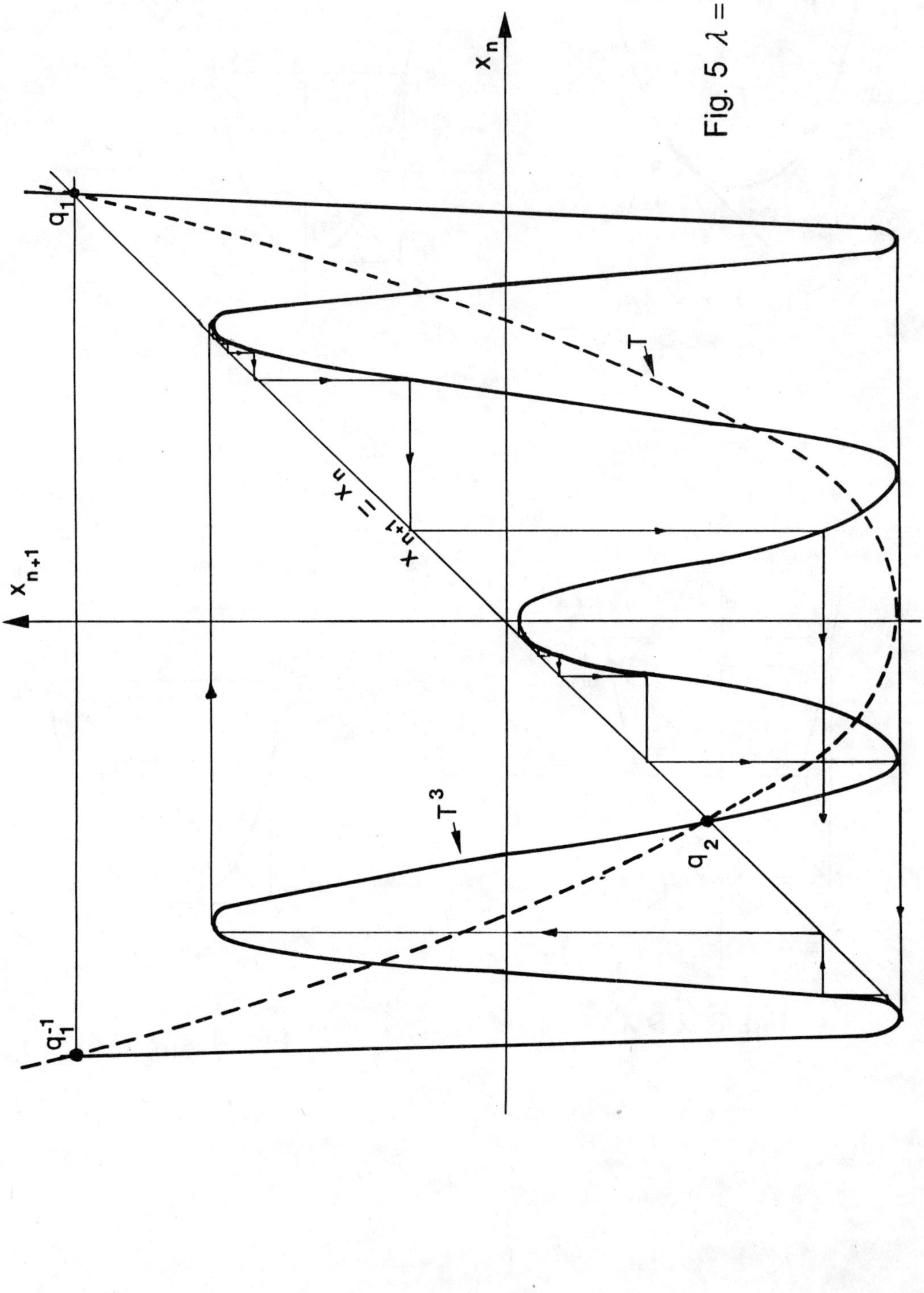

Fig. 5 $\lambda = \lambda_{(3)_0}$

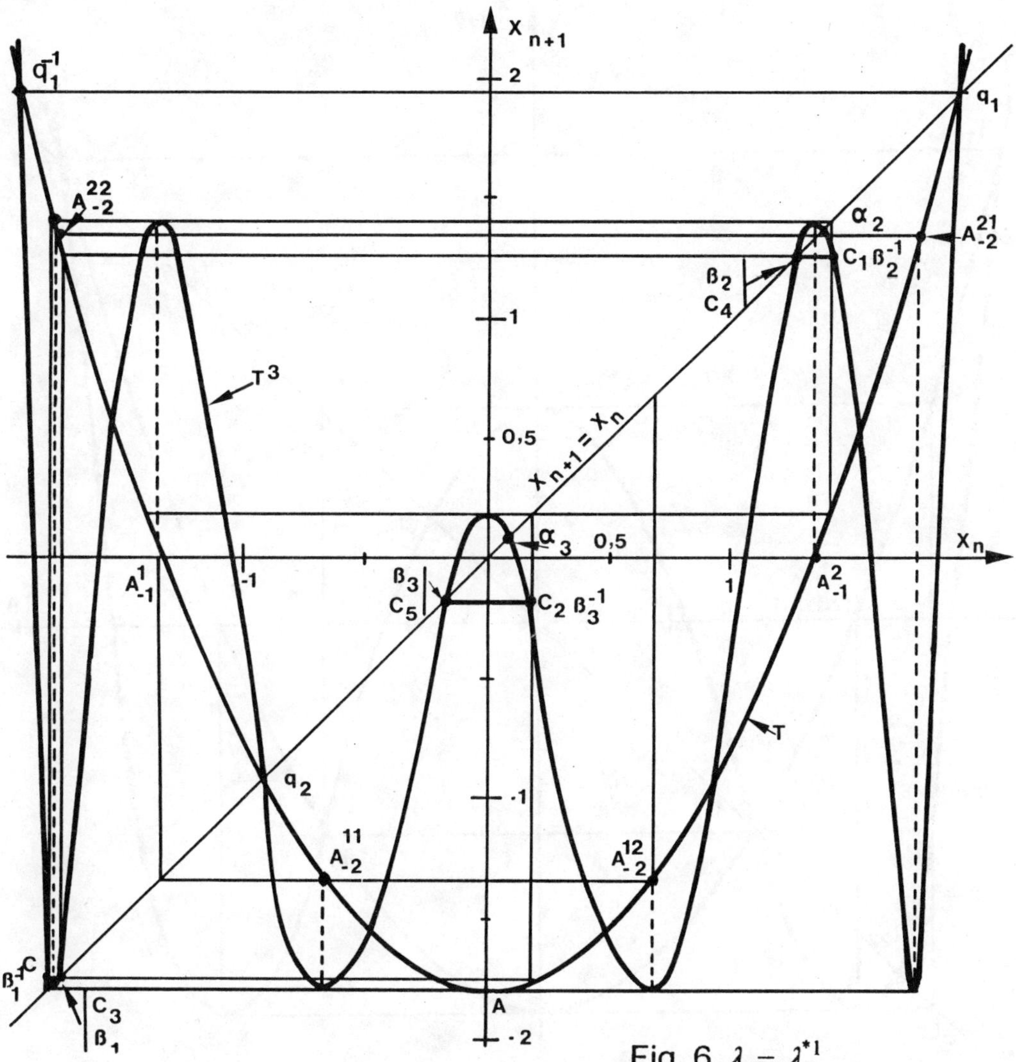

Fig. 6 $\lambda = \lambda_3^{*1}$

$\alpha_i, \beta_i, i = 1, 2, 3$, are respectively the 3 points of the cycle k = 3 with S < 1, and of the cycle k = 3 with S > 1. C_j, j = 0, 1, ..., 5, ($C_0 \equiv C$), is the consequent of rank j of the minimum A. The projections of the parabolic segments (C_ℓ), ℓ = 1, 2, 3, of T on x_n - axis are respectively $\overline{CC_3}, \overline{C_2C_5}, \overline{C_1C_4}$. ($C_1$) has a minimum, ($C_2$), ($C_3$) have each one a maximum.

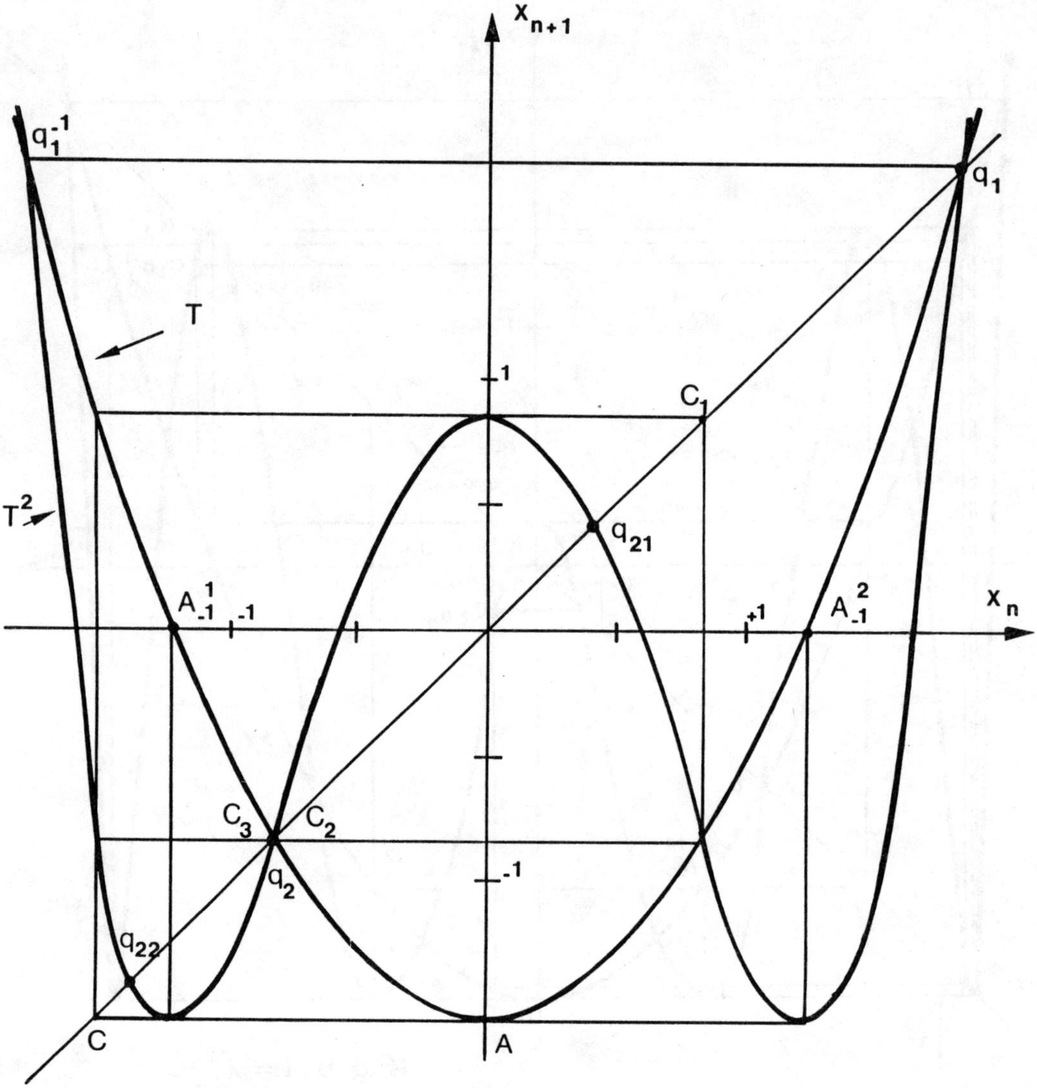

Fig. 7 $\lambda = \lambda^*_{2^1}$

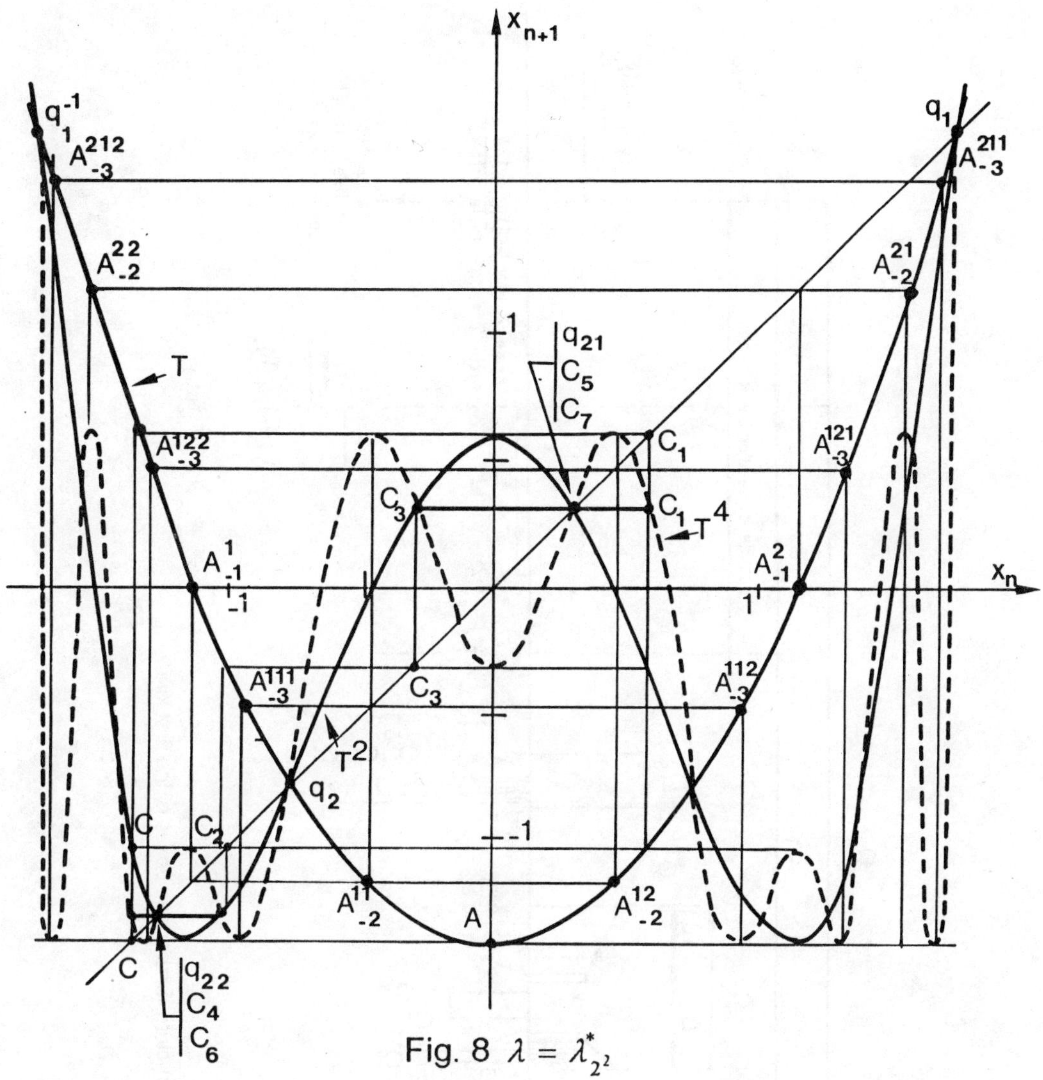

Fig. 8 $\lambda = \lambda^*_{2^2}$

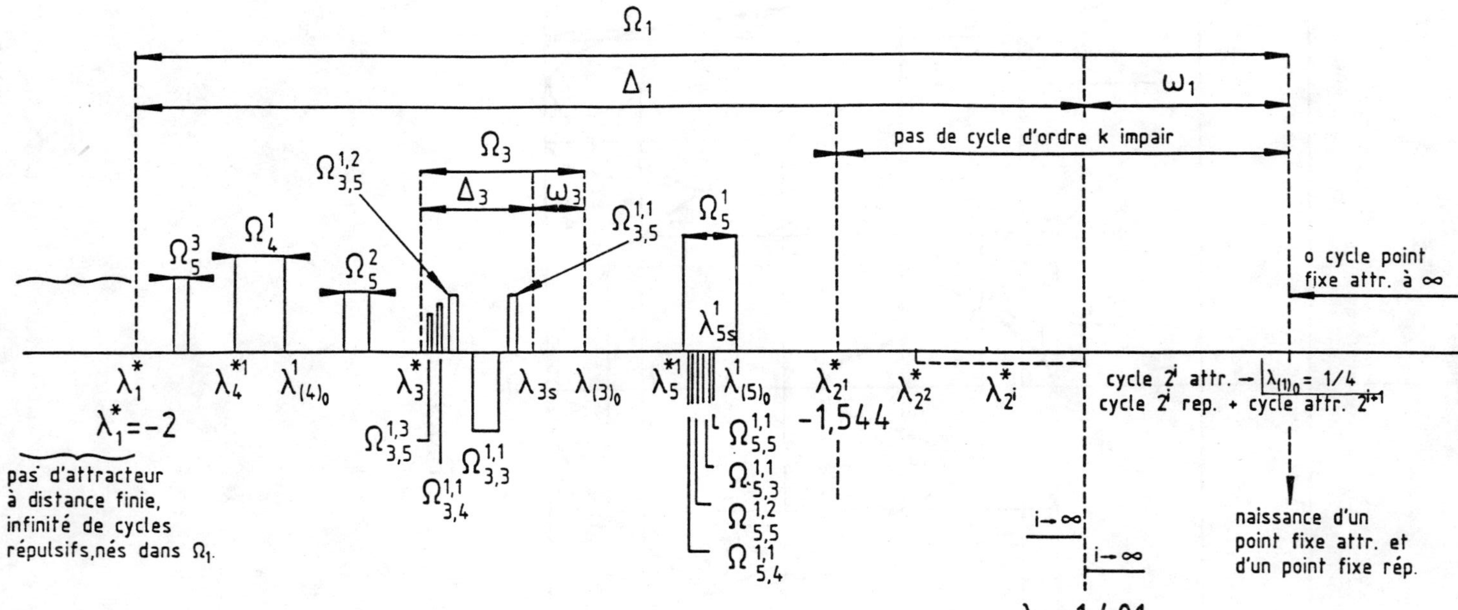

Fig. 9

The box-within-a-box bifurcation structure. Embedded boxes of the first kind.

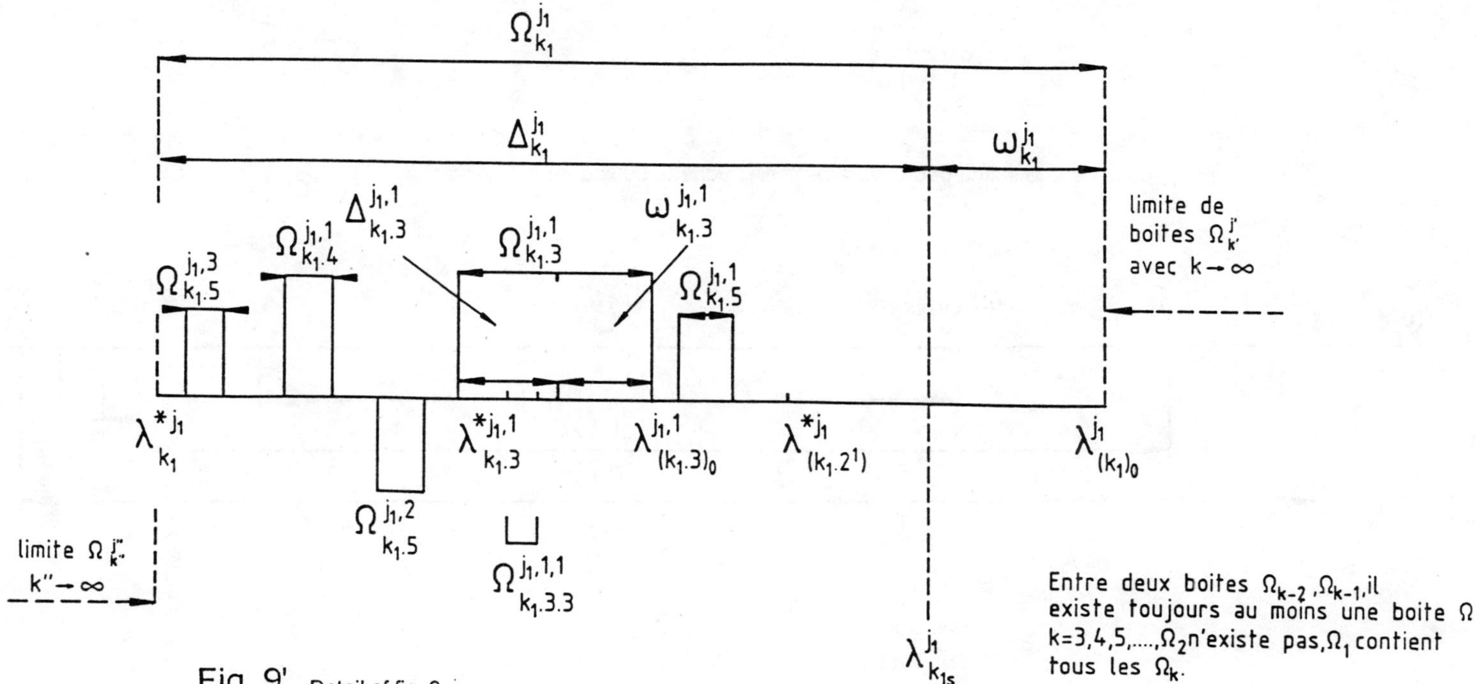

Fig. 9' Detail of fig. 9

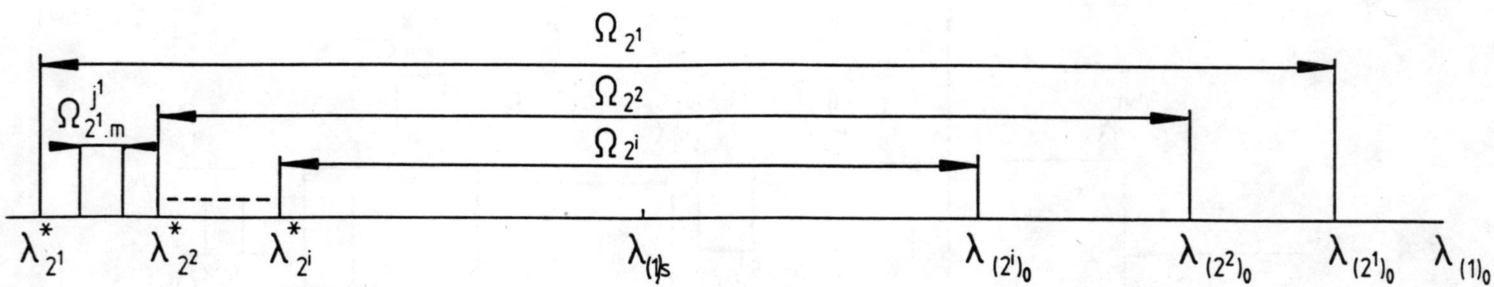

Fig. 10 The box-within-a-box bifurcation structure. Embedded boxes of the second kind.

INVITED LECTURES

RECURRENCE IN KEYNESIAN MACROECONOMIC MODELS

VOLKER BÖHM[1]
Lehrstuhl für Volkswirtschaftslehre, Wirtschaftstheorie
Universität Mannheim
Postfach 10 34 62, D–W–6800 Mannheim

1 Introduction

The development of new mathematical techniques in the theory of nonlinear dynamic systems has greatly enlarged the analytical basis for modern business cycle theory in economics. The elaborate theory of one–dimensional systems offers a large spectrum of methods and results indicating a great degree of different dynamic phenomenae which were not known before. Its impact on dynamic economics can already be found in a large number of recent publications. One of the most surprising class of results is given by the long list of contributions examining chaotic behavior in one–dimensional competitive systems (see for example the contributions in [10]).

In spite of the formal elegance and the portrayal of new and interesting results, competitive business cycle theory analyses intertemporal allocation problems within market clearing models, which, in general, cannot describe dynamic processes (see Grandmont [9]). The equilibrium requirement and the perfect foresight assumption together generate infinite sequences of equilibrium prices and allocations only, for which a forward recursive time map cannot be constructed in many cases.

Modern contributions to non–market clearing theories also applied the new techniques (see the recent survey by Lorenz [14]). One of the models studied frequently in that literature is the one originally proposed by Kaldor[13] in 1940. Dana/Malgrange [5] performe extensive simulations for a Kaldor type model. They show that varying a parameter of the model changes a stable fixed point to a closed orbit which, after a further increase of the parameter, becomes unstable itself. Thus, strange attractors or possibly chaos occur. In contrast to the competitive business cycle theory, however, these Keynesian models seldom are built on the same level of microeconomic basic principles. To some they are therefore considered too much ad hoc and unacceptable. Moreover, a comparison of the two types of models or their results is essentially futile since different methodologies are used for different economic models which leaves no room for a meaningful comparison.

[1] I am indebted to Markus Lohmann for his priceless assistance in computational matters at all stages of this research. Generous financial support by the University of Melbourne is gratefully acknowledged.

The present paper represents an attempt to overcome some of these fundamental disparities. It uses features of Keynesian disequilibrium in an overlapping generations model. Thus, the same natural microeconomic basis as in competitive business cycle theory is used. In this way, some of the fundamental difficulties of the market clearing approach are avoided while the advantages of the demographic structure of overlapping generations models is maintained. Moreover, the market clearing situation becomes a special case of the disequilibrium. Thus, it is hoped that a meaningful comparison of the results of the two classes of models becomes possible.

Here the prototype model proposed in [4], is developed further. There the dynamic elements of the model were fully described, but no dynamic analysis was carried out. However, it was shown that for a two class consumer model the properties of the set of steady states imply that stable monotonic trajectories cannot be expected in many cases. Here the dynamic analysis will be presented for a one class consumer model. This model resembles most closely the standard Keynesian AD–AS model in its temporary form.

2 The Model

Consider an economy which evolves over time $t = 1, 2, \ldots$. In each period t one homogeneous output is produced from homogeneous labor as the only input factor. Labor and output are not storable and output is produced instantaneously. Fiat money is the only store of value between periods. Its price is equal to one in all periods. Thus money serves as a unit of account and as a store of value. Let p_t and w_t denote the price of output and the wage rate in period t respectively in terms of money.

The set of agents in the economy consists of a government, a firm, and of consumers. The government and the firm are both infinitely lived. The set of consumers has the overlapping generations structure.

- **Government**

  The government purchases a quantity $g \geq 0$ of the commodity in each period at the market price $p_t \geq 0$, and it raises revenue by levying a proportional income tax on young consumers at the rate tax, $0 \leq tax \leq 1$. Since economic activity determines the level of tax revenue, budget deficits and surpluses will typically occur. These are financed through money creation or destruction which constitutes the only source for changes in the money stock held by consumers. Thus their net asset position changes if and only if the deficit of the government is nonzero. There are no monetary transfers or lump sum taxes.

- **Consumers**

Each generation of consumers consists of one consumer only, who lives and consumes for two consecutive periods. Each consumer supplies a fixed amount of labor $L_{max} > 0$ during the first period of his life and receives wage income as well as profit. An old consumer neither receives any income nor any government transfers, so that all consumption during the second period of a consumer's life has to be financed through savings.

Let $M_t \geq 0$ denote the amount of money held by an old consumer at the beginning of period t. Then, given the current commodity price p_t, consumption demand of the old consumer is given by M_t/p_t.

Preferences of young consumers over consumption plans $(x_t, x_{t+1}) \geq 0$ are given by an intertemporal utility function $u : \mathbb{R}^2_+ \to \mathbb{R}$, which satisfies the following assumption:

Assumption C: (Preferences)

1. $u : \mathbb{R}^2_+ \to \mathbb{R}$
2. u is C^2, strictly monotonic, strictly quasi–concave, homothetic
3. for any $(x^n_t, x^n_{t+1}) \gg 0$
$$\frac{\partial u}{\partial x_t}(x^n_t, x^n_{t+1}) \to +\infty \quad \text{if} \quad x^n_t \to 0$$
$$\frac{\partial u}{\partial x_{t+1}}(x^n_t, x^n_{t+1}) \to +\infty \quad \text{if} \quad x^n_{t+1} \to 0$$

Given the preferences of a young consumer, his consumption/savings decision will depend on his net income Y^{net} in the first period of his life and on his price expectations for the second period. These will be taken to be point forecasts which the cosumer makes on the basis of past prices. Given his forecast p^e_{t+1} for the price in period $t+1$, define $\theta^e_t = p^e_{t+1}/p_t$. Then, an optimal consumption and savings plan is given by the solution of

$$\max\{u(x_t, x_{t+1}) \mid p_t x_t + p^e_{t+1} x_{t+1} \leq Y^{net}\}.$$

Because of **Assumption C**, the solution of the consumers optimization problem yields the notional commodity demand x^*_t in the first period of his life as

$$x^*_t = \arg\max \left\{ u\left(x_t, \frac{Y^{net} - p_t x_t}{p^e_{t+1}} \right) \right\},$$

which can be written as

$$x^*_t = c\left(\frac{p^e_{t+1}}{p_t}\right) \frac{Y^{net}}{p_t} = c(\theta^e_t)\,\frac{Y^{net}}{p_t}.$$

His notional savings, i. e. his demand for money then is

$$S_t^* = (1 - c(\theta_t^e))\,Y^{net}.$$

The homotheticity of the utility function implies the particular form of the demand function. The function $c(\theta_t^e)$ is the average and marginal propensity to consume which depends on relative expected prices only, and lies strictly between zero and one. Thus consumption demand and the demand for money will always be positive as long as current, expected prices, and net income are positive.

For an analysis of the temporary structure of the model expected prices are essentially a parameter for the economy at time t. However, for a full dynamic analysis an explicit description has to be given of how young consumers make a particular forecast. Here it is assumed that the expected prices by consumers depend on observed prices over some finite past and that all generations use the same expectations function with an identical length of memory.

Let $\tau = 0, 1, 2, 3, \ldots$ denote the number of periods before t for which generation t considers past prices to be relevant for their forecast. Then, the expected price p_{t+1}^e for period $t+1$ will be a function of the vector of past and current prices $(p_t, p_{t-1}, p_{t-2}, \cdots, p_{t-\tau})$ which will be of the following general form:

$$p_{t+1}^e = p_t\,\Psi\left(\frac{p_t}{p_{t-1}}, \cdots, \frac{p_{t+1-\tau}}{p_{t-\tau}}\right).$$

Written more compactly one obtains

$$\theta_t^e = \Psi(\theta_{t-1}, \cdots, \theta_{t-\tau}),$$

in other words, generations of consumers make a point forecast of the inflation rate from t to $t+1$ on the basis of the past τ inflation rates. Apart from continuity and inflation/deflation confirmation no further specific assumption will be imposed on Ψ.

Assumption E: (Expectations)

1. $p_{t+1}^e = p_t\,\Psi\left(\frac{p_t}{p_{t-1}}, \cdots, \frac{p_{t+1-\tau}}{p_{t-\tau}}\right)$

2. $\Psi : \mathbb{R}_{++}^{\tau} \rightarrow \mathbb{R}_{++}$ continuous

3. $\Psi(\theta, \ldots, \theta) = \theta \qquad \forall \theta > 0$

4. $\Psi \equiv 1 \quad$ if $\tau = 0$.

- **Producer**

In each period t the production of output is instantaneous from labor. There is no inventory holding. The capital stock of the economy is constant and one firm produces all output while attempting to maximize current profits. Let $F : \mathbb{R}_+ \to \mathbb{R}_+$ denote the production function of the firm in each period, so that output $y_t = F(z_t)$ where z_t denotes labor input. Then, given the current wage rate w_t and the current commodity price p_t, the firm solves the problem

$$\max\{p_t y_t - w_t z_t | y_t \leq F(z_t)\}.$$

The following standard assumptions will be made:

Assumption F: (Production)

1. $F : \mathbb{R}_+ \to \mathbb{R}_+ \quad ; \quad y = F(z)$
2. F is C^2, strictly monotonic, strictly concave
3. $$\begin{array}{ll} F(0) = 0 & \lim_{z \to \infty} F(z) = \infty \\ F'(0) = \infty & F'(\infty) = 0 \end{array}$$

Let $\alpha_t = w_t/p_t$ denote the real wage in period t. Then, one obtains as notional labor demand of the firm

$$z_t^* = h(\alpha_t) = \arg\max\{F(z) - \alpha_t z\},$$

and as notional commodity supply

$$y_t^* = F(h(\alpha_t)).$$

Clearly, under **Assumption F** labor demand and commodity supply are strictly positive at all positive real wages α_t.

3 Temporary Feasible States

For the simple macroeconomic model considered here, the market structure and the set of agents imply for any period t the same type and number of feasible situations as in all well known macroeconomic models built as general equilibrium models with quantity rationing. Thus for any given pair of the wage rate and the commodity price, feasibility and the one–sidedness assumption of rationing imply that there may exist three distinct disequilibrium situations labeled Keynesian unemployment, classical unemployment, repressed inflation, or one of the four possible boundary cases. Since labor supply is fixed and exogenously given at all prices and wages, the determination of these states can be carried out in the same simple fashion as in the traditional AD–AS model. This means that the feasibility considerations can be decoupled from the spillover structure of demand and supply behavior of the agents.

- **Aggregate Demand**

  Consider the situation on the commodity market first. Any level of feasible output y_t has to be equal to the sum of the quantities demanded by the government, the young consumer, and by the old consumer, i. e.

$$y_t = \frac{M_t}{p_t} + c\,(\theta_t^e)\,(1 - tax)\,y_t + g.$$

  Let $m_t = M_t/p_t$ denote real balances. Solving for y_t yields the aggregate demand function $D\,(m_t, \theta_t^e, g, tax)$ given by

$$y_t^D = D\,(m_t, \theta_t^e, g, tax) = \frac{m_t + g}{1 - c\,(\theta_t^e)\,(1 - tax)}.$$

- **Aggregate Supply**

  Aggregate supply in this economy is described by the profit maximizing behavior of the firm and by the availability of labor, i. e. by the minimum of the notional supply of the firm at any real wage and the productive capacity of the economy $F(L_{max}) = y_{max}$:

$$y_t^s = \min\left\{F\left(h\left(\alpha_t\right)\right), F(L_{max})\right\}.$$

Feasibility for the economy as a whole requires that actual output is determined by the minimum of aggregate demand and aggregate supply. Thus, for any period t, given government parameters (g, tax), current prices and wages, expected prices, and money holdings of the old consumer, a state of the economy in period t is uniquely defined by actual output y_t given by

$$y_t = \min\left\{y_t^D, y_t^*, y_{max}\right\} = \mathcal{Y}\left(p_t, w_t, M_t, p_{t+1}^e, g, tax\right),$$

and by employment L_t given by

$$L_t = F^{-1}\left(\mathcal{Y}\left(p_t, w_t, M_t, p^e_{t+1}, g, tax\right)\right) = \mathcal{L}\left(p_t, w_t, M_t, p^e_{t+1}, g, tax\right).$$

Here $\mathcal{Y}$ and $\mathcal{L}$ denote the associated functions. It is straightforward to verify the statements made in the following theorem.

Theorem: Given **Assumptions C, F**, then:

$$\forall\,(p_t, w_t, p^e_{t+1}) \gg 0, \quad \forall\,(M_t, g) > 0, \quad \forall\, 0 \leq tax \leq 1:$$

1. $\exists$ unique positive feasible output and employment levels given by the two functions $\mathcal{Y}$ and $\mathcal{L}$,
2. the type of temporary feasible state is either

   C – classical

   K – Keynesian

   I – repressed inflation

   or one of the 4 boundary cases[2],
3. the functions $\mathcal{Y}$ and $\mathcal{L}$ are continuous and homogeneous of degree zero in $(p_t, w_t, M_t, p^e_{t+1})$.

Hence, using the homogeneity property, one may write

$$y_t = \mathcal{Y}(\alpha_t, m_t, \theta^e_t, g, tax)$$

and

$$L_t = \mathcal{L}(\alpha_t, m_t, \theta^e_t, g, tax).$$

The important implication of the theorem is that temporary feasible states are uniquely defined by real wages, real balances, expected inflation rates, and by government parameters. Thus, the dynamic development of the economy can be described in a unique way by sequences of these same variables.

4 Steady States and Perfect Foresight

Consider the economy in period $t \gg 1$, assuming that economic activity started at some initial point $t = 1$. Then, given the values for $(p_t, w_t, M_t, p^e_{t+1}, g, tax)$ of period t, the functions $\mathcal{L}$ and

[2]See for example Böhm[4] for the definitions of the disequilibrium types.

$\mathcal{Y}$ determine the current disequilibrium situation of period t. Assume that government activity is stationary, i. e. the tax rate as well as government demand is constant over time. Then, the dynamic development of the economy is described by a sequence $\{p_t, w_t, M_t, p^e_{t+1}\}$ of prices, wages, money balances, and expected prices for each $t \geq 1$.

Expected prices are determined by the expectation function Ψ. Money balances are determined by the savings behavior of the young generation in each period. The possibility of forced savings under demand rationing of young consumers makes it necessary to describe actual savings of the young as a function of actual output and employment. Demand rationing situations on the commodity market in any period t may involve rationing of three different agents, namely the government, the old consumer, or the young consumer. For a determinate outcome, therefore, it is necessary to define a specific rationing rule for the commodity market. It will be assumed here that under demand rationing the government is served first, then the old consumer, and then the young consumer. This implies that actual consumption of the young consumer in period t for given output y_t is given by

$$x_t = \max\left\{0, y_t - g - \frac{M_t}{p_t}\right\}.$$

As a consequence, actual savings of the young, i. e. initial money balances at the beginning of the next period are

$$M_{t+1} = (1 - tax)\, p_t y_t \quad - \quad p_t x_t = p_t \left[\min\left\{y_t, \frac{M_t}{p_t} + g\right\} - tax\ y_t\right].$$

This equation corresponds to the usual government budget constraint and constitutes one of the difference equations of the model. If there is no demand rationing of the old consumer, i. e. if $M_t/p_t \leq y_t - g$, then the change in the money stock is equal to the government deficit. Otherwise young agents are demand rationed to zero and savings is equal to total net income. Thus possible amounts of money unspent by the old consumer are destroyed and not distributed to the young.

The government budget constraint, the expectations function, and the allocation function $\mathcal{Y}$ can now be used to define steady states with perfect foresight, in spite of the fact that a specific price and wage adjustment process has not been defined. In general, sequences of temporary feasible states would be given by sequences of prices, wages, money balances, and price expectations. Due to the homogeneity of the allocation function, a three dimensional state space suffices with the coordinates for real wages, real money balances, and expected inflation rates.

Def.: A sequence $\{\alpha_t, m_t, \theta_t^e\}_{t=1}^{\infty}$ of real wages, real money balances, and expected inflation rates is called a path with quantity rationing, or simply a path, if

1. $m_{t+1}\theta_t \;=\; \min\{y_t, m_t + g\} - tax\, y_t,$

2. $\theta_t^e \;=\; \Psi(\theta_{t-1}, \ldots, \theta_{t-T}),$

3. $y_t \;=\; \mathcal{Y}(\alpha_t, m_t, \theta_t^e, g, tax).$

Steady states imply constant allocations, i. e. constant levels of employment, production and consumption. These are generated by constant sequences of real wages, of real balances, and of expected inflation rates.

Def.: A path $\{\alpha_t, m_t, \theta_t^e\}_{t=1}^{\infty}$ is called quasi–stationary if

$$\forall\, t, t' : \; \alpha_t = \alpha_{t'} \;,\; m_t = m_{t'} \;,\; \theta_t^e = \theta_{t'}^e.$$

The associated steady state is also called quasi–stationary. It is called stationary if $\theta_t^e = 1$. It is immediately apparent that agents' price expectations are fulfilled at any quasi–stationary state, i. e. expected and actual inflation coincide. Moreover, non zero inflation ($\theta \neq 1$) implies, of course, that nominal money balances grow or shrink at the same rate as prices and wages. Thus, for such states the government deficit has to be non zero. Conversely, the only steady states with a balanced government budget are those with zero inflation, i. e. $\theta = 1$.

One of the striking results derived in [4] is that, in a slightly more general model, the set of steady states is a piecewise differentiable manifold which possesses a double fold. With this information it was conjectured that not all trajectories can be monotonically converging. The same property of the set of steady states holds here as well for the model with a more aggregate consumption sector and a proportional income tax.

Theorem: Given **Assumptions C, E, F**, let $y_{max} = F(L_{max})$ denote capacity output and $\alpha^* = F'(L_{max})$ the full employment real wage. Then

$\forall\, g > 0$ and $\forall\, 0 \leq tax \leq 1$ one has:

1. $\forall\, (\theta, \alpha) \gg 0,$
   $\exists\, m > 0$ s.t. $(\alpha,\, m,\, \theta)$ is quasi–stationary;

2. $\forall\, (\theta, \alpha) \gg 0$ and $\theta > 1$ or $g > [1 - c(\theta)(1 - tax)]\, y_{max}$
   $\exists$ unique $m > 0$ s.t. (α, m, θ) is quasi–stationary;

3. if $g < tax\, y_{max}$:

   $\exists$ an open set $B \subset (0,1) \times (0,\alpha^*)$

   s.t.$\forall\, (\theta,\alpha) \in B \quad \exists\, m_1 < m_2 < m_3$

   with (α, m_i, θ) quasi–stationary, $i = 1,2,3,$

   and

   $(\alpha, m_1, \theta) \in \mathbf{K},$

   $(\alpha, m_2, \theta) \in \mathbf{I} \setminus \mathbf{I}_0,$

   $(\alpha, m_3, \theta) \in \mathbf{I}_0.$

The set $\mathbf{I}_0$ denotes those states of repressed inflation where young consumers are rationed to zero. The multiplicity of steady states as given in property 3 of the theorem is again one primary source for the possibility of nonmonotonic, cyclical, or chaotic behavior. The numerical analysis of the last section indicates that the curvature of the double fold decreases with the degree of concavity of the production function. However, this is only one crucial parameter for the qualitative results obtained.

5 Disequilibrium Price Adjustment – The Law of Supply and Demand

For a complete description of the dynamic process the wage and price adjustment mechanisms have to be defined. In [4] a general class of market specific adjustment rules was proposed which transform disequilibrium signals on each market into an associated price or wage adjustment. The general principle is straightforward. Supply (demand) rationing in any particular period leaves a potential seller (buyer) unsatisfied, who then would be willing to sell for a lower (buy for a higher) price, leading to lower (higher) prices in the respective market in the next period. Such a rule corresponds most closely to an adjustment mechanism typically associated with a non–tâtonnement process. In this context it is immaterial whether this rule is implemented by an anonymous auctioneer, the government, or whether the producer and the worker follow it. Such a rule is essentially myopic. It is defined using exclusively information provided by the economy at date t through the disequilibrium configuration on each market. Hence it does not take any past history of states or prices nor any expectations for the future into account.

Formally, the price and wage adjustment mechanism consists of two parts, namely the function determining the disequilibrium signals and the function determining the price and wage adjustment. Let (s^c, s^ℓ) denote a pair of numbers between minus one and plus one, describing disequilibrium measures or signals for the commodity and for the labor market respectively. They are best interpreted to indicate percentages of unsatisfied desired transactions, but other monotonic transformations could be used as well. Negative numbers mean supply rationing, positive numbers mean demand rationing. Thus, for example, $s^\ell = -0.3$ could indicate an unemployment rate of 30 per cent. These measures depend on the disequilibrium state in every period, i. e. on the three variables (α, m, θ^e). Therefore, the two associated signaling functions σ^c and σ^ℓ generating the measures are defined on the state space $\mathbb{R}^3$ of the economy.

$$\sigma^c : \mathbb{R}^3_{++} \to [-1, +1] \quad ; \quad s^c = \sigma^c(\alpha, m, \theta^e)$$

$$\sigma^\ell : \mathbb{R}^3_{++} \to [-1, +1] \quad ; \quad s^\ell = \sigma^\ell(\alpha, m, \theta^e)$$

The signaling functions are consistent with the disequilibrium state if the following assumption is satisfied.

Assumption P Part 1: (Disequilibrium Signaling)

$$\sigma^c(\alpha, m, \theta^e) = \begin{cases} > 0 & (\alpha, m, \theta^e) \in \text{int}\,(C \cup I) \\ < 0 & (\alpha, m, \theta^e) \in \text{int}\,K \\ = 0 & (\alpha, m, \theta^e) \in K \cap C, \end{cases}$$

$$\sigma^\ell(\alpha, m, \theta^e) = \begin{cases} > 0 & (\alpha, m, \theta^e) \in \text{int}\,I \\ < 0 & (\alpha, m, \theta^e) \in \text{int}\,(C \cup K) \\ = 0 & (\alpha, m, \theta^e) \in C \cap I, \end{cases}$$

$$\sigma^\ell(\alpha, m, \theta^e) > \sigma^c(\alpha, m, \theta^e) = 0 \quad \text{if}\,(\alpha, m, \theta^e) \in (K \cap I) \setminus WE,$$

$$\sigma^\ell, \sigma^c \quad \text{continuous except on} \quad K \cap I.$$

The first two sets of conditions present the natural notion of disequilibrium, i. e. indicating actual rationing if and only if the measure is nonzero. Continuity seems to be a normal requirement. However, in the present model, this cannot be guaranteed on the boundary $K \cap I \setminus WE$. This results exclusively from the structural asymmetry of the model with intertemporal consumption decisions and atemporal production decisions. This discontinuity would not arise in a model where both sectors have a true intertemporal decision problem.

The price and wage adjustment functions now map the disequilibrium signals of any period in a continuous and sign preserving fashion into rates of price or wage change as discussed above, a rule which may be called the Law of Supply and Demand.

Assumption P Part 2: (The Law of Supply and Demand)

$$\mathcal{P}: [-1,1] \to (-1,+\infty) \qquad p_{t+1} = p_t \left(1 + \mathcal{P}(s_t^c)\right)$$

$$\mathcal{W}: [1,1] \to (-1,+\infty) \qquad w_{t+1} = w_t \left(1 + \mathcal{W}(s_t^\ell)\right)$$

$$\mathcal{P}(0) = 0 \quad \mathcal{W}(0) = 0$$

$$\mathcal{P}, \mathcal{W} \quad \text{continuous, monotonically increasing .}$$

A price and wage adjustment rule satisfying **Assumption P** Parts 1 and 2 will be called consistent. With these specifications the description of the dynamic system is now complete. There are essentially two equivalent functional forms which can be used to describe the dynamic process. One form considers the expected inflation rate θ_t^e as the third state variable whereas the other one considers the actual inflation rate θ_t. In either case the difference equation is of order τ from $\mathbb{R}_+^3$ to itself. If $\tau = 0$, or in some other special cases where expectations 'don't matter', the dynamic system reduces to a first order difference equation from $\mathbb{R}_+^2$ to itself. Here, the formulation with expected inflation rates is given.

Def.: A sequence $\{\alpha_t, m_t, \theta_t^e\}_{t=1}^\infty$ is called a consistent path, i. e. a disequilibrium path with consistent price adjustment, if

$$\alpha_{t+1} = \alpha_t \frac{1 + \mathcal{W}(s_t^\ell)}{1 + \mathcal{P}(s_t^c)},$$

$$m_{t+1} = \frac{1}{\theta_t} [\min\{y_t, m_t + g\} - tax\ y_t],$$

$$\theta_{t+1}^e = \Psi(\theta_t, \ldots, \theta_{t+1-\tau}),$$

such that

$$y_t = \mathcal{Y}(\alpha_t, m_t, \theta_t^e, g, tax),$$

$$s_t^j = \sigma^j(\alpha_t, m_t, \theta_t^e) \qquad j = c, \ell,$$

$$\theta_t = 1 + \mathcal{P}(s_t^c).$$

It is straightforward to verify the following properties of consistent steady states. If (α, m, θ) is consistent and quasi–stationary, then

1. $\theta^e = \theta$,

2. $(\alpha, m, \theta) \notin C$,

3. $\theta > 1$ iff , $(\alpha, m, \theta) \in I$,

$\theta = 1$ iff $(\alpha, m, \theta) \in WE$,

$\theta < 1$ iff $(\alpha, m, \theta) \in K$.

Expectations are fulfilled in consistent steady states and states can never be of the classical unemployment type. Keynesian unemployment states must be deflationary, whereas states of repressed inflation must have a positive inflation rate. Moreover, as the following theorem indicates, the type of steady state strictly depends on the production characteristics of the economy and on the relative sizes of government demand to taxes, but neither on the adjustment speeds on any of the markets nor on consumer characteristics.

Theorem: If **Assumptions C, E, F, P** hold, then there exists a unique steady state (α, m, θ), such that

$$(\alpha, m, \theta) \in K \quad \text{iff} \quad g < tax\, F(L_{max})$$

$$(\alpha, m, \theta) \in WE \quad \text{iff} \quad g = tax\, F(L_{max}).$$

$$(\alpha, m, \theta) \in I \quad \text{iff} \quad g > tax\, F(L_{max})$$

6 Simulation Results

In spite of the fact that the uniqueness of steady states and their qualitative properties are obtained quite easily, the dynamic properties of the system seem intractable on the general level of the model so far. Even for the simplest case with no expectations memory ($\tau = 0$), the resulting planar system of a first order difference equation has a sufficient amount of complexity, so that only numerical techniques are capable of generating global dynamic results. Therefore a class of parametric specifications of the assumptions **C,E,F,P** is chosen for which some of the simulation results are presented in this section.

Assumption C: For $\delta > 0$ and $-\infty < \rho < 1$:

$$u(x_t, x_{t+1}) = \begin{cases} \frac{1}{\rho}[x_t^\rho + \delta\, x_{t+1}^\rho] & \rho \neq 0 \\ \ln\, x_t + \delta\, \ln\, x_{t+1} & \rho = 0. \end{cases}$$

C is the standard CES intertemporal utility function with substitution parameter ρ and time discount parameter δ. The Cobb-Douglas case, i. e. $\rho = 0$, implies that current demand is independent of expected prices. In this situation the dynamics are independent of expectations. Thus the system is two–dimensional and of first order regardless of the length of memory τ and of the expectations function Ψ.

Assumption E: For $\tau = 0, 1, 2, 3, \ldots$ and $T = \min\{t-1, \tau\}$:

$$\theta_t^e = \frac{p_{t+1}^e}{p_t} = \begin{cases} \frac{1}{T}\sum_{k=1}^{T}\theta_{t-k} & T > 0 \\ 1 & T = 0. \end{cases}$$

This expectations function is a simple unweighted averaging procedure. No attempt has been made to match a sophisticated econometric forecasting method.

Assumption F: For $A > 0$ and $1 > B > 0$:

$$y_t = \frac{A}{B}\, z_t^B .$$

Assumption P: For $0 < \gamma < 1$, $0 < \kappa < 1$:

$$P_{t+1} = P_t \begin{cases} 1 + \gamma \frac{y_t^D - y_t}{y_t^D} & y_t^D > y_t \\ 1 + \kappa \frac{y_t - y_t^*}{y_t^*} & \text{otherwise,} \end{cases}$$

and for $0 < \mu < 1$, $0 < \lambda < 1$:

$$w_{t+1} = w_t \begin{cases} 1 + \lambda \frac{L_t - L_{\max}}{L_{\max}} & L_{\max} > L_t \\ 1 + \mu \frac{z_t^* - L_t}{z_t^*} & \text{otherwise.} \end{cases}$$

Here the disequilibrium measures are the usual effective excess demand percentages, and the adjustment functions $\mathcal{P}$ and $\mathcal{W}$ are linear with constant parametrically chosen adjustment coefficients.

Apart from the two government parameters (g, tax), the assumptions **C,E,F,P** require the numerical specification of ten parameter values: $(\delta, \rho, \tau, L_{max})$ for the consumer, (A, B) for the producer, and the adjustment coefficients $(\gamma, \kappa, \lambda, \mu)$ for the two markets. L_{max} and A are essentially scaling parameters which can be set equal to one without loosing too much structural information. As a consequence the real wage α^* which clears the labour market is also equal to one for all other possible parameter values. This leaves eight parameters plus (g, tax) to be chosen.

The available numerical results so far represent the characteristics of the model for a partial range of parameter variations only. However, they show four distinct structural features which are not attributed usually to standard macroeconomic models of the Keynesian kind and which imply the possibility of a wide range of endogenous business cycles. Judging these features from the point of view of modern dynamic theory, they supply a consistent picture of a highly complex nonlinear system which is capable of generating a multitude of different dynamic paths.

- First, there are large sets of parameter values for which the unique steady state is stable and others for which it is unstable. There seems to be no immediate heuristic or economically intuitive arguments which make stability or instability more plausible for certain sets than others.

- Second, there are large sets of values for some parameters such that there exist stable cycles of order 2, 3, 4, 5, 7, 9, and higher, as well as their multiples, depending on the values of the remaining parameters. For example, for a set of $(\delta, \rho, \tau, B, \gamma, \kappa, \lambda, \mu)$ different values of (g, tax) generate the above mentioned cycles. Thus, an economist may conclude, that, other things being equal, different economic policies 'cause' business cycles of different degrees.

- Third, continuous changes of some parameters generate the typical bifurcation phenomenon of period doubling. This is to be expected knowing that there exist stable cycles of different order depending on the values of one parameter, other things being equal. Hence, for small changes of some parameters the stability of a cycle of order k is lost and the system changes to a stable cycle of order $2k$ or $k/2$, as the case may be.

- Fourth, for open sets of parameter values, no stable cycles exist and long iterated sequences show all features of irregular, possibly chaotic, orbits. The associated trajectories form so called strange attractors which are independent of initial conditions.

The following set of parameter values can be considered as a benchmark which may serve as a reference point for the discussion:

$$\rho = 0, \ \delta = 1, \ \ B = .5, \ \ \gamma = \kappa = \lambda = \mu = .5, \ \ g = 1, \ tax = .5.$$

There are no deep economic reasons for chosing these values. The Cobb-Douglas utility function with no time preference, i. e. $\rho = 0$ and $\delta = 1$, is an economic benchmark. The next six values are just the midpoints of their allowable intervals. Given these, $g = 1$ yields a Walrasian steady state with half of total output consumed by the government. All numerical experiments with these values show convergence to the WE for any initial conditions (p_1, w_1, M_1). The same is true for parameter values 'close by' with any memory between zero and twenty. No cycles of higher order were found. Thus, the steady state seems globally stable for all values near the benchmark case.

The experiments also revealed that all of the four features listed above can be obtained for systems with $\rho = 0$, i. e. for the simplest two dimensional system where expectations and memory do not matter. On the other hand no specific features have been detected in experiments with values for $\rho \neq 0$ and $\tau > 0$ which were not reproducible for a model with $\rho = 0$. Therefore, all further results reported here deal with the case of $\rho = 0$ only. It is still an open question left for further experimentation to what extent expectations and memory matter, especially given the sensitivity of many standard macroeconomic models to those two elements.

Among the many situations for which the unique steady state is unstable the results of three experiments are reported here. These were designed to answer the following questions:

1. Do high price and wage adjustment coefficients lead to instability whereas low coefficients do not?

2. To what extent are the features of the technology, i. e. the concavity of the production function, responsible for instability, cycles, and possibly chaos?

3. What role do the government parameters play for instability, cycles, and possibly chaos?

No decisive answer seems possible from the experiments so far with respect to the values of the adjustment coefficients. Cycles appeared for values higher than 0.6, but also for values lower than 0.2. In other cases stability could be exhibited for these values. More experiments are necessary to determine whether adjustment coefficients alone can control stability or instability.

The production parameter B is a measure for the concavity of the production function which decreases with increasing values for B. Preliminary experiments show that for $B < 0.6$ instability of the steady state does not occur. However, for values between 0.75 and 0.95 many stable cycles of higher order exist. A full range analysis of the role of the production parameter still has to be carried out. The preliminary results seem to suggest that low values for B, i. e. strong curvature, eliminate cycles. But it is unclear whether these results are decisive.

The following four diagrams show some of the typical situations where the steady state is unstable. They depict the set of parameters, the time paths for the employment level and for the two state variables (α_t, m_t), plus the attractor in state space.

Model my3cycle		
A: 1.000	gamma: 0.600	delta: 1.000
B: 0.900	kappa: 0.600	rho: 0.000
Lmax: 1.000	lambda: 0.600	w0: 3.000
g: 0.270	my: 0.600	p0: 5.000
tax: 0.270	tau: 10.000	m0: 20.000

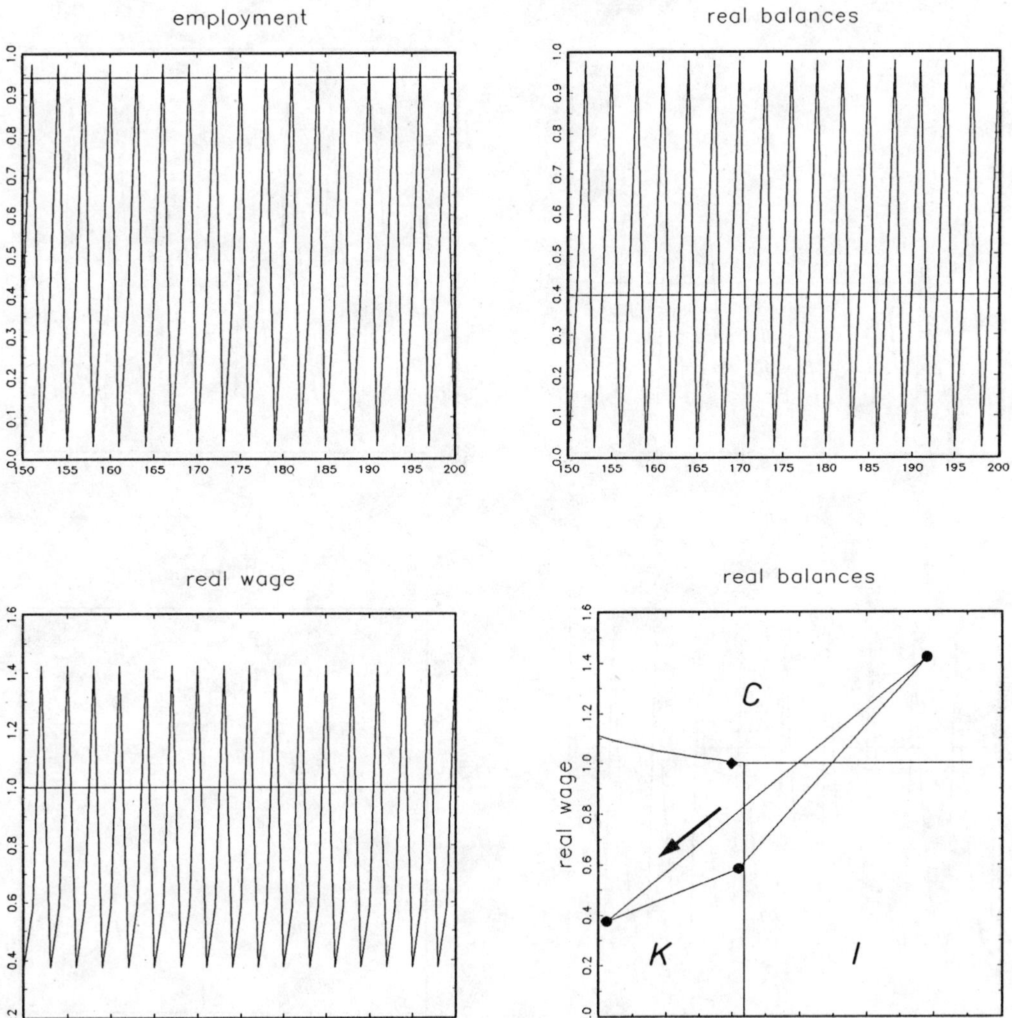

Figure 1: A three cycle

Model my5cycle		
A: 1.000	gamma: 0.600	delta: 1.000
B: 0.900	kappa: 0.600	rho: 0.000
Lmax: 1.000	lambda: 0.600	w0: 3.000
g: 0.040	my: 0.600	p0: 5.000
tax: 0.270	tau: 10.000	m0: 20.000

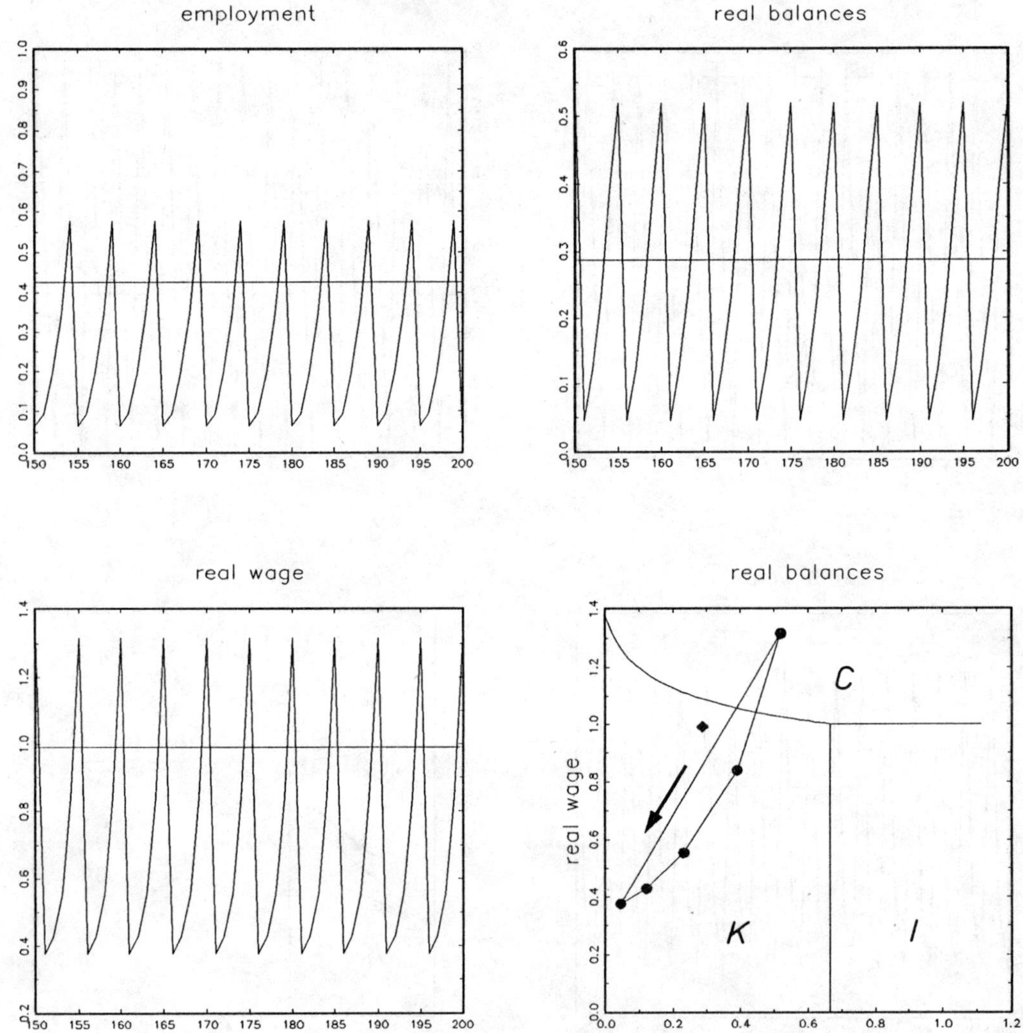

Figure 2: A five cycle

Model my9cycle		
A: 1.000	gamma: 0.600	delta: 1.000
B: 0.900	kappa: 0.600	rho: 0.000
Lmax: 1.000	lambda: 0.600	w0: 3.000
g: 0.323	my: 0.600	p0: 5.000
tax: 0.270	tau: 10.000	m0: 20.000

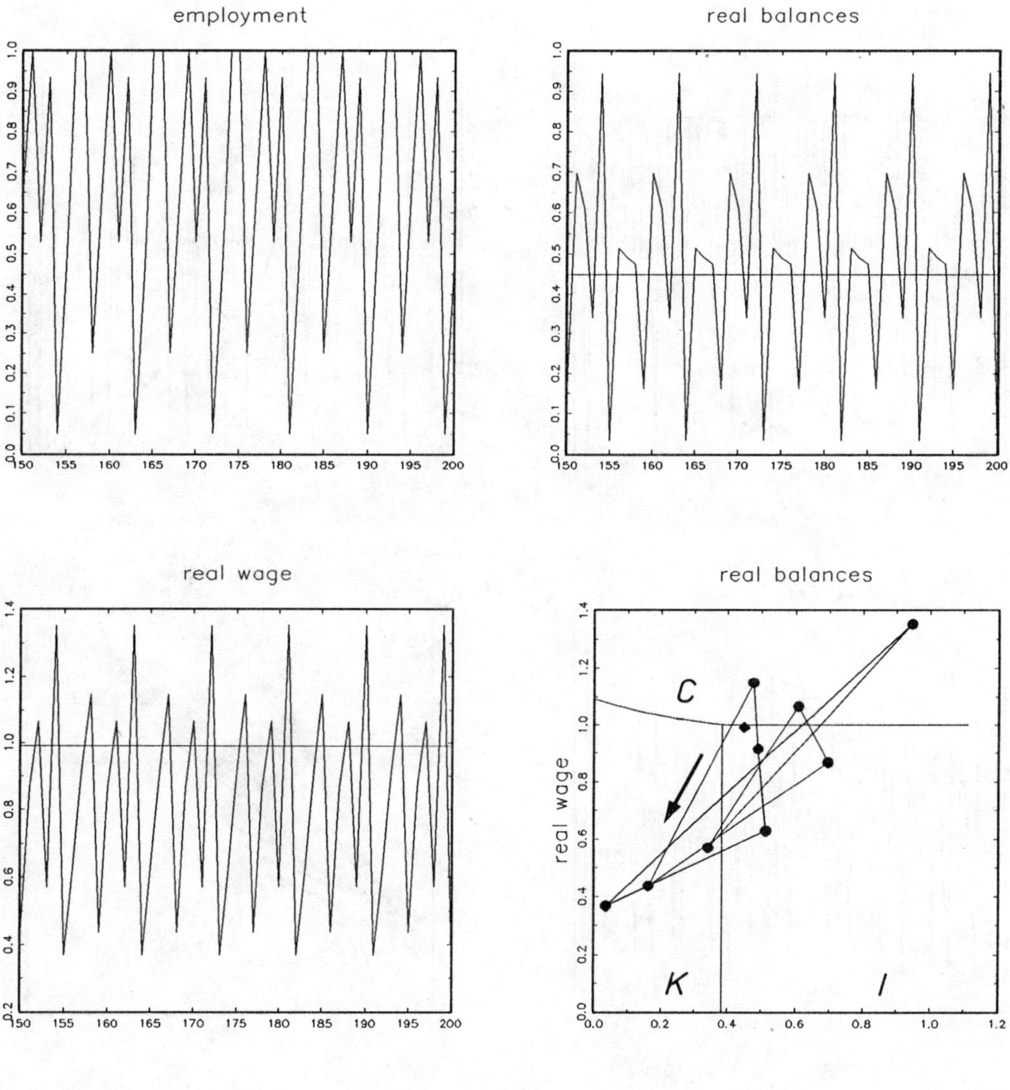

Figure 3: A nine cycle

Model mychaosa					
A:	1.000	gamma:	0.600	delta:	1.000
B:	0.900	kappa:	0.600	rho:	0.000
Lmax:	1.000	lambda:	0.600	w0:	3.000
g:	0.300	my:	0.600	p0:	5.000
tax:	0.270	tau:	10.000	m0:	20.000

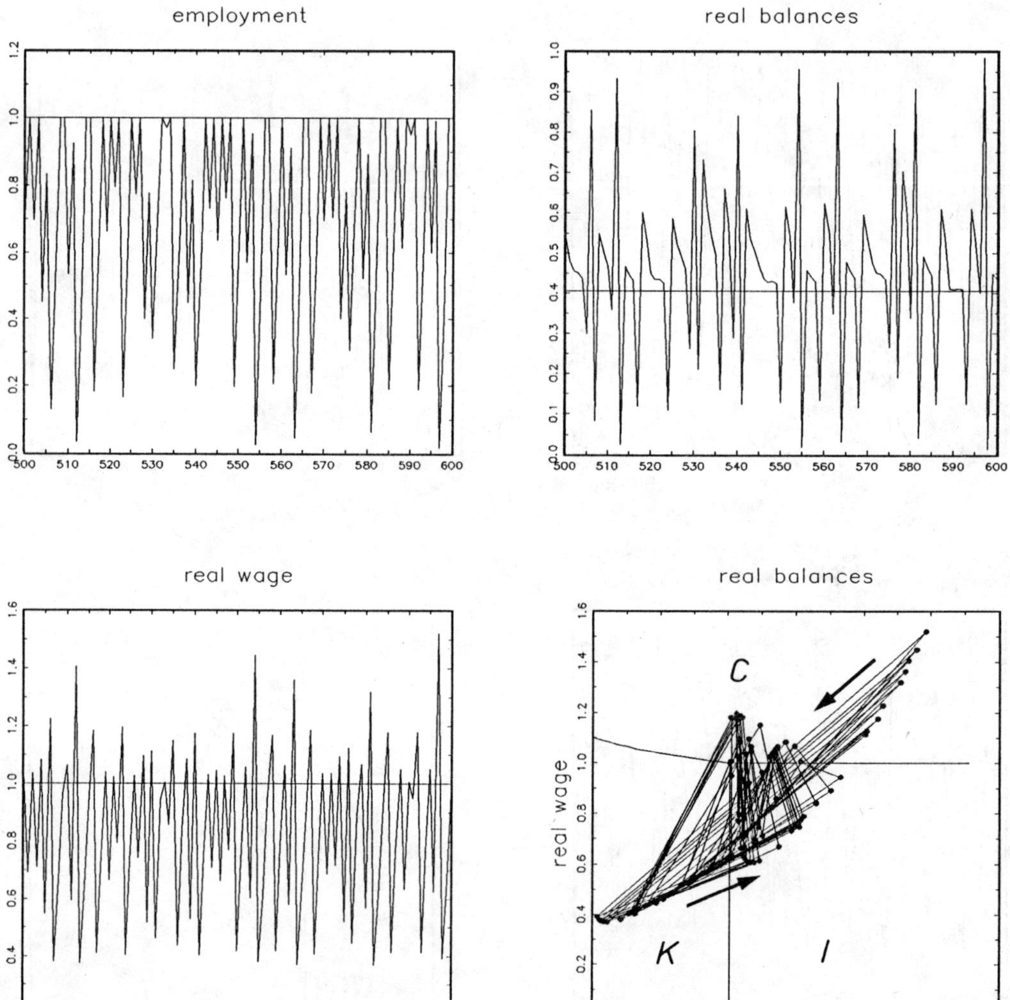

Figure 4: Irregular behavior

The square dot marks the location of the steady state and the arrows indicate the orientation of the cycles. The first three figures show cycles of order 3, 5, and 9. Since they are converging relatively fast, iterations of less than 100 periods were sufficient to obtain exact cycles. The time series plotted show the values for periods 150 to 200.

All three cycles exhibit a counterclockwise orientation. The pattern of regime switching is quite different between them, as is the location of the steady state. Notice, however, that the parameter sets differ only in the level of government demand and not in the adjustment coefficients $(\gamma, \kappa, \lambda, \mu)$, as one might have expected. The parameters for the fourth model presented in the next diagram differ again only in the value of government demand. They are such that the steady state is a Walrasian equilibrium. The values for periods 500 to 600 are shown. The time series show quite strikingly that the behavior is non–cyclical, and the lines connecting the points in state space (the lower right hand box) reveal the complexity of the orbit. Figure 5 shows the values for periods 50,000 to 500,000 (!!) without the connecting lines which provides an indication of the shape of the attractor.

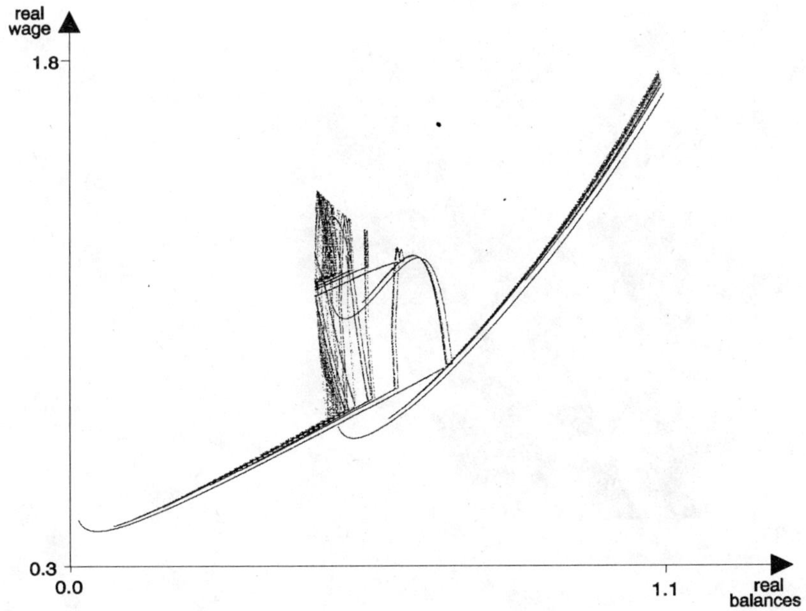

Figure 5

Figures 6, 7 and 8 display bifurcation graphs for changes of government demand keeping all other parameters as before. Since the state space is $\mathbb{R}^2_+$, a bifurcation graph is a subset of $\mathbb{R}^3_+$. Any graphical representation of such an object is some projection into the plane which, in general, cannot reveal the full dimensionality of the true graph, as can be seen from Figure 6. Therefore, the real wage variable is plotted separately in Figure 7 and 8. The first graph shows the whole range of g between zero and one, while the second one shows an enlarged window for $0.25 \leq g \leq 0.55$. For each parameter value of g an iteration of 2,000 periods has been carried out and the values for the last 700 periods are plotted.

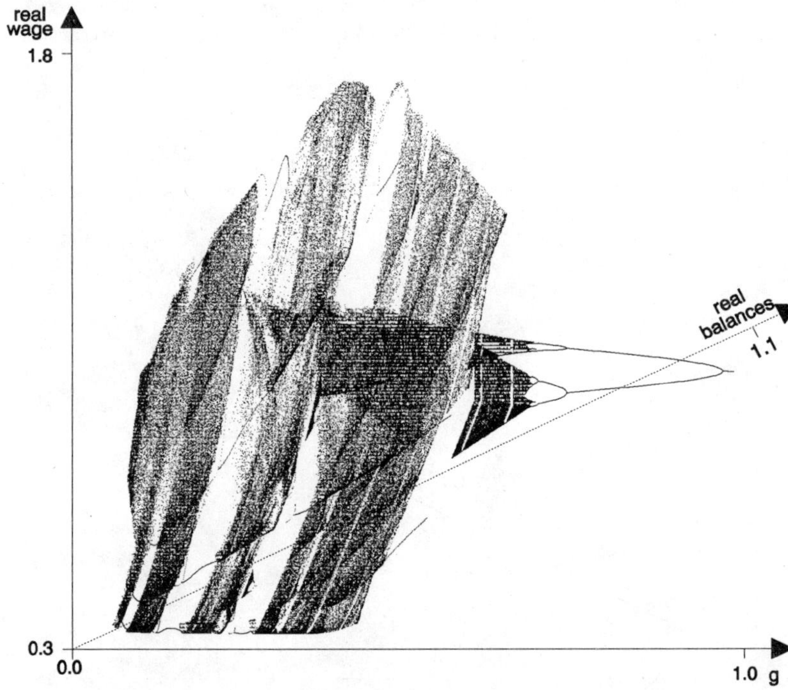

Figure 6: A 3D bifurcation

The last two diagrams show the typical bifurcation phenomenon known from the one–dimensional logistic map, like period doubling, but also the window structure for ranges of cycles of different integer order between the ones with irregular orbits. Since the parameter sets between the first four diagrams and the bifurcation map coincide, it is easy to identify the location of the values of government demand which show the corresponding cycles as well as the value for the irregular attractor. The enlargement provides a finer view of the windows with cycles, including the one of order nine.

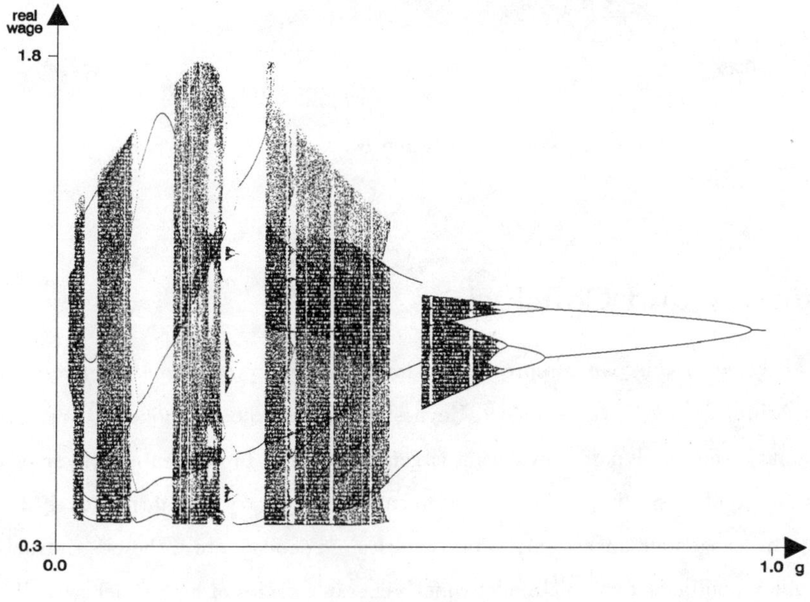

Figure 7

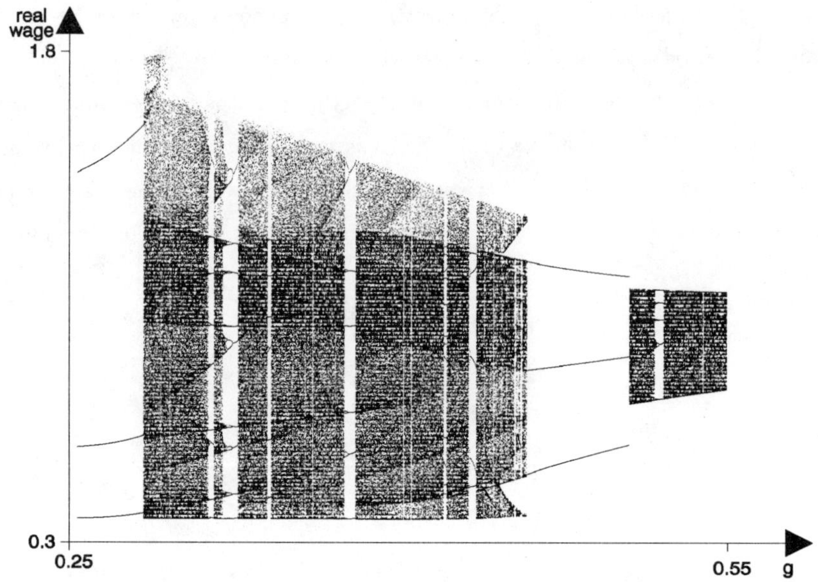

Figure 8

7 Summary and Conclusions

The model analysed in this paper represents a simple prototype of a consistent dynamic and full general equilibrium version of the standard Keynesian macroeconomic model. Its structure is completely stationary and its dynamic evolution is generated from fundamental principles of national income accounting, of feasibility, and of basic elements of temporary equilibrium analysis. In spite of its simplicity (no exogenous uncertainty, no inventories, no capital, etc.), the basic structure implies a highly complex nonlinear dynamic model which generates cycles of high order as well as irregular behavior endogenously. This shows that the Keynesian model, whether in this simple or in more extensive versions does supply a theoretical framework for studies of the business cycle.

This paper supplies only a first view of the dynamic features of the standard Keynesian model. It suggests that government demand for goods is a crucial bifurcation parameter. Further experiments should be designed to determine whether there are others and what their relationship is. One issue related to the question of the role of government is whether the model behaves in the same way if there is no government activity at all. From an economic point of view it also remains an intriguing question whether and why expectations in this model seem to play such a secondary role, a fact which contrasts sharply with current macroeconomic folklore. This question should be examined in a larger setting than here, including in particular different expectations functions.

References

[1] Blanchard, O. J. and Fischer, S. 1989: *Lectures on Macroeconomics.* MIT Press.

[2] Blinder, A. S. and Solow, R. M. 1973: 'Does fiscal policy matter'. *Journal of Public Economics*, 2, 319–37.

[3] Böhm, V. 1978: 'Disequilibrium dynamics in a simple macroeconomic model'. *Journal of Economic Theory*, 17, 179–99.

[4] Böhm, V. 1989: *Disequilibrium and Macroeconomics.* Oxford: Basil Blackwell.

[5] Dana, R. A. and Malgrange, P. 1984: 'The Dynamics of a Discrete Version of a Growth Cycle Model'. in: J. P. Ancot (ed.), *Analysing the Structure of Economic Models*, The Hague: Martinus Nijhoff, 205–222.

[6] Day, R. H. 1984: 'Disequilibrium Economic Dynamics'. *Journal of Economic Behaviour and Organisation*, 5, 57–76.

[7] Day, R. H. and Shafer, W. 1986: 'Keynesian Chaos'. *Journal of Macroeconomics*, 7, 277–295.

[8] Grandmont, J.-M. 1985: 'On Endogenous Competitive Business Cycles'. *Econometrica*, 53, 995–1045.

[9] Grandmont, J.-M. 1988: 'Introduction'. In: J.-M. Grandmont (ed.), *Temporary Equilibrium — Selected Readings*, Academic Press, London, xiii–xxiv.

[10] Grandmont, J.-M. and Malgrange, P. 1986: 'Nonlinear Economic Dynamics: Introduction'. *Journal of Economic Theory*, 40, 3–12.

[11] Hahn, F. 1982: *Money and Inflation.* Oxford: Basil Blackwell.

[12] Hénin, P. Y. and Michel, P. 1982: *Croissance et accumulation en déséquilibre.* Paris: Economica.

[13] Kaldor, N. 1940: 'A Model of the Trade Cycle'. *Economic Journal*, 50, 78–92.

[14] Lorenz, H.-W. 1993: 'Complexity in Deterministic, Nonlinear Business-Cycle Models — Foundations, Empirical Evidence, and Predictability'. *this volume.*

[15] Picard, P. 1983: 'Inflation and growth in a disequilibrium macroeconomic model'. *Journal of Economic Theory*, 30, 266–95.

[16] Tobin, J. and Buiter, W. 1976: 'Longrun effects of fiscal and monetary policy on aggregate demand'. In: J. Stein (ed.), *Monetarism*, Amsterdam: North Holland, 273–309.

ECONOMIC NONLINEAR DYNAMIC DEVELOPMENT

Richard M. Goodwin

Dipartimento di Economia Politica
Università di Siena
Piazza San Francesco, 17
53100 Siena

The conception of a limit cycle was formulated towards the end of the last century. A practical, usable form was first developed by van der Pol and widely used in the physical sciences. The first qualitative model in economics was proposed by Kalecki in the early thirties but, being linear, was seriously criticized by Frish on the grounds that it was structurally unstable. Then came the dramatic impact of the Keynes General Theory, which led to an altered perception of the problem.

The most important result of this was a graphical, nonlinear model of the business cycle formulated by the late Lord Kaldor. Unfortunately it was only published in 1941, during the war, and hence only came to the notice of economists much later. After much difficulty in finding a satisfactory formulation, I was able to arrive at a quantitative model which was structurally stable and produced a limit cycle, thus yielding an explanation of how and why industrial capitalism has tended to function in waves for two centuries.

All the early models were of an alternation about a constant level of output (not unnaturally in the 1930's). Somewhat later I realized that by defining variables in ratios, it is possible to arrive at and discuss a model represented in simple, finite form, but which, at the same time, can represent unlimited growth. Thus if $x(t) = a/b$, one can have

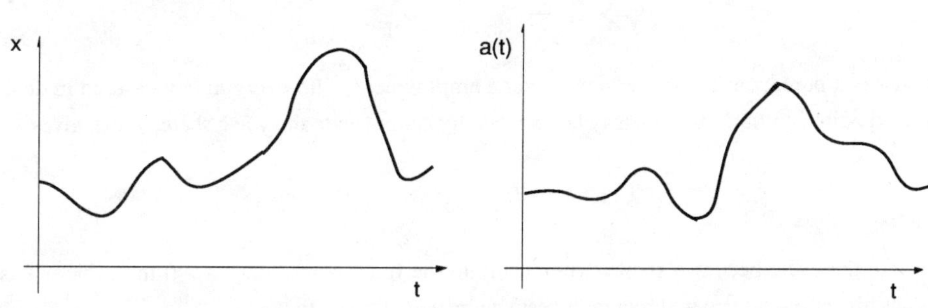

Thus behavior in state space can be totally different from functions of time. This result became useful for analysis in the 1960's, 1970's and 1980's.

The decade of the 1930's was dominated by the Great Depression: economic variables exhibited little growth, so models were about stationary levels. Then in the post war period came the greatest growth rates over the longest periods of time ever recorded, so that growth became the dominant preocupation. Then in the 1980's it was no longer possible to consider only growth; for this reason it is helpful to define ratios of economic quantities as the relevant variables.

Even more important was the discovery of 'strange attractors', or Chaos. As everyone knows, economic variables show highly irregular time series, with no precisely identifiable periodicity, in spite of having an obvious tendency to alternating rising and falling behavior. Frisch persuaded economists to believe this was entirely due to exogenous shocks, which, being unexplained, could explain anything. Now, as a result of this remarkable new conception, it has become clear that some large part (how large is unclear) of the irregularity of economic data over both short and long run periods can be the result of the internal economic structure and need not be solely the effect of unexplained external shocks.

Traditionally economists have assumed a fixed point equilibrium and have studied the conditions for dynamical stability to that point. Poincaré long ago proposed a fixed closed curve of equilibrium motion, but this had little or no impact on economic studies. Now as a result of chaos theory, the concept of a stable closed curve has been dramatically broadened to a stable closed region to which all variables will tend or, if initially within the region, will remain there. Thus the notion of a stable equilibrium point has undergone a staggering generalization from a single point to a well defined region in state space.

For the analysis of short and long run behavior, it is helpful to use ratios of the basic variables. Define u as the unit cost of labour, which will then in this simple model be proportional to the share of wages in output. With a_L as the quantity of labour per unit of output, $u = a_L w$, where w is the wage rate and share of wages in output. Measure employment v as the ratio of employment, L, to the total available labour force, N, i.e. $v = L/N = a_L q/N$. To keep the analysis as simple as possible, assume N constant, with all variables in dimensionless form. Then the central oscillatory nature of industrial capitalism can be represented by

$$\dot{v} = -u$$
$$\dot{u} = +v$$

where the wage share rises with the degree of employment and the ratio of employment declines with the decline in profit share, yielding

$$\ddot{v} = -\dot{u} = -v,$$

which produces a pure, constant cycle in output and employment, with everything measured in deviations from the fixed point equilibrium. This may be enriched by adding au to the wage share, which gives

$$\ddot{v} - a\dot{v} + v = 0.$$

If $a < 0$, the cycle becomes stable dynamically to the fixed point, but it $a > 0$ the cycle is unstable, which means higher output and will require investment in added capacity.

To come closer to long run reality, one needs to consider k, the measure of capacity to produce, in deviations from the fixed point. Thus one must consider investment in added capacity, of which the necessity investment raises demand and output requiring increased capacity to allow the rising output. Innovations in products and methods of production tend to follow a logistic pattern: they begin slowly, are little understood, and then rise rapidly as the advantages become known and hence widely adopted; then as the potential becomes fully realized, the investment gradually ceases. The process can thus be represented by

$$\dot{k} = b + k(v - c).$$

The complete system can then be represented in dimensionless form (to show the logic but not the details of the dynamic) as

$$\dot{v} = -u - k,$$
$$\dot{u} = +v + au,$$
$$\dot{k} = b + k(v - c).$$

For small values of a, b and c there will result a limit cycle, but with slighly larger values of c the cycle grows in amplitude, which requires a larger accumulation of k. The consequence is two distinct cycles alternating over time. Then for higher values of c, more and more different cycles appear and succeed one another in complicated ways. This shows how chaotic behavior can arise endogenously; there are succeeding waves but each one is different from the others; simple prediction becomes impossible.

Growth come from technological innovation either in new products or better methods of production, the main result of which is increased labour productivitiy. To model this call k new innovative capacity and assume it can be represented by a logistic functioning over a long period of around 50 years. A major innovation like steam or electricity takes a long time to become completely integrated into the economic structure. Thus it can be represented by an appropriate logistic. At first crudely designed and little understood; then it gains recognition and is rapidly integrated into the production process. As this process is completed, the special growth stimulus gradually declines to zero.

For more realism one can formulate in dimensional form: let $\dot{v} = -du + fv$ and $\dot{u} = +hv$. The term fv represents the fact that growth is stimulated by a growing economy, yielding unstable cycles. Given an unstable cycle about equilibrium, the usual procedure was to assume upper and lower bounds which gave global stability. Instead, assume a dynamical control parameter, z, which provides downward pressure for positive values and a growing upward one for negative values, thus

$$\dot{z} = b + gz(v - c).$$

Labour productivity is assumed to grow proportionately to the innovative capacity, thus $m\dot{k} / k = -\dot{a}_L / a_L$. One assumes an historical half century logistic of innovation: $\dot{k} = jk(1 - sk)$. This means that innovative investment peaks at around 25 years and approaches zero as k approaches 1/s. With a constant labour force

$$\dot{v} / v = \dot{L} / L = \dot{q} / q + \dot{a}_L / a_L, \quad \text{giving}$$
$$\dot{q} / q = \dot{v} / v - \dot{a}_L / a_L.$$

The complete system then is:

$$\dot{v} = -du + fv - ez$$
$$\dot{u} = +hv$$
$$\dot{z} = +b + gz(v - c)$$
$$\dot{k} = +jk(1 - sk)$$
$$\dot{q} / q = (-du + fv - ez) / (v + \hat{v}) + mj(1 - sk),$$

where $\hat{v}$ is an equilibrium value of v, thus avoiding division by zero.

Imposing a 50 year logistic on a cyclical mechanism means that the cycle is first much attenuated by the investment in innovatory technology, and then, as the logistic completes its course, the cycle will again predominate. Such a model can give a great variety of behaviour types, depending on the parameters. Thus in the middle of the logistic the cycle practically disappears, except in terms of growth rates. Then as the logistic gradually subsides, the cycle again dominates.

In the model there is no assumption of full employment; as innovatory investment ceases, one should expect output to decline to its original level, since the innovations are laboursaving. Here there is the assumption that the competition of producers for a given supply of labour raises the real wage and generates demand for output, thus compensating for the lower input of labour per unit of output. Hence the buoyancy of wages is not harmful but rather is crucial for achieving growth, providing that the buoyancy is neither too weak nor too strong.

Random Walk vs. Chaotic Dynamics in Financial Economics

A. G. MALLIARIS

Department of Economics, Loyola University of Chicago
820 N. Michigan Avenue, Chicago, IL 60611

G. PHILIPPATOS

College of Business Administration, The University of Tennessee
432 Stokely Management Center, Knoxville, TEN 27990

1. INTRODUCTION

During the past three decades, financial economists have studied in detail the behavior of stock market prices and the prices of derivative securities issued on such stocks. By price behavior we mean the dynamic, period by period, change in the price level of a given stock, such as, the daily closing price of an IBM share and the daily settlement price of the corresponding put or call. The extensive literature that addresses these twin problems is known as the market efficiency theory and the option pricing theory. Both theories constitute significant pillars of modern financial economics and despite various puzzles and anomalies, such as the October 1987 stock market crash, that cannot be explained by market efficiency, there are currently no competing theories that are widely accepted.

We do not wish to review here market efficiency or option pricing. Both are well known and can be found readily in textbooks such as Lee, Finnerty, and Wort (1990). Ross (1987) gives an insightful and comprehensive overview of the field of finance and dedicates a significant portion of his essay on efficient markets and options. Rather, we propose to contrast the random walk behavior of stock prices and of derivative securities to chaotic dynamics. Although we plan to give a precise definition of chaotic dynamics later on, the methodological intuition of this concept is motivated by the notion that stock prices follow a deterministic, dynamic and nonlinear process which generates a very complex time series that although it looks like the random walk it actually is not.

In other words, in this essay we address the question: is it possible for stock prices and their derivative instruments to appear to be random but not to be really random? Put differently, we ask: do there exist nonrandom functions whose time series characteristics are similar to random walk? We hasten to inform the reader that the answer to both questions is affirmative. In other words, there are nonrandom functions whose time characteristics appear as complicated as those of the random walk and by implication it is, at least theoretically, possible for stock prices to be generated by such functions.

In section 2 we describe the meaning of random walk and reformulate the two questions in a technically more precise way. In section 3 we give an example of a deterministic (nonstochastic) dynamic (indexed by time) and nonlinear function whose time series not only appears (visually) to be random, but actually fails to reject the null hypothesis of a random walk. We also give a precise definition of chaotic dynamics and explain it in detail. We dedicate section 4 to some recent techniques used in distinguishing between random and nonrandom time series and report some available empirical evidence. In this section we also address the theoretical and practical implications of these two alternative modelling approaches to asset pricing. The last section summarizes our ideas and offers suggestions for future research.

2. RANDOM WALK

Random walk is a statistical term which financial economics uses to describe the dynamic behavior of stock market and other asset prices. In its simplest formulation we define the sequence of prices, denoted by $\{\mathbf{p(t)} : \mathbf{t} = 0, 1, 2, \ldots\}$, to follow a random walk if

$$p(t + 1) = p(t) + \epsilon(t + 1), \tag{2.1}$$

where $\boldsymbol{\epsilon}(\mathbf{t} + 1)$ is the value obtained from sampling with replacement from a given distribution with a given population mean μ_ϵ and a variance of σ^2_ϵ. In (2.1) we express tomorrow's price as a random departure from today's price, or equivalently, we express the price change between today and tomorrow, i.e. $\mathbf{p(t + 1) - p(t)}$, as random. It is usually assumed that $\mu_\epsilon = 0$. In our analysis we concentrate on price changes denoted as $\mathbf{dp(t + 1) = p(t + 1) - p(t)}$.

As a mathematical model, the notion of random walk has its methodological foundation in probability theory. Recall that probability theory analyzes events whose outcome is uncertain in contrast to deterministic calculus where the relationship between the dependent and independent variable is exact. Long before the efficient market hypothesis was conceived, formulated and tested, the random walk model in (2.1) was utilized to convey the notion that stock prices cannot be systematically forecasted. Over fifty years ago Cowles (1933) asked rhetorically the question: can stock market forecasters forecast? Roberts (1959) reviews several early papers on stock market price behavior and challenges the relevance of technical analysis in anticipating price changes.

Roberts uses the term technical analysis to describe the search for patterns in stock market prices and argues that such patterns may actually be nothing more than statistical artifacts. Although Roberts does not use the term random walk, he constructs a "chance model" and argues that weekly changes of a typical stock market index behave as if they were independent sample observations from a normal distribution with mean + 0.5 and standard deviation 5.0.

The early observations of the random behavior of stock market prices and their modelling using the random walk paradigm, eventually directed finance researchers to seek explanations for such a statistical phenomenon. Thus, the efficient market hypothesis was developed to rationalize the random walk behavior claiming that the current price **p(t)** fully and correctly reflects all relevant information and because the flow of information between now and next period cannot be anticipated, price changes are serially uncorrelated. Fama (1970) skillfully reviews the earlier theoretical and empirical literature on efficient capital markets.

During the last twenty years, the theory of market efficiency has been refined analytically, mathematically and statistically. Analytically, the concept of information was made precise and its meaning was clarified. Mathematically, the notion of random walk was generalized to martingales and Itô processes; and finally, numerous sophisticated statistical tests were employed to test the theory. In such an intense scientific activity it was not surprising to find, along with numerous studies confirming market efficiency, several studies rejecting it.

This rapid overview allows us to conclude that currently, the random walk behavior of stock market price changes is the orthodoxy of financial economics. Needless to say, this orthodoxy is not undisputed, nor have analysts given up their search for alternative modelling. Actually we wish to propose such an alternative modelling here and in order to do so we claim that Figure 1 can be utilized as a metaphor of the random walk and the market efficiency theory. This figure illustrates a sequence of 101 random numbers between 0 and 1. Obviously, market price changes range over a much larger subset of the real numbers rather than the subset of [0, 1]. However, this is a simple issue of scaling. What matters in Figure 1 and in the theory of market efficiency is not so much the range of price changes but the fact that knowing, let us say, the first 10 numbers, does not enable us to predict the 11th number and in general knowing all the numbers up to a given number does not allow us to predict the next one. Thus, Figure 1 is a numerical representation of the random walk and what market efficiency theory does is to provide a rationale for such a statistical behavior.[1]

---

[1]The 101 numbers in Figure 1 were obtained from the random number generator of LOTUS 1-2-3. Their mean and variance are **.502435** and **.076573** respectively. Each element of the set $\{\epsilon(t) : t = 0, 1, 2, ..., 100\}$ represents a numerical random price change. Note that if instead of the simple random walk in (2.1) an Itô equation were used to describe price changes of the form $dp(t) = \mu dt + \sigma dZ(t)$, assuming μ and σ as constant parameters, it would also generate a graph similar to the one in Figure 1. This is so because an Itô equation is driven by its random term **dZ** which in discrete time is approximated by sampling from a normal distribution with zero mean and variance equal to one. Therefore, there is no loss of generality in analyzing the random walk in its numerical representation in Figure 1 instead of Itô processes or martingales. A methodological analysis of martingales is presented in Malliaris (1981) and of Itô processes in Malliaris (1990).

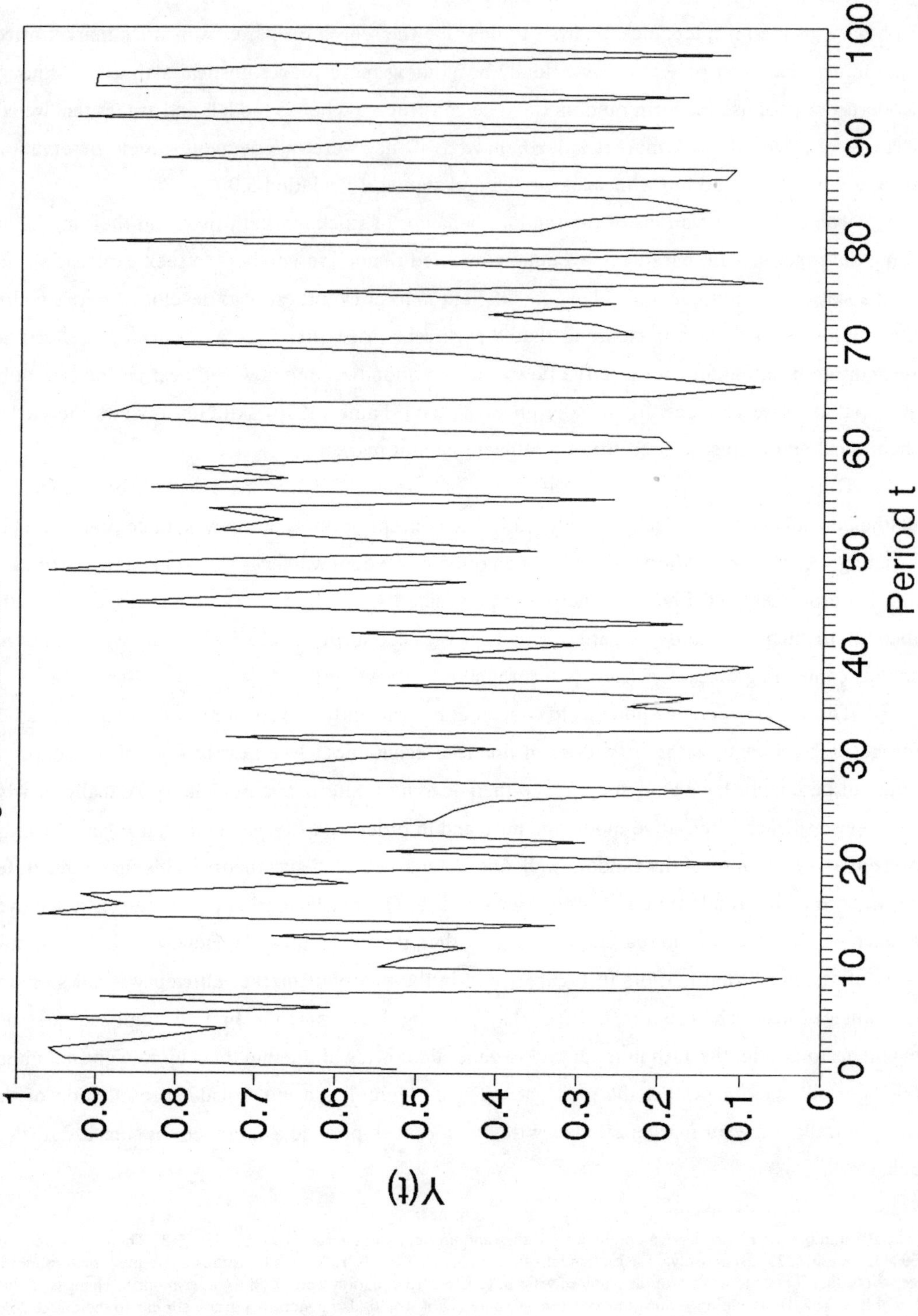

Figure 1: Random Walk

Focusing on Figure 1 we now ask the question: can a graph similar to the one in Figure 1 be constructed from a nonrandom methodology? In other words, does there exist a deterministic (nonrandom) function with an exact relationship between dependent and independent variable that generates a graph like the one in Figure 1? These are purely mathematical questions with significant implications for market efficiency. In sharp contrast to the random walk, the existence of an exact, deterministic equation would imply perfect predictability of all future prices. Market efficiency would argue that such a clairvoyant knowledge would alter today's price because market participants would take appropriate positions today to benefit from such knowledge about the future and in so doing would alter this deterministic equation. In other words a deterministic equation and market efficiency are not compatible, provided that the deterministic stock price model is common across investors and furthermore, it is common knowledge.

To briefly recapitulate, consider the random behavior in Figure 1 as a paradigm of stock market price changes. On the basis of casual observation and more formally, on the basis of traditional statistical tests, can we manufacture a similar graph from a nonrandom equation? This is the topic presented in the next section.

3. CHAOTIC DYNAMICS

Consider the nonlinear deterministic equation

$$dp(t+1) = 3.89\, dp(t)\,[1 - dp(t)], \tag{3.1}$$

with initial condition **dp(0) = .52**. The value selected for the initial condition is that of the first value of the random walk in Figure 1. It is used to coordinate the starting value of the random walk and the logistic map and has no significance. Any value in [0, 1] will yield similar results.

Suppose that stock price changes are generated by (3.1). How does the time series of such price changes look like? Figure 2 illustrates such a time series for **t = 0, 1, 2, ...100.** Notice that for each **t = 1, 2, ...100**, equation (3.1) precisely yields a stock price change denoted as **dp(t).** Furthermore, all that is needed to calculate the stock price change next period is the current price change. Randomness does not enter equation (3.1) and therefore we can say that stock price changes are not uncertain. Knowing today's price change, (3.1) allows us to calculate all future price changes precisely.

We do not propose that (3.1) is an actual mathematical expression of stock price changes. We simply wish to illustrate that (3.1) generates a time series that exhibits complex dynamics that resemble actual stock price changes. If Figure 2 appeared in a business publication it would not surprise anyone; yet its time series comes from an exact, deterministic, nonrandom, and nonlinear

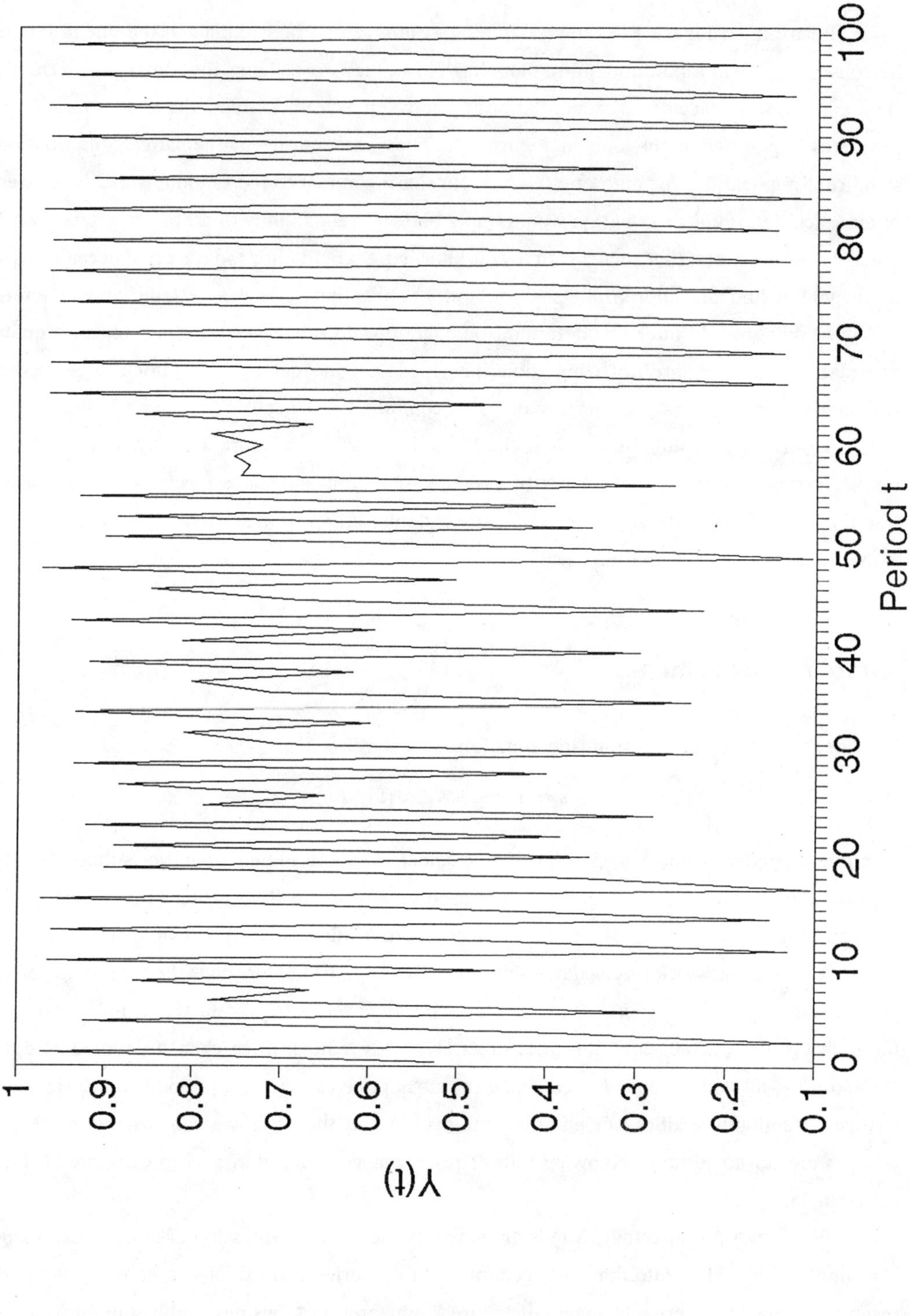

Figure 2: Logistic Map

equation that generates random-like behavior.

Obviously the existence of a deterministic equation such as (3.1) does not disprove that stock market price changes follow a random walk, it only casts a strong doubt that the random walk cannot be the only and exclusive mathematical model for such price changes. It is true, that the random walk is supported by an elaborate theory of efficient markets and by numerous empirical studies. However, the existence of an alternative mathematical paradigm invites our intellectual consideration.

At this point we could digress to explain the chaotic dynamics associated with (3.1). Brock and Malliaris (1989) give an introduction to chaos and explain how the work of physicists on turbulence has offered financial economists new ways of modelling complicated time series. Hsieh (1991) gives a detailed analysis of chaos and nonlinear dynamics in financial markets. It suffices for our purpose to simply say that (3.1) is a specific example of a chaotic function, known as the logistic map, and that it has been studied extensively not only by physicists but has also been reviewed in economics by Baumol and Benhabib (1989) and in futures markets by Savit (1988). The remarkable characteristic of the logistic map is not so much its exact quadratic (therefore nonlinear) expression but, rather, the fact that by changing the values of the coefficient 3.89 in (3.1), this equation can generate a rich variety of time series behavior. Figures 3a and 3b give a small sample of few time series obtained by simply changing the coefficient **w** in

$$dp(t+1) = w\,dp(t)\,[1 - dp(t)]. \tag{3.2}$$

Savit (1988) and Baumol and Benhabib (1989) devote essentially their entire articles in analyzing, illustrating and explaining the behavior of (3.2) for parameter values[2] of **w** in various subintervals of **[0, 4]**. The important point, however, is that (3.1) as a special case of (3.2) invites the financial analyst to reflect on the question: could it be that actual stock price changes are generated by nonlinear, deterministic, dynamic equations? As much as our intuition, guided by the orthodoxy of efficient market theory[3], might object such a consideration, academic curiosity encourages us to proceed.

The logical way to proceed in the analysis of chaotic dynamics is to give a precise definition. The definition we give is purely mathematical and can be found in several books such as Devaney

---

[2]The important paper that proposed the use of differential equations depending upon a parameter for the modelling of turbulence is Ruelle and Takens (1971). For an elegant review of the mathematical properties of the logistic map and of other maps known to mathematicians for their complicated time series see May (1976). In Figures 3a and 3b we illustrate how the behavior of (3.2) and its graphical representation change as the parameter value changes. For **w = 3** we obtain a series that is convergent; for **w = 3.3** the map generates a two-period cycle while for **w = 3.4495** we have a four-period cycle. For **w = 3.5** we generate a long cycle while for **w = 3.935** and **w = 3.99** we obtain chaotic behavior. More specifically note that for $w \leq 3$, the system is stable while for $3 < w \leq 3.57$ the system is periodic. Finally, for $3.57 < w < 4$, the system is mostly chaotic.

[3]Notice that our approach is to contrast the paradigms of random walk and that of chaotic dynamics instead of attacking the efficient market hypothesis. For a recent attack see Shleifer and Summers (1990).

Figure 3a: Selected Logistic Maps

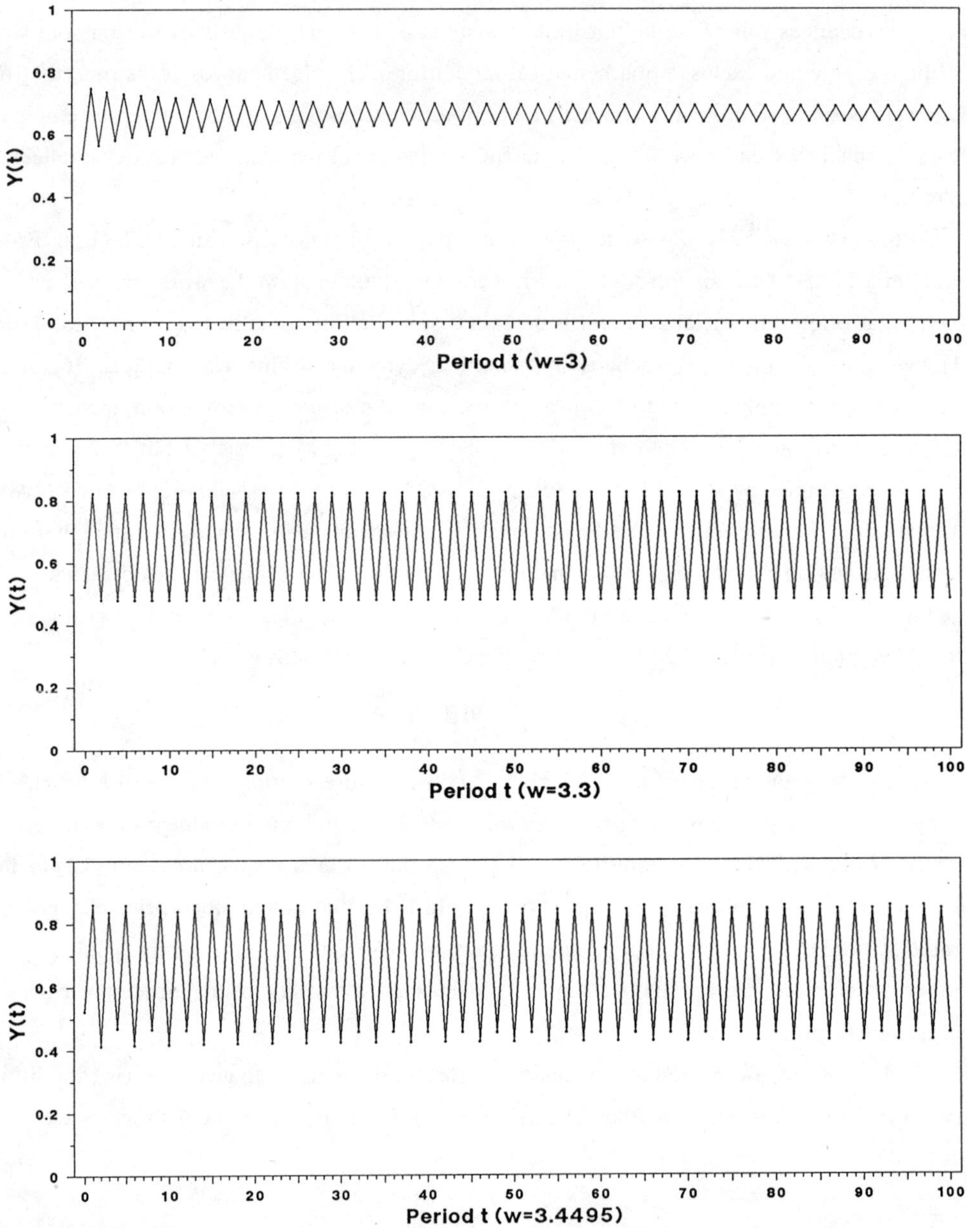

Figure 3b: Selected Logistic Maps

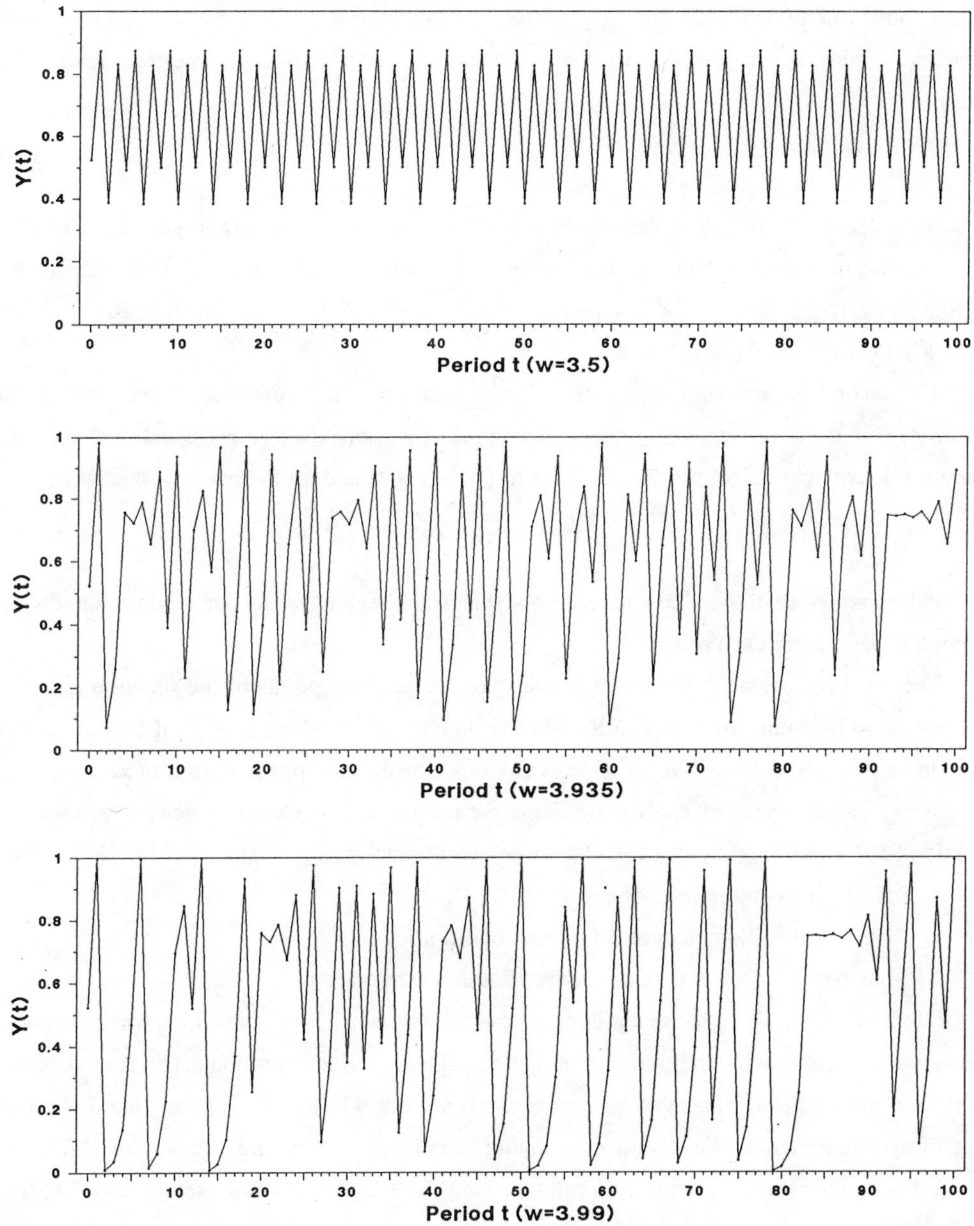

(1986). It requires, first, to explain a few terms. We do this next.

Consider a real-valued function $\mathbf{f}: \mathbf{R} \rightarrow \mathbf{R}$. We are interested in the time series generated by this function starting from some arbitrary $\mathbf{x}_0 \in \mathbf{R}$. Denote by $\mathbf{f}^2 \equiv \mathbf{f}[\mathbf{f}(\mathbf{x})] \equiv \mathbf{f} \circ \mathbf{f}(\mathbf{x})$ where $\mathbf{o}$ means composition and in general let $\mathbf{f}^n = \mathbf{f} \circ \mathbf{f} \circ \ldots \circ \mathbf{f}(\mathbf{x})$ mean $\mathbf{n}$ compositions. The time series takes the values

$$x_o,\ f(x_o),\ f^2(x_o),\ \ldots, f^n(x_o),\ \ldots, \tag{3.3}$$

for $\mathbf{t} = \mathbf{0}, \mathbf{1}, \mathbf{2}, \ldots, \mathbf{n}$. For (3.3) to describe a chaotic function it must satisfy three requirements.

First it must sample infinitely many values. To make this idea precise we say that $\mathbf{f}: \mathbf{R} \rightarrow \mathbf{R}$ is <u>topologically transitive</u> if for any pair of open sets $\mathbf{U}$ and $\mathbf{V}$ in the real line $\mathbf{R}$ there is an integer $\mathbf{k} > \mathbf{0}$ such that $\mathbf{f}^k(\mathbf{U}) \cap \mathbf{V} \neq \phi$.

The second requirement is sensitive dependence on initial conditions. We say that the function $\mathbf{f}: \mathbf{R} \rightarrow \mathbf{R}$ has <u>sensitive dependence</u> on initial conditions if there exists a $\delta > \mathbf{0}$ such that for any $\mathbf{x} \in \mathbf{R}$ and any neighborhood $\mathbf{N}$ of $\mathbf{x}$, there is a $\mathbf{y} \in \mathbf{N}$ and an integer $\mathbf{n} > \mathbf{0}$ such that

$$|f^n(x) - f^n(y)| > \delta. \tag{3.4}$$

This condition says that there are time series that start very close to each other but diverge exponentially fast from each other.

The third requirement involves a property of the periodic points of the function $\mathbf{f}$, namely that these periodic points are dense in $\mathbf{R}$. We say that a point $\mathbf{x} \in \mathbf{R}$ is <u>periodic</u> if for $\mathbf{n} > \mathbf{0}$, $\mathbf{f}^n(\mathbf{x}) = \mathbf{x}$. The least positive integer $\mathbf{n}$ for which $\mathbf{f}^n(\mathbf{x}) = \mathbf{x}$ is called the <u>prime period</u> of $\mathbf{x}$.

We can summarize our analysis by giving the definition of a chaotic function. We say that a function $\mathbf{f}: \mathbf{R} \rightarrow \mathbf{R}$ is <u>chaotic</u> if it satisfies three conditions:

1. f is topologically transitive.
2. f has sensitive dependence on initial conditions.
3. f has periodic points that are dense in the real numbers.

Observe that this is a precise mathematical definition which is not motivated by stock market price behavior. Yet, each condition can be given a financial interpretation. The first condition requires the time series dynamics to be rich in the sense that (3.1) takes infinitely many different values. This condition makes a chaotic map similar to random walk because each value is different from all the previous ones. Of course, in random walk this happens because we are sampling from an infinite population. On the other hand, in chaotic dynamics we do not have sampling; instead we have a nonlinear equation that generates many different values. Note that for both the random walk and for the chaotic dynamics it is possible for certain values to occur more than once in the time series. What we are emphasizing is that such a repetition is very unlikely. Put differently the first condition of topological transitivity, requires the time series to be rich in the sense that it takes infinitely many different values. Intuitively, such a map can move under iteration, i.e. through time, from one arbitrarily small neighborhood to any other. Since the space cannot be decomposed into two disjoint open sets which are invariant under the map (by definition) the points not only can wander anywhere (since they can't be blocked) but actually will wander everywhere.

The second condition casts serious difficulties in forecasting. Although a chaotic map is deterministic and knowing today's value immediately allows one to compute tomorrow's price, the same exact equation can generate very dissimilar time series if we are uncertain about when the series got started and at what initial value $\mathbf{x}_o$. To contrast with a random walk, recall that the past and future values are independent because we are sampling from an infinite population of values. The inability to forecast is due precisely to this statistical independence. In a chaotic function, however, we know exactly the relationship between the past and the future but we are unable to predict because we cannot be sure as to when we started and with what value. Put differently, in a chaotic function, only if we know exactly $\mathbf{x}_o$ can we then generate the sequence (3.1). Figure 4 illustrates the time series of errors generated from a very small error in the initial value for the logistic map. In this graph the top two time series, **y(t)** and **v(t)**, are generated with the same parameter value **w = 3.89** but two slightly different initial conditions, **y(0) = .52** and **v(0) = .51**. The third graph depicts the deviations due to the insignificant difference in the initial value. It should be, however, noted that not all points near $\mathbf{x}_0$ need eventually separate from $\mathbf{x}_0$ under iteration; rather it must be emphasized that there must be at least one such point in every neighborhood of $\mathbf{x}_0$.

The third condition gives a chaotic function structure. It essentially requires that the chaotic function exhibit important regularities. However, these regularities are hidden in the sense that no researcher could explore the infinitely many patterns of the periodic points and their limits. In an analogous manner, the random walk can be said to have some structure given to it by the properties of the distribution that characterizes the population. Again, no researcher could explore the infinitely many sample paths that a random walk process can generate. This analogy between the structure of a chaotic function and a random walk should not be understood as meaning that both have exactly the same structure. Although we do not know how to compare correctly the structure of a chaotic function to that of a random walk, it suffices to remark that (3.1) involves infinitely many iterations of a nonlinear function and therefore its structure could be viewed as being more complex compared to the structure of a random walk generated from a simple equation as (2.1). More technically, one can argue that in chaotic dynamics because the set of periodic points is dense in **R**, for any point in **R**, there exists a sequence of periodic points which converges to this point. Thus, it appears intuitively that not only a structure exists because of the mere existence of the periodic points, but moreover because they are clustered around each point in the domain. Therefore, due to the fact that periodic points are dense, each point in the domain can be identified

Figure 4: Sentitive Dependence on Initial Conditions

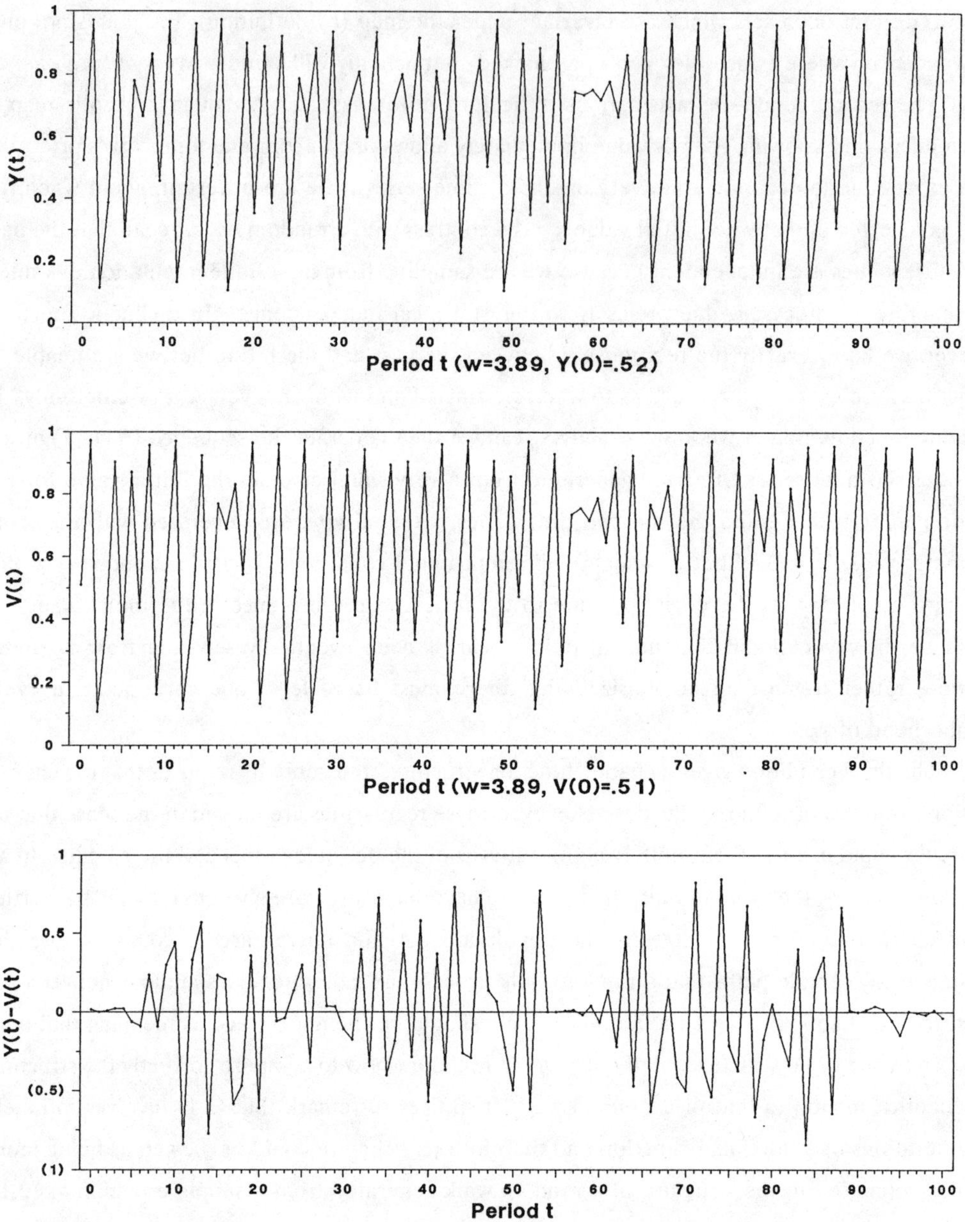

by a sequence of periodic points, which converges to it. However, in the random walk case, each point is identified by its probability of occurrence which is described by the normal density function.

Having presented and explained the definition of a chaotic function, there are at least two ways to proceed. First, one can take the road of mathematics and present theorems about chaotic dynamics. The second possibility is to return immediately to financial economics and reflect the appropriateness of chaotic dynamics in representing stock market price changes and price changes of derivative assets. The first possibility, although informative, becomes rapidly very technical. The second possibility has limited potential because we only have one tool: the definition of a chaotic process. Therefore we suggest a third alternative: we will describe an interesting mathematical result instead of rigorously stating and proving theorems, and use it for our main purpose of contrasting the methodologies of random walk vs. chaotic dynamics in financial economics.

The mathematical result that makes chaotic dynamics very interesting is the existence of strange attractors. In studying various chaotic maps, mathematicians discovered that as time increases, despite the turbulent behavior of such maps that looks like random, the time series values indeed converge to a set. Furthermore, the set which, of course, depends on the specific map is not one of the standard sets of stability theory such as a point, a circle, or a torous. Because the attractors of chaotic maps are not as the regular attractors of ordinary differential equations, they were named strange.

A precise mathematical definition of a strange attractor is given in Guckenheimer and Holmes (1983) along with several beautiful illustrations. We will use a simple definition and say that a strange attractor of a chaotic dynamical system is a compact set, denoted **S**, such that almost all initial conditions in the neighborhood of **S** converge to **S**. The neighborhood of **S** from where almost all initial conditions yield time series that converge to **S** is called the basin of the strange attractor.

Instead of reproducing graphically strange attractors of famous chaotic maps we generated 5000 points of the logistic map and graphed in Figure 5 not the time series $\{y(t) : t = 0, 1, 2, 5000\}$ but instead its phase diagram, that is $\{[y(t), y(t+1)] : t = 0, 1, 2, ..., 5000\}$. Observe that although Figure 2 shows that the logistic map with $w = 3.89$ as in (3.1) behaves randomly (only the first 101 points are illustrated but the same is true for the entire time series) as time increases the values of this map stay within a set that has a specific shape and looks like a parabola. From a mathematical standpoint we cannot decide the strange attractor with only 5000 iterations but it is nevertheless instructive that even so early the limit set begins to take shape.

In sharp contrast to Figure 5 now examine Figure 6. It is generated from a random walk with 5001 drawings. As in Figure 1, which depicts the first 101 points we continued the process for 5001 drawings and then graphed the pairs $\{[y(t), y(t+1)], t = 0, ... 5000\}$ as explained in footnote 1. Figure 5 illustrates that chaotic maps settle down to structured sets while Figure 6 illustrates that

Figure 5: Strange Attractor

Y(0)=.52, w=3.89

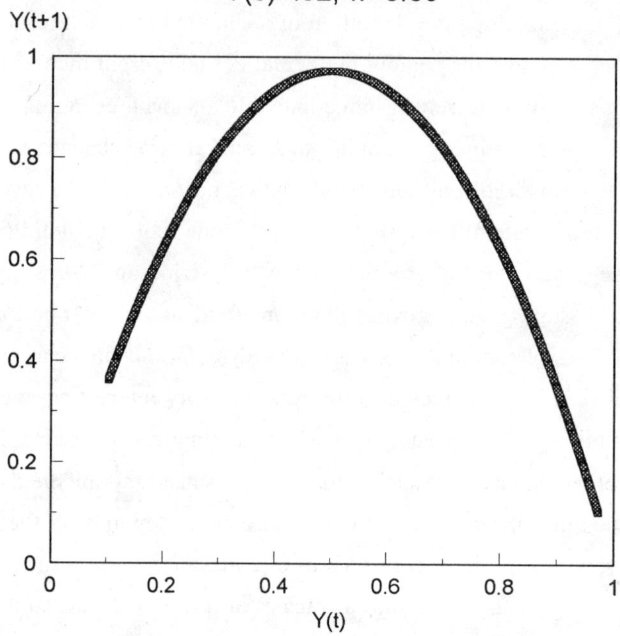

Figure 6: Random Walk - Scatter Diagram

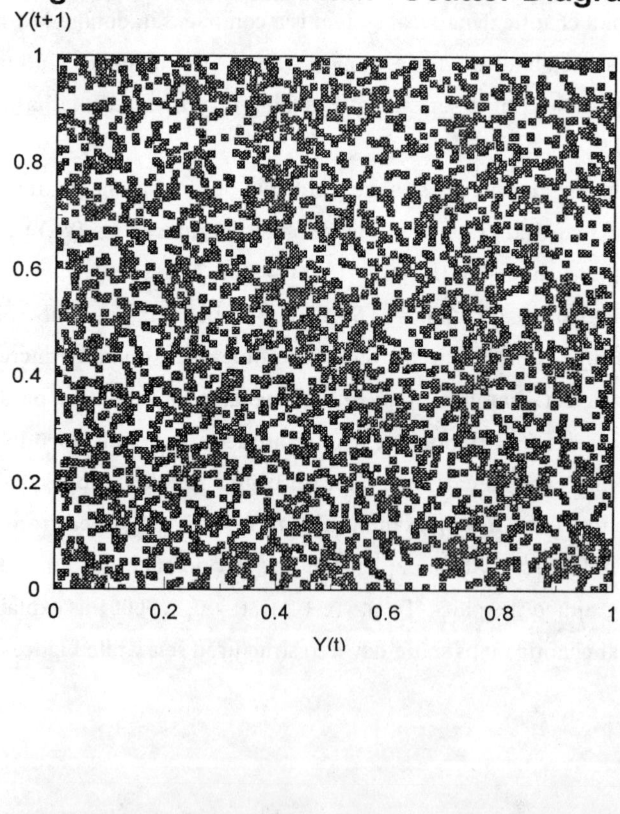

random walks do not settle down. One conclusion we can draw from the examination of Figures 5 and 6 is that a random walk fills all the space and continues to wander around (as time increases) while chaotic dynamics (despite their appearance as random and turbulent) fill much less space and have strange attractors.

4. DETECTING CHAOTIC DYNAMICS

The reader has by now, most likely, understood our message: given a time series of actual stock price changes how can it be analytically modelled? We have argued that the random walk paradigm, despite its wide popularity is only one way. Another model is chaotic dynamics. Furthermore we have contrasted the definitions and graphical representations of these two approaches and concluded that the random walk wanders for ever while chaotic dynamics wanders also but in a narrower range. Put differently, the randomness of random walk has no structure while the randomness of chaotic dynamics has significant hidden structure. In other words, random walk describes uncertainty in a more extreme way than chaotic dynamics. Naturally, the important question is: Given a time series how can we distinguish whether it is generated by a random walk or a chaotic process?

In an important paper Brock (1986) reviewed an extensive literature in physics that addresses precisely this question. He also evaluated the various methods used by the physicists and reported some preliminary results using such methods in economic and financial data. Brock and Malliaris (1989, Chapter 10) present a pedagogical exposition of some similar ideas.

What we plan to do in this section is to intuitively explain one method, i.e. correlation dimension[4], for detecting whether the data are random or chaotic and then apply it to the two sets of data that generated Figures 5 and 6. Since we manufactured both sets and already know from these two figures the nature and structure of these data, our procedure would allow us to evaluate the effectiveness of the detecting methodology.

The correlation dimension was originally proposed by Grassberger and Procaccia (1983). We first give an intuitive motivation and then proceed to describe the methods more carefully. The intuition behind this method is guided by Figures 5 and 6. A system that is random is space filling as in Figure 6 while a system that is chaotic has a strange attractor that fills less space. Instead of just examining pairs $\{[y(t), y(t+1)] : t = 0, 1, 2, ...\}$ in two dimensional figures as in 5 and 6, suppose that we consider triplets $\{[y(t), y(t+1), y(t+2)] : t = 0, 1, 2, ...\}$ and in general M-

[4]There are at least three methods used by nonlinear scientists in distinguishing random from deterministic systems: correlation dimension, Liapunov exponents and Kolmogorov entropy. These methods are reviewed and evaluated in Eckmann and Ruelle (1985), Brock (1986) and Brock and Malliaris (1989). There is general agreement that the correlation dimension has emerged as the most useful method, among these three.

histories $\{[y(t), y(t+1), \ldots y(t+M-1)] : t = 0, 1, 2, \ldots\}$. The same way the pairs of a random walk filled the 2-dimensional space, one would expect the M-histories of a random walk to fill the M-dimensional space while the chaotic system's attractor may not spread over too many dimensions. In other words the dimension of a chaotic system tends to stabilize.

Let us now translate this intuition into careful analysis. Suppose that we are given a time series of price changes $\{dp(t) : t = 0, 1, 2, \ldots T\}$. Suppose that **T** is large enough so that a strange attractor has begun to take shape. Use this time series to create pairs, i.e. $dP^2(t) \equiv \{[dp(t), dp(t+1)] : t = 0, 1, 2, \ldots T\}$ and then triplets and finally M-histories, i.e. $dp^M(t) \equiv \{[dp(t), \ldots dp(t+M-1)] : t = 0, 1, 2, \ldots T\}$. In other words we convert the original time series of singletons into vectors of dimension **2, 3, ... M**. In generating these vectors we allow for overlapping entries. For example if $M = 3$ we have a set of the form $\{[dp(0), dp(1), dp(2)], [dp(1), dp(2), dp(3)], \ldots, dp(T-2), dp(T-1), dp(T)\}$. Such a set will have $(T + 1) - (M - 1)$ vectors. Mathematically, the process of creating vectors of various dimension from the original series is called an <u>embedding</u>.

Suppose that for a given embedding dimension, say **M**, we wish to measure if these **M**-vectors fill the entire **M**-space or only a fraction. For a given $\epsilon > 0$ define the <u>correlation integral</u>, denoted by

$$C^M(\epsilon) = \frac{\textit{the number of pairs } (s, t) \textit{ whose distance } \| dp^M(s) - dp^M(t) \| < \epsilon}{T^2_M}$$
$$= \frac{\textit{the number of } (s, t),\ 1 \le t,\ s \le T,\ \| dp^M(s) - dp^M(t) \| < \epsilon}{T^2_M}, \tag{4.1}$$

where $T_M = (T + 1) - (M - 1)$, and as before

$$dp^M(t) = [dp(t), dp(t+1), \ldots, dp(t+M-1)].$$

Observe that $||\cdot||$ in (4.1) denotes vector norm. Using the correlation integral we can define the <u>correlation dimension</u> for an embedding dimension **M** as

$$D^M = \lim_{\substack{\epsilon \to 0 \\ T \to \infty}} \frac{\ln C^M(\epsilon)}{\ln \epsilon}. \tag{4.2}$$

In (4.2) **ln** denotes natural logarithm. Finally, the correlation dimension **D** is given by

$$D = \lim_{M \to \infty} D^M. \tag{4.3}$$

We remark that technical accuracy requires that D^M in (4.2) is a double limit, first in terms of $T \to \infty$ and then in terms of $\epsilon \to 0$. However, in practice **T** is usually given and it is impossible to increase it to infinity. Thus the limit $T \to \infty$ is meaningless in practice and moreover **M** is practically bounded by T. Therefore, we only consider the limit $\epsilon \to 0$ in (4.2).

Tables 1 and 2 illustrate the use of (4.1), (4.2) and (4.3). For our two sets of data, each with 5001 points, we proceed as follows. Since **T** is fixed, our two variables are the embedding

TABLE 1: CORRELATION DIMENSION FOR LOGISTIC DATA

EMBEDDING DIMENSION	VALUES OF ϵ				
	ϵ (.3366)	ϵ^2 (.1133)	ϵ^3 (.03814)	ϵ^4 (.01284)	ϵ^5 (.004321)
2	1.00	.94	.93	.93	.92
3	1.34	1.16	1.09	1.05	1.02
4	1.67	1.36	1.22	1.14	1.10
5	1.99	1.55	1.35	1.25	1.19
6	2.28	1.73	1.48	1.34	1.27
7	2.60	1.92	1.60	1.44	1.35
8	2.88	2.10	1.73	1.54	1.42
9	3.16	2.27	1.85	1.63	1.50
10	3.44	2.45	1.97	1.73	1.59
11	3.72	2.62	2.10	1.82	1.66

dimension **M** and the distance of neighboring points. We consider the values of **M = 2, 3, ..., 11**. Obviously one could consider many more. For ϵ we consider the first five powers of the standard deviation of the original data sets. Therefore the entries in Table 1 correspond to specific values of (4.1). The limit (4.2) corresponds to the limit of a given row of this Table, while **D** corresponds to the limit of the last column.[5]

A review of tables 1 and 2 is quite revealing. Table 1 presents in a matrix form the correlation dimension calculated for a given embedding dimension and a given value of ϵ for the 5001 points of the logistic map. For example, for **M = 2** and ϵ = **.3366** the calculations in (4.1) yield **1.00**, while for **M = 10** and ϵ^4 = **.01284** the value of (4.1) is **1.73**. Notice that for a given embedding dimension as $\epsilon \to 0$ the values converge so that D^M in (4.2) has a limit. Also notice that as we hold ϵ or its powers fixed and increase the embedding dimension the numbers increase very slowly, again implying convergence. From our limited calculations we conclude that the correlation dimension **D** in (4.3) approaches **1.66** which is a small and finite number.

In contrast to Table 1, observe the results generated using the 5001 random data with a very similar mean and standard deviation to those of the logistic map. For a given embedding dimension as $\epsilon \to 0$, (4.1) now yields values that diverge. Furthermore, as you examine the values in a given cell as the embedding dimension increases holding ϵ or its powers fixed there is an increase which is faster than that of the logistic data. In conclusion, Table 2 shows that because random data fills the space even as the embedding dimension increases the correlation dimension **D** in (4.2) is not defined. In other words, the quantitative description of figures 5 and 6 is given quantitative expressions in calculating **D** in (4.3) confirming that the correlation dimension of the strange attractor is smaller than that of the random set.

Thus far the correlation dimension was applied to the 5001 points of the two sets: random and logistic. Actually, the entire article is an exposition of these two paradigms. However, we wish now to briefly report that the same methodology has been applied to actual data[6]. Scheinkman and LeBaron (1989) present preliminary evidence that indicates the presence of chaotic dynamics in stock market data. They used an initial data set of at least 5200 daily returns on the value-weighted portfolio of the Center for Research in Security Prices at the University of Chicago (CRSP). Because daily returns are usually noisy, these authors constructed a weekly return series of 1226 observations. Using embedding dimension from **M = 1, 2, ... 14** and letting their $\epsilon \to 0$ they observe that the correlation dimension **D** in (4.3) is about **6.3**. Of course this number is small but one cannot be absolutely confident that this is conclusive evidence of chaos. The authors provide,

---

[5]All the calculations in Tables 1 and 2 were performed using Professor Dechert's software for calculating BDS statistics. We thank Professor Dechert for supplying us with his helpful program.

[6]It is of historical significance to note that two decades ago Philippatos and Wilson (1971, 1972, 1974), Philippatos and Martell (1974) and Philippatos and Nawrocki (1973) used entropy measures to study time dependency in stock market prices.

TABLE 2: CORRELATION DIMENSION FOR RANDOM DATA

		VALUES OF ϵ				
		ϵ (.2902)	ϵ^2 (.08422)	ϵ^3 (.02444)	ϵ^4 (.0071)	ϵ^5 (.002058)
EMBEDDING DIMENSION	2	1.14	1.48	1.63	1.72	1.77
	3	1.71	2.21	2.45	2.50	2.74
	4	2.28	2.94	3.26	*	*
	5	2.84	3.66	4.11	*	*
	6	3.41	4.38	*	*	*
	7	3.97	5.07	*	*	*
	8	4.53	6.04	*	*	*
	9	5.09	*	*	*	*
	10	5.65	*	*	*	*
	11	6.21	*	*	*	*

* : An asterisk denotes that calculations do not yield a finite number.

however, a yardstick for comparison: they create scrambled data in the following manner. First, returns were regressed on past returns. Then, they sampled with replacement from the residuals and rebuilt the data set using the estimated linear system and the same initial values as the real data. This way they created data that seemed much more random than the initial 1226 observations. For the scrambled data, they found that the correlation dimension almost doubled in value to **11.2**. Furthermore, Scheinkman and LeBaron (1989) compute the correlation dimension of Abbot Labs and find that for both the original data of this stock and for the scrambled data the numbers are higher than for the index. One implication of these findings is that individual stock returns could be more random than the value-weighted index.[7]

Although these early findings are encouraging, much more work needs to be done. A tentative conclusion is that as research reveals that the random walk paradigm is extreme, such findings would encourage financial economists to reformulate the theories of market efficiency[8].

5. SUMMARY AND CONCLUSIONS

We have contrasted two paradigms of stock market price changes: random walk and chaotic dynamics. The analysis emphasized the definitions of these two concepts and graphical presentations illustrated their behavior. Instead of casting the analysis in a form of a debate by attacking the random walk model, we chose to clarify the issues involved. Namely, both random walk and chaotic dynamics are mathematical concepts whose time series generate graphical representations resembling actual stock market price changes. However the scientific foundations of these two models are radically different: one is probabilistic while the other is deterministic.

Because chaotic dynamics is a relatively new concept it is developed here in a little more detail and the method of correlation dimension is explained and illustrated with two data sets. Our conclusions include the following.

First, despite its general acceptability, substantial empirical evidence and analytical simplicity, the random walk model of stock price changes does not command currently the popularity it once had. Therefore the profession is searching for alternative models.

Second, various generalizations of the random walk, theoretically such as martingales and Itô processes or empirically, such as ARCH, GARCH, bilinear models, or theoretical deviations

---

[7]Ramsey and Yuan (1989) and Ramsey, Sayers and Rothman (1988) evaluate the Scheinkman and LeBaron results using various simulations. Brock, Dechert and Scheinkman (1986) develop a test that is better grounded on statistical theory. For details see these references and Brock, Hsieh and LeBaron (1991). Finally, applications of chaotic techniques to derivative and other financial markets is currently available. Few representative studies among several others are: Savit (1989) for options, Hsieh (1989) for foreign currencies, Blank(1991) for futures markets and Van Der Ploeg (1986) for bonds.

[8]Brock (1988) discusses the theoretical implications of chaotic dynamics in economics and finance.

from market efficiency, such as noise trading, share common probabilistic foundations and therefore are not radical departures from the old methodology.

Third, chaotic dynamics offers an important alternative paradigm. The time series of a chaotic dynamic system appears random but actually contains significant structure. In other words its randomness is not extreme. Financial economists can learn a great deal from physicists who have researched this area extensively.

Fourth, random walk is supported by an elaborate theory of market efficiency. Chaotic dynamics has no companion theory. Market efficiency is inconsistent with the deterministic foundation of chaos and nonlinearity. For chaotic dynamics to gain further ground, appropriate theories of market behavior must be developed to offer theoretical support.

Fifth, initial empirical evidence of actual stock market data has provided partial support for chaotic dynamics and nonlinearity. A further challenge for chaotic dynamics is the development of an appropriate theory of statistical inference. The work of Brock, Dechert, and Scheinkman is very encouraging. See also the forthcoming book of Brock, Hsieh and LeBaron (1992).

Finally, the use of the logistic map or other well known chaotic maps, only serves as a metaphor of the actual map that drives stock market price changes. The actual map, if it is chaotic, is unknown. Even worst, the nonlinear scientist has currently no methods for discovering it. Available methods only distinguish between chaos and randomness. Simply put, we may have more models of the behavior of stock market but the "market is still a fascinating mystery."

ACKNOWLEDGEMENT

We owe a significant intellectual debt to Professor William Brock for his pioneering work in this area, for his continued support and valuable comments on an earlier draft. Parts of this paper were presented by A. G. Malliaris at the Citicorp Seminar of the Economics Department at Brown University. We wish to thank Professor Jerome Stein and various seminar participants for their valuable comments. We are grateful to Professor L. Geronazzo for the invitation to contribute this paper to the present volume. All errors are our own responsibility.

BIBLIOGRAPHY

Baumol, W., and J. Benhabib, (1989), "Chaos: Significance, Mechanism, and Economic Applications", Journal of Economic Perspectives, Vol. 3, 77-105.

Blank, S., (1991), "Chaos In Futures Markets? A Nonlinear Dynamical Analysis", Journal of Futures Markets, 11, 711-728.

Brock,W., (1986), "Distinguishing Random and Deterministic Systems: Abridged Version", Journal of Economic Theory, Vol. 40, 168-194.

Brock, W., (1988), "Nonlinearity and Complex Dynamics in Economics and Finance", in THE ECONOMY AS AN EVOLVING COMPLEX SYSTEM, SFI Studies in the Sciences of Complexity, Addison-Wesley Publishing Company.

Brock, W., W. Dechert, and J. Scheinkman, (1986), "A Test for Independence Based on the Correlation Dimension", Working Paper, Department of Economics, University of Wisconsin, University of Chicago and University of Houston.

Brock, W., D. Hsieh and B. LeBaron (1991), NONLINEAR DYNAMICS, CHAOS AND INSTABILITY : STATISTICAL THEORY AND ECONOMIC EVIDENCE, Cambridge, Massachusetts : The MIT Press.

Brock, W., and A.G. Malliaris, (1989), DIFFERENTIAL EQUATIONS, STABILITY AND CHAOS IN DYNAMIC ECONOMICS. Advanced Textbooks in Economics, North-Holland Publishing Company, Amsterdam.

Brock, W., and C. Sayers,(1988), "Is the Business Cycle Characterized by Deterministic Chaos", Journal of Monetary Economics, Vol. 22, 71-90.

Cowles, A., (1933), "Can Stock Market Forecasters Forecast?", Econometrica, Vol. 1, 309-324.

Devaney, R., (1986), AN INTRODUCTION TO CHAOTIC DYNAMICAL SYSTEMS, Menlo Park, California, Benjamin/Cummings Publishing.

Eckmann, J., and D. Ruelle, (1985), "Ergodic Theory of Chaos and Strange Attractors", Review of Modern Physics, Vol. 57, 617-656.

Fama, E., (1970), "Efficient Capital Markets: A Review of Theory and Empirical Work", Journal of Finance, Vol. 25, 383-417.

Frank, M., and T. Stengos, (1989), "Measuring the Strangeness of Gold and Silver Rates of Return", Review of Economic Studies, Vol. 56, 553-567.

Grassberger, P. and I. Procaccia, (1983), "Measuring the Strangeness of Strange Attractors", Physics, Vol. 9-D, 189-208.

Guckenheimer, J., and P. Holmes, (1983), NONLINEAR OSCILLATIONS, DYNAMICAL SYSTEMS AND BIFURCATIONS OF VECTOR FIELDS, Springer-Verlag, New York.

Helms, B., and T. Martell, (1985), "An Examination of the Distribution of Futures Price Changes", The Journal of Futures Markets, Vol. 5, 259-272.

Hsieh, D., (1989), "Testing for Nonlinear Dependence in Daily Foreign Exchange Rates", Journal of Business, Vol. 62, 339-368.

Hsieh, D. (1991), "Chaos and Nonlinear Dynamics : Application to Financial Markets", The Journal of Finance, Vol. 46, 1839-1877.

Lee, C., J. Finnerty, and D. Wort, (1990), SECURITY ANALYSIS AND PORTFOLIO MANAGEMENT, Scott, Foresman/Little, Brown Higher Education, Glenview, Illinois.

Malliaris, A.G., (1981), "Martingale Methods in Financial Decision-Making", Society for Industrial and Applied Mathematics, Vol. 23, 434-443.

Malliaris, A.G., (1990), "Itô's Calculus: Derivation of the Black-Scholes Option-Pricing Model", in SECURITY ANALYSIS AND PORTFOLIO MANAGEMENT by C.F. Lee, J. Finnerty and Donald Wort, 737-763.

May, R., (1976),"Simple Mathematical Models With Very Complicated Dynamics", Nature, Vol. 261, 459-467.

Melese, F., and W. Transue, (1986), "Unscrambling Chaos Through Thick and Thin", The Quarterly Journal of Economics, Vol. 101, 419-423.

Philippatos, G., and T. Martell, (1974), "Adaptation, Information, and Dependence in Commodity Markets", The Journal of Finance, Vol. 29, 493-498.

Philippatos, G., and D. Nawrocki, (1973), "The Information Inaccuracy of Stock Market Forecasts: Some New Evidence of Dependence of the New York Stock Exchange", Journal of Financial Quantitative Analysis, 445-458.

Philippatos, G., and C. Wilson, (1971), "Entropy As A Measure of Dispersion in The Portfolio Selection Problem", American Institute for Decision Sciences, 142-152.

Philippatos, G., and C. Wilson, (1972), "Entropy, Market Risk, and The Selection of Efficient Portfolios", Applied Economics, Vol. 4, 209-220.

Philippatos, G., and C. Wilson, (1974), "Information Theory and Risk in Capital Markets", Omega, The International Journal of Management Science, Vol. 2, 523-532.

Ramsey, J. B., C. Sayers, and P. Rothman (1988), "The Statistical Properties of Dimension Calculations using Small Data Sets : Some Economic Applications", International Economic Review, Vol. 31, 991-1020.

Ramsey, J. B., and H. Yuan, (1989), "Bias and Error Bars in Dimension Calculations and their Evaluation in Some Simple Models", Physics Letters A, Vol. 134, 287-297.

Roberts, V., (1959), "Stock-Market 'Patterns' and Financial Analysis: Methodological Suggestions", The Journal of Finance, Vol. 14, 1-10.

Ross, S., (1987), "Finance", in THE NEW PALGRAVE, Vol. II.

Ruelle, D., and F. Takens, (1971), "On the Nature of Turbulence", Communications of Mathematical Physics, Vol. 20, 167-192.

Savit, R., (1988), "When Random is Not Random: An Introduction to Chaos in Market Prices",

The Journal of Futures Markets, Vol. 8, 271-289.

Savit, R., (1989), "Nonlinearities and Chaotic Effects in Options Prices", The Journal of Futures Markets, Vol. 9, no. 6, 507-518.

Scheinkman, J., and B. LeBaron, (1989), "Nonlinear Dynamics and Stock Returns", Journal of Business, Vol. 62, 311-337.

Sheifer, A., and L. Summers, (1990), "The Noise Trader Approach to Finance", The Journal of Economic Perspectives, 4, 19-33.

Van der Ploeg, F., (1986), "Rational Expectations, Risk and Chaos in Financial Markets", The Economic Journal, 151-162.

CONTRIBUTED PAPERS

A New Keynesian Model of the Business Cycle and Financial Fragility

Domenico Delli Gatti
Dipartimento di Economia, Università Cattolica di Milano
largo Gemelli 1, 10123 Milano, Italy

Mauro Gallegati
Dipartimento di Metodi Quantitativi ed Economia Politica, Università "G.D'Annunzio"
viale Pindaro 42, 65127 Pescara, Italy

1. Introduction

Two competing procedures are currently adopted in modelling the cyclical dynamics of output. According to the first one, output movements must be conceived of as responses of a linear system to stochastic disturbances (Frisch, 1933; Slutstky, 1937; Lucas, 1975). Alternatively, the second one interprets the oscillating path of income as a built-in feature of a non-linear deterministic system (Kaldor, 1940; Hicks, 1950; Goodwin, 1982; Grandmont, 1985). According to us, there is no reason why these two explanations should not co-exist: in this paper output dynamics is determined by a non-linear system of difference equations which takes into account also stochastic shocks (similar attempts in this direction have been recently carried out by Greenwald and Stiglitz, 1988a; Day and Lin, 1991; Delli Gatti et al., 1992). In our model the basic ingredients of both explanations are incorporated in the investment equation. Infact the propensity to invest is modelled as a non-linear function of income affected by a stochastic disturbance. Stochastic disturbances enter the process of income determination also through the capital assets price equation. Therefore the dynamics of the main macro-variables is jointly determined by the deterministic non-linear difference equations system and the random process which generates "clouds" around a deterministic cycle (when the shock is additive), and "jumps" from a cycle to another (when the shock affects the value of the parameters).

In section 2 we describe the model. Income determination is investment driven through entrepreneurial expectations (note that, since the model generates chaotic dynamics, the assumption of adaptive expectations is not sub-optimal (Lorenz, 1989)). Because of asymmetric information, firms are assumed to be equity-rationed so that their equity position strictly depends on internally generated cash flow and, since debt accumulates slowly, there can be persistence in the response of output to aggregate demand disturbances. Following recent literature on asymmetric information, we assume that credit availability is supply driven on the basis of internal finance, given the current rate of interest (Calomiris and Hubbard, 1990).

The behavior of output in the model depends on the financial conditions of the firms, described by their equity level. This is a well known result in the New Keynesian literature (Greenwald and Stiglitz, 1988a, 1988b). A deterministic path around a critical point arises since the propensity to invest can be above or below the propensity to save and therefore the flows of internal finance and debt commitments will change, affecting investment demand, as pointed out by Eckstein and Sinai (1986). We model the shifts of the propensity to invest according to a white noise random process which recalls the "animal spirits" argument by Keynes. Since a different limit cycle is associated to each level of this propensity, a *continuum* of cycles can be detected (see also Gallegati and Stiglitz, 1993).

Section 3 is devoted to an analysis of the mathematical properties of the model. We state: 1. the conditions upon which *deterministic chaos* occurs; 2. the emergence of *stochastic chaos* due to the presence of random processes affecting the capital asset price; and, 3. the emergence of *aperiodic cycles* due to the random process affecting the propensity to invest.

Section 4 describes the dynamic behaviour of the system. Depending on the evolution of the propensity to invest the model can generate: i) stationary states; ii) bounded cycles with chaotic behavior; and, iii) crises of a financial nature. Moreover, since the financial side is a main determinant of the business cycle (Bernanke and Gertler, 1990) monetary policy can be effective.

Finally, we draw some conclusions in section 5.

2. A Short Run Macro Model

In this model we analyze a closed economic system without public sector, with three types of agents: firms, banks and households. Households supply labor services and demand consumption goods and supply banks' liabilities (that is they demand deposits). Firms supply (consumption and investment) goods and demand labor services, investment goods and banks' assets, i.e. loans. Finally, banks demand liabilities (deposits) and supply assets (loans).

There are three markets: labor, credit and goods. in order to simplify the argument as much as possible, we assume that the labor market is "residual". Employment is a positive function of effective demand and the real wage is given (for instance at the level of the "efficiency wage"). Moreover, we assume that the price level is given and normalize it to 1, for the sake of simplicity. Equity rationing characterizes the Stock market while credit is supplied by banks on the basis of firms' internal finance.

Income in real terms (Y) is equal to:

$$Y_t=C_t+I_t \tag{1}$$

where: C is consumption; I is investment.

The consumption function is modelled according to Hendry's empirical investigation (Hendry, 1983),

$$C_t=c_0+ c_1 Y_t + c_2 Y_{t-1} \tag{2}$$

where c_1 is the propensity to consume ($0<c_1<1$) out of current income; c_2 is the propensity to consume ($0<c_2<1$) out of lagged income, and c_0 is autonomous consumption ($c_0>0$).

Since neither technical change nor capital depreciation occur in the short run, the aggregate demand for investment can be written as:

$$I_t = a\, v_t + bIF_t \tag{3}$$

where a,b>0 represent the sensitivity of investment to Tobin's q and firms' cash flow respectively, v is the price of capital assets (in our context the price of current output is given and normalized to 1 so that average q boils down to the Stock price) and IF is internal finance, which, in turn is defined as the difference between lagged, profits and debt commitments:

$$IF_t=\pi Y_{t-1}- r\, D_t \tag{4}$$

where: r is the (given and constant) interest rate on corporate debt (loans extended by the banking system), and π is the (given and constant) share of profits in national income; $r,p \in (0,1)$.

In modelling investment expenditure, we rely upon recent theoretical results and empirical evidence. Abel and Blanchard (1986) show that internal finance plays a central role in investment activity on the assumption that alternative sources of finance are not perfect substitutes. Following a similar line of reasoning, Fazzari et al. (1988) regress investment expenditure on Tobin's average q and firms' cash flow. Blanchard et al. (1990) argue that average q represents a white noise random process. Therefore we model the price of capital assets as an autoregressive process:

$$v_t = v_{t-1} + \varepsilon_v$$

Fazzari's empirical investigation implies a pro-cyclical propensity to invest due to a sort of "composition effect". According to his data, small (large) firms are characterized by a small (large) capital stock, a high (low) real sales and capital growth rate, a high (low) retention ratio and a high (low) propensity to invest out of internal finance. The aggregate propensity to invest is a weighted average of the propensity to invest of small firms and large firms, with weights equal to the share of the total cash flow generated by small firms and large firms respectively. Since during the ascending phase of a business cycle the population of small firms increases, the propensity to invest out of internally generated funds, b, goes up, too. Therefore, we model the propensity to invest as a non-linear increasing function of lagged profits πY_{t-1} (figure 1):

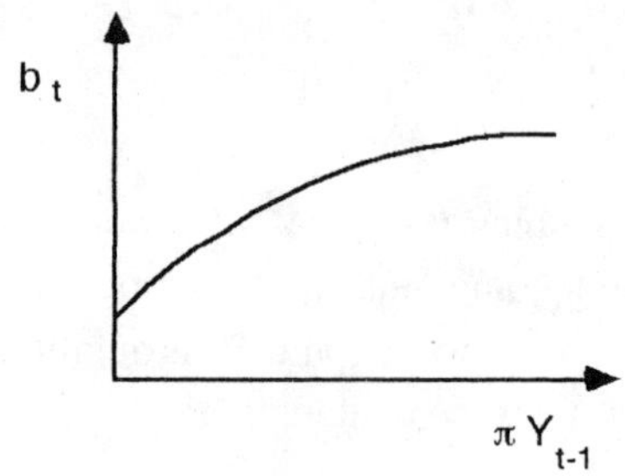

figure 1

The propensity to invest is represented by the function:

$$b(Y)=b_1 \text{ arctg } (Y) + \varepsilon_b \quad Y \geq 0; \qquad b_1>0$$

where ε_b is white noise. According to this function agents' expectations continuously shift from a "wary" state, captured by a low b, to an "euphoric" state, represented by a high b, with an upper level which constitutes a ceiling. Figure 2 shows two different b curves, as determined by a white noise process which guides the "animal spirits" of entrepeneurs.

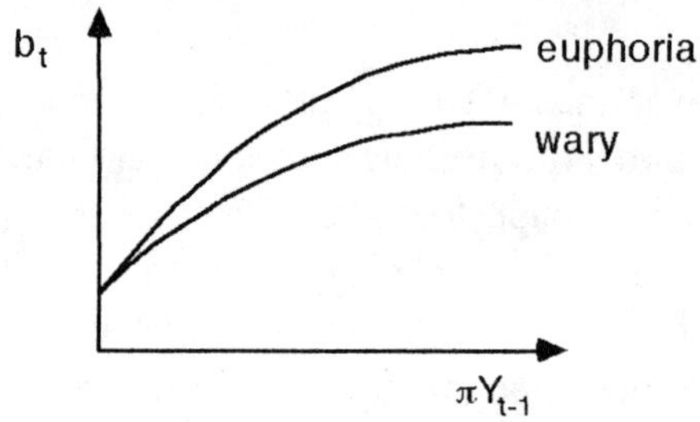

figure 2

The existence of asymmetric information implies that investment is constrained by the availability of external finance. In particular, we assume that the supply of finance is a linear function of internal finance which is assumed to be the most relevant screening device for the banking system (Calomiris and Hubbard, 1990). The law of motion of debt is:

$$D_t=D_{t-1}+F_t \tag{5}$$

where D represents the stock of corporate debt (bank loans) and F the flow-supply of credit extended by the banking system. The availability of external finance is an increasing function of internal finance, that is:

$$F_t=\beta IF_t \tag{6}$$

Substituting equations (2)-(3)-(4) into equation (1), we get:

$$Y_t=\frac{1}{1-c_1}[c_0+av_{t-1}+a\varepsilon_v+c_2Y_{t-1}+b(\pi Y_{t-1}-rD_t)] \tag{7}$$

All other things being equal, an increase in b produces an excess of investment with respect to saving, and therefore must be accompanied by an increase in ouput to keep equilibrium in the goods market. An increase in output stimulates investment less than savings and eliminates excess investment when the elasticity of investment to internal finance is smaller than the propensity to save. If $b \gg (1-c_1)$, a financial crisis will emerge. In fact, in this case an increase in output would stimulate investment more than saving, thereby widening the gap between the former and the latter.

Substituting equations (4) and (6) into equation (5) we get:

$$D_t=\frac{1}{1+\beta r}(D_{t-1}+\beta\pi Y_{t-1}) \tag{8}$$

Substituting (8) into (7) we obtain a bidimensional non-linear map, let us say, map F:

$$\begin{aligned} Y_t &= \phi_0+\phi_1Y_{t-1}+\phi_3\left(\phi_2Y_{t-1}-\frac{r}{a}D_{t-1}\right) \\ D_t &= \frac{1}{a}(D_{t-1}+\beta\pi Y_{t-1}) \end{aligned} \tag{F}$$

where: $\phi_0=\frac{1}{1-c_1}(c_0+av_{t-1}+a\varepsilon_v)$; $\phi_1=\frac{1}{1-c_1}c_2$; $\phi_3=\frac{1}{1-c_1}$; $\phi_2=\pi-\frac{b}{a}\pi$; $a=1+\beta r$.

3. Nonlinear Dynamics

The analysis of the dynamic behavior of map F in the deterministic assumption ($v_t=v_{t-1}$, and $\varepsilon_b=0$), will be the object of subsection 3.1, and the results will be used in subsection 3.2 where we discuss the dynamics of the stochastic map F ($v_t=v_{t-1}+\varepsilon_b$ and $\varepsilon_b=0$); subsection 3.3 will be devoted to an analysis, through numerical simulation, of the map F when $v_t=v_{t-1}$, and $\varepsilon_b\neq 0$.

In the following we derive the conditions for the existence of an economically meaningful stationary equilibrium, i.e. an equilibrium point on the positive orthant of the (Y,D) plane, which we will label $E=(Y^*,D^*)$, and list sufficient conditions for the local asymptotical stability of E. The equilibrium point E may become unstable via Hopf-bifurcation. Note that even if the equilibrium point is unstable, the oscillating paths tend towards another stable attractor, which

Corollary 3:

We can perform the bifurcation analysis as a function of b. In such a case, condition (jj) becomes: $f(Y^*)<b^H$, $b_1 < \frac{b^H}{arctg(Y^*)}$

Proposition 2:

Let

(j) $r(1-f_1)>0$

(jjj) $\frac{d}{db_1} f(Y^*) \neq 0$

then at b_1^H *the equilibrium point E becomes unstable via Hopf bifurcation.*

Proof: When (j) holds and $b_1 = b^H$ the eigenvalues of J are complex of unitary modulus: $|\lambda|^2 = \det J = 1$, and $\frac{d}{db_1}|\lambda| = \frac{1}{2}\pi\phi_3 \frac{d}{db_1} f(Y^*)$. Under assumption (jjj) the transversality condition of the Hopf's theorem for maps (Iooss, 1979; Guckenheimer and Holmes, 1983; Lorenz, 1989) is satisfied.

Corollary 4:

Because $\frac{d}{db_1}$, $f(Y^*) = arctg\,(P^*) > 0$, when the equilibrium point E is unstable, the dynamic behavior of the model depends on the type of Hopf-bifurcation, i.e. subcritical or supercritical, which in turn depends on the values of the economic parameters.

For reasonable values of the parameters we have detected a supercritical Hopf-bifurcation. When the Hopf-bifurcation is supercritical there exists an invariant attractive curve Γ, on which the orbits are quasiperiodic. Several examples of plane nonlinear maps (Mira, 1987) suggest that the invariant curve Γ may disappear on varying b_1, and other bounded attractors may appear. We shall briefly discuss some of the numerical results obtained as a function of b_1 in the range of instability of E.

For values of $b_1 > b^H$, b_1 "near" b^H, we have detected a closed invariant curve Γ, locally attractive, on which the orbit are quasi-periodic (an example is given in figure 3).

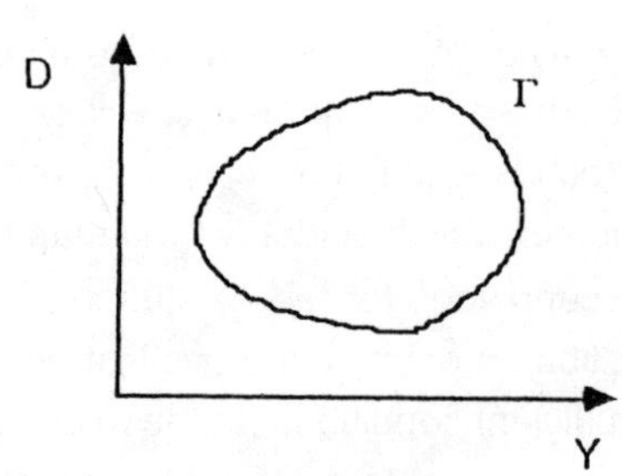

figure 3

may be regular (a cyclic or periodic path), or something more complex, but with structure and bounds which may be analyzed.

3.1 Deterministic Chaos

In Proposition 1 we list conditions for the existence of an economically meaningful equilibrium point $E=(Y^*,D^*)$ of the deterministic map F (i.e. $Y^*>0$ and $D^*>0$). In Proposition 2 we detect sufficient conditions for the local stability of E and the Hopf-bifurcation values.

Proposition 1:
Let

(j) $r(1-f_1)>0$

(jj) $f(Y^*)<b^H, \qquad b^H=\dfrac{a-f_1}{a\pi\phi_3}$

then the unique equilibrium point E is positive and stable.

Proof. From (j) it follows immediately that E is positive. Let J be the jacobian matrix of F evaluated at the equilibrium point, and $P(\lambda)$ its characteristic polinomial. Sufficient conditions for the local asymptotic stability of E are:

$$P(1)=\frac{b}{a}r\,(1-\phi_1)>0$$

$$P(-1)=2\,(\frac{1}{a}+\phi_1)+2\pi\phi_3\phi(Y^*)+\frac{b}{a}(r(1-\phi_1)>0 \qquad (9)$$

$$\det J=\frac{\phi_1}{a}+\pi(\phi_3\phi(Y^*))<1$$

where det stands for determinant. From the assumptions on r and j_2 it follows $P^*>0$, $P(1)>0$ and $P(-1)>0$, while the last condition in (9) follows from assumption (jj).

Corollary 1:
The equilibrium point E does not depend on b but on the exogenous constants, while the local stability of E depends only on b.

Corollary 2:
Under assumption (j) the first two conditions in (9) are always satisfied and the equilibrium point E cannot become a saddle point with an associated real eigenvalue greater than 1, neither become unstable via Flip-bifurcation. It may become an unstable focus via a Hopf-bifurcation, as it is shown in the following.

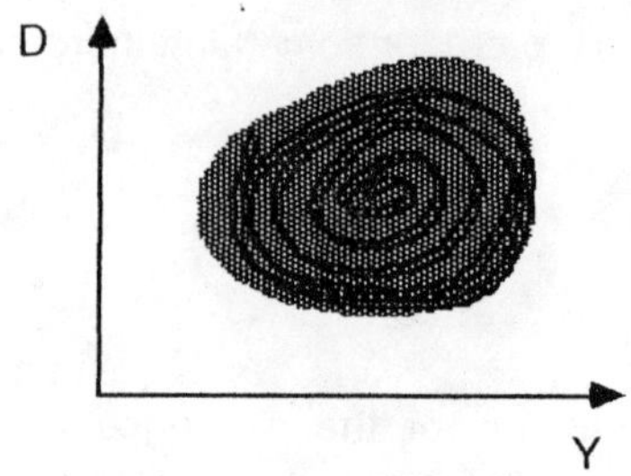

figure 4

Increasing b_1, further bifurcations occur, and other bounded attractors, either regular or chaotic, may appear (see figure 4) until b_1 reaches a critical value, b^M, beyond which all the numerically computed orbits are found to be divergent (i.e. an "explosion" occurs).

3.2 Stochastic Chaos

The model characterized by the assumption

$$v_t = v_{t-1} + \varepsilon_v,$$

does not have an equilibrium point or an attracting invariant curve any more, due to the presence of the stochastic variable ε_v. Let us write the stochastic map as

$$X_{t+1}=F(X_t,\varepsilon_t) \qquad (10)$$

to denote that ϕ_0 contains the variable ε_v whose value ε_t at each t is chosen randomly in the interval R_v.

We can figure out that each point determined by (10) belongs to a particular trajectory of a deterministic map, obtained with a fixed constant value ε for ε_v, say

$$X_{t+1}=F_\varepsilon(X_t).$$

Let X_0, ε_0 be the initial values, then

$$X_1=F(X_0,\varepsilon_0),\ X_2=F(X_1,\varepsilon_1),\ X_3=F(X_2,\varepsilon_2), ...$$

is the trajectory of the stochastic map (10). If we consider the deterministic map $F_\varepsilon(X_t)$ with ε_v= s, a constant value at any t, then it is also

$$X_1=F_{\varepsilon 0}(X_0),\ X_2=F_{\varepsilon 1}(X_1),\ X_3=F_{\varepsilon 2}(X_2), ...$$

The stochastic trajectory X_t can be viewed as a sequence of points belonging to different deterministic trajectories. When each of the deterministic map $F_\varepsilon(X)$, $\varepsilon \in R_V$, has an attracting set A_ε, we may expect that the asymptotic state of the trajectories of the stochastic map (10) are random points which belong to a bounded region W of the phase-plan, containing all the attractors A_ε for each $\varepsilon \in R_V$.

Remark 1:
When conditions (j) and (jj) are satisfied for each $\varepsilon \in R_V$, then all the deterministic maps F_e, have an attracting fixed point E_ε, that is $A_\varepsilon = E_\varepsilon$ for each $\varepsilon \in R_V$. In this case we have found that the qualitative shapes of the orbits is a bounded *cloud* of points (figure 5).

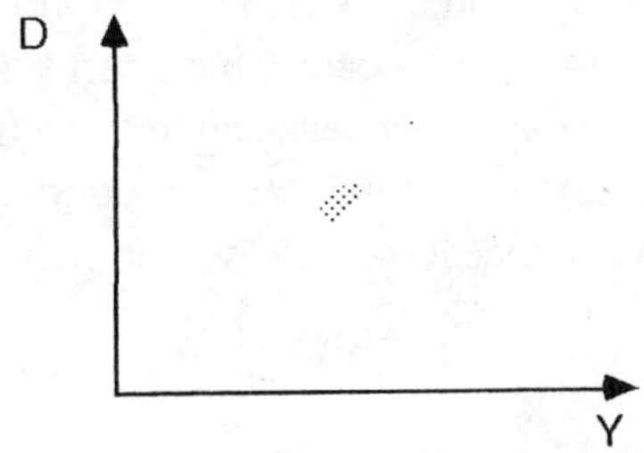

figure 5

Remark 2:
When condition (jj) is not satisfied for some (or all the) ε in R_V, and $A_\varepsilon = \Gamma_\varepsilon$ for these ε, $A_\varepsilon = E_\varepsilon$ for the other ε, the qualitative shape of the orbits is a band structure, which resembles the Γ_ε curves (figure 6).

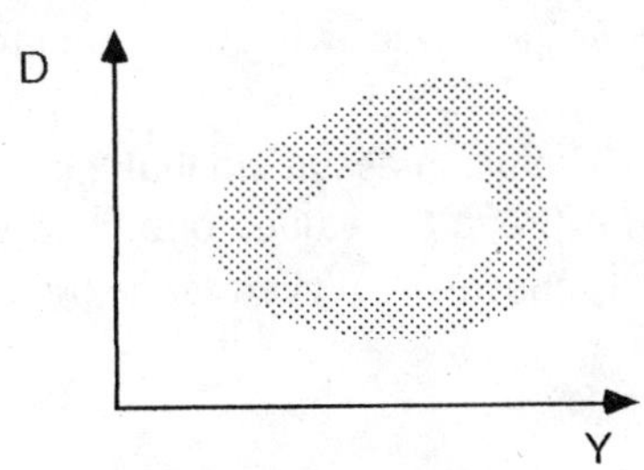

figure 6

Remark 3:
When $A_\varepsilon = E_\varepsilon$ for some (or all the) e in R_V, $A_\varepsilon = G_\varepsilon$ or $A_\varepsilon = E_\varepsilon$ for the other ε, a stochastic-chaotic area is observed which is qualitatively similar to that of the deterministic maps (figure 7).

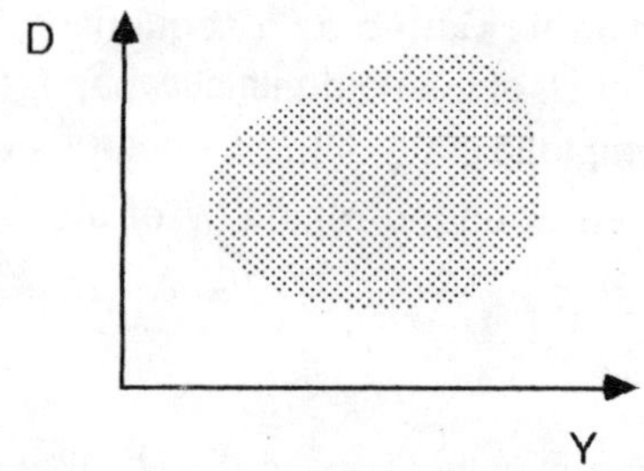

figure 7

Remark 4:

When a stochastic disturbance hits the system in the neighborhood of the critical values, a different configuration of parameters may occur which can bring about dynamic paths of a different nature. In other words, the same stochastic shock may have wholly different outcomes as far as the dynamics of the system is concerned depending on the degree of financial "fragility" of it as captured by the value assumed by the parameter b.

3.3 Aperiodic Cycles with Shifting Regimes

Let assume that attractive cycles $\Gamma(b)$ exist as a function of b, such that from whatever initial conditions the trajectory will converge to Γ. Let assume two values of b exist (w, i.e. wary, and e, euphoria, see figure 2) respectively b_w and b_e to which two limit cycles will correspond, Γ_w and Γ_e, within a region B. Then if the parameter b randomly assumes the values b_w and b_e, every initial condition has trajectories converging to an annular region A (it is drawn as an envelope of the trajectories escaping from Γ_w and Γ_e in which the trajectories themselves "jump" in a random way from cycle Γ_w to cycle Γ_e, as showed in figure 8a). By plotting the time series of income versus time, we generate a highly irregular behavior, which apparently follows a random pattern (figure 8b).

We can generalize the previous intuition assuming that the parameter b assumes a random value in the interval $I = (b_w$ and $b_e)$, and the values of b change randomly at each interval of time Δt (being on its turn randomly chosen in a given range $[\Delta t_{min}, \Delta t_{max}]$).

Let's assume that:

(j) $\forall\, b \in I, \exists$ a limit cycle $\Gamma(b)$

(jj) $\exists\, B \neq \emptyset$

(jjj) $B \supset \Gamma(b); \forall\, b \in I$

then every initial condition within B has a trajectory entering into a connected region A. As previously observed, region A can be obtained from the envelope of the trajectories escaping from the border of the area s, being s the minimal area enclosing $\Gamma(b)$, $\forall\, b \in I$. Within A the trajectory continuously jumps from a cycle to another one for each random change of b, without leaving the region A.

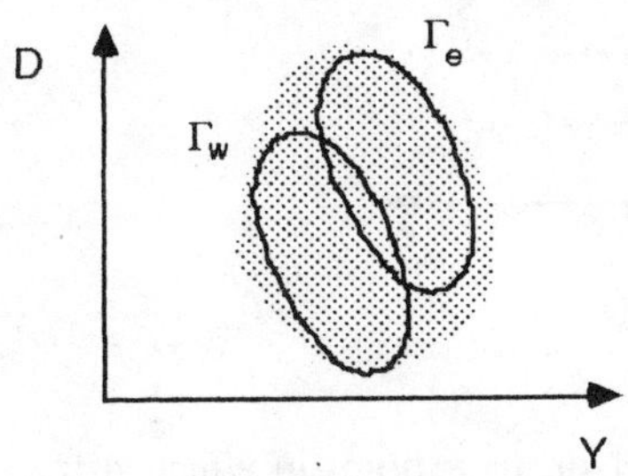

figure 8a

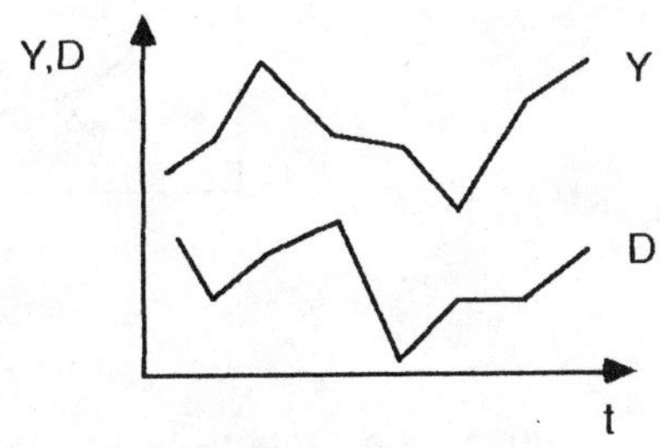

figure 8b

In figure 8b we can appreciate the interaction between the self sustained different cycles and the random process which governs the shifting from one cycle to another. Evidently, every deterministic path is lost and fluctuations appear to be without any precise periodicity.

4. The Business Cycle

On the (Y,D) plane, the system follows a counterclockwise motion along an asymmetric orbit (the upswing of business fluctuations lasts more than the downswing). When the sensitivity of investment to internal finance is "low" ($b<b^H$), the steady state is locally stable as shown in proposition 1. The dynamic paths of income and debt converge to their steady-state long-run values. Fluctuations can be traced back to the stochastic shock to the price of capital assets while the stock of debt works as a transmission mechanism. When the value of b increases ($b^H<b<b^M$), the system enters a phase characterized by bounded cycles and chaotic dynamics. Only when b overreacts to the internal finance ($b>b^M$) a financial crisis occurs.

Let us suppose that the system is in equilibrium with expectations in a "wary" state, i.e. the propensity to invest is smaller than the marginal propensity to save. Investment expenditure drives income and profits through the working of the keynesian multiplier. The growth of income brings about an increase in retained profits which in turn stimulates investment. Since the propensity to invest is smaller than the propensity to save, retained earnings and households' savings increase more than investment , thus reducing the need for external finance. As a consequence, the burden of debt commitments becomes lighter (period (i)).

This scenario describes a virtuous circle in which the growth of investment, income and cash flow is paralleled by the decline in the stock of debt (see figure 9).

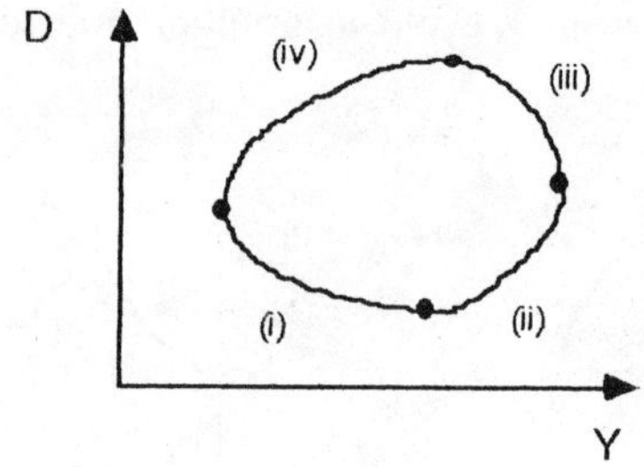

figure 9

Income growth drives the propensity to invest up to a point in which a transition to an "euphoric" state of expectations occurs. In such a state the propensity to invest is greater than the propensity to save so that income feeds upon investment in a spiralling boom of profits and capital accumulation, while the supply of external finance goes up increasing the burden of debt commitments (period (ii)). This scenario describes a vicious circle of growing indebtedness which parallels the growth of investment and income. When the flow of retained earnings does not suceed in catching up with the growing burden of debt commitments, a turning point in the business cycle will occur.

If a downswing occurs, a change in entrepreneurial state of confidence is likely to happen. The recession will be characterized by the same structure of parameters which was typical of the first stage of the upswing. The decline of income would bring about a decrease in retained earnings higher than the decline in investment and therefore cause an increase in the demand for external finance. In other words, by adopting a more cautious investment strategy in order to reduce indebtedness entrepreneurs would worsen the financial situation of their firms (period (iii)). This scenario describes a situation of debt-depression (see figure 10). Only when declining investment expenditure falls short of declining internal funds is the lower turning point of the cycle reached (period (iv)).

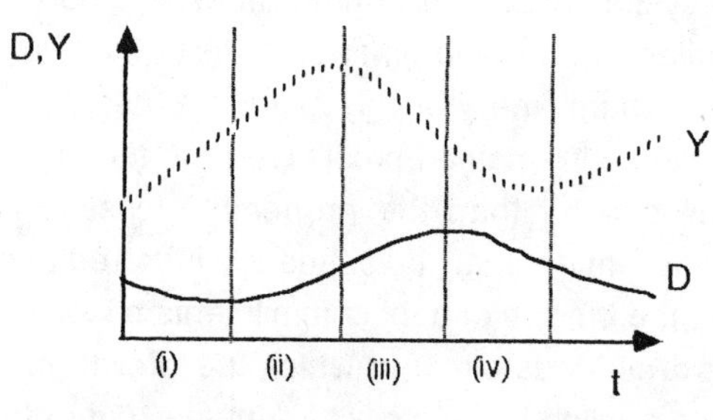

figure 10

Further, if the state of expectations is "euphoric", a situation of financial crisis is likely to occur when the propensity to invest goes beyond a critical upper level. In such a case, the growth of debt commitments is so fast that the system experiences financial distress with widespread falls in income, investment and employment (of course, policy intervention can prevent the system to fall in such a state, through imposing ceilings and floors).

Random shocks increase the irregularity of business fluctuations brought about by the deterministic structure of the model, but do not alter their fundamental stability properties. It is worth mentioning that a stochastic disturbance in the neighborhood of the critical values (b^H or b^M) can help moving the system to a different configuration of parameters which brings about dynamic paths of a different nature. In other words, the same stochastic shock may have wholly different outcomes as far as the dynamics of the system is concerned depending on the degree of its "fragility".

5. Conclusion

In this paper we have shown how to derive endogenous business cycles in a macroeconomic system characterized by asymmetric information. In particular, we have detected the conditions upon which i) a stationary state; ii) bounded cycles with deterministic chaotic behavior; and, iii) crises of a financial nature may occur. These conditions essentially consists of different values of the propensity to invest.

Moreover, we have superimposed stochastic shocks to the non-linear deterministic structure of the model. The fundamental stability properties of the reduced form are not altered but the degree of "irregularity" of the time series generated by the model is significantly increased as it was to be expected. A dynamic configuration of stochastic chaos can be detected.

The paper, therefore, can be thought of as an attempt to bridge the gap between linear-stochastic and nonlinear-deterministic explanations of the cycle: the fundamental tools of both modelling procedures are incorporated in the propensity to invest , which is treated as a non-linear function of income affected by a stochastic disturbance. Therefore the dynamics of the main macro-variables is jointly determined by the deterministic non-linear difference equations system and the random process which affects them.

References

ABEL A. and BLANCHARD O. (1986), The Present Value of Profits and Cyclical Movement in Investment, *Econometrica*.

BERNANKE B. and GERTLER M. (1990), Financial Fragility and Economic Performance, *Quarterly Journal of Economics*.

BLANCHARD O., RHEE C. and SUMMERS L. (1990), *The Stock Market, Profit and Investment*, NBER, working paper.

CALOMIRIS C. and HUBBARD G. (1990), Firm Heterogeneity, Internal Finance and Credit Rationing, *Economic Journal*.

DAY R. and LIN T. (1991), *A Keynesian Business Cycle*, in Nell E. and Semmler W. (eds.), *Nicolas Kaldor and Mainstream*, New York: Macmillan.

DELLI GATTI D., GALLEGATI M. and GARDINI L. (1992), Investment Confidence, Corporate Debt and Income Fluctuations, *Journal of Economic Behavior and Organization*.

ECKSTEIN O. and SINAI A. (1986), The Mechanism of the Business Cycle in the Postwar Era, in Gordon R. (ed.), *The American Business Cycle*, Chicago: University of Chicago Press.

FAZZARI S., HUBBARD G. and PETERSEN B. (1988), Financing Constraints and Corporate Investment, *Brooking Papers on Economic Activity*.

FRISCH, R. (1933), Propagation Problem and Impulse Problem in Dynamic Economics, in *Economic Essays in Honour of Gustav Cassel*, London: Allen & Unwin.

GALLEGATI M. and STIGLITZ J. (1993), Stochastic and Deterministic Fluctuations in a Non-linear Model with Equity Rationing,*Giornale degli Economisti*.

GOODWIN, R.M. (1982), *Essays in Economic Dynamics*, London: Macmillan.

GRANDMONT J.M. (1985), On Endogenous Competitive Business Cycles, *Econometrica*.

GREENWALD B. and J.E.STIGLITZ (1988a), *Imperfect Information, Finance Constraints and Business Fluctuations*, NBER working paper.

GREENWALD B. and STIGLITZ J.E. (1988b), *Money, Imperfect Information and Economic Fluctuation*, in M.Kohn and S.Tsiang (ed.), *Finance Constraints, Expectations and Macroeconomics*, Oxford: Oxford University Press.

GUCKENHEIMER J. and HOLMES P.H. (1983), *Nonlinear Oscillations, Dynamical Systems and Bifurcation of Vector Fields*, New York: Springer.

HENDRY D. (1983), Econometric Modelling: The "Consumption Function" in Retrospect, *Scottish Journal of Political Economy*.

HICKS, J. (1950), *A Contribution to the Theory of the Trade Cycle*, Oxford: Clarendon Press.

IOOSS G. (1979), *Bifurcation of Maps and Applications*, Amsterdam: North Holland.

KALDOR N. (1940), A Model of the Trade Cycle, *Economic Journal*.

LORENZ H. (1989), *Nonlinear Dynamical Economic and Chaotic Motion*, New York: Springer.

LUCAS R.E.jr. (1975), An Equilibrium Model of the Business Cycle, *Journal of Political Economy*.

MIRA C. (1987), *Chaotic Dynamics*, New York: World Scientific.

SLUTSTKY E. (1937), The Summation of Random Causes as the Source of Cyclic Processes, *Econometrica*.

Abstract

In this paper we demonstrate the existence of fluctuations due to the integration of deterministic and stochastic elements in a macroeconomic system with asymmetric information and interdependence between loan and goods markets. In particular, we list the conditions upon which i) a stationary state; ii) bounded cycles with deterministic chaotic behavior; iii) crises of a financial nature; iv) aperiodic cycles with switching regimes can occur.

NON-WALRASIAN EQUILIBRIA IN A LABOUR-MANAGED ECONOMY *

ANGELA DE SANCTIS

Universita' "G. D'Annunzio" di Chieti
Viale Pindaro 42, I-65127 Pescara

GERD WEINRICH

Universita' Cattolica del Sacro Cuore
Largo Gemelli 1, I-20123 Milano

Abstract

This paper studies the existence and stability of non-Walrasian equilibria in a labour-managed economy. The main finding is that non-Walrasian equilibria exist and constitute a one-dimensional smooth manifold; they are stable but not asymptotically stable.

1. Introduction

Varian (1977) has studied the existence and stability of non-Walrasian equilibria in a standard profit maximizing economy (PME). He has shown that, with respect to a specific continuous time dynamic system assumed, the Walrasian equilibrium is unstable whereas the non-Walrasian equilibrium (NWE) is stable. With regard to traditional general equilibrium and welfare analysis this is somewhat disturbing since the NWE involves lower output and employment, and thus in general lower welfare, than the WE. A way of organizing productive activity alternative to the one commonly related to a PME is labour management. There, workers themselves decide on the production plans and on their remuneration. In theoretical literature, this has been translated in maximization of value added per unit of labour by firms. An economy in which firms behave in this way is called a labour-managed economy (LME). The present paper investigates, using an approach inspired by that of Varian, the existence and

*This research has been performed as part of a national research project on Non Linear Dynamics in Economics and Social Sciences M.P.I. 40%. The authors are grateful to anonymous referees for helpful comments.

stability of NWEs in a LME. The main finding is that, under the conditions of our model, there is a smooth one-dimensional manifold of stable (but not asymptotically stable) NWEs.

The way we come to the above conclusion is as follows. In section 2 we model the economy as consisting of one consumer-worker (called household in the sequel) and one labour-managed firm. There are three types of goods, a composite consumption good (=output), and labour and capital (=inputs). The household provides the inputs and buys the output. The firm uses the inputs to produce and it sells the output. The firm's objective is to maximize value added per working hour. Under standard regularity assumptions, this economy possesses a general (=Walrasian) equilibrium. In order to investigate the economy's behaviour out of Walrasian equilibrium, we first study the household's and the firm's behaviour in the presence of quantity constraints. In section 3, then, we formulate a three-dimensional continuous time dynamic system which is supposed to reflect the dynamic behaviour of the rental rate of capital, r , the expectation of the household's effective demand as held by the firm, y , and of the price of output, p . We call a stationary point (r,y,p) of this system a dynamic equilibrium[1]. We show that the Walrasian equilibrium (r^*,y^*,p^*) is one, but not the only, dynamic equilibrium. More precisely, there exist $r_0 < r^*$ and $y_0 < y^*$ such that (r_0,y_0,p^*) is a dynamic equilibrium but not a Walrasian equilibrium. Such an equilibrium is therefore called a non-Walrasian equilibrium. We use the regular value theorem to prove that there is a continuum of NWEs (r,y,p) which, around the point (r_0,y_0,p^*), has the structure of a one-dimensional smooth manifold.

Regarding stability of non-Walrasian equilibria, this is a delicate issue due to the fact that the NWEs constitute a one-dimensional manifold. We procede in two steps. We first show that the NWE (r_0,y_0,p^*) is an asymptotically stable point with respect to the truncated two-dimensional system where the equation of motion regarding p is removed and p is held fixed at p^*. To this end, since we have not been able to calculate the sign of the determinant of the Jacobian matrix at the NWE directly, we first demonstrate that the determinant of the Jacobian of the truncated system has negative sign at the Walrasian equilibrium. We then invoke the Poincare'-Hopf index theorem to conclude that at (r_0,y_0,p^*) the sign of the

[1] This is for brevity only; in dynamical systems literature such a point is usually called a fixed point of the flow, or of the dynamical system.

Jacobian's determinant is positive. As the Jacobian's trace is negative, this completes the argument. In the second step we extend the analysis to the full system and show that the manifold of NWEs in a neighborhood of (r_0, y_0, p^*) is stable, but not asymptotically stable.

2. The Model

The Model can be seen as a special case of Drèze's (1985) general equilibrium model of a LME. There are two types of economic agents, firms and worker-households. All firms are identical and produce a composite consumption good from inputs labour, marketed (variable) capital and non-marketed (fixed) capital. All households are identical and supply the inputs and demand the consumption good. All agents take the prices for the consumption good (p), marketed capital (r) and non-marketed capital (s) as given.

Firms

Denoting with ℓ, k and q the quantities of inputs labour, marketed capital and non-marketed capital, respectively, and with c the quantity produced, a typical firm has a production technology $c=\tilde{F}(\ell,k,q)$. Assuming that labour, marketed and non-marketed capital are *all* inputs used, $\tilde{F}$ has necessarily constant (or, in some initial range, increasing) returns to scale. However, we assume that q is fixed at some value $\bar{q}$, say, which we may without loss of generality normalize to $\bar{q}=1$. Then the function $F(\ell,k)=\tilde{F}(\ell,k,1)$ has (eventually) decreasing returns. This justifies the following assumption:

(F) $F(\ell,k) = G(H(\ell,k))$, where $H(\ell,k) = \ell^{\alpha}k^{1-\alpha}$, $0<\alpha<1$; G is twice differentiable, increasing and strictly concave, $G(0) = 0$, $\lim_{h\to\infty} G(h)=\infty$ and $\lim_{h\to\infty} G'(h)=0$.

A firm's problem is to maximize value added per working hour[2], that is

[2] A reader not familiar with the rationale for the objective of maximizing value added per working hour may consult Drèze (1985).

$$\frac{pF(\ell,k)-rk-s}{\ell} =: V(\ell,k)$$

Solutions are denoted $\ell^{d*}(r/p,s/p)$ and $k^{d*}(r/p,s/p)$. Moreover, we use $c^{s*}(r/p,s/p) = F(\ell^{d*}(r/p,s/p),k^{d*}(r/p,s/p))$ for the optimal output quantity.

Lemma 1: (i) For any $p>0$, $r>0$ and $s>0$ there exists a unique solution to the firm's problem; (ii) $c^{s*}(r/p,s/p) = c^{s*}(s/p)$, that is, it is independent of r/p; (iii) $k^{d*}(r/p,s/p) = (1-\alpha)\frac{p}{r}[c^{s*}(s/p) - s/p]$.

Proof: (i) Necessary conditions for a solution are

$$pF_{\ell}(\ell,k) = V(\ell,k) \quad (1)$$

$$pF_{k}(\ell,k) = r \quad (2)$$

Using the definitions of F and V and inserting (2) in (1), we can write (1) as

$$pG'(H(\ell,k))H_{\ell}(\ell,k)\ell = pG(H(\ell,k)) - pG'(H(\ell,k))H_{k}(\ell,k)k - s$$

which implies

$$G'(H(\ell,k))[H_{\ell}(\ell,k)\ell + H_{k}(\ell,k)k] = G(H(\ell,k)) - s/p .$$

Since H has constant returns to scale, the term in square brackets is equal to $H(\ell,k)$. Writing $h=H(\ell,k)$, we show next:

For every $s/p>0$ there exists a unique solution, denoted $h(s/p)$, to the equation

$$G(h) - G'(h)h = s/p \quad (3)$$

Write $M(h) = G(h) - G'(h)h$. It is a continuous function with domain $]0,\infty[$. To prove (3) we show that M is monotone and has image $]0,\infty[$. The first fact is immediate since $M'(h) = - G''(h)h > 0$ by concavity of G. Again by concavity, we have for any fixed $h_0>0$

$$G(h) + G'(h)(h_0 - h) \geq G(h_0)$$

for every $h>0$. For $h_0 \to 0$ this yields $G(h) - G'(h)h \geq 0$, and since $G(0)=0$, $\lim_{h\to 0} M(h)=0$. On the other hand it is true for any $h > 0$ that $\lim_{h\to\infty} M(h) = \lim_{h\to\infty} [G(h) + G'(h)h_0 - G'(h)h] = \lim_{h\to\infty} [G(h) + G'(h)(h_0 - h)] \geq G(h_0)$. Since $G(h_0) \to \infty$ for $h_0 \to \infty$, this implies $\lim_{h\to\infty} M(h) = \infty$. Since M is continuous, this proves that M is onto.

From the above and (2) it is clear that $\ell^{d*}(r/p,s/p)$ and $k^{d*}(r/p,s/p)$ are determined as solution to

$$\begin{aligned} H(\ell,k) &= h(s/p) \\ H_k(\ell,k) &= \frac{r}{p}\,\frac{1}{G'(h(s/p))} \end{aligned} \tag{4}$$

Since $H(\ell,k)$ is assumed to be Cobb-Douglas, the unique existence of a solution to (4) is immediate.

(ii) From (4) follows

$$\begin{aligned} c^{s*}(r/p,s/p) &= G(H(\ell^{d*}(r/p,s/p),k^{d*}(r/p,s/p)) \\ &= G(h(s/p)) \ . \end{aligned}$$

(iii) Dividing equations (1) and (2) yields

$$\frac{H_\ell(\ell,k)}{H_k(\ell,k)} = \frac{F_\ell(\ell,k)}{F_k(\ell,k)} = \frac{V(\ell,k)}{r}$$

and, using that H is Cobb-Douglas,

$$\frac{\alpha k}{(1-\alpha)\ell} = \frac{pF(\ell,k)-rk-s}{r\ell} \quad .$$

Solving for k one obtains

$$\begin{aligned} k^{d*}(p,r) = k &= (1-\alpha)\,\frac{p}{r}\,[F(\ell,k) - s/p] \\ &= (1-\alpha)\,\frac{p}{r}\,[c^{s*}(s/p) - s/p]. \end{aligned}$$ ■

A firm's behaviour is illustrated in Figure 1.

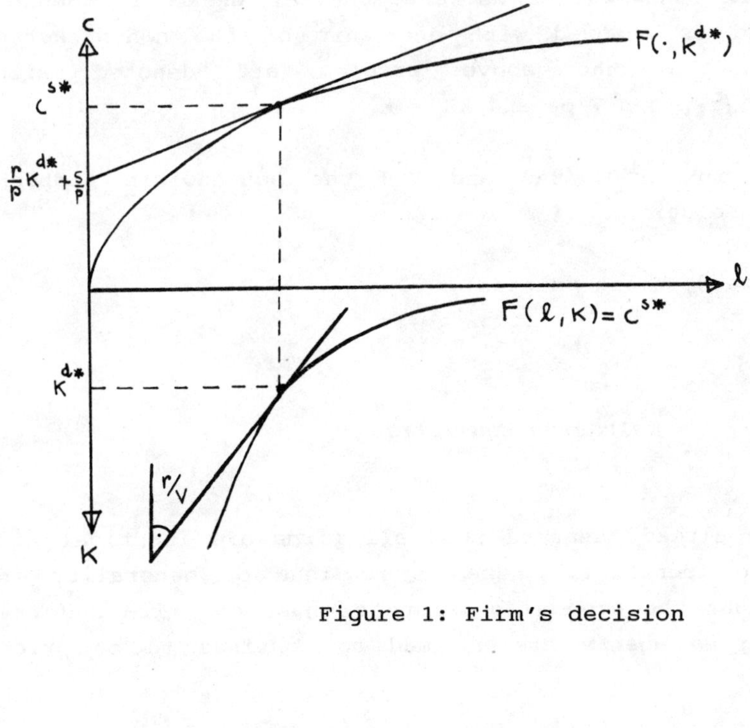

Figure 1: Firm's decision

Households

A typical household's income stems from labour income and the income from the lease of marketed and non-marketed capital. Capital supply is assumed to be fixed but the labour supply/consumption demand decision depends on V, p, r and s. This means that, to the household, V is a given datum. This is reasonable since firms, by maximizing V, determine it in such a way that it is optimal for households anyway. A household's preferences are assumed to be representable by a utility function $U(c,L-\ell)$, where $L>0$ denotes the maximum time available.

(H) U is non-decreasing, differentiable, strictly quasi-concave and such that neither consumption c nor leisure $L-\ell$ is an inferior good; moreover, $U(c,L-\ell) > U(0,L-\ell')$ for any $c>0$, $0 \le \ell,\ell' \le L$.

The last requirement in (H) says that leisure is not a perfect substitute for the consumption good. The household's problem is

$$\max_{c,\ell} U(c,L-\ell)$$
$$\text{s.t. (i)} \quad c\ge 0,\ 0 \le \ell \le L$$
$$\text{(ii)} \quad pc \le V\ell + rk^s + s$$

where k^s denotes the endowment of marketed capital and it is assumed that the household is endowed with one unit of the non-marketed capital. Solutions to the above problem are denoted with $\ell^{s*}(r/p,s/p,V/p)$, $c^{d*}(r/p,s/p,V/p)$ and $k^{s*} = k^s$.

Lemma 2: For any $p>0$, $r>0$, $s>0$ and $V>0$ the household's problem possesses a unique solution.

Proof: Straightforward, hence omitted. ∎

Walrasian Equilibrium

Since we have already assumed that all firms are identical and all households are identical, there is no loss of generality in further assuming that the economy consists of just one firm and one household, as long as agents are assumed to continue to be price takers. We make this assumption since it avoids an otherwise more complicated notation. Moreover, it will enable us to illustrate our analysis graphically.

Definition 1: A list (p^*, r^*, s^*, V^*) is a *Walrasian equilibrium* (or a general equilibrium) if it satisfies the following conditions:

$$\text{(i)} \quad k^{d*}(r/p, s/p) = k^s$$

$$\text{(ii)} \quad c^{s*}(s/p) = c^{d*}(r/p, s/p, V/p)$$

$$\text{(iii)} \quad V/p = \frac{c^{s*}(s/p) - (r/p)k^{d*}(r/p, s/p) - s/p}{\ell^{d*}(r/p, s/p)}$$

Whereas (i) and (ii) are market clearing conditions, (iii) requires the consistency of the value added per hour realized by the firm with the value added communicated to the household. The labour market does not appear in the above definition since the household's budget equality implies that the labour market clears whenever (i) to (iii) hold.

Proposition 1: Under assumptions (F) and (H) there exists a Walrasian equilibrium.

Proof: For notational convenience we write $R=r/p$ and $S=s/p$. Using Lemma 1 (iii), condition (i) can be written as

$$R = \Phi(S) =: \frac{1-\alpha}{k^s}\,[c^{s*}(S) - S]\ .$$

Using Φ and condition (i), we can express (iii) as

$$V/p = \frac{c^{s*}(S) - \Phi(S)k^s - S}{\ell^{d*}(\Phi(S), S)} =: (V/p)^*(S)\ .$$

Since $G(H(\ell^{d*}, k^{d*})) = c^{s*}$ and H is Cobb-Douglas, we can solve for ℓ^{d*} to obtain

$$\ell^{d*} = \left[G^{-1}(c^{s*})\right]^{1/\alpha} \cdot \left[k^{d*}\right]^{\frac{\alpha-1}{\alpha}}\ .$$

Inserting this in the expression for $(V/p)^*(S)$ we obtain

$$(V/p)^*(S) = \frac{c^{s*}(S) - \Phi(S)k^s - S}{\left[G^{-1}(c^{s*}(S))\right]^{1/\alpha} \cdot \left[k^s\right]^{\frac{\alpha-1}{\alpha}}}$$

$$= \frac{c^{s*}(S) - (1-\alpha)[c^{s*}(S) - S] - S}{\left[h(S)\right]^{1/\alpha} \cdot \left[k^s\right]^{\frac{\alpha-1}{\alpha}}} = \frac{\alpha[c^{s*}(S) - S]}{\left[h(S)\right]^{1/\alpha} \cdot \left[k^s\right]^{\frac{\alpha-1}{\alpha}}} .$$

Using (3) and $c^{s*}(S) = G(h(S))$ this yields

$$(V/p)^*(S) = \frac{\alpha G'(h(S))h(S)}{\left[h(S)\right]^{1/\alpha} \cdot \left[k^s\right]^{\frac{\alpha-1}{\alpha}}} = \alpha\left[\frac{k^s}{h(S)}\right]^{\frac{1-\alpha}{\alpha}} G'(h(S)) .$$

Since $c^{d*}(R,S,V/p) = (V/p)\ell^{s*}(R,S,V/p) + Rk^s + S$, we can use the expression found for $(V/p)^*(S)$ to write c^{d*} in dependence of S only:

$$c^{d*}(S) = \alpha\left[\frac{k^s}{h(S)}\right]^{\frac{1-\alpha}{\alpha}} G'(h(S))\ell^{s*}(\Phi(S),S,(V/p)^*(S)) + (1-\alpha)[c^{s*}(S) - S] + S \tag{5}$$

$$= \alpha\left[\frac{k^s}{h(S)}\right]^{\frac{1-\alpha}{\alpha}} G'(h(S))\ell^{s*}(\Phi(S),S,(V/p)^*(S)) + (1-\alpha)c^{s*}(S) + \alpha S .$$

It remains to show the existence of $S>0$ such that $c^{d*}(S) = c^{s*}(S)$ which will follow from

$$\lim_{S\to\infty} [c^{d*}(S) - c^{s*}(S)] < 0 \tag{6}$$

$$\lim_{S\to 0} [c^{d*}(S) - c^{s*}(S)] > 0 \tag{7}$$

and the continuity of the functions involved.

To show (6), we use (3) to conclude

$$\lim_{S\to\infty} [G(h(S)) - G'(h(S))h(S)] = \lim_{S\to\infty} S = \infty$$

which implies $\lim_{S\to\infty} h(S) = \infty$ by monotonicity of $G(h) - G'(h)h$. From (5) we obtain

$$c^{d*}(S) - c^{s*}(S) = \alpha\left[\frac{k^s}{h(S)}\right]^{\frac{1-\alpha}{\alpha}} G'(h(S))\ell^{s*}(\Phi(S),S,(V/p)^*(S)) - \alpha\,[c^{s*}(S) - S]$$

$$= \alpha\left[\frac{k^s}{h(S)}\right]^{\frac{1-\alpha}{\alpha}} G'(h(S))\ell^{s*}(\Phi(S),S,(V/p)^*(S)) - \alpha G'(h(S))h(S)$$

$$= \alpha G'(h(S))\left\{\left[\frac{k^s}{h(S)}\right]^{\frac{1-\alpha}{\alpha}} \ell^{s*}(\Phi(S),S,(V/p)^*(S)) - h(S)\right\} .$$

Since $\ell^{s*}(\cdot) \le L$ and $h(S) \to \infty$ for $S \to \infty$, this implies (6).

Regarding (7), observe that $\lim_{S\to 0} h(S) = 0$. Indeed, if it were true that $\lim_{S\to 0} h(S) = c > 0$, then take c_1 such that $0 < c_1 < c$. The assumptions made on G would yield

$$G(c_1) - G'(c_1)c_1 < G(c) - G'(c)c = 0$$

which is impossible. This implies

$$\lim_{S\to 0} c^{s*}(S) = 0 \quad \text{and} \quad \lim_{S\to 0} (V/p)^*(S) = \infty .$$

Since by assumption (H) the consumption plan $c=0$ is always dominated by a positive consumption, the fact that $(V/p)^*(S)$ does not converge to zero for $S\to 0$ means that also $c^{d*}(S)$ stays away from zero. Thus $c^{d*}(S) - c^{s*}(S) > 0$ for S sufficiently small. ■

Since all behavioural functions depend only on the *real* prices r/p, s/p and V/p, it is clear that a Walrasian equilibrium (p^*,r^*,s^*,V^*) is determined only up to multiplication by a positive scalar. Denote the Walrasian real prices by $(r/p)^*$, $(s/p)^*$ and $(V/p)^*$. Then we can normalize s to one and set $p^* = 1/(s/p)^*$, $r^* = (r/p)^*p^*$ and $V^* = (V/p)^*p^*$. Moreover, we can define, by a slight abuse of notation,

$$\ell^{d*}(r,p) = \ell^{d*}(r/p,1/p) \; , \; k^{d*}(r,p) = k^{d*}(r/p,1/p)$$
$$c^{s*}(p) = c^{s*}(1/p)$$

and

$$\ell^{s*}(r,p,V) = \ell^{s*}(r/p,1/p,V/p) \; , \; c^{d*}(r,p,V) = c^{d*}(r/p,1/p,V/p).$$

Behaviour in Disequilibrium

For the analysis of the dynamic behaviour of the economic system out of Walrasian equilibrium we need to study the economic agents' behaviour in the presence of quantity constraints. To this end we denote by y the quantity of consumption good that the firm expects to be able to sell. Its decision problem becomes then

$$\max_{\ell,k} \frac{pF(\ell,k) - rk - 1}{\ell}$$

$$\text{s.t.} \quad F(\ell,k) \le y$$

We denote solutions by $(\ell^d(r,p,y),\ k^d(r,p,y))$.

Lemma 3. For $y>1/p$, $\ell^d(r,p,y)$ and $k^d(r,p,y)$ exist and are determined by

$$pF_\ell(\ell,k) = V(\ell,k) + \rho F_\ell(\ell,k)\ell \tag{8}$$

$$pF_k(\ell,k) = r + \rho F_k(\ell,k)\ell \tag{9}$$

where ρ is the non-negative Lagrange multiplier for the output constraint. For $1/p < y \le c^{s*}(p)$ this results in

$$k^d(r,p,y) = \frac{1-\alpha}{r}\,(py - 1) \tag{10}$$

$$\ell^d(r,p,y) = [G^{-1}(y)]^{1/\alpha} \cdot [k^d(r,p,y)]^{\frac{\alpha-1}{\alpha}} \ . \tag{11}$$

Proof: The Lagrangian $\mathcal{L} = V(\ell,k) + \rho[y-F(\ell,k)]$ gives rise to the first order conditions

$$\frac{\partial \mathcal{L}}{\partial \ell} = \frac{\ell pF_\ell(\ell,k) - [pF(\ell,k) - rk - 1]}{\ell^2} - \rho F_\ell(\ell,k)$$

$$= \frac{1}{\ell}\,[pF_\ell(\ell,k) - V(\ell,k)] - \rho F_\ell(\ell,k) = 0$$

$$\frac{\partial \mathcal{L}}{\partial k} = \frac{pF_k(\ell,k) - r}{\ell} - \rho F_k(\ell,k) = 0$$

which are obviously equivalent to (8) and (9). To show (10) we divide (8) by (9) and obtain $H_\ell/H_k = F_\ell/F_k = V/r$. Using that H is Cobb-Douglas this yields

$$\frac{\alpha k}{(1-\alpha)\ell} = \frac{pF(\ell,k) - rk - 1}{r\ell} = \frac{py - rk - 1}{r\ell}$$

which can be solved for k to yield (10). From this follows that k^d is positive if and only if $y>1/p$. In that case the equation $G(H(\ell,k^d(r,p,y))) = y$ can be solved for ℓ and, using that H is Cobb-Douglas, this yields (11). ■

We next study the *expansion path*

$$C(r,p) = \left\{(\ell^d(r,p,y),k^d(r,p,y)) \mid y > \frac{1}{p}\right\} .$$

This is a locus in ℓ-k-plane and traces out all input combinations corresponding to alternative values of y. From (10) we obtain

$$\frac{\partial k^d}{\partial y}(r,p,y) = \frac{1-\alpha}{r}\, p > 0 \tag{12}$$

(11) yields

$$\frac{\partial \ell^d}{\partial y}(r,p,y) = \frac{1}{\alpha}\left[G^{-1}(y)\right]^{\frac{1-\alpha}{\alpha}} G^{-1\prime}(y)(k^d)^{\frac{\alpha-1}{\alpha}}$$

$$+ \left[G^{-1}(y)\right]^{1/\alpha} \frac{\alpha-1}{\alpha}(k^d)^{-1/\alpha} \cdot \frac{\partial k^d}{\partial y}$$

and thus

$$\frac{\partial \ell^d}{\partial y}(r,p,y) =$$

$$\frac{1}{\alpha}\left[\frac{G^{-1}(y)}{k^d(r,p,y)}\right]^{1/\alpha} \cdot \left[\frac{G^{-1\prime}(y)}{G^{-1}(y)}\, k^d(r,p,y) - (1-\alpha)^2 \frac{p}{r}\right] \tag{13}$$

For $y = c^{s*}(p)$ the firm is unconstrained and therefore by (8) $pF_\ell = V$ which entails $G'(H(\ell,k)) = (1/\alpha)\ell V/(pH(\ell,k))$. Using this and $G^{-1}(y) = H(\ell,k) = \ell^\alpha k^{1-\alpha}$, (13) becomes

$$\frac{\partial \ell^d}{\partial y}(r,p,c^{s*}(p)) = \frac{1}{\alpha}\frac{\ell^{d*}}{k^{d*}}\left[\frac{\alpha p k^{d*}}{\ell^{d*}V} - (1-\alpha)^2 \frac{p}{r}\right]$$

$$= \frac{p}{\alpha}\frac{\ell^{d*}}{k^{d*}}\left[\frac{\alpha k^{d*}}{\ell^{d*}V} - (1-\alpha)^2 \frac{1}{r}\right].$$

Therefore we have

$$\frac{\partial \ell^d}{\partial y}(r,p,c^{s*}(p)) > 0 \iff \alpha r k^{d*}(r,p) > (1-\alpha)^2\, V\, \ell^{d*}(r,p,y)$$

$$\iff pc^{s*}(p) - rk^{d*}(r,p) - 1 < \frac{\alpha}{(1-\alpha)^2}\, rk^{d*}(r,p)$$

$$\iff pc^{s*}(p) - 1 < \left[\frac{\alpha}{(1-\alpha)^2} + 1\right] rk^{d*}(r,p)$$

Using (iii) of Lemma 1 this is equivalent to

$$pc^{s*}(p) - 1 < \frac{1-\alpha+\alpha^2}{(1-\alpha)^2}[pc^{s*}(p) - 1]$$

$$\Leftrightarrow \quad 1-2\alpha+\alpha^2 < 1-\alpha+\alpha^2$$ which is true. Therefore we have shown

$$\frac{\partial \ell^d}{\partial y}(r,p,c^{s*}(p)) > 0 \qquad (14)$$

(12) and (14) mean that if, starting from the unconstrained optimum $c^{s*}(p)$, y is decreased, then both k^d and ℓ^d decrease. Thus, for y close to $c^{s*}(p)$, there is a positive correlation between k^d and ℓ^d along the expansion path. This allows to define a function $\ell = f(k)$ by the requirement that $(\ell,k) \in C(r,p)$, for (ℓ,k) close to $(\ell^{d*}(r,p),k^{d*}(r,p))$. f is a parameterfree representation of a piece of the expansion path and we have shown that

$$f'(k) = \frac{\frac{\partial \ell^d}{\partial y}(r,p,y)}{\frac{\partial k^d}{\partial y}(r,p,y)} > 0 \quad \text{for y close to } c^{s*}(p). \qquad (15)$$

However, as $y \rightarrow 1/p$, $k^d(r,p,y) \rightarrow 0$ and therefore by (11) $\ell^d(r,p,y) \rightarrow \infty$. Taking these facts together we can sketch the expansion path as shown in Figure 2.

A firm may not only be constrained on the output marked but also on the capital and labour market. For the subsequent analysis it is necessary to study the firm's labour decision if it is rationed on the

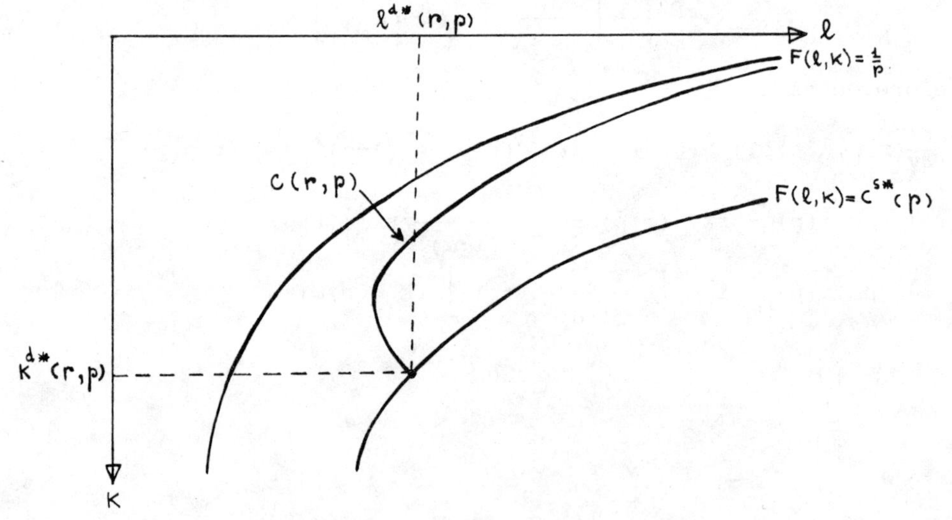

Figure 2: Firm's expansion path

capital market as well. Thus denote with $\ell^d(r,p,y,\bar{k})$ the ℓ-component of the solution to the problem

$$\max_{\ell,k} \frac{pF(\ell,k) - rk - 1}{\ell}$$
$$\text{s.t.} \quad \text{(i)} \quad F(\ell,k) \le y$$
$$\text{(ii)} \quad k \le \bar{k}$$

There are three possibilities regarding the dependence of ℓ^d on y and $\bar{k}$. These are classified by means of Figure 3. There are shown, among

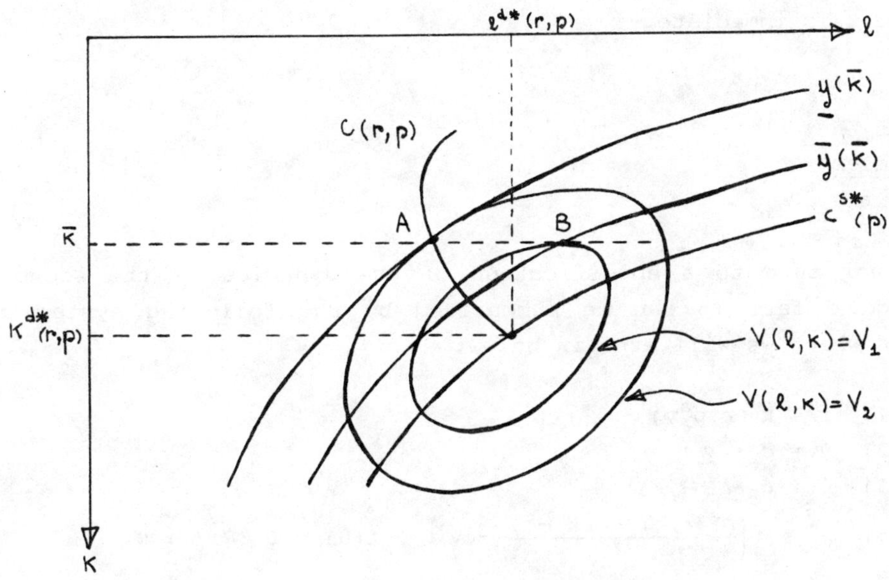

Figure 3: Various regimes of firm's effective labour demand

others, two iso-value-added loci, $V(\ell,k) = V_1$ and $V(\ell,k) = V_2$. Of course, $V_1 > V_2$. The expansion path C(r,p) is the locus of all points of tangency between some iso-value-added locus and some isoquant. There are also shown three isoquants, belonging to output levels denoted by $\underline{y}(\bar{k})$, $\bar{y}(\bar{k})$ and $c^{s*}(p)$. The meaning of the first two is as follows . If $y < \underline{y}(\bar{k})$, then only y is binding , and we may express this by writing $\ell^d(r,p,y,\bar{k}) = \ell^d(r,p,y)$. If $y > \bar{y}(\bar{k})$, then only $\bar{k}$ is binding $\ell^d(r,p,y,\bar{k}) = \ell^d(r,p,\bar{k})$. For $\underline{y}(\bar{k}) < y < \bar{y}(\bar{k})$ both y and $\bar{k}$ are binding, and in this case $\ell^d(r,p,y,\bar{k})$ is simply equal to $F(\cdot,\bar{k})^{-1}(y)$.

Regarding the household's behaviour out of Walrasian equilibrium it will be sufficient for our purposes to consider the case that the household is constrained on the capital market. We will denote by $\ell^s(r,p,V,\bar{k})$ and $c^d(r,p,V,\bar{k})$ the solution to

$$\begin{aligned} &\max \quad U(c,L-\ell) \\ &\text{s.t.} \quad \text{(i)} \quad c \geq 0 \ , \ 0 \leq \ell \leq L \ , \ 0 \leq k \leq k^s \\ &\qquad\ \ \text{(ii)} \quad pc \leq V\ell + rk + 1 \\ &\qquad\ \ \text{(iii)} \quad k \leq \bar{k} \end{aligned}$$

This differs from the unconstrained problem only in that k may be smaller than k^s. The existence of a unique solution for given positive p,r,V and $\bar{k}$ is immediate.

3. Dynamics

We now turn to a specification of the dynamics of the economy described so far. It can be summarized by the following system of equations which we will explain below:

$$\text{(D.1)} \quad \dot{r} = k^d(r,p,y) - k^s$$

$$\text{(D.2)} \quad \dot{y} = c - y$$

$$\text{(D.3)} \quad \dot{p} = c - F(\ell,k)$$

$$\text{(D.4)} \quad \dot{V}^e = f\left(\frac{pF(\ell,k) - rk - 1}{\ell} - V^e\right) \ , \ f(0) = 0 \ , \ f' \geq 0$$

where

$$\text{(E.1)} \quad k = \min\{k^d(r,p,y),k^s\}$$

$$\text{(E.2)} \quad \ell = \min\{\ell^d(r,p,y,k),\ell^s(r,p,V^e,k)\}$$

$$\text{(E.3)} \quad c = \frac{V^e}{p}\ell + \frac{r}{p}k + \frac{1}{p}$$

(D.1)-(D.4) are differential equations which describe how the state variables r, y, p and V^e vary where V^e denotes the value added expected by workers; (E.1)-(E.3) are used to determine certain variables appearing in (D.1)-(D.4). Consider a given vector of state variables (r,y,p,V^e). The firm accordingly formulates its capital demand $k^d(r,p,y)$. This is confronted with capital supply k^s on the capital market to determine the feasible transaction quantity k (equ. (E.1)) and the change in r (equ. (D.1)). The firm and the household, both taking into account the situation on the capital market, then meet on the labour market, and the feasible labour quantity ℓ is determined (equ.(E.2)). At this point the household is in a position to voice its effective consumption goods demand c (equ. (E.3)). This is confronted with the expected demand y to determine the adjustment in y (equ. (D.2)). Moreover, c is compared with the effective supply $F(\ell,k)$, giving rise to an adjustment in p (equ. (D.3)). Finally, the expected value added V^e is compared with the actual value added $[pF(\ell,k)-rk-1]/\ell$ to determine a possible change in V^e (equ. (D.4)).

The system (D.1)-(D.4), (E.1)-(E.3) is in a position of rest if r, y, p and V^e are such that $\dot{r} = \dot{y} = \dot{p} = \dot{V}^e = 0$. We then speak of a *dynamic equilibrium* in order to distinguish it from the Walrasian equilibrium.

Observe that any vector (r,y,p,V^e) satisfying $\dot{r} = \dot{y} = \dot{p} = 0$ and (E.1)-(E.3) is a dynamic equilibrium. Thus to describe dynamic equilibria, condition (D.4) is not needed. This entails also that the Walrasian equilibrium is a dynamic equilibrium. The behaviour of V^e and thus of the dynamic system out of equilibrium depends of course on the specification of the function f in (D.4). We will adopt here a trivial form of f which is in part dictated by the complexity of the system considered so far, namely that f is constant (which implies of course $f \equiv 0$). This reduces the dimensionality of the dynamic system from four to three. Moreover, since we want our system to continue to be compatible with Walrasian equilibrium, we then have to assume $V^e = V^*$, where V^* is the value added realized in the Walrasian equilibrium. Since the Walrasian equilibrium is our main point of reference , this choice seems natural. Economically it means that workers continue to believe that they will be paid V^* even if the system is out of Walrasian equilibrium. This is of course a strong assumption but our subsequent analysis remains qualitatively valid as long as V^* is not very responsive to changes in the other variables, that is, as long as f is sufficiently "flat"[3].

---

[3]The present treatment of the value added as expected by households is analogous to that of Varian (1977) with respect to the profit payments expected by households. Varian assumes that they are constant and equal to the profits in Walrasian equilibrium.

The Manifold of Non-Walrasian Equilibria

We will call those dynamic equilibria which are not a Walrasian equilibrium *non-Walrasian equilibria.* Due to our specification of f and $V^e = V^*$, in any non-Walrasian equilibrium workers will expect and realize the same value added per working hour as in the Walrasian equilibrium. This raises the question whether non-Walrasian equilibria exist. To address this problem rigorously, we first recall the system to be analyzed:

$$\text{(D.1)} \quad \dot{r} = k^d(r,p,y) - k^s$$

$$\text{(D.2)} \quad \dot{y} = c - y$$

$$\text{(D.3)} \quad \dot{p} = c - F(\ell,k)$$

$$\text{(E.1)} \quad k = \min\{k^d(r,p,y),k^s\}$$

$$\text{(E.2)} \quad \ell = \min\{\ell^d(r,p,y,k),\ell^s(r,p,V^*,k)\}$$

$$\text{(E.3)} \quad c = \frac{V^*}{p}\,\ell + \frac{r}{p}\,k + \frac{1}{p}$$

We denote the set of non-Walrasian equilibria by E, that is

$$E = \{(r,y,p) \in \mathbb{R}^3_+ \mid \dot{r} = \dot{y} = \dot{p} = 0\}/\{(r^*,y^*,p^*)\}$$

where (r^*,y^*,p^*) refers to the Walrasian equilibrium. We will proceed in two steps : we will first fix p at p^* and delete (D.3) from our system. This will enable us to show the existence of at least one non-Walrasian equilibrium. In the second step we will return to the full system and use the regular value theorem to show that E extends as a smooth one-dimensional manifold around the non-Walrasian equilibrium found in the first step.

Setting $p = p^*$ and deleting (D.3) gives us the system

$$\text{(RS)} \quad \begin{cases} \dot{r} = k^d(r,p^*,y) - k^s \\ \dot{y} = c - y \\ k = \min\{k^d(r,p^*,y),k^s\} \\ \ell = \min\{\ell^d(r,p^*,y,k),\ell^s(r,p^*,V^*,k)\} \\ c = \dfrac{V^*}{p^*}\,\ell + \dfrac{r}{p^*}\,k + \dfrac{1}{p^*} \end{cases}$$

We call this system the real system (RS). Due to the min-operators, (RS) is not differentiable. Because we want to apply concepts from differentiable topology, we therefore have to introduce so-called virtual systems. They will be differentiable and, by "glueing" them together in an appropriate way, will give us back the real system. There are two virtual systems relevant for the study of E. They both refer to the case that $\ell^d(r,p^*,y,k) < \ell^s(r,p^*,V^*,k)$ and then one will deal with the case $k^d(r,p^*,y) \le k^s$ and the other case $k^d(r,p^*,y) \ge k^s$. More precisely, let (VS.a) and (VS.b) denote the following systems:

$$\text{(VS.a)} \quad \begin{cases} \dot{r} = k^d(r,p^*,y) - k^s \\ \dot{y} = c^a - y \\ c^a = \dfrac{V^*}{p^*}\,\ell^d(r,p^*,y) + \dfrac{r}{p^*}\,k^d(r,p^*,y) + \dfrac{1}{p^*} \end{cases}$$

$$\text{(VS.b)} \quad \begin{cases} \dot{r} = k^d(r,p^*,y) - k^s \\ \dot{y} = c^b - y \\ c^b = \dfrac{V^*}{p^*}\,F(\cdot,k^s)^{-1}(y) + \dfrac{r}{p^*}\,k^s + \dfrac{1}{p^*} \end{cases}$$

Both systems coincide with (RS) in certain regions of the r-y-plane. The division of that plane in different regions is indicated in Figure 4. (VS.a) coincides with (RS) in regions A and B , while (VS.b) coincides with (RS) in regions C and D. Point W indicates the Walrasian equilibrium while point Z indicates a non-Walrasian equilibrium. More precisely, the loci and regions shown in Figure 4 have the following meaning.

<u>Loci</u>:

I: $k^d(r,p^*,y) = k^s$

IIa: $c^a = y$

IIb: $c^b = y$

III: $\ell^d(r,p^*,y,k^s) = F(\cdot,k^s)^{-1}(y) = \ell^d(r,p^*,k^s)$

IV: $\ell^d(r,p^*,k^s) = \ell^{s*}(r,p^*,V^*)$

V: $\ell^d(r,p^*,y) = \ell^s(r,p^*,V^*,k^d(r,p^*,y))$

<u>Regions</u>:

A: $k^d(r,p^*,y) < k^s$

$\ell^d(r,p^*,y,k^s) = \ell^d(r,p^*,y) < \ell^s(r,p^*,V^*,k^d(r,p^*,y))$

$c^a > y$

B: $k^d(r,p^*,y) < k^s$

$\ell^d(r,p^*,y,k^s) = \ell^d(r,p^*,y) < \ell^s(r,p^*,V^*,k^d(r,p^*,y))$

$c^a < y$

C: $k^d(r,p^*,y) > k^s$

$\ell^d(r,p^*,y,k^s) = F(\cdot,k^s)^{-1}(y) < \ell^d(r,p^*,k^s) < \ell^{s*}(r,p^*,V^*)$

$c^b < y$

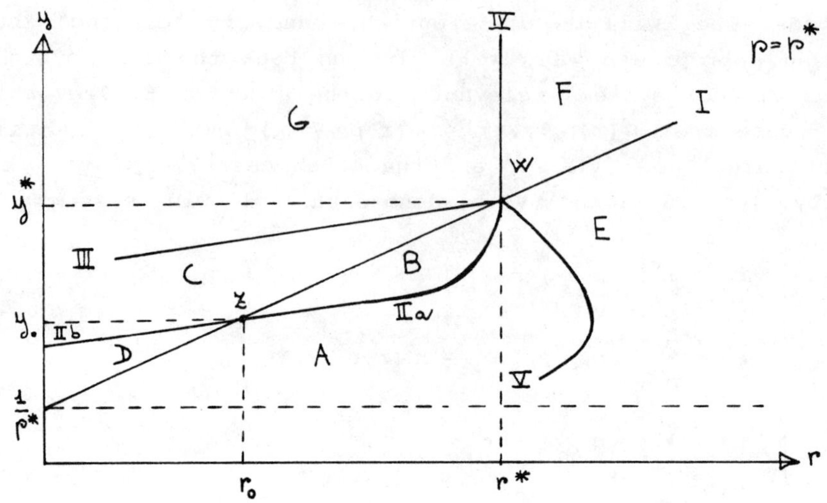

Figure 4: Division of r-y-plane in regions A to G

D: $k^d(r,p^*,y) > k^s$
$\ell^d(r,p^*,y,k^s) = F(\cdot,k^s)^{-1}(y) < \ell^d(r,p^*,k^s) < \ell^s(r,p^*,V^*)$
$c^b > y$

E: $k^d(r,p^*,y) < k^s$
$\ell^d(r,p^*,y,k^s) = \ell^d(r,p^*,y) > \ell^s(r,p^*,V^*,k^d(r,p^*,y))$

F: $k^d(r,p^*,y) > k^s$
$\ell^d(r,p^*,y,k^s) = \ell^d(r,p^*,k^s) > \ell^{s*}(r,p^*,V^*)$

G: $k^d(r,p^*,y) > k^s$
$\ell^d(r,p^*,y,k^s) = \ell^d(r,p^*,k^s) < \ell^{s*}(r,p^*,V^*)$

Our task in the sequel is to derive these facts and, most importantly, to show the claimed intersection of the loci IIa/IIb with locus I at some (r_0,y_0) with $0 < r_0 < r^*$, $1/p^* < y_0 < y^*$.

To start with, consider the locus $k^d(r,p,y) = k^s$. By (10) it can be given explicitly as

$$y = \frac{k^s}{(1-\alpha)p}\, r + \frac{1}{p} \tag{16}$$

Moreover, since by (10)

$$\frac{\partial k^d(r,p,y)}{\partial r} = -\frac{k^d(r,p,y)}{r} < 0 \qquad , \tag{17}$$

$k^d < k^s$ to the right of locus I and $k^d > k^s$ to the left of it. Furthermore, $k^d(r,p,y) < k^s$ is equivalent to $\ell^d(r,p,y,k^s) = \ell^d(r,p,y)$ because in that case (and only in that case) $k \le k^s$ is not a binding constraint for the firm. This means also that locus I represents the borderline between the regions in which, regarding the determination of ℓ^d, only y is binding and both y and k^s are binding.

Next consider locus III. It is the borderline between the regions in which both y and k^s are binding and only k^s is binding. Referring back to Figure 3 it means that the firm is in a position shown by point B. The corresponding y is bigger than the one belonging to point A, a situation resulting from some $(r,y) \in I$, $r < r^*$. Thus III lies above I for $r < r^*$. Moreover, from $F(\cdot,k^s)^{-1}(y) = \ell^d(r,p,k^s)$ we can obtain its slope as

$$\frac{dy}{dr} = \frac{\partial \ell^d}{\partial r}(r,p,k^s)\cdot F_\ell(\ell^d,k^s) \quad .$$

$\ell^d(r,p,k^s)$ is determined from maximizing $[pF(\ell,k^s)-rk^s-1]/\ell$ which yields the condition

$$pF_\ell(\ell,k^s)\ell - pF(\ell,k^s) + rk^s + 1 = 0 \quad .$$

This implies

$$\frac{\partial \ell^d(r,p,k^s)}{\partial r} = -\frac{k^s}{pF_{\ell\ell}(\ell,k^s)\ell} > 0 \qquad . \tag{18}$$

Thus locus III has a positive slope. This discussion also shows that in regions C and D $\ell^d = F(\cdot,k^s)^{-1}(y)$ whereas in region G and F $\ell^d = \ell^d(r,p^*,k^s)$.

Consider now locus IV. There $\ell^d(r,p^*,k^s) = \ell^{s*}(r,p^*,V^*)$. Indeed, $r = r^*$ satisfies this equation , and it is independent of y. Thus IV is vertical. Moreover, if $r < r^*$, then by (18) $\ell^d(r,p^*,k^s) < \ell^d(r^*,p^*,k^s)$. On the other hand, the household's wealth is smaller for r than for r^*,

$$\frac{r}{p^*} k^s + \frac{1}{p^*} < \frac{r^*}{p^*} k^s + \frac{1}{p^*}$$

Since we have assumed that leisure is not an inferior good, this implies

$$L - \ell^{s*}(r,p^*,V^*) \le L - \ell^{s*}(r^*,p^*,V^*) \quad .$$

From this we can conclude $\ell^d(r,p^*,k^s) < \ell^{s*}(r^*,p^*,V^*) \le \ell^{s*}(r,p^*,V^*)$. This completes the explanation of regions F and G.

Regarding locus V, we calculate its slope as

$$\frac{dy}{dr} = - \frac{\frac{\partial \ell^d}{\partial r} - \frac{\partial \ell^s}{\partial r} - \frac{\partial \ell^s}{\partial k}\cdot\frac{\partial k^d}{\partial r}}{\frac{\partial \ell^d}{\partial y} - \frac{\partial \ell^s}{\partial k}\cdot\frac{\partial k^d}{\partial y}}$$

Again since leisure is non-inferior, $\frac{\partial \ell^s}{\partial k} \le 0$. Together with (12) and (14) this implies that the denominator of the above expression is positive for y not too far away from y^*.

Regarding the numerator, observe that $\frac{\partial \ell^s}{\partial r} + \frac{\partial \ell^s \partial k^d}{\partial k\, \partial r} = 0$

since a change in r does not change the household's budget constraint. Indeed,

$$\frac{\partial}{\partial r}\left[\frac{r}{p} k^d(r,p,y)\right] = \frac{k^d}{p} + \frac{r}{p}\cdot\frac{\partial k^d}{\partial r} = 0$$

by (17). By (18) $\frac{\partial \ell^d}{\partial r} > 0$, so altogether $\frac{dy}{dr}$ is negative for y close to y^* and positive as y approaches $1/p^*$.

Consider now $y = y^*$ and $r > r^*$. Then ℓ^s is equal to the Walrasian ℓ^{s*} whereas $\ell^d(r,p^*,y^*) > \ell^d(r^*,p^*,y^*)$. Thus $\ell^d > \ell^s$ in region E and $\ell^d < \ell^s$ in regions A and B.

The discussion so far justifies to work with systems (VS.a) in regions A and B and with (VS.b) in regions C and D. It remains to explain the shape of locus IIa $\cup$ IIb. To this end let us consider the virtual system (VS.b) and more precisely the equation $c^b - y = 0$, or

$$\frac{V^*}{p^*} F(\cdot,k^s)^{-1}(y) + \frac{r}{p^*} k^s + \frac{1}{p^*} - y = 0 \qquad (19)$$

For $r = r^*$ it possesses the (Walrasian) solution $y = y^* = c^{s*}(p^*)$. As r decreases, $\frac{r}{p^*} k^s$ decreases, and since $F(\cdot,k^s)^{-1}$ is increasing in y, y has to decrease. More precisely,

$$\frac{dy}{dr} = - \frac{k^s/p^*}{\frac{V^*}{p^*} \frac{1}{F_\ell(F(\cdot,k^s)^{-1}(y),k^s)} - 1} .$$

Thus $dy/dr > 0 \Leftrightarrow V^*/p^* < F_\ell(F(\cdot,k^s)^{-1}(y),k^s)$. But since

$$\frac{d}{dy}\left[F_\ell(F(\cdot,k^s)^{-1}(y),k^s)\right] = F_{\ell\ell}(\cdot)\frac{1}{F_\ell(\cdot)} < 0 \quad ,$$

$V^*/p^* < F_\ell(F(\cdot,k^s)^{-1}(y),k^s) \Leftrightarrow y < y^*$. This implies $dy/dr > 0$ for $y < y^*$ and $dy/dr = \infty$ for $y = y^*$. For $r = 0$, (19) becomes

$$\frac{V^*}{p^*} F(\cdot,k^s)^{-1}(y) + \frac{1}{p^*} - y = 0 \quad .$$

This entails $y > 1/p^*$ for $r = 0$. The locus $c^b - y = 0$ is shown in Figure 5. Part AZ of it coincides with locus IIb in Figure 4.

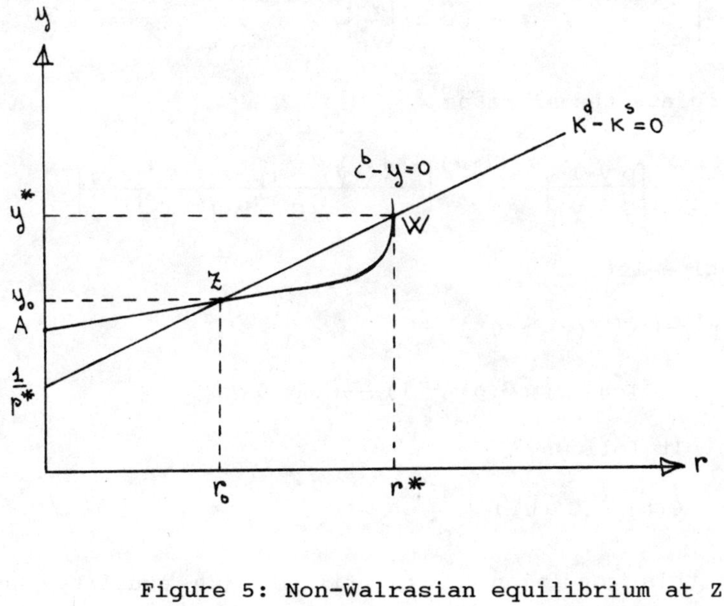

Figure 5: Non-Walrasian equilibrium at Z

Since (19) defines a continuous function between y and r, the facts established above imply an intersection between the loci $c^b - y = 0$ and $k^d(r,p^*,y) - k^s = 0$ at some $Z=(r_0,y_0)$ with $0 < r_0 < r^*$ and $0 < y_0 < y^*$. Since in that point $k^d(r,p^*,y) = k^s$, (VS.b) coincides there with the virtual system (VS.a). Therefore (r_0,y_0) is a (non-Walrasian) equilibrium for (VS.a) and (VS.b), and thus also for the real system (RS). We have thus established the following

<u>Proposition 2</u>: There exists a non-Walrasian equilibrium (r_0,y_0,p^*) with $r_0 < r^*$ and $y_0 < y^*$. ■

To complete the discussion of Figure 4, we have to explain locus IIa. It derives from the equation

$$\frac{v^*}{p^*}\,\ell^d(r,p^*,y) + \frac{r}{p^*}\,k^d(r,p^*,y) + \frac{1}{p^*} - y = 0 \tag{20}$$

which is part of (VS.a). Using (10) and (11) this yields

$$v^*\left[G^{-1}(y)\right]^{1/\alpha}\left[\frac{1-\alpha}{r}(p^*y-1)\right]^{(\alpha-1)/\alpha} + (1-\alpha)(p^*y-1) + 1 - p^*y = 0$$

$$\Leftrightarrow \qquad v^*\left[\frac{r}{1-\alpha}\right]^{(1-\alpha)/\alpha} = \alpha\left[\frac{p^*y-1}{G^{-1}(y)}\right]^{1/\alpha} \qquad \Leftrightarrow$$

$$r = \gamma\left[\frac{p^*y-1}{G^{-1}(y)}\right]^{1/(1-\alpha)}, \quad \gamma = (1-\alpha)\left(\frac{\alpha}{v^*}\right)^{\alpha/(1-\alpha)} \tag{21}$$

From this we calculate the slope as

$$\frac{dr}{dy} = \left(\frac{\alpha}{v^*}\right)^{\alpha/(1-\alpha)}\left[\frac{p^*y-1}{G^{-1}(y)}\right]^{\alpha/(1-\alpha)}\left[\frac{p^*G^{-1}(y) - (p^*y-1)G^{-1\prime}(y)}{[G^{-1}(y)]^2}\right].$$

This is non-negative iff

$$p^*G^{-1}(y) - (p^*y-1)G^{-1\prime}(y) \geq 0$$

$$\Leftrightarrow \qquad p^*h - (p^*G(h) - 1)\frac{1}{G'(h)} \geq 0$$

where $h = G^{-1}(y)$. It follows

$$\frac{dr}{dy} \geq 0 \quad \Leftrightarrow \quad G(h) - G'(h)h \leq \frac{1}{p^*}$$

For $h^* = G^{-1}(y^*)$ this condition is fullfilled with equality whereas for $h < h^*$, by concavity of G, we have the inequality.

To sum up, we have shown that the locus IIa passes through points Z and W, is strictly positively sloped in between them and has slope infinity at W. This concludes our discussion of Figure 4.

The above Proposition 2 shows that the set of non-Walrasian equilibria E is non-empty. More precisely we have demonstrated the existence of a non-Walrasian equilibrium (r_0, y_0, p^*) at the Walrasian price of output $p = p^*$. By varying p we now want to show that E has the structure of a smooth one-dimensional manifold, at least around the equilibrium (r_0, y_0, p^*). To this end we return to the three-dimensional dynamic system (D.1)-(D.3), (E.1)-(E.3). Observe, however, that at (r_0, y_0, p^*) the firm is rationed in its sales, that is $y_0 < y^*$. Therefore, also in a neighborhood of (r_0, y_0, p^*) it is true that $y < y^*$, which implies that the firm always satisfies its constraint $F(\ell, k) \leq y$ with equality. (D.1)-(D.3) therefore simplify to

(D.1) $\dot{r} = k^d(r,p,y) - k^s$

(D.2)′ $\dot{y} = \dot{p} = c - y$

We are now in a position to prove

<u>Proposition 3</u>: There exists a neighborhood of the non-Walrasian equilibrium (r_0, y_0, p^*) in which the set of non-Walrasian equilibria E is a smooth one-dimensional manifold.

<u>Proof</u>: The system defined by (D.1), (D.2)′, (E.1)-(E.3) gives rise to a function $f: \mathbb{R}_+ \times (1/p, \infty) \times \mathbb{R}_+ \longrightarrow \mathbb{R}^2$,

$$f(r,y,p) = (k^d(r,p,y) - k^s, c(r,p,y) - y)$$

with $c(r,p,y) = \frac{V^*}{p} \ell + \frac{r}{p} k + \frac{1}{p}$

and ℓ and k determined by (E.1) and (E.2), respectively. The counterimage of $(0,0) \in \mathbb{R}^2$, $f^{-1}(0,0)$, is E. If (0,0) is a regular value of f (i.e. $Df(r,y,p)$ has maximal rank for any $(r,y,p) \in f^{-1}(0,0)$) then by the regular value theorem $f^{-1}(0,0)$ is a one-dimensional manifold.

In showing this, a problem is that f is not necessarily differentiable at points in E. This is due to the min-operators in (E.1) and (E.2). Therefore we consider instead the smooth functions

$$f^a(r,y,p) := (k^d(r,p,y) - k^s, c^a(r,p,y) - y)$$

$$f^b(r,y,p) := (k^d(r,p,y) - k^s, c^b(r,p,y) - y)$$

with

$$c^a(r,p,y) := \frac{V}{p}\,\ell^d(r,p,y) + \frac{r}{p}\,k^d(r,p,y) + \frac{1}{p}$$

$$c^b(r,p,y) := \frac{V^*}{p}\,F(\cdot,k^s)^{-1}(y) + \frac{r}{p}\,k^s + \frac{1}{p}$$

For $(r,y,p) \in E$, $k^d(r,p,y) = k^s$ which implies $\ell^d(r,p,y) = \ell^d(r,p,y,k^s) = F(\cdot,k^s)^{-1}(y)$. Moreover, in a neighborhood of (r_0,y_0,p^*) $\ell^d(r,p,y,k) < \ell^s(r,p,V^*,k)$. Therefore $f^a|_E = f^b|_E = f|_E$. It is thus sufficient to study one of the functions f^a and f^b, say f^b.

The Jacobian of f^b is

$$Df^b = \begin{pmatrix} \frac{\partial k^d}{\partial r} & \frac{\partial k^d}{\partial y} & \frac{\partial k^d}{\partial p} \\ \frac{\partial c^b}{\partial r} & \frac{\partial c^b}{\partial y} - 1 & \frac{\partial c^b}{\partial p} \end{pmatrix}$$

Taking the minor defined by the first and the third column of Df^b and using that in equilibrium $k^d = k^s$ and $c^b = y$, one calculates, using (10),

$$\det \begin{pmatrix} -\frac{k^d}{r} & \frac{(1-\alpha)y}{r} \\ \frac{k^s}{p} & -\frac{c^b}{p} \end{pmatrix} = \frac{yk^d}{rp} - (1-\alpha)\frac{yk^s}{rp} = \frac{\alpha y k^s}{rp} > 0 \quad .$$

Thus Df^b has maximal rank at any point of $f^{-1}(0,0)$. ∎

Stability

Our analysis so far has established the existence both of a Walrasian equilibrium and of a one-dimensional manifold of non-Walrasian equilibria. The latter contains a non-Walrasian equilibrium with $p = p^*$. We now turn to the stability features of these equilibria. We start with the analysis of the truncated system (RS), that is where (D.3) is deleted and p is held fixed at its Walrasian value p^*.

<u>Lemma 4</u>: The Walrasian equilibrium is unstable in the real system (RS).

<u>Proof</u>: Since the system (RS) is not differentiable at the Walrasian

equilibrium, it is necessary (and sufficient) to work with a "virtual" system. We consider the Jacobian matrix of (VS.b)

$$Df^b = \begin{pmatrix} \frac{\partial k^d}{\partial r} & \frac{\partial k^d}{\partial y} \\ \frac{\partial c^b}{\partial r} & \frac{\partial c^b}{\partial y} - 1 \end{pmatrix} = \begin{pmatrix} a_{11} & a_{12} \\ a_{21} & a_{22} \end{pmatrix}$$

The eigenvalues are the solutions of the characteristic polynomial:

$$(a_{11}-\lambda)(a_{22}-\lambda) - a_{12}a_{21} = 0 \Leftrightarrow \lambda^2-\lambda(a_{11}+a_{22})+a_{11}a_{22}-a_{12}a_{21} = 0.$$

The discriminant of this second order equation is

$$\begin{aligned} \Delta &= (a_{11} + a_{22})^2 - 4(a_{11}a_{22} - a_{12}a_{21}) \\ &= (a_{11} - a_{22})^2 + 4a_{12}a_{21} \end{aligned}$$

From (12) $a_{12} = \frac{1-\alpha}{r} p > 0$ and $a_{21} = k^s/p > 0$. Thus $\Delta > 0$ which implies two distinct real valued eigenvalues λ_1 and λ_2. Moreover,

$$\lambda_1\lambda_2 = \begin{vmatrix} a_{11} & a_{12} \\ a_{21} & a_{22} \end{vmatrix} = -\frac{k^s}{p}\cdot\frac{(1-\alpha)p}{r} < 0$$

since $a_{22} = \frac{V^*}{p}\cdot\frac{1}{F_\ell} - 1 = 0$ at the Walrasian equilibrium by (1). Therefore either $\lambda_1 > 0$ or $\lambda_2 > 0$ which implies instability. ■

To investigate the stability of the non-Walrasian equilibrium (r_0,y_0,p^*) (whose existence we have shown in Proposition 2) with respect to the system (RS), we introduce some concepts from differential topology.

Given a smooth dynamic system $\dot{x} = f(x)$ on a bordered manifold M, we can, provided $f(x) \neq 0$ on the boundary of M , define the *Gauss map on the boundary of* M by $g(x) = f(x)/\|f(x)\|$, where $\|\cdot\|$ is the ordinary Euclidean norm. The Gauss map is *nullhomotopic* if it is not onto the unit sphere, that is if there is some direction such that $\dot{x}$ never points in that direction along the boundary of M. In these circumstances one can invoke the following elementary consequence of the Poincaré-Hopf theorem:

Theorem: Let $\dot{x} = f(x)$ be a smooth dynamic system on the bordered manifold M with the Gauss map nullhomotopic on the boundary of M and such that there exist a finite number of isolated equilibria $x_1,\dots,x_n$ with $\det(Df(x_i)) \neq 0$ for $i = 1,\dots,n$. Then one can define the index of each equilibrium as follows:

$$\text{index}(x_i) = \begin{cases} +1 & \text{if } \det(-Df(x_i)) > 0 \\ -1 & \text{if } \det(-Df(x_i)) < 0 \end{cases}$$

and furthermore,

$$\sum_{i=1}^{n} \text{index}(x_i) = 0$$

The proof of this theorem is an easy modification of the Hopf lemma on page 36 of Milnor (1972).

The application of this result to our problem requires again to work with a virtual system instead of the real system (RS) in order to avoid the nondifferentiability of the latter. More precisely we consider again the system (VS.b),

$$\begin{aligned} \dot{r} &= k^d(r,p^*,y) - k^s =: f_1(r,y) \\ \dot{y} &= \frac{V^*}{p^*} F(\cdot,k^s)^{-1}(y) + \frac{r}{p^*} k^s + \frac{1}{p^*} - y =: f_2(r,y) \end{aligned} \tag{22}$$

The discussion regarding equations (16) and (19) had revealed the following qualitative shapes of the loci $\{(r,y) \mid \dot{r} = 0\}$ =: I and $\{(r,y) \mid \dot{y} = 0\}$ =: II :

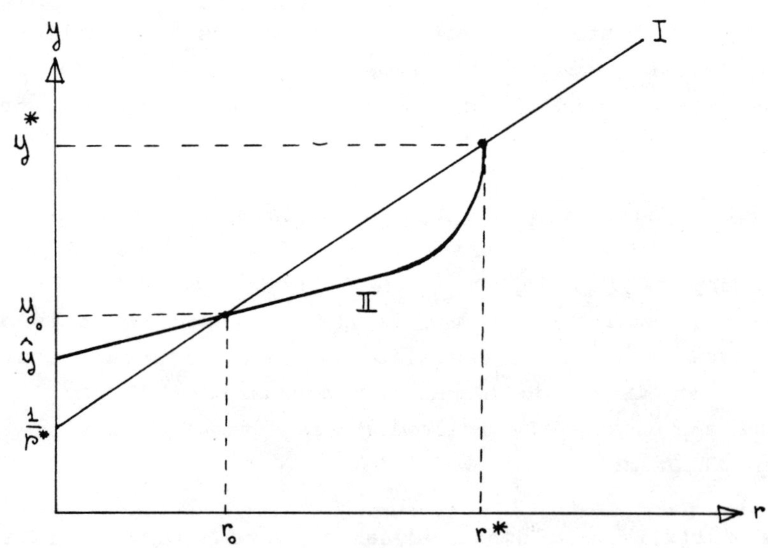

Figure 6: Shape of loci I and II

In particular locus II intersects the y-axis at a value $\hat{y}$ for which $1/p^* < \hat{y} < \overset{*}{y}$ holds. Also, the slope of II at (r^*,y^*) is infinite. From this it is clear that there exist $\underline{r}$, $\overline{r}$, $\underline{y}$ and $\overline{y}$ such that $(\underline{r},\underline{y}) \in I$, $(\overline{r},\overline{y}) \in I$ and $1/p^* < \underline{y} < \hat{y}$. Use these to consider, as natural state space, the rectangle

$$\{(r,y) | \underline{r} \le r \le \overline{r},\ \underline{y} \le y \le \overline{y}\} \quad .$$

Since, however, we actually need the state space to be a *smooth* manifold with boundary, we round off the corners of the above rectangle and call the resulting set M. By construction, there is no point on the border of M for which $\dot{r} = 0$ and $\dot{y} = 0$. Thus the Gauss map $f(x)/\|f(x)\|$ is well defined. Moreover it is nullhomotopic because there is no point on the border of M for which $\dot{r} < 0$ and $\dot{y} < 0$. This is shown in Figure 7.

In order to be able to apply the above theorem to the system (22) acting on M, we still have to show that it admits a finite number of equilibria only. To this end we use (10) and $\dot{r} = 0$ to express y as function of r:

$$y = \frac{rk^s}{p^*(1-\alpha)} + \frac{1}{p^*}$$

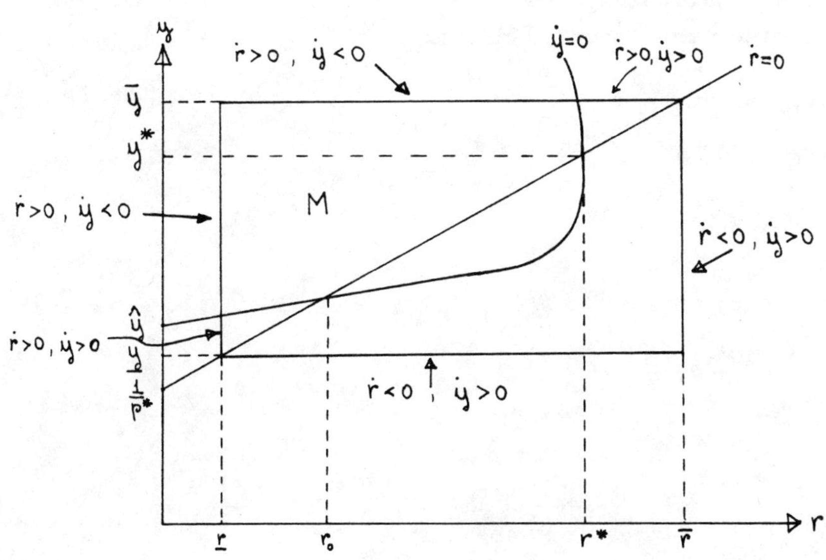

Figure 7: The bordered manifold M

Inserting this in the equation $\dot{y} = 0$ of (22) yields

$$V^*F(\cdot,k^s)^{-1}\left(\frac{rk^s}{p^*(1-\alpha)}+\frac{1}{p^*}\right) = rk^s\left(\frac{1}{1-\alpha}-1\right)$$

$$\Leftrightarrow \qquad F(\cdot,k^s)^{-1}\left(\frac{rk^s}{p^*(1-\alpha)}+\frac{1}{p^*}\right) = \frac{\alpha}{1-\alpha}\cdot\frac{rk^s}{V^*}$$

$$\Leftrightarrow \qquad \frac{rk^s}{p^*(1-\alpha)}+\frac{1}{p^*} = F\left(\frac{\alpha}{1-\alpha}\cdot\frac{rk^s}{V^*},k^s\right)$$

The left hand side of this equation can be seen as a linear function of r; the right hand is, due to assumption (F), strictly concave as function of r. Thus there are at most two solutions. Since we have already shown (Propositions 1, 2) that there are at least two equilibria of our dynamical system, it follows that (22) has exactly two equilibria. We can now demonstrate the following

Lemma 5: The non-Walrasian equilibrium (r_0,y_0,p^*) is an asymptotically stable equilibrium of the system (RS).

Proof: Since the real system coincides with the virtual systems (VS.a) and (VS.b) in the respective regions, and all three systems coincide on E, it is necessary and sufficient to show the stability with respect to the two virtual systems.
(VS.a) : We consider the Jacobian matrix

$$Df = \begin{pmatrix} a_{11} & a_{12} \\ a_{21} & a_{22} \end{pmatrix}$$

where, using (10) and (11),

$$a_{11} = \frac{\partial k^d}{\partial r} = -\frac{k^d}{r}$$

$$a_{12} = \frac{\partial k^d}{\partial y} = (1-\alpha)\,\frac{p^*}{r}$$

$$a_{21} = \frac{V^*}{p^*}\frac{\partial \ell^d}{\partial r} + \frac{k^d}{p^*} + \frac{r}{p^*}\frac{\partial k^d}{\partial r} = \frac{V^*}{p^*}\left[\,G^{-1}(y)\right]^{1/\alpha}\ \frac{1-\alpha}{\alpha}\ \frac{\left(k^d\right)^{\frac{\alpha-1}{\alpha}}}{r}$$

$$a_{22} = \frac{V^*}{p^*}\frac{\partial \ell^d}{\partial y} + \frac{r}{p^*}\frac{\partial k^d}{\partial y} - 1 =$$

$$\frac{V^*}{p^*}\frac{1}{\alpha}\left[G^{-1}(y)\right]^{1/\alpha}\left(k^d\right)^{-1/\alpha}\left\{\frac{\left[G^{-1}(y)\right]'}{G^{-1}(y)}k^d - (\alpha-1)^2\frac{p^*}{r}\right\} - \alpha$$

Since in the Walrasian equilibrium

$$G^{-1}(y^*) = H(\ell^*,k^s) \quad e \quad G'(H(\ell^*,k^s)) = \frac{\ell^* V^*}{\alpha p^* H(\ell^*,k^s)}$$

it follows that

$$a_{11} = -\frac{k^s}{r^*} \qquad a_{12} = (1-\alpha)\frac{p^*}{r^*}$$

$$a_{21} = \frac{V^*}{p^*}\ell^*\left(k^s\right)^{\frac{1-\alpha}{\alpha}}\frac{1-\alpha}{\alpha}\left(k^s\right)^{\frac{\alpha-1}{\alpha}}\frac{1}{r^*} = \frac{1-\alpha}{\alpha}\frac{V^*\ell^*}{p^*r^*}$$

$$a_{22} = \frac{V^*}{p^*}\frac{1}{\alpha}\frac{\ell^*}{k^s}\left\{\frac{\alpha p^*}{\ell^* V^*}k^s - (1-\alpha)^2\frac{p^*}{r^*}\right\} - \alpha =$$

$$1 - \alpha - \frac{(1-\alpha)^2}{\alpha}\frac{V^*\ell^*}{k^s r^*}$$

Therefore

$$\det(Df(r^*,p^*,y^*)) = -\frac{k^s}{r^*}(1-\alpha)\left\{1 - \frac{1-\alpha}{\alpha}\frac{V^*\ell^*}{k^s r^*}\right\} -$$

$$- \frac{(1-\alpha)^2}{\alpha}\frac{V^*\ell^*}{(r^*)^2} = -\frac{1-\alpha}{r^*}k^s < 0$$

Thus we can apply the Poincare'-Hopf theorem to conclude that the Jacobian has positive determinant at the non-Walrasian equilibrium (r_0,Y_0,p^*). As in the proof of Proposition 4, the eigenvalues of $Df(r_0,Y_0,p^*)$ are the solutions to

$$\lambda^2-\lambda(a_{11}+a_{22})+a_{11}a_{22}-a_{12}a_{21}=0.$$

The associated discriminant is

$$\Delta = \left(a_{11} - a_{22}\right)^2 + 4\, a_{12}a_{21} > 0$$

as in the proof of Proposition 4. Therefore both eigenvalues are real-valued and distinct. Moreover,

$$\lambda_1 + \lambda_2 = tr(Df(r_0,y_0,p^*)) = a_{11} + a_{22} = -\frac{k^d}{r_0} +$$

$$\frac{v^*}{p^*}\frac{1}{\alpha}[G^{-1}(y_0)]^{1/\alpha}(k^d)^{-1/\alpha}\left\{\frac{[G^{-1}(y_0)]'}{G^{-1}(y_0)}k^d - (\alpha-1)^2\frac{p^*}{r_0}\right\} - \alpha$$

To determine the sign of this expression, we first show

$$\frac{[G^{-1}(y)]'}{G^{-1}(y)} \le \frac{1}{y - \frac{1}{p}} \tag{23}$$

From (3) we know that there is $h(p) = c(p)^{s^*}$ such that

$$G'(h(p))h(p) = G(h(p)) - \frac{1}{p} .$$

Since G is a concave function, we deduce that

$$G(h(p)) + G'(h(p))(\bar{h} - h(p)) \ge G(\bar{h})$$

and $G'(\bar{h}) \ge G'(h(p))$, for every $\bar{h} \le h(p)$ with $G(\bar{h})=y$. It follows that

$$\frac{1}{p} + G'(\bar{h})\bar{h} \ge \frac{1}{p} + G'(h(p))\bar{h} =$$

$$G(h(p)) - G'(h(p))h(p) + G'(h(p))\bar{h} \ge G(\bar{h}) = y$$

Using

$$[G^{-1}(y)]' = \frac{1}{G'(\bar{h})}$$

we obtain (23) , where the equality is true only at h(p).

Using now (23) , we deduce

$$\lambda_1 + \lambda_2 \le \frac{v^*}{p^*}\frac{1}{\alpha}[G^{-1}(y_0)]^{1/\alpha}(k^d)^{-1/\alpha}\left\{(1-\alpha)\frac{p^*}{r_0} - (1-\alpha)^2\frac{p^*}{r_0}\right\} - \alpha - \frac{k^d}{r_0}$$

$$= v^*\,[\,G^{-1}(y_0)/k^d\,]^{1/\alpha}\,\frac{1-\alpha}{r_0} - \alpha - \frac{k^d}{r_0} =$$

$$v^*\,[\,\ell^d / k^d\,]\,\frac{1-\alpha}{r_0} - \alpha - \frac{k^d}{r_0}$$

From (8) and (9) follows

$$\frac{(p - \rho \ell)\, F_\ell\, (\ell,k)}{(p - \rho \ell)\, F_k\, (\ell,k)} = \frac{V(\ell,k)}{r} \Leftrightarrow \frac{\alpha k}{(1-\alpha)\ell} = \frac{pF(\ell,k) - rk - 1}{r\ell}$$

As we have argued at the beginning to chapter 3, the value added $V(\ell,k)$ realized by the firm in a non-Walrasian equilibrium is equal to the Walrasian value added V^*, thus

$$\lambda_1 + \lambda_2 = V^* \frac{\alpha \ell^d}{p_0 y_0 - r_0 k^s - 1} - \alpha - \frac{k^d}{r_0} = \alpha - \alpha - \frac{k^d}{r_0} < 0.$$

This shows $\lambda_1 < 0$ and $\lambda_2 < 0$, thus (r_0, y_0, p) is an asymptotically stable equilibrium with respect to the system (VS.a).

(VS.b) : In the proof of Proposition 4 we had shown that the Jacobian matrix

$$Df = \begin{pmatrix} \frac{\partial f_1}{\partial r} & \frac{\partial f_1}{\partial y} \\ \frac{\partial f_2}{\partial r} & \frac{\partial f_2}{\partial y} \end{pmatrix} = \begin{pmatrix} a_{11} & a_{12} \\ a_{21} & a_{22} \end{pmatrix}$$

of (22) has negative determinant at the Walrasian equilibrium (r^*, y^*, p^*). Thus we can apply the Poincaré-Hopf theorem to conclude that the same Jacobian has positive determinant at the non-Walrasian equilibrium (r_0, y_0, p^*). As in the proof of Proposition 4, the eigenvalues of $Df(r_0, y_0, p^*)$ are the solutions to

$$\lambda^2 - \lambda \left(\frac{\partial f_1}{\partial r} + \frac{\partial f_2}{\partial y} \right) + \frac{\partial f_1}{\partial r} \cdot \frac{\partial f_2}{\partial y} - \frac{\partial f_1}{\partial y} \cdot \frac{\partial f_2}{\partial r} = 0$$

The associated discriminant is

$$\Delta = \left(\frac{\partial f_1}{\partial r} - \frac{\partial f_2}{\partial y} \right)^2 + 4 \frac{\partial f_1}{\partial y} \cdot \frac{\partial f_2}{\partial r} > 0$$

as in the proof of Proposition 4. Therefore both eigenvalues are real-valued and distinct. Moreover,

$$\lambda_1 + \lambda_2 = \mathrm{tr}(Df) = \frac{\partial f_1}{\partial r} + \frac{\partial f_2}{\partial y} = - \frac{k^d}{r} + \left(\frac{V^*}{p^*} \cdot \frac{1}{F_\ell} - 1 \right) .$$

As before the value added $V(\ell,k)$ realized in a non-Walrasian equilibrium is equal to the Walrasian value added V^*. Thus we can invoke (8) to conclude $(V^*/p^*)(1/F_\ell)-1 \le 0$, and therefore $\lambda_1 + \lambda_2 < 0$. Since $\lambda_1 \lambda_2 = \det(Df(r_0, y_0, p^*)) > 0$, this shows $\lambda_1 < 0$ and $\lambda_2 < 0$. Thus

(r_0, Y_0, p^*) is an asymptotically stable equilibrium with respect to the system (VS.b) . ∎

We can illustrate the above stability result recurring to Figure 5 and completing it with arrows indicating the directions of change of r and y, according to the definition of the regions A, B, C and D. This is shown in Figure 8.

We finally come to the stability analysis of dynamic equilibria with respect to the full system (D.1)-(D.3),(E.1)-(E.3). To prepare this we first observe the following fact. Let A' denote a 3x3 matrix whose second and third row coincide,

$$A' = \begin{pmatrix} a_{11} & a_{12} & a_{13} \\ a_{21} & a_{22} & a_{23} \\ a_{21} & a_{22} & a_{23} \end{pmatrix}$$

Since $\det(A') = 0$, one of its eigenvalues, say λ'_3, is zero. Developping $\det(A'-\lambda' I) = 0$, one can see that the other two eigenvalues λ'_1 and λ'_2 have to satisfy the equation

$$\lambda^2 - \lambda(a_{11} + a_{22} + a_{33}) + a_{11}a_{22} - a_{12}a_{21} + a_{11}a_{23} - a_{21}a_{13} = 0.$$

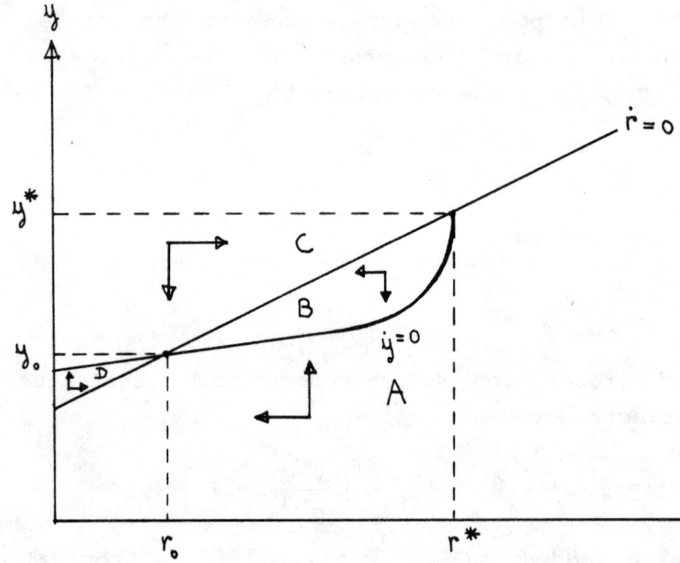

Figure 8: Stability of the non-Walrasian equilibrium (r_0, Y_0, p^*) with the respect to real system

Consider next the submatrix of A′

$$A = \begin{pmatrix} a_{11} & a_{12} \\ a_{21} & a_{22} \end{pmatrix}$$

Then the eigenvalues λ_1 and λ_2 of A satisfy

$$\lambda^2 - \lambda(a_{11} + a_{22}) + a_{11}a_{22} - a_{12}a_{21} = 0.$$

Comparing this with the equation for λ_1' and λ_2' yields

$$\left.\begin{aligned} \lambda_1' + \lambda_2' &= a_{11} + a_{22} + a_{23} = \lambda_1 + \lambda_2 + a_{23} \\ \lambda_1' \lambda_2' &= a_{11}\, a_{22} - a_{12}a_{21} + a_{11}a_{23} - a_{21}a_{13} = \\ &\qquad \lambda_1\lambda_2 + a_{11}a_{23} - a_{21}a_{13} \end{aligned}\right\} \qquad (24)$$

Regarding the stability analysis of the non-Walrasian equilibria, this is a complex issue since due to Proposition 3 there is a continuity of them. Intuitively it should be clear that, starting from any point (r_0, y_0, p_0) of the manifold E of the non-Walrasian equilibria, any arbitrary small disturbance of the system to some point $(\hat{r}, \hat{y}, \hat{p}) = (r_0+\Delta r, y_0+\Delta y, p_0+\Delta p) \notin E$ will set off a dynamics for which there is no reason to expect that the system returns to the very point (r_0, y_0, p_0) to which the disturbance was applied. Indeed, $(r_0+\Delta r, y_0+\Delta y, p_0+\Delta p)$ could have equally been obtained from some disturbance applied to some $(r_1, y_1, p_1) \in E$ arbitrarily close to (r_0, y_0, p_0). But then, to which of the points (r_0, y_0, p_0) and (r_1, y_1, p_1) (if at all) should the system move to, considering that both of them are equilibria? All we can hope for is that the system returns to *some* point in E. Although our intuition suggests that that be the case, we have not succeeded so far to demonstrate this conjecture.

Although it is clear that no point in the manifold of non-Walrasian equilibria can be asymptotically stable, (non-asymptotic) stability holds as a consequence of Lemma 5:

<u>Proposition 4</u>: The non-Walrasian equilibrium (r_0, y_0, p^*) is stable with respect to the dynamic system (D.1)-(D.3),(E.1)-(E.3).

<u>Proof.</u>: The discussion preceding Proposition 3 has shown that in some

neighborhood of (r_0,y_0,p^*) the system (D.1)-(D.3) becomes (D.1)-(D.2)′, which is

$$\dot{r} = f_1(r,y,p) = k^d(r,p,y) - k^s$$
$$\dot{y} = f_2(r,y,p) = c - y$$
$$\dot{p} = f_2(r,y,p)$$

where c is either

$$c^a = \frac{V^*}{p}\,\ell^d(r,p,y) + \frac{r}{p}\,k^d(r,p,y) + \frac{1}{p}$$

or

$$c^b = \frac{V^*}{p}\,F(.,k^s)^{-1}(y) + \frac{r}{p}\,k^s + \frac{1}{p}\,.$$

If $c = c^a$, then (D.1)-(D.2)′ gives rise to a 3x3 Jacobian matrix A′ whose second and third row coincide and whose elements a_{11}, a_{12}, a_{21} and a_{22} are as in part (VS.a) of the proof of Lemma 5 (and with p in place of p^*). Moreover

$$a_{13} = \frac{\partial k^d}{\partial p} = (1-\alpha)\frac{y}{r}$$

$$a_{23} = \frac{\partial c^a}{\partial p} = -\frac{c^a}{p} + \frac{V^*}{p}\frac{\partial \ell^d}{\partial p} + \frac{r}{p}\frac{\partial k^d}{\partial p}$$

In a point of equilibrium, a_{23} becomes by (11) and (10),

$$a_{23} = -\frac{y}{p} - \frac{V^*}{p}\,[G^{-1}(y)]^{1/\alpha}\,\frac{(1-\alpha)^2}{\alpha}\,(k^s)^{-1/\alpha}\,\frac{y}{r} + (1-\alpha)\frac{y}{p}$$
$$= -\frac{y}{p}\left\{\alpha + \frac{V^*}{r}\,[G^{-1}(y)]^{1/\alpha}\,\frac{(1-\alpha)^2}{\alpha}\,(k^s)^{-1/\alpha}\right\} < 0.$$

Using the expressions found in part (VS.a) of the proof of Lemma 5, we have that in equilibrium

$$a_{11}a_{23} - a_{21}a_{13}$$
$$= \alpha\,\frac{yk^s}{rp} + \frac{V^*}{r}[G^{-1}(y)]^{1/\alpha}\,\frac{(1-\alpha)^2}{\alpha}\,(k^s)^{(\alpha-1)/\alpha}\,\frac{y}{rp}$$
$$- \frac{V^*}{r}\,[G^{-1}(y)]^{1/\alpha}\,\frac{(1-\alpha)^2}{\alpha}\,(k^s)^{(\alpha-1)/\alpha}\,\frac{y}{r^2} = \frac{\alpha y k^s}{rp} > 0.$$

By (24), the eigenvalues of A′ satisfy $\lambda_3' = 0$ and

$$\lambda_1' + \lambda_2' = \lambda_1 + \lambda_2 + a_{23}$$

$$\lambda_1'\lambda_2' = \lambda_1\lambda_2 + a_{11}a_{23} - a_{21}a_{13}$$

By Lemma 5, $\lambda_1<0$ and $\lambda_2<0$. Thus we conclude $\lambda_1' + \lambda_2' < 0$ and $\lambda_1'\lambda_2' > 0$ which implies $\lambda_1' < 0$ and $\lambda_2' < 0$.

If $c = c^b$, (D.1) - (D.2)' implies

$$a_{11} = \frac{\partial k^d}{\partial r} = -\frac{k^d}{r}, \quad a_{21} = \frac{\partial c^b}{\partial r} = \frac{k^s}{p}, \quad a_{13} = \frac{\partial k^d}{\partial p} = (1-\alpha)\frac{y}{p}$$

$$a_{23} = \frac{\partial c^b}{\partial p} = -\frac{c^b}{p} \quad .$$

In an equilibrium this yields $a_{23} = -\frac{y}{p} < 0$ and $a_{11}a_{23} - a_{21}a_{13} = \frac{\alpha yk}{rp} > 0$. Since by Lemma 5 $\lambda_1 < 0$ and $\lambda_2 < 0$, it follows from (24) that $\lambda_1' < 0$ and $\lambda_2' < 0$.■

<u>Proposition 5</u>: There exists a neighborhood of (r_0,y_0,p^*) relative to the manifold E such that any equilibrium in that neighborhood is stable with respect to the system (D.1) - (D.3) , (E.1) - (E.3).

<u>Proof</u>.: We have shown in the proof of Proposition 4 that in some neighborhood of (r_0,y_0,p^*) relative E any point in that neighborhood implies a Jacobian for which the eigenvalue λ_3' is zero. The eigenvalues λ_1' and λ_2' relative to the point (r_0,y_0,p^*) had satisfied:

$$\lambda_1' + \lambda_2' = \text{tr } A' < 0$$

$$\lambda_1'\lambda_2' = \det A + \det B > 0$$

where

$$B = \begin{pmatrix} a_{11} & a_{13} \\ a_{21} & a_{23} \end{pmatrix}$$

By continuity of the functions trace and determinant, they preserve their respective signs in a suited neighborhood of (r_0,y_0,p^*) . Thus in that neighborhood all points give rise to eigenvalues $\lambda_1' < 0$ and $\lambda_2' < 0$. Together with $\lambda_3' = 0$, this proves the assertion. ■

4. Conclusion

In this paper we have studied the dynamic behaviour of a labour managed economy. To this end we have set up a continuous time dynamic system specifying the movement in prices and sales expectations of firms. We have shown that this system gives rise to a continuum of dynamic equilibria which we have distinguished in non-Walrasian equilibria and a Walrasian equilibrium. In the non-Walrasian equilibria the firm has pessimistic expectations regarding its sales and thus economic activity is depressed relative to the Walrasian equilibrium.

The stability analysis of the non-Walrasian equilibria has been complex since they constitute a smooth manifold. This has implied that any non-Walrasian equilibrium cannot be asymptotically stable in the traditional sense. We have shown however that if the output price is fixed at its Walrasian value, the corresponding non-Walrasian equilibrium is asymptotically stable with respect to the truncated dynamic system. This is relevant for labour managed economies where consumption goods prices are frozen by the government as has indeed been the case, for example, in Yugoslavia in the '70s.

We have shown moreover that, with respect to the full dynamic system, the non-Walrasian equilibria under consideration are stable (although not asymptotically stable). This means that, starting from any point in a suitable neighborhood of the manifold of non-Walrasian equilibria, the system remains in that neighborhood. It does not mean that the system actually converges to some point on the manifold. This would be a stronger assertion the correctness of which is yet unclear.

A crucial assumption has been that workers continue to believe that they will be paid the value added per unit of labour belonging to the Walrasian equilibrium even if the economy is outside of Walrasian equilibrium. This assumption has been adopted mainly to reduce the complexity of the system from four to three dimensions. The analysis would continue to hold even if workers are allowed to change their expectations as long as these changes are slow enough. It is clear, however, that this is a delicate point and further work on this topic is called for to assess more reliably the dynamic behaviour of a labour managed economy.

References

Bartlett, W. and G. Weinrich (1992): "Instability and Indexation in a Labour-Managed Economy", Advances in the Economic Analysis of Participatory and Labor-Managed Firms, Vol. 4, pp. 93-112.

Brock, W.A. and A.G. Malliaris (1989): Differential Equations, Stability and Chaos in Dynamic Economics, Amsterdam: North-Holland.

Domar, E. (1966): "The Soviet Collective Farm as a Producer Cooperative", American Economic Review, 56(4), pp 737-757.

Drèze, J.H. (1985): "Labour Management and General Equilibrium", Advances in the Economic Analysis of Participatory and Labor-Managed Firms, Vol.1, pp. 3-20.

Drèze, J.H. (1989): Labour Management, Contracts and Capital Markets, Oxford, Basil Blackwell.

Guillemin, V. and A. Pollack (1974): Differential Topology, Englewood Cliffs, N.J.: Prentice-Hall.

Meade, J.E. (1972): "The Theory of Labour-Managed Firms and of Profit Sharing", The Economic Journal, pp. 402-428.

Milnor, J. (1972): Topology from the Differentiable Viewpoint, Charlottesville: University Press of Virginia.

Saldanha, F.B. (1989): "Fixprice Analysis of Labor-Managed Economies", Journal of Comparative Economics, pp. 227-253.

Vanek, J. (1970): The General Theory of Labour-Managed Market Economies, Ithaca, Cornell University Press.

Varian,. H.R. (1977): "Non-Walrasian Equilibria", Econometrica, Vol. 45, pp. 573-590.

Ward, B (1958): "The Firm in Illyria: Market Syndacalism", American Economic Review, 48, pp. 566-589.

Weinrich, G.(1992): "Instability of General Equilibrium in a Labour Managed Economy", Contributi di Ricerca in Matematica, Economia Matematica ed Econometria, Anno 1992 No. 7, Università Cattolica d.S.C. di Milano, forthcoming in Journal of Comparative Economics.

ENDOGENOUS CYCLES, INCREASING RETURNS AND GLOBAL BIFURCATIONS IN AN IMPERFECTLY COMPETITIVE ECONOMY[1]

Jean Pierre DRUGEON

Laboratoire M.A.D. ; Université de Paris 1-Panthéon-Sorbonne ; 90, rue de Tolbiac ; 75634 Paris Cédex 13 ; FRANCE

1. INTRODUCTION

The purpose of this paper is firstly to analyze the possibility and secondly to characterize the consequences of aggregate externalities of increasing returns to scale in a decentralized growth model specialized to incorporate aggregate externalities of stock which are intended to stylize in a convenient way natural limits on expansion on the economy.
The present model starts from the analysis of HAMMOUR [1988] but is concerned with search for an integrated theory of business cycles and economic growth. Its originality lies in the fact that it is explicitly based on a nonlinear perspective of economic dynamics. In other words, it tries to establish a tentative articulation between the short run and the long run that hinges on increasing returns to scale and indeterminacy — local or global — of equilibrium.

During many decades, the role of increasing returns to scale has been quite completely ignored or even dismissed by what is commonly refered as *mainstream economics*. This absence of any explicit consideration was partly due to the intricate character of their incorporation in general equilibrium settings — mainly because of the associated non-convexities —, but also related to a kind of intellectual *cumfort* that is traditionnally confered by the commonly used *well-behaved functional forms* with regular properties.
However, this state of the play has been questioned since the beginning of the eighties by, first, the pioneering article of WEITZMAN [1982] that has profoundly renewed the traditional ways of understanding the functioning of the labor market by conceiving this market with considerations based on increasing returns to scale and, secondly, by the celebrated model of ROMER [1986] that has reconciled the neoclassical theory of economic growth with the possibility of increasing returns to scale at the social level.
Although the preceeding parallel seems quite revelant, it should in fact be considered as being of a rather limited interest since the effective influence of these highly novative contributions in their respective areas — roughly, short-run fluctuations and long-run growth — is far from being the same.

---

[1]Preliminary versions of the present contribution have been presented at the first Summer School of the European Economic Association held at Lisbon in September 1990 and at the IInd Workshop on Nonlinear Dynamics in Economics held at the Certosa di Pontignano in Sienna in May 1991. I would like to thank for useful comments and suggestions A. d'AUTUME, A. CHENCINER, P.Y. GEOFFARD, J. GLACHANT, F. PORTIER, S. REBELO, P. REICHLIN, D. VERNER, M. WOODFORD and one of the referees. I am particularly grateful to B. WIGNIOLLE for a careful reading and for many improvements. The responsability for any errors is mine.

First, there has been a great development of contributions that have been concerned with, in the line of WEITZMAN [1982], the essential role that might be played in short-run fluctuations by the occurrence of increasing returns to scale. Seminal papers in this short-run perspective are, e.g., the ones by KIYOTAKI [1988], HOWITT & MCAFEE [1988], HAMMOUR [1988], DIAMOND & FUDENBERG [1989] or BOLDRIN, KIYOTAKI & WRIGHT [1992].

Briefly, the proof of the connection between the occurrence of increasing returns to scale and the indeterminacy of equilibrium can admittedly be considered as the strongest result of this whole class of models. In fact, all these contributions depart only from the ones which are more standardly used by the very proof of the multiplicity of equilibria that they allow. This should be perceived as an essential advantage of this approach in that, by the sole adoption of an assumption that, from an empirical point of view, seems to be an essential feature of short-run fluctuations[2] , these models might give rise to the possibility of *endogenous dynamics*[3] and then provide a consistent *alternative* theory of short-run fluctuations. At the opposite, the so-called *new models of endogenous growth* that have grown exponentially in the recent years, have not relied — from a dynamical point of view — to the *increasing returns feature* of ROMER [1986].

In fact, they have commonly been essentially interested in the other *message* that was still implicit in ROMER [1986], the possibility of the occurrence of a growth process at a constant rate in the long run without requiring any resort to ususal mathematical artefacts such as exogenous technical progress or assumed positive rates of population growth.

As ROMER [1989] remarked, the abandonment of increasing returns to scale should be considered as harmful since the examination of long-run data seems to favour the *increasing rates of growth* thesis. From a technical point of view, the very abandonment of the original motivation of the understanding of the close connection between increasing returns to scale and increasing rates of growth should be also perceived as prejudicious to the actual content of the new growth literature. In fact, it can be shown that the assumption of increasing returns might lead to a finite set of multiple equilibrium-paths which do possess specific properties and can be pareto-ranked. Apart from a very limited set of examples in this huge literature — namely AZARIADIS & DRAZEN [1990] and some related contributions —, all the new growth models restrain to the stability of the unique constant growth rate.

Finally, it should be noticed that some related models which are more closely concerned with the problem of economic development do exhibit the multiplicity result in the long run[4] They are of interest by the renewal of old ideas rigorously formalized that they often provide, but they usually refer to settings that depart too strongly from the usual standard models of business cycle and economic growth to really allow for comparison and, then, for the generality of the results.

This set of general considerations provides further motivation for an improved understanding of the role that increasing returns to scale should play in a *integrated nonlinear theory of business cycles and economic growth*. In fact, a similar interest in a global understanding of short-run fluctuations and long-run paths belongs to the current agenda of research of the Real Business

---

[2]See, among others, HALL [1988].

[3]See, e.g., DIAMOND & FUDENBERG [1989] or HAMMOUR [1988].

[4]E.g., MATSUYAMA [1991].

Cycles literature[5] but is admittedly still in its very enfancy. The first notable contribution in this line was SHLEIFER [1986], that is often considered as remaining the more convincing and thorough model in this vein, while two related ones in the line of this celebrated paper are the preliminary work of AGHION & HOWITT [1988] and CORRIVEAU [1988] ; although these are essentially growth models in that they do not provide any convincing explanation for the cycle that appears to be a mere curiosity of their structure.

In this line, the present contribution starts from a short-run perspective, but does explicitly incorporate aggregate externalities of stock which mainly make sense in the long run. It first establishes the existence of multiple stationary equilibria, before proving the possibility of endogenous fluctuations from a local point of view. At this stage, it is merely in position to formulate conjectures about both the long run and the global dynamics at the large from the finite set of stationary equilibria.
Secondly, it establishes the possibility of a complete understanding of the global dynamics in a special case where these latter ones are of the *conservative* variety.[6] It is essentially similar in this aspect to the MATSUYAMA [1991]'s sectoral adjustment-industrialization model but enlarges his results from three essential points of view :

(i) It is not crucially based on assumptions about *irreversibility of career decisions* which gives rise to the possibility of a one state variable — whose motion does also exhibit highly specific microfoundations — two-dimensional system with an associated jump variable or about nonsense values for the discount rate.

(ii) It proves that, contrary to MATSUYAMA [1991]'s assertion, local and global bifurcations results — hence the short run and the long run — are closely connected — a related point is made by CHIAPPORI & GUESNERIE [1989].

(iii) It restrains to a commonly used and admittedly very general model. This should imply that the present results do correspond to an unusual, but effective possibility in a standard economic setting.

The plan of the contribution is as follows : a general model is fully specified in 2, the equilibrium is realized in 3, local short-run dynamics are studied in 4 and global dynamics are characterized in 5.

2. THE MODEL

The basic setting is the general equilibrium model under monopolistic competition of KIYOTAKI [1988] modified to infinite horizon both for the identical households and for the firms, each of these latter ones producing a specific product. The following analysis will first describe their static program in terms of consumption of each good before studying their intertemporal behavior. Hence, it is assumed that a *non-entry condition* applies at each period, so that the number of firms — denoted as F — is fixed. This latter one is finally supposed to be sufficiently large so that each product is an imperfect substitute for the remaining ones.

[5] See, e.g., KING & REBELO [1988].

[6] The classical reference in economics for such systems is GOODWIN [1967].

2.1. HOUSEHOLDS

2.1.1. PREFERENCES

In the sake for simplicity, the number N of households in the economy will henceforth be normalized to 1. More specifically :

ASSUMPTION C1 : The global consumption index of the representative consumer — denoted as c — is a C.E.S. function of the DIXIT & STIGLITZ [1977]'s variety given by :

$$c = F^{1/(1-\epsilon)}\left(\sum_{f=1}^{F} c_f^{(\epsilon-1)/\epsilon}\right)^{\epsilon/(\epsilon-1)}, \tag{1}$$

with c_f as the level of consumption of the fth product and ϵ as the elasticity of consumption between the different goods.

Taking the vector $\{P_f\}_{f=1}^{F}$ of sectoral prices as given, the representative household will characterize his optimal consumption for each good by minimizing his total expenditure according to his preferences as specified in (1). The first order conditions of this optimization problem produce his demand for consumption of a good $f \in [1, F]$:

$$c_f = \left(\frac{P_f}{P}\right)^{-\epsilon} \frac{c}{F}, \tag{3}$$

with $P = \left(F^{-1}\sum_{f=1}^{F} P_f^{\epsilon-1}\right)^{1/(\epsilon-1)}$ as the global price index.

2.1.2. INTERTEMPORAL BEHAVIOR

The representative household solves a problem of the RAMSEY [1928] type. It is assumed that each household in the economy supplies his labor endowment — denoted as $z(t)$ at time t — with an infinite elasticity up to an upper bound z_M : $z(t) \leq z_M, \forall t \in [0, +\infty)$.

The level of his real wealth at time t is denoted as $H(t)$. Its law of motion should be understood as the household's intertemporal budget constraint :

$$\dot{H}(t) = r(t)H(t) + \omega(t)z(t) - c(t), \tag{3}$$

with $r(t)$ and $\omega(t) = w(t)/P(t)$ respectively the real interest rate and the real wage rate.

The felicity function of the representative consumer can be characterized as follows

ASSUMPTION C3 : The preferences of the representative consumer verify :

$$U : \mathbb{R}_+ \longrightarrow \mathbb{R}_+, c \longmapsto U(c), U_c(c) > 0, U_{cc}(c) < 0,$$
$$U_c(c)/U_{cc}(c) < \infty, \forall c \in [0, +\infty).$$

Under assumptions C1-3, the household's decision problem at time t will be to choose a time-path of consumption $\{c(t)\}_{t=0}^{+\infty}$ and wealth $\{H(t)\}_{t=0}^{+\infty}$ so as to solve the following program :

$$\begin{aligned} &\max_{\{c(x)\}} \int_t^{+\infty} U(c(x)) \exp(-\rho x) \\ &\text{s.t. } (3) \text{ and } H(t) = H_0, \end{aligned} \tag{P(c)}$$

taking as given the time-path of $\{r(t)\}_{t=0}^{+\infty}$, $\{\omega(t)\}_{t=0}^{+\infty}$, with $0 < \rho < 1$ as his rate of time preference. Defining $\zeta(c) = -U_c(c)/(U_{cc}(c)c)$ as the inverse of the negative of the intertemporal elasticity of substitution of the consumer, the necessary and sufficient conditions in order for a maximum are given by (3),

$$\dot{c}(t) \,/\, c(t) = \zeta(c(t))\,(r(t) - \rho), \tag{4}$$

and $\lim_{t \to +\infty} \exp(-r(t))\lambda(t)H(t) = 0$, with $\lambda(t)$ as the value at time t of the *shadow price* of consumption associated to the constraint (3) in (P(c)).

2.2. Entrepreneurs and Firms

2.2.1. Preferences

Firms accumulate capital by the use of a set of goods. This latter one is characterized by :

Assumption T1 : The firms total demand of goods is described by a C.E.S. function of all the products $f \in [1, F]$:

$$\gamma = F^{1/(1-\epsilon)} \left(\sum_{f=1}^{F} \gamma_f^{(\epsilon-1)/\epsilon} \right)^{\epsilon/(\epsilon-1)}, \tag{5}$$

with γ_f as the firm's demand for accumulation of the fth good.

Subject to a given accumulation expenditure γ, the optimal demand of each product by the firm derives as :

$$\gamma_f = \left(\frac{P_f}{P} \right)^{-\epsilon} \frac{\gamma}{F}. \tag{6}$$

2.2.2. Intertemporal Value Optimization

Although the model, from an intertemporal point of view, should merely be considered as a *classic* decentralized one, assumption C2 on the strict upper-boundedness of labor supply, exhibits specific properties once incorporated in a *general equilibrium* setting. Indeed, if an assumption about potential connections between the complementarities of factors in the production function and the nature of the returns to scale is added to this first scheme, the binding of the constraint in assumption C2 will reveal to be essential in the nature of the dynamics.

2.2.2.1. Profit Maximization

Assumption T2 : The firm has access at each period of time to a production function with the following properties :

(i) $F : \mathbb{R}_+ \times \mathbb{R}_+, \longrightarrow \mathbb{R}_+, (k, z) \longmapsto F(k, q(\omega)z), F_k > 0, F_z > 0, F_{kk} < 0,$
$F_{zz} < 0, F_{kz} > 0, F(0,0) = 0, \lim_{k \to \infty} F_k = 0, \lim_{k \to 0} F_k = +\infty, \lim_{z \to 0} F_z = +\infty,$

with $q : \mathbb{R}_+ \longrightarrow \mathbb{R}_+, \omega \longmapsto q(\omega), q_\omega > 0, q_{\omega\omega} > 0, \forall \omega \in [0, \omega_c),$
$q_{\omega\omega} < 0, \forall \omega \in [\omega_c, +\infty),$

(ii) $F(\Upsilon k, \Upsilon q(\omega)z) > \Upsilon F(k, q(\omega)z)$, for $\Upsilon > 1$, with ω_c in assumption T2 (i) a a unique *critical level* of the real wage rate.

REMARK 1 : As this will be shown in the subsequent analysis, assumption T2 (ii) should be interpreted as the holding of increasing returns to scale at the firm level up to the binding of the constraint established by assumption C2. ◇

The incorporation of the level of the real wage rate ω in the production function refers to the *qualitative* nature of labor supply. It should merely be understood here as a technical device used to fix the real wage rate at a level that departs from the *walrasian* one.
For simplicity, the following *modified* COBB-DOUGLAS formulation will from now on be adopted for $F(\cdot)$ under assumption T2 :

$$F(k, q(\omega)z) \stackrel{\text{def}}{=} k^{\alpha}\left(q(\omega)z\right)^{\beta} - \varsigma Y; \varsigma > 0, 0 < \alpha < 1, 0 < \beta < 1, 1 < \alpha + \beta, \tag{7}$$

where ς is a positive parameter that is supposed to give the size of an *external diseconomy of expansion* induced by the level of the gross national product Y. The intuitive idea behind this assumption could be stated as follows : certain kinds of ressources, essential for the capital accumulation process, might necessitate more time for being accumulated than this latter one. Thus, at each point of time, the bigger the accumulation process, the higher the induced gross national product, and finally the stronger the prevailing external *diseconomies of scale*. The essential argument is that such a specification seems to be more appealing from a long-run perspective — agents are faced with a kind of *finite ressources constraint*.
Taking as given its capital stock, assuming that each firm will select an identical amount of employment — without loss of generality, only symmetric equilibria will be considered in the sequel —, the firm will first have to solve the following *instantaneous optimization problem* :

$$\begin{aligned} &\operatorname*{Max}_{\{z,w\}} \left(\frac{P_f}{P}\right) \mathcal{P}(k_f, q(\omega)z_f) - \omega_f z_f \\ &\text{s.t. assumption T1, } (2) \text{ and } (6), z_f \leq z_M, \end{aligned} \tag{P(f_s)}$$

with $z_M = Z_M/F$ and $\mathcal{P}(k_f, \omega, z_f) \stackrel{\text{def}}{=} F(k_f, q(\omega)z_f) - \omega z_f, \forall f \in [1, F]$. The first order conditions with respect to the amount of employment and nominal wage setting's decisions of the firm derive as :

$$\begin{aligned} q(\omega)\left(\frac{P_f}{P}\right)(1-\epsilon)\, F_z(k_f, q(\omega)z_f) - \omega + \eta \leq 0 \\ q_\omega(\omega)(1-\epsilon)\left(\frac{P_f}{P}\right) P^{-1} z_f F_z(k_f, q(\omega)z_f) - z_f = 0, \end{aligned} \tag{8}$$

with η as the costate variable associated to the constraint of assumption C2 in (P(f_s)) and where the first component of (8) holds with equality if and only if $\eta = 0$. Intuitively, the marginal efficiency associated to a supplementary unit of the wage rate equals its mean efficiency.

LEMMA 1. *Defining* $\varepsilon_{q(\omega)/\omega} = q_\omega(\omega)\omega \;/\; q(\omega)$ as the elasticity of the «quality» of labor with respect to the real wage rate, the optimal real wage rate $\widehat{\omega}$ associated to (P(f_s)) is is given by $\varepsilon_{q(\widehat{\omega})/\widehat{\omega}} = 1$.

PROOF : Immediate from $\left(\mathrm{P}(f_s)\right)$ and (8). $\square$

Owing to assumption T2 (ii), the implicit function theorem applies for $q(\cdot)$ on $\mathbb{R}_+ \setminus \{\omega_c\}$, so that the *unitary elasticity condition* from lemma 1 defines an optimal wage rate denoted as $\widehat{\omega}$.

COROLLARY 1. *If $z = z_M = Z_M/F$ holds, a given firm trying to take advantage of the complementarity assumption* T2 (i) *between the production factors, that is of increasing returns — assumption* T2 (ii) *—, will be required to increase its nominal wage to maintain the holding of* (8), *so that the real wage rate will depart from* $\widehat{\omega}$.

Recalling the assumed — T2 (ii) — holding of increasing returns to scale at the firm level, it is of interest to further consider the *marginal properties* of the instantanteous profit function $\mathcal{P}(k, q(\omega)z)$.[7] Taking account of the first component of (8) and of $(\mathrm{P}f_s)$, it is possible to derive what should be refered as a *measure of profit incentives* for the firm :

$$\mathcal{P}_k\left(k_f, q(\omega)z_f\right) = \epsilon\alpha k_f^{\alpha-1}\left(q(\omega)z_f\right)^{\beta}\left(\frac{P_f}{P}\right)\left(1-\epsilon^{-1}\right)^{-1}. \tag{9}$$

PROPOSITION 1. *Under assumptions* C1-3 *and* T1-2, *an individual firm has no «local incentives» to unilateraly increase its holding of capital.*

PROOF : It suffices to characterize the properties of $\mathcal{P}_k\left(k_f, q(\omega)z_f\right)$. They can be derived from the total differenciation of (9) with respect to time :

$$\frac{d\mathcal{P}_k}{dk} = \left(1-\epsilon^{-1}\right)P\left(\frac{(\alpha+\beta)-(\epsilon/(\epsilon-1))}{-\beta+(\epsilon/(\epsilon-1))}\right), \tag{10}$$

The R.H.S. of (10) must be negative owing to assumption T2 for admissible values of ϵ. $\square$

Hence, the existence of increasing returns to scale does not allow for the convexity of the *profit function* with respect to the stock of capital held by the firm.

2.2.2.2. INTERTEMPORAL ENTREPRENEUR'S PROBLEM

To characterize their optimal time-path in terms of capital accumulation, firms will have to intertemporally maximize a criterion — based on their previous instantaneous profit maximization — with the following features :

ASSUMPTION T3 : Firms will take into account a *cost function* $J(\cdot)$:

$$J(\cdot) : \mathbb{R} \times \mathbb{R}_+ \longrightarrow \mathbb{R}_+; (\gamma, K) \longmapsto J(\gamma, K); J_\gamma > 0, J_{\gamma\gamma} > 0, J_K > 0, J(0, K) = 0$$
$$J(\gamma, K) > 0, \forall (\gamma, K) \in \mathbb{R} \times \mathbb{R}_{++},$$

where γ denotes the rate of capital accumulation.

[7] Profitability properties under increasing returns to scale are more generaly characterized in HAMMOUR [1990].

REMARK 2 : The convexity of $J(\cdot)$ with respect to γ can be proved to be a necessary condition for the concavity of the maximand of the intertemporal value maximization problem. ◊

The cost function $J(\cdot)$ refers to the existence of internal as well as to external — market structures, finite stocks of non durable goods — problems. In the present imperfectly competitive setting, the latter one seems more appealing and hence will be retained in the sequel.
The other argument of $J(\cdot)$ provides a stylization of the existence of *negative aggregate externalities of stocks*. Such a class of phenomena makes more sense in the long run than in the immediate short run where firms cannot be seriously supposed to instantaneously perceive these *diseconomies of expansion* : their role will indeed be proved to be essential in the long-run dynamics characterized in 5.
In order for tractablility, but also to provide a convenient measure of the strength of the aforementioned effects, the subsequent analysis restrains to a functional form for $J(\cdot)$:

$$J(\gamma, K) = \upsilon(\gamma) + \psi K\gamma, \upsilon_\gamma > 0, \upsilon_{\gamma\gamma} > 0, \psi > 0. \tag{11}$$

The *gross* nature adopted for the formulation of the adjustment cost function (T3) allows a simple law of motion for the capital stock :

$$\dot{k}(t) = \gamma(t). \tag{12}$$

Assumption T3, (11) and (12) complete the characterization of the set over which the entrepreneur will maximize his criterion. Indeed, it will be to choose a time-path for the capital stock $\{k(t)\}_{t=0}^{+\infty}$ and for capital accumulation $\{\gamma(t)\}_{t=0}^{+\infty}$ so as to solve the following problem at date t :

$$\begin{aligned}&\underset{\{k(x)\}}{\text{Max}} \int_t^{+\infty} \Big(\mathcal{P}(x) - J(\gamma(x), K(x))\Big) \exp\Big(-\int_t^x r(v)dv\Big)dx \\ &\text{s.t. } (12) \text{ and } k(t) = k_0,\end{aligned} \tag{P(f_s)}$$

with $\mathcal{P}(x) \stackrel{\text{def}}{=} \mathcal{P}(k(x), K(x), z(x), Z(x))$, under assumptions C1-3 and T1-3 and given the time-path of the aggregate capital stock $\{K(t)\}_{t=0}^{+\infty}$. Owing to the PONTRYAGIN's maximum principle and having realized the substitution of the shadow price of capital, denoted as $\chi(t)$ at time t, it is posssible to assert that the necessary and sufficient conditions in order for a maximum are (12), $k(0) = k_0$ and :

$$\begin{aligned}&\dot{\gamma} = \left(\frac{J_\gamma(\gamma, K)}{J_{\gamma\gamma}(\gamma, K)}\right)\left(r - \frac{\mathcal{P}_k(k, K, z, Z) + J_{\gamma K}(\gamma, K)\Gamma}{J_\gamma(\gamma, K)}\right) \\ &\lim_{t\to\infty} \exp(-r(t))\chi(t)k(t) = 0.\end{aligned}$$

with $\Gamma(t)$ defined as the aggregate amount of capital accumulation at date t.

3. EQUILIBRIA

This section will first characterize the features of the static macroeconomic equilibrium and then complete the derivation of an autonomous dynamical system in $\mathbb{R}^2$.

3.1. Market Equilibria

Since all firms were assumed to be identical, they will all undertake similar employment decisions. Furthermore, they all face the same form of demand curve which can be derived by summing its consumption — (2) — and accumulation — (5) — components, taking into account the expression of the effective amount of this latter one, i.e. $J(\gamma, K)$ as given in (11). Thus, the total demand addressed to a firm f can be expressed as :

$$\mathcal{D}_f = \left(\frac{P_f}{P}\right)^{-\epsilon} \frac{C + J(\Gamma, K)}{F}, \tag{14}$$

with C and $J(\Gamma, K)$ as the respective amount of aggregate demand for consumption and aggregate effective demand for accumulation.

Proposition 2. *The market equilibrium of the economy characterized by assumptions* C1-3, T1-2 *holds under monopolistic competition.*

Proof : See Dixit & Stiglitz [1977] or Kiyotaki [1988]. □

The following assumption is going to substiantially simplifies the expression of the equilibrium.

Assumption T4 : Under assumptions C1-3 and T1-3, the equilibrium is symmetric and $P_{f'} = P_{f''}; \forall f', f'' \in [1, F]; f' \neq f''$.

The equilibrium amount of labor derives from the aggregate counterpart of (8) :

$$\begin{aligned} q(\omega)F_z(K, q(\omega)Z) - \omega + \eta &\leq 0 \\ q_\omega(\omega)ZP^{-1}F_w(K, q(\omega)Z) - Z &= 0, \end{aligned} \tag{8'}$$

where the first part of (8') is binding if and only if $\eta = 0$. Since from proposition 2, the instantaneous amount of capital will be identical across firms at the market equilibrium, i.e., $Fk_f = K$, the aggregate level of employment is given by :

$$Z = K^{\alpha/(1-\beta)}\left(\beta(q(\widehat{\omega}))^{\beta}\left((1-\epsilon^{-1})\widehat{\omega}F^{\alpha+\beta-1}\right)^{-1}\right)^{1/(1-\beta)}, \tag{15}$$

with $Fz_f = Z \leq Z_M$. The expression of $\mathcal{P}_K$ is going to allow to derive the same class of results of conclusions as in 2, but it characterizes *profitability properties* from an aggregate point of view.

Proposition 3. *Under assumptions* C1-3 *and* T1-4, *the economy is characterized by an increasing marginal profitability when* $Z < Z_M$ *and by a decreasing one as soon as this inequality does not hold and the constraint on employment is binding.*

Proof : Taking account of (8'), (15), assumptions C1-3 and T1-4 and (P(f_s)), the aggregate counterpart of the *private shadow return* derives as :

$$\begin{aligned} \mathcal{P}_K(K) &= \alpha K^{(\alpha/(1-\beta))-1}\left(\frac{\beta(q(\widehat{\omega}))^{\beta+1}}{(1-\epsilon^{-1})^{(1+\beta)/\beta}F^{\alpha+\beta-1}\widehat{\omega}}\right)^{\beta/(1+\beta)}, \forall K \in [0, K_M], \\ \mathcal{P}_K(K) &= \alpha K^{\alpha-1}K_M^{\alpha\beta/(1-\beta)}\left(\frac{\beta(q(\widehat{\omega}))^{\beta}(1-\epsilon^{-1})^{-1}}{(q(\widehat{\omega}))^{(1+\beta)/\beta}F^{(\alpha+\beta-1)/\beta}\widehat{\omega}}\right)^{\beta/(1+\beta)}, \forall K \in [K_M, +\infty), \end{aligned} \tag{16}$$

with

$$K_M \stackrel{\text{def}}{=} \left(Z_M \left(\beta (q(\widetilde{\omega}))^{\beta} \left((1-\epsilon^{-1}) F^{\alpha+\beta-1} \widehat{\omega} \right)^{-1} \right)^{1/(\beta-1)} \right)^{(1-\beta)/\alpha},$$

where $\widetilde{\omega}$ is the real wage rate that permits to the second part of the optimality conditions to be still verified once $Z = Z_M$ and $K > K_M$ — 1this does of course imply that $\widetilde{\omega} > \widehat{\omega}$ —, and K_M is the amount of capital that precisely corresponds to full employment without requiring any depart from the *efficient* real wage $\widehat{\omega}$. In other words, this corresponds to the threshold level of capital that *exactly fits* full employment and the binding of the constraint of *finite ressources*. Conducting the same procedure as for the individual problem, it derives :

$$\frac{d\mathcal{P}_K(K)}{dK} = \alpha K^{\alpha-1} (q(\omega) Z)^{\beta} \left(\frac{\alpha+\beta-1}{1-\beta} \right) > 0. \qquad \square$$

COROLLARY 2. *The main result of proposition 3 could be stated as follows :*

$$\begin{aligned} \mathcal{P}_{KK}(K) &\geq 0, \forall K \in [0, K_M), \\ \mathcal{P}_{KK}(K) &< 0, \forall K \in (K_M, +\infty). \end{aligned} \tag{17}$$

REMARK 3 : Corollary 2 could have similarly been derived from (7) and (16). ◊

The convexity of $\mathcal{P}(K)$ with respect to K will henceforth be refered as the existence of *aggregate externalities of increasing returns to scale* : the *uniform* and *coordinated* increase of the capital stock at the aggregate level will induce a rise in the level of profits which, once redistributed, will imply a subsequent rise in demand by the households, so that at the firm level, each one will benefit from an aggregate externality of increasing returns to scale. This phenomenon will be shown in the following to have strong consequences on the aggregate dynamics, in the short run, but also in the long run.

3.2. INTERTEMPORAL EQUILIBRIUM

Due to proposition 2, the law of motion governing the time-path of the aggregate capital accumulation process is simply given by :

$$\dot{\Gamma} = \left(\frac{J_{\Gamma}(\Gamma, K)}{J_{\Gamma\Gamma}(\Gamma, K)} \right) \left(r - \frac{\mathcal{P}_K(K) + J_{\Gamma K}(\Gamma, K)\Gamma}{J_{\Gamma}(\Gamma, K)} \right). \tag{18}$$

In order to obtain a tractable two-dimensional closed form for the dynamics, it is first necessary to derive an expression for the equilibrium interest rate and then to incorporate the obtained value into the *dynamical system* whose components are the aggregate counterpart of the law of motion of the capital stock (11) and (18). This proceeds in two successive steps. First, under assumptions C1-3 and T1-4, for any $K \in [0, +\infty)$, there does exist a unique level of Z such that the results of corollary 2 hold, so that it is possible to express the aggregate ressource constraint $C + J(\Gamma, K) = Y$ in the (K, Γ) space. Differentiating the aggregate ressource identity with respect to time and taking into account the first order conditions of (P(c)) — (4) —, it is possible to derive the equilibrium value of the interest rate as :

$$r(K, \Gamma) = \left(\left(\frac{(J_{\Gamma})^2}{J_{\Gamma\Gamma}} - \frac{U_c}{U_{cc}} \right)^{-1} (Y_K - J_K) \dot{K} - \frac{\rho U_c}{U_{cc}} + (\mathcal{P}_K + J_{K\Gamma}\Gamma) \left(\frac{J_{\Gamma}}{J_{\Gamma\Gamma}} \right) \right).$$

Finally :

DEFINITION 1 : Under assumptions C1-3 and T1-4, an intertemporal symmetric equilibrium under imperfect competition is a sequence of quantities $\{K(t), Z(t), \Gamma(t)\}_{t=0}^{+\infty}$ and prices $\{P(t), w(t), r(t)\}_{t=0}^{+\infty}$ such that :

$$\begin{cases} \dot{K} = \Gamma \\ \dot{\Gamma} = \dfrac{J_\Gamma}{J_{\Gamma\Gamma}}\left(\left(\dfrac{(J_\Gamma)^2}{J_{\Gamma\Gamma}} - \dfrac{U_c}{U_{cc}}\right)^{-1}\left((Y_K - J_K)\Gamma - \dfrac{U_c}{U_{cc}}\left(\rho - \dfrac{\mathcal{P}_K + J_{K\Gamma}\Gamma}{J_\Gamma}\right)\right)\right). \end{cases} \tag{19}$$

DEFINITION 2 : The preceeding economy is henceforth going to be refered as $\dot{\kappa}(t) = \Phi(\kappa(t))$, with $\kappa \in \Omega \subset \mathbb{R}^2$ and $\Phi(\kappa(t)) = \big(\Phi_1(K(t), L(t)), \Phi_2(K(t), L(t))\big)$. ◊

To summarize, it has been shown that the preceeding economy can be described by a two-dimensional dynamical system. This latter one is also known to exhibit specific properties — the existence of aggregate externalities of increasing returns to scale — up to a threshold level K_M.

4. LOCAL DYNAMICS

4.1. INTUITIVE ANALYSIS

In the sake for compactness, the following notation will henceforth be adopted for the set of stationary solutions :

DEFINITION 3 : $\text{Fix}(\Phi) \stackrel{\text{def}}{=} \big\{\kappa \in \mathbb{R}_{++} \times \mathbb{R} \mid (\Phi_1(\kappa), \Phi_1(\kappa))' = (0, 0)'\big\}$.

LEMMA 2. *Under assumptions* T1-3, $\text{Fix}(\Phi) = \big\{(K, \Gamma) \in \mathbb{R}_{++} \times \mathbb{R} \mid \Gamma = 0 \text{ and } (\mathcal{P}_K / J_\Gamma) = \rho\big\}$.

PROOF : Derives from the values of $J(\cdot)$ and $J_\Gamma(\cdot)$ at $\Gamma = 0$. □

The introduction, through assumption C2, of an upper bound on labour supply has been proved in proposition 3 to give rise to an *increasing marginal profitability* up to the binding of the constraint on employment. More precisely, from corollary 2, it derives that $\mathcal{P}_{KK}$ is a strictly increasing positive-valued function on $(0, K_M)$ and a strictly decreasing one on domain $(K_M, +\infty)$. Although of interest, this result does not allow for any definite conclusion about the cardinality of Fix(Φ). Nevertheless, this latter one can be characterized for sufficiently strong aggregate externalities of increasing returns to scale.

LEMMA 3. *If* $\alpha/2 + \beta > 0$, $\text{Fix}(\Phi) \cap \mathbb{R}_{++}$ *is a pair.*

Proof : From (16), $\alpha/2+\beta>0 \iff \mathcal{P}_{KKK}(K)>0$, $\forall K \in [0, K_M)$. Thus, $\mathcal{P}_K$ will cross the 45 degrees line once on $(0, K_M)$ and once on $(K_M, +\infty)$. See figure 1. □

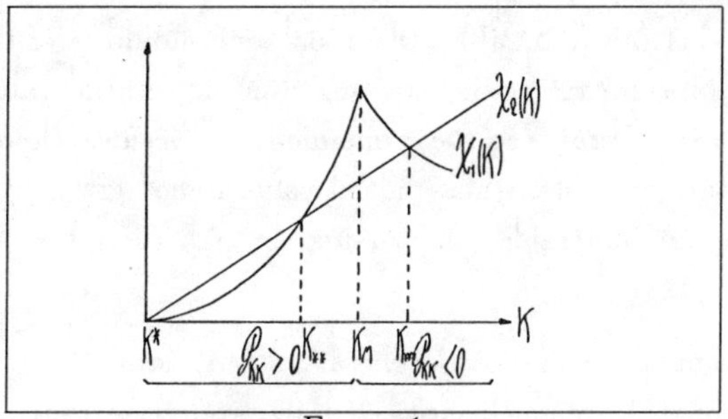

Figure 1

In other words, under this condition , the locus $\chi_1(K) \stackrel{\text{def}}{=} \{(K,\Gamma) \mid \dot{\Gamma}=0\}$ becomes convex with respect to the capital stock K up to the critical level K_M. In the sequel, conditions of lemma 3 will always be assumed to hold. Furthermore, and owing to assumption C2, only *finite* values of the *curvature* of the utility function are allowed at the origin : this latter one is to be considered as a *degenerated stationary equilibrium*. It will be refered as K_* in the subsequent anlysis, whereas K_{**} and K_{***} will respectively denote the unique element of $\mathrm{Fix}(\Phi)$ where the convexity of $\mathcal{P}_K$ prevails and the unique one where it is the case of concavity.

4.2. Local Analysis

If the elements of $\mathrm{Fix}(\Phi)$ are hyperbolic, the behavior of the dynamical system in their close neighborhood can be analyzed and also fully characterized by the means of a jacobian matrix :

$$D\Phi(\kappa(s))\big|_{s\in\mathrm{Fix}(\Phi)} = \begin{pmatrix} 0 & 1 \\ \mathcal{X} & \mathcal{Y} \end{pmatrix}, \tag{20}$$

with

$$\mathcal{X} = \frac{(J_\Gamma/J_{\Gamma\Gamma})\big((-U_c/U_{cc})\mathcal{P}_K\big)}{(J_\Gamma/J_{\Gamma\Gamma})^2-(U_c/U_{cc})}$$

$$\mathcal{Y} = \frac{(J_\Gamma/J_{\Gamma\Gamma})\big(((\mathcal{P}_K-Y_K)/J_\Gamma)-(J_{K\Gamma}/J_{\Gamma\Gamma})\big)}{(J_\Gamma/J_{\Gamma\Gamma})^2-(U_c/U_{cc})},$$

whereas its expression at the degenerate stationary equilibrium derives as :

$$D\Phi(\kappa(s))\big|_{s\in\mathrm{Fix}(\Phi)} = \begin{pmatrix} 0 & 1 \\ J_{K\Gamma} & 0 \end{pmatrix}. \tag{21}$$

As a first approach, (20) and (21) allow to conclude about the status of the hyperbolic equilibria of the dynamical system :

Proposition 4. *Under assumptions* C1-3 *and* T1-4, *the saddlepoint property holds for* K_* *and* K_{***}, *whereas it fails for* K_{**}.

PROOF : Derives from the properties of $J(\cdot)$ under assumption C3 and from proposition 3. □

REMARK 4 : Locally, in the respective neighborhoods of K_* and K_{***}, there will just exist a one dimensional manifold leading either to K_* or to K_{***}. In the present context, and as was early pointed out by LIVIATHAN & SAMUELSON [1969], one should refer to *saddlepoint stability* : if there is a unique equilibrium trajectory starting from any initial value of the state variable, then the saddlepoint is *locally stable in the economic sense* because the *second dimension* of the system is merely a costate variable, whose initial value is not given by history but adjusts to put the economy on the unique stable arm passing through the given initial value of the state variable. ◇

Although a careful examination of the *degenerate steady state* — an *economic catastrophe* (HOWITT & MCAFEE [1988]) — might be criticized, its properties overcome such a view. It could in effect be associated to what has recently been refered in the *new growth theory* literature as an *underdevelopment trap*. More explicitly, although the *aggregate return* $\mathcal{P}_K(K)$ of a higher aggregate stock of capital might be high, the private economic incentive for capital accumulation remains too low to support a positive amount of investment by any of the decentralized agents and therefore the escape from the trap or the *jump* to another stationary equilibrium possibly associated with a higher income level cannot be achieved.

The status of the remaining element of Fix(Φ) — namely the one associated to the occurrence of aggregate externalities of increasing returns to scale — although being more intricate since — as will be rigorously proved in the sequel, its local stable manifold might fail to be tangent to the linear plane in its neighborhood, allowing a *major role for non linearities* — it is not hyperbolic, is interesting in its relation to non-convexities.

THEOREM 1. *If the measure of the aggregate externality of scale denoted as ψ passes by a critical value ψ_{**} implicitly defined by :*

$$J_K - Y_K + \left(\frac{U_c}{U_{cc}}\right)\left(\frac{\mathcal{P}_K}{J_\Gamma} - \frac{\psi}{J_{\Gamma\Gamma}}\right) = 0, \qquad (22)$$

where $Y_K, J_K, \mathcal{P}_K, J_\Gamma, J_{\Gamma\Gamma}$ are defined in a close neighborhood of K_{**}, the economy characterized by assumptions C1-3, T1-3 *undergoes a* HOPF *bifurcation in the neighborhood of (K_{**}, Γ_{**}), allowing for the existence of at least one closed orbit.*

PROOF : The proof consists of an application of the HOPF bifurcation theorem for flows[8] in $\mathbb{R}^2$ The holding of (22) corresponds to the crossing of the imaginary axis by the eigenvalues associated to the vector field $\Phi(\kappa)$. Since it is two dimensional, their unicity is obvious. The bifurcation value of ψ can easily be computed as $\psi_{**} = (J_\Gamma/J_{\Gamma\Gamma})\left(((-Y_K U_c)/U_{cc}) + (\mathcal{P}_K/J_\Gamma)\right)$ — where all functions are defined at (K_{**}, Γ_{**}). The remaining part of the proof is concerned with a *nonzero speed* for this crossing. It can be derived that $d\Re(\mu(\psi))/d\psi|_{\psi=\psi_{**}} = (U_c/U_{cc})((-\rho/\psi) - 1)$ that must belong to $\mathbb{R}_{++}$ owing to the concavity assumptions made on $U(c)$. Hence, there exists a unique three-dimensional manifold passing through $\kappa(\psi_{**})$ and a smooth system of coordinates

[8] See, e.g., GUCKENHEIMER & HOLMES [1986].

for which the TAYLOR expansion of degree 3 of the center manifold is given by the following normal form :

$$\dot{r}(t) = \iota_\psi r + v(0)r^3 + \mathcal{O}(\psi^2 r, \psi r^3, r^5)$$
$$\dot{\theta}(t) = \delta(0) + \delta_\psi(0)r + \phi(0)r^2 + \mathcal{O}(\psi^2, \psi r^2, r^4),$$

with $\iota \stackrel{\text{def}}{=} \Re(\mu(\psi))$ and $\delta \stackrel{\text{def}}{=} \Im(\mu(\psi))$. It can be proved[9] that, if $\iota(\psi) \neq 0$ and $\phi(\psi) \neq 0$, the solutions lie along a parabola $\psi = v(0)r^2/\iota_\psi(0)$, which thus gives rise to a paraboloid of revolution as the shape of the surface in the 3D extended center manifold, containing the periodic orbit. □

Further information is available about the actual relevance of this curve.

PROPOSITION 5. *Assuming that the dynamical system under consideration, namely* $\dot{\kappa}(t) = \Phi_\psi(\kappa)$, $\kappa \in \mathbb{R}^2, \psi \in \mathbb{R}$, *can be reexpressed in the eigenspace associated to* $\mid \mu(\psi_{**}) \mid$ *and* $\overline{\mid \mu(\psi_{**}) \mid}$ *so that its jacobean at the critical — bifurcation — value of* ψ *is of the following form :*

$$D\Phi_\psi(\kappa)|_{\psi=\psi_{**}} = \begin{pmatrix} 0 & \mid \mu(\psi_{**}) \mid \\ - \mid \mu(\psi_{**}) \mid & 0 \end{pmatrix}.$$

Assuming further that $(\Lambda_1(\cdot), \Lambda_2(\cdot))$ *denotes the two-dimensional associated vector field in the new coordinates base* (a, b) *; then, defining the functional form* $\Xi(\psi_{**})$ *as :*

$$\begin{aligned}\Xi(\psi_{**}) \stackrel{\text{def}}{=} & (\Lambda_{1,aaa} + \Lambda_{1,abb} + \Lambda_{2,aab} + \Lambda_{2,bbb}) \\ & - (|\mu(\psi_{**})|)^{-1} (\Lambda_{1,ab}(\Lambda_{1,aa} + \Lambda_{1,bb}) - \Lambda_{2,ab}(\Lambda_{2,aa} + \Lambda_{2,bb}) \\ & - \Lambda_{1,aa}\Lambda_{2,aa} + \Lambda_{1,bb}\Lambda_{2,bb}),\end{aligned}$$

there does exist a limit cycle in the neighborhood of ψ_{**} *if* $\Xi(\psi_{**}) < 0$.

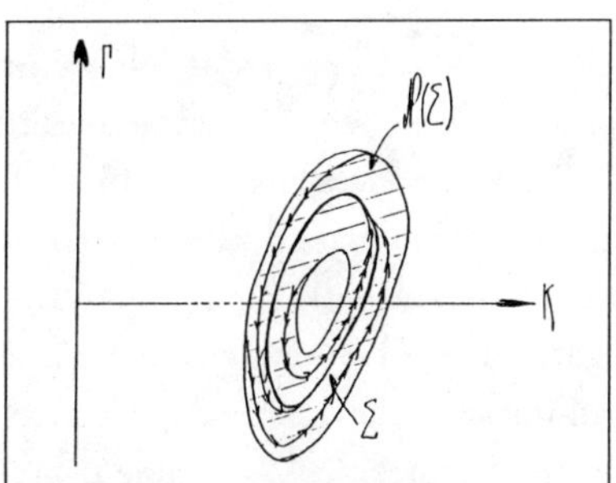

Figure 2 : Bassin of attraction of a limit cycle

PROOF : Recall first the actual definition of a *limit cycle*. First, a *point* K will be on a *closed curve* Σ if there does exist a $t \neq 0$ that verifies for a given flow denoted $\aleph$ the equality $\aleph_t(K) = K$. This orbit will be attracting and refered as a *limit cycle* if there does exist a neighborhood $\mathcal{N}(\Sigma)$ such that, for any $K \in \mathcal{N}(\Sigma)$, the flow $\aleph_t(K)$ approaches the closed orbit, i.e. $\lim_{t\to+\infty} d(\aleph_t(K), \Sigma) = 0$, with $d(\cdot)$ the distance between the flow and the trajectory.

The rigorous proof of the relevance of the preceeding — implicit in the statement of the proposition — algorithm for *detecting a limit cycle* is given in MARSDEN & MCCRACKEN [1976].

[9] Details are available in appendix 1 of DRUGEON [1990].

Here, it suffices to transform the original dynamical system into the required form. Recalling that the expression of the jacobean at the bifurcation value was given by :

$$\mathrm{D}\Phi_{\psi}(\kappa)\Big|_{\psi=\psi_{**}} = \begin{pmatrix} 0 & 1 \\ \left(-\left|\mu\left(\psi_{**}\right)\right|\right)^{2} & 0 \end{pmatrix},$$

it appears that the original dynamics do not authorize the convenient form given in proposition 4. Nevertheless, this latter one can easily be attained after the following change of coordinates : $a = K \times \mid \mu(\psi_{**}) \mid$, $b = \Gamma$. The *truncated* form of the dynamics can from now on be expressed as :

$$\begin{cases} \dot{a} = \Phi(a,b) = b \\ \dot{b} = \Lambda(a,b) = \dfrac{(J_b/J_{bb})(\mid \mu(\psi^{**}) \mid)^{-1}}{(J_b/J_{bb})^2 - (U_c/U_{cc})}\left(\sigma + \dfrac{(Y_a - J_a)}{(-U_c/U_{cc})^{-1}} - \dfrac{\mathcal{P}_a + J_{ab}b}{J_b}\right) \end{cases}$$

Obviously, at this level of generality and without admitting precise functional forms, the exact value of $\Xi(\psi_{**})$ cannot be precisely computed. Nevertheless, it allows to assess that since the jacobean of the vector field $(\Lambda_1(a,b), \Lambda_2(a,b))$ belongs to the convenient class at the critical value ψ_{**}, the associated value of $\Xi(\psi_{**})$ would give rise to the possibility to conclude about the stability of the closed orbit in the neighborhood of ψ_{**}. A negative value of $\Xi(\psi_{**})$ has been proved by MARSDEN & MCCRACKEN [1976] to correspond to the occurrence of the HOPF bifurcation, and then of the closed orbit, after the passage of ψ by its critical value. In other words, the orbit arises in the domain where the real part of the roots are strictly positive, so that the stationary steady state equilibrium K_{**} would *repel* trajectories which, once entered in the *bassin of attraction* of the closed orbit, all converge to this latter one, determining the possibility of a limit cycle. □

The possibility of a periodic cycle can be interpreted as follows : the existence of an increasing marginal profitability of the capital stock — which itself derives from aggregate externalities of increasing returns to scale — implies an *accelerating* rate of investment from the entrepreneurs. But the convexity of $J(\cdot)$ with respect to γ and the existence of *negative diseconomies of expansion* imply accelerating costs at a sufficiently high level of the capital stock and then firstly a decelerating and secondly a negative rate of investment. After a time, the economy will be back in the *increasing returns* area and initiate another cycle.

In the economics literature, only the supercritical — stable orbit — case is usually considered as being of interest since it should lead to an *observable limit cycle.* An exception is BENHABIB & MIYAO [1981] who consider the concept of *bassin of attraction* that has to be associated to a closed orbit to interpret the unstable subcritical case in terms of *corridor stability* (LEIJONHUFVUD [1973]) : as long as the initial value of the state variable — $K(0) = K_0$ in the present context — is located inside the elliptic area Ω composed by a closed orbit and its interior , it will stay in the corridor defined by $\partial\Omega$ and will eventually converge to K_{**}.

However, with respect to the stability of the orbits, and thus to the actual locus where the HOPF bifurcation holds , economics should be considered as a rather specific field. More precisely, whereas in physics or theoretical biology or any other science where there has recently been a significant interest in dynamical systems theory and nonlinear phenomena, researchers are often faced with *truly* two state variables whose initial values can have been independently given by history, the economics literature concerned with bifurcation theory in a continuous time setting has usually avoided such systems. The rationale for this comes from the fact that the autonomous form of the dynamical system is merely a *truncated* expression of the motion of the costate variable. In other words, this latter one will be either a price or a control variable, so that its path can be *adjusted* by the agents to conform with their expectations, e.g., their *degree of optimism*. To get a clearer perception of the actual importance of the occurence of a *deterministic* cycle, whether stable or unstable, the careful graphical examination of these two possibilities illustrated in figure 3 — that is adapted from Woodford [1984] — reveals to be useful.

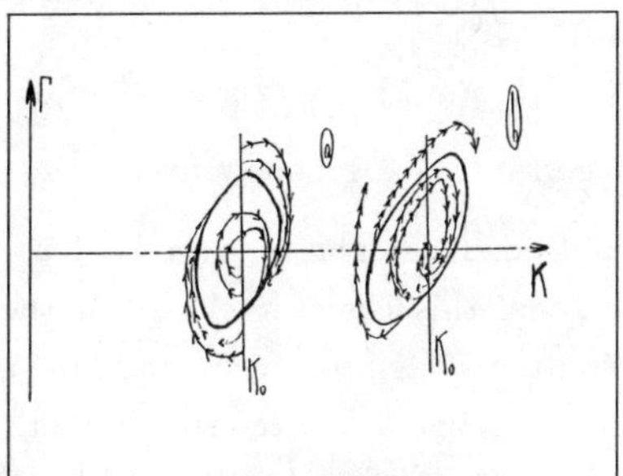

Figure 3 : Supercritical (a) and Subcritical (b) cases

In one state variable systems, even if the HOPF bifurcation is of the subcritical type, there will generally exist two levels for the jump variable, that could be interpreted [18] as an optimistic one — $\Gamma > 0$ — and as a pessimistic one — $\Gamma < 0$. With this regard, it should also be pointed out that there does still remain many *indeterminacy results*, e.g., learning schemes, that, although being well understood from an intuitive point of view, are yet far from having received any relevant formalisation in continuous time settings. This is detrimental to the search for an improved understanding of the actual implications of such a class of phenomena in the sense that continuous time dynamics, at least in low-dimensional cases, are much more tractable than discrete ones.
To summarize, it has been proved that the dynamical system is characterized by a triple of stationnary equilibria among which two exhibit the *classical* saddlepoint property whereas the third one, associated to the occurrence of aggregate externalities of increasing returns to scale, gives rise to a periodic orbit.

5. GLOBAL DYNAMICS

Despite the relevance of the problems that have been put forth at the end of the preceeding section, the usual way macroeconomics have had to deal with has been, the most part of the time, to omit their explicit consideration. This is prejudicial since it restricts strongly both the significance of the results and the general character of the analysis. Still more importantly, by the explicit omission of any consideration about global behavior, it *de facto* rules out what could have provided a *natural connection between the short run and the long run*. More explicitly, the

purpose of the present section will be to prove that, starting from a *short-run* model, long-run *growth problems* can also be addressed in an original way.
The model is the same as the one that has been developed and analyzed along 2, 3 and 4, but it makes explicit use of functional forms — which are admittedly recognized of general use in economics — in order to derive explicit analytical results. The set of assumptions concerning these forms can be summarized as follows :

ASSUMPTION C4 : $U(c)$ is characterized by an infinite intertemporal elasticity of substitution.

ASSUMPTION T5 : $J(\gamma, K)$ and $F(k, q(\omega)z)$ are as given in 2, but $v(\cdot)$ is explicitly of the quadratic variety :

$$J(\gamma, K) = \frac{1}{2}\gamma^2 + \gamma\psi K$$
$$F(k, q(\omega)z) = \epsilon k^{\alpha}(q(\omega)z)^{\beta} - \varsigma Y.$$

ASSUMPTION T6 : The real wage rate is exogenously fixed at $\check{\omega}$.

REMARK 5 : Although assumption T6 might be perceived as a significant alteration of the generality of the previous analysis, this is not the case in the present model. In fact, since the sole effect of the assumption that was previously made to restrict consideration to *efficient amounts of labor* was to fix the real wage at a level associated to the existence of a positive rate of unemployment, it will appear in the sequel that it is by far simpler to assume that this real wage rate is exogenously fixed at a level strictly superior to the walrasian one. Furthermore, it will be proved to preserve all the preceeding results. ◇

In order for clearity, let us recall that, since the equilibrium is of the symmetric class and the number of firms and households in the economy is normalized to unity, the incorporation of assumptions C4, T5-6 into definition 2 and the resulting simplifications produce a formal definition of an intertemporal equilibrium as a pair of time-paths $\{K(t), \Gamma(t)\}_{t=0}^{+\infty}$ such that :

$$\begin{aligned} \dot{K} &= \Gamma \\ \dot{\Gamma} &= r(\Gamma + \psi K) - \mathcal{P}_K - \psi\Gamma \\ r &= \rho \\ 0 &\leq z_f(t) \leq Z(t)/F, K(t) \geq 0, \forall t \in [0, +\infty) \\ \lim_{t\to+\infty} & \exp(-r(t))\chi(t)K(t) = 0. \end{aligned} \tag{23}$$

This section will be organized as follows : it will first be proved that the particularly simple *truncated* model that is described exhibits exactly the same features as the previous general form from a local point of view. Furthermore, its extreme tractability will extand the analysis by explicitly deriving all the critical values already mentioned, e.g., to conclude about the stability properties of the HOPF bifurcation.
Unfortunately, this analysis — although detailed — will not allow any depart from local results which do not authorize any rigorous conclusion concerning the global behavior on the half-plane of equilibrium trajectories. This motivates for the second part of this section which will provide a global analysis of the dynamics that will be proved to allow a large class of results concerning the long run.

5.1. Local Features and Global Conjectures

First, since it would be possible to conduct the same kind of *intuitive analysis* as in 3, the system (23) still admits a pair of nondegenerate stationary equilibria and another degenerate stationary equilibrium. Moreover, a simple examination of the dynamical system reveals that, taking K as given and since the following equality $\mathcal{P}_K = r\psi K$ will hold at each of the stationary equilibria, the slope of the isocline $\dot{\Gamma} = 0$ at K_*, K_{**}, K_{***} entirely derives from the sign of $(r - \psi)$ so that, at a tentative level, three kinds of configurations can be conjectured. In fact, the equation of the isocline $\dot{\Gamma} = 0$ is given by $\Gamma = (r\psi K - \mathcal{P}_K) \,/\, (\psi - r)$. Owing to the *strong convexity* of $\mathcal{P}_K$ that has been assumed in lemma 3, the following set of inequalities will hold :

$$\begin{cases} r\psi K - \mathcal{P}_K < 0 \text{ for } K \in (K_*, K_{**}) \\ r\psi K - \mathcal{P}_K > 0 \text{ for } K \in (K_{**}, K_{***}) \\ r\psi K - \mathcal{P}_K < 0 \text{ for } K \in (K_{***}, +\infty). \end{cases} \tag{24}$$

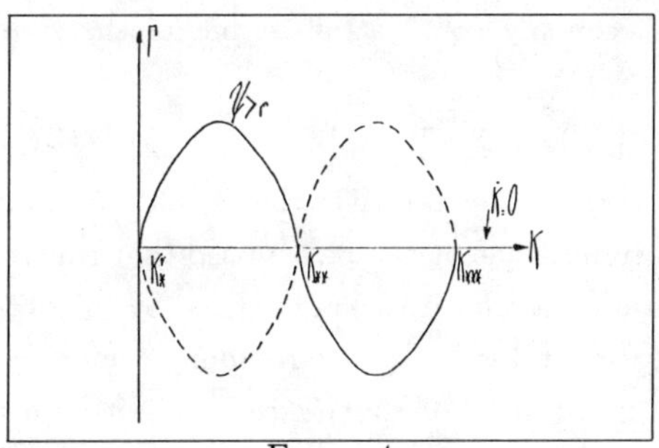

Figure 4

This implies that the sign of the slope of the isocline is entirely given by the one of $r - \psi$ on each of the previous intervals.

For $r - \psi > 0$, it is straightforward to verify that it is negative at K_*, positive at K_{**} and negative at K_{***}, whereas opposite conclusions hold for $r - \psi < 0$. Finally, for $r - \psi = 0$, the slope of the isocline $\dot{\Gamma} = 0$ is infinite at each of the stationary equilibria. This allows for the possibility of a first tentative perception of the eventualities which are illustrated in figure 4.

Let us now conduct a rigorous analysis of the stability properties of the stationary equilibria. Despite the apparent simplicity of the figure 4, it will reveal that, even locally, the system exhibits very interesting properties.

The straightforward expression for the jacobean is given by :

$$D\Phi_\psi(\kappa(s))\Big|_{s,s\in \mathrm{Fix}(\Phi)} = \begin{pmatrix} 0 & 1 \\ -\mathcal{P}_{KK} + r\psi & r - \psi \end{pmatrix}. \tag{25}$$

Case 1 : $r - \psi > 0$

In this first case, the Liviathan & Samuelson [1969] result applies. There does exist an alternance between two saddlepoint stable stationary equilibria $(K_*$ and $K_{***})$ and an unstable one (K_{**}).

Generally speaking, if there does not occur sufficiently strong aggregate externalities of stock, this *nonsaddle equilibrium* will reveal to be unobservable under small perturbations — this is the essence of the LIVIATHAN & SAMUELSON [1969] result. Thus, apart from this steady state itself, there does not exist any other trajectory starting anywhere else than at the low level nondegenerate stationary equilibrium that converges to it.

Nevertheless, it must be noticed that this result does not completely characterize the dynamics near K_{**}. In fact, it straightforwardly derives that if the following inequality holds :

$$r^2 + 2\psi r + \psi^2 < 4\mathcal{P}_{KK} \; ; \tag{26}$$

that is, if the aggregate externalities of increasing returns are sufficiently strong — in other words, if the degree of convexity of $\mathcal{P}(K)$ with respect to K is high enough —, the system does admit a simple pair a complex roots and the dynamics should be understood as being *initially indeterminate*. More precisely, in the neighborhood of the unstable low level non degenerate steady state (K_{**}, Γ_{**}), the economy could attain either of the saddlepoint stable stationary equilibria.

Its actual long-run position should then depend on the features of the initial expectations of the other agents : if $\mathcal{P}_{KK}$ is sufficiently positive, they could coordinate on the high level non degenerate stationary equilibrium. Thus, it can be assessed that this case in fact reveals to be far from *traditional* features in the sense that it is characterized by the overcoming of the *historically given position* of the aggregate capital stock by *self-fulfilling prophecies* — i.e., unfounded perfect foresights paths based, e.g., on *optimism* or *confidence*. The initial position of the economy with respect to the unstable low level non degenerate stationary equilibrium does not play any role any more in the long-run outcome. See figure 5 for a global perspective and figure 6a for a local one.

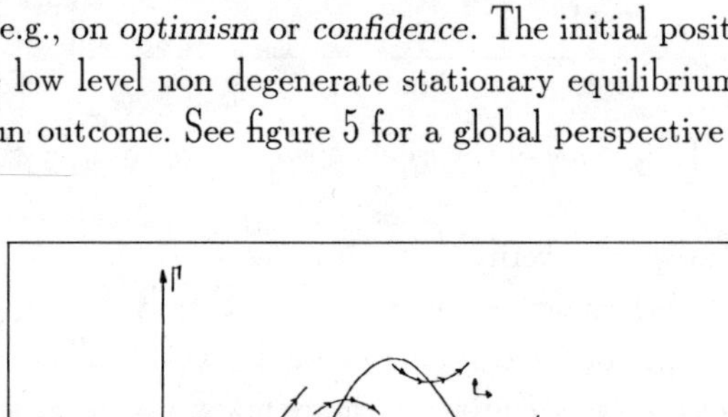

Figure 5

On the contrary, if the reverse of (26) holds, the initial position of the economy completely determines its long-run one. The intuition behind this result is closely related to the one of KRUGMAN [1989] in an adjustment model. If the entrepreneurs sufficiently discount the future, aggregate externalities of increasing returns to scale are surpassed and the behavior of the economy should be understood as a *classic* one — it is the one described by A. MARSHALL at the beginning of the century — in the sense that the long-run outcome derives from the initial position. See figure 6b.

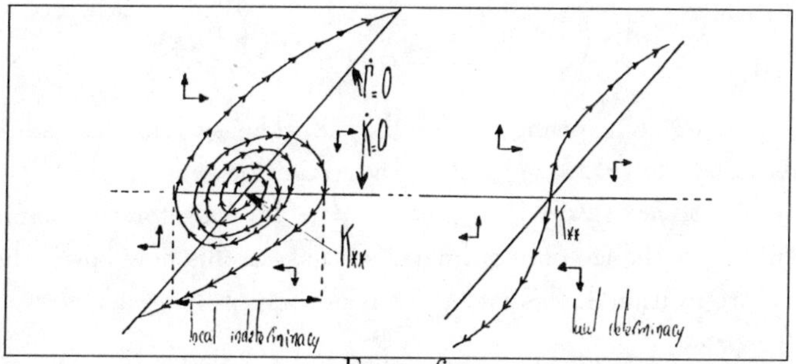

Figure 6

Local indeterminacy (a) and determinacy (b) of the Steady State

CASE 2 : $r - \psi < 0$

Under this *strong aggregate externalities of stock* — or *low discounting* — *case*, owing to the jacobean (25), the stationary equilibrium becomes a sink. The main consequence of this new shape is that, for any initial value of the state variable K_0, in the neighborhood of the stationary equilibrium, there will exist continuum many equilibrium-paths starting with an aggregate stock equal to K_0 and converging to K_{**}. Furthermore, if (26) holds, that is if the aggregate externalities of increasing returns to scale are sufficiently pronounced, the *indeterminacy result* will be even stronger in that K_{**} becomes a spiraling sink.

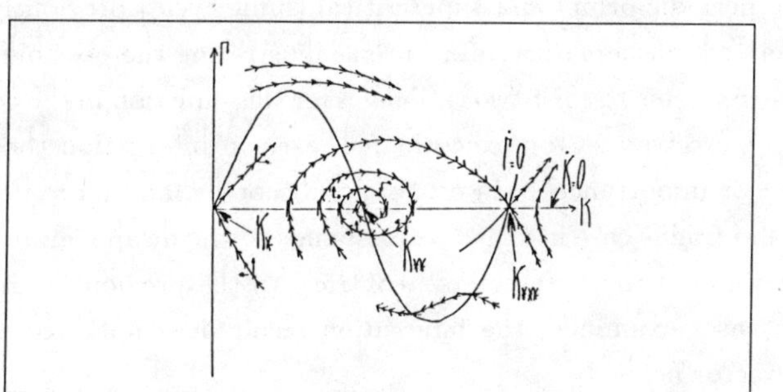

Figure 7

CASE 3 : $r - \psi = 0$

This limit case is rather special in that it corresponds to an isocline $\dot{\Gamma} = 0$ which reduces to $\psi r K = \mathcal{P}_K$. Thus, this latter one does not depend anymore on Γ and admits three solutions for this equation, namely K_*, K_{**}, K_{***}. In other words, the slope of this isocline will verify :

$$\lim_{r \to \psi} \left(\frac{\mathcal{P}_K - r\psi}{r - \psi} \right) = +\infty.$$

Whereas the the status of the saddleproperty of the two extremal stationary equilibria remains obvious, it seems possible to conjecture that the dynamical system should still undergo a HOPF bifurcation in the neighborhood of (K_{**}, Γ_{**}). This can indeed easily be verified. Furthermore, the simplicity of (21) is going to allow us to conclude about the stability of the periodic orbits.

First, it is straightforward to notice that the product of the real parts of the roots is given by :

$$\det\left(D\Phi(\kappa)\Big|_{\psi=\psi_{**}}\right) = -\psi_{**}r + \mathcal{P}_{KK},$$

that must be positive for K_{**} owing to corollary 2. The system still admits a single pair of imaginary eigenvalues for $\psi = \psi_{**}$ and the condition (ii) of the HOPF bifurcation is straightforward since $(d\Re(\mu(\psi))/d\psi)|_{\psi=\psi_{**}} = -r \neq 0$. Looking for the stability of the closed curve and proceeding to a change of coordinates so that, in this new basis, the system satisfies the requirements of proposition 4, this latter one is now given by :

$$\begin{cases} \dot{a} = b \\ \dot{b} = \left(\mu(\psi_{**})\right)^{-1}\left(r(b+\psi_{**}a) - \mathcal{P}_a - \psi b\right). \end{cases}$$

Explicitly computing the coefficients of the index of stability the orbits given by $\Xi(\psi_{**})$ in proposition 4, these ones verify $\Phi_{aa} = \Phi_{abb} = \Phi_{ab} = \Phi_{aaa} = \Phi_{bb} = 0, \Lambda_{aab} = \Lambda_{bbb} = \Lambda_{ab} = 0$, $\Lambda_{aa} = -\mathcal{P}_{aa}$, so that, finally :

$$\Xi(\psi_{**}) = 0.$$

This surprising result is sometimes refered in the literature as a *critical* HOPF *bifurcation*. A few words should be said about this limit case of the HOPF bifurcation that has, to our obest knowledge, never been explicitly considered in economics. It is the one that lies *between* the subcritical (unstable periodic orbit) and supercritical (limit cycle) previously mentioned and is also refered in the related mathematical literature as illustrating the possibility of a *degenerated* HOPF bifurcation. There seems to exist two rationales for this omission in the concerned economics literature. First, it is perceived as too exceptionnal, even in bifurcation theory, for having any actual significance — or importance — in economics. Secondly, and more fundamentally, it is a *highly degenerated and fragile* case in that is corresponds to the disappearance of all these closed orbits for any other value of the parameters : contrary to the previous *standard* — subcritical and supercritical — cases examined, the bifurcation result does not hold any more after any perturbation of the vector field.

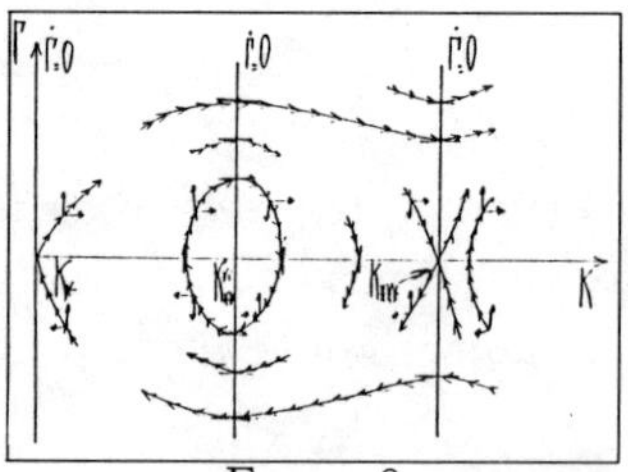

Figure 8

Heuristically, it should correspond to a bifurcation that holds exactly at $\psi = \psi^{**}$: it is highly special in the sense that there does exist a continuum of periodic cycles. As has been pointed out by BENHABIB & RUSTICHNI [1991], for any initial conditions, the optimal trajectory is periodic provided the feasibility constraints are satisfied.

Unfortunately, such a result might also come from the omission of higher order nonlinear terms that has been used for deriving the form $\Xi(\psi_{**})$. Finally, as it is illustrated in the graphical representation of this case, very little can be said about the potentiality of orbits in the large from K_{**}. Many conjectures and possibilities are admissible — for example, in case 2, HOWITT & MCAFEE [1988] argue that since there does only exist a unique equilibrium-path leading to the saddlepoint whereas there does exist continuum many which lead to a sink, the latter is highly likely —, but one cannot at this stage derive any general rigorous conclusion about the global behavior of the equilibrium-paths.

5.2. HAMILTONIAN DYNAMICS

5.2.1. PURE HAMILTONIAN DYNAMICS

LEMMA 4. *Under assumptions* C4, T5-6, the system (23), denoted as $d\kappa/dt = \Phi(\kappa)$, with $\kappa \in \Omega \subset \mathbb{R}^2$, $\kappa = (K, \Gamma)'$ and $\Phi(\kappa) = (\Phi_1(\kappa), \Phi_2(\kappa))'$ does not admit any closed orbit on its domain Ω.

PROOF : If $r \neq \psi$, the following equation holds :

$$\frac{\partial \Phi_1(K,\Gamma)}{\partial K} + \frac{\partial \Phi_2(K,\Gamma)}{\partial \Gamma} \in \mathbb{R} \setminus \{0\}. \tag{27}$$

Owing to the fact that the dynamical system is defined on $\mathbb{R}_+ \times \mathbb{R}$, that it is simply connected on $\mathbb{R}^2_+$ and that (27) holds, it becomes possible to notice that for any solution curve of this dynamical system, the following equation also holds :

$$\frac{d\Gamma}{dK} = \frac{\Phi_2(K,\Gamma)}{\Phi_1(K,\Gamma)},$$

so that, defining A as the closed set composed by a solution curve and its interior $\mathring{A}$— with $\oint_{\partial A}$ as the line integral along this closed curve ∂A (the boundary of the set) — :

$$\oint_{\partial A} \Big(\Phi_1(K,\Gamma) d\Gamma - \Phi_2(K,\Gamma) dK \Big) = 0.$$

It follows, owing to the GREEN-STOKES' theorem :

$$\iint_{\mathring{A}} \left(\frac{\partial \Phi_1(K,\Gamma)}{\partial K} - \frac{\partial \Phi_2(K,\Gamma)}{\partial \Gamma} \right) dK\, d\Gamma = 0. \tag{28}$$

If $r - \psi \neq 0$, it will not be possible to find a bounded area $A \subseteq \Omega$ such that (28) holds. Hence there cannot exist closed curves entirely in Ω . ▯

In other words, in any open area Ω of $\mathbb{R}^2$, $\partial\Phi_1(K,\Gamma)/\partial K - \partial\Phi_2(K,\Gamma)/\partial\Gamma$ is not identically zero and does not reverse its sign, the system defined by (23) will not admit fully developed closed orbits in Ω. This gives rise to the possibility of establishing a result which will reveal to play an essential role with respect to the global dynamics of the economy.

LEMMA 5. *Under assumptions* C4, T5-6, the system (23) corresponds to a one degree of freedom hamiltonian system for $r = \psi$.

PROOF : If $r = \psi$, owing to the continuity properties of $\mathcal{P}_K(K)$, there does exist a function $\mathcal{H}(\cdot)$ of class C^1, $(K, \Gamma) \longmapsto \mathcal{H}(K, \Gamma)$ such that the vector field (23) satisfies the so-called *Hamiltonian equations* :

$$\begin{cases} \dot{K} = +\dfrac{\partial \mathcal{H}(K,\Gamma)}{\partial \Gamma} \\ \dot{\Gamma} = -\dfrac{\partial \mathcal{H}(K,\Gamma)}{\partial K}. \end{cases} \tag{29}$$

It can be defined as :

$$\mathcal{H}(K,\Gamma) = \frac{1}{2}\Gamma^2 - r\psi K^2 + \int_0^K \mathcal{P}_K(K(x)). \tag{30}$$ □

THEOREM 2. *Under the assumptions* C4, T5-6, the following equality holds for all the equilibrium paths of the dynamical system (23) :

$$\mathcal{H}(K,\Gamma) = I, I \in \mathbb{R},$$

where I is a constant term.

PROOF : Since $\mathcal{H}(\cdot)$ is of class C^1, it is possible to differentiate with respect to time its functional form as given by (30) :

$$D\mathcal{H}(K,\Gamma) = \left(\frac{\partial \mathcal{H}(K,\Gamma)}{\partial K}\right)\dot{K} + \left(\frac{\partial \mathcal{H}(K,\Gamma)}{\partial \Gamma}\right)\dot{\Gamma}.$$

Recalling that, under the conditions of lemma 5, the dynamical system (23) does verify the *Hamiltonian equations* (29), it straightforwardly follows that :

$$D\mathcal{H}(K,\Gamma) = \left(-\dot{\Gamma}\dot{K}\right) + \left(\dot{\Gamma}\dot{K}\right) = 0.$$

So, that the stationary equilibrium-paths of (23) do correspond to the constancy of the functional form $\mathcal{H}(K,\Gamma)$ defined in (30). □

Heuristically, the occurrence of a dynamical system that is of the Hamiltonian variety allows the indexing of any point on the half-plane $\mathbb{R}_+ \times \mathbb{R}$ by a level curve of the Hamiltonian function defined above.

Before a more thorough examination of the large set of admissible economic configurations that result from this *strong* property of the dynamical system, it is useful to characterize formally the actual shape of the hamiltonian.

LEMMA 6. $\mathcal{H}(K,\Gamma)$ admits three critical points with respect to the capital stock , namely K_*, K_{**}, K_{***}.

PROOF : It is immediate to notice that $\partial \mathcal{H}(K,\Gamma)/\partial K|_{K=K_*} = 0$. Furthermore, owing to the properties of $\mathcal{P}_K(K)$ and to the holding $\mathcal{P}_K(K) = r\psi K$ at the stationary equilibria :

$$\begin{cases} \partial \mathcal{H}(K,\Gamma)/\partial K < 0, \forall K \in (K_*, K_{**}) \\ \partial \mathcal{H}(K,\Gamma)/\partial K > 0, \forall K \in (K_{**}, K_{***}) \\ \partial \mathcal{H}(K,\Gamma)/\partial K < 0, \forall K \in (K_{***}, +\infty). \end{cases}$$ □

A further result will imply that, for $r = \psi$, the dynamics give rise to a phase diagram that is well-known in physics, namely one of the *pendulum variety*.

LEMMA 7. $\mathcal{H}(K, \Gamma)$ does admit a strict mimimum with respect to the capital stock at the low level nondegenerate stationary equilibrium K_{**}.

PROOF : It is straightforward owing to the convexity — corollary 2 — properties of $\mathcal{P}_K(K)$ on the open interval (K_{**}, K_{***}) :

$$\left.\frac{\partial \mathcal{H}(K, \Gamma)}{\partial K}\right|_{K=K_{**}} = 0, \quad \left.\frac{\partial \mathcal{H}^2(K, \Gamma)}{\partial K^2}\right|_{K=K_{**}} > 0. \qquad \square$$

It has to be recalled — see ARNOLD [1981a] — that a one degree of freedom hamiltonian is always defined up to a constant term. This is precisely the sign of this latter one that is going to index the whole half-plane by the level curves of (30).

The very fact that K_{**} is a minimum for the hamiltonian deserves further comments. In a physical system with two state variables, e.g. the pendulum, such a stationary point would have been strongly attractive. This is not the case in the present model, precisely because it is concerned with economics, which is interested in agents that formulate expectations about the future. In other words ; whereas such a case would no doubt have been the *good one*, in physics because one always holds a set of initial conditions, it might well correspond to the *bad one* in our case — and more generally, in economics — because it might lead to an indeterminacy of the equilibrium.

More precisely and as will soon become clear, the crucial result concerning the kind of *Hamiltonian dynamics* that actually prevails will lie in the level curve that passes by the high level nondegenerate stationary equilibrium K_{***}.

PROPOSITION 6. *If the following condition holds :*

$$0 < (r\psi)^{-\alpha/(2-\alpha)} K_M^{2\alpha\beta/(1-\beta)(2-\alpha)} \mathcal{B}^{2/(2-\alpha)} \left(\frac{2-\alpha}{2\alpha}\right) - \left(\frac{\mathcal{F}}{\alpha} \beta K_M^{\alpha/(1-\beta)}\right), \qquad (31)$$

with $\mathcal{B} = \alpha\Big((\beta) \;/\; ((1+\tau)^{(1+\beta)/\beta} F^{\alpha+\beta-1}\breve{\omega})\Big)^{\beta/(1+\beta)}$ and $\mathcal{F} = \alpha K_M^{\alpha\beta/(1-\beta)} (\beta(1+\tau)^{-1}/\ \breve{\omega}$ $F^{(\alpha+\beta-1)/\beta})^{\beta/(1+\beta)}$, *where* $\epsilon = (1+\tau)/\tau$, *as the constant term that applies to* $K^{\alpha-1}$ *to the expression* (9) *of* $\mathcal{P}_K(K)$ *for* $K \in (K_M, +\infty)$, *but adapted to allow for rigid wages ; then* $\mathcal{H}(K_{***}, \Gamma_{***})$ *is a strict maximum for the hamiltonian as given in* (30) *and the following inequality holds :*

$$\mathcal{H}(K_{***}, \Gamma_{***}) > \mathcal{H}(K_*, \Gamma_*) > \mathcal{H}(K_{**}, \Gamma_{**}). \qquad (32)$$

PROOF : The proof essentially consists of a cumbersome computation whose details are given in an appendix available on request. For $K > K_M$, it has to be recalled that the third term on the R.H.S. of the hamiltonian (30) writes as :

$$\begin{aligned} \int_0^K \mathcal{P}_K(K(x))dx &= \int_0^{K_M} \mathcal{P}_K(K(x))dx + \int_{K_M}^K \mathcal{P}_K(K(x))dx \\ &= \int_0^K \mathcal{F}K(x)^{\alpha-1}dx + \text{constant term.} \end{aligned} \qquad (33)$$

Owing to the continuity of the hamiltonian at K_{**}, it derives that, since at K_{***}, the first term on the R.H.S. of (33) will just be equal to $r\psi K_{***}$, the sign of the hamiltonian at this point will be the one of the constant term that can be proved to be the R.H.S. of (31). If this latter one is strictly positive, so is the hamiltonian, so that (30) holds. ∎

To get a first perception of the actual possible shapes of the hamiltonian function, it seems interesting to use 3D graphs. As has already been proved, and since there must exist a unique level curve between two points which correspond to the same value of the hamiltonian function, owing to the signs of $\partial\mathcal{H}(K,\Gamma)/\partial K$ that have been derived in the proof of lemma 6, this gives an interesting first intuition about what the *actual dynamics* might be.

CASE 1 : $\mathcal{H}(K_{***},\Gamma_{***}) < \mathcal{H}(K_*,\Gamma_*)$.

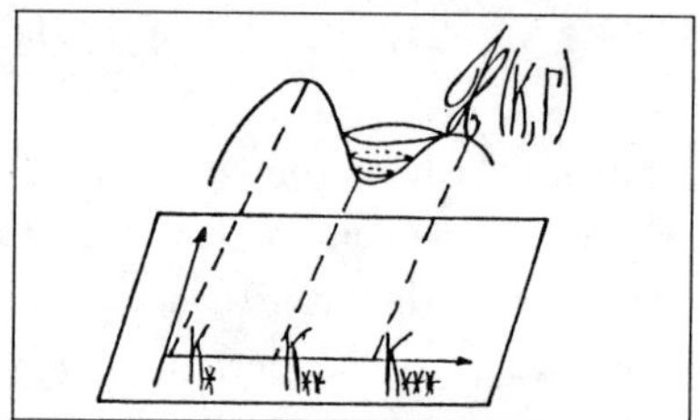

Figure 9

The hamiltonian does here admit a strict minimum at K_{**} and a strict maximum at K_*. The main point is that it is always possible to construct a one-parameter family of hamiltonians which will correspond to the intercrossing with the plane (K,Γ).

CASE 2 : $\mathcal{H}(K_{***},\Gamma_{***}) = \mathcal{H}(K_*,\Gamma_*)$.

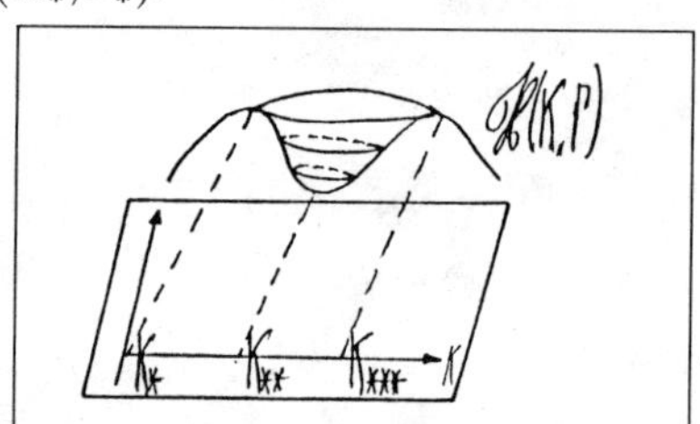

Figure 10

In this second case, the hamiltonian still admits a strict minimum at K_{**} but only local maxima. It is a limit case in the sense that it corresponds to a zero-value for the constant term given by the R.H.S. of (31).

CASE 3 : $\mathcal{H}(K_{***},\Gamma_{***}) > \mathcal{H}(K_*,\Gamma_*)$.

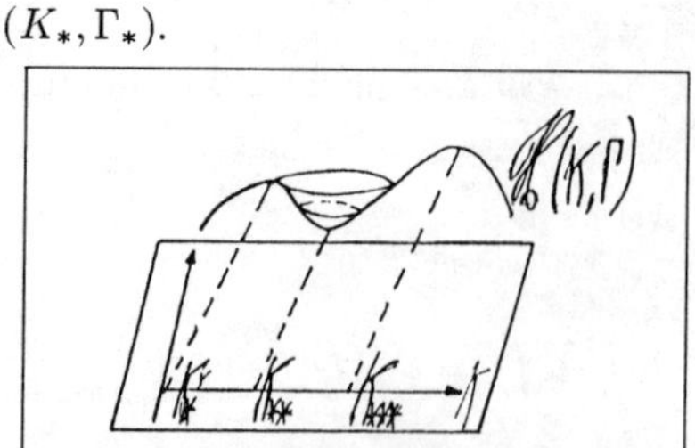

Figure 11

This last case is the exact opposite of the former one : the hamiltonian still admits a strict minimum at K_{**}, but takes its maximum value at K_{***}.
Although this hamiltonian function seems to be potentiallly interesting from the dynamic point of view, it might seem quite difficult to fully articulate its features with the economic content of the model that has previously been analyzed. In fact, its very interest can be understood in a very intuite manner by conducting the same kind of intuitive analysis as the one used in 4.1 for the local dynamics. Let us first recall that the dynamics of (23) can be completely understood after a detailed examination of the isoclines $\chi_1(K)$ and $\chi_2(K)$ defined by :

$$\chi = \chi_1(K) = \frac{\mathcal{P}_K}{r}$$
$$\chi = \chi_2(K) = \psi K.$$

It seems useful to conduct a more thorough examination on the graphical representation of this system. At the opposite of what happened in 4.1, here we are not interested in the number of equilibria, but we look for *actual understanding of the features* of this system.

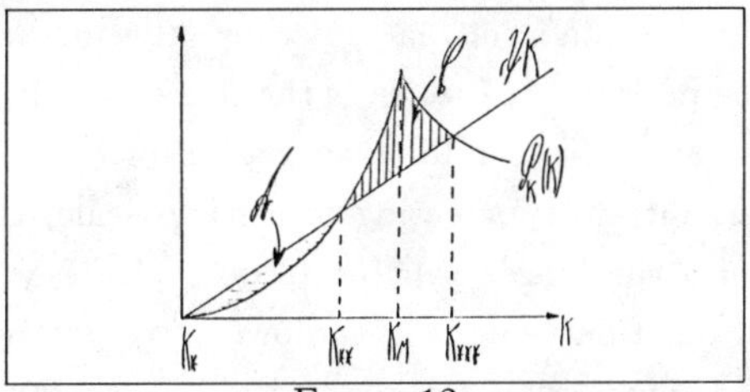

Figure 12

Denoting $\mathcal{A}$ and $\mathcal{C}$ as :

$$\mathcal{A} = \int_{K_*}^{K_{**}} \Big(\mathcal{P}_K(K(x)) - r\psi K(x)\Big)dx$$
$$\mathcal{C} = \int_{K_{**}}^{K_{***}} \Big(\mathcal{P}_K(K(x)) - r\psi K(x)\Big)dx.$$

PROPOSITION 7. *If* $\mathcal{C} \gtrless \mathcal{A}$, *then* $\mathcal{H}(K_{***}, \Gamma_{***}) \gtrless \mathcal{H}(K_*, \Gamma_*)$.
PROOF : The proof derives from the definition (30) of the hamiltonian functional form. Its level curves will take the following values at K_* and K_{***} :

$$\mathcal{H}(K_*, \Gamma_*) = 0$$
$$\mathcal{H}(K_{***}, \Gamma_{***}) = -r\psi\,(K_{***})^2 + \int_0^{K_{***}} \mathcal{P}_K(K(x)) + \text{ constant term.}$$

Owing to the continuity at K_M of the Hamiltonian function defined by (29)-(30), it immediatly follows that :

$$\mathcal{H}(K_{***}, \Gamma_{***}) > \mathcal{H}(K_*, \Gamma_*) \quad \text{iif} \quad \text{constant term} > 0,$$

which is exactly the required condition of proposition 6 — (31). □

This property allows to derive an *economic* interpretation of the characteristics of the hamiltonian function. That is, the larger will be the area of aggregate increasing returns to scale and the smaller will be the level of the curve of this function that passes by K_{***}. Although, the intuition underlying a large area $\mathcal{A}$ might not be obvious at this stage, it suffices to remind about the condition (31) of proposition 6 to get it.

In fact, more generally, proposition 7 gives rise to the possibility of an economic understanding of the actual significance of (31) and to derive some conclusions about the consequences of some *variational effects on the shape of the hamiltonian functions.* Despite its rather complicated form, three important results appear :

(i) The first is concerned with the level K_M which is associated with the *exact binding* of the full employment condition $Z = Z_M$. If it is increased, the economy will asymptotically tend toward the case where $\mathcal{A} < \mathcal{C}$ — characterized by «strong» aggregate externalities of increasing returns to scale. The underlying intuition is quite clear and is closely related to the conjecture about fixed ressources in the concluding remarks of HOWITT & MCAFEE [1988] : if the fixed factor, i.e., qualified labor, is increased, the *capacity constraints* on the economy are loosened, and the level of welfare of the representative entrepreneur is improved.

(ii) Secondly, if the number F of firms is increased, the economy also tends toward the case where $\mathcal{A} < \mathcal{C}$ holds. The intuition is immediate, because the bigger F, the closer the market structure to the perfectly competitive case which is the *first best* with respect to welfare.

(iii) On an intuitive mode and by a careful examination of the subsequent figure (13) : the stronger the aggregate externalities of increasing returns to scale, the faster will the loci K_{**} and K_M be attained, but also the longer will the form $\chi_1(K) - \chi_2(K) = \mathcal{P}_K(K) - r\psi K$ — respectively the hamiltonian function — need to go down — respectively to climb again. Briefly, *strong aggregate externalities of increasing returns to scale clearly favour the existence of a strict maximum at K_{***} for the hamiltonian function.*

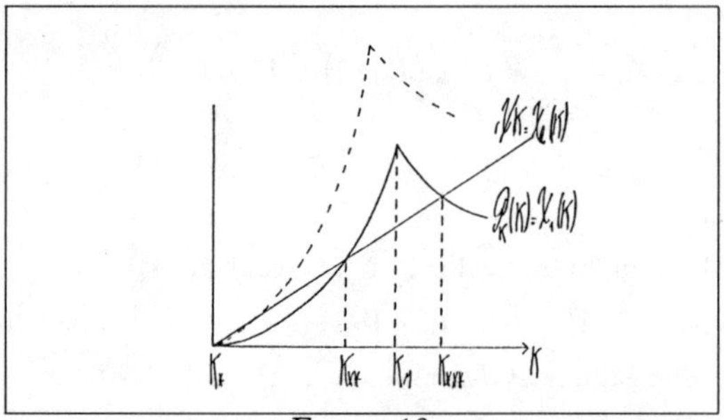

Figure 13

This allows a more thorough and rigorous examination of the possibilities that were intuitively shown in the 3D-analysis.

DEFINITION 4 : A *homoclinic orbit* or *saddle loop* that starts from K_{***} — see figure 14 — can be defined as :

$$\mathcal{O}_{***} = \left\{ (K_o, \Gamma_o) \in \mathbb{R}_{++} \times \mathbb{R} \mid \lim_{t \to \infty} \aleph_t(K_o, \Gamma_o) \in \mathcal{W}^s(K_{***}, \Gamma_{***}) \cap \mathcal{W}^u(K_{***}, \Gamma_{***}) \right\},$$

with $\mathcal{W}^s(K_{***}, \Gamma_{***})$ $\left(\mathcal{W}^u(K_{***}, \Gamma_{***})\right)$ as the *stable* and $\left(\textit{unstable}\right)$ *manifold* of (K_{***}, Γ_{***}) and $\aleph_t(\cdot, \cdot)$ the *flow* associated to the vector field (23) for $r = \psi$.

See figure 14. Furthermore :

PROPOSITION 8. *If* $\mathcal{A} > \mathcal{C}$, $\mathcal{O}_{***} \neq \emptyset$ and there does exist a saddle loop that starts from (K_{***}, Γ_{***}).

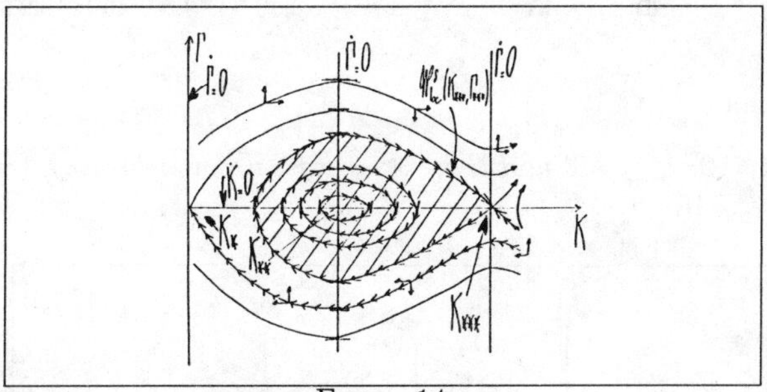

Figure 14

PROOF : Suppose $(K_o, \Gamma_o) \in \mathcal{W}^u(K_{***}, \Gamma_{***})$ with $K_o < K_{***}$ and $\mathcal{H}(K_o, \Gamma_o) = \mathcal{H}(K_{***}, \Gamma_{***})$. Then, owing to the fact that the trajectory-path defined by the eigenvector associated with the jacobean matrix at (K_{***}, Γ_{***}) is only defined for negative values of Γ when $K < K_{***}$, it derives that $\Gamma_o < 0$. That is (K_o, Γ_o) belongs to the left arm of $\mathcal{W}^u(K_{***}, \Gamma_{***})$ or, in other words, it is on the south-west from (K_{***}, Γ_{***}). If $\mathcal{A} > \mathcal{C}$ holds, then, owing to proposition 4 and the continuity of $\mathcal{H}(\cdot)$ characterized by lemma 5, $\mathcal{H}(K_{**}, \Gamma_{**}) < \mathcal{H}(K_o, \Gamma_o) = \mathcal{H}(K_{***}, \Gamma_{***}) < \mathcal{H}(K_*, \Gamma_*)$, with $\Gamma_* = \Gamma_{***} = 0$. Hence, there does exist a value $K_T \in (K_*, K_{**})$ such that $\mathcal{H}(K_{**}, 0) < \mathcal{H}(K_T, 0) = \mathcal{H}(K_o, \Gamma_o) < \mathcal{H}(K_*, 0)$. At this stage, let us remark first that even if this trajectory crosses $\dot{K} = 0$, the precise locus where this occurs needs not and cannot be a stationary point since $K_T \notin \{K_*, K_{**}, K_{***}\}$ so that this crossing is not characterized by a zero speed. Secondly, at $\dot{K} = 0$, the slope of the tangent to the hamiltonian curve needs to be $+\infty$. This follows from the fact that since (23) is an autonomous two-dimensional system, as long as $K_o \neq K_T$, there will always exist a neighborhood $\mathcal{N}(K_o)$ such that it is possible to define a function $\Gamma(K)$ which does not depend on time, such that $\Gamma_K(K) = d\Gamma/dK = (d\Gamma/dt)((dt/dK) = \dot{\Gamma}/\dot{K}$ and which verifies : $\lim_{K \to K_T} \Gamma_K(K) = +\infty$. Furthermore, such a reasoning obviously works both for $\Gamma < 0$ and for $\Gamma > 0$. Thus, K_T will correspond to an inflexion point for the hamiltonian function ; owing to the continuity of $\mathcal{H}(\cdot)$, the level curve of $\mathcal{H}(K_o, \Gamma_o)$ will then have to be associated with positive values of Γ. Owing to the one-dimensional feature of $\mathcal{W}^s(K_{***}, \Gamma_{***})$, it follows that $\lim_{t \to +\infty} \Phi_t(K_o, \Gamma_o) \in \mathcal{W}^s(K_{***}, \Gamma_{***})$. Thus, if $\mathcal{A} > \mathcal{C}, \mathcal{O}_{***} \neq \emptyset$. The proof proceeds along similar lines for the case $\mathcal{A} < \mathcal{C}$. □

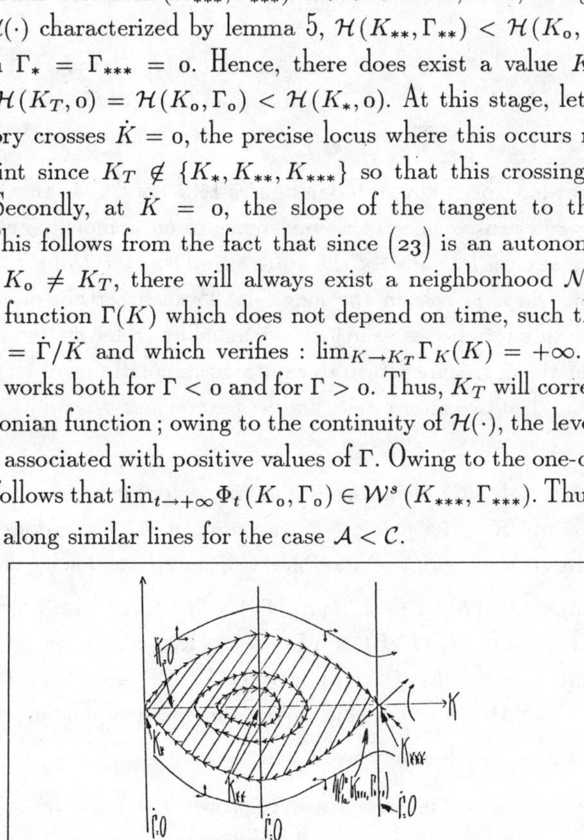

Figure 15

DEFINITION 5 : A *homoclinic cycle* — which is made of *heteroclinic orbits* — including K^* and K^{***} can be defined, for $i, j = (*, ***), i \neq j$, by :

$$\mathcal{E}^*_{***} = \left\{ (K_o, \Gamma_o) \in \mathbb{R}_{++} \times \mathbb{R} \mid \lim_{t \to \infty} \aleph_t (K_o, \Gamma_o) \in \mathcal{W}^s (K_i, \Gamma_i) \cap \mathcal{W}^u (K_j, \Gamma_j) \right\},$$

The following result holds :

PROPOSITION 9. *If $\mathcal{A} = \mathcal{C}$, $\mathcal{E}^*_{***} \neq \emptyset$ and there does exist a homoclinic cycle that is composed of K_* and K_{***}. See figure* 16.

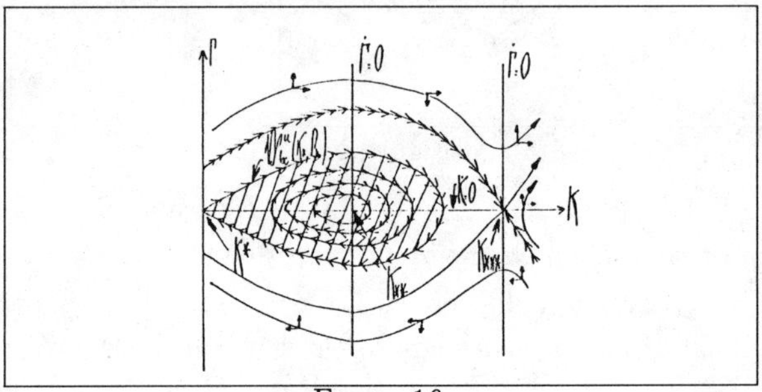

Figure 16

PROOF : If $\mathcal{A} = \mathcal{C}$, by theorem 2, $\mathcal{H}(K_*, \Gamma_*) = \mathcal{H}(K_{***}, \Gamma_{***})$. Then, $\forall (K_o, \Gamma_o) \in \mathcal{W}^u (K_*, \Gamma_*), \lim_{t \to +\infty} \aleph_t (K_o, \Gamma_o) \in \mathcal{W}^s (K_{***}, \Gamma_{***})$. Similarly, $\forall (K_o, \Gamma_o) \in \mathcal{W}^u (K_{***}, \Gamma_{***})$, $\lim_{t \to +\infty} \aleph_t (K_o, \Gamma_o) \in \mathcal{W}^s (K_*, \Gamma_*)$. Thus, $\mathcal{E}^*_{***} \neq \emptyset$. ▯

The previous results that have been illustrated in figures 14, 15 and 16 in the (K, Γ) space deserve some comments. The main consequence of the existence of an homoclinic cycle would be, at a heuristic level, that *for any initial value of the state variable, everything can happen*. In other words, *initial conditions play no role in the long run*. From a certain point of view, it is an extreme case of self-fulfilling prophecies : the locus attained by the economy derives entirely from the expectations in that the aggregate return to capital accumulation will be higher the higher is the rate of accumulation. The two alternative, and less extreme, cases do justify a more detailed examination.

PROPOSITION 8. *If $\mathcal{A} < \mathcal{C}$, $(\mathcal{A} > \mathcal{C})$, denoting K_T as the locus where the saddle loop $\mathcal{O}_*$ $(\mathcal{O}_{***})$ crosses the isocline $\dot{K} = 0$, $\forall K_o \in (K_T, K_{***})$ $(\forall K_o \in (K_*, K_T))$, there does just exist a unique equilibrium path leading to the high (low) level non degenerate stationary equilibrium.*

PROOF : Owing to lemma 7, $\mathcal{H}(K_T, \Gamma_T) = \mathcal{H}(K_*, \Gamma_*) < \mathcal{H}(K_{***}, \Gamma_{***})$ holds for $\mathcal{A} < \mathcal{C}$. Since, owing to the proof of lemma 6, $\mathcal{H}_K(K, \Gamma) > 0$ for $K \in (K_{**}, K_{***}), \forall K_o \in (K_T, K_{***})$, there does exist at least a simple couple (K_o, Γ_o) such that $\aleph_t (K_o, \Gamma_o) \longrightarrow (K_{***}, \Gamma_{***})$ for $t \longrightarrow +\infty$. Thus, $\lim_{t \to +\infty} \aleph_t (K_o, \Gamma_o) \in \mathcal{W}^s (K_*, \Gamma_*)$ which is one-dimensional. The uniqueness follows. The proof proceeds along similar lines for the case $\mathcal{A} > \mathcal{C}$. ▯

Thes case $\mathcal{A} < \mathcal{C}$ is of a crucial interest since it proves the importance of both aggregate externalities of increasing returns to scale and self-fulfilling prophecies in the long run. If external economies are strong enough, an initially badly endowed economy might well *take-off* if the entrepreneurs are sufficiently optimistic. On the contrary, if they do not take advantage from the existence of these externalities, they might also *plug* the economy into a *vicious circle* where disparate initiatives cannot allow the depart from the *underdevelopment trap*. Here, see figure 16, indeterminacy of equilibrium seems to be associated with an inferior outcome from the welfare point of view.

This case is also of interest — see figure 15 — in that it appears to be quite difficult to conclude about its status concerning welfare. At a tentative level, indeterminacy of the long-run outcome — in the sense that a *sunspot* variable could authorize the jump from one level of the hamiltonian curves to another one in a range of values for the state variable — is mostly associated to favorable outcomes. But this case also gives rise to the possibility of a *degeneration equilibrium path*. For high levels of the aggregate stock of capital, since aggregate externalities of increasing returns to scale are weak, it might well be the case that these latter ones are in a sense completely *surpassed* by the negative aggregate externalities of stock. Furthermore, recalling that in the hamiltonian case, those ones are higher the higher the entrepreneurs discount the future, this impossibility of taking off for economies which suffer both from poor endowments and from the lack of a class of entrepreneurs is very close to SKIBA [1978]'s result about the stability of an underdevlopment equilibrium. As a conclusion for this section, it becomes possible to assess that, although aggregate externalities of increasing returns to scale were previously — in 4 — proved to be closely related to the *local indeterminacy of equilibrium*, this does not impinge in any manner on the role that they play in the long run. Briefly, they give rise to the possibility of an *endogenous selecting process* — starting from the expectations and the subsequent behavior of the agents — of the long-run equilibrium attained by the economy.

5.2.2. Degenerated — Nearby — Hamiltohian Dynamics : Positive Divergence of the Vector Field[10]

One of the more striking properties of the *hamiltonian dynamics* lies in the fact that they do not only autorize to establish some global dynamics statements in the *pure Hamiltonian case* — in the present model, it is $r = \psi$ —, but they also provide results give rise to the possibility of obtaining results *near* this one with *degenerated* — the appropriate term is *nearby hamiltonian dynamics*. More explicitly, in the neighborhood of the previous case, the dynamics still belong to a specific class that is well understood. Nevertheless, it should be mentioned that these are refered as coming from the *structural instability* of *nonhyperbolic dynamical systems* admitting *nonhyperbolic equilibria* and, more precisely, as the results of a *homoclinic bifurcation*. This latter class of phenomena, although of global character, is not too intricate as long as one restrains, as in the present case, to the analysis of flows on the half-plane $\mathbb{R}_+ \times \mathbb{R}$: it merely corresponds to the breaking of the homoclinic orbits which where previously proved to occur in the hamiltonian case for values of ψ which lie in a close neighborhood of ψ_{**}. Formally, this can be understood

[10] See DRUGEON [1990] for a characterization of the possibilities that derive from a negative divergence of the vector field, the main result of this case being the possibility of a local, but also of a global, indeterminacy of the perfect foresight equilibrium.

in a rather simple manner by refering to the concept of *divergence of vector fields* as given by :

$$\mathrm{D}v(\Phi_1(K,\Gamma),\Phi_2(K,\Gamma)) = \frac{\partial\Phi_1(K,\Gamma)}{\partial K} + \frac{\partial\Phi_2(K,\Gamma)}{\partial\Gamma}.$$

It can then be stated that, for any level curve of the hamiltonian system, the following holds :

$$\mathrm{D}v(\Phi_1(K,\Gamma),\Phi_2(K,\Gamma)) = 0 + (r-\psi) = 0 \text{ on } \Omega.$$

Thus, and for low enough values of $|r-\psi|$, it remains possible to characterize the global dynamics. This is of interest since, although it was perfectly possible in 5.1 to completely characterize the shapes of the isoclines $\dot{K}=0$ and $\dot{\Gamma}=0$ in all the admissible cases, it was not at the opposite possible to conclude about the ones of the equilibrium trajectories on the half-plane $\mathbb{R}_+\times\mathbb{R}$. Since in these cases , the stationary equilibria were of the hyperbolic variety, the usual *linearization techniques* remained valid, but only allowed for conclusions in a close neighborhood of the steady states. Concerning the global behavior of the system, it was necessary to restrain to qualitative conjectures among the numerous admissible possibilities.

CASE $\mathcal{A} < \mathcal{C}, r-\psi > 0$

PROPOSITION 11. *If an economy is characterized by* $\mathcal{A} < \mathcal{C}, r-\psi > 0$ *and* $K_0 \notin (K_*, K_T)$, *with* K_T *defined as the unique solution to* $\mathcal{W}_*^u \cap \chi_1(K) \neq \emptyset$, *the unique long-run position is* K_{***}.

PROOF : Denoting $\mathfrak{B}(K_*,\Gamma_*)$ as the *bassin of attraction* of (K_*,Γ_*), since (K_{**},Γ_{**}) *repels* trajectories for $r-\psi>0$,$K_0 \notin (K_*,K_T)$ implies that there does not exist any $\Gamma\in\mathbb{R}$ such that $(K_0,\Gamma_0)\cap\mathcal{W}_*^u \neq \emptyset$. Thus, the fact that $\lim_{t\to\infty}\aleph_t(K_0,\Gamma_0)$ does not belong to $\mathfrak{B}(K_*,\Gamma_*)$ implies that $\lim_{t\to+\infty}\aleph_t(K_0,\Gamma_0)$ differs from (K_*,Γ_*) ∎

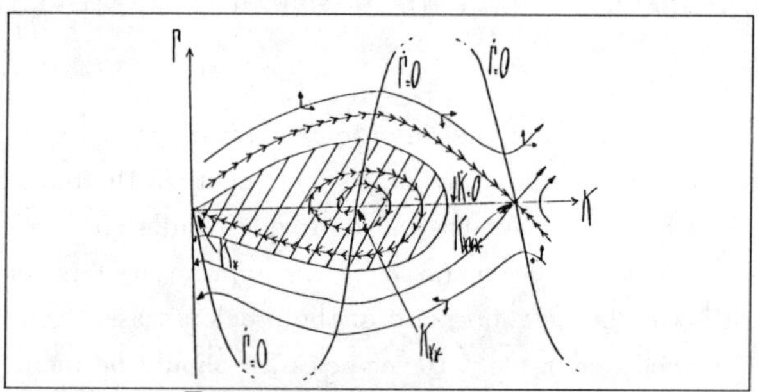

Figure 17 : $\mathcal{A} < \mathcal{C}, r-\psi > 0$

It is needless to say that this case is the less favorable one in that, for a large range of admissible values of K and for reasonable values of the rate of accumulation, the only admissible position in the long run will be the *degenerate equilibrium* : there does not anymore exist any alternative path. Thus, contrary to the local conjectures formulated in 5.1 for this case, when the entrepreneurs sufficiently discount the future, the economy will converge to the *worst equilibrium.* Even if the economy initially locates at $K_0 > K_{**}$, if this initial position belongs to a sufficiently small neighborhood of K_{**}, it will asymptotically stay on the stable manifold of the degenerate stationary equilibrium. Furthermore, it should also be pointed out that, at the opposite, it reveals to be extremely favourable for initially well endowed economies in that their only admissible long-run position will be the high level nondegenerate steady state equilibrium. This could be interpreted as the result of the aggregate externality of increasing returns to scale, which are not too strong and whose consequences play no role for low values of the aggregate stock of capital, due to the *convexo-concavity* of $\mathcal{P}(K)$ with respect to K, but provide incentives for higher ones.

CASE $\mathcal{A} > \mathcal{C}, r - \psi > 0$

PROPOSITION 12. *If an economy is characterized by* $\mathcal{A} > \mathcal{C}, r - \psi > 0$ *and* $K_0 \notin (K_T, K_{***})$, *with* K_T *defined as the unique solution to* $\mathcal{W}^u_{***} \cap \chi_1(K) \neq \emptyset$, *the only long-run position is* K_*.

PROOF : The proof proceeds along similar lines as the one of proposition 10. □

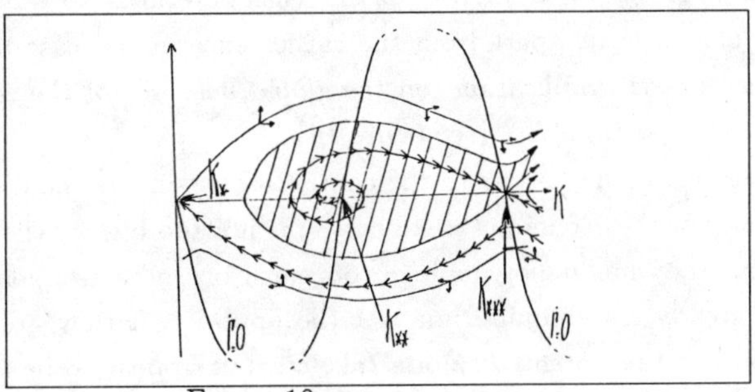

Figure 18 : $\mathcal{A} > \mathcal{C}, r - \psi > 0$

This case appears to be an extremely favourable one in that, for sufficiently well initially endowed economies and for a large range of plausible levels of the rate of accumulation — for a *smooth shape of these latter ones* —, the only long-term position where the economy can end by is the high level nondegenerate steaty state equilibrium. Indeed, this latter one, far from being an exceptional case as when $\mathcal{A} < \mathcal{C}, r - \psi > 0$, becomes the usual one. In fact, even if the entrepreneurs' behavior might initially be unstable in the vincinity of K_{**}, due to the convexity of $\mathcal{P}(K)$ with respect to K, they will asymptotically locate on the stable manifold of K_{***} and converge to the highest equilibrium. It should also be noticed that if the economy is initially too poorly endowed, the sole existence of strong aggregate externalities of returns to scale, probably because of the high discount of the future, will reveal to be unsufficient for actually providing any opportunity of *taking-off*.

CASE $\mathcal{A} = \mathcal{C}, r - \psi > 0$

This case does not really justify thorough an examination, since it appears to correspond to a too limit one. Nevertheless, it deserves two sets of comments, firstly with respect to the *linearized cases* analyzed in 5.1 and secondly about the actual influence of the aggregate externalities of increasing returns to scale.

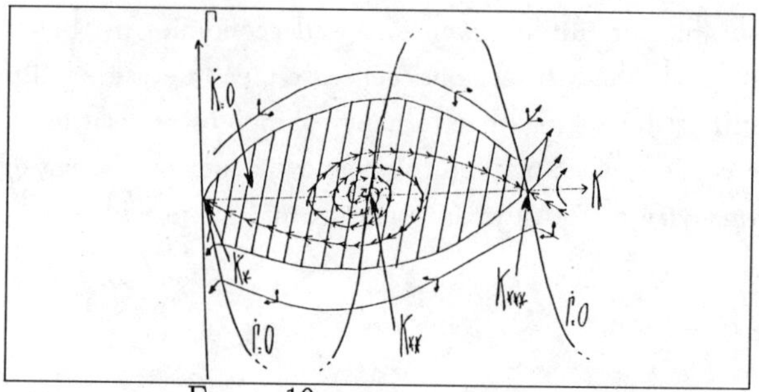

Figure 19 : $\mathcal{A} = \mathcal{C}, r - \psi > 0$

First, it reveals that the result of 5.1, see figure 6a, far from being a *satisfying approximation*, does in fact correspond to a highly exceptional case in that it is associated with a very strong set of assumptions on the dynamics.

Secondly, the role of aggregate externalities of increasing returns to scale reveals to be an extremely *asymetric* one in that, apart from the rather exceptional case of cyclicity, its *local strength will have very drastic implications on the global behavior of the economy, even if this latter one locates at the large from* K_{**} (see figure 13).

If they are not too big but if they occur in the context of sufficiently cautious — with respect to the actual possiblities of the economy (ψ), agents r, is not too big — who do adopt a smooth shape of accumulation, they might not impinge too much on the convergence toward the high level non degenerate steady state equilibrium. At the opposite, if they are sufficiently strong, they mainly correspond to the *potentiality* of a take-off, but appear to be a rather exceptional case due to the high discounting of the future by the agents, which could be interpreted as the lack of a class of entrepreneurs.

6. CONCLUSION

The purpose of this paper was firstly to understand the consequences of aggregate externalities of increasing returns to scale in a decentralized growth model specialized to include aggregate externalities of stock.

At a first, general level of the analysis, it was possible — following HAMMOUR [1988] — to endogenously prove the eventuality of a HOPF local bifurcation for the dynamical system. Although the proof of the existence of a finite set of stationary equilibria enlarged the *traditional* perception of dynamics, the very occurrence of a closed orbit did not allow to derive any statement about the actual economic significance of such a result. In fact, due to the *one state variable* feature of the dynamical system, it was highly conjectural to assess the importance of the cyclicity result : even if the convergence to either of the admissible two other stationary equilibria, that were proved to occur, implies the locating on a specific one-dimensional manifold on the half-plane, it would have been possible to argue that, for any level of the state variable — the capital stock —, the agents always had the opportunity to adjust on this curve by the very choice of the required value of the jump variable — the accumulation of capital.

The other main conjecture at this stage lied in the actual significance of the local indeterminacy of equilibrium that is well-known to occur in the neighborhood of a closed orbit. More particularly, does there exist any possibility in this indeterminacy area for departing such an equilibrium to jump to the more favourable case ? Although many possibilities seemed equally plausible, the local analysis did not autorize the statement of supplementary conclusions concerning equilibrium-paths on the plane and then of the long run attained by the economy.

The allowance of explicit functional forms for the components of the dynamical system gave also rise to the possibility of concluding about the stability of the closed orbit. The result revealed to be an extremely unusual one in that it was shown that, for a unique value of the bifurcation parameter, there did exist a continuum of orbits.

The second part of the dynamical analysis revealed firstly, that the dynamical system could in a critical case be characterized from a global point of view. Secondly, it permitted to explicitly establish that, whereas for a certain range of values of the state variable, there existed *determinate outcomes with multiple equilibria* (HOWITT [1989]), for others, the local indeterminacy result previously shown revealed to depart from its originally local character to extand to very large values of the state variable.

It was possible to conclude about the crucial role played by the aggregate externalities of increasing returns to scale in such a nonlinear setting.

They provide an interesting and seemingly natural connection between the short run and the long run by the very allowance of extanding a standard local analysis to more ambitious global results.

Even if the actual empirical evidence is still under examination and thus under debate, they allow to capture a much more general class of phenomena than the usual stability results, and then to provide original points of view about old problems or even new results.

They are crucially connected with the existence of indeterminate equilibria. Although this was not formalized, they provide a rationale for sunspot phenomena which enlarges their very interest far beyond their *usual overlapping generations setting*. In the very case of multiple long-run paths, the initial selection of a specific one by the economy might result phenomena which are not entirely founded on objective criteria but also result from waves of mood. Once initiated, such phenomena, such paths will become *self-reinforcing ones* and remain optimal from the point of view of the agents.

One of the main results of the contribution lies in the closed connections which exist between the local dynamics and the global behavior of the dynamical system once one departs from the hyperbolic cases to enter in the lands of bifurcation and stuctural instability.

Finally, mention should be made of the promising work of CHIAPPORI & GUESNERIE [1989] who proved the existence of specific equilibrium-paths between the sunspots that were conjectured in the present setting and derive strong conclusions about money neutrality. As this has been pointed out by SHLEIFER [1986], self-fullfilling prophecies might well correpond to a crucial determinant of both the short run and the long run. These two examples provide further motivation for an actual understanding of this class of phenomena in continuous time[11] , which might well reveal their essential importance once one loosens all the necessary conditions for the existence of the turnpike results.

7. REFERENCES

ARNOLD, V.W. [1981a]. *Equations différentielles ordinaires*. Moscou : MIR.

ARNOLD, V.W. [1981b]. *Chapitres supplémentaires de la théorie des équations différentielles ordinaires*. Moscou : MIR.

AZARIADIS, C. [1988]. «Threshold Externalities and Underdevelopment Traps», seminar R. ROY held at the Ecole Nationale des Ponts et Chaussées, Paris, May 16.

AZARIADIS, C. & A. DRAZEN [1990]. «Threshold Externalities and Economic Development», *Quarterly Journal of Economics* 105 : 501-526.

BENHABIB, J. & T. MIYAO [1981]. «Some new results on the Dynamics of the Generalized Tobin Model», *International Economic Review* 22 : 589-596.

BENHABIB, J. & K. NISHIMURA [1979]. «The Hopf Bifurcation and the Existence and Stability of Closed Orbits in Multisector Models of Optimal Economic Growth», *Journal of Economic Theory* 21 : 421-444.

BENHABIB, J. & A. RUSTICHNI [1990]. «Equilibrium Cycling with Small Discounting», *Journal of Economic Theory* 52 : 423-432.

CHENCINER, A. [1984]. «Systèmes dynamiques différentiables». In : *Encyclopaedia Universalis*. Paris : Le Livre de Paris.

CHIAPPORI, A. & R. GUESNERIE [1989]. «Self-Fulfilling Theories : The Sunspot Connection», working paper # 8919, D.E.L.T.A.

CHOW, S.N. & J.K. HALE [1982]. *Methods of Bifurcation Theory*. New York, New York, Heidelberg, Berlin : Springer-Verlag.

CORRIVEAU, L. [1988]. «Entrepreneurs, Growth and Cycles», manuscript, University of Western Ontario.

DIXIT, A. & J.E. STIGLITZ [1977]. «Monopolistic Competition and Optimum Product Diversity», *American Economic Review* 67 : 297-308.

DRUGEON, J.P. [1990]. «An Equilibrium Model with Endogenous Cycles and Global Bifurcations in the Long Run», unpublished, University of Paris 1-Panthéon-Sorbonne.

DRUGEON, J.P. & B. WIGNIOLLE [1991]. «A Model of Growth with Self-Fulfilling Prophecies», unpublished, University of Paris 1-Panthéon-Sorbonne.

GOLUBITSKY, M. & D.J. SCHAEFFER [1985]. *Singularities and Groups in Bifurcation Theory, Volume* 1. New York : Springer-Verlag.

[11]See DRUGEON & WIGNIOLLE [1991] for a first result in this line.

GUCKENHEIMER, J. & P. HOLMES [1986]. *Nonlinear Oscillations, Dynamical Systems and Bifurcations of Vector Fields, Second Printing, Revised and Corrected.* New York : Springer-Verlag.

HALL, R.E. [1988]. «Increasing Returns : Theory and Measurement with Industry Data», manuscript, Stanford University.

HAMMOUR, M. [1988]. «Increasing Returns and Endogenous Business Cycles», manuscript, Massachussets Institute of Technology.

HAMMOUR, M. [1990]. «Social Increasing Returns to Scale in Macro Models with External Effects», manuscript, Columbia University.

HIRSCH, M.W. & S. SMALE [1974]. *Differential Equations, Dynamical Systems, and Linear Algebra.* New York, London : Academic Press.

HOWITT, P. [1989]. «Determinate Outcomes with Multiple Equilibria», manuscript, University of Western Ontario.

HOWITT, P. & MCAFEE [1984]. «Stable Low Level Equilibrium», manuscript, University of Western Ontario.

HOWITT, P. & MCAFEE [1988]. «Stability of Equilibria with Externalities», *Quarterly Journal of Economics* 103 : 261-163.

KING, R.G. & S.T. REBELO [1988]. «Business Cycles with Endogenous Growth», unpublished, University of Rochester.

KIYOTAKI, N. [1988]. «Multiple Expectational Equilibria under Monopolistic Competition», *Quarterly Journal of Economics* 103 : 261-277.

KRUGMAN, P. [1991]. «History versus Expectations», *Quarterly Journal of Economics* 106 : 651-666.

LEIJONHUFVUD, A. [1973]. «Effective Demand Failures», *Swedish Journal of Economics* 75 : 27-48.

LIVIATHAN, N. & P.A. SAMUELSON [1969]. «Notes on Turnpikes : Stable and Unstable», *Journal of Economic Theory* 1 : 454-475.

MARSDEN, J.E. & M. MCCRACKEN [1976]. *The Hopf Bifurcation and its Applications.* New York-Berlin-Heidelberg-Tokyo : Springer-Verlag.

MARSHALL, A. [1920]. *Principle of Economics.* Londres : MacMillan Press.

MATSUYAMA, K. [1991]. «Increasing Returns, Industrialization and Indeterminacy of Equilibrium». *Quarterly Journal of Economics* 106 : 617-650.

RAMSEY, F.P. [1928]. «A Mathematical Theory of Saving», *The Economic Journal* 38 : 543-559.

ROMER, P.M. [1986]. «Increasing Returns and Long-Run Growth», *Journal of Political Economy* 94 : 1002-37.

ROMER, P.M. [1989]. «Increasing Returns and the New Theories of Economic Growth», manuscript, University of Chicago.

SKIBA, A. [1978]. «Optimal Growth With a Convex-Concave Production Function», *Econometrica* 46 : 527-540.

WEITZMAN, M.L. [1982]. «Increasing Returns and the Foundations of Unemployment Theory», *The Economic Journal* 92 : 787-804.

WOODFORD, M. [1984]. «On Indeterminacy of Equilibrium in the Overlapping Generations Model», manuscript, Columbia University.

The Dynamics of Real Wages

PIERO FERRI

Department of Economics, University of Bergamo
Via Salvecchio 19, 24100 Bergamo, Italy

and

EDWARD GREENBERG[1]

Department of Economics, Washington University
One Brookings Drive, St. Louis MO 63130, USA

1 Introduction

Within the subject of labour market dynamics, controversies about the relationship between employment and real wages over the business cycle have a long history. In this perspective they raise theoretical and empirical issues, as is witnessed by the lack of well established "stylized facts." To the traditional dichotomy between those who believe in a countercyclical movement typically ascribed to Keynes (1936) and the supporters of the procyclical pattern (among others, Keynes (1939) himself),[2] a new attitude is emerging that believes this pattern to be very complex. The complexity derives either from the influence of stochastic elements or from the presence of factors that play different roles in different historical contexts. As Zarnowitz (1985, p. 543) points out: "The evidence is mixed and not conclusive. It varies with the choice of the deflator, the characteristics of the period covered, methods and dates."

According to Greenwald and Stiglitz (1988), three competing theories attempt to interpret these facts. The Real Business Cycle theories attribute these results to the functioning of a labour market that is essentially in equilibrium. The alternative theories, by stressing the role of imperfections and institutions, belong either to the traditional Keynesian perspective or to its new-Keyensian variety, where the latter attempts to supply microfoundations for the rigidities.

From a dynamic point of view, however, these theories belong to the same genus: they are mainly driven by exogenous shocks. This research strategy encounters difficulties even at the empirical level where these theories are supposed to have a decisive advantage over their rivals. For example, it is difficult to identify both the nature of the shocks (it is now fashionable to attribute them to the real sphere) and the forces that assure persistence of the phenomenon in time.

---

[1]We acknowledge financial support from the Italian Ministry of University and Scientific Research.

[2]Keynes's various opinions have been reconsidered in Hicks (1989, Chapter 4).

In what follows we consider the possibility that the stylised facts can be generated by endogenous forces. It is well known that one way to generate the cycle endogenously is to introduce some form of nonlinearity. In the present model, regime switching is used to introduce a piece-wise linear model that can generate complex dynamic behavior, similar to models based upon ceilings and floors. (See Hicks, 1950.) The revival of these models and the development of new nonlinear techniques (see Baumol and Benhabib, 1989, for a review) have started to challenge the dominant paradigm based upon linear models plus random shocks, even though empirical applications are still at a primitive stage. It is important to stress that our goal is not so much to disprove the role of exogenous forces as it is to understand whether endogenous forces can contribute to the explanation of facts. Moreover, important economic policy issues are involved: fluctuations attributed to economic policy measures that would destabilize an otherwise stable world may be the result of deeper economic forces.

We develop our research along two lines. First, we consider a shock-driven business cycle model to serve as a benchmark. In a series of papers, Nickell and coauthors (1986, 1988, 1989, and 1990) reach important conclusions about the pattern of real wages, the impact of different types of shocks, and the role of various kinds of rigidities. From the analysis of a small-scale macroeconomic model Dimsdale, Nickell, and Horsewood (1989, p. 275) conclude that "... the most interesting fact which emerges is that there is no necessary relation whatever between the depth of the recession induced by any given adverse shock and the movement of real wages." In order to understand this result it is essential to introduce the price equation explicitly into the discussion. In other words, the labour market alone is not sufficient to explain stylised facts about the labour market.

This lesson is accepted and further developed in our second line of research: to specify a model that can generate stylised facts by means of endogenous forces. The results confirm the richness of the dynamic patterns that emerge from a labour market considered within a small scale macroeconomic model and highlight the possible role of different kinds of rigidities in shaping historical results.

In the next section of the paper we consider some stylised facts and the challenges they pose to various theories. In section 3 we consider Nickell's model with particular emphasis on the relationship between real wages and economic activity, considered both asymptotically and dynamically. In Section 4 we justify and develop a regime-switching model that generates endogenously driven cycles. In section 5 we analyze the model, and in section 6 we examine the pattern of real wages that emerges from these models. Section 7 contains economic policy considerations, and Section 8 offers general conclusions.

Table 1: Relative variability of employment and real wages in manufacturing. (Monthly data)

		Standard deviations		Correlations
		Employment	Real Wages	
Austria	1965-83	0.614	1.785	0.126
Canada	1947-86	0.802	0.645	0.055
Japan	1952-85	0.543	1.332	0.056
U.K.	1953-83	0.387	1.375	-0.013
U.S.	1947-86	0.949	0.501	0.196

Source: Kennan (1988), pp. 162–63. (The log of each series was first differenced and regressed on a constant and monthly dummies.)

2 Facts and Theories

The main stylised facts about the relationship between real wages and employment can be summarised by their relative variability and contemporaneous correlation; these have been examined by Kennan (1988), whose results are cited in Table 1. Although these figures are very sensitive to the choice of the deflator and to the period considered, it is worth pointing out some general findings: i) The empirical association between employment and real wages is very weak. The correlation coefficients are generally close to zero, which confirms that the pattern is acyclical. This weak correlation is also found between real wages and output. (See Greenwald and Stiglitz, 1988.) ii) As far as relative variability is concerned, the results are not uniform. Employment is more variable than real wages in Canada and in the U. S. but not in the other countries. Because of the near zero correlation, scatter diagrams of the two variables typically assume one of two forms: either vertical ellipses, as in the case of the U.K. where the variability of real wages (on the y-axis) is greater than that of employment (on the x-axis), or horizontal ellipses, as in the case of the U.S where the opposite has occurred.

The second kind of pattern is disturbing to the Real Business Cycle theories, which consider shifts in labor demand to be the driving force of employment fluctuations and assume a stable, elastic supply curve. Studies based upon micro data, however, show that the supply curve is rather inelastic. As Greenwald and Stiglitz (1988, p. 241) put it: "To reconcile the data with the hypothesis that firms operate along the labor supply curve, one must argue that the cross-sectional studies are wrong or that there are important shifts in the short-run labor supply curve." That the vertical ellipse type of pattern can be considered compatible with these theories shows the difficulty of having a single framework applicable across different countries. Possibly, institutional features should be considered, and this is precisely where the Keynesian theories come in: the rejection of an auction labour market in favour of some form of imperfect competition is one of the main alternative research strategies.

3 A Small Scale Macroeconomic Model

Nickell (1988) specifies a three-equation, log linear model, where the unknowns are the level of economic activity (y), prices (p), and nominal wages (w) :

$$\begin{aligned} y &= \alpha_0 + \alpha_1(m-p) + \alpha_2 g & (1)\\ p - w &= \beta_0 - \beta_1(p - p_e) + \beta_2 y & (2)\\ w - p &= \gamma_0 - \gamma_1(p - p_e) + \gamma_2 y + z. & (3) \end{aligned}$$

Equation (1) is the demand equation, where y is total final expenditures, m is money, and g is exogenous real demand factors. The parameter α_1 synthesises the interest elasticity of demand for money and the impact of the rate of interest and real wealth on the level of final expenditures.

Equations (2) and (3) determine prices and wages, and their formulation is sufficiently general to encompass several mechanisms and institutions. In equation (2), prices are a function of the expected competitors' prices p_e and the level of activity. It is interesting to note the role of β_1 and β_2. The former is equal to zero if there is a competitive regime, while the latter is equal to zero if there is normal cost pricing. If there are decreasing returns, β_2 is greater than zero.

Equation (3) states that wage setting depends positively on expected prices and the level of activity. In addition, the wage bargain may depend on such factors as the strength of trade unions, the generosity of unemployment benefits, or changes in the terms of trade; these are included in z. The values of the parameters are chosen to impose long run homogeneity; β_1 and γ_1 reflect what is usually called nominal inertia, while β_2 and γ_2 measure (inversely) real rigidity.[3]

Equations (1), (2), and (3) form a complete model that determines wages, prices, and output for given levels of m, g, z, and p_e. The asymptotic behavior (i.e. the long run equilibrium) of the model is obtained when price expectations are fulfilled ($p = p_e$) so that:

$$\begin{aligned} y^* &= -\frac{\beta_0 + \gamma_0 + z}{\beta_2 + \gamma_2} & (4)\\ p^* &= m + \frac{\alpha_0 + \alpha_2 g - y*}{\alpha_1} & (5)\\ w^* - p^* &= \frac{\beta_2\gamma_0 - \gamma_2\beta_0 + \beta_2 z}{\beta_2 + \gamma_2}. & (6) \end{aligned}$$

[3]According to Blanchard (1987), who uses a similar model, in the case of imperfectly competitive firms these functions can no longer be interpreted as the usual supply and demand functions. Equation (2) is not an output supply equation but describes instead the joint movements of markups and output in response to shifts in demand. A small coefficient of the activity level in this equation implies that firms require a small increase in the markup to increase output. Equation (3) describes the joint movements of employment and real wages in response to shifts in the demand for labour. A low value of γ_2 in this equation has been justified in different ways by the New-Keynesians, for example by bargaining theories. For a review of these theories, see Blanchard and Fischer (1989).

The following points are worth noting. First, all parameters are nonnegative, except the constants in (4) in order to assure positive values for y^*. Second, the smaller are β_2 and γ_2, the larger is y^*. In other words, greater rigidity is associated with larger output. Third, demand side factors have no effect on the real equilibrium, and the model has the standard natural rate property despite the fact that no assumptions about clearing markets have been made. This occurs because equations (2) and (3) generate an equilibrium level of activity where the feasible real wage allowed by price setting behavior is made consistent with that emerging from wage bargaining.

The fact that demand shifts have no real effect in the long run equilibrium does not imply that they have no short run effects. To see this, assume $p_e = p(t-1)$.[4] In this case, the previous system becomes

$$\begin{aligned} y(t) &= \alpha_0 + \alpha_1(m - p(t)) + \alpha_2 g & (7)\\ p(t) - w(t) &= \beta_0 - \beta_1(p(t) - p(t-1)) + \beta_2 y(t) & (8)\\ w(t) - p(t) &= \gamma_0 - \gamma_1(p(t) - p(t-1)) + \gamma_2 y(t) + z, & (9)\end{aligned}$$

and we examine how real wages respond to a change in the money supply. In terms of deviations from asymptotic values, equations (6) through (9) yield

$$\hat{w}(t) - \hat{p}(t) = \frac{\gamma_2\beta_1 - \gamma_1\beta_2}{\beta_1 + \gamma_1}\alpha_1\omega^t\, dm, \qquad (10)$$

where

$$\omega = \frac{\beta_1 + \gamma_1}{\beta_1 + \gamma_1 + \alpha_1(\beta_2 + \gamma_2)}.$$

Some points are worth stressing. First, if $\gamma_2 + \beta_2 > 0$, then the system is stable and real wages tend to asymptotic values. Second, the pattern of real wages during recession (if dm is negative) depends on the values of the parameters. In particular, with

$$\rho = \frac{\gamma_2\beta_1 - \gamma_1\beta_2}{\beta_1 + \gamma_1},$$

then real wages tend to fall during recession if $\rho > 0$ or $\beta_1/\gamma_1 > \beta_2/\gamma_2$, "that is if prices are sticky relative to wages and if the impact of economic activity on prices is low relative to that on wages." (See Dimsdale, Nickell, and Horsewood, 1989, p. 275.) It is straightforward to see that nominal rigidities slow the return to equilibrium and that the opposite is true for the size of the activity effects in both the price and wage equations. Finally, note an interesting feature of this model: greater real rigidities lead both to a larger equilibrium output and to a slower rate of convergence to it.

In contrast to changes in the money supply, the results are different for exogenous shocks to the wage equation (z), which have long run effects. Nickell (1988,

[4]Dimsdale, Nickell, and Horsewood (1989) claim that the assumption of static expectations makes no difference to the basic results, which are essentially the same even under rational expectations.

p. 71), having shown that one obtains different results depending on parameter values, concludes: "...studying real wage movements will not, in general, reveal anything about the real consequences of adverse supply shocks even though the shocks themselves originate from the labour market."

In conclusion, one can say that the links between real wage dynamics and the level of economic activity depend on the nature of the shock affecting the economy and on the degree of nominal and real inertia characterising the wage and price equations. Two lessons are worth repeating in view of the analysis we intend to develop. The first is that the dynamics of real wages result from the interaction of wages and the price behaviour of firms, an interaction that integrates labour and product markets. The second is that different countries or the same country at different periods of time may experience different real wage patterns depending on parameter values.

4 The Economics of Regime Switching

Let us next consider what happens to the above results when we introduce regime switching, which appears to be the simplest device that is capable of generating persistent endogenous cycles.[5] There are two places in recent economics literature in which this tool of analysis has been employed and reasons for switching are given.[6] One is in the area of economic disequilibrium, where Keynesian, Walrasian, or repressed inflation situations can be found. (See, for instance, Malinvaud, 1980.) In this context regime switching means changes in parameter values as a function of the nature of the unemployment. A second place is the type of regime switching linked to changes in monetary policy, where institutional considerations are important.[7]

Our use of regime switching differs from the way it is used in the literature mentioned above. It differs from the first type in that changes in the parameters or shifts in the functions are linked to a threshold level of unemployment (or to some indicator linked to unemployment, such as the level of activity) rather than to the nature of unemployment. It differs from the second type in that these

[5] See Ferri and Greenberg (1989, 1990a) for additional discussion and applications of regime switching in macro models.

[6] An economic regime has been defined as a set of rules and institutions that embody the overall framework for economic activity and determine the behaviour patterns of economic agents.

[7] The most appropriate reference for our purposes is Lucas (1987), who argues that models should be based upon first principles in order to avoid these shifts. Other authors do not accept this conclusion, although stressing the importance of regime changes. See, for instance, Leijonhufvud (1987). The concept of regime switching has been extended beyond the realm of monetary policy to such areas as exchange rates (where changes from fixed, managed and flexible exchange rates are possible), the political environment (see Sachs, 1989), industrial relations, employment functions, and technological change (see Ferri and Greenberg, 1990b).

switches can take place even without policy changes.

Returning to Nickell's model of section 3 and concentrating on the wage equation (3), we can hypothesize three channels through which a regime switch can be generated, each associated with a change in a parameter:[8] γ_1, z, or γ_2. We concentrate on why γ_2 might change at a particular level of output; it should, however, also be noted that γ_1, which measures nominal rigidity, is particularly sensitive to changes in monetary regimes,[9] and z, which measures the impact of exogenous terms, can vary with the expected productivity gain and changes in industrial relations.[10] Keynes (1936, p. 301) suggested reasons to expect discontinuous changes in γ_2: "In actual experience the wage-unit does not change continuously in terms of money in response to every small change in effective demand, but discontinuously. These points of discontinuity are determined by the psychology of the workers and by the policies of employers and trade unions."

Subsequent research suggests nonlinearity, but not necessarily discontinuity, in the relation between wages and unemployment. Phillips (1958, p. 283) stated that "...the relation between unemployment and the rate of change of wage rates is ...likely to be highly nonlinear." Phillips stressed an asymmetry between a wage increase and a wage reduction as an explanation. Lipsey (1960) emphasized, within the same theoretical framework, the role of sectoral imbalances to justify the presence of nonlinearity.

Wage equations estimated more recently, however, are different from the original Phillips curve. They are mainly concerned with the real wage level,[11] and their paradigm of reference is usually union-firm bargaining mechanisms. Nickell (1987) considers the effect of the changing proportion of recently unemployed persons who are both more active in looking for work and more attractive to employers. Since this proportion tends to fall as the level of unemployment becomes higher, the

[8]Many authors have found empirically that the wage equation changes in time and that these changes may take the form of shifts in the intercept or changes in the slope. (For a discussion of this distinction, see Medoff and Abraham, 1982.) According to Gordon (1988, p. 282) "...the results are consistent with those who claim that the decade of the 1980s has witnessed a 'new regime' in wage formation." (Gordon's remarks are not entirely pertinent to our model in two respects. First, we consider a wage equation expressed in real terms and second, we are particularly interested in changes in the parameter measuring the impact of activity.)

[9]In this perspective, Okun (1981, p. 310) claims: "...it becomes reasonable for people to change their secular inflation expectations less in response to periods of prolonged slack (like 1958–63) than to periods of prolonged boom (like 1965–69)."

[10]Perry (1986, p. 141) says that "...the most useful way to characterize what goes on at the macroeconomic level is to view the short-run response of wage (and price) inflation to cyclical fluctuations in output as operating around a relatively stable norm for wage increases that only changes in response to extreme or prolonged departures of the economy from what is typical."

[11]See Christofides and Oswald (1989) for a discussion of the changing nature of the estimated wage equation.

wage-unemployment relationship is nonlinear.[12] Finally, Manning (1990) hypothesizes a wage equation like (3) that is based on a nonlinear bargaining model.

We conclude from this discussion that a nonlinear relation between real wages and economic activity, whether measured by unemployment or output, is to be expected.[13]

In the model presented in the next section we utilize a discontinuous relationship in the spirit of Keynes. It should be noted that discontinuities may also arise in the form of piece-wise approximations to continuous nonlinear functions. (See Medio, 1978.)

5 A Regime-Switching Model

Before presenting our model formally, we discuss the form of the nonlinear relationship between wages and economic activity that was mentioned in the previous section. Although very little direct econometric work has been done on the question whether slopes of wage and price equations switch as functions of economic activity, some indirect evidence may be cited. Dimsdale, Nickell, and Horsewood (1989, p. 286) estimate price and wage equations for Britain in the 1930s, a period when economic activity was clearly depressed. They find a coefficient of -0.054 on log unemployment, which would indicate a coefficient of the opposite sign on output. In contrast, for the period 1954–1983, when the economy spent at least part of the time at high levels of economic activity, Layard and Nickell (1986, p. S152) find a coefficient of -0.621, which would indicate an upward shift in the relation between real wages and economic activity. Moreover, the price equation for the 1930s fails to include a term for economic activity (p. 286), while the price equation for the second period (p. S151) contains a positive and statistically significant coefficient on a variable representing 'real demand relative to potential output.' Although this evidence is far from conclusive and is based on the extreme situation of the 1930s, it is consistent with the hypothesis of a discontinuous shift of the relationship. (Note that a concurrent shift in the intercept would be required to produce a continuous function after a shift in the slope.) It is important to note that our analysis is basically unaffected if the price and wage curves switch at different values of activity, if the switch point depends on whether activity is increasing or decreasing (a form of hysteresis), or if there is a stochastic component

[12]Pissarides (1990) stresses the relevance of unemployment duration from a firm hiring point of view. If unemployed workers with short duration are more profitable to firms, hiring rates exhibit highly nonlinear dynamics.

[13]If a labour market indicator is also introduced, it would be possible to consider two different thresholds, one for the product market and one for the labour market. In this case, firms may be supposed not to supply whatever is demanded, and dynamics with rationing would be introduced. For a discussion, see Nickell (1990).

to the switch point. For our purposes, however, at least one of the curves must have a discontinuity.

In our model, therefore, we assume that when $y(t-1) \geq y_0$, γ_2 is increased by ψ in period t, and, for simplicity, that the coefficient measuring the impact of activity in the price equation is supplemented at y_0 by δ.[14] Equations (2) and (3) become, respectively,

$$\begin{aligned} p - w &= \beta_0 - \beta_1(p - p_e) + (\beta_2 + \delta)y & (11) \\ w - p &= \gamma_0 - \gamma_1(p - p_e) + (\gamma_2 + \psi)y + z. & (12) \end{aligned}$$

It follows that the asymptotic values in regime 2 of output, prices and real wages are

$$\begin{aligned} y^{**} &= -\frac{\beta_0 + \gamma_0 + z}{(\beta_2 + \delta) + (\gamma_2 + \psi)} & (13) \\ p^{**} &= m + \frac{\alpha_0 + \alpha_2 g - y^{**}}{\alpha_1} & (14) \\ w^{**} - p^{**} &= \frac{(\beta_2 + \delta)\gamma_0 - (\gamma_2 + \psi)\beta_0 + (\beta_2 + \delta)z}{(\beta_2 + \delta) + (\gamma_2 + \psi)}. & (15) \end{aligned}$$

From equations (4), (8), and (9), we obtain the dynamics of output when $y(t-1) < y_0$:

$$y(t) = (1 - \omega_1)y * + \omega_1 y(t-1), \tag{16}$$

where

$$\omega_1 = \frac{\beta_1 + \gamma_1}{\beta_1 + \gamma_1 + \alpha_1(\beta_2 + \gamma_2)},$$

which is the ω of equation (10). For $y(t-1) \geq y_0$, one obtains from equations (11), (12), and (13)

$$y(t) = (1 - \omega_2)y^{**} + \omega_2 y(t-1), \tag{17}$$

where

$$\omega_2 = \frac{\beta_1 + \gamma_1}{\beta_1 + \gamma_1 + \alpha_1[(\beta_2 + \delta) + (\gamma_2 + \psi)]}.$$

Figure 1 depicts the long-run relationship (when $p = p_e$) between real wages and output. From equation (2) a decreasing curve is obtained, while equation (3) is increasing in the level of output for $\gamma_2 > 0$. Their intersection is $(y^*, w^* - p^*)$, given by equations (4) and (5). The graph shows another wage curve (12), steeper than the original, which results from the increasing pressure of labour market forces for the reasons discussed in the previous section; there is also a second price curve (11), whose slope reflects increasing pressure on prices as economic activity increases. The latter two curves intersect at $(y^{**}, w^{**} - p^{**})$, given by equations

[14]Mutatis mutandis, changes in the values of the parameters in the price equation can be justified along the same lines as the wage equation. See Blanchard and Fischer (1989) for a general discussion. See also Rotemberg and Saloner (1989).

(13) and (15). The threshold value of output y_0 separates the two regimes: regime 1 is the regime associated with a level of activity less than y_0, and regime 2 is associated with a greater level. It must be stressed that this threshold level has no equilibrium properties and, as will be explained below, its role depends not only on its absolute value, but also on the values of other parameters and the structure of the model. There are several ways of interpreting y_0: in the context of the Phillips curve, y_0 corresponds to that level of unemployment at which the curvature of the wage-unemployment relation changes sharply; and in the context of wage-bargaining models, it corresponds to that level of unemployment at which the relative bargaining power of firms and unions changes.

Our model, therefore, contains multiple equilibria; to be precise there is have one equilibrium for each regime. This is not a novelty; multiple equilibria have been found for other models.[15] In the present model these points are not necessarily reached even in the long run, because of the switch in regimes. In fact, if $\delta+\psi > 0$, which can be interpreted as an increase in overall real rigidity, $y^{**} < y^*$ (while the opposite is true for prices); if this condition holds and if y_0 is between y^{**} and y^*, a cycle can be generated. The fundamental mechanism governing the cycle is that y^{**}, which is the equilibrium for regime 2, lies in regime 1, and y^* is in regime 2. Thus, a system initially in regime 2 is driven by equation (17) toward y^{**} and eventually enters regime 1, at which time it is driven by equation (16) back towards y^*, which lies in regime 2. We might interpret these two equilibria as corresponding to two different natural rates of unemployment, neither of which is reached because of the regime switch. The regime switch occurs because the rigidity parameters in regime 1 generate a larger equilibrium output than the threshold value. Of course, with different values of parameters one of these equilibria might be reached, but then cycles would not persist.

The parameters affect the cycle through their impacts on the positions of the asymptotic values relative to the threshold and on the values of the ω_i. Note that a small (large) value of ω_i increases (decreases) the speed of convergence to equilibrium and therefore generates a short (long) cycle. The parameters measuring the impact of activity (γ_2 and ψ) play an essential role because they affect the equilibrium values and the ω_i, but this is not true for z and γ_1. A large value of z can reduce y^{**} relative to y_0, a necessary condition to obtain a cycle, but z does not affect the ω_i. In contrast, γ_1 affects the ω_i but not the asymptotic values. In general, the higher β_1 and γ_1, the longer the cycle. In other words, nominal rigidities lengthen the cycle.

[15] For instance, Manning (1990) obtains multiple equilibria with a Nickell type of model by introducing the hypothesis of increasing returns to scale. He then studies the dynamics by means of a quadratic cost adjustment function. See Blanchard and Fischer (1989) both on the relationship between multiple equilibria and economic fluctuations and on ways of obtaining multiple equilibria in the labor market, for instance, through the interrelationships between transaction costs and the labor supply. On this point, see also Pissarides (1990).

6 The Pattern of Real Wages

To study the dynamics of real wages in regime 1, substitute equation (1) into (8) and (9) and then use equations (4) and (6) to obtain

$$w(t) - p(t) = (w^* - p^*) + \rho_1(y(t) - y^*), \tag{18}$$

where

$$\rho_1 = \frac{\beta_1\gamma_2 - \beta_2\gamma_1}{\beta_1 + \gamma_1}.$$

From the corresponding equations for regime 2, one obtains

$$w(t) - p(t) = (w^{**} - p^{**}) + \rho_2(y(t) - y^{**}), \tag{19}$$

where

$$\rho_2 = \frac{\beta_1(\gamma_2 + \psi) - (\beta_2 + \delta)\gamma_1}{\beta_1 + \gamma_1}.$$

If we assume that the price equation does not switch, i.e. $\delta = 0$, implications of the model for wage dynamics can be compared with those of Nickell. First, suppose that the product market has no nominal rigidities, i.e. $\beta_1 = 0$; then it is apparent from (18) and (19) that we move on the price equation. The correlation between real wages and output is negative, and the relative variability of wages and output depends on the slope. A simulation exercise for this case yields a 5-period cycle that remained in regime 1 for four periods and in regime 2 for one.[16] Next, assume also a normal cost pricing strategy, i.e. $\beta_2 = 0$; then the price line becomes horizontal. In this case there is no correlation between the variables, with output experiencing variability and real wages remaining fixed. A higher value of z results in a greater equilibrium output, but not in higher real wages.

The dynamics of real wage are pictured in Figure 2, which is built upon equations (18) and (19), respectively, depending on regime. Movement is along the two lines in the direction of the arrows; for the situation portrayed in Figure 2 it is in a counterclockwise direction. Since the vertical intercept is equal for both lines,[17] the direction of movement is clockwise when $\rho_1 > \rho_2$; in that case, $(y(t), w(t)-p(t))$ moves to the right when in regime 1 and to the left when in regime 2. It is counterclockwise otherwise. The correlation between real wages and output over the cycle, however, cannot be inferred from the direction of movement in this discrete-time model, because it depends on the actual values assumed by these variables.

This result differs from Nickell's, where, in the case of an adverse demand shock, real wages fall with activity only if the value of ρ is positive. In the present case, the values of the ρ_i in the two regimes are important, not just their sign.

---

[16] Parameter values used to simulate the system composed of equations (16), (17), (18), and (19) are the following: $\alpha_0 = 0.099$; $\alpha_1 = 0.6$; $\alpha_2 = 0.1$; $\beta_0 = -0.3$; $\beta_1 = 0$; $\beta_2 = 0.1$; $\gamma_0 = 0.2$; $\gamma_1 = 0.5$; $\gamma_2 = 0.2$; $\delta = 0$; $\psi = 0.4$; $w(0) = 51$; $p(0) = 50$; $m = 50$; $g = 0.05$; $z = 0$; $y_0 = 0.30$.

[17] This requires that z does not change between regimes, which we assume for convenience.

As we shall see shortly this is not the only difference from Nickell's analysis. The main conclusion, however, is the same: there cannot be a precise stylised pattern, because the pattern depends on the historical conditions influencing both the labour and the product market.

To reinforce this conclusion let us consider the results of other simulation exercises. Figure 3 displays an eight-period cycle that spends seven periods in regime 1 and one period in regime 2 and moves counterclockwise.[18] Additional simulations reveal that both positive and negative correlations are possible and that the relative variability between activity and real wages depends on parameter values.[19] What matters in this model is not only the relative rigidity in the product market with respect to the labour market, but also differences across regimes.

7 Policy Considerations

Conclusions about economic policy that might be drawn from our analysis depend very much on the nature of the benchmark model that we have utilized. In a model that generates a natural rate of unemployment, the long-run effect of monetary policy (changes in m) and of fiscal policy (changes in g) can have an impact on prices but not on output. (See equations (4) and (5)). In the short run, monetary policy is transmitted by α_1: a lower α_1 implies a larger ω and a longer cycle. This result also appears in our variant of the benchmark model.[20]

Policy could be treated in a broader perspective if the present framework were extended by introducing alternative hypotheses. For example, a different hypothesis about price expectations would introduce more links between nominal and real variables, and policy issues associated with the Phillips curve debate could be considered. Moreover, if one introduces hysteresis, which, according to Nickell (1988, p. 73), "... always tends to weaken the equilibrating forces in the economy," a rich context for the application of economic policy is created.

The version of the regime switching model that we have analysed has some implications for policy issues in general and more specifically. First, the model is characterised by multiple equilibria that can be interpreted as different natural rates of unemployment. In this context the role of policy becomes different than in those models that have one equilibrium. (See Manning, 1990.) Second, the

[18] In this simulation we emphasise changes in the parameters affecting the level of activity in the wage and price equations. With respect to the simulation carried out under footnote 16, we change the following values: $\beta_1 = 0.6$ and $\delta = 0.2$.

[19] For instance, if the values of δ and ψ in the previous simulation are reversed ($\delta = 0.4$ and $\psi = 0.2$), a clockwise movement is obtained (ρ_1 becomes greater than ρ_2). With $\delta = 0.2$, one obtains a counterclockwise movement but with a greater variability in real wages than in output. In both cases, there is a positive correlation between wages and output.

[20] It is worth stressing that these results depend on the model with which we have been dealing. Hahn and Solow (1986) find in another framework that wage flexibility may lead to erratic adjustments.

fact that the model can generate an endogenous cycle implies that instability is not necessarily related to economic policy measures but may reflect the working of the economy. Third, in our model the role of the threshold is strategic. The closer is the value of the threshold to y^*, the longer is the cycle and the time spent in regime 1,[21] which justifies our assertion that the role of the threshold depends not only on its absolute value but also on the other parameters of the model. It follows that the parameters of the model or values of exogenous variables might be manipulated to eliminate the cycle or to remain longer in regime 2. Policy instruments to accomplish this include an income policy to control the switching in behavior and a policy toward productivity to reduce conflict over distribution.

8 Concluding Remarks

In this paper we have investigated the behaviour of labour market variables from a business cycle perspective through a simple regime switching model. In endogenizing the cycle by adding a regime switch to Nickell's benchmark equations, we strengthen his results and at the same time find some differences.

In these models real wage movements are, in general, not related systematically to movements in activity as a result of either demand shocks or shocks to the wage equation: reasons must be found in how prices are set. It follows that the empirical results can be "period" or "country" specific, and it is not surprising that it has been so difficult to find a consistent stylised pattern. These results are confirmed by our analysis, but two main differences are worth stressing. First, the model can generate endogenous cycles. Second, nominal and real rigidities play different roles. An increase in nominal rigidities, which emphasises the role of demand shocks, can lengthen the cycle, but changes in the parameters concerned with output affect both the length of the cycle and whether or not the model generates a cycle. In our model, the strategic role is played by the relative rigidity in the two regimes.

The analysis can be extended beyond the benchmark model. If the main lesson of the benchmark model is the necessity of integrating the labour market with the product market, a further step could be that of integrating both these aspects with aggregate demand analysis. In this perspective, there are two main consequences. First, the pattern of aggregate demand cannot be considered independent of what happens in the labour market. Second, the broader the perspective becomes, the more unsatisfactory it is to regard exogenous shocks as the Archimedes lever governing dynamics.

[21] The length of the cycle and the number of periods spent in regime 1 change in the following way as functions of the threshold value y_0 in the simulation of footnote 16:

y_0	Length of cycle	Periods in regime 1
0.1	no cycle	0
0.15	5	2
0.18	2	1
0.31	11	9

BIBLIOGRAPHY

Baumol, W. J. and Benhabib, J. (1989). 'Chaos: significance, mechanism, and economic applications.' *Journal of Economic Perspectives,* vol. 3, pp. 77–105.

Blanchard, O. J. (1987). 'Aggregate and individual price adjustments.' *Brookings Papers on Economic Activity,* pp. 57–109.

Blanchard, O. J. and Fischer, S. (1989). *Lectures on Macroeconomics.* Cambridge: MIT Press.

Christofides, L. N. and Oswald, A. J. (1989). 'Real wage determination in collective bargaining agreements.' Cambridge: NBER Working Paper No. 3188.

Dimsdale, N. N., Nickell, S. J., and Horsewood, N. (1989). 'Real wages and unemployment in Britain during the 1930s.' *The Economic Journal,* vol. 99, pp. 271–292.

Ferri, P. and Greenberg, E. (1989). *The Labor Market and Business Cycle Theories.* New York: Springer-Verlag.

Ferri, P. and Greenberg, E. (1990a). 'A wage-price regime switching model.' *Journal of Economic Behavior and Organization,* vol. 13, pp. 77–95.

Ferri, P. and Greenberg, E. (1990b). 'Technical change and the wage-share fluctuations in a regime-switching model.' Mimeo.

Gordon, R. J. (1988). 'The role of wages in the inflation process.' *American Economic Review Papers and Proceedings,* vol. 78, pp. 276–283.

Greenwald, B. C. and Stiglitz, J. E. (1988). 'Examining alternative macroeconomic theories.' *Brookings Papers on Economic Activity,* pp. 207–260.

Hahn, F. H. and Solow, R. M. (1986). 'Is wage flexibility a good thing?' In *Wage Rigidity and Unemployment.* Beckerman, W. (ed). London: Duckworth.

Hicks, J. R. (1950). *Trade Cycles.* Oxford: Clarendon Press.

Hicks, J. R. (1989). *A Market Theory of Money.* Oxford: Clarendon Press.

Kennan, J. (1988). 'Equilibrium interpretations of employment and real wage fluctuations.' In *NBER Macroeconomics Annual.* Fischer, S. (ed). Cambridge: MIT Press.

Keynes, J. M. (1936). *The General Theory of Employment, Interest and Money.* London: Macmillan.

Keynes, J. M. (1939). 'Relative movements of real wages and output.' *Economic Journal,* vol. 49, pp. 34–51.

Layard, P. R. G. and Nickell, S. J. (1986). 'Unemployment in Britain.' *Economica,* vol. 53, pp. S121–S170.

Leijonhufvud, A. (1987). 'Rational expectations and monetary institutions.' In *Monetary Theory and Economic Institutions.* (De Cecco, M. and Fitoussi, J. P. (eds). London: Macmillan.

Lipsey, R. G. (1960). 'The relation between unemployment and the rate of change of money wage rates in the United Kingdom 1862-1957: a further analysis.' *Economica,* vol. 27, pp. 1–31.

Lucas, R. E. (1987). *Models of Business Cycles.* Oxford: Basil Blackwell.

Malinvaud, E. (1980). *Profitability and unemployment.* Cambridge: Cambridge University Press.

Manning, A. (1990). 'Imperfect competition, multiple equilibria and underemployment policy.' *The Economic Journal,* vol. 100, pp. 151–162.

Medio, A. (1978). *Teoria Nonlineare del Ciclo Economico.* Bologna: Societa Editrice il Mulino.

Medoff, J. L. and Abraham, K. G. (1982). 'Unemployment, unsatisfied demand for labor, and compensation growth, 1956-80.' In *Workers, Jobs, and Inflation.* Baily, M. N. (ed). Washington: The Brookings Institution.

Nickell, S. J. (1987). 'Why is wage inflation in Britain so high.' *Oxford Bulletin of Economics and Statistics,* vol. 49, pp. 103–128.

Nickell, S. J. (1988). 'Wages and economic activity.' In *Keynes and Economic Policy: The Relevance of the General Theory after Fifty Years.* Eltis, W. and Sinclair, P. (eds). London: Macmillan.

Nickell, S. J. (1990). 'Unemployment: a survey.' *The Economic Journal,* vol. 100, pp. 391–439.

Okun, A. M. (1981). *Prices and Quantities: A Macroeconomic Analysis.* Washington: The Brookings Institution.

Perry, G. L. (1986). 'Policy lessons from the postwar period.' In *Wage Rigidity and Unemployment.* Beckerman, W. (ed). London: Duckworth.

Phillips, A. W. (1958). 'The relation between unemployment and the rate of change of money wage rates in the United Kingdom, 1861-1957.' *Economica,* vol. 25, pp. 283–299.

Pissarides, C. A. (1990). 'Unemployment and the persistence of employment shocks.' London: Centre for Labour Economics Discussion Paper No. 377.

Rotemberg, J. J and Saloner, G. (1986). 'A supergame-theoretic model of price wars during booms.' *American Economic Review,* vol. 76, pp. 390–407.

Sachs, J. (1989). 'Social conflict and populist policies in Latin America.' Cambridge: NBER Working Paper No. 2897.

Zarnowitz, V. (1985). 'Recent work on business cycles in historical perspective: a review of theories and evidence.' *Journal of Economic Literature,* vol. XXIII, pp. 523–580.

Figure 1: A Two-regime model

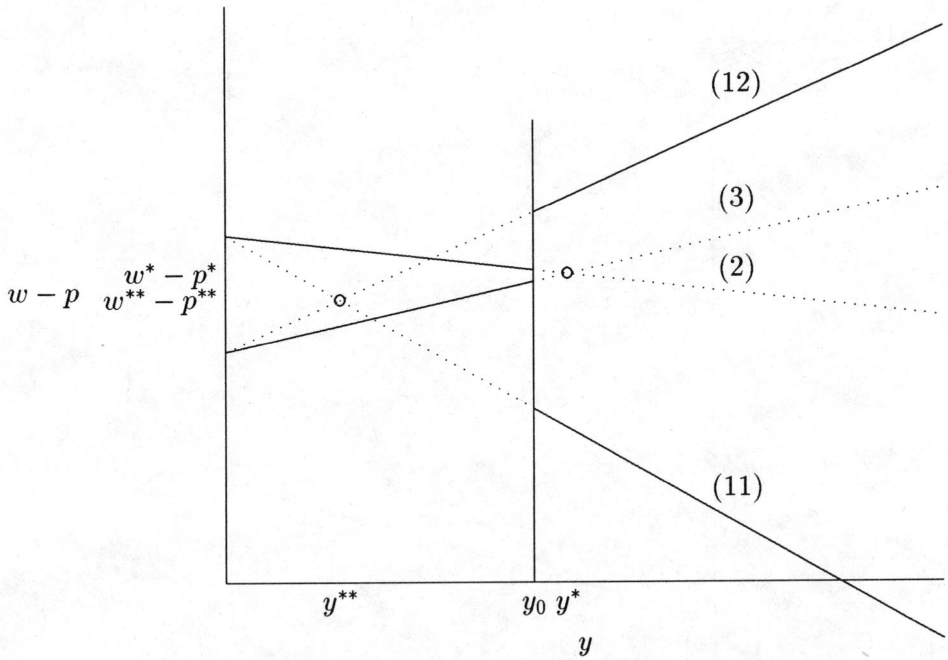

Numbers in parentheses refer to numbered equations in text.

Figure 2: Real wages and output.

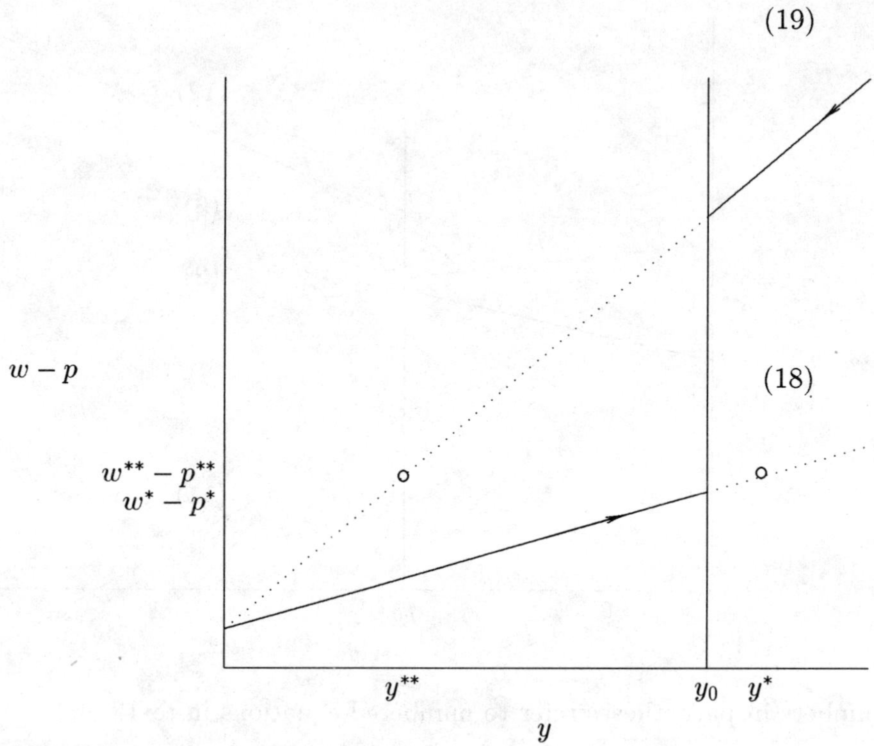

Numbers in parentheses refer to numbered equations in text.

Figure 3: Cycle in real wages and output.

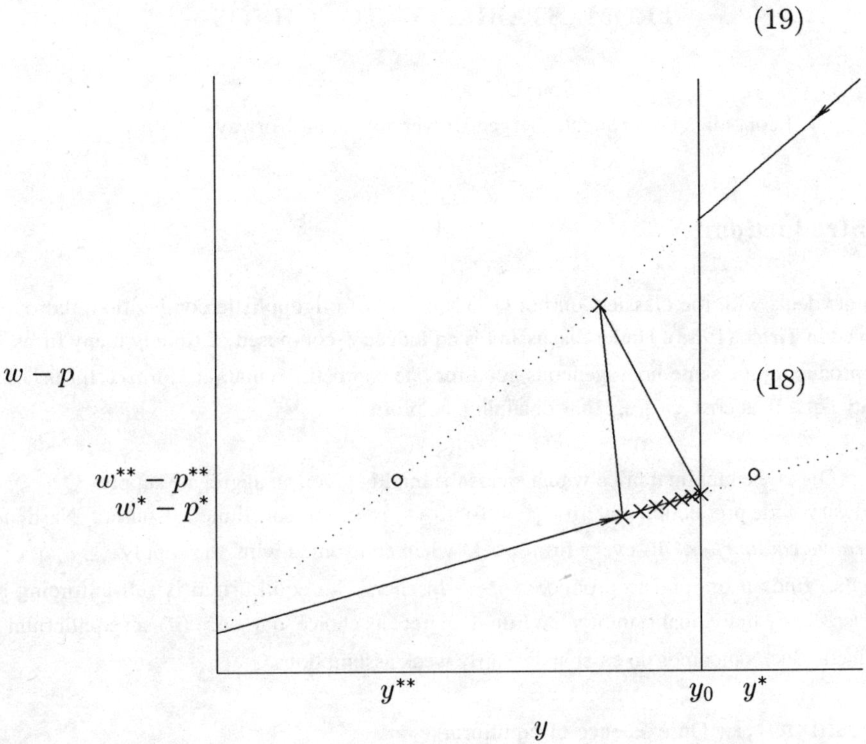

Numbers in parentheses refer to numbered equations in text.

OLIGOPOLISTIC COMPETITION; FROM STABILITY TO CHAOS

Sjur D. Flåm,
Economics Department, Bergen University, 5008 Norway

1. Introduction.

This note deals with the classic Cournot (1838) model of oligopolistic competition, thoroughly reviewed in Tirole (1988). Under discussion is an industry composed of finitely many firms $i \in I$, all producing the same homogeneous good for one competitive market. Firm i furnishes the quantity $q_i \geq 0$ at cost $c_i(q_i)$, thus obtaining the profit

$$\pi_i = p(Q)q_i - c_i(q_i).$$

Here $p(Q)$ is the maximal price which clears the market given an aggregate supply $Q := \Sigma_i q_i$. An industry-wide production pattern $q^* = (q^*_i)_{i \in I}$ is said to constitute a Cournot -Nash *non-cooperative equilibrium* iff every firm $i \in I$, when confronted with the supply $\Sigma_{\iota \neq i} q^*_\iota$ of its rivals, finds it optimal to produce q^*_i. In short, an equilibrium is self-enforcing and characterized by individual stability; no firm i regrets its choice q^*_i once (if) an equilibrium q^* is attained. Such outcomes do exist under fairly weak assumptions.

Proposition 1.1.(On existence of equilibria)
Suppose every profit function π_i *is concave upper semicontnuous with respect own production* q_i *and that the inverse demand* $p(.)$ *is continuous. Also suppose that each* q_i *is bounded above. Then there exists at least one equilibrium.*
This is a direct corollary of (Aubin, 1984, Thm.12.2). To reckognize equilibria when they come about, it is convenient to record, without proof, the following

Proposition 1.2. (On characterization of equilibria)
Assume the marginal profit $m_i := \partial\pi_i/\partial q_i$ *is well defined as long as* $q \geq 0$. *If all profit functions* π_i *are concave with respect to own production* q_i, *then* q^* *is an equilibrium iff one of the following equivalent assertions hold:*

(1) $m_i(q^*) \leq 0$, $q_i^* \geq 0$, *and* $m_i(q^*) q_i^* = 0$ *for all* i;

(2) *for all* i, $m_i(q^*) = 0$ *whenever* $q_i > 0$, *otherwise the positive part* $m_i(q^*)^+ = 0$;

(3) $\Sigma_{i \in I} m_i(q^*)(q_i - q_i^*) \leq 0$ *for all* $q = (q_i)_{i \in I} \geq 0$.

Our concern here is not with equilibrium responses or their characterizations, but rather with *disequilibrium behavior*. Specifically, we shall consider two paradigms.

First, in Section 2, we explore a quite natural, continuous-time process, designed via (2), that goes as follows. Each firm $i \in I$ starts with some non-negative production $q_i(0)$ and updates this at every instant of time $t \geq 0$, guided by its current marginal gain $m_i = \partial\pi_i/\partial q_i$. Specifically, given a smooth, non-negative function $s(Q)$ bounded away from zero, let

$$dq_i(t)/dt = s(Q)\, m_i(q(t)) \quad \text{as long as } q_i(t) > 0, \qquad (1.1)$$

Otherwise, replace (1.1) by

$$dq_i(t)/dt = s(Q)\, m_i(q(t))^+, \quad \text{when } q_i(t) = 0. \qquad (1.2)$$

In short, (1.1) says that as long as a firm earns profit on the last unit sold (i.e. $m_i > 0$), it produces even more. Else, if the last unit brought a loss ($m_i < 0$) , production is reduced. Only at $m_i = 0$, is output stabilized. The modification in (1.2) ensures that $q_i(t) \geq 0$ througout. A simple example is illustrated in Fig. 1 below.

Second, in Section 3, we investigate the following discretized version of (1.1-2):

$$q_i^{k+1} = \{ q_i^k + s_k(Q^k)\, m_i(q^k) \}^+, \quad k = 0,1,.... \qquad (1.3)$$

where $s_k(Q^k) > 0$ is the stepsize at stage k.

Remark. In Prop. 1.2, and in much of what follows, we can accomodate for instances where $m_i = \partial\pi_i/\partial q_i$ stands for the partial (super)differential in the generalized sense of convex analysis (Rockafellar, 1970)). Then (1.1-2) would read

$$dq_i(t)/dt \in s(Q)\, m_i(q(t)) \quad \text{if} \quad q_i(t) > 0, \qquad (1.1)'$$

$$dq_i(t)/dt \in s(Q)\{g_i^+ : g_i \in m_i(q(t))\} \text{ otherwise.} \qquad (1.2)'$$

Although such situations, involving non-smooth data, occur often in practice, we shall refrain from this generality in the subsequent analysis. For more on this see instead Flåm & Ben-Israel (1990).

2. Continuous convergence.

The main issue is whether equilibrium will be attained or approached over time. For this we focus on instances where a unique equilibrium is known to exist. It is convenient then to invoke some monotonicity in one form or another.

Definition. (Monotonicity)
The correspondence $m(q) := (m_i(q))_{i\in I} = (\partial\pi_i(q)/\partial q_i)_{i\in I}$ *of marginal profits is said to be monotone (decreasing) if for all* $q, q' \geq 0,\ q \neq q'$, *we have*

$$\Sigma_{i \in I} [m_i(q) - m_i(q')] (q_i - q_i') \leq 0. \qquad (2.1)$$

If, on such occasions, strict inequality holds in (2.1), *then* m *is called* strictly monotone. *A monotone* m *is called* maximal *if its graph is not properly contained in that of another monotone correspondence.*

Therorem 2.1. (Global asymptotic stability of (1.1-2))

1.(Existence and uniqueness of trajectories) *Suppose the correspondence* $m(q)$ *of marginal profits is maximal monotone. Then, from very initial production pattern* $q(0) \geq 0$, *there emanates a unique, infinitely extendable, absolutely continuous trajectory* $q(t), t \geq 0$, *solving* (1.1-2) *almost everywhere. Also, if there exists at least one equilibrium, then the trajectory* $q(t), t \geq 0$, *is bounded.*

2.(Uniqueness and stability of equilibria) *Suppose* m *is strictly monotone. Then there exists at most one equilibrium* q^*. *If moreover,* m *is strictly monotone with respect to such a* q^* *(now assumed to exist) with modulus* μ *in the sense that*

$$\Sigma_i [m_i(q) - m_i(q^*)] (q_i - q_i^*) \leq -\mu(\|q - q^*\|) \quad \textit{for all} \quad q \geq 0, \qquad (2.2)$$

then for any trajectory solving (1.1-2), *we have that* $\lim q(t) = q^*$. *Here* μ *is a continuous, non-negative function vanishing only at* 0.

3.(Rate of convergence) *In fact, if* μ *is purely quadratic (linear), then* $q(t)$ *tends to* q^* *at an exponential rate (in finite time, respectively).*

Proof. Statement 1 is results from (Aubin & Cellina, 1984, Thm.3.2.1). Indeed, the solution of (1.1-2) is, up to a change of time scale, the same as the one which emerges when the term $s(Q)$ is dropped. Omitting $s(Q)$, system (1.1-2) assumes the form

$$dq_i(t)/dt = Pm_i((q(t)) \quad \text{for all } i, \qquad (2.3)$$

where P denotes the projection onto the tangent cone of the half-line $[0,\infty)$ at the point $q_i \geq 0$. But by (Aubin & Cellina, op. cit.) the latter system (2.3) has a unique solution which is non-expansive with respect to equilibria.

Statement 2 and 3 concerning convergence are immediately verified by considering the Lyapunov function $L(t) := \|q(t) - q^*\|^2/2$ defined along the trajectory. Specifically, we get that

$$dL(t)/dt \leq \Sigma_i (q_i(t) - q_i^*) s(Q(t)) m_i(q(t))$$

$$\text{(by (2.2))} \qquad \leq \Sigma_i (q_i(t) - q_i^*) s(Q(t)) m_i(q^*(t)) - s(Q(t)) \mu(\|q(t) - q^*\|)$$

(by Prop.1.1(3)) $\leq$ - $s(Q(t))\,\mu(\,\|q(t) - q^*\|\,)$ $\leq$ - $\sigma\mu(\,\|q(t) - q^*\|\,)$

where σ is a positive lower bound on $s(Q(t)), t \geq 0$. Whence the conclusion is immediate.•

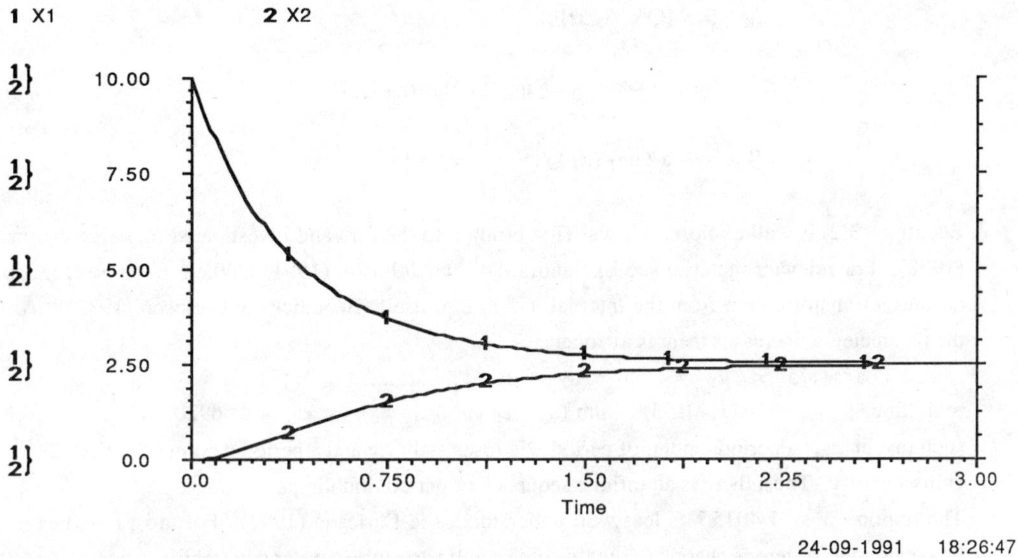

Fig.1. Depicted here are the system trajectories $q_1(t), q_2(t), t \geq 0$, marked 1 and 2 respectively of (1.1-2) for a duopoly with marginal costs $c_i{}'(q_i) = q_i$, inverse demand $p(Q) = 10 - Q$, scale function $s(Q) = 1$, and initial point $q(0) = (10, 0)$. The equilibrium $q^* = (2.5, 2.5)$. The trajectories result from simple numerical integration using Euler´s method with stepsize dt = .0125.

3. Discrete-time dynamics.

We turn now to system (1.3) which seems more realistic than (1.1-2). In fact, the discrete-time formulation (1.3) captures the fact that the market does not meet or adjust at every time instant. Rather, only at separate epochs, say every morning, will transactions take place. This introduces a lag structure, whence the system, if and when non-linear, is prone to exhibit complex behavior. To bring this out, let us simplify (1.3) by assuming that the positive part operation there is superfluous within the range we are discussing. Then, adding (1.3) over players we arrive at

$$Q^{k+1} = Q^k + s_k(Q^k)\,[p'(Q^k)Q^k + n\,p(Q^k) - \Sigma_i c_i{}'(q_i{}^k)], \quad k = 0,1,.... \quad (3.1)$$

where $n := /I/$ denotes the cardinality of the set I.

To have a handy grip of (3.1) we specialize, supposing that all cost functions $c_i(q_i) = c_{io} + c_{i1}q_i$ are linear, and likewise that $s_k(Q) = hQ$, $p(Q) = p_o - p_1Q$, all constants being positive. Simple algebra then provides us with the difference equation

$$x_{k+1} = 1 - a(x_k)^2, \tag{3.2}$$

where $a := [h^2(np_o - \Sigma_i c_{i1})^2 - 1]/4,$

$$x_k := [Q^k - \alpha]/\beta,$$

$$\alpha := [1 + h(np_o - \Sigma_i c_{i1})] / 2hp_1(n+1),$$

$$\beta := a / hp_1(n+1).$$

Equation (3.2) is well explored. It was first brought to the fore and investigated by Feigenbaum (1978). For relevant material see Ekeland(1984) and Johnson (1991). When $0 < a < 2$, (3.2) defines a transformation from the interval (-1,1) into itself (Benedicks & Carleson (1985)). As the parameter a increases there is a sequence

$$a_o = .75 < a_1 = 1.25 < a_2 < a_3 < \ldots\ldots\ldots\ldots$$

with $\lim a_n =: a^* \approx 1.40155$, $\lim (a_n - a_{n-1})/(a_{n+1} - a_n) =: \delta \approx 4.66920$,
such that at a_n a periodic point of period 2^n loses stability and a periodic point of period 2^{n+1} gains stability. Thus, there is an infinite sequence of period doublings.
The region $a > 1.40155$ is less well understood, see Carleson (1991). For most a-values in this region the system is chaotic except in some small parts where order and stability reign.

With no loss of generality we may set $np_o - \Sigma_i c_{i1} = 1$, so as to have $a = (h^2 - 1)/4$. Hence, increasing h above $(1 + 4a^*)^{1/2}$ is most likely to cause completely random system behavior in (3.2). Even for smaller h-values cycles may emerge with exceedingly long periods. In both cases the long run, "ergodic" system image of (3.2) will be a non-degenerate, invariant measure. This shows that high sensitivity to profit signals (i.e., relatively large h), on the part of each firm, may very much destabilize the community. Moreover, since the profit functions π_i often are jointly concave in q, everybody will lose: The resulting fluctuations are less profitable on the average than their mean. Clearly, if only one or few producers are reacting strongly out of equilibrium, it can happen that stability is preserved, and that these firms gain short term profit. But, if all firms have high speeds of adjustment, stability disappears and they may all be worse off.

4. Conclusion.

The Cournot model of oligopolistic competition offers, of course, a highly stilized scenario. In essence, and from its origin, the game is one-shot, static. By contrast, we have emphasized dynamic, out-of-equilibrium behavior, and in doing so, we gave no account for foresigth or conjectural variations. The myopic mode of play not withstanding, it should be noted that (1.1-2) and (1.3) are very much decentralized. Indeed, to drive either system there is essentially no need for communication; everybody can contend with observing only his own marginal profit and the aggregate supply. Also, (1.1-2), (1.3) have good meaning even when players are quite ignorant about market demand and the cost functions of their rivals.

In this setting we have indicated that, even when there is a unique equilibrium, aggregate production may fluctuate wildly. This is likely to happen when all firms have high velocities in their adaptation to profit posssibilities. The instability is, as usual, the joint result of non-linearity and lags. If there are no lags, the analysis of Section 1 shows that the non-cooperative equilibrium is a global attractor. These findings may be relevant for industries with insignificant cost for changing the output volume; for others more stability is likely to pertain.

References.

J.-P.Aubin, *L'analyse non linéaire et ses motivations économiques,* Masson, Paris (1984).

J.-P.Aubin and A. Cellina, *Differential inclusions,* Springer Verlag, Berlin (1984).

M. Benedicks and L. Carleson, "On iterations of 1- ax^2 on (-1,1)", *Annals of Mathematics,* 122,1-25 (1985):

L. Carleson, "Stochastic behavior of deterministic systems", *Journal of Economic Behavior & Organization,* vol. 16, no. 1-2, 85-92 (1991).

A. Cournot, *Recherches sur les Principes Mathématiques de la Théorie des Richesses,* Paris (1838).

I.Ekeland, *Le Calcul, L'imprévu; Les Figures du temps de Kepler a Thom,* Seuil, Paris (1984).

M.Feigenbaum, "Quantitative universality for a class of non-linear transformations", *Journal of Stat. Phys,* 19,25-52 (1978).

S.D. Flåm and A. Ben-Israel, "A continuous approach to oligopolistic market equilibrium", *Operations Research,* vol. 38,6, 1045-1051 (1990).

R.A.Johnson, "Loss of stability and emergence of chaos in dynamical systems",*Journal of Economic Behavior & Organization,* vol. 16, no. 1-2, 93-113 (1991).

R.T. Rockafellar, *Convex snalysis,* Princeton University Press, New Jersey (1970).

J.Tirole, *The theory of industrial organization,* MIT Press, Cambridge (1988).

Abstract. We consider a Cournot oligopoly involving finitely many quantity-setting producers. Each producer adjusts his output in response to current marginal profit. Given fairly weak market interaction, and *continuous* adjustments, such behavior leads the industry to a Nash non-cooperative equilibrium. The same dynamic process remains globally stable if *discretized* with small stepsizes. However, if all oligopolists react swiftly and strongly to profit signals (large stepsizes), the industry may be cornered in an impasse: Stability disappears, chaos may even emerge, and often everybody stands at loss. This finding sheds some doubt about alledged benefits in firms being quick in their adaptation to profit possibilities.

NEAREST NEIGHBOR FORECASTS OF PRECIOUS METAL RATES OF RETURN

Murray Frank*

Faculty of Commerce and Business Administration, University of British Columbia
Vancouver, B.C., Canada V6T 1Z2

Thanasis Stengos

Department of Economics, University of Guelph
Guelph, Ontario, Canada N1G 2W1

1. Introduction

In 1953 Kendall presented the results of a statistical study intended to separate out regular price cycles in the time-series of certain assets. Surprisingly he was not able to find such patterns. Kendall's discovery had been anticipated by Bachelier, Working and probably others. The observation that asset prices appear to behave randomly stimulated a great deal of empirical and theoretical research. Kendall expected opposition to his findings by economists. However under the label of the "efficient markets hypothesis," it is now well understood that such randomness is not evidence of irrationality in the market processes. As a result, such terms as martingale, random walk and fair game have become standard textbook material in finance. For a classic presentation of the development of these ideas see Fama (1970, 1991).

Recent developments have undermined the prevously wide acceptance of the martingale hypothesis. The theoretical assumptions used to generate the martingale hypothesis turn out to be quite restrictive. For example in the well known model of Lucas (1978) the twin assumptions of market clearing and rational expectations are not sufficient to generate the theoretical prediction of a martingale in asset prices. One needs to correct for dividends, discounting and then either assume that the agents are risk neutral[1] or else that there is no aggregate risk. Such added assumptions reduce the theoretical appeal.

Empirically too there are difficulties. A variety of anomalies such as the "January effect," the "small firm effect" and the "weekend effect" are by now well known, even if not well explained, see Thaler (1987a, 1987b). From a different perspective, evidence consistent with significant nonlinear structure has been found by Scheinkman and LeBaron (1989) and by Frank and Stengos (1989) in financial time series. All these developments reopen the possibility of there being usefully predictable structure in such time series.

As emphasized by Zellner (1988) prediction is central both in econometrics and in other sciences. Difficulty in obtaining satisfactory forecasts has however proved a problem for

---

*We would like to thank J.D. Farmer for helpful criticisms. The first author would like to thank the Centre for International Business Studies, U.B.C. for financial support, the second author acknowledges financial support from SSHRC grant number 879-11. Any deficiencies in the work rest with the authors.

[1] Even in a risk-neutral equilibrium world, transaction costs can also lead to the failure of prices to follow a martingale, see Hughson (1988) for example.

economists. In the physical sciences, where the systems are often simpler, and the theories are more complete there may be less of a problem. One can sometimes carefully measure the initial conditions and then use the equations of the model to produce forecasts. Without a convincing set of equations this method does not work so well. One may then take recourse to ad hoc statistical models. Predictions are generated by assuming that the future is a parametric stochastic function of the past. Recently the troubling nature of the functional form assumptions have received increased attention, see Gallant and White (1988), Priestley (1988) and Ullah (1988).

One usually employs a statistical model in place of a theoretical model due to an absence of well established knowledge about the system. Accordingly one would like to impose little prior structure since the status of such structure is uncertain. It is the lack of well established prior knowledge which necessitates the use of ad hoc methods. Such methods are then assessed according to how well they work.

We evaluate a simple approach to forecasting using the nearest neighbor method of Stone (1977). Applications of nearest neighbor methods include the work of Robinson (1987) in a regression context as well as the work of Yakowitz (1987) and of Farmer and Sidorowich (1987, 1988a, 1988b) in a forecasting context. It uses the embedding technique employed in empirical investigation of chaotic dynamics.[2] This approach imposes little prior structure on the problem.[3]

Apart from a natural desire for riches derived from beating the market, there are at least two reasons to pursue this question. Farmer and Sidorowich (1987, 1988b) report some success in using this approach to forecast simple chaotic systems. Given the results of Scheinkman and LeBaron (1989) and Frank and Stengos (1989) one might conjecture that such methods could potentially aid in forecasting financial rates of return. Furthermore Sims (1984) has argued that there is a theoretical case for the martingale hypothesis as a local property of asset prices for short time intervals such as a week.

LeBaron (1988) reports the results of similar tests for some financial indices, the tent map and the Mackey-Glass data fit with an AR (10). He considers embedding dimensions ranging from one through four. On the value weighted CRSP (Center For Research in Security Prices) index between July 1962 and March 1974 a very limited degree of forecastability was found. On other indices and other periods no forecastability was found. The tent map was readily forecasted while the Mackey-Glass data had a moderate degree of forecastable structure. Farmer and Sidorowich (1988a) indicate that a limited attempt to forecast financial time series yielded little advantage over conventional (linear) methods. One difficulty they indicate was that their series had 1000 or fewer observations. In contrast to the Dow-Jones Industrial Average or to IBM stock, our data has exhibited properties consistent with chaos under other tests. Furthermore we have roughly three times as many observations in each time series. Larger data sets should improve the prospects for the nearest neighbor technique to work.

The balance of the paper is organized as follows. Section 2 provides a statement of the

---

[2] The embedding idea has been used in rapidly growing number of papers in economics. Examples of the use of this idea include Barnett and Chen (1988), Brock, Hsieh and LeBaron (1991), Brock and Sayers (1988), Frank, Gencay and Stengos (1988), Frank and Stengos (1988a), Lorenz (1989), Mayfield and Mizrach (1992), Sayers (1986) and Scheinkman and LeBaron (1989).

[3] However, in order to derive some appealing convergence properties for nearest neighbor methods Yakowitz (1987) does make some assumptions. Yakowitz assumes the process is stationary, ergodic and Markov. These assumptions are also commonly employed in asset pricing theory.

problem. Section 3 describes the data and reports the empirical forecasts for gold, silver and platinum rates of return. Both traditional linear methods and nearest neighbor methods are shown to provide extremely limited forecasting ability.

Section 4 considers possible reasons for the limited forecastability observed empirically. Computer experiments forecasting data generated from known systems are reported. The small sample performance of nearest neighbor forecasting is the focus. To generate the data we used the mock martingale, the Henon map, and the tent map. For one and two dimensional systems, one step ahead forecasting is successful even with quite limited sample size. However the data requirements seem to rise exponentially in the extrapolation time. A brief conclusion is provided in Section 5.

2. The Problem

The true system takes the following form: $X_{t+1} = F(X_t)$, $F:R^n \rightarrow R^n$. The law of motion for the system X_t is represented by F. Our information set is assumed to be restricted to a time series of scalar observations $\{x_t\}_{t=1}^{T}$, where $x_t = h(X_t)$, $h:R^n \rightarrow R$. An empirical model for the system takes the form

$$x_t = g(x_{t-1}, x_{t-2}, \ldots, x_0). \tag{1}$$

A statistical model is a choice of assumptions concerning $g(\bullet)$. Commonly $g(\bullet)$ is assumed decomposable into signal and error components.

Particularly popular have been the autoregressive model (AR) and the autoregressive moving average (ARMA) model. The ARMA (k, ℓ) model is given as

$$x_t = \sum_{i=1}^{k} \alpha_i x_{t-i} + \sum_{j=1}^{l} \beta_j \varepsilon_{t-j} + \varepsilon_t \tag{2}$$

The error term in (2) is assumed to be identically and independently distributed (iid). In that sense the systematic part in (2) captures all the relevant structure of the process. Forecasting then requires selection of values for k and ℓ followed by statistical estimation of the α_i and β_j values. From our perspective it is the linear functional form assumption that is particularly troubling.

The nearest neighbor method can be viewed as an alternative specification of the autoregressive function in (1). Take the time series and convert it into a series of M-histories as $x_t^M = (x_t, x_{t-1}, \ldots, x_{t-M+1})$. For a theoretical explanation of this embedding technique see Takens (1981). For M sufficiently long there is generically a diffeomorphism between the data generating process and the M-histories. The nearest neighbor forecast method is carried out as follows. To each M-history attach a 1-future to get a vector with M+1 entries, i.e., $(x_{t+1}; x_t, x_{t-1}, \ldots, x_{t-M+1})$. The problem is to forecast x_τ from the information available at $\tau - 1$. Take the most recent M-history $(x_{\tau-1}, x_{\tau-2}, \ldots, x_{t-M})$ and search over the set of all M-histories to find the k nearest neighbors. We focus on the case k=1 where this means

$$\underset{s\ <\ \tau-1}{\text{minimize}} \| x^M_{\tau-1} - x^M_s \| . \tag{3}$$

If x_j^M solves (3) then x_{j+1} is the prediction for x_τ . To do this analysis requires a commitment to a choice of a metric. We use the Euclidean distance. LeBaron (1988) used the sup norm. If the system is not purely deterministic then the sup norm will not be quite as efficient. The sup norm is sensitive to individual entries in the histories which happen to be close simply by accident.

3. Empirical Results

We consider three daily time series of precious metals prices, traded on the London exchange. from the mid-1970s to the mid-1980s. The silver contract is denominated as British pense per troy ounce, gold is U.S. $ per fine ounce, while platinum is in British pounds per ounce. If the original prices are denoted as P^i , i = silver, gold and platinum; then the daily rate of return is $x_t^i = (P_t^i - P_{t-1}^i)/P_{t-1}^i$.

There are alternative ways in which to evaluate the quality of forecasts, see Maddala (1977). We proceeded as follows. For each system we constructed 250 forecasts. The following regression is run

$$x_t^i(\text{actual}) = \beta x_t^i(\text{forecast}) + \varepsilon_t. \tag{4}$$

If the forecasts are of good quality then $\hat{\beta}=1$ and it will be highly significant. The R^2 should be near unity if there is good explanatory power. If there is no explanatory power it will be near zero.

In Table 1 we report the outcomes of the forecast evaluations corresponding to (4). The results are clearly disappointing. For gold and silver the nearest neighbor forecasts are slightly better than an AR(6) while for platinum they are slightly worse. An ARMA(3,3) produced even worse predictive ability than did the AR(6). Increasing the number of nearest neighbors to include had essentially no impact (we used an arithmetic average of the k nearest neighbors to produce the point forecast). From an economic perspective however we see that for all intents and purposes the rates of return are not forecastable with these methods. There is virtually no explanatory power present.

4. Simulations

With the precious metal rates of return the true data generating process is not observable. Given the inability of the methods to forecast real data we felt it worthwhile to see how these methods perform on data generating processes that are known, see also Farmer and Sidorowich (1987, 1988b). Such simulations can aid in putting the results from Section 3 into context. Three sorts of systems were analyzed, iterated tent maps, the Henon map, a mock martingale.

The tent map is represented by $x_{t+1} = F^1(x_t)$, x_0 given and where

$$F^1(x) = \begin{cases} 2x & \text{if } 0 < x < 1/2 \\ 2(1-x) & \text{if } 1/2 \leq x < 1 \end{cases} \tag{5}$$

The function $F^2 = F^1(F^1(x))$ and in general iterations are created as $F^N(x) = F^1\ (F^{N-1}(x))$. The tent map is a one dimensional system. By using the iterations more complex systems can be created in a natural and systematic fashion. Farmer and Sidorowich (1987) refer to such iterations as the extrapolation time.

The Henon map, is a particularly popular example of a nonlinear dynamic system. It is known to be approximately 1.25 dimensional, see Grassberger and Procaccia (1983).

$$x_{t+1} = 1 + y_t - 1.4x_t \tag{6}$$

$$y_{t+1} = 0.3x_t$$

In order to illustrate some of the issues in chaos Frank and Stengos (1988b) used the logistic map to create data reminiscent of financial time series. The mock martingale is given as

$$P_{t+1} = P_t + x_t - 0.5 \tag{7}$$

$$x_{t+1} = 4x_t(1-x_t)\ .$$

Each of these examples was used to create both the data set as well as the data to be forecast. Only observations prior to date t are used in an attempt to forecast x_t. We report forecasts generated by the nearest neighbor approach, ARMA as well as AR models.

The basic findings from the simulations are set out in Tables 2 and 3. Linear time series models such as AR(k) and ARMA (k,ℓ) have no success in forecasting these nonlinear systems. This is to be expected since they assume functional forms that are not valid. The inability of familiar parametric models to forecast does not mean that the systems are lacking in predictable structure.

The nearest neighbor technique works well in simple systems. The mock martingale and the Henon map were readily forecasted even from fairly small data sets. Call the extrapolation time N. Once and twice iterated tent maps (N=1,2) were also readily forecasted. When N=3 the data requirements rise rather abruptly. When N=4 even using a data set of 60,000 observations only led to an $R^2 = 0.52$. For N = 5 we do not know how many observations would be needed. We suspect it would require at least 10^6 observations to work in a satisfactory manner. For economic applications such a volume of data without structural change seems inconceivable. Data requirements seem to rise sharply in the extrapolation time. This is consistent with Farmer and Sidorowich (1987).

The correspondence between extrapolation time in a simulation and the timing of empirical observations is a bit unclear. In light of Hughson (1988) it may be the case that many individual trades alter the public information set. Such a change could correspond to an iteration. This interpretation suggests that there may be a huge number of iterations per day.

Even if much of the observed variability is due to nonlinear structure it will not be discernable with the methods used here if such an interpretation is correct. In this respect the results of Mayfield and Mizrach (1992) are quite suggestive.

It should be noted that we tried using more than a single nearest neighbor. This did not improve the quality of the forecasts produced. It seemed rather to reduce predictive accuracy in the simulated systems. The use of larger embedding dimensions ($M > N$) also did nothing but somewhat degrade forecast quality.

5. Conclusions

The main conclusion is that the nearest neighbor approach to forecasting is able to work on some simple systems for which traditional models do not work. The nearest neighbor approach is a nonparametric approach to forecasting. As such it is successful on some simple systems for which linear parametric methods fail. The data requirements rise quite sharply as the true complexity of the underlying data generating process rises. This may account for our inability to successfully forecast precious metals rates of return. For successful economic forecasting it seems necessary to use an approach which imposes a bit more *a priori* structure than does the nearest neighbor method, see Gallant and White (1988) and Priestly (1988). Only further work will tell whether some more parametric methods that allow for nonlinearity will make progress.

Table 1
Forecast Accuracy For Precious Metal
Rates of Return

Silver

Forecast Technique	Nearest Neighbor	Nearest Neighbor	AR(6)
$\hat{\beta}$	-0.1345	-0.1244	0.1231
S.E.	0.0989	0.1011	3.5171
R^2	0.0118	0.0133	0.0032
M	6	15	-
k	1	1	-

Gold

Forecast Technique	Nearest Neighbor	Nearest Neighbor	AR(6)
$\hat{\beta}$	-0.0441	-0.0450	-1.2135
S.E.	0.0798	0.0810	2.1531
R^2	0.0019	0.0019	0.0002
M	6	15	-
k	1	1	-

Platinum

Forecast Technique	Nearest Neighbor	Nearest Neighbor	AR(6)
$\hat{\beta}$	-0.0516	-0.0522	-2.3171
S.E.	0.1371	0.1531	2.1731
R^2	0.0031	0.0029	0.0041
M	6	15	-
k	1	1	-

Table 1 (continued)

Silver

Forecast Technique	Nearest Neighbor	Nearest Neighbor	ARMA(3,3)
$\hat{\beta}$	-0.1438	-0.1343	-0.7351
S.E.	0.1032	0.1032	3.1271
R^2	0.0163	0.0130	0.0001
M	6	15	-
k	5	5	-

Gold

Forecast Technique	Nearest Neighbor	Nearest Neighbor	ARMA(6)
$\hat{\beta}$	-0.0432	-0.0417	-1.1012
S.E.	0.0812	0.0731	1.6542
R^2	0.0017	0.0021	0.0001
M	6	15	-
k	5	5	-

Platinum

Forecast Technique	Nearest Neighbor	Nearest Neighbor	ARMA(6)
$\hat{\beta}$	-0.0617	-0.0571	2.4172
S.E.	0.1531	0.1621	1.9135
R^2	0.0032	0.0023	0.0003
M	6	15	-
k	5	5	-

$\hat{\beta}$ = estimated coefficient as in equation (4)
T = total number of data points created
M = embedding dimension
k = number of nearest neighbors included to produce the point forecast

Table 2
Nearest Neighbor Forecast Quality on the Henon Map
and the Mock Martingale

Henon Map

Forecast Variable	x_t	y_t	x_t	y_t
$\hat{\beta}$	0.9643	0.9733	0.9989	1.0096
t-statistic	26.10	26.13	242.14	190.60
R^2	0.7026	0.7213	0.9997	0.9953
T	500	500	2500	2500
M	2	2	2	2

Mock
Martingale

Forecast Variable	P_t	P_t	P_t	P_t
$\hat{\beta}$	0.9971	0.9989	0.9913	1.0085
t-statistic	212.51	348.20	251.17	333.67
R^2	0.9531	0.9716	0.9731	0.9987
T	500	1,000	500	1,000
M	3	3	3	3

$\hat{\beta}$ = estimated coefficient as in equation (4)
T = total number of data points created. The last 250 observations were forecasted using the earlier observations as the data set.
M = embedding dimension.

Table 3
Forecast Accuracy on Iterated Tent Map

N = the degree of iteration of the tent map, i.e., F^N (x) as in (5). Also known as the extrapolation time.

N = 1

Forecast Technique	Nearest Neighbor	AR(1)	ARMA(1,1)
$\hat{\beta}$	1.0021	0.9785	1.0015
t-statistic	128.13	18.78	18.58
R^2	0.9744	0.0041	0.0037
T	500	2500	2500
M	2	---	---

N = 2

Forecast Technique	Nearest Neighbor	AR(2)0	ARMA(1,1)
$\hat{\beta}$	1.0417	0.9996	0.8841
t-statistic	87.08	18.74	17.35
R^2	0.9227	0.0009	0.0006
T	500	2,500	2,500
M	2	---	---

Table 3 (continued)

N = 3

Forecast Technique	Nearest Neighbor	Nearest Neighbor	Nearest Neighbor	Nearest Neighbor
$\hat{\beta}$	0.9352	1.0051	1.0139	1.0178
t-statistic	20.16	38.26	38.47	46.16
R^2	0.1420	0.6431	0.7393	0.7766
T	500	2,500	5,000	7,500
M	3	3	3	3

Forecast Technique	Nearest Neighbor	AR(3)	ARMA (2,1)
$\hat{\beta}$	1.0116	1.0053	1.0031
t-statistic	102.57	16.73	16.54
R^2	0.9591	0.0021	0.0001
T	15,000	2,500	2,500
M	3	---	---

N = 4

Forecast Technique	Nearest Neighbor	Nearest Neighbor	Nearest Neighbor	Nearest Neighbor
$\hat{\beta}$	0.9124	0.9824	0.9178	1.0035
t-statistic	15.53	16.35	17.17	26.25
R^2	0.0001	0.0031	0.0042	0.5173
T	5,000	7,500	15,000	60,000
M	4	4	4	4

Forecast Technique	AR(4)	ARMA (2,2)
$\hat{\beta}$	0.9931	1.0081
t-statistic	18.54	17.54
R^2	0.0071	0.0051
T	2,500	2,500
M	---	---

References

Barnett, W./Chen, P. (1988): The aggregation-theoretic monetary aggregates are chaotic and have strange attractors. In: **Barnett, W./Berndt, E./White, H.** (eds.): *Dynamic Econometric Modelling*, pp. 247-265. Cambridge: Cambridge University Press.

Brock, W.A./Hsieh, D.A./LeBaron, B. (1991): *Nonlinear Dynamics, Chaos, and Instability.* Cambridge, Mass.: The MIT Press.

Brock, W./Sayers, C. (1988): Is the business cycle characterized by deterministic chaos? *Journal of Monetary Economics 22*, pp. 71-90.

Fama, E. (1970): Efficient capital markets: a review of theory and empirical work. *Journal of Finance 25*, pp. 383-417.

Fama, E. (1991): Efficient capital markets: II. *Journal of Finance 46*, pp. 1575-1617.

Farmer, J.D./Sidorowich, J.J. (1987): Predicting chaotic time series. *Physical Review Letters 59*, pp. 845-848.

Farmer, J.D./Sidorowich, J.J. (1988a): Can new approaches to nonlinear modelling improve economic forecasts? In: **Anderson, P./Arrow, K./Pines, D.** (eds.): *The Economy as an Evolving Complex System*, pp. 99-114. Reading, Mass.: Addison-Wesley.

Farmer, J.D./Sidorowich, J.J. (1988b): Exploiting chaos to predict the future and reduce noise. Theoretical Division and Center for Nonlinear Studies, Los Alamos National Laboratory. Technical Report LA-UR-88-9O1.

Frank, M./Gencay, R./Stengos, T. (1988): International chaos? *European Economic Review 32*, pp. 1569-1584.

Frank, M./Stengos, T. (1988a): Some evidence concerning macroeconomic chaos. *Journal of Monetary Economics 22*, pp. 423-438.

Frank, M./Stengos, T. (1988b): Chaotic dynamics in economic time-series. *Journal of Economic Surveys 2*, pp. 103-133.

Frank, M./Stengos, T. (1989): Measuring the strangeness of gold and silver rates of return. *Review of Economic Studies 56*, pp. 553-567.

Gallant, A.R./White, H. (1988): A unified theory of estimation and inference for nonlinear dynamic models. Oxford: Basil Blackwell.

Grassberger, P./Procaccia, I. (1983): Measuring the strangeness of strange attractors. *Physica D 9*, pp. 189-208.

Hughson, E. (1988): Intraday trades in dealership markets. Mimeo. Graduate School of Industrial Administration, Carnegie Mellon University.

Kendall, M. (1953): The analysis of economic time-series, part I: prices. *Journal of the Royal Statistical Society (part I) 96*, pp. 11-25.

LeBaron, B. (1988): Stock return nonlinearities: Some initial tests and findings. Unpublished doctoral dissertation. Department of Economics, University of Chicago.

Lorenz, H.-W. (1989): *Nonlinear Dynamical Economics and Chaotic Motion*, Berlin: Springer-Verlag.

Lucas, R.E., Jr. (1978): Asset prices in an exchange economy. *Econometrica 46*, pp. 1429-1445.

Maddala, G. (1977): *Econometrics*, New York: McGraw-Hill.

Mayfield, E.S./Mizrach, B. (1992): On determining the dimension of real-time stock-price data, *Journal of Business & Economic Statistics 10*, pp. 367-374.

Priestley, M.B. (1988): Current developments in time series modelling. *Journal of Econometrics 37*, pp. 67-86.

Robinson, P.M. (1987): Asymptotically efficient estimation in the presence of heteroscedasticity of unknown form. *Econometrica 55*, pp. 875-891.

Sayers, C. (1986): Workstoppages exploring the nonlinear dynamics. Mimeo Economics, University of Wisconsin.

Scheinkman, J./LeBaron, B. (1989): Nonlinear dynamics and stock returns. *Journal of Business 62*, pp. 311-337.

Sims, C.A. (1984): Martingale-like behavior of prices and interest rates. Discussion Paper 205. Economics, University of Minnesota.

Stone, C.J. (1977): Consistent nonparametric regression (with discussion). *Annals of Statistics 5*, pp. 595-645.

Takens, F. (1981): Detecting strange attractors in turbulence. In: **Rand, D./Young, L.** (eds.): *Dynamical systems and turbulence, Warwick 1980*, pp. 366-381. Berlin: Springer-Verlag.

Thaler, R. (1987a): Anomalies: The January effect. *Journal of Economic Perspectives 1*, pp. 197-201.

Thaler, R. (1987b): Anomalies: seasonal movements in security prices II: weekend, holiday, turn of the month, and intraday effects. *Journal of Economic Perspectives 1*, pp. 169-177.

Ullah, A. (1988): Non-parametric estimation of econometric functionals. *Canadian Journal of Economics 21*, pp. 625-658.

Yakowitz, S. (1987): Nearest-neighbor methods for time series analysis. *Journal of Time Series Analysis 8*, pp. 235-247.

Zellner, A. (1988): Bayesian analysis in econometrics. *Journal of Econometrics 37*, pp. 27-50.

Abstract

In a series of papers Farmer and Sidorowich (1987, 1988a, 1988b) have used the nearest neighbor technique to forecast chaotic time series. Precious metal rates of return have certain features consistent with chaos. Hence the applicability of the nearest neighbor approach is investigated. Spot returns for gold, silver and platinum are analyzed from the mid-1970s to the mid-1980s. Neither traditional methods nor nearest neighbor methods provide much forecasting ability. Simulations reporting forecasts for known chaotic data generating processes are reported. Nearest neighbor methods seem to require too much data for successful economic application.

On a model of financial crisis: critical curves as new tools of global analysis

LAURA GARDINI
Istituto di Scienze Economiche, Università di Urbino, Piazza della Repubblica 3, 61029 Urbino (PS), Italia

1. Introduction

Many models applicable to several fields are mathematically described by a nonlinear system of two difference equations, or map of the plane $\mathbb{R}^2$ into itself. This is particularly true in the economic context, where the variables often change at discrete times by their own nature or definition. Generally, in these models, the nonlinearities are such that the resulting map is one with a non-unique inverse, that is, an endomorphism. Examples can be found in [1-4]. The model described in [3] is a particular case of the more general one presented in [4]. They interpret "economic cycles" and "financial crisis" endogenously generated from the nonlinear interaction between the "goods market" and the "money market". We use this model to illustrate how new analytical tools, the critical curves, can be used to study (in endomorphisms) the local-global attractivity of fixed points, invariant curves, cycles or of other attracting sets (regular and chaotic), as well as to determine and characterize global bifurcations which cause changes in the structure of invariant sets, or in the structure of trajectories.

Many studies are devoted to the description of the dynamical behavior (mechanisms of bifurcation and transitions to chaos), in one-dimensional endomorphisms (maps with a non-unique inverse) and two-dimensional homeomorphisms (maps with a unique inverse) (see [5] as a review of the main results), while only a few works are devoted to n-dimensional endomorphisms with $n \geq 2$. However, a powerful tool for the study of global dynamics and bifurcations in endomorphisms has been introduced by Gumowski and Mira [6]: the "critical curve". The critical curve is the natural generalization of the critial points of a one-dimensional endomorphism which are local extrema. We recall that with the consequents of the critical points it is possible to determine absorbing intervals, and to characterize the global bifurcations occurring in one-dimensional endomorphisms. Thus, we may expect this to occur also in two-dimensional endomorphisms. Indeed, critical curves have been used to determine absorbing and chaotic areas and their basins of attraction (we recall below their definitions, while their properties can be found in [6-12]).

In our opinion, however, the potentiality of this analytical tool (the critical curves) is much wider. They have been used in [13] to study global dynamics and bifurcations occurring in the macroeconomic model described in [14]. In the analysis of the model presented in [3, 4], which is the object of this communication, they enable us to prove that if the fixed point is locally attracting, then it is globally attracting, while if it is a repelling focus and other stable attractors exist, then the attractors belong to well defined absorbing areas, which are globally attracting. The proofs of these propositions and others given in the following, as well as the detailed description of the bifurcations occurring in the dynamical behaviour of the model, can be found in [15, 16].

We briefly recall now some definitions [6]. The critical curve of rank 1, denoted by LC, of a plane endomorphism $P_{t+1}=F(Pt)$, is the locus of points of the plane having at least two coincident preimages. Let LC_{-1} denote the locus of coincident preimages. In maps defined by continuously differentiable functions, LC_{-1} is generally the set of points satisfying the following equation:

$$|J(P)| = 0; \quad P \in \mathbb{R}^2$$

J(P) being the jacobian matrix of F, and $|J|$ its determinant. The critical curve of order (i+1) of F, $i \geq 0$, is $LC_i=F^{i+1}(LC_{-1})$ (denoting $LC_0=LC$).

An absorbing area d' is a closed and bounded area of the plane, whose boundary consists of arcs of critical curves, such that $F(d')\subseteq d'$, and there exists a basin of attraction $\mathcal{D}$, with $\mathcal{D}\supset d'$. A chaotic area d is an invariant area $d\subseteq d'$, $F(d)=d$, bounded by elements of critical curves, such that d includes aperiodic orbits. We refer to [6-12] for the determination of these areas and related properties.

2. The model

The macroeconomic model we consider, is described by the following nonlinear system of two difference equations in the independent variables Y and D, which represent income and debts, respectively, in a closed economy:

$$F\begin{cases} Y_t = \phi_0 + \phi_1 Y_{t-1} + \phi_2 D_{t-1} + \phi_3(\theta\eta Y_{t-1} - rD_{t-1})b; \; b = b_1 \operatorname{arctg}(Y_{t-1}) \\ D_t = \dfrac{1}{\alpha}\{D_{t-1} + \beta\theta\eta Y_{t-1}\} \end{cases} \qquad (1)$$

where

$$\begin{aligned} &\phi_0 = [h(c_0 + c_2B) + k_2(Hc_0 - Ba) + hv^e(c_2H + a)] / \gamma \\ &\phi_1 = c_1'(k_2H + h)/\gamma && >0 \\ &\phi_2 = (c_2H + a)/\gamma && >0 \\ &\phi_3 = (k_2H + h)/(\gamma\alpha) && >0 \\ &\gamma = k_1(c_2H + a) + (1 - c_1)(k_2H + h) > 0 \end{aligned} \qquad (2)$$

The constitutive equations and the derivation of system (1), which define the map F, are given in the appendix in concise form (we refer to [3, 4] for more details).

We are interested in the dynamical behaviour of the trajectories of the map F as a function of the parameter b_1, for $b_1>1$ (the coefficient b in (1) represents the "investment confidence"). The values of the parameter b, at the bifurcations that we describe are expressed (explicitly or implicitly) as a function of the other economic parameters, or are determined in terms of the geometrical configuration of critical curves which characterize the bifurcation.

Let us first note that if the coefficient b in (1) is assumed constant, then the map becomes linear. It is shown in [4] that the fixed point of the linear map, say P*=(Y*, D*), explicitly given by:

$$P^* = (Y^*, D^*) = \left(\frac{r\phi_0}{r(1-\phi_1)-\theta\eta\phi_2}, \frac{\theta\eta}{r}Y^*\right) \tag{3}$$

is positive and (globally) attracting if

$$\begin{aligned} &(\text{i})\ \ \phi_0 > 0,\ r(1-\phi_1) > \theta\eta\phi_2 \\ &(\text{ii})\ \ b < b^h;\ b^h = \frac{\beta\phi_2}{\alpha\phi_3} + \frac{\alpha-\phi_1}{\alpha\theta\eta\phi_3} \end{aligned} \tag{4}$$

As b crosses b^h, the fixed point changes from a stable focus to an unstable focus. The model thus possesses endogenously generated "cyclical paths". However, the explosive trends which occur when the fixed point is unstable are not quite satisfactory in the economic interpretation of the model. Things go better with the nonlinear map F. It is easy to see that there is only one fixed point of F, the same given in (3), which is positive under condition (i) in (4), and locally attracting if (sufficient condition):

$$(\text{iii})\ \ b_1 < b_1^*;\ b_1^* = \frac{b^h}{\operatorname{arctg}(Y^*)} \tag{5}$$

As b_1 crosses b_1^*, the fixed point undergoes a Neimark-Hopf bifurcation, changing from a locally attracting focus to a repelling focus and generating an attracting invariant closed curve.

3. P* globally attracting

Making use of the critical curves it is possible to show that when b_1 belongs to the interval $[1, b_1^*]$, the fixed point is globally attracting (i.e. its basin of attraction is the whole plane). However, several bifurcations occur in this regime of stability of P* which characterize the qualitative behavior of the trajectories. The critical curve of order 1 of the map F is determined by $LC = F(LC_{-1})$, where LC_{-1} is the curve of equation $|J(P)| = 0$, that is:

$$(LC_{-1})\quad D = \frac{\theta\eta}{r}Y + \frac{1+Y^2}{\phi_3 b_1}\{\phi_1 - \beta\theta\eta\phi_2 + \alpha\phi_3\theta\eta b_1 \operatorname{arctg}(Y)\}$$

LC separates the plane in two regions, Z_0 and Z_2, the points of which have 0 preimages and 2 distinct preimages of order one, respectively. We take the images of $\overline{Z}_2, \overline{Z}_2 = Z_2 \cup LC$ until we determine a closed set V such that F(V)=V. The set V is globally attracting. As b_1 varies, changes in the geometrical configuration of V denote changes in the qualitative structure of the trajectories, and in the stable invariant manifolds of P* (which is obtained, in part or at all, as a limit of the images of the critical curve LC, or of some of its arcs). Increasing b_1 from 1, the critical curve LC intersects LC_{-1} at one point, c_0, until the first bifurcation takes place, after which LC intersects LC_{-1} at two points, c_0 and a_0. In Figure 1a is shown an example in the first regime, in which the fixed point is an attracting node, and in Figure 1b an example in which the fixed point is an attracting focus.

The figures included in this note are obtained with the following values of the economic parameters (the values of b_1 are given in the figures):

$$\begin{aligned} &a = 0.1,\ \theta = 0.5,\ \frac{\omega}{\lambda} = 0.7,\ \beta = 0.8,\ r = 0.08,\ H = 0.6,\ B = 100,\ k_1 = 0.7 \\ &k_2 = 0.4,\ C_0 = 100,\ c_1 = 0.5,\ c_1' = 0.2,\ c_2 = 0.1,\ h = 0.8,\ v^e = 100. \end{aligned} \tag{6}$$

We denote $c_i = T^i(c_0)$, $a_i = T^i(a_0)$ for $i \geq 1$. The branch L_{-1} (resp. L'_{-1}) in Fig.1a is the halfcurve of LC_{-1} below (resp. above) the critical point c_0; L_i (resp. L'_i) denote their images. ∂V is made up of the branch L (which contains the arc c_0c_1), of all the images of the arc c_0c_1, that is $\bigcup_{i\geq 1} c_ic_{i+1}$, $c_ic_{i+1} = F^i(c_0c_i)$ for $i \geq 0$ (which are arcs converging to the fixed point P*). When LC intersects LC_{-1} in two points, we denote as L_{-1} the branch of LC_{-1} below c_0 and as L'_{-1} the branch of LC_{-1} above a_0; L_i and L_{-1} denote their images. The points of the arc c_0a_0 converge to P* (when P* is attracting). The branches L and L' belong to ∂V and the remaining part of the boundary of V is obtained with the images of the arcs c_0c_1 and a_0a_1. If these images do not intersect the critical curve LC_1 then ∂V contains $\bigcup_{i\geq 1} c_ic_{i+1}$ and $\bigcup_{i\geq 1} a_ia_{i+1}$, $a_ia_{i+1} = F^i(a_0a_1)$ (the qualitative shape of V is shown in Fig.1b). Otherwise, ∂V contains also an arc of L_1, as it is shown in Fig.2.

After this first bifurcation, other bifurcations occur: (i) when the attracting node becomes an attracting focus; (ii) when the images of the arc c_0c_1 intersect LC_1; (iii) when the images of the arc a_0a_1 intersect LC_1; (iv) when the images of the arc c_0c_1 intersect LC_{-1}. This last one is particularly important because it is followed by a complex structure of the stable invariant manifold of F. This is because invariant curves connecting P* to points at infinity are tangent to the critical arcs c_ic_{i+1} and a_ia_{i+1} for $i \geq 0$. When both the images of the arcs c_0c_1 and a_0a_1 intersect LC_{-1} then the arcs c_ic_{i+1} and a_ia_{i+1} wing around the attracting set (P*, or an invariant curve Γ, or another attractor) and intersect each other infinitely many times. However, from now on the determination of this manifold is no longer relevant, as an absorbing area $\tilde{d}$ can be constructed with the images of the arc c_0c_1 of LC. Let m be the first integer such that c_mc_{m+1} intersect LC_{-1} in a point, say h_0. Then the boundary of $\tilde{d}$ consists of the arc h_1c_1 of LC ($h_1 = F(h_0)$) and of the critical arcs c_ic_{i+1}, $i = 1, \ldots, (m-1)$, c_mh_0, h_0h_1. This area $\tilde{d}$ is globally absorbing, and the trajectories of its points are convergent to P*, when P* is attracting (see Fig.2a).

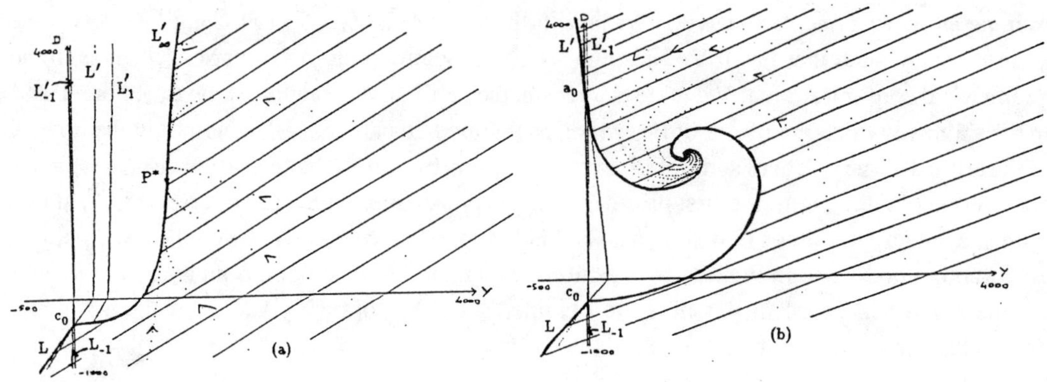

Fig.1 Region V (hatched). P* is an attracting node in (a), b_1=1.25; an attracting focus in (b), b_1=1.7.

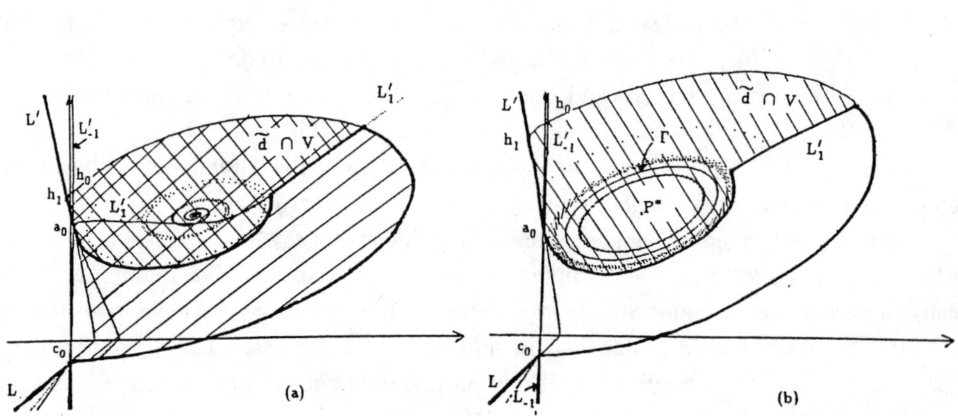

Fig.2 (a) b_1=1.9, P* is an attracting focus in the absorbing area $\tilde{d} \cap V$.
(b) b1=1.976, Γ is attracting in $\tilde{d} \cap V$.

4. Neimark-Hopf bifurcation

With global arguments (that is without making use of the eigenvalues of the jacobian matrix of F evaluated at the fixed point) we can see that the Neimark bifurcation gives rise to an invariant closed curve, say Γ, globally attracting. In fact, when $b_1 \leq b_1^*$, then $\lim_{k\to\infty} F^k(\tilde{d}) = P^*$; while for $b_1 > b_1^*$ ($b_1^* \approx 1.975008$), until a successive bifurcation, it results $\lim_{k\to\infty} F^k(\tilde{d}) = \mathcal{A}$, where $\mathcal{A}$ is invariant, with invariant boundary, that is $\partial\mathcal{A} = \Gamma$ (see Fig.2b).

5. Bifurcations of Γ

The first bifurcation involving the closed invariant curve Γ occurs at a value b_1^{g1} when Γ becomes tangent to the curve LC_{-1} (and thus to the critical curves LC_i, for all $i \geq 0$). This first bifurcation of Γ causes the appearance of smooth ascillations in the geometrical shape of the invariant curve, due to the tangency of Γ with the critical arcs $a_i a_{i+1}$ in the images of the points p_0 and q_0, being $\{p_0, q_0\} = \Gamma \cap LC_{-1}$. In this regime the points p_0 and q_0 belong to the arc $a_{-1}a_0$, unique preimage of the arc $a_0 a_1$ of LC (see Fig.3a).

After this bifurcation, that is for $b_1 > b_1^{g1}$, the area enclosed by Γ is no longer invariant. However, from now on, until the "final bifurcation" take place, it is possible to determine an absorbing area d', $d' \subset \tilde{d}$, bounded by critical arcs belonging to the images of the arc $a_0 a_1$ of LC, and before the occurrence of the bifurcation called "snap-back repeller", an annular absorbing area d_a', $d_a' \subset d'$ exists (the procedure to determine d_a' and d' is described in [17]). Apart from the fixed point, the points of $\tilde{d}$ (globally absorbing) have an image of finite order in d_a', and the images of this annular absorbing area shrink to Γ, until Γ is globally attracting.

The second bifurcation involving the closed invariant curve Γ occurs at a value b_1^{g2} when Γ crosses LC_{-1} in the point a_{-1}, so that Γ becomes tangent to the critical curves LC_i in the images a_{i+1} of the point a_{-1}, for $i \geq 0$. This bifurcation causes the appearance of "non smooth oscillations" on the geometrical shape of the curve as foldings are crated, for $b_1 > b_1^{g2}$, due to the tangency of Γ to the critical arcs LC_i in the images of the points p_0 and q_0, $\{p_0, q_0\} = \Gamma \cap LC_{-1}$, and now p_0 is external to the arc $a_{-1}a_0$ (while q_0 belongs to the arc $a_{-1}a_0$). The mechanism is illustrated in Fig.3b. In this regime, as well as in the previous one, the invariant curve may or not possess periodic orbits (if cycles exist on Γ attracting then they are necessarily two, a repelling one and an attracting one). When periodic orbits are absent, then the trajectories on Γ are quasiperiodics.

6. "Cyclical behavior", regular and complex

Examples of annular absorbing areas d_a' and of stable attractors contained therein are shown in Fig.4. Increasing b_1 (the nonlinearity increases), we observe the transition from a cyclical regime (due to attracting periodic orbits, of several periods), to a complex regime (see Fig.5). However, all of the attracting and repelling cycles are located inside the annular absorbig area, which becomes an annular chaotic area, globally attracting (apart from the repelling fixed point).

We note that this regime, in which there exists an annular globally absorbing area, inside which the trajectories (asymptotically periodic or aperiodic) follow a cyclical trend, is perhaps the more interesting one for the interpretation of the model in the economic context.

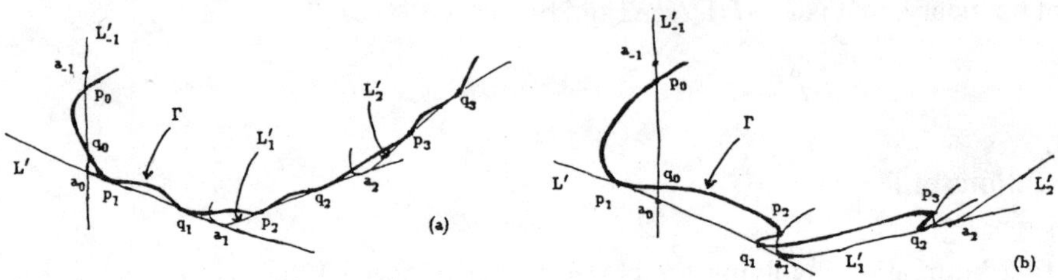

Fig.3 (a) $b_1^{g_1} < b1 < b_1^{g_2}$; (b) $b_1 > b_1^{g_2}$

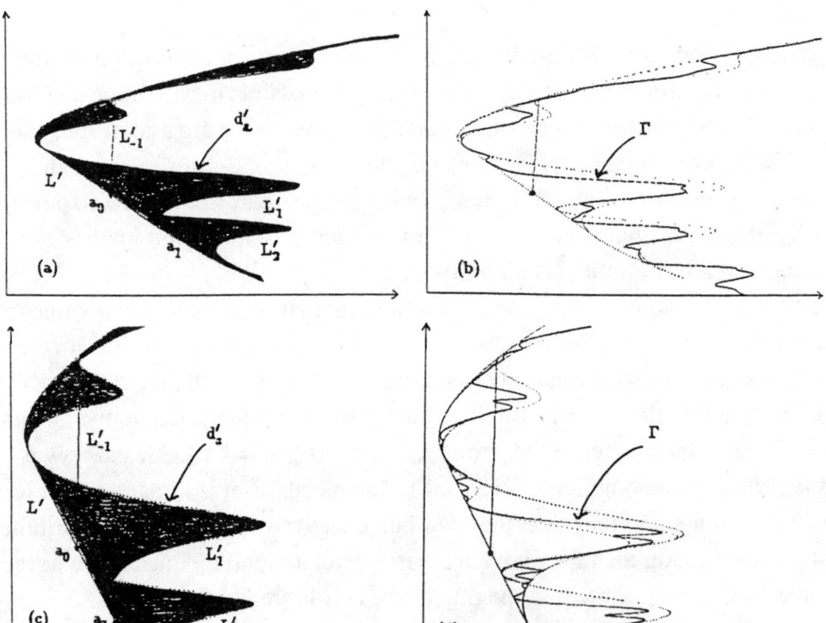

Fig.4 (a) b_1=1.9859, a portion of the anular absorbing area d'_a;
(b) a portion of the curve Γ inside the area reported in (a);
(c) b_1=1.9863, a portion of the annular absorbing area d'_a;
(d) a portion of the curve Γ inside the area reported in (c).

7. "Snap-Back Repeller" bifurcation

The "regularity" which can be observed in the presence of an annular chaotic area (see the attractors of Fig.5a and Fig.5c), is not maintained when the chaotic area becomes simply connected. This transition occurs at a global bifurcation, which has been studied and characterized in terms of critical curves in [11]. That is, it occurs when the preimage of the fixed point, distinct from the fixed point, belongs to the boundary of the absorbing area d'. Moreover, it is proved in [16] that this is also the necessary and sufficient condition to have the transition of the fixed point P* from "expanding" to "snap-back repeller" (we refer to [16,18,19] for the meaning of these terms). Thus, the existence of an orbit homoclinic to P* (which implies the existence of infinitely many repelling cycles of F) can be taken as the signal of a stochastic regime. This complex behavior however occurs inside the absorbing area d', with known geometrical shape and structure, and whose structure also determines the aperiodic behavior of the generic trajectory (putting in evidence zones more frequently "visited" by the points of a generic trajectory).

8. Stochastic regime

Bifurcations which change the structure of the absorbing area d' occur whenever there are changes in the order of the first image of the arc a_0a_1 which intersects LC_{-1} (examples of different attractors are shown in Fig.5d and Fig.5e).

The "final bifurcation", which causes the disappearance of the attractor, can also be characterized by the critical curves. From Mira [5], we know that generally this occurs when the boundary of the chaotic area has a contact with the boundary of its basin of attraction. As regards the example under examination, the construction of the chaotic area d' is possible for any value of b_1 until the fixed point is a focus. Also a wider absorbing area $\tilde{d}$ can be constructed, with the chaotic area d' strictly included in $\tilde{d}$. Thus, we may expect that a contact of the boundary of d' with the boundary of its basin of attraction cannot occur at a finite point. Indeed, by analyzing the points at infinity on the "Equator of Poincaré", it can be seen [15] that, in our example, the absorbing area $\tilde{d}$ (and d') is globally absorbing, as long as it exists. We can thus conclude that the contact causing the destruction of the attractor takes place at infinity, when the repelling focus P* becomes a repelling node.

To be more precise, we recall that this final bifurcation makes repelling an invariant set, which is attracting before bifurcation, and still exists after bifurcation: it is called a "strange repellor" [5, 6]. The generic trajectory of the plane is divergent after bifurcation, and the frequently observed chaotic transient is due to the presence of the "strange repellor". As noted in [3], this last regime is also susceptible of interesting economic interpretations (e.g. a financial crisis).

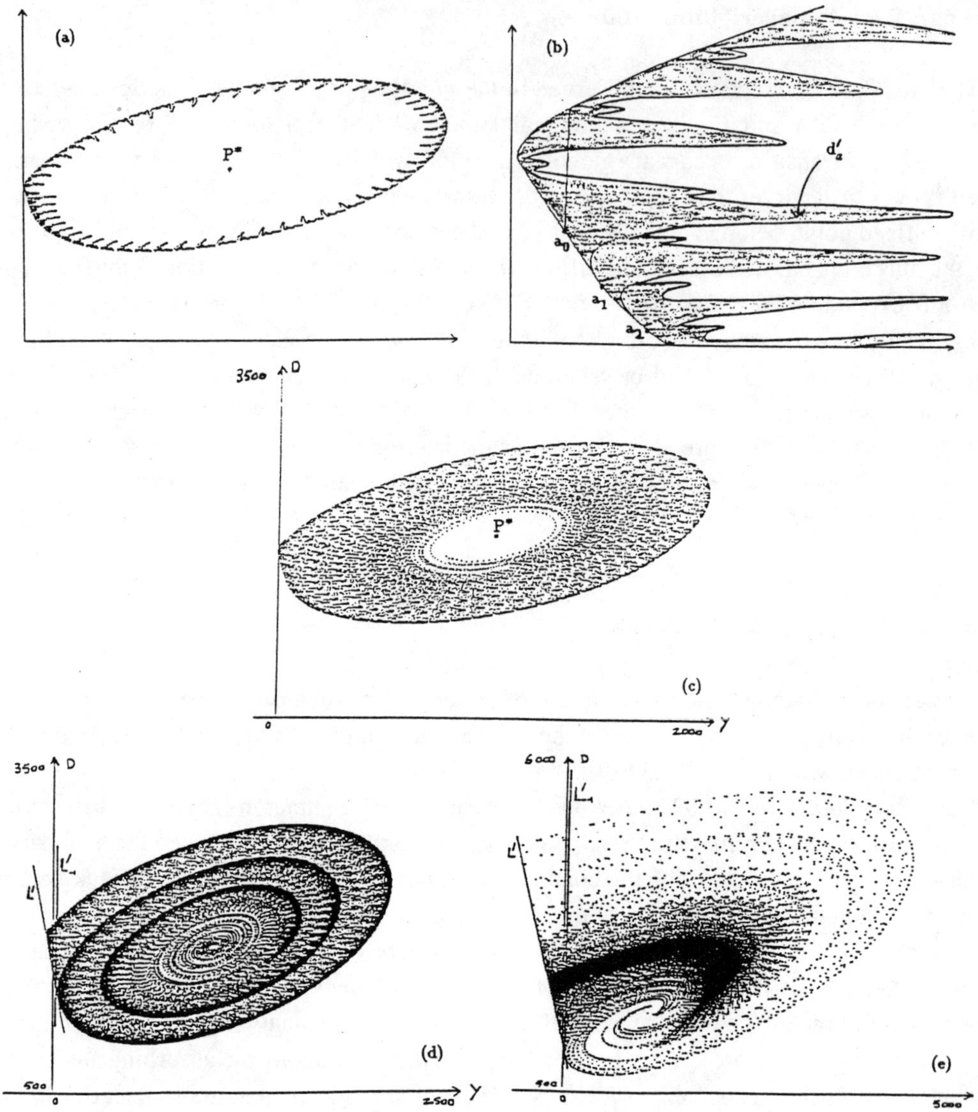

Fig.5 (a) b_1=1.987, an attracting set; (b) a portion of the annular absorbing area d'_a containing the attracting set reported in (a); (c) b_1=1.99, P* is expanding; (d) b_1=1.201, P* is a snap-back repeller; (e) b_1=2.2.

Appendix

We give in concise form the constitutive equations of the model presented in [4], and the derivation of the system of equations (1) in the text.

- GOOD MARKET.

The meaning of the economic variables is the following: Y=income, C=consumption, I=investment, Π=profit, N=employment, W=wealth, v=price of capital stock, IF=internal finance, EF=external finance, D=debt.

(A.1) $Y_t=C_t+I_t$

(A.2) $Y_t=\omega N_t+\Pi_t$; $0<\omega<1$

(A.3) $N_t=(C_t+I_t)/\lambda$; $0<\omega<\lambda<1$

From (A.3) and (A.1) we get: $Y_t=\lambda N_t$ and,
defining $\eta=1-\frac{\omega}{\lambda}(0<\eta<1)$, with (A.2) we get: $\Pi_t=\eta Y_t$.

(A.4) $C_t=c_0+c_1Y_t+c_1'Y_{t-1}+c_2W_t$; $c_1,c_1',c_2\in(0,1)$, $c_0>0$

(A.5) $W_t=Hv_t+B$; $H>0$, $B>0$

(A.6) $I_t=av_t+bIF_t$; $a>0$, $b=b_1\mathrm{arctg}(Y_{t-1})$, b_1

(A.7) $IF_t=\theta\eta Y_{t-1}-rD_t$; $0<\theta<1$, $0<r<1$

(A.8) $D_t=D_{t-1}+EF_t$

(A.9) $EF_t=\beta IF_t$; $0<\beta<1$

From equations (A.1), (A.4-A.9) it follows the equation for the variable debt:

$$\text{(A.10)}\quad D_t=\frac{1}{\alpha}\{D_{t-1}+\beta\theta\eta Y_{t-1}\}$$

where we have defined $\alpha=1+r\beta$, and the following IS-equation:

$$\text{(A.11) (IS)}\quad Y_t=\frac{1}{(1-c_1)}\{(c_0+c_2B)+(a+c_2H)v_t+c_1'Y_{t-1}+\frac{1}{\alpha}(\theta\eta Y_{t-1}-rD_{t-1})b\}$$

- MONEY MARKET

M^d=demand of money, M^s=supply of money, TR=transactive demand, SP=speculative demand.

(A.12) $M_t^d=M_t^s$ (equilibrium condition)

(A.13) $M_t^s=D_t$

(A.14) $M_t^d=TR_t+SP_t+EF_t$

(A.15) $TR_t=k_1Y_t+k_2W_t$; $0<k_1<1$, $0<k_2<1$

(A.16) $SP_t=h(v_t-v^e)$; $h>0$, $v^e>0$

From the equilibrium condition (A.12), after algebraic substitions, we get the following LM-equation:

$$\text{(A.17) (LM)} \quad Y_t = \frac{1}{k_1}\{D_{t-1} - (k_2H + h)v_t + (hv^e - k_2B)\}$$

From the two equations IS and LM, equating the second members, we get the explicit formulation of v_t as a function of (Y_{t-1}, D_{t-1}):

$$\text{(A.18)} \quad v_t = \frac{1}{\gamma}\{-\psi_0 - k_1c_1'Y_{t-1} + (1-c_1)D_{t-1} - \frac{k_1}{\alpha}(\theta\eta Y_{t-1} - rD_{t-1})b\}$$

where:

$$\gamma = k_1(c_2H + a) + (1-c_1)(k_2H + h)$$
$$\psi_0 = k_1(c_0 + c_2B) + (1-c_1)(k_2B - hv^e)$$

Substituting v_t, given in (A.18), into the LM-equation, the equation of Y_t, as a function of (Y_{t-1}, D_{t-1}) is obtained, which coupled to equation (A.10) of D_t, closes the model (all the other economic variables being explicitly expressed in terms of (Y_{t-1}, D_{t-1})). Mathematically, it is represented by a nonlinear system of two difference equations:

$$\begin{cases} Y_t = \phi_0 + \phi_1 Y_{t-1} + \phi_2 D_{t-1} + \phi_3(\theta\eta Y_{t-1} - rD_{t-1})b; \; b = b_1 \operatorname{arctg}(Y_{t-1}) \\ D_t = \frac{1}{\alpha}\{D_{t-1} + \beta\theta\eta Y_{t-1}\} \end{cases} \tag{1}$$

where the coefficients are defined in (2) in the text.

Acknowledgements

The author thanks professors C. Mira and R. Abraham for having corrected the first draft of this communication, and an anonimous Referee for useful suggestions.

References

[1] M. Gallegati and L. Gardini "A nonlinear model of the business cycle with money and finance", Metroeconomica, 42, pp 1-32, 1991.

[2] R. A. Dana and P. Malgrange "The dynamics of a discrete version of a growth cycle model", in J. P. Ancot (ed.) "Analysing the Structure of Economic Models", Martinus Nijhoff, The Hague,

Cap.7, pp 115-142, 1984.

[3] D. Delli Gatti, M. Gallegati and L. Gardini "Investment confidence, corporate debt and income fluctuations", J. of Economic Behavior and Organization (in press), 1991.

[4] M. Gallegati "Fluttuazioni del reddito e crisi finanziarie", Ed. N.I.S., Roma (in press), 1992.

[S] C. Mira "Chaotic Dynamics", World Scientific, Singapore, 1987.

[6] I. Gumowski and C. Mira "Dynamique Chaotique", Cepadues Editions, Toulouse, 1980.

[7] C. Mira "Complex dynamics in two-dimensional endomorphisms", Nonlinear Analysis, T. M. & A., vol. 4, n. 6, pp. 1167-1187, 1980.

[8] A. Barugola "Determination de la frontiere d'une zone absorbante relative a une recurrence du deuxieme ordre, a inverse non unique", C. R. Acad. Sc. Paris, t. 290, Serie B, pp. 257- 260,1980.

[9] A. Barugola "Quelques proprietes des lignes critiques d'une recurrence du second ordre a inverse non unique. Determination d'une zone absorbante", R.A.I.R.O., Numerical Analysis, vol. 18, n. 2, pp. 137-151,1984.

[10] A. Barugola "Sur certains zones absorbantes et zones chaotiques d'un endomorphisme bidimensionnel", Int. J. Non-Linear Mechanics, vol. 21, n. 2, pp. 165-168, 1986.

[11] A. Barugola, J. C. Cathala and C. Mira "Annular chaotic areas", Nonlinear Analysis, T. M. & A., vol. 10, n. 11, pp. 1223-1236,1986.

[12] J. C. Cathala "On some properties of absorptive areas in second order endomorphisms", European Conference on Iteration Theory, Batschuns, Australia, Sept. 1989.

[13] L. Gardini "Some global bifurcations of two-dimensional endomorphisms by use of critical lines", Nonlinear Analysis, T. M. & A. Vol.18, n.4, pp.361-399, 1992.

[14] L. Gardini "Dinamiche complesse in una classe di modelli IS-LM", Atti XIII Convegno AMASES, 1989.

[15] L. Gardini "Insiemi invarianti globalmente attrattivi nell'interazione fra il mercato dei beni ed il mercato della moneta", submitted for publication, 1992.

[16] L. Gardini "Homoclinic bifurcations in n-dimensional endomorphisms due to expanding periodic points", submitted for publication, 1992.

[17] L. Gardini and C. Mira "A procedure to determine chaotic and absorbing areas in two-dimensional endomorphisms", Quaderno N. 9002, Gruppo Nazionale MURST "Modelli Nonlineari in Economia e Dinamiche Complesse", Urbino, 1990.

[18] J. R. Marotto, "Snap-back repellers imply chaos in R^n", J. Math. Analysis Applic. vol. 63, pp. 199-223,1978.

Phase-Locking in a Goodwin Model

Christian Haxholdt
Institute of Theoretical Statistics
Copenhagen Business School
Julius Thomsens Plads 10
DK-1366 Frederiksberg C, Denmark

Erik Reimer Larsen and Mich Tvede
Institute of Economics
Copenhagen Business School
DK-1366 Copenhagen K, Denmark

Erik Mosekilde
Physics Laboratory III
The Technical University of Denmark
DK-2800 Lyngby, Denmark

1. Introduction

Mode-locking is a phenomenon that arise in nonlinear dynamical systems, when two or more cyclic motions interact with one-another. In the first place mode-locking means that the oscillations adjust to each other so as to get in step. However, the adjustment is more complicated than this because each mode contains harmonics and subharmonics which may also try to get in step. Many economic phenomena can be thought of as coupled oscillators. Examples are the interaction between seasonal fluctuations and the business cycle, the interaction between different sectors in an economy (Lorenz, 1987a), and the interaction between different national or regional economies (Lorenz, 1987b).

We consider the simplest case of coupled oscillators, namely a model that consists of an independent oscillator which acts as a forcing on an internally generated cyclic motion. The internal motion is produced by a Goodwin model of economic business cycles (Goodwin, 1951). Perhaps, the Goodwin model does not meet the standards of business cycle models of today. However, it is easy to illustrate mode-locking with this model, and mode-locking can arise in more popular models as well through the same channels as illustrated here. Mode-locking has at least one important empirical implication: If a model with mode-locking is estimated by standard econometric techniques, the obtained parameter values will typically be in error because the observed behaviour is influenced in a complicated manner by the nonlinear interaction between the cycles. This has important consequences for policy formulation.

2. The model

The examined model will only be sketched here. A more detailed presentation may be found in Goodwin (1951).

The model is a nonlinear accelerator-multiplier model. The consumption function is of the traditionally Keynesian type with an extra term that depends negatively on the growth in income. This term can be interpreted as an adjustment of consumption to changes in levels of income. The desired stock of capital is proportional to the level of income, and the investment function is piecewise linear. In general, the investment is equal to lagged changes in the desired stock of capital. For particular small or large changes in the desired stock of capital, this linear function is truncated so that investment is fixed at lower and upper bounds, respectivly. These bounds can be interpreted as arising from adjustment costs and from bottlenecks associated, for instance, with finasial constrains and limitations in labor availability. Income is equal to the sum of consumption and investment.

In the present treatment, the model is represented by a second order Taylor-expansion in order to deal with the lag in the investment function, and the piecewise linear investment function is approximated by a smooth function to avoid numerical errors in the simulations. With these modifications we obtain the following second order differential equation:

$$\epsilon\theta\ddot{z} + [\epsilon + (1-\alpha)\theta]\dot{z} - \phi(\dot{z}) + (1-\alpha)z = 0 \tag{1}$$

where z represents deviations in income from it's steady-state value. ε is the factor by which changes in income affects consumption, α the marginal propensity to consume, θ the length of the lag. The investment function ϕ is given by:

$$\phi(\dot{z}) = 12\,\frac{\arctan(\dot{z})}{\pi} + 3 \tag{2}$$

This nonlinear model produces a limit cycle with a period of 8.5 years. The assumed parameters are ε = 0.50 years, α = 0.6, θ = 10.00 years.

We now perturb the model by a periodic external forcing so that the marginal propensity to consume becomes

$$\alpha = \alpha_0(1 + A\sin(2\pi t/P)) \tag{3}$$

where A is the amplitude and P the period of the forcing. This modulation can be interpreted as a cyclical variation in investments arising, for instance, from seasonal factors, from variations in interest rate or from other factors outside the boundary of the model.

3. Simulation with the Model.

All models that can produce a spontaunous oscillations, like the Goodwin model presented above, will basically behave in the same way if they are perturbed by a periodic external forcing. The external forcing changes the internally generated cycle, and mode-locking tends to occur. This phenomenon has a number of characteristics which we will go through in the following. The internally generated cycle has a tendency to lock into a period which is commensurate with the external forcing, i.e., when the external wave has completed precisely p cycles, the internal wave will have completed q, where p and q are integers. For example if the ratio between the two waves is close to a 1:2 (1 internal for each 2 external), the internal cycle will change its period so that the ratio becomes precisely 1:2. Figure 1 shows an adjustment process of this type, the first 50 years are simulated with a constant rate of income to consumption, generating an 8.5 year cycle. At t = 50 years an external cycle is introduced in income for consumption with a period $P = 6.56$ years and a relative amplitude $A = 0.20$. The internally generated cycle now changes its period to 26.24 years corresponding to precisely 4 external cycles. However, each cycle can be viewed as taking 8.74 years (26.24/4) which might still be considered as the fundamentel period of the internal cycle. This indicates that the model has changed its period by 3 percent to get in step with the external cycle in a 3:4 mode-locked solution. Although the change in actual period is small, the change in the appearance of the endogenous cycle is large. Before there was a simple limit cycle. After the external cycle was introduced, however, the internal cycle has changed both amplitude and form significantly.

Mode-locking occurs around all rational ratios between the two periods. It may be characterized by a so called winding number $W = p/q$ where $p,q \in N$. On figure 2 the winding number is plotted against the forcing period P. The forcing amplitude is kept constant at $A = 0.15$. The figure shows the main series of mode-locked solutions, with other more complicated solutions as 2:3, 5:6 to be found between these. A structure like this is known as a devil's staircase (Mandelbrot 1977). A devil's staircase has a fractal structure (it is possible to find a new rational number between two given rational numbers) and show self-similarity under magnification. As an example of this the region between the 1:2 and 2:3 mode-locked solutions is magnified and shown as the insert on figure 2. Here, solutions such as 5:8 and 8:11 can be found. The organization of the devil's staircase is

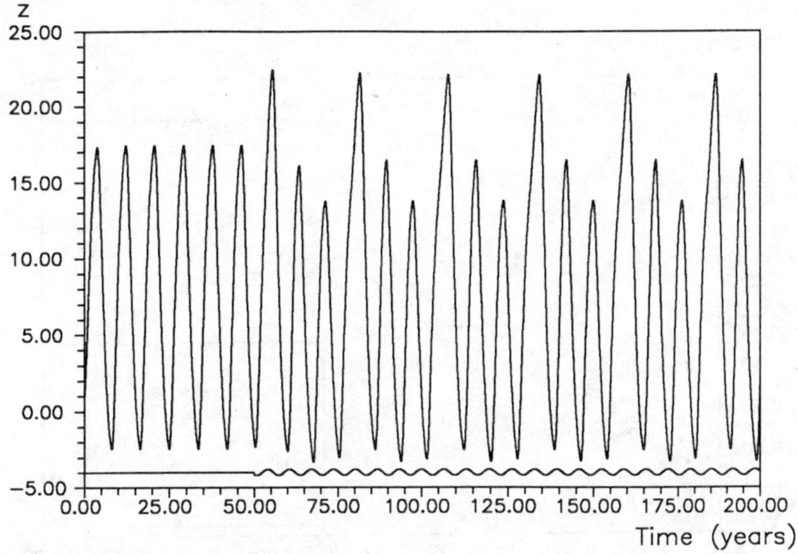

Figure 1. An example of mode-locking. For the first 50 years the external forcing is constant. A cyclic modulation is then applied with an relative amplitude of A = 0.20, and a driving period P =6.56 years. The internally generated cycle hereby changes form and amplitude to adjust its period to the external cycle, the final result being a 3:4 mode-locked solution.

similar to the structure of a Farey tree (Schuster 1988), and it can be shown that it is the irrational numbers that separate the 'steps' in the staircase (Bergé et al. 1984).

The interval over which a certain mode-locking occurs depends on the strength of the nonlinear interaction, i.e., on the size of the forcing amplitude A, as well as on the winding number. Simple mode-locked solutions, such as 1:1 are more pronounced than complicated ones such as, e.g., 5:7. If the forcing amplitude A is changed, the interval over which mode-locking can be found will also change. Figure 3 shows an example. Here, both the amplitude A and the forcing period P are changed, and the figure shows the main mode-locked solutions. The areas in which mode-locking can be found are known as Arnol'd tongues. The tongues widen as the forcing amplitude A is increased, and in this case the 1:2 tongue seems to expand at the expense of the other less pronounced solutions, including the 1:1 solution. The tongues cannot continue to grow, however. At some point they start to overlap, or certain tongues may be suppressed so that the corresponding solutions no longer exist. In the case of the Goodwin model, forcing periods P which do not produce a mode-locked solution will give quasiperiodic behaviour. This can be shown by calculating the largest Lyapunov exponent λ, which in the case of quasiperiodic behaviour is 0. For mode-locked

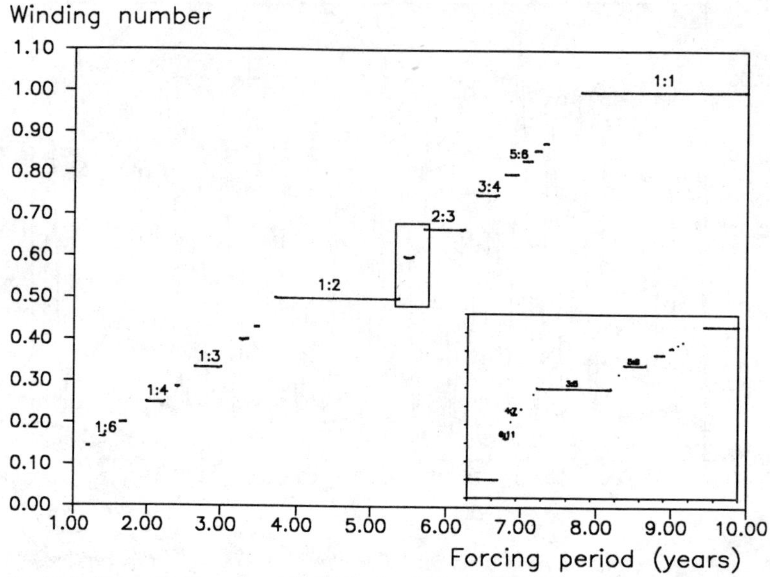

Figure 2. A devil's staircase of mode-locked solutions. The figure shows the intervals over which the mode-locked solutions can be observed for a forcing amplitude A = 0.15. The small box shows a magnification of the region between two major 'steps' in the staircase.

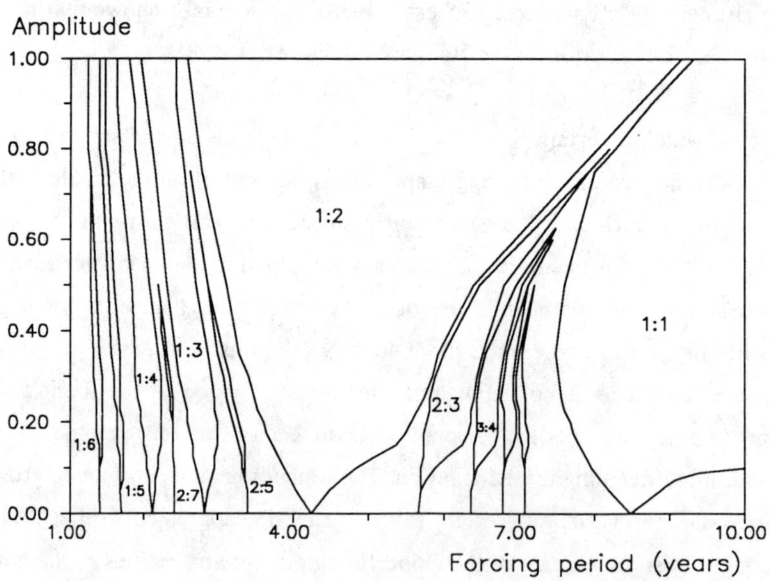

Figure 3. Arnol'd tongue diagram showing where mode-locked solutions can be found as a function of the forcing period P and the forcing amplitude A. As with the devil's staicase, the simple ratios are most pronouced. It seems as if the 1:2 tongue expands at the expense of the other tongues, including the 1:1.

solutions $\lambda < 0$ (Wolf 1986). The model thus provides an example of nonchaotic transition from quasi-periodicity to complete mode-locking (Alstrøm et al. 1988).

To characterize the behavior in the model, Lyapunov exponents are calculated for different values of the forcing amplitude. The Goodwin model has two state variables z and v. Figur 4 shows the variation of the largest Lyapunov exponent as a function of the period of the external drive. When we speak about the mode-locked solutions we refer to the stationary behavior of the system after transients have died out. If the system is excited by random external events, the picture becomes somewhat more complex. Each disturbance will knock the system out of its stationary orbit and at and, at least as long as the disturbance is sufficiently small, a new approach to the orbit will then begin. This approach will be characterized by a time constant, which is equal in magnitude to the reciprocal of the largest Lyapunov exponent. This time constant can be written as follows

$$\tau = \frac{1}{|\lambda|} \tag{4}$$

This formally expresses how rapid the solution mode-locks, and hereby the "strength" of the entrainment.

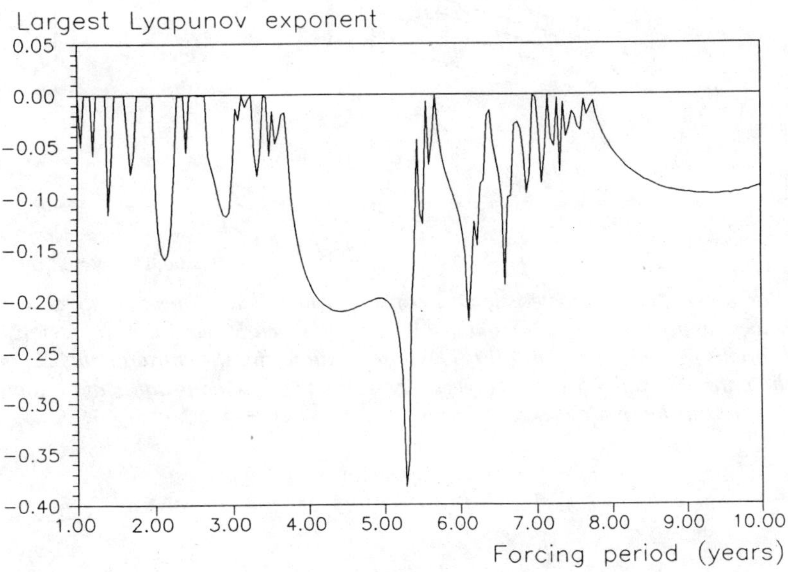

Figure 4. Variation of the largest Lyapunov exponent for the Goodwin model, as a function of the external drive. One can note that the intervals where the largest exponent is negative and compare it with mode-locked solutions in the Arnol'd tongue diagram. We do not see overlaps between the tongues, and the model thus provides an example of non-chaotic transition to complete mode-locking.

Figur 5 shows the variation of the lock-in time as a function of the period of the external forcing. We clearly recognize the regions in which the various periodic solutions exist. The time constants for entrainment into the 1:2 and 2:3 solutions is of the order 2.5 and 4.5 years, respectively, while time constants of more than 5 years an found for the rest of the mode-locked solutions. In practice, this presumably implies that only the entrainment 1:2 can be observed. The system will never have time enough to settle down into one of the other mode-locked solutions before a new external excitation again knocks it away from its orbit. The question of whether one can identify a particular mode-locked solution in a time series is also related to how much the transient resembles the stationary solution.

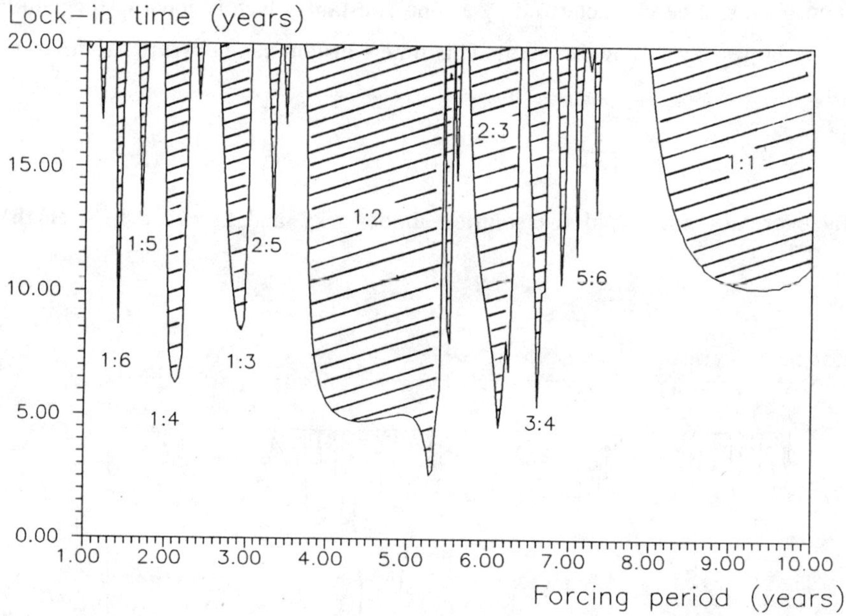

Figure 5. Variation of the characteristic time constant which determines the rate at which the model locks onto the various periodic solutions. We clearly recognize the regions in which the various periodic solutions exist. The time constants for the entrainments 1:2 and 2:3 is of the order 2.5 and 4.5 years, respectively, while the time constant is more than 5 years for the rest of the mode-locked solutions.

4. Conclusion

We have presented a set of methods which are useful in the study of comovements in economic models arising from interaction between different cycles. We used a simple Goodwin model to illustrate the results but it is important to realize that most of the phenomena presented here can be found in any nonlinear model where different cycles interact.

Acknowledgment

This work was partly supported through a grant from the Danish Social Science Research Council.

References

Alstrøm, P., B. Christiansen and M.T. Levinsen, 1988, Nonchaotic Transition from Quasiperiodicity to Complete Phase-Locking, Physical Review Letters 61, pp. 1679-1682.

Arrowsmith, D.K. and C.M. Place, 1990, An Introduction to Dynamical Systems (Cambridge University Press, Cambridge, UK).

Bergé, B., Y. Pomeau and C. Vidal, 1984, Order within Chaos (John Wiley & Sons, New York).

Goodwin, R.M., 1951, The Nonlinear Accelerator and the Persistence of Business Cycles, Econometrica, Vol. 19, No. 1, pp. 1-17.

Lorenz, H.- W., 1987a, Strange Attractors in a Multisector Business Cycle Model, Journal of Economic Behavior and Organization 8, pp. 397-411.

Lorenz, H.- W., 1987b, International Trade and the Possible Occurrence of Chaos, Economic Letters 23, pp. 135-138.

Mandelbrot, B.B., 1977, Fractals: Form, Chance and Dimension (Freeman, San Francisco).

Schuster, H.W., 1988, Deterministic Chaos (VCH Verlagsgesellschaft, Weinheim)

Wolf, A., 1986, Quantifying Chaos with Lyapunov Exponents in A.V. Holden, ed., Chaos, Nonlinear Science: Theory and Applications (Manchester University Press, UK).

Abstract

To investigate how mode-locking and other highly nonlinear dynamic phenomena may arise in economic models, we have considered a traditional business cycle model subjected to an external forcing. When varying the period of this forcing the model is found to produce a devil's staircase of mode-locked cycles. The overall behaviour of the model is delineated in terms of an Arnol'd tongue diagram.

Complexity of Optimal Paths in Strongly Concave Problems[1]

LUIGI MONTRUCCHIO

Istituto di Matematica Finanziaria, Università di Torino
Via Assarotti 3, 10122 Torino, Italy

1. Introduction

Several economic problems are often formulated in terms of a dynamic optimization model. Although a broad variety of mathematical models have been studied, the optimal capital accumulation model originated in RAMSEY (1928) has played a prominent role. From the mathematical point of view, it can be formulated as a discrete-time, infinite-horizon concave optimization problem:

(P) $\quad W_\delta(x_0) = \sup_{(x_t)} \sum_{t=0}^{\infty} V(x_t, x_{t+1})\delta^t \quad$ s.t.

$(x_t, x_{t+1}) \in D$ and x_0 is fixed,

where $V : D \to R$ is a concave function defined over a convex and closed set $D \subset X \times X$, and the initial condition x_0 belongs to $X = pr_1(D) \subset R^n$.

The recent book by STOKEY and LUCAS (1989) is an excellent source of references. There, the reader can find both the basic results on this model and a huge variety of examples arising in modern economic dynamics which can be studied by using particular specifications of the above problem P.

Even if the basic problems, such as the existence of optimal solutions and their characterization, have been extensively studied in literature, our insight into long-term behavior of optimal paths is poor and several issues are still open.

Our concern in this paper is to present recent results which point in this direction. More specifically, we shall present results on the relationship between the asymptotic properties of optimal solutions to P and the discount factor δ viewed as a parameter varying over the interval (0,1).

Known results in the dynamics of P can be roughly summarized in the following two facts:

i) any dynamic behavior is possible whenever the discount factor is small enough.

ii) turnpike theorems assure that, under suitable conditions related to the curvature of the short-run utility V and for discount factors near 1 enough, all the optimal trajectories shrink and converge to a unique fixed point. So, for low discounting the dynamic behavior is simple.

It is worth pointing out the different nature of these two facts to avoid misinterpretations. In fact, the first says that, given a dynamical system $x_{t+1} = h(x_t)$, there is a discount factor $\delta^*(h)$, which depends on h, such that for any fixed $0 < \delta < \delta^*(h)$ there exists some well-behaved problem P having the optimal paths generated by the dynamical system $x_{t+1} = h(x_t)$.

[1]This research was partially supported by M.U.R.S.T. "National Group on Non-Linear Dynamics in Economics and Social Sciences".

This was proved in BOLDRIN and MONTRUCCHIO (1986) where an estimate from below for $\delta^*(h)$ was also given. This theorem does not provide any information as to which discount factors the dynamics $x_{t+1} = h(x_t)$ is not optimal for any problem P. Actually, some chaotic behavior may coexist for discount factors arbitrary close to 1.

Note that this fact does not contrast with the turnpike results claimed at (ii). Indeed, (ii) affirms that, given a problem P, there exists a discount factor $\delta(V)$, depending on V, such that the optimal dynamics are simple for any $\delta > \delta(V)$. As $\delta(V)$ depends on the curvature of V, the turnpike discount factor may be relegated arbitrary near 1.

In Section 2 we discuss point (i) concerning the occurrence of any kind of dynamic behavior for small discount factors. Theorem 1, stated in MONTRUCCHIO (1992,b) is a new improved version of the BOLDRIN and MONTRUCCHIO (1986) theorem.

Section 3 contains two interesting results due to SANTOS (1991) and SORGER (1992,a) that prove the existence of a relationship between the dynamic complexity of the solutions to P and the discount factor.

Section 4 recalls briefly the mathematics of strong concavity. Actually all the results described in this paper make use of notions related to the strong concavity for the short-run function V(x,y).

Section 5 provides a general theorem on the Holder (Lipschitz) continuous dependence of the solutions to P with respect to the initial condition. This is possible by regarding the solution to P as an element of Hilbert space $\ell_2(\delta)$.

Section 6 is devoted to finding the maximal discount factor in order that a given dynamics can be optimal or, in dual manner, the minimal discount factor in order to avoid a dynamics as optimal. Theorem 6 shows that a map with positive topological entropy cannot be an optimal dynamics for any strongly concave problem whenever the discount factor is large enough. Furthermore, a uniform estimate based on its topological entropy is given.

In the last section we provide a few new turnpike results which are strictly related to Theorem 5 on Lipschitz dependence of optima. The basic idea is that of adopting a new distance on the state space. Theorem 7 proves that, for regular problems, the policy function is a global contraction whenever the discount factor is greater than $1 - (\alpha + \beta)/\gamma$. The number $\alpha + \beta$ can be seen as a measure of lower curvature of the utility function V(x,y), while γ can be taken as a measure of upper curvature for V(x,y). Theorem 8 is a theorem of local turnpike which drops the strong assumption of regularity used in Theorem 7. Theorem 8 can be seen as a generalization of the local turnpike result given by SCHEINKMAN (1976) without adopting differentiability assumptions for V(x,y).

2. Complicated Solutions for Small Discount Factors

It has already been recognized (see BOLDRIN and MONTRUCCHIO (1986), DENECKERE and PELIKAN (1986)) that chaotic paths can be solutions to concave problems (P). In BOLDRIN and MONTRUCCHIO (1986) we showed that the dynamic behavior of the solutions to P can be of any kind whenever the discount factor δ is small enough. The proof of this fact is based on Dynamic Programming method which relates P to the functional equation:

(B) $$W_\delta(x) = \sup_{y \in D(x)} (V(x,y) + \delta W_\delta(y))$$

where $D(x) = (y; (x,y) \in D)$ and $W_\delta(x)$ is the value function.

It is also very well-known that, under assumptions of existence and uniqueness of optimal solutions for all initial data, one can derive from the Bellman equation B the optimal policy $y' = h(x)$ defined as the unique point y' where the optimal value is attained, i.e., $W_\delta(x) = V(x,h(x)) + \delta W_\delta(h(x))$.

Of course, the policy $h(x)$ completely describes the dynamic behavior of the optimal paths (x^*_t) because they are generated by the discrete dynamical system: $x^*_{t+1} = h(x^*_t)$ with initial point $x^*_0 = x_0$.

In the sequel the policy $h(x)$ will often be denoted with $h_\delta(x)$ for emphasizing its dependence on the discount factor.

Below, we quote a new version of Boldrin and Montrucchio's theorem given in MONTRUCCHIO (1992,b). It contains an improvement on the estimate of the discount factor.

Theorem 1. *Let $h: X \to X$ be any $C^{1,1}$ map which satisfies $(x,h(x)) \in D$ for all x in X and where X is a convex subset of R^n. There exists an interval $[0, \delta^*(h)]$, such that for any fixed discount factor $\delta \in (0, \delta^*(h))$, one can find a bounded concave utility function $V_\delta(x,y)$, defined on $X \times X$, so that h turns out to be the optimal policy for the problem P with short-run utility $V_\delta(x,y)$ and discount factor δ. Moreover, one has:*

$$\delta^*(h) \geq (k_1 + (k_0 k_2)^{1/2})^{-2}$$

where: $k_0 = Max\ |x - y|$, $k_1 = Max\ |Dh(x)|$ and k_2 is a Lipschitz constant for $Dh(x)$, i.e., $|Dh(x_1) - Dh(x_2)| \leq k_2 |x_1 - x_2|$ for x_1, x_2 in X.

Also, $V_\delta(x,y)$ can be chosen strongly concave, of class $C^{1,1}$, increasing in x and decreasing in y.

Here a map of class $C^{1,1}$ means that it is defined and differentiable over an open set containing X and its derivative is Lipschitz continuous over X. All the norms $|.|$ in this theorem are Euclidean norms.

The extension of Theorem 1 to policy functions that are not $C^{1,1}$ is not known. The embedding of some C^0 functions has been provided by NEUMANN et ALII (1988). On the other hand, the existence of C^1 policies, which are not C^2, has been observed by ARAUJO (1990) for problems P with short-run utilities of class C^2. Analogous results for the continuous time version of model P have been provided by SORGER (1990) and, independently, by MONTRUCCHIO (1988, 1992,a).

It should be noted that Theorem 1 is a constructive one and it provides an estimate from below, δ^*, for the "maximal" discount factor. Unfortunately, such an estimate may sometimes prove the existence of optimal paths just for very small discount factors. For instance, in BOLDRIN and MONTRUCCHIO (1986) it is given a neoclassical two-sector model where the optimal capital stocks are generated by the logistic function $x_{t+1} = 4x_t(1 - x_t)$. This requires a high discounting. In fact, $k_0 = 1$, $k_1 = 4$ and $k_2 = 8$. Thus $\delta^* = (1/8)(3 - 8^{1/2}) \approx 0.02$.

On the other hand, the same theorem suggests also that some chaotic behavior can occur for discount factors close to 1, if the problem P has at least three state variables. This can be easily seen by using the following argument.

Take a continuous three dimensional dynamical system $x' = f(x)$ which is of class C^2. Let $x(t) = \Phi(t,x) = \Phi^t(x)$ be the flow generated by the dynamical system. Let us suppose that the flow $\Phi^t(x)$ is "chaotic" and $\Phi^t(X) \subseteq X$ for all $t \geq 0$ for some compact an convex set X. If we now take the map $h(x) = \Phi^{t_0}(x)$ with $t_0 > 0$ small enough, it is readily checked that the amount k_1 can be made close to 1 while k_2 close to 0, so $\delta^*(h)$ is arbitrarily near 1. On the other hand, the dynamic behavior of the map $h(x) = \Phi^{t_0}(x)$ turns out to be chaotic.

The existence of ergodic chaos in a two-sectors economic growth model for small discounting has recently been studied by NISHIMURA and YANO (1992).

3. Complicated Solutions and Discount Factors

The brief discussion of Section 2 raises a few interesting questions. Is it $\delta^*(h) < 1$, at least for a large class of problems P? Is the lower bound $\delta^*(h) \geq (k_1 + (k_0k_2)^{1/2})^{-2}$ a good estimate? Is it possible to give upper bounds for $\delta^*(h)$?

A first result in this direction turns out to be as a consequence of the SANTOS (1991) theorem on the differentiability of the policy function (see also ARAUJO, 1991).

Theorem 2. *(SANTOS,1991) Let $V(x,y)$ be of class C^2 and the policy $h_\delta(x)$ be interior, i.e., $h_\delta(x_t) \in Int\, D(x_t)$ for all $t \geq 0$. If $V(x,y)$ is $(0,\beta)$-concave and $\beta > 0$, then:*
(i) the policy $h_\delta(x)$ is of class C^1 and the value function $W_\delta(x)$ is C^2.
(ii) there exists a constant N such that: $|Dh^t_\delta(x)| \leq N\delta^{-t/2}$ for all t and all x in X.

The assumption of $(0,\beta)$-concavity of Theorem 2 is a condition of strong concavity. Details will be given in the next section. Just an example is needed to understand how to use Theorem 2 to our end. Take the logistic map $h(x) = 4x(1 - x)$. We have seen that it can be an optimal policy for discount factor less than 0.02. It is not difficult to see that $|Dh^t| = 4^t$. From (ii) of Theorem 2, it follows that $\delta^*(h) \leq 1/16 \approx 0.063$ (at least for strongly C^2 - problems P).

Recently, SORGER (1992,a,b) provided a result in the characterization of optimal sequences which gives an insight into the role played by the discount factor. He proves that in the class of strictly concave problems P the initial data cannot be represented as the weighted average of the future sequence, when the weights are required to decrease at least as fast as the discount factor. He uses this general result to obtain uniform upper bounds on the discount factor in all strictly concave problems P which can possess a given sequence as its optimal solution. The paper contains also an extension to the continuous time model. We refer to Sorger's paper for details. Here we give just his main theorem that can be proved by using Dynamic Programming.

Theorem 3. (SORGER,1992,a) *Let $\mathbf{x} = (x_0,x_1,x_2,\ldots)$ be any fixed sequence with $x_0 \neq x_1$. Let us suppose that there exists a number $\delta_1 \in (0, 1)$ and a scalar sequence $\mathbf{z} = (z_1,z_2,\ldots)$ with $z_1 \geq z_2 \geq \ldots$, such that:*

$$i) \quad \sum_{t=1}^{\infty} z_t\delta_1^t = 1 \qquad ii) \quad \sum_{t=1}^{\infty} z_t\delta_1^t x_t = x_0 \quad .$$

Then the path $\mathbf{x} = (x_0,x_1,x_2,\ldots)$ cannot be an optimal solution to any strictly concave problems whenever the discount factor is $\delta \geq \delta_1$.

By this theorem, Sorger computes upper bounds of the maximal discount factor $\delta^*(h)$ for several classes of maps h.

4. Strongly Concave Problems

Sorger's approach consists in looking at a single path. On the contrary, in MONTRUCCHIO (1992,b) we took into account the relationship between the sensitivity to initial conditions and the discount factor in the direction suggested by Santos' result. Of course the strong assumptions of differentiability and interiority, which are present in his theorem, are dropped, while the assumption of strong concavity for the utility function V(x,y) is maintained.

We list some basic definitions which are perhaps not completely standard.

Let $X \subset H$ be a convex subset of a Hilbert space H, and α be a real number. A function $f: X \to R \cup (-\infty)$ is termed α-concave if the function $f(x) + (1/2)\alpha|x|^2$ is concave over X. If a positive number $\alpha > 0$ exists such that the previous condition is fulfilled, then we shall say that f is strongly concave. See ROCKAFELLAR (1976), SCHAIBLE and ZIEMBA (1981) and VIAL (1983).

For a function U(x,y), depending on two groups of variables, we shall say that U is (α,β)-concave if $U(x,y) + (1/2)\alpha|x|^2 + (1/2)\beta|y|^2$ is concave.

Given a function $f: X \to R$, we shall say that f is concave-γ if $f(x) + (1/2)\gamma|x|^2$ is convex over X.

5. Sensitivity to Initial Conditions

The idea behind this approach is to look at the map $x_0 \to (x^*_1, x^*_2, x^*_3, \ldots)$, sending the initial point $x_0 \in X$ to the optimal path $(x_1^*, x_2^*, x_3^*, \ldots)$ starting at x_0, as a map $X \to \ell_2(\delta)$, where $\ell_2(\delta)$ is a suitable Hilbert space of sequences weighted by the discount factor δ. We recall that the idea of looking at problem P as programming over sequence spaces goes back to ARAUJO and SCHEINKMAN (1977). By using the space ℓ_∞, they gave interesting turnpike results.

A bit of additional notation is now needed.

For a given δ in (0,1), let $\mathbf{x} = (x_1, x_2, x_3, \ldots)$, with $x_t \in R^n$, be a sequence satisfying $\Sigma^\infty_{t=1} |x_t|^2 \delta^t < \infty$. The space of all such sequences will be denoted with $\ell_2(\delta)$. It is a Hilbert space with inner product defined as: $<x,y> = \Sigma^\infty_{t=1} x_t \cdot y_t \delta^t$.

Given now a map $h: X \to X$, where X is compact, we can associate to h the map $\mathbf{h}: X \to \ell_2(\delta)$ defined as $\mathbf{h}(x_0) = (h(x_0), h^2(x_0), h^3(x_0), \ldots)$, i.e., the map which sends any initial point in X to the trajectory generated by iterating h. Of course, if $h_\delta(x)$ is the policy of some problem P then $\mathbf{h}_\delta(x)$ is the optimal trajectory, starting at x, seen as a sequence of $\ell_2(\delta)$. This is obvious if we only consider problems P in which the initial condition belongs to a compact set X. If X is unbounded, it is not obvious whether the optimal paths $(x^*_t) \in \ell_2(\delta)$. Although the bounded case is important enough, it is worthy of note that this is the case under assumptions of strong concavity for the utility function V(x,y).

We quote a theorem given in MONTRUCCHIO (1990) which shows the natural role played by the space $\ell_2(\delta)$ in strongly concave problems.

Theorem 4. *Let problem P be given with $D = R^n \times R^n$ and $V: D \to R \cup (-\infty)$. Under the assumptions:*

i) $W(x_0) > -\infty$

ii) $V(x,y)$ is upper semicontinuous;

iii) $V(x,y)$ is (α,β)-concave, with a and $\beta > 0$;

there exists a unique optimal path $(x_0,\mathbf{x}) = (x_0,x_1,x_2,x_3,\ldots)$ starting at x_0. Moreover, $\mathbf{x} \in \ell_2(\delta)$, where δ is the discount factor.

The theorem is still true under weaker assumption $\alpha + \beta > 0$, provided that $\sup_{(x,y)} V(x,y) = V(x^*,y^*)$ for some (x^*,y^*).

The next theorem has been established in MONTRUCCHIO (1992,b).

Theorem 5. *Let problem P be given. If $V(x,y)$ is (α,β)-concave on D with α, $\beta \geq 0$ and $\alpha + \beta > 0$, then the map $x \rightarrow \mathbf{h}_\delta(x)$, from X to $\ell_2(\delta)$, satisfies the following properties:*

i) $(1/2)[\alpha + (\beta/\delta)]\,|\mathbf{h}_\delta(x_0) - \mathbf{h}_\delta(x)|^2 \leq W_\delta(x_0) - W_\delta(x) + p.(x - x_0)$

for all $x \in X$, $x_0 \in Int(X)$ and all $p \in \partial W_\delta(x_0)$.

ii) for any $x_0 \in Int(X)$, there exists a constant H and a neighborhood $V(x_0)$ such that $|\mathbf{h}_\delta(x_1) - \mathbf{h}_\delta(x_2)| \leq H\,|x_1 - x_2|^{1/2}$ holds for all x_1,x_2 in $V(x_0)$.

iii) if in addition the value function $W_\delta(x)$ is concave-γ over X, then the following Lipschitz condition holds:

$$|\mathbf{h}_\delta(x) - \mathbf{h}_\delta(x_0)| \leq K^{1/2}\,|x - x_0|$$

for all $x_0 \in Int(X)$, $x \in X$ and with $K = \delta(\gamma - \alpha)(\alpha\delta + \beta)^{-1}$.

Some comments are in order.

1) Statements *(ii)* and *(iii)* prove the Holder continuous dependence and Lipschitz dependence, respectively, of the optimal paths in the strong topology of $\ell_2(\delta)$. This implies a sort of restriction to the sensitivity to initial conditions as the discount factor increases. In the next section we shall discuss this aspect further.

2) Statement *(iii)* of Theorem 5 requires that the value function be concave-γ. Such a property is not always valid, at least globally. Subclasses of problems P which enjoy this property are known [see Proposition 4.2 in MONTRUCCHIO (1992,b)].

6. Upper Bounds for the Maximal Discount Factor of Maps

Theorem 5 is able to provide upper bounds for the maximal discount factor $\delta^*(h)$ within the class of strongly concave problems. The intuition behind this is due to the fact that the Holder dependence, with respect to the initial condition, binds the rate of divergence of trajectories. In MONTRUCCHIO (1992,b) we related this property to the topological entropy of a map, which is a measure of complexity of the dynamical system generated by iterating the map.

We recall that the topological entropy H(h) of a map h measures the growth rate of the number of orbits of h that can be distinguished by increasingly better observations (for details and a formal definition we refer to GUCKENHEIMER and HOLMES, 1986).

We report here the main result established in MONTRUCCHIO (1992,b). Let $h: X \rightarrow X$ be a map where X is a compact and convex subset of R^n. Let Λ be a compact set, contained in the interior to X, which is positively invariant for h, i.e., $h(\Lambda) \subseteq \Lambda$. Let us denote with H(h) the topological entropy of h on Λ.

Theorem 6. *A necessary condition in order that h be a policy for some strongly concave problem is that the discount factor is not greater than exp(-H/n), where H is its topological entropy and n = dim X. In other words, the estimate $\delta^*(h) \leq \exp(-H/n)$ holds.*

Of course Theorem 6 shows that a map with positive entropy cannot be a policy for discount factors near 1. Moreover, an upper bound of $\delta^*(h)$ can be obtained through its topological entropy. Other more stringent upper bounds can be given by slightly restricting the class of problems P. We refer to MONTRUCCHIO (1992,b) for a few results in this direction.

7. Turnpike Results

In this section we prove new results on the stability of optimal solutions to P by exploiting Theorem 5 on Hölder and Lipschitz dependence of optimal solutions on initial conditions. All these results will have the feature of pointing out the extent of discount factors for which this property holds. This is achieved by giving an estimate of the interval on which the turnpike property is assured, as a function of the parameters of curvature for the short-run function *V(x,y)*. For basic turnpike results the reader is referred to CASS and SHELL (1976), McKENZIE (1986), ROCKAFELLAR (1976) and SCHEINKMAN (1976).

The first result presented here covers only partially the models of interest in economics. Its interest is due to its extreme simplicity. We need to restrict the class of problems *P* under study by introducing the class defined below.

Definition 1. A problem *P* will be said to be regular if

i) V(x,y) is continuous and there exist numbers $\alpha,\beta \geq 0$, with $\alpha + \beta > 0$, so that V(x,y) is (α,β)-concave over D;

ii) the correspondence $x \to D(x)$ is continuous;

iii) for every discount factor $\delta \in (0,1)$, the value function $W_\delta(x)$ is concave-γ over X for some non-negative number γ independently of δ.

We shall make use of the following new distance on the state space X:

$$\text{(M)} \qquad d(x,y) = \left(\Sigma^{\infty}_{t=0}|h^t_\delta(x) - h^t_\delta(y)|^2\delta^t\right)^{1/2}$$

where h_δ is the policy function.

Theorem 7. *Let problem P be regular, then:*

i) the distance M is equivalent to the Euclidean metric, more precisely:

$$|x - y|^2 \leq d^2(x,y) \leq (1 + K)|x - y|^2$$

holds for all x, y in X, with $K = \delta(\gamma - \alpha)(\alpha\delta + \beta)^{-1}$.

ii) the policy is a contraction for the metric M, whenever $\delta > 1 - (\alpha + \beta)/\gamma$.

Proof. If h: $X \to X$ is any continuous map where X is a compact set, then the associated map **h**: $X \to \ell_2(\delta)$ is continuous in the strong topology of $\ell_2(\delta)$, for any weight $\delta \in (0, 1)$. On the other hand, assumptions *(i)-(ii)* of Definition 1 imply that the policy h_δ is continuous [see for example STOKEY and LUCAS (1989)]. Thus **h**: $X \to \ell_2(\delta)$ is continuous. From *(iii)* of Theorem 5, we know that

$$| \mathbf{h}_\delta(x_1) - \mathbf{h}_\delta(x_2)| \leq K^{1/2} | x_1 - x_2 | \quad (1)$$

holds for all $x_1, x_2 \in \text{Int } X$ and where $K = \delta (\gamma - \alpha)(\alpha\delta + \beta)^{-1}$.
From the continuity of $\mathbf{h}_\delta$ we can deduce that (1) holds for all $x_1, x_2 \in X$ as well. Now from (1) we have

$$| x - y |^2 \leq d^2(x,y) = |x - y|^2 + |\mathbf{h}_\delta(x) - \mathbf{h}_\delta(y)|^2 \leq (1 + K)|x - y|^2 ,$$

and statement (i) is proved.
Next, by definition of the distance *M* it follows:

$$\delta d^2(h_\delta(x), h_\delta(y)) + |x - y|^2 = d^2(x , y).$$

Thus, $d^2(x , y) \geq \delta d^2(h_\delta(x), h_\delta(y)) + (1 + K)^{-1}d^2(x , y)$, that leads to

$$d^2(h_\delta(x), h_\delta(y)) \leq \delta^{-1}K(1 + K)^{-1}d^2(x , y).$$

Since $K = \delta(\gamma - \alpha)(\alpha\delta + \beta)^{-1}$, it follows

$$d^2(h_\delta(x), h_\delta(y)) \leq (\gamma - \alpha)(\beta + \gamma\delta)^{-1} d^2(x , y).$$

Thus, by adopting this new metric, the new Lipschitz constant decreases as δ increases and it turns out to be less than one when $(\gamma - \alpha)(\beta + \gamma\delta)^{-1} < 1$, i.e., when $\delta > 1 - (\alpha + \beta)/\gamma$.

Remark. If the policy is a contraction for the metric M, then there is an iterate of the policy which is a contraction for the Euclidean distance. This implies the existence of a unique globally attracting fixed point for the policy. This is a global turnpike property.

Indeed, several growth models may have some stationary optimal solutions placed at the boundary which never converge to the modified optimal steady state. That implies that the policy function is never a contraction in this kind of model. In other words Theorem 7 fails because some relevant problems are not regular. To get around this difficulty, we adopt the device used by SCHEINKMAN (1976). First we prove a local turnpike theorem, which shows that all the optimal paths in a neighborhood of the optimal steady state go asymptotically to the stationary state. The idea behind the proof is that, at least locally around the optimal steady state, the property of contraction for the policy function still holds. It will be sufficient to use a Liapunov function which is strictly related to the new distance used in proving the global turnpike Theorem 7.

It is worth noting that our proof of local stability is completely different from that of SCHEINKMAN (1976). In fact, he assumed V(x,y) to be at least three times continuously differentiable and furthermore, assumed a saddle property for the the undiscounted linearized Euler difference system. His proof then goes on by using the stable manifold theorem and proving the continuous dependence of the stable manifold on the discount factor. His proof is quite involved and does not provide a evaluation of the range of discount factors for which the local stability holds.

Let us suppose that there exists a family of stationary solutions x^*_δ as δ runs over a subinterval $(\delta', 1)$ of $(0 , 1)$.

Theorem 8. *Let Y be a closed convex set such that:*
$Y \subset \text{Int } X$, $Y \times Y \subset D$ and there is an ε-neighborhood $U_\varepsilon (x^*_\delta)$ of x^*_δ which is contained in Y and with radius ε independent of δ, for all $\delta \in (\delta',1)$.
Under additional assumptions:
(i) V(.,y) is concave-γ over Y for any y in Y,

(ii) $V(x,y)$ is $(\alpha,,\beta)$-concave over D, with $\alpha + \beta > 0$,
then the stationary point x^*_δ is locally asymptotically stable for discount factors $\delta > Max\,[\delta', 1 - (\alpha + \beta)/\gamma]$. Furthermore, the basin of attraction of x^*_δ contains a circular neighborhood with a radius which is a non-decreasing function of the discount factor δ.

The proof of this theorem needs the following lemma.

Lemma 1. *Under the same assumptions of Theorem 8, the value function $W_\delta(x)$ turns out to be concave-γ over a neighborhood $U_\eta\,(x^*_\delta) \subset U_\varepsilon\,(x^*_\delta)$. Moreover, the radius η of $U_\eta\,(x^*_\delta)$ can be chosen to not decrease as δ increases.*

Proof of Lemma 1. By the strong concavity of $V(x,y)$ and interiority of x^*_δ, it follows from *(i)* of Theorem 5 that

$$(1/2)[\alpha + (\beta/\delta)]\,|\mathbf{h}_\delta(x^*_\delta) - \mathbf{h}_\delta(x)|^2 \leq W_\delta(x^*_\delta) - W_\delta(x) + p.(x - x^*_\delta) \qquad (2)$$

for all $p \in \partial W_\delta(x^*_\delta)$.
On the other hand, we have $W_\delta(x^*_\delta) = (1 - \delta)^{-1}V(x^*_\delta,x^*_\delta)$, being x^*_δ a steady state optimal solution to P. Furthermore, it holds $W_\delta(x) \geq V(x,x^*_\delta) + \delta W_\delta(x^*_\delta)$, for all $x \in U_\varepsilon(x^*_\delta)$. This is valid because $U_\varepsilon(x^*_\delta)\times U_\varepsilon(x^*_\delta) \subset D$. It will be sufficient using the Bellman equation. Thus (2) becomes:

$$(1/2)[\alpha + (\beta/\delta)]\,|\mathbf{h}_\delta(x^*_\delta) - \mathbf{h}_\delta(x)|^2 \leq V(x^*_\delta, x^*_\delta) - V(x, x^*_\delta) + p.(x - x^*_\delta)\,.$$

From BENVENISTE and SCHEINKMAN's (1979) result, $p \in \partial W_\delta(x^*_\delta)$ implies $p \in \partial_1 W_\delta(x^*_\delta,x^*_\delta)$.
If one denotes by M a Lipschitz constant of $V(x,y)$ over $Y\times Y$ and by N an upper bound $|p| \leq N$, for $p \in \partial W_\delta(x_\delta)$ and $x \in Y$, we get

$$V(x^*_\delta, x^*_\delta) - V(x, x^*_\delta) + p.(x - x^*_\delta) \leq (M + N)\,|\,x - x^*_\delta\,|$$

for every $\delta \in (\delta', 1)$ and where M and N are independent of δ.
Thus we can write

$$(1/2)[\alpha + (\beta/\delta)]\,|\mathbf{h}_\delta(x^*_\delta) - \mathbf{h}_\delta(x)|^2 \leq (M + N)\,|\,x - x^*_\delta\,|.$$

In particular,

$$|h_\delta(x) - x^*_\delta\,| \leq H(\delta)\,|x - x^*_\delta\,|^{1/2}$$

holds for all x in $U_\varepsilon(x^*_\delta)$ and with $H(\delta) = 2^{1/2}(M + N)^{1/2}(\alpha\delta + \beta)^{-1/2}$.
Note that the Holder constant $H(\delta)$ turns out to be a decreasing function of δ.
Now take $\eta = \mathrm{Min}\,(\varepsilon, \varepsilon^2/H^2(\delta))$. It follows that $x \in U_\eta(x^*_\delta)$ implies $h_\delta(x) \in U_\varepsilon(x^*_\delta)$. From Proposition 4.2 of MONTRUCCHIO (1992,b), applied to $U_\eta(x^*_\delta)\times U_\varepsilon(x^*_\delta)$, it follows that the value function $W_\delta(x)$ turns out to be concave-γ on $U_\eta(x^*_\delta)$ for all δ. The radius η increases as δ increases.

Proof of Theorem 8. Define the function S: $X \rightarrow R$ as

$$S(x) = \Sigma^\infty_{t=0}\,|h^t_\delta(x) - x^*_\delta\,|^2\,\delta^t$$

for all $\delta > \delta'$. In view of Lemma 1 and (iii) of Theorem 5, there exists a neighborhood $U_\eta(x^*_\delta)$ of x^*_δ, with η independent of δ, so that

$$\Sigma^\infty_{t=1}\,|h^t_\delta(x) - x^*_\delta\,|^2\,\delta^t \leq K\,|x - x^*_\delta\,|^2$$

holds for any $x \in U_\eta(x^*_\delta)$.

We have

$$S(x) \geq |x - x^*_\delta|^2 \tag{3}$$

for all x in X and

$$S(x) \leq (1 + K)|x - x^*_\delta|^2 \tag{4}$$

for all $x \in U_\eta(x^*_\delta)$.

By construction, one has $S(x) = \delta S(h_\delta(x)) + |x - x^*_\delta|^2$.

Given now any x in $U_\eta(x^*_\delta)$ and by using (4), the same method adopted in the proof of Theorem 7 leads to $S(h_\delta(x)) < S(x)$, whenever $\delta > 1 - (\alpha + \beta)/\gamma$ and $\delta > \delta'$.

Replacing x with $h_\delta(x)$ in (3), we get

$$|h_\delta(x) - x^*_\delta|^2 \leq S(h_\delta(x)) < S(x) \leq (1 + K)|x - x^*_\delta|^2.$$

So that, if we take a point x in the ω-neighborhood of x^*_δ where $\omega = \eta\,(\alpha + \beta)^{1/2}(\beta + \gamma)^{-1/2}$, we have $S(h_\delta(x)) < S(x)$ and $h_\delta(x) \in U_\eta(x^*_\delta)$.

Thus we have: $S(h^2_\delta(x)) < S(h_\delta(x)) < S(x)$ and once again

$$|h_\delta(x) - x^*_\delta|^2 \leq (K + 1)\,|x - x^*_\delta|^2 \text{ , i.e., } |h_\delta(x) - x^*_\delta| < \eta.$$

Iterating this procedure, we get that all the orbit $(x, h_\delta(x), h^2_\delta(x), h^3_\delta(x),\ldots)$ lies in $U_\eta(x^*_\delta)$ whenever the initial condition starts at $U_\omega(x^*_\delta)$. Furthermore, one has $S(x) > S(h_\delta(x)) > S(h^2_\delta(x)) > S(h^3_\delta(x)) > \ldots$.

By standard arguments adopted in Liapunov theory, it follows that the orbit $(x, h_\delta(x), h^2_\delta(x), h^3_\delta(x),\ldots)$ converges to x^*_δ and this completes the proof of the local stability of the fixed point x^*_δ.

Remark. From Theorem 8 we could get a global turnpike result by using the same argument adopted by SCHEINKMAN (1976). In fact, the existence of a neighborhood of x^*_δ, with radius independent of the discount factor and on which the solutions go asymptotically to the stationary solution x^*_δ, permits to use the Visit Lemma. Details will be given in a next paper.

References

Araujo, A., The once but not twice differentiability of the policy function, Econometrica, 59, 1383-1393, 1991.

Araujo, A., J.A.Scheinkman, Smoothness, Comparative Dynamics and the Turnpike Property, Econometrica, 45, 601-620, 1977.

Benveniste, L.M., J.A. Scheinkman, On the Differentiability of the Value Function in Dynamic Models of Economics, Econometrica, 47, 727-732, 1979.

Boldrin, M., L.Montrucchio, On the indeterminacy of capital accumulation paths, Journal of Economic Theory, 40, 26-39, 1986.

Cass,D., K.Shell, The structure and stability of competitive dynamical systems, Journal of Economic Theory, 12, 31-70, 1976.

Deneckere,R., S.Pelikan, Competitive Chaos, Journal of Economic Theory, 40, 13-25, 1986.

Guckenheimer, J., P.Holmes, Nonlinear Oscillations, Dynamical Systems, and Bifurcations of Vector Fields, Springer-Verlag, New York, 1986.

McKenzie, L.W.. Optimal Economic Growth and Turnpike Theorems. In "Handbook of Mathematical Economics", Vol. III, K.J. Arrow and M. Intrilligator (eds.), Amsterdam, North Holland, 1986.

Montrucchio, L., The occurrence of erratic fluctuations in models of optimization over infinite horizon, in "Growth Cycles and Multisectoral Economics: the Goodwin Tradition",G.Ricci and K.Velupillai (eds.), Springer Verlag, Berlin, 1988.

Montrucchio, L., Problemi matematici nei modelli di ottimizzazione intertemporale, Atti del Convegno A.M.A.S.E.S., Pescara, 1990.

Montrucchio, L., Dynamical Systems that Solve Continuous-Time Concave Optimization Problems: Anything Goes, in "Cycles and Chaos in Economic Equilibrium", J.Benhabib (ed.), New Jersey, Princeton University Press, 1992,a.

Montrucchio, L., Dynamic Complexity of Optimal Paths and Discount Factors for Strongly Concave Problems, Journal of Optimization Theory and Applications, 1992,b, forthcoming.

Nishimura, K. and M. Yano, Non-Linear Dynamics and Chaos in Optimal Growth, University of Southern California, mimeo, 1992.

Neumann, D.A., O'Brien, T. e Kim, K., Policy Functions for Capital Accumulation Paths, Journal of Economic Theory, 46, 205-214, 1988.

Ramsey, F., A Mathematical Theory of Saving, Economic Journal, 38, 543-559, 1928.

Rockafellar, T.R., Saddle points of Hamiltonians systems in convex Lagrange problems having a nonzero discount rate, Journal of Economic Theory, 12, 71-113, 1976.

Santos, M.S., Smoothness of the Policy Function in Discrete Time Economic Models, Econometrica, 59, 1365-1382, 1991.

Schaible, S., W.T.Ziemba(eds.), Generalized Concavity in Optimization and Economics, New York, Academic Press, 1981.

Scheinkman, J.A., On Optimal Steady States of n-Sector Growth Models when Utility is Discounted, Journal of Economic Theory, 12, 11-30, 1976.

Sorger, G., On the optimality of given feedback controls, Journal of Optimization Theory and Applications, 65, 321-329, 1990.

Sorger, G., On the Minimum Rate of Impatience for Complicated Optimal Growth Paths, Journal of Economic Theory, 56, 160-179, 1992,a.

Sorger, G., Minimum Impatience Theorems for Recursive Economic Models, Springer-Verlag, Berlin, 1992,b.

Stokey, N.L., R.E. Lucas, and E. Prescott, Recursive Methods in Economic Dynamics, Harvard University Press, Cambridge, 1989.

Vial, J.P., Strong and Weak Convexity of Sets and Functions, Mathematics of Operation Research, 8, 231-259, 1983.

Acyclicity of Optimal Paths

Luigi Montrucchio * Nicola Persico

University of Turin

Abstract

It is well known that the stability of optimal paths for infinite horizon concave problems is not assured for all discount factors. Along the ideas developed in Boldrin and Montrucchio (IER, 1988), we provide new results of stability which are related to the notion of acyclicity. Some order relations are introduced which can be seen as generalizations of Liapunov theory. Our results are quite complete for one-dimensional case. In higher dimensions we state some new results.

1 Introduction

This paper is concerned with the dynamics of optimal policy functions. The matter is interesting since the contributions of some authors (see for example Boldrin–Montrucchio [2], where it is shown that any kind of erratic behaviour is possible, provided the discount factor is low enough). Classical turnpike theorems, on the other hand, show that regular behaviour is forced when the discount factor gets close to one. In the middle there should be some kind of bifurcation, but little is known in general.

The purpose of this paper is to give results about the regular behaviour of the policy function, based on properties of the primitives of the problem, and independently of the magnitude of the discount factor.

The results obtained are based on the notion of acyclicity of a binary relation, and lie in the line of research started by Montrucchio [7] and developed in Boldrin and Montrucchio [3]. One of the advantages of this approach is that the analysis is carried out without assumptions of differentiability, although further characterizations can be provided in case the primitives are differentiable.

The results we obtain are quite complete for the one-dimensional case and, when compared with the alternative unimodularity approach, prove more general.

In Section 2 we recall some brief definitions concerning dynamical systems. Section 3 is devoted to the exposition of a general theorem and of additional results for one-dimensional systems. Section 4 contains the application of the theorems above to the standard problem of dynamic programming over infinite horizon. The results about the dynamics of the policy function are derived, and the one-dimensional case is examined in detail. Furthermore, we show the connections between acyclicity and unimodularity. In the last subsection we show how, using our method, it is possible to allow only low-period cycles in one dimension, ruling out more complicated dynamics.

* The first author was partially supported by a grant from M.U.R.S.T., National Group on Nonlinear Dynamics in Economics and Social Sciences

2 Definitions and notation

In this section we will develope some notation, and revise some knowledge that we will need later on.

Suppose X is a complete metric space. A discrete dynamical system is a continuous mapping $f : X \to X$. It is well known that the solution to the initial value problem $x_t = f(x_{t-1}), \quad x_0 = x^0$ is given by $x_t = f^t(x^0)$ where f^t denotes the t-th iterate of f.

Denote with

$$\text{Fix}(f) = \{x \in X; f(x) = x\}$$

and

$$\text{Per}(f) = \{x \in X; f^n(x) = x \text{ for some } n \in \mathbf{N}\}.$$

Let us recall some classical definitions related to the asymptotic behaviour of the trajectories $f^n(x)$.

For any $x \in X$ define the ω-limit set $\omega(x)$ as the set of all limit points of the sequence $f^n(x)$. An alternative definition (see [6]) is:

$$\omega(x) = \bigcap_{n\geq 0} \overline{\bigcup_{k\geq n} f^k(x)}.$$

The basic properties of limit sets are summarized in

Fact 1 *Every limit set $\omega(x)$ is closed and positively invariant. If in addition the sequence $f^n(x)$ is relatively compact, then $\omega(x)$ is nonempty, compact, invariant and invariantly connected.*

We refer to [5, 6] for details. Here, we just recall that a set $H \subset X$ is said to be *positively invariant* if $f(H) \subseteq H$, and *invariant* if $f(H) = H$.

Furthermore, H is said to be *invariantly connected* if it is not the union of two nonempty, disjoint closed invariant sets. It should be noted that the motion $f^n(x)$ is relatively compact when X is compact. Analogoulsy it is possible to introduce the α-limit set. Given $x \in X$, the set $\alpha(x)$ is defined as the collection of points $y \in X$ such that there exist two sequences x_n and $\alpha_n \geq 0$ satysfying

$$x_0 = x, \quad x_n \to y \quad \text{as } n \to +\infty \quad \text{and } f^{\alpha_n}(x_{n+1}) = x_n.$$

In the sequel we shall denote

$$\omega(f) = \cup_{x\in X}\omega(x) \text{ and } \alpha(f) = \cup_{x\in X}\alpha(x).$$

Let us introduce the second concept which is related to the recurrence property.

Definition 1 *A point $p \in X$ is a* **wandering point** *for f if there exists a neighbourhood V of p and a positive integer t_0 such that $f^t(V) \cap V = \emptyset$, for all $t > t_0$. Otherwise we say that p is a* **non–wandering point**. *The collection of all such p's is the* **non–wandering set** $\Omega(f)$.

Since the space X is metric, we can give a simpler definition for $\Omega(f)$. A point x is in $\Omega(f)$ iff there exist two sequences $x_k \to x$ and $y_k \to x$ as $k \to +\infty$, and a sequence of integers $n_k \to +\infty$ such that $f^{n_k}(x_k) = y_k$.

For every $x \in X$ it is possible to write the following relation:

$$\text{Fix}(f) \subseteq \text{Per}(f) \subseteq \omega(f) \cup \alpha(f) \subseteq \Omega(f).$$

A classical discussion of the set Ω for discrete and continuous dynamical systems is in [9]. Informally, we can say that Ω contains equilibria, α-limits and periodic orbits, and also all other points of X which keep coming back near themselves under iteration of f: Ω is the dynamically interesting part of X. If we were able to show that $\Omega(f) = \mathrm{Fix}(f)$, then we would say that the map f is "simple", in the sense that no periodic points, "chaos" or topologic transitivity is allowed. If $\Omega(f) = \mathrm{Fix}(f)$ and $\mathrm{Fix}(f)$ is finite then $\omega(x) = \{p\}$ for some $p \in \mathrm{Fix}(f)$. This follows from Fact 1 in addition with the remark that a finite invariantly connected set is a periodic orbit.

Now, let us turn to some algebraic notion we use in the sequel. We define a binary relation over X, called P; that is, P is a subset of $X \times X$. We will write yPx for $(x, y) \in P$. Moreover, thinking of P as a correspondence, we will denote with $P(x)$ the set $P(x) = \{y \in X : yPx\}$, and we will feel free to use the terminology of correspondences. For example, we will say that P is lower-hemicontinuous if the correspondence defined by P is lower-hemicontinuous.

Now, let us turn to the notion of *acyclicity.*

Definition 2 *A binary relation P over X is called* **cyclic** *if for some $n \geq 2$ there exists a sequence $(x_1 \dots x_n)$ of distinct points in X such that x_2Px_1, $x_3Px_2, \dots$, x_nPx_{n-1}, x_1Px_n. P is said to be* **acyclic** *if it is not cyclic.*

REMARK: If we define the *transitive completion* as the set $P^* = \{(x, y) \in X \times X$ such that there exists a finite sequence $(x_1 \dots x_n)$ of points in X satisfying x_1Px, $x_2Px_1, \dots$, x_nPx_{n-1}, yPx_n $\}$, then Definition 2 simply states that P is acyclic if and only if P^* is irreflexive. ◇

3 Binary relations

3.1 The general case

We give immediately the main theorem of this paper.

Theorem 3.1 *Let $f : X \to X$ be a continuous map and P a binary relation over X. Assume that f and P satisfy the following conditions*

1. *$f(x)Px$ for all $x \in X$ such that $f(x) \neq x$*

2. *P is open and acyclic.*

Then we have:

$$\Omega(f) = Fix(f).$$

Proof: See [3] and [7]: □

Theorem 3.1 might well be interpreted as a fixed-point theorem whenever X is compact. In fact, by Lemma 1 we are sure $\omega(f)$ is nonempty, and since the theorem establishes the equality $\omega(f) = \mathrm{Fix}(f)$, we know that in this case the set of fixed points is nonempty, without requiring any convexity of the space X.

3.2 The one–dimensional case

In this subsection we are concerned with the case when X is an interval of the real line. The one–dimensional case yelds particularly good results with our approach, due to the completeness of the natural order structure on $\mathbf{R}$, and to the use of Sarkovsky's powerful theorem (see [8]) on the ranking of cycles.

Let us assume the following regularity conditions for the relation P.

i) P is lower-hemicontinuous.

ii) The set $P(x)$ is convex for every $x \in X$.

iii) If, for a particular point $x' \in X, P(x') = \emptyset$, then for any sequence $x_n \rightarrow x'$ such that $P(x_n) \neq \emptyset$ there exists a sequence $y_n \rightarrow x'$ with $y_n \in P(x_n)$.

Definition 3 *A binary relation P on X is said to be* **n–cyclic** *if there exists a set of distinct points $x_1 \ldots x_n \in X$ such that x_2Px_1,x_3Px_2,$\ldots x_nPx_{n-1}$, x_1Px_n. The relation will be called* **n-acyclic** *if it is not n-cyclic.*

Lemma 1 *Assume a binary relation P satisfies the regularity conditions i),ii),iii). Then for every sequence of distinct points $\{x_1 \ldots x_n\} \in X$, such that $x_{i+1}Px_i$ $(n+1=1)$ there exists a continuous map $\mu : X \rightarrow X$ with the following properties:*

1. $\mu(x_i) = x_{i+1}$
2. $\mu(x)Px$ *for every* $x \neq \mu(x)$

Proof: See [3]. □

Theorem 3.2 *Suppose P is m–acyclic, and P satisfies Assumptions i)-iii) above. Then P is n–acyclic for $n \succ m$ in the Sarkovsky ordering of the natural numbers.*

Proof: Assume P is m–acyclic, and suppose there exists a cycle $y_1, \ldots y_n$ with $y_{i+1}Py_i\,(n+1 = 1)$ and with $n \succ m$.

If P satisfies i)–iii) then, by Lemma 1, a continuous map $\mu : X \rightarrow X$ exists such that $\mu(y_i) = y_{i+1}$ and $\mu(x)Px$. But then we can apply Sarkovsky's theorem. In fact, the existence of a period–n cycle forces the existence of a period–m cycle, denoted by $\{x_1 \ldots x_m\}$. But this, by Lemma 1, implies x_2Px_1, x_3Px_2,$\ldots x_mPx_{m-1}$ and x_1Px_m, contradicting the assumption. □

The consequence of Theorem 3.2 is that it is sufficient to exclude 2-acyclicity in order to rule out acyclicity.

4 Optimal paths

4.1 The problem

The optimization problem is the usual one, described by (1) and by assumptions A1—A3 below (see for example [10]).

$$W_\delta(x) = \max \sum_{t=0}^{\infty} V(x_t, x_{t+1})\delta^t$$

$$\text{s. t. } (x_t, x_{t+1}) \in D \qquad (1)$$
$$x_0 \text{ given in } X$$

A1 $X \subset \mathbf{R}^n$ is compact and convex.

A2 D is a convex subset of $X \times X$, and the correspondence $D : X \to X$ defined by $D(x) = \{y \in X : (x, y) \in D\}$ is a continuous and compact–valued correspondence, such that $x \in D(x)$ for all $x \in X$.

A3 $V : X \times X \to \mathbf{R}$ is a continuous and concave function, and $V(x, \cdot)$ is strictly concave for every $x \in X$.

We recall here some well-known properties of (1) that we will use in the sequel.

The function $W_\delta : X \to \mathbf{R}$ is the value function associated to (1). It is concave and continuous, and satisfies the Bellman equation

$$W_\delta(x) = \max_{y \in D(x)} \{V(x, y) + \delta W_\delta(y)\}. \qquad (2)$$

Define $\tau_\delta : X \to X$ the continuous mapping solving (2), i. e.

$$W_\delta(x) = V(x, \tau_\delta(x)) + \delta W_\delta(\tau_\delta(x)). \qquad (3)$$

We call τ_δ the *policy function* of (1), and we will often omit in what follows the subscript δ. It can be shown, using Bellman's optimality principle, that $\{x_t\}_{t=0}^{\infty}$ is a feasible sequence realizing the maximum of (1) if and only if it satisfies $x_{t+1} = \tau_\delta(x_t)$. The hypotheses made above have the goal of assuring the existence of a well-behaved policy function (for details see [10]).

It is well known (see [2]) that very complicated dynamic behaviour is possible for the function τ. Then it is interesting to obtain stability conditions for τ that do not depend on the explicit knowledge of τ.

4.2 Bellman's equation: the n–dimensional case

We will now provide the application of the general theorems provided in Section 3. Informally, we start from the fact that the function $\tau(x)$ is seen to be the maximizer of the right-hand side of (2), and is therefore "preferred" to any other point in X, including the linear combination of itself with the point x.

Definition 4 *Let* $U : X \times X \to \mathbf{R}$ *be continuous, with* U, X *and* D *satisfying A1-A3. For a given number* $\theta \in [0, 1)$ *define the binary relation* P_θ *over* X *as*

$$y P_\theta x \Leftrightarrow U(x, (1-\theta)x + \theta y) < U(x, y)$$

for $(x, y) \in X \times X$.

The relation P_θ is open in $X \times X$ because U is continuous.

We are interested in the case in which the function $U(x, y)$ is defined as

$$U(x, y) = V(x, y) + \delta W_\delta(y),$$

where V and W_δ are as in problem (1). In other words, one wants to study the acyclicity of the relation

$$yP_\theta x \Leftrightarrow V(x,(1-\theta)x+\theta y)+\delta W_\delta((1-\theta)x+\theta y) < V(x,y)+\delta W_\delta(y) \quad (4)$$

for $\theta \in [0,1)$, and $(x,y) \in X \times X$.

Since $\tau(x) = \text{argmax}_{y\in D(x)} U(x,y)$ for some suitable U, it is true that $\tau(x)P_\theta x$ when $\tau(x) \neq x$, because of the strict concavity of $U(x,\cdot)$, and because $(x,x) \in D$. We are then in the conditions to apply Theorem 3.1, except for the acyclicity of the relation P_θ.

Before turning to the acyclicity of P_θ, let us establish some properties of this relation following [4], where it was first introduced.

Proposition 1 *$\theta > \theta'$ implies $P_\theta \subset P_{\theta'}$, where P_θ is now considered as a subset of $X \times X$.*

Proof: Let $(x,y) \in P_\theta$. Then $U(x,(1-\theta)x+\theta y) < U(x,y)$. For fixed x and y, consider the function $\phi : [0,1) \to \mathbf{R}$ defined as $\phi(\theta) = U(x,(1-\theta)x+\theta y)$. Then $(x,y) \in P_\theta$ is equivalent to $\phi(\theta) < \phi(1)$. The concavity of $U(x,\cdot)$ guarantees that ϕ is concave, and therefore $\theta > \theta'$ implies $\phi(\theta') \leq \phi(\theta) < 1$, i. e. , $U(x,(1-\theta')x+\theta' y) < U(x,y)$, and thus $(x,y) \in P_{\theta'}$. □

Corollary 4.1 *If P_θ, defined as in Definition 4, is acyclic for $\theta = \bar{\theta}$, then it is also acyclic for all $1 > \theta > \bar{\theta}$.*

In the following we will convene to call ***θ*-acyclic** any U that induces a relation P_θ which is acyclic.

Looking at Definition 4 it is immediate to verify that

Proposition 2 *If V is θ-acyclic for some $\theta \in [0,1)$ then the new function $U(x,y) = V(x,y)+\psi(x)$ is also θ-acyclic for any function $\psi : X \to \mathbf{R}$.*

Definition 5 *Let $V(x,y)$ be as in A3. We say that it is* **additively *θ*-acyclic** *iff the functions $U(x,y) = V(x,y)+W(y)$ are θ-acyclic for any concave $W(\cdot)$.*

We know that the policy function satisfies (4) for any admissible θ, whenever $\tau(x) \neq x$, because of assumptions A2 on D. Then Theorem 3.1 applies. Obviously, if V is additively θ-acyclic for some $\theta \in [0,1)$, then the policy function τ is "simple" *for every* $\delta \in [0,1)$. Let us now turn to a sufficient condition that guarantees the additively θ-acyclicity of V.

Theorem 4.2 *Let $V(x,y)$ be as in A3, and τ_δ be as defined in (3). If there exists a θ such that for any N and for any sequence of distinct points $\{x_1 \ldots x_N\}$ one has*

$$\sum_{t=1}^{N} V(x_t,(1-\theta)x_t+\theta x_{t+1}) \geq \sum_{t=1}^{N} V(x_t,x_{t+1}) \quad (5)$$

with $x_{N+1} = x_1$, then V is additively θ-acyclic and τ_δ is "simple".

Proof: We will proceed by contradiction. Let (5) be satisfied for some $0 \leq \theta < 1$ and assume that P_θ as defined in (4) is not acyclic for some concave W. This means that there exists a sequence of points $\{x_1 \ldots x_N\}$ such that $x_{t+1}P_\theta x_t$ with $t = 1 \ldots N$ and $x_{N+1} = x_1$. In other words, for the given θ and chosen W one has

$$V(x_t,(1-\theta)x_t+\theta x_{t+1})+W((1-\theta)x_t+\theta x_{t+1}) < V(x_t,x_{t+1})+W(x_{t+1}) \quad \text{for t=1...N.}$$

Summing over t:

$$\sum_{t=1}^{N}[V(x_t,(1-\theta)x_t+\theta x_{t+1})+W((1-\theta)x_t+\theta x_{t+1})]<\sum_{t=1}^{N}[V(x_t,x_{t+1})+W(x_{t+1})]. \quad (6)$$

As W was assumed concave, we have

$$\sum_{t=1}^{N}W((1-\theta)x_t+\theta x_{t+1})\geq(1-\theta)\sum_{t=1}^{N}W(x_t)+\theta\sum_{t=1}^{N}W(x_{t+1})=\sum_{t=1}^{N}W(x_t).$$

The latter inequality implies that Equation (6) may be rewritten as:

$$\sum_{t=1}^{N}V(x_t,(1-\theta)x_t+\theta x_{t+1})<\sum_{t=1}^{N}V(x_t,x_{t+1})$$

which contradicts the hypothesis (5). □

REMARK: Theorem 2 of [3] is obtained as a special case of Theorem 4.2 by taking $\theta=0$. ◇

Obviously, we have the following propositions.

Proposition 3 *If a function V satisfies condition (5) for $\theta=\bar{\theta}$, then V satisfies condition (5) for all $\theta>\bar{\theta}$.*

Proof: The same argument used in the proof of Proposition 1 may be applied to the function $\phi:[0,1)\to\mathbf{R}$ defined by $\phi(\theta)=\sum_{t=1}^{N}[V(x_t,(1-\theta)x_t+\theta x_{t+1})]$ for every given sequence $\{x_1\ldots x_N\}$. □

Proposition 4 *If a function V satisfies (5) for some $\theta\in[0,1)$ then for any function $\psi:X\to\mathbf{R}$ and any concave function $\phi:X\to\mathbf{R}$, the new function $V^+(x,y)=V(x,y)+\psi(x)+\phi(y)$ also satisfies condition (5).*

Proof: One needs only to replicate the argument in the proof of Theorem 4.2. □

Proposition 4 may be quite misleading: in fact, the addition of a function $\phi(y)$ may render additively θ-acyclic a function that is not 0-acyclic. To show this, we have to remind the notion of α-concavity.

A function $V(x,\cdot)$ is said to be α-concave if

$$V(x,(1-\theta)y+\theta z)\geq(1-\theta)V(x,y)+\theta V(x,z)+\frac{1}{2}\alpha\theta(1-\theta)\|y-z\|^2,$$

for all $\theta in[0,1]$, y,z.

Proposition 5 *Take a $V(x,y)$ such that $V(x,\cdot)$ is α-concave for some $\alpha>0$. Suppose*

$$\sum_{t=1}^{N}V(x_t,x_t)\geq\sum_{t=1}^{N}V(x_t,x_{t+1})-\frac{1}{2}\alpha_1\sum_{t=1}^{N}\|x_t-x_{t+1}\|^2 \quad (7)$$

for some $0<\alpha_1<\alpha$, for every N and for every sequence of distinct points $\{x_1\ldots x_N\}$ in X with $x_{N+1}=x_1$. Then $V(x,y)$ turns out to be additively θ-acyclic for $\theta=\alpha_1/\alpha$.

Proof: By contradiction as usual, let $\{x_1 \dots x_N\}$ be a sequence of distinct points in X with $x_{N+1} = x_1$ which realizes a cycle for $\theta = \alpha_1/\alpha$. Then we have

$$V(x_t, (1-\theta)x_t + \theta x_{t+1}) + W((1-\theta)x_t + \theta x_{t+1}) <$$
$$V(x_t, x_{t+1}) + W(x_{t+1}) \quad \text{for i=1...N.} \tag{8}$$

If $V(x, \cdot)$ is α-concave,

$$V(x_t, (1-\theta)x_t + \theta x_{t+1}) \geq (1-\theta)V(x_t, x_t) + \theta V(x_t, x_{t+1}) + \frac{1}{2}\alpha\theta(1-\theta)\|x_t - x_{t+1}\|^2,$$

and comparing with (8)

$$(1-\theta)V(x_t, x_t) + \theta V(x_t, x_{t+1}) + \frac{1}{2}\alpha\theta(1-\theta)\|x_t - x_{t+1}\|^2 + W((1-\theta)x_t + \theta x_{t+1}) <$$
$$V(x_t, x_{t+1}) + W(x_{t+1}),$$

or

$$V(x_t, x_t) + W((1-\theta)x_t + \theta x_{t+1}) < V(x_t, x_{t+1}) - \frac{1}{2}\alpha\theta\|x_t - x_{t+1}\|^2 + W(x_{t+1}).$$

Summing up over t, because of the concavity of W, we have

$$\sum_{t=1}^{N} V(x_t, x_t) < \sum_{t=1}^{N} V(x_t, x_{t+1}) - \frac{1}{2}\alpha\theta \sum_{t=1}^{N} \|x_t - x_{t+1}\|^2$$

which contradicts (7), being $\alpha\theta = \alpha(\alpha_1/\alpha) = \alpha_1$. □

Finally, if V is differentiable in the second set of arguments, we have the following criterion to detect acyclicity, which is very useful from the computational point of view (we use the notation $V_2(x, y) \equiv \nabla_y V(x, y)$).

Proposition 6 *Assume V is as in A3, and differentiable in the second set of arguments. Then V is additively θ-acyclic for some $0 < \theta < 1$ if and only if*

$$\sum_{t=1}^{N} V_2(x_t, x_{t+1}) \cdot (x_{t+1} - x_t) \leq 0 \tag{9}$$

for every sequence of distinct points $\{x_1 \dots x_N\}$ in X with $x_{N+1} = x_1$, for every N.

Proof: Let the set $\{x_1 \dots x_N\}$ satisfying the assumptions of the proposition be given in X, and set $\phi(\theta) = \sum_{t=1}^{N} V(x_t, \theta x_{t+1} + (1-\theta)x_t)$. ϕ is strictly concave on $[0, 1]$ since $V(x, \cdot)$ is concave by assumption. Also, $\phi(\theta) \geq \phi(1)$ because V is acyclic. Hence $\phi'(1) \leq 0$, which is

$$\phi'(1) = \sum_{t=1}^{N} V_2(x_t, x_{t+1}) \cdot (x_{t+1} - x_t) \leq 0.$$

Conversely, suppose that (9) is satisfied for the generic suitable $\{x_1 \dots x_N\}$. Since $V(x, \cdot)$ is concave and differentiable, we have

$$V(x_t, x_{t+1}) \leq V(x_t, \theta x_{t+1} + (1-\theta)x_t) + (1-\theta)V_2(x_t, \theta x_{t+1} + (1-\theta)x_t)(x_{t+1} - x_t).$$

Summing up over t we have

$$\sum_{t=1}^{N} V(x_t, x_{t+1}) \leq \sum_{t=1}^{N} V(x_t, \theta x_{t+1} + (1-\theta)x_t) + Q$$

where

$$Q = (1-\theta)\left[\sum_{t=1}^{N} V_2(x_t, \theta x_{t+1} + (1-\theta)x_t)(x_{t+1} - x_t)\right].$$

But the quantity between brackets is nonpositive by (9), and so

$$\sum_{t=1}^{N} V(x_t, x_{t+1}) \leq \sum_{t=1}^{N} V(x_t, \theta x_{t+1} + (1-\theta)x_t)$$

holds, which implies the additively θ-acyclicity of V. □

Example 1. Take X a convex subset of $\mathbf{R}^n$, and $D = X \times X$. Let $V(x,y) = \phi(x) + \psi(y) + \mu\langle x, y\rangle$, with $\phi(x)$ α-concave on X, $\psi(y)$ β-concave on X and $\langle \cdot, \cdot \rangle$ denotes the inner product.

One may easily check that V will be concave iff $\mu^2 \leq \alpha\beta$, and will be strictly concave in the second argument if $\beta > 0$.

If $\mu \geq 0$, V is 0-acyclic. In fact, exploiting the relation

$$\|x_t - x_{t+1}\|^2 = \|x_t\|^2 + \|x_{t+1}\|^2 - 2\langle x_t, x_{t+1}\rangle$$

we get

$$\mu \sum_{t=1}^{N} \langle x_t, x_{t+1}\rangle \leq \mu \sum_{t=1}^{N} \|x_t\|^2,$$

which is the sufficient condition (5) if $\mu \geq 0$ (with $\theta = 0$).

If $\mu < 0$ one has, always using the above relation,

$$\mu \sum_{t=1}^{N} \langle x_t, x_{t+1}\rangle = \mu \sum_{t=1}^{N} \|x_t\|^2 - \frac{\mu}{2} \sum_{t=1}^{N} \|x_t - x_{t+1}\|^2,$$

or

$$\mu \sum_{t=1}^{N} \|x_t\|^2 = \mu \sum_{t=1}^{N} \langle x_t, x_{t+1}\rangle + \frac{\mu}{2} \sum_{t=1}^{N} \|x_t - x_{t+1}\|^2.$$

Then, if $-\beta < \mu$, V is acyclic with $\theta = |\mu|/\beta$ by Proposition 5. ◇

4.3 Bellman's equation: the one–dimensional case

As in the n–dimensional case, the relation we will consider is

$$y P_\theta x \Leftrightarrow V(x, (1-\theta)x + \theta y) + \delta W_\delta((1-\theta)x + \theta y) < V(x,y) + \delta W_\delta(y). \tag{10}$$

But now, due to Theorem 3.2, we have more information. For example, we need not check a total acyclicity of the relation P_θ, since it is enough to rule out odd periodic points to ensure a certain degree of dynamical regularity of the map τ. The icing on the cake is that, to rule out periodic points of any period, it is sufficient to check that the relation P_θ is not 2-periodic. Making use of Theorem 4.2 we get

Proposition 7 *Let X be an interval in* $\mathbf{R}$. *If, for some $\theta \in [0,1)$, V satisfies*

$$V(x,(1-\theta)x+\theta y)+V(y,(1-\theta)y+\theta x)\geq V(x,y)+V(y,x)$$

for all $(x,y),(y,x)\in X\times X$ with $x\neq y$, then V is additively θ-acyclic.

Proof: We are going to use Theorem (3.2). First, one must check that P satisfies the regularity conditions i)-iii) of Subsection 3.2.

i) is satisfied because of the continuity of V (and consequently of W).

ii) is true because of the concavity of $V(x,\cdot)$.

iii) holds because the strict concavity of V and the fact that $\theta<1$ imply that $P(x)\neq 0$ for all $x\in X$.

Now the proof is immediate, stemming from the comparison of Theorem 4.2 and Theorem 3.2. □

Now, let us define the *unimodularity property*, and show its connections with acyclicity (see [4]).

Definition 6 *A function $V(x,y)$ defined over $X\times X$ is called*

- **supermodular** *if for any two pairs x_1,x_2 and y_1,y_2 in X with $x_1\leq x_2$, $y_1\leq y_2$ we have* $V(x_1,y_1)+V(x_2,y_2)\geq V(x_1,y_2)+V(x_2,y_1)$
- **submodular** *if in the same situation we have* $V(x_1,y_1)+V(x_2,y_2)\leq V(x_1,y_2)+V(x_2,y_1)$

Proposition 8 *Let X be an interval, and $V:X\times X\to\mathbf{R}$ be unimodular. Then*

- *if V is supermodular the policy function τ_δ is non-decreasing*
- *if V is submodular the policy function τ_δ is non-increasing*

Proof: One should note, first of all, that $V(x,y)$ unimodular implies that $U(x,y)=V(x,y)+\delta W_\delta(y)$ is also unimodular. Let us consider the supermodular case, the other one being completely symmetric. Set $x_1<x_2$ and suppose, by contradiction, that $\tau_\delta(x_1)>\tau_\delta(x_2)$. Set $y_2=\tau_\delta(x_1)>y_1=\tau_\delta(x_2)$. Supermodularity gives: $U(x_1,\tau_\delta(x_2))+U(x_2,\tau_\delta(x_1))\geq U(x_1,\tau_\delta(x_1))+U(x_2,\tau_\delta(x_2))$. Strict concavity together with the optimality principle give

$$U(x_1,\tau_\delta(x_1))+U(x_2,\tau_\delta(x_2))>U(x_1,\tau_\delta(x_2))+U(x_2,\tau_\delta(x_1)),$$

a contradiction. □

We are now ready to show that supermodularity implies acyclicity, that is, acyclicity is a weaker condition that permits to have regular behaviours.

Proposition 9 *Consider problem 1 with $dim(X)=1$. In this case, if V is supermodular then it is additively θ-acyclic.*

Proof: We need only show that the conditions of Proposition 7 are satisfied. Let x and y be two points in X with, say, $x<y$. In the definition of supermodularity set $x_1=y_1=x$ and $x_2=y_2=y$.

This gives $V(x,x)+V(y,y)\geq V(x,y)+V(y,x)$, which is the desired inequality. □

REMARK: The converse is not true. See Example 2 ◇

An important class of return functions is that of the functions $V(x,y) = U(f(x) - g(y))$, where U is concave and f and g are nondecreasing functions. The relevance of this class of one–period return functions is that it covers the standard model of one–sector growth. It turns out that functions in this class are supermodular.

To prove our claim, suppose $x_1 \leq x_2$. One has

$$f(x_2) - g(y_1) \geq f(x_1) - g(y_1) \geq f(x_1) - g(y_2)$$

and

$$f(x_2) - g(y_1) \geq f(x_2) - g(y_2) \geq f(x_1) - g(y_2).$$

If we denote $\Delta f = f(x_2) - f(x_1)$, using the above inequalities and the fact that U is concave we get

$$\frac{U(f(x_2) - g(y_1)) - U(f(x_1) - g(y_1))}{\Delta f} \leq \frac{U(f(x_2) - g(y_2)) - U(f(x_1) - g(y_2))}{\Delta f},$$

or

$$U(f(x_2) - g(y_1)) + U(f(x_1) - g(y_2)) \leq U(f(x_2) - g(y_2)) + U(f(x_1) - g(y_1)),$$

which is the definition of supermodularity.

In the case of differentiability, we can say (see Proposition 6)

Proposition 10 *Assume V is as in A3 and C^1. Then V is additively θ-acyclic for some $0 < \theta < 1$ if and only if*

$$[V_2(x,y) - V_2(y,x)]\,(y - x) \leq 0 \qquad \forall (x,y),(y,x) \in X \times X. \tag{11}$$

When V is twice differentiable the (11) implies $V_{12}(x,x) \geq V_{22}(x,x)$.

Example 2. Consider $V(x,y) = ax + by - (1/2)\,Ax^2 - y^2 - xy - (1/2)\,Bxy^2$ defined on any set $D \subseteq [0,1] \times [0,1]$. For the following set of parameters V satisfies Assumption A3: $A \geq 1/2$, $B \geq -2$, and $(2A-1) \geq B(B+2)$. This function also satisfies Condition (11), and is therefore acyclic because of Proposition 10. Furthermore, when $B > 0$, $V(x,y)$ is submodular, whereas for $B < 0$ V is neither sub- nor supermodular. This proves the claim that acyclicity does not imply supermodularity. ◇

4.4 Low–period cycles

As an application of our approach, which we regard as a field in which work has yet to be done, in this section we tackle the problem of excluding not all cycles, but just those of high period. Again, we have to restrict ourselves to the case of X a subset of the real line. A first step in this direction was Theorem 3.2 on the ranking of the cycles of a relation. But the theorem has the practical problem that it is difficult, for many relations, to exclude cycles of higher order once one has ascertained the presence of period–two cycles. Moreover, the discount factor plays no role, in the sense that the acyclicity of a relation is independent of the magnitude of δ.

One could then think to study another relation, that we could call P_θ^2. This relation would be satisfied by the second iterate of τ. If P_θ^2 was acyclic, then we would know that τ has no periodic points of period 4. But this, by Sarkovsky's theorem, would exclude periodic points of any period other than 2. Moreover, it is our hope that further work in this direction may highlight the role of the discount factor δ.

Let us define a new function V^2, defined as

$$V^2(x,y) = \max_u V(x,u) + \delta V(u,y) \quad \text{such that } (x,u),(u,y) \in D. \tag{12}$$

Now, let $D^2 = \{(x,y)|$ there is a u such that $(x,u),(u,y) \in D\}$. A little reflection shows that, if D satisfies A2, then D^2 satisfies A2 too. On the other hand, if V satisfies A3, then V^2 satisfies A3. Then the problem

$$W(x) = \max_{y \in D^2(x)} V^2(x,y) + \delta^2 W(y) \tag{13}$$

yelds a well-behaved function, which is the second iterate of τ.

The relation P_θ^2 is defined as

$$yP_\theta^2 x \Leftrightarrow V^2(x,(1-\theta)x + \theta y) + \delta W((1-\theta)x + \theta y) < V^2(x,y) + \delta W(y),$$

where $W(\cdot)$ is some concave function. To exclude periodic points of period 4, we need to check the acyclicity of V^2. Moreover, since V^2 depends from δ, we hope to exploit this dependence.

Example 3. Set

$$V(x,y) = -\frac{y^3}{3} - byx + k\frac{x^2}{2} - \frac{y^2}{2},$$

with $X = [0,1]$ and $D = X \times X$.

One may check that V is concave iff $k \leq -b^2$. If $b > 1$, then using Proposition 10 we find that V is not additively θ-acyclic for any θ in (0,1).

Calculating V^2 yelds

$$V^2(x,y) = k\frac{x^2}{2} - \delta\frac{y^3}{3} - \delta\frac{y^2}{2},$$

and again using Proposition 10 one finds that V^2 is acyclic. Hence, although V is cyclic, the only possible cycles are of period two. This result is, again, valid for any value of the discount factor.

Theorem 3.2, applied to this case, produces cumbersome calculations that we have not tried to manage. ◇

Example 4. Set

$$V(x,y) = -x^2 - y - xy - y^3x^2(yx+1)$$

with $X = [0,1]$ and $D = X \times X$.

One readily calculates that V is cyclic, but computing V^2, one finds that $V_2(x,y) = -x^2 - \delta y$ is acyclic. ◇

The preceding examples all had the feature that the value of u maximizing expression (12) was on the boundary of the admissible values. In fact, a little reflection shows that, if such a feature is verified, then V^2 is acyclic, since it is the sum of two functions respectively of x and y. But it is not true that, in case the value of u is internal to the feasible set, then V^2 is cyclic. This is the argument of the following

Example 5. Set $V(x,y) = \mu x^2 - y - xy + \mu x$, with $X = [0,1]$, $D = X \times X$ and μ a positive parameter. The same calculations performed in the example above yeld that V is cyclic. Working out V^2, one finds that if $\mu > 1 + (2/\delta)$ then u is interior to X, and

$$u = 1 - \frac{\delta y + x + 1}{\delta \mu}.$$

Substituting, after long–lasting algebra one gets

$$V_2^2(x,y) = -\delta,$$

which shows that V^2 is acyclic. ◇

Note that the function V used in this last example is strictly concave in the first variable rather than in the second. In fact, this hypothesis could have been made in A3 with no harm for the properties of the policy function, except for the case in which the discount factor equals 0.

References

[1] J.P. Aubin and A. Cellina, "Differential Inclusions", *Springer-Verlag* 1984.

[2] M. Boldrin and L. Montrucchio, "On the Indeterminacy of Capital Accumulation Paths", *Journal of Economic Theory* 40 (1986), 26–39.

[3] M. Boldrin and L. Montrucchio, "Acyclicity and Stability for Intertemporal Optimization Models", *International Economic Review* 29(1) (1988), 137–146.

[4] M. Boldrin and L. Montrucchio, "Acyclicity and Dynamical Stability: Generalizations and Economic Applications", *MIMEO* 1990.

[5] J. Hale, "Asymptotic Behavior of Dissipative Systems", *American Mathematical Society* Rhode Island, Providence 1988.

[6] J. P. LaSalle, "The Stability of Dynamical Systems", *Society for Industrial and Applied Mathematics* Philadelphia, Pennsylvania 1976.

[7] L. Montrucchio, "Optimal Decisions Over Time and Strange Attractors: an Analysis by the Bellman Principle", *Mathematical Modelling* 7 (1986), 341–352.

[8] A. N. Sarkovsky, "Coexistence of Cycles of a Continuous Map of the Line into Itself", *Ukr. Mat. Z.* 16 (1964), 61–71.

[9] S. Smale, "Differential Dynamical Systems", *Bulletin of the American Mathematical Society* 1967

[10] N. Stokey and R. Lucas and R. Prescott, "Recursive Methods in Economic Dynamics", *Harvard University Press* 1989.

Expected and Unexpected Distributive Shocks: an Analysis of Short and Long Run Effects

Franco Nardini

Dipartimento di Matematica dell'Università di Bologna
Piazza di Porta San Donato, 5 - I-40127 Bologna

1 - Introduction.

The theory of economic growth has faced the problem of shocks since its very beginning: a shock is a sudden change of one or several relevant parameters of the economic system which perturbs the growth path and sometimes significantly changes its direction.

In this paper we analyze the effects of a sudden rise of the real wage rate under the alternative assumptions that it occurs unexpectedly and that it is foreseen in advance. We carry out this program in the framework of the Neo-Austrian theory of Sir John Hicks (1973)[1] which has been introduced with "the hope of being able to trace through time the impact of each new change in economic environment on equilibrium prices and quantities" (Malinvaud (1986) § 4).

The paper is divided into six sections which are organized as follows:

1 Introduction.
2 Short account of the model and summary of the basic standard assumptions.
3 Description of the relation between investment and consumption and introduction of a hypothesis on their evolution.
4 Basic equation for the activity level of the system, description of the structure of its solutions (thm. 1) and their asymptotic behaviour (thm. 2)
5 Qualitative description of the short and long run evolution of the main economic variables after the unexpected shock.
6 Outline of the short and medium run consequences of an expected and anticipated shock.

---

[1] The theory has been first established by Hicks (1973) in his pioneering book "*Capital and Time*" ; Hicks himself has then given further contributions (see Hicks (1977) ch. 1 e 2 and (1985) ch.14); a rigourous and sound mathematical framework for it has been then provided by Belloc (1980).Beyond the above cited works, we remember the papers by Gozzi- Zamagni (1982), Zamagni (1984), Violi (1984), and Nardini (1990) and (1992).

The results in sections 4 and 5 have been established in a slightly different context in NARDINI (1992): here we state the theorems 1 and 2 without going into further mathematical details for which we refer to NARDINI (1992) § 3.2 and § 3.3; also for the description in sect. 5 we refer to NARDINI (1992) § 3.4.

The case of the expected shock in section 6 has no counterpart in NARDINI (1992)

2 - The Model

One of the main features of the Neo-Austrian model[2] is the description of the productive system viewed as a set of differently aged elementary production processes[3]. These processes describe how a flow of input of labour[4] $a:[0,D]\to\mathbb{R}$ generates a flow of output of consumer goods which we assume produced in fixed proportions $b:[0,D]\to\mathbb{R}$. We assume that both functions a , b are continuously differentiable in their domain and that

$$\begin{aligned} &a(0) > 0 && \text{and} \quad a(u) \geq 0 \quad \forall\ u \in [0,D] \ , \\ &b(u) = 0 \quad \forall\ u \in [0,d] && \text{and} \quad b(u) > 0 \quad \forall\ u \in (d,D] \ . \end{aligned} \tag{1}$$

D is the optimal duration of the process while d is the delay between the beginning of the flow of input and the beginning of the flow of output and may be viewed as the capital good making period[5].

---

2 For an exhaustive description of the theory and its foundations we refer to HICKS (1973) and to BELLOC (1980). For a critical discussion on the economic significance of the theory we remember the papers of BERNHOLTZ (1974), SOLOW (1974), SCAZZIERI (1983), BALDONE (1984), FABER (1986), and MALINVAUD (1986).

3 The general features of the model are obviously the same described in our previous papers (see NARDINI (1990) §1.1 and NARDINI (1992) sect. 1).

4 Labour is the only productive factor.

5 The optimal life of the process D depends on many economic and technical factors such as physical wearing out, antiqueness, rate of interest, and wage-rate: "We may presume that the above mentioned factors, namely physical wearing out, moral wearing out and the period of amortization, in most cases will *cooperate* in determining the time at which the replacement takes place" (see EINARSEN (1938_2) Part II, ch.1 § 5-B).

We assume that the elementary processes are arbitrarily divisible and have constant return to scale, so if at time t the total employment $L(t)$ is the sum of the employment required by all processes with age less than or equal to D

$$L(t) = \int_0^D a(u)\, x(t-u)\, du. \tag{2}$$

Analogously the total output $Q(t)$ is

$$Q(t) = \int_0^D b(u)\, x(t-u)\, du \tag{3}$$

We assume that at every moment there is equilibrium on the market of the consumer goods and that the output is completely consumed (full performance assumption[6])

$$Q(t) = C(t) + w(t)\, L(t)\,,$$

where $w(t)$ denotes the real wage rate at time t. Obviously $w(t)\, L(t)$ stands for workers' consumption[7] while $C(t)$ denotes thc take out which includes not only consumption out of profits but also consumption of public bodies etc.[8].

We assume that also the capital market is in equilibrium at every moment t : if $w_e(t,s)$ is the real wage rate that at time t is expected to prevail at time $s>t$ then

$$q_e(t,s,u) = b(u) - w_e(t,s)\, a(u) \tag{4}$$

is the net revenue that at time t a process of age u is expected to give at time $s>t$.

The interest rate $i_e(t,s)$ that at time t is expected to prevail at time s satisfies

$$\int_0^D e^{i_e(t,t_0+u)u}\, q_e(t,t_0+u,u)\, du = 0 \qquad \text{for every } t \leq t_0 \tag{5}$$

and the actual interest rate is $i(t) = i_e(t,t)$. Equation (5) means that an elementary process starting at moment t_0 is expected to yield no extra profit. A standard

---

6 A discussion of the meaning of the full performance path can be found in HICKS (1973) ch. 5 § 4.

7 This means that workers has no propensity for saving; this restriction is not a serious one since the case of a positive propensity for saving can be treated with minor changes following GOZZI-ZAMAGNI (1982) § III.

8 See HICKS (1977) § 1.

hypothesis in traverse analysis is that before the shock occurs the economic system moves on a steady state growth path with growth rate g^*

$$x^*(t) = x^* e^{g^* t} \quad , \tag{6}$$

$$Q^*(t) = Q^* e^{g^* t} \quad , \tag{7}$$

$$L^*(t) = L^* e^{g^* t} \quad , \tag{8}$$

$$C^*(t) = C^* e^{g^* t} \quad ^{9}. \tag{9}$$

3 - Evolution of Investment and Take Out

In order to close the model we need an assumption on the dynamic of the take out. By the full performance assumption (3) this amounts to introduce an hypothesis on the dynamic of investment; namely the term $w(t)\,L(t)$ can be viewed also as the sum of the cost of the wages payed to the workers employed in already productive plants plus the investment required to produce capital goods. Since both the total output $Q(t)$ and the amount of the workers employed in already productive plants do not depend on the choices to be made at time t, but on these made in the interval $[t\text{-}D,t\text{-}d]$, the evolution of the take out determines that of the investment and conversely.

We assume that the take out is proportional to a wealth index measuring not only profits at time t but also all foreseeable future gains and losses[10].

The actual value at the moment t of the expected output of all existing processes is

$$B_e(t) = \int_{t-D}^{t} x(s) \left(\int_{t}^{D+s} e^{-i_e(u,t)(t-u)}\, b(u-s)\, du \right) ds \quad . \tag{10}$$

Analogously the expected input required to produce $B_e(t)$ is

9 Obviously (7), (8), and (9) follows from (6) and (2), (1), and (3) respectively.

10 This index has been introduced in NARDINI (1990) § 1.2 to which we refer for further details and comments.

$$A_e(t) = \int_{t-D}^{t} x(s) \left(\int_{t}^{D+s} e^{-i_e(u,t)(t-u)} w_e(t,u)\, a(u-s)\, du \right) ds \quad . \tag{11}$$

We define the difference

$$V(t) = B_e(t) - A_e(t) \, , \tag{12}$$

wealth index of the system and assume that the take out is proportional to this index

$$C(t) = \beta \, V(t) \quad , \tag{13}$$

where β is a positive constant.

We remark explicitly that a rise of the expected interest rate generally causes a diminishing of $V(t)$ and hence a contraction of the take out; this is the well known substitution effect: a part of present consumption is shifted to the future when the interest rate rises[11].

4 - Unexpected Shock

The unexpected shock occurs when the expectations on the wage rate are static and the present wage rate is expected to prevail also in the future

---

11 We recall that, among the motivations which have led us to introduce this hypothesis, the following remark has played an important role "for the study of the traverse, Hicks only considers models in which economic growth is absolutely myopic, even blind: the condition of the current period fully determine the investment, without conditions in the subsequent period playing any role" (MALINVAUD (1986)). We are perfectly aware that this hypothesis has not a complete microeconomic foundation as somebody could wish; however "We economists should, according to them, recognize only constraints, behaviour and equilibrium conditions. Clearly such a stand is too dogmatic ....If we correctly identify elementary behaviour, this is perfect; but when we cannot, we have to stick to observing results of a more complex sort and we should not impose on the data an unfounded preconception" MALINVAUD (1988_1) §1. The likelihood of our hypothesis relies on the fact that it describes a consumption behaviour which satisfies a basic assumption: "Sous des hypothèses classiques, on sait qu' une augmentation du taux d' interêt entraînera, a partir de la date 0 , une substitution de consommation future à la consommation présente, c' est-a-dire un basculement vers le futur des projets de consommation" BELLOC (1980) ch. 6 sect. 1 sous sect. 1 §3.

$$w_e(t,s) = w(t) = \begin{cases} w^* & \text{for } t < 0 \quad \text{and} \quad s \geq t \\ w & \text{for } t \geq 0 \quad \text{and} \quad s \geq t \end{cases} ; \tag{14}$$

where $0 < w < w^*$. If we denote by a^* b^* the elementary production process maximizing profits when the wage rate is w^* and by a b the maximizing process for the wage rate w, the assumptions on the efficiency of the capital market and on the expectations (14) yield that the for $t < 0$ only old-type processes a^* b^* are started, while for $t \geq 0$ only new-type ones a b are.

We define the function

$$q(u) = b(u) - w\, a(u) \tag{15}$$

net revenue of the process a b at the wage rate w. The function q^* is defined analogously, moreover we consider also the net revenue of the old type process a^* b^* at the new wage rate w

$$q^+(u) = b^*(u) - w\, a^*(u)\,. \tag{16}$$

We assume that the functions q^*, q^+, and q are non decreasing[12].

From (14) we obtain easily the expected net revenue (4) in terms of the functions (15) and (16) for the case under consideration

$$q_e(t,s,u) = \begin{cases} q^*(u) & \text{for } t < 0, \quad s \geq t \quad u \in [0,D^*] \\ q^+(u) & \text{for } t \geq 0, \quad s \geq t \quad D^* > u > s \\ q(u) & \text{for } t \geq 0, \quad s \geq t \quad 0 < u < \min\{s,D\} \end{cases} ; \tag{17}$$

so the expected interest rate is

$$i_e(t,s) = i(t) = \begin{cases} r^* & \text{for } t < 0, \quad s \geq t \\ r & \text{for } t \geq 0, \quad s \geq t \end{cases} ; \tag{18}$$

where r^* is the internal rate of return of the process a^* b^* for $t < 0$. We recall that is the internal rate of return r^* [resp. r^+, r]of the process a^* b^* for $t < 0$

---

12 A comment on this (unessential) assumption can be found in NARDINI (1990) § 3.5 where it is shown to what extent it can be removed.

[resp. of the process a^* b^* for $t > 0$, of of the process a b for $t > 0$]defined to be the unique positive real solution of the equation

$$\int_0^D \theta(u)\, e^{-r^*u}\, du = 0 \quad ; \tag{19}$$

with $\theta = q^*$ [resp. $\theta = q^+$, $\theta = q$]. We assume that

$$r^+ < r < r^* \, . \tag{20}$$

The first inequality of (20) simply means that the new-type process is more profitable than the old-type one when the wage rate is w ; the second one means that the fall of profitability caused by the rise of the wage rate can be limited, but not annulled by a different choice of the type of productive processes.The assumption that r is positive means that the new distributive configuration is technically tenable.

Now we can compute the wealth index introducing (7) and (8) into (12) and taking into account (6)

$$V(t) = \tag{21}$$

$$\begin{cases} = \displaystyle\int_{t-D^*}^{t} x^* e^{g^*s} \left(\int_t^{D^*+s} e^{-r^*(u-t)}\, q^*(u-s)\, du \right) ds & \text{for } t < 0 \\[2ex] = \displaystyle\int_{\min\{t-D^*,0\}}^{0} x^* e^{g^*s} \left(\int_t^{D^*+s} e^{-r(u-t)}\, q^+(u-s)\, du \right) ds + & \text{for } t \geq 0 \, . \\[2ex] \quad + \displaystyle\int_{\max\{t-D^*,0\}}^{t} x(s) \left(\int_t^{D+s} e^{-r(u-t)}\, q(u-s)\, du \right) ds & \end{cases}$$

We are now in position to obtain an equation for the rate of start $x(t)$ for $t \geq 0$;

to this aim we introduce the r. h. s. of (21) into the expression yielding the take out (13) and then we substitute (13) into the full performance equation (3) and get

$$\int_{\min\{t-D^*,0\}}^{0} x^* \, e^{g^* s} \left(\beta \int_{t}^{D^*+s} e^{-r(u-t)} q^+(u-s)\, du - q^+(t-s) \right) ds \quad = \qquad (22)$$

$$= \int_{\max\{t-D,0\}}^{t} x(s) \left(q(t-s) - \beta \int_{t}^{D+s} e^{-r(u-t)} q(u-s)\, du \right) ds \ .$$

The two following theorems yield fairly detailed informations on the structure and the asymptotic behaviour of the solution of the equation (22).

THEOREM 1. *The equation* (22) *has a solution* $x(t)$ *in the space of the Laplace transformable Schwartz distributions*[13]*; it has the form*

$$x(t) \;=\; \frac{h}{q(0)} \sum_{j=0}^{\infty} \left(\frac{q(D)}{q(0)} \right)^{j} \delta_{t-jD} + x_1(t) \ . \qquad (23)$$

where $x_1(t)$ *is the derivative of a continuous function supported in* $[0,+\infty)$, δ *denotes the Dirac distribution, and* h *is a positive constant*[14].

THEOREM 2. *Assume that the function* $x_1(t)$ *appearing in (23) is non negative in* $(0,+\infty)$ *and that every zero of the Laplace transform* $L(\bar{K})(z)$ *but* r *lies in the halfplane* $\mathrm{Re}\, z < g$ *,where*

$$g \;=\; r - \beta \ , \qquad (24)$$

then the function $x_1(t)$ *displays the following asymptotic behaviour*

$$x_1(t) \sim e^{gt} \qquad as \qquad t \to +\infty \ . \qquad (25)$$

---

13 See SCHWARTZ (1966), for the theory of distributional Laplace transform see MISRA-LAVOINE (1986) and ZEMANIAN (1965).

14 The constant h is positive if r is in a (right) neighbourhood of r^+ , h is negative if $r^+ < r^* < r$; this latter case can be interpreted as occurrence of a technical progress allowing a rise in productivity that overtakes the effects of the upwards jump of the wage rate. We shall steadily assume that such a miracle does not take place and that r^+ and r are close to each other.

5 - Main Features of the Traverse Following the Unexpected Shock

The evolution described by (23) is the result of the overlapping of a cyclical component $\frac{h}{q(0)} \sum_{j=0}^{\infty} (\frac{q(D)}{q(0)})^j \; \delta_{t-jD}$ and a trend one $x_1(t)$. the cyclical component alternatively determines sudden falls and rises of the number of productive processes started after the time $t = 0$: namely for $t = 0$ we observe the first contraction (since $\frac{h}{q(0)} < 0$). Since a negative elementary process yields a net (positive) output in the first part of its life (say $[0,d]$) and requires a net input in the subsequent period, we interpret a sudden fall of the number of processes as a resort to the foreign credit in the interval $[0,d]$ followed by a repayment period (including interest) up to the the maturity $t = D$ when the debt is completely sunk[15]

This interpretation makes the meaning of the cyclical component completely clear: at the time $t = 0$ the upward jump of the purchasing power of the workers causes a sudden relevant rise of the total consumption; on the other hand the total output goes on slowly growing along the steady state growth path as long as $t = d$; so an excess demand for consumer goods emerges which can be satisfied only by borrowing from abroad (or exploiting existing stocks). The subsequent period is characterized by the payment of instalments inclusive of both capital and interest; as soon as the debt is sunk ($t = D$) a relevant amount of resources become available for investment causing the first upwards jump of the number of processes; such jump comes with a rise of employment (in the sector of capital goods) and is followed at $t = D+d$ by a quick expansion of the total production.

At $t = 2D$ all the processes started at $t = D$ reach the end of their productive life and are scraped; this causes a fall of employment and production and again the latter does not cope with the demand for consumer goods. So a new resort to the credit can not be avoided (and a new contraction of the number of processes is observed at $t = 2D$) and a new oscillation begins[16].

The amplitude of the jth oscillation is tuned by the factor $(\frac{q(D)}{q(0)}))^j$; since a reasonable assumption is that $0 < q(D) < -q(0)$, the oscillation is damped and eventually peters out allowing the trend component $x_1(t)$ to come to the fore; the estimate (24) guarantees that the system converges to a new steady state growth rate given by (25).

---

15 Another possible interpretation is the resort to stocks in the interval $[0,d]$ followed by their reconstruction to be completed at $t = D$.

16 In NARDINI (1990) connection of this cyclical oscillation with the reinvestment cycle analyzed by EINARSEN (1939_1) and (1939_2) is discussed.

6 - Expected Anticipated Shock

The main difference of the present case from the preceding one is the beginning of the traverse path. The traverse does not begin when the shock occurs ($t=0$), but as soon as the expectation for the shock is formed ($t=-\sigma$) because of the anticipation of its consequences. In particular, if the expectation is formed before $t = -D^*$ (i.e. $\sigma > D^*$) all processes starting in the interval $[-D^*,0]$ are expected to undergo a fall of the net revenue in the second part of their productive life, this may result in many changes of the choice of the productive technology in order to maximize profitability; however, in order to simplify the discussion we assume that in the interval $[-D^*,-\tau]$ the most profitable elementary process is the old-type one a^* b^* while in the interval $[-\tau,0]$ the process maximizing profits is the new-type one a b [17]; this is to say that there exist no different types of processes which are more profitable at any time $t \in [-D^*,0]$.

We first consider the case

$$w_e(t,s) = \begin{cases} w^* & \text{for } t < -\sigma \quad s \geq t \\ & \text{and for } t \geq -\sigma \quad t < s < 0 \\ w & \text{for } t \geq -\sigma \quad s \geq \max\{t,0\} \end{cases} \quad ; \tag{26}$$

where $\sigma \in (0,\tau)$; this means that the expectation of the upwards jump of the wage rate is formed at time $-\sigma$. Obviously before $t = -\sigma$ the system remains on the steady state growth path and only old-type processes are started; after $t = -\sigma$ the steady state breaks down and new-type processes are started, so the expected net revenue is

$$q_e(t,s,u) = \tag{27}$$

$$= \begin{cases} b^*(u) - w^* a^*(u) & \text{for } t < -\sigma \quad s \geq t \quad u \in [0,D^*] \\ & \text{and for } t \geq -\sigma \quad s \in [-\sigma,0) \quad u \in [\max\{0,s+\sigma\},D^*] \\ b(u) - w^* a(u) & \text{for } t \geq -\sigma \quad -\sigma \leq s < 0 \quad u \in [0,\min\{s+\sigma,D\}] \\ b^*(u) - w\, a^*(u) & \text{for } t \geq -\sigma \quad s \geq 0 \quad u \in [\max\{0,s+\sigma\},D^*] \\ b(u) - w\, a(u) & \text{for } t \geq -\sigma \quad s \geq 0 \quad u \in [0,\min\{s+\sigma,D\}] \end{cases}$$

---

17 The constant τ is positive and smaller than D^* .

If the expectations are formed late and the profitability gain achieved by shifting from the old-type process to the new-type one is small, then[18] $\lim_{t \to -\sigma-} V(t) > V(-\sigma)$. Hence the wealth index jumps downwards as soon as the imminent rise of the wage rate is foreseen causing a proportional contraction of the take out and a shift of resources from consumption to investment. So at the time $t = -\sigma$ the reconversion of the productive system begins and many new-type processes start letting the employment grow (in the capital goods sector); at the time $t = d-\sigma$ these processes enter their productive life and a phase of fast growth of the production begins.

On the other side at the time $t = 0$ workers' purchasing power and consumption jumps up together with the wage rate while production and take out mantain their previous trends; a resort to the foreign credit (or to stocks) cannot be avoided just as in the case of the unexpected shock, however in this case the repayment of debts is made easier by the growth of production beginning at $t = d-\sigma$.

In full analogy with the previous case the upward ($t = -\sigma$) and downward ($t = 0$) jumps propagate in the future, hence for $t = D-\sigma$ the processes started at $t = -\sigma$ are scraped and the corresponding contraction of the production has no counterpart in the evolution of the consumption causing a new resort to the foreign credit (or to stocks), while at the time $t = D$ the end of the repayment of debts allows a new boom of investment with a sudden growth of the employment and a somewhat delayed ($t = D+d$) fast growth of the total output: the growth of the employment ($t = D$) roughly compensate the previously observed contraction at $t = D-\sigma$ while the growth of the output will easy the repayment of the loans obtained in the interval $[D-\sigma, D-\sigma+d]$. (See fig. 1 and 2)

Turning to the case of an early expectation formation, we discover a deeply different scenario. For instance we perform our analysis in the case in which the expectation is formed at $t = -D^*$ (i.e. $\sigma = D^*$); under this assumption all processes starting in the interval $[-D^*, 0]$ are expected to undergo a fall of the net revenue in the second part of their life because of the expected rise of the wage rate at $t = 0$: precisely

$$q_e(-D^*, s, u) \; =$$

18 This can be infered by continuity examining the limit case $\sigma = 0$ and $r^* = r$ (no expectation is formed before the shock and no alternative technology is available); in this case $\lim_{t \to -\sigma-} V(t) - V(-\sigma) = x^* \frac{1}{r^*-g^*} \int_0^{D^*} e^{-g^*v} \, q^*(v) \, dv \; - \; x^* \int_0^{D^*} e^{r^+v} \, v \; q^+(v) \, dv \quad (1+O(r^= - g^*))$. The positivity follows since the first term is positive and large due to the factor $\frac{1}{r^*-g^*}$.

$$= \begin{cases} b^*(u) - w^* a^*(u) & \text{for } -D^* \leq s < 0 \quad u \in [max\{0,s+\tau\},D^*] \\ b(u) - w^* a(u) & \text{for } s \in [-D^*,0) \quad u \in [0,min\{s+\tau,D\}] \\ b^*(u) - w\, a^*(u) & \text{for } s \geq 0 \quad u \in [max\{0,s+\tau\},D^*] \\ b(u) - w\, a(u) & \text{for } s \geq 0 \quad u \in [0,min\{s+\tau\},D\}] \end{cases} \quad . \tag{28}$$

Hence the expected internal rate of return of these processes continuously decreases from r^* (at $t = -D^*$) to r (at $t = 0$), so also the interest rate $i(t)$ will display an analogous evolution and in general we may assume that

$$i(t) < r^* \qquad \text{for} \quad t \in [-D^*,0) \; . \tag{29}$$

Since

$$i_e(t,s) = \begin{cases} r^* & \text{for } t < -D^* \quad s \geq t \\ i(t) & \text{for } t \in [-D^*,0) \quad s \in [t,0) \\ r & \text{for } t \in [-D^*,0) \quad s \geq 0 \\ & \text{and for } t \geq 0 \quad s \geq t \end{cases} \quad , \tag{30}$$

it is easy to verify that $\lim_{t \to -D^*-} V(t) < V(-D^*)$. Hence the expectation for a falling interest rate causes a rise of consumption due to the substitution effect of future consumption by present one; on the other hand the production grows on the steady state path at least until $t = d\text{-}D^*$; so borrowing is the only chance to preserve equilibrium on the consumer goods market; in the repayment period the rate of starts will be compressed.

At the time $t = 0$ the boom of workers' consumption will be compensated by the end of the repayment of debts, thus reducing or even annulling the difficulties observed at $t = 0$ in all preceding cases.

REFERENCES

Atsumi, H. (1988): "On the Rate of Interest in a 'Neo-Austrian' Theory of Capital". Paper presented at the conference *'Value and Capital- Fifty years later'* . Bologna, September 1988.

Baldone, S.(1984): "Integrazione verticale, struttura temporale dei processi produttivi e transizione fra le tecniche". *Economia Politica* **1** ,79.

Belloc, B.(1980): *Croissance economique et adaptation du capital productif.* Economica Paris .

Bernholtz, P.(1974): "Review on J. Hicks Capital and Time. A Neo-Austrian Theory". *Kyklos* **24**, 410.

Einarsen, J. (1938_1): "Reinvestment Cycles". *Review of Economic Statistics* **20** , 1.

Einarsen, J. (1938_2): *Reinvestment Cycles.* J. Ch. Grundersen. Oslo.

Faber, M.(1986): "On the Development of Austrian Capital Theory".In: *Studies in Austrian Capital Theory, Investment and Time.*Faber, M. ed. Springer Verlag. Berlin .

Gozzi, G.; Zamagni, S.(1982): "Crescita non uniforme e struttura produttiva: un modello di traversa a salario fisso". *Giornale degli Economisti ed Annali di Economia* **41** , 305.

Hicks, J.(1973): *Capital and Time: a Neo-Austrian Theory.* Oxford University Press, Oxford .

Hicks, J.(1977): *Economic Perspectives: Further Essays on Money and Growth.* Clarendon Press, Oxford .

Hicks, J.(1985): *Methods of Dynamic Economics.* Clarendon Press, Oxford .

Malinvaud, E.(1986): "Reflecting on the Theory of Capital and Growth". *Oxford Economic Papers* **38** , 376.

Malinvaud, E.(1988_1): "Observations in Macroeconomic Theory Building". Presidential Address at the *European Economic Association Third Annual Congress* Bologna, August 1988.

Malinvaud, E.(1988_2): "Incomplete Market Clearing". Paper presented at the conference *'Value and Capital- Fifty years later'.* Bologna, September 1988

Misra, O. P.; Lavoine, J. L.(1986): *Transform Analysis of Generalized Functions.* North Holland, Amsterdam .

Nardini, F.(1990): "Cycle-Trend Dynamics in a Fixwage Neo-Austrian Model of Traverse". *Journal for Structural Change and Economic Dynamic* **1** (1), 165.

Nardini, F. (1992): "Traverse and Convergence in the Neo-Austrian Model: the Case of a Distributive Shock". To appear in: *Structural Change and Economic Dynamics.*

Scazzieri , R.(1983): "The Production Process: General Characteristics and Taxonomy". *Rivista Internazionale di Scienze Economiche e Commerciali* **30** , 597.

Schwartz, L.(1966): *Theorie des Distributions.* Hermann, Paris .

Solow, R. M.(1974): "Review on J. Hicks Capital and Time. A Neo-Austrian Theory". *The Economic Journal* **84** ,189.

Violi, R.(1984): "Sentiero di traversa e convergenza". *Giornale degli Economisti ed Annali di Economia* **43** , 153.

Zamagni, S.(1984): "Ricardo and Hayek Effect in a Fixwage Model of Traverse". *Oxford Economic Papers* **36** , 135.

Zemanian, A. M.(1965): *Distribution Theory and Transform Analysis.* Mc Graw Hill, New York.

Fig. 1
total output

Case of the Expected Shock

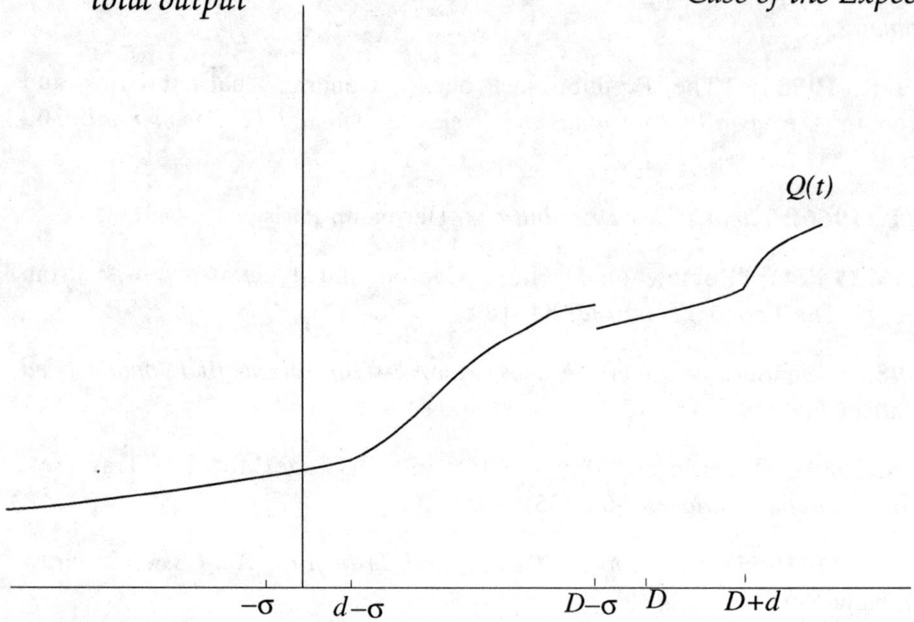

Fig. 2
total employment

Case of the Expected Shock

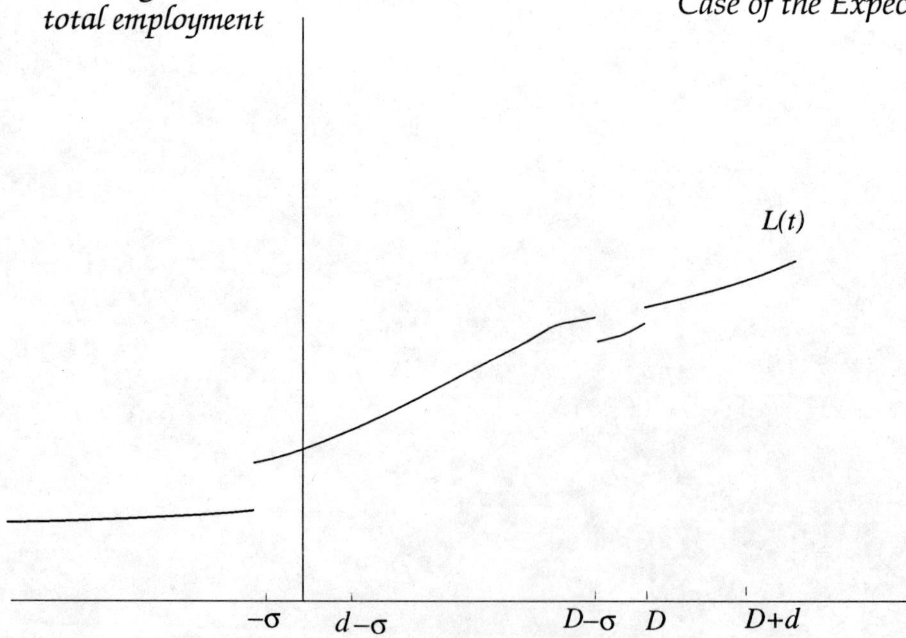

Nonstandard General Equilibrium

Pier-Carlo Nicola

Department of Mathematics, University of Milan
via Saldini 50, 20133 Milan, Italy

1. Introduction

When writing his book Walras (1874–1877) had no mathematical tools, actually the so called *fixed points theorems*, to prove the existence of economically meaningful solutions to his *one period competitive general equilibrium models*, from now on shortly called *walrasian models* or *abstract models*. But he felt reasonably sure that (substantially) he had solved the existence problem in two ways, distinct both conceptually and practically. The first way was by counting the number of (independent) equations forming the model and the number of unknowns, to show that these numbers are equal. The second way discovered by Walras, a more practical one, was to make a conceptual experiment consisting in assuming that there is a particular agent, called by Walras *auctioneer*, who chooses "at random" one positive price vector and then records market demand and market supply of every good. In a second step, once ordered all markets in some sequence, the auctioneer rises prices in markets in which the excess demand is positive and decreases prices in those markets for which excess demand is negative. Walras felt sure that in the end all excess demands would be reduced (in absolute value) to zero, so obtaining a vector of equilibrium prices for his one–period models. During the whole process of manipulating prices no agent is allowed to produce or to consume: economic operators must only inform the auctioneer about their supplies and demands at the various prices, as if those prices where equilibrium ones; so 'tâtonnements' do not work in calendar time: time is here merely logical time. Moreover, to introduce an auctioneer means to assume that walrasian general equilibrium has a lot of structure.

For many years after Walras there was no rigorous mathematical analysis of the 'tâtonnement' process, until Samuelson (1941–42) formalized the problem by means of a system of differential equations. But, as it is well known, convergence of actual prices to equilibium prices (when they exist) may be more problematic than 'a priori' one may hope for, as stressed, for instance, by Kirman (1989). Since then the literature on the subject has grown considerably [see, for instance, Hahn (1982)]. Actually, the problem of the *stability of a general equilibrium* solution is not a very lively one, for more than one reason. At a formal level the (sufficient) assumptions needed to insure the existence of a general equilibrium are not sufficient to insure its stability too, as proved by the counter–examples produced by Scarf (1960) and by Gale (1963). At a substantial level it is impossible to give flesh and bones to the auctioneer, whose job is indeed that of a 'deus ex machina', introduced with the only aim of bringing to an end a "human comedy" which would be difficult to conclude otherwise. Thirdly, it is frankly difficult, even in our times of powerful and hig speed computers, both to think that 'tâtonnements' can work outside calendar time and to embody into the computations the many thousands of goods and millions of agents belonging to a modern market economy. Not to speak of the problem of the truthful transmission of data from individual agents to the auctioneer.

At least formally, it is possible to give up the process of walrasian 'tâtonnement', without being compelled to put aside the whole representation of an economy as is the picture offered by walrasian models. If we limit ourselves to prove the existence of equilibria then the fixed point theorems are ready to bear the burden. Even more, today there are efficient algorithms, the first of which was introduced by Scarf (1967), to approximate fixed points of functions and multifunctions, capable to solve small and medium size models. Why then not to give up definitely every research on 'tâtonnement' processes ? Indeed in actual economics prices, for the great majority of goods, are not calculated by an auctioneer but are essentially chosen, period after period, by firms. Hence it seems to be very interesting to study general many–persons models, as an alternative to walrasian models, where prices in every period are chosen by individual agents, as if they were imitating some 'tâtonnement'. In many instances this of course was done in a successful way. Think of duopoly and oligopoly models, introduced by Cournot since 1838, well before Walras worked out his models. Or think of the extension of oligopoly models, with differentiated products, so widely studied today by economists. A very interesting paper is the one by Hart (1982). These models are very singular ones [exceptions being the pioneering paper by Negishi (1961) and in part the monograph by Nikaido (1975)], whose working asks for numerous exchanges of informations among agents, and where the very nature of general equilibrium is truly compressed. For instance, households'choices are usually aggregated in a naive way, and very often demand functions are assumed to be almost linear. One verifies this, for instance, by examining the book by Tirole (1988).

The model by Edgeworth (1881) too is an alternative to walrasian models. It is well known [see, for instance, the book by Hildenbrand–Kirman (1988)], that models obtained from Edgeworth, as general as walrasian models are, do not contain prices but operate directly and exclusively on quantities of goods. Such models seem to be less structured than the walrasian ones, but it is not so. Indeed in Edgeworth–type models it is 'a priori' assumed that every possible coalition among agents can be formed. But the amount of information needed to form coalitions does not seem to be less demanding than the amount required by the walrasian auctioneer to steer prices.

Nonstandard general equilibrium, which has nothing in common with "nonstandard analysis" introduced long ago by the mathematician Robinson, is defined in the following pages and is rooted in some previous papers by the present writer [Nicola (1986), (1989a), (1989b)]; it can be considered as an intermediate form between Walras– and Edgeworth–type models. Nonstandard equilibrium contains prices as do walrasian models; but all prices are chosen directly by economic agents, in each time period, with the intervention of no outside agent, exactly as in Edgeworth's model coalitions seem to be directly formed by agents. It is also to be noted that in the following model information is dispersed among agents, because agents are communicating among themselves only by means of prices (which are common knowledge) and quantities (direct knowledge only of every pair of meeting agents), so that nonstandard general equilibrium features an economy which is incentives compatible, according to Hurwicz (1960, 1986).

2. Some remarks on general competitive equilibrium

To simplify the following developments and comparisons, let us start from a very naive framework, to put us in a position capable to clearly show the main elements under analysis. We study a one period general equilibrium model allowing for both production and consumption, and we assume that all goods are named goods, meaning that different agents 'a priori' produce different goods, because generally households consider as different the outputs produced by distinct firms. This means, assuming no joint productions, that in this model economy there are as many firms as there are goods. Let there are n agents $(j = 1, 2, ..., n)$ and outputs $(i = 1, 2, ..., n)$. Outputs are such that every good is perfectly durable from the beginning to the end of the time period in which it is produced, but suddenly disappears at the end of the period. Let there be also one type of labour. Agent j at the start of the period is endowed only with a positive amount of labour, l_j, useful merely to produce good j, according to some (continuous and strictly increasing) production function $\phi_j(.)$, namely

$$y_j = \phi_j(z_j),$$

where y_j means the maximum output of good j instantly produced by the amount z_j of labor. Because labor, by assumption, has no utility as leisure, it is wholly used in production; so output of good j is

$$\bar{y}_j = \phi_j(l_j).$$

By a choice of units for outputs, we may put $\bar{y}_j = 1$ for every j.

Economically, we may also depict this situation as one in which individual agents have a starting endowment, $\bar{c}^j$, given by vectors

$$\bar{c}^j = (\delta_{1j}, ..., \delta_{nj}), \tag{1.j}$$

where δ_{ij} are the Kronecker's numbers. In so doing we can say that the model is an equilibrium exchange model. Both interpretations are equally possible, but looking at the model as a production model it becomes more palatable to followers of the classical schools.

To show in detail how the model works in a walrasian framework and then is generalized to nonstandard equilibrium, let agents have preferences expressed by the following utility indicators, considered long ago by Amoroso:

$$c^j \mapsto u_j(c^j) = \sum_{i=1}^{n} \alpha_{ij} \log(1 + \beta_{ij} c_{ij}). \tag{2.j}$$

All parameters α_{ij}'s are nonnegative and verify the conditions $\sum_i \alpha_{ij} = 1 (\forall j)$; all β_{ij}'s associated to positive α_{ij}'s are also positive, because it is useless to have an α_{ij} positive coupled to a zero β_{ij} or viceversa. Utility functions (2) are generalizations of the usual Cobb–Douglas functions; every good i individually contributes to household j's utility, of course when $\alpha_{ij} > 0$. Indeed in every modern economy there are thousands of consumption goods, each one having some "substitutes", so that it is very difficult to think that there may be one good giving $u_j(c) = 0$ when this good is not consumed, independently of the amounts consumed of all other goods. Only the air we are breathing is essential to our lives, but up to now it is not yet an economic good !

Households'endowments are given by vectors (1); if $p \in \Re^n_{++}$ is the vector of prices, measured in some numeraire, the individual incomes, m_j, are simply

$$m_j = p_j. \tag{3.j}$$

By maximizing his utility (2.j) under the budget constraint $p \cdot c = m_j$, agent j finds his demand functions. To write these functions let us put $I_j = \{i | \alpha_{ij} > 0\}$ and

$$x_{ij} = \alpha_{ij}(p_j + \sum_{h \in I_j} p_h/\beta_{hj})/p_i - 1/\beta_{ij} \qquad (i \in I_j).$$

When all x_{ij}'s are nonnegative then we obtain $c_{ij} = x_{ij}$, while in case at least one x_{ij} is negative then we have $c_{ij} = 0$ for all such i's and we must determine new values α'_{ij} to calculate the nonnegative values c_{ij}'s as follows. Let $I_j(p) = \{i | x_{ij} \geq 0\}$ and write

$$\alpha'_{ij} = \frac{\alpha_{ij}}{\sum_{h \in I_j(p)} \alpha_{hj}};$$

the formulae for the nonnegative c_{ij}'s are now similar to the previous formulae, but with the α'_{ij}'s taking the place of the values α_{ij}'s and with the indexes h's running on $I_j(p)$, namely:

$$c_{ij} = \alpha'_{ij}\left[p_j + \sum_{h \in I_j(p)} p_h/\beta_{hi}\right]/p_i - 1/\beta_{ij} \qquad (i \in I_j(p)). \tag{4.i, j}$$

If, after this step, some element of the consumption vector is still negative, then the step is reiterated, as many times as needed to have all consumptions non-negative. Of course, in the end there is always at least one positive consumption.

The one period model of general competitive equilibrium is formed by the system:

$$\sum_{j=1}^{n} c_{ij} = 1 \tag{5.i}$$

or, inserting functions (4) into (5):

$$\sum_{j=1}^{n} \left[\alpha'_{ij} p_j/p_i + \alpha'_{ij} \sum_h (p_h/\beta_{hj})/p_i - 1/\beta_{ij}\right] = 1. \tag{6.i}$$

Multiplying both sides of (6.i) by p_i and rearranging terms we have

$$\sum_j \alpha'_{ij} p_j + \sum_h \sum_j (\alpha'_{ij}/\beta_{hj}) p_h = (1 + \sum_j \beta_{ij}^{-1}) p_i \qquad (\forall i)$$

or, interchanging indexes h and j in the double sum on the left hand side:

$$\sum_j \alpha'_{ij} p_j + \sum_j \sum_h (\alpha'_{ih}/\beta_{jh}) p_j = (1 + \sum_j \beta_{ij}^{-1}) p_i \quad (\forall i),$$

which is a linear homogeneous system with p_i's as unknowns. The last equations are written also

$$\sum_j \left[\alpha'_{ij} + \sum_h (\alpha'_{ih}/\beta_{jh})\right] p_j = (1 + \sum_j \beta_{ij}^{-1}) p_i \qquad (\forall i).$$

To put the system in matrix form, let:

$$m_{ij} = \alpha'_{ij} + \sum_h (\alpha'_{ih}/\beta_{jh}) \quad (\forall i, \forall j) \quad ; \quad d_i = 1 + \sum_j \beta_{ij}^{-1},$$

$$M = [m_{ij}] \quad ; \quad D = diag[d_i],$$

where both M and D are nonnegative square matrices. Then we have

$$Mp = Dp. \tag{7}$$

Equation (7) shows p as a fixed point of the nonnegative linear operator $D^{-1}M$, namely as a column latent vector associated to the latent root $\lambda^* = 1$ of $D^{-1}M$.

Let us denote by $\hat{p}$ this vector; the values $\hat{p}_i$ are of course equilibrium relative prices.

It is important to note that in a walrasian equilibrium generally the 'quid pro quo' condition among all pairs of agents, namely $\hat{p}_i\hat{c}_{ij} = \hat{p}_j\hat{c}_{ji}$ does not hold, as remembered by Ostroy–Starr (1990, pp.30-36). See also the paper by Clower–Friedman (1986). This paves the road to nonstandard equilibrium analysis, introduced in §3, and also to money in general equilibrium.

Who is charged by the task of choosing prices and in which way are determined equilibrium prices ? The second question is easily answered: by making every market demand equal to its market supply. Who is in charge of this task we do not know: certainly no agent. The model is not a picture of a noncooperative game, in which prices act as strategic variables. Surely it is compelling to assume that there is some exchange of (truthful) informations among all agents; but it is unlikely, if not by 'fiat', that there is voluntary and full cooperation among all agents, as is needed to form coalitions according to the theories of cooperative games.

The traditional answer about who settles competitive equilibrium prices, already mentioned, is the *walrasian auctioneer.* Assuming *the law of supply and demand* to be at work, may be the only existing law in economics (it is possible sometimes to keep it inoperative, but only temporarily), if there were an auctioneer then he could use the following system of differential equations to manipulate prices:

$$\dot{p}(t) = dp(t)/dt = (M - D)p(t) = D(D^{-1}M - I)p(t). \tag{8}$$

When $M - D$ has negative and dominant main diagonal elements then the trajectories of system (8) are globally stable with respect to walrasian prices $\hat{p}$. It is true that whenever one has $p(0) \neq \lambda\hat{p}$ then convergence to equilibrium of $p(t)$ happens only for $t \to \infty$; but this is not at all a negative result, because here calendar time is absolutely at rest.

Once $\hat{p}$ is known, the economy is not yet in a position to dismiss the auctioneer and to operate autonomously by means of bilateral exchanges among agents. This would be possible, as previously remembered, if for every pair (i, j) in equilibrium we had $\hat{p}_i\hat{c}_{ij} = \hat{p}_j\hat{c}_{ji}$. But generally these relations cannot be fully satisfied so it is compelling to assume [see, for instance, Nicola (1989a)] that the auctioneer is still in charge to manage a *trade center*, in which agent j lays down th amount $1-\hat{c}_{jj}$ of his output and subsequently, after everybody has made the same operation, takes up the amounts of goods $\hat{c}_{ij}$ $(i \neq j)$. Hence even for an economy in walrasian equilibrium all exchanges are based on reliance in the auctioneer. Were an agent refusing to use the trading center then no walrasian equilibrium colud be implemented. Of course, as we shall see, a 'fiat' money colud act as a substitute of the trading center; this means, contrary to the beliefs of many economists, that money plays an essential role even in walrasian equilibrium: no Clower–type constraint is really needed.

3. Bilateral Nonstandard General Equilibrium

Let us again consider the very simple economy of the previous §, about which economy we know everything, provided there is somebody, as the auctioneer, having the power to manage it from the outside. Assuming the existence of an auctioneer is tantamount to assume that in the economy there is a complex network of information, used by the auctioneer to get informations from agents in order to perform his task of centralizing decisions about prices and to manage the trade center. The following model does not contain any auctioneer because all choices are directly made by individual agents, including the choice of prices in every time period. A solution to the following economic model is called *bilateral nonstandard general equilibrium.* A quite different bilateral model was studied by Feldman (1973). Because the present model is much less structure demanding than walrasian models, instead of "nonstandard" we could call it "pre–walrasian" or perhaps, in some good sense, even "post–walrasian".

From here on time becomes calendar time, formally an integer variable: t means the time period running from dates $t-1$ and t. The value $t=0$ is the starting date; before, everything belongs to history, now definitely past. The only agents on the stage are the n households of §2 (n is a large integer), possessing the same economic features there considered: each period can be thought of as a "Hicksian week", namely it is short enough so that each agent incurs a "psychological cost" in revising his choices before the end of the period. In other words, agents choose their best actions only once at the start of each period and they feel committed to their choices.

There is no auctioneer and it is assumed that each agent has an healthy diffidence with respect to all other agents, so nobody thinks it is useful for himself to promote coalitions among agents, up to the point of giving rise to an auctioneer. This assumption simulates what happens in a real economy, where there are millions of agents and, were it ideally possible, it would be very costly both to exchange full (and truthful) informations, and to build a framework to do this.

In our model–economy it is both impossible and useless to solve directly equations (6), because each equation contains variables regarding all agents. This means that no agent by himself can calculate walrasian prices, whose knowledge is needed to determine all other equilibrium values. But each household must choose the price for his good in every time period, by using everything he knows, namely his output, one unit in the present situation, while he does not know the market demand function for his output. Let the unknown market demand functions be conjectured by agent j to be:

$$c_j = \varphi_j(p). \tag{9.j}$$

It is reasonable to assume that every agent perceives his market demand function as continuous, positively homogeneous of degree zero, decreasing in its own price and (generally) increasing in all other prices. Obviously, there is an infinity of such functions; it is only by means of a temporal sequence of distinct observations that it is possible to correctly estimate such functions. Some points are made in Nicola (1989a). At present there is no need to take up this problem, because after the first period here each household modifies his current price by means of the following equations (27); for present purposes it is enough to clearly perceive where and how the estimation problem of market demand functions enters the agent current choices.

With prices given in some commonly agreed numeraire, let us start by examining how agent j chooses his current price p_j, of course fully ignoring the present prices chosen by all other agents while, were this of some help, it is assumed that everybody knows all prices in all past periods. Once produced its output, agent j maximizes his utility indicator, $u_j(.)$, for the running period, under two constraints: i) it is impossible to satisfy a market demand greater than actual output; ii) current expenditure cannot exceed presently expected income. With the previous notations the expected income is $m_j(t) = p_j(t)\varphi_j[p(t)]$; so the two constraints are written:

$$\varphi_j[p(t)] \leq 1, \tag{10.j}$$

$$\sum_{i=1}^{n} p_i(t)c_{ij}(t) \leq p_j(t)\varphi_j[p(t)]. \tag{11.j}$$

All prices $p_i(t)$ $i \neq j$ are exogenous to agent j, because they are determined by other agents; assuming the differentiability of constraint (10.j) and its convexity with respect to p_j, as (11.j) is, from strict quasi concavity of $u_j(.)$ its maximum under constraints is the saddle point of the following Lagrangian (to simplify notations written with no time indications):

$$L_j(c^j, p_j, \lambda_j, \mu_j) = \sum_i \alpha_{ij} \log(1 + \beta_{ij}c_{ij}) + \lambda_j[1 - \varphi_j(p)] + \mu_j[p_j\varphi_j(p) - p \cdot c^j].$$

Of course, in equilibrium the whole income is spent, while if p_i were such that (10.j) hold as a strict inequality then the utility could not be maximized. This means the optimum consumption vector and p_j solve the following system:

$$\alpha_{ij}\beta_{ij}/(1 + \beta_{ij}c_{ij}) - \mu_j p_i \leq 0, \quad c_{ij}\partial L_j/\partial c_{ij} = 0, \tag{12.i, j}$$

$$-\lambda_j \partial\varphi_j/\partial p_j + \mu_j[\varphi_j(p) + p_j\partial\varphi_j/\partial p_j - c_{jj}] = 0, \tag{13.j}$$

$$1 - \varphi_j(p) = 0, \tag{14.j}$$

$$p_j\varphi_j(p) - \sum_i p_i c_{ij} = 0. \tag{15.j}$$

From system (12)–(15), introducing time and remembering what we said with reference to formulae (4), we have:

$$c_{ij} = \alpha'_{ij}\Big[p_j(t) + \sum_{h\in I_j(p(t))} p_h(t)/\beta_{hj}\Big]/p_i(t) - 1/\beta_{ij}, \tag{16.i,j}$$

$$\mu_j(t) = \frac{1}{p_j(t) + \sum_h [p_h(t)/\beta_{hj}]}, \tag{17.j}$$

$$\lambda_j(t) = \Big[\frac{1 + p_j(t)\partial\varphi_j/\partial p_j}{p_j(t) + \sum_h p_h(t)/\beta_{hj}} - c_{jj}(t)\Big](\partial\varphi_j/\partial p_j)^{-1}. \tag{18.j}$$

Now let us put $p_{-j} = (p_1, ..., p_{j-1}, p_{j+1}, ..., p_n)$ and assume that (14.j) can be written as follows:

$$p_j(t) = \psi_j[\tilde{p}_{-j}(t)], \tag{19.j}$$

where a "tilde" means estimations, made by agent j, about actual prices chosen by all other agents. Note that in the previous formulae $\varphi_j(.)$ has no direct impact in determining output, income and individual demand functions for agent j. This so happens only in the present model, because here output is given in advance, while in more general situations $\varphi_j(.)$ is needed to chose the optimal current price as a function of the estimated prices chosen by agents. See, for instance, Nicola (1989b).

3.1 Existence of bilateral nonstandard general equilibrium

Every agent solves a problem such as the one previously considered; in particular, agents have conjectures to choose their optimal current prices as functions of prices chosen by other households. If the conjectured functions $\varphi_j(.)$ are such that we have

$$p(t) = \lambda\hat{p} \qquad (\lambda > 0), \tag{20}$$

then a walrasian equilibrium would obtain as in §2. Plainly, the nature of actual equilibrium entirely rests upon prices satifying (20) or not ! If (20) is fulfilled then we are in a walrasian equilibrium state. In this instance, a wholly fortuitous one, all agents find their expectations to be completely satified so that, in all future periods, they have only to replicate their present choices and the economy would reach a stationary equilibrium, as all fundamentals on which it is built are stationary.

By assumption, all prices are public knowledge; assume also, generically, that actual prices don't fulfil (20); in what follows all present values are denoted by appending an asterisk to the defining variables, whose values now differ from the walrasian ones. Hence there are at least two goods having non zero excess demands (one positive and the other negative because desired demands satisfy Walras's law). So a temporary equilibrium entails at least one rationed good. To go on, it is useful to calculate the values of the goods to be exchanged. In the next few pages, for notational clarity, time is suppressed when there is no possibility of misunderstanding. The values of goods to be exchanged bilaterally is given by $p_{ij}^* c_{ij}^*$ $(\forall i, \forall j)$. At actual prices, because by assumption p^* are non walrasian prices, at least one pair of indices are such that we have $p_i^* c_{ij}^* \neq p_j^* c_{ji}^*$. Indeed if equalities are true for all pairs (i, j) then we must have $\sum_j p_i^* c_{ij}^* = \sum_j p_j^* c_{ji}^*$ $(\forall i)$, namely

$$p_i^* \sum_j c_{ij}^* = \sum_j p_j^* c_{ji}^* = p_i^*, \tag{21.i}$$

due to the budget constraint for consumer i. From (21) we obtain $\sum_j c_{ij}^* = 1$ $(\forall i)$; hence p^* is a walrasian equilibrium prices vector, contrary to the supposition made.

Observe now that under freedom of exchange the amounts bilaterally exchanged are determined by the minimum between pairs of values. Placing a "tilde" on symbols to mean effective values, the amounts of goods effectively exchanged are:

$$\tilde{c}_{ij} = \min\{c_{ij}^*, p_j^* c_{ji}^* / p_i^*\} \qquad (i \neq j). \tag{22.i,j}$$

To call "effective" these values anticipates the conditions to be satified in order that a nonstandard equilibrium is actually obtained. Formally, a *nonstandard general equilibrium* is defined by the following system:

$$\sum_j \tilde{c}_{ij} = 1 \qquad (\forall i), \tag{23.1}$$

$$p_i^* \tilde{c}_{ij} = p_j^* \tilde{c}_{ji} \qquad (i \neq j, \forall i, \forall j), \tag{23.2}$$

$$\tilde{c}_{ii} \geq c_{ii}^* \qquad (\forall i), \tag{23.3}$$

$$\tilde{c}_{ij} \leq c_{ij}^* \qquad (i \neq j, \forall i, \forall j). \tag{23.4}$$

Inequalities (23.3) say that every agent must be able to consume, of his output, an amount at least equal to what he wishes to consume, while (23.4) mean that effective exchanges are *voluntary*, namely nobody is compelled to buy, of some goods, an amount greater than he wishes to buy.

We must show that system (23) is satisfied by the set of values

$$\tilde{c}_{ij} \quad (i, j = 1, 2, ..., n)$$

. From (22) it is seen directly that relations (23.2) are verified. Now let us write

$$\tilde{c}_{ii} = 1 - \sum_{j \neq i} \tilde{c}_{ij}; \tag{24.i}$$

from individual budget constraints, $p_j^* = \sum_i p_i^* c_{ij}^* \geq \sum_i p_i^* \tilde{c}_{ij}$, we have

$$1 \geq \sum_i p_i^* \tilde{c}_{ij} / p_j^* = \sum_i \tilde{c}_{ji}. \tag{25.j}$$

Relations (24), (25) show that (23.1) hold true, while (23.3) are obtained as follows:

$$c_{ii}^* = 1 - \sum_{j \neq i} p_j^* c_{ji}^* / p_i^* \leq 1 - \sum_{j \neq i} p_j^* \tilde{c}_{ji} / p_i^* = 1 - \sum_{j \neq i} \tilde{c}_{ij} = \tilde{c}_{ii}.$$

Hence the following is true:

Proposition 1. *Under the previous assumptions the model formed by relations (23) has a bilateral nonstandard equilibrium.*

Such an equilibrium, contrary to a walrasian equilibrium, generally cannot be Pareto efficient (see, for instance, Silvestre 1985), because it is plain that there are many bilateral exchanges that could prove profitable to numerous pairs of agents but cannot be implemented owing to the need of balancing bilaterally the values exchanged. This type of inefficiency very likely is, at least conceptually, the most important reason to introduce a 'fiat' money in many agents models. Indeed a money, if it is used as a means of exchange by all agents, becomes a powerful aid to overcome the need to bilaterally pairing exchanged values, because money may become part of every exchange, as we shall see in §6.

3.2 Dynamics of nonstandard equilibrium

From now on time is again explicitly noted, to study the behavior of agents in a sequence of time periods. The previously calculated values in a nonstandard equilibrium are generically associated to period t. At prices $p_i^*(t)$ desired demands to agent i are $c_i^*(t) = \sum_j c_{ij}^*(t)$, to which demands there correspond unitary outputs by choice of units. This means that excess demands are:

$$e_i[p^*(t)] = \sum_j c_{ij}^*(t) - 1, \tag{26.i}$$

whose values are $p_i^*(t) e_i[p^*(t)] = \sum_j p_i^*(t) c_{ij}^*(t) - p_i^*(t)$. Which is an economically meaningful reaction by agent i to his present situation ? When his excess demand is negative it is reasonable to think that he will decrease his price in period $t+1$, and viceversa in the opposite situation. Indeed, when the excess demand happens to be negative the agent was unable to sell his whole output; hence, because his production cost is independent from output, 'a priori' he finds useful to decrease his price. On the contrary, when there is a positive excess demand it may prove profitable to increase the price, because this decision very likely will increase his total revenue, namely income, as far as the price is not so much increased as to decrease demand drastically under output. To prevent this unfavorable possibilty, use of the conjectured demand function $\varphi_i(.)$ may prove useful. But at present we shall not dwell on this point, in order to make things as simple as possible. We simply assume that the rule, followed by all agents, to change prices is formally given by

$$\Delta p_i^*(t) = p_i^*(t+1) - p_i^*(t) = p_i^*(t) \frac{e_i(p^*(t))}{1 + |e_i(p^*(t))|}. \qquad (27.i)$$

Economically, the dynamics of prices is governed by the value of the corresponding excess demands; the denominators ensure that all prices are always positive, of course when starting from positive prices.

The dynamic process generated by the difference equations (27), with the starting condition $p(0) \gg 0$, has trajectories of strictly positive price vectors, which in general may not converge to some vector. But when there is convergence, surely the limit is λp^*, for some positive λ. Indeed, were the limit be different from walrasian prices then at least two excess demands would be non zero, and at least two prices would undergo further changes. So we have the following

Proposition 2. *In the previous model of bilateral nonstandard general equilibrium actual prices are always positive. When they converge, such convergence is to walrasian prices, whatever is* $p(0) \gg 0$.

Of course, this result rests on the assumption that agents behave, in manipulating their prices, according to rule (27). While it is true that this type of behavior someway limits our conclusion, it is equally true that the rule looks very plausible. Anyway, some rule has to be assumed at work.

The previous proposition does not allow one to think there is a positive probability of convergence to walrasian prices. But even when such a convergece occurs, it would be only for time going to infinity, namely never on practical grounds. Nonstandard general equilibrium does not suffer any loss for this, because here time is calendar time and households implement their "relative optimal" choices period after period, being not at all compelled to wait until an abstract equilibrium is reached. This feature is another element in favor of nonstandard equilibrium as compared to the traditional walrasian equilibrium.

4. Generalization

The previous model aims at presenting, in a very simple setting, the idea of bilateral nonstandard general equilibrium and some of its properties. Is it possible to generalize it ? Here we consider the possibility to employ general utility indicators, namely general demand functions, of course satisfying all the assumptions usually made in traditional walrasian equilibrium. To simplify the presentation, and at no loss of generality, let us work directly on demand functions, mantaining all other assumptions previously made. Let the demand function for agent j be:

$$f^j : \Re^n_{++} \to \Re^n_+ \quad ; \quad p \mapsto f^j(p) = c^j, \tag{28.j}$$

continuous, positively homogeneous of degree zero and satisfying the budget constraint

$$p \cdot f^j(p) = p_j. \tag{29.j}$$

Assume also that all functions (28) satisfy the assumption:

$$\textit{either } f^j_i(p) = 0 \textit{ or } \lim_{p_i \to 0+} f^j_i(p) = +\infty \qquad (\forall p \in \Re^n_{++}), \tag{30.i, j}$$

namely, if good i is wanted by agent j then its demand becomes unbounded when p_i goes to zero.

Under the stated assumptions, after introducing the market demand functions

$$f : \Re^n_{++} \to \Re^n_+ \quad ; \quad p \mapsto f(p) = \sum_j f^j(p),$$

we know that there is one walrasian equilibrium to the following model:

$$e(p) = f(p) - s \leq 0, \tag{31}$$

where $e(.)$ satisfies *Walras 'law*, namely $p \cdot e(p) = 0$, and $s = (1, 1, \dots, 1)$. Walrasian prices for model (31) are still denoted by $\hat{p}$; of course actually there may be many equilibria.

4.1 Bilateral nonstandard equilibrium

Let p^* be the vector of prices presently chosen by agents, using their conjectured demand functions $\varphi_j(.)$ $(j = 1, ..., n)$. While individual desired demands are $c^*_{ij} = f^j_i(p^*)$, agents effective exchanges, $\tilde{c}_{ij}$, must satisfy:

$$\tilde{c}_{ij} = \min(c^*_{ij}, p^*_j c^*_{ji} / p^*_i). \tag{32.i, j}$$

Formally, relations (23) still define the nonstandard model, to which all developments presented in §3 apply; this proves

Proposition 3. *Under the previous assumptions model (23) has a bilateral nonstandard general equilibrium.*

4.2 Dynamics of nonstandard equilibrium

Inserting time in the following formulae, assume as in §3 that agents use the following rule to change their prices:

$$p_i^*(t+1) = p_i^*(t)\left\{1 + \frac{e_i(p^*(t))}{1+|e_i(p^*(t))|}\right\}. \tag{33.i}$$

Introducing the variables

$$g_i(p) = \frac{f_i(p) + |f_i(p) - 1|}{1 + |f_i(p) - 1|} \qquad (\forall i),$$

and

$$G = diag[g_1, \ldots, g_n]$$

in matrix notations equations (33) are written $p^*(t+1) = G[p^*(t)]p^*(t)$. When agents start the dynamic process from any $p(0) \gg 0$ then, owing to assumption (30) on functions $f^j(.)$, every price is always positive. Obviously the conclusion that a nonstandard equilibrium may be globally unstable remains true; but when there is global stability the sequence $\{p^*(t)\}$ does converge to a walrasian equilibrium, for the same considerations put forward in §3. So we have

Proposition 4. *Under the previous assumptions $p^*(t)$ is positive for every t. If the sequence $\{p^*(t)\}$ is a convergent one then its limit is a walrasian equilibrium for any $p(0)$.*

It is of some interest to observe that difference equations similar to (33) are applicable also to stability analysis of equilibria in walrasian models which are more general than the ones here examined. It is always true that prices are positive and that when prices converge then convergence is to walrasian prices.

5. Multilateral nonstandard equilibrium

The previous definition of nonstandard general equilibrium is dubbed *bilateral nonstandard equilibrium* because it assumed that exchanges occur between pair of agents, as the equality among values of goods exchanged must hold bilaterally. It is possible to generalize nonstandard equilibrium by assuming that values may be equalized trilaterally, or in general multilaterally. In such nonstandard models we could reach a walrasian equilibrium when prices are $\lambda\hat{p}$ and exchanges become n–lateral. Concretely, let us exemplify by considering a situation in which all trilateral exchanges are possible, according to presently given prices p^*. Let generically i, j, k be the indexes of three distinct agents (and of their outputs); then the amounts effectively exchanged, namely $\tilde{c}_{ij}, \ldots, \tilde{c}_{ki}$ must satisfy relations like $p_i^*\tilde{c}_{ij} + p_k^*\tilde{c}_{kj} = p_j^*\tilde{c}_{ji} + p_j^*\tilde{c}_{jk}$, obtained by interchanging indices i, j, k. In defining a trilateral nonstandard equilibrium these relations take the place of the previous relations (23.2), while all other relations (23) are still valid. Moreover, the quantities exchanged must satisfy relations analogous to (22), but holding as inequalities because now expenditures must balance only trilaterally. For agent j these relations are

$$p_i^* \tilde{c}_{ij} \leq \min(p_i^* c_{ij}^*, p_j^* c_{ji}^* + p_j^* c_{jk}^*) \qquad ; p_k^* \tilde{c}_{kj} \leq \min(p_k^* c_{kj}^*, p_j^* c_{ji}^* + p_j^* c_{jk}^*).$$

Actually there are nine relations to solve for six unknowns, meaning that there may be an infinity of solutions, due to the fact that each agent has some freedom to distribute his income in buying the outputs of the other two agents. But there are further difficulties to cope with. Even if every triple of agents were able to find an acceptable agreement about their exchanges, it is quite possible that generically relations (23.1) are not satisfied, because trilateral exchanges do not implement any automatic rationing as assured by relations (22). Essentially, if one tries to overcome the bilaterality of exchanges then one enters immediately the realm of rationing, useless only in the very singular case where actual prices are walrasian prices. Hence we see that by trying to overcome the narrow horizon of bilateral exchanges we are immediately confronted by new and more fundamental questions. Of course, these last considerations apply 'a fortiori' to multilateral exchanges: multilaterality cannot work as it stands.

6. Exogenous "money"

The path followed up to now aimed at fully abolishing any need to take into consideration a super–individual operator such as the walrasian auctioneer. But modern societies are always assisted by some global authorities; in the economic field the most typical of such authorities is the one charged by the task of issuing and managing money, presently to be thought of as exogenous or 'fiat' money. In the previous models is there any space to be filled by money ? Of course the answer is a positive one, corroborated by the practical impossibility, undelined in §5, for individual agents to implement multilateral exchanges. To motivate the existence of "money" as a medium of exchanges and numeraire, it is not necessary to assume that there are transaction costs, or that there is some "cash in advance" constraint, as introduced for instance by Clower; we do not even need to use overlapping generations models, in which households maximize intertemporal utility indicators and employ money to transfer their wealth among different time periods.

An exogenous money is able to implement bilateral exchanges, usually necessary to get a walrasian equilibrium, as previously remembered. Apart of all considerations about historic–institutional elements from which the actual western monetary systems arose, let us limit ourselves to assume that the institution of a monetary authority is founded on a "social contract freely subscribed by all agents" active when this authority was introduced. Because every conclusion is already fully contained in the premises, a mathematical model cannot produce a historical sequence capable to end with such a social contract. Once introduced, let us assume that the monetary authority is the only agent endowed with the power of issuing money, for instance in the form of banknotes put into circulation under many face values, from small ones on: it is even possible to think of an electronic money. The only aim given to the monetary authority is to promote (bilateral) exchanges among agents. To this aim, at the start of period t let agent j be endowed with a "sufficient" amount of money, $m_j(t) > 0$. For instance, assume that the monetary authority endows each agent with whatever (finite) sum of money he asks for, let us say:

$$m_j(t) = p^*(t) \cdot \bar{c}^j; \tag{34.j}$$

from (34), even when consumer j is compelled to do all his purchases before selling his output, his starting money's endowment is enough to let him execute all possible exchanges. In this setting there is no Milton Friedman's problem, about determining an optimum quantity of money, as extensively discussed by Woodford (1990).

Let the social contract giving birth to the monetary authority state also: i) every end of period money must be returned to the monetary authority (namely in each period new banknotes are issued while all old banknotes are no more current money); ii) every seller must agree to receive money in payment for his sales; iii) every price must always be quoted in the same units chosen to name money. Owing to this general norms, we assume that every agent in each period feels compelled to satisfy his "non monetary" budget constraint:

$$p^*(t) \cdot c(t) = p^*(t) \cdot \bar{c}^j, \tag{35.j}$$

while obviously there is no more need for goods bilaterally exchanged to be of equal values; namely, relations (23.2) are substituted by the following ones:

$$p_i^*(t)\tilde{c}_{ij}(t) = p_j^*(t)\tilde{c}_{ji}(t) + m_{ji}(t), \tag{36.i, j}$$

where $m_{ij}(t) = -m_{ji}(t)$ is the sum of money transferred from agent i to agent j if $m_{ij}(t)$ is positive, and viceversa for $m_{ij}(t)$ negative.

Apparently, the social contract on money seems to open the road to an increased efficiency (in a paretian meaning) in multilateral nonstandard general equilibrium; but actually the situation may be very different. Indeed, as we saw in §5 on multilateral exchange, if on one side money breaks the iron chain imposed by the bilateral pairing of values, on the other side it compels to ration outputs every time actual prices are not proportional to a walrasian equilibrium price vector. Namely, if it is true that money is a powerful lubricant for exchanges, it is also true that money must be supported by rationing, because money 'per se' is not a tool to make exchanges globally consistent.

Because the monetary authority is the only super–individual agent, rationing must be directly implemented by individuals. A rationing scheme which is simultaneously individual, efficient and non manipulable is the scheme based on the principle of the waiting queue, where buyers are served, up to full depletion of the output, on a basis of "first arrived first served". Formally, with respect to good i, let$(1_i, 2_i, ..., j_i, ..., n_i)$ with $1_i = i$ be the permutation of the first n integers giving the arrivals of potential buyers of output i. Then for every i we have $\tilde{c}_{ii} = c^*_{ii}$, while the amounts effectively got by agents, $\tilde{c}_{ij}$ $(j \neq i)$, are determined by the formulae:

$$\tilde{c}_{ij_i} = \min\left\{c^*_{ij_i}, \max\left[0, 1 - \sum_{h=1_i}^{(j-1)_i} \tilde{c}_{ih}\right]\right\} \qquad (j_i \neq i). \qquad (37.i,j)$$

It is useful to assume that each agent records all customers orders got at prices $p^*(t)$, so that he is able to apply, in the following period, rule (33.j) to choose his price for the next period. Of course, because a rationing scheme is needed, it is impossible to prove generally that nonstandard general equilibrium points to increased efficiency, in a paretian sense, of the solution obtained. Namely, it is difficult in this framework to prove that introducing money surely improves the efficiency of an economy; but at an individual level agents have no tools to verify this. Surely money enormously widens the exchanges possibilities, because money breaks the iron condition of 'quid pro quo', but at the same time the very existence of money asks for the introduction of some rationing scheme. Note that, owing to the randomness of the adopted rationing scheme, from the same starting data one obtains in general different results, unless by chance prices are walrasian prices. So in a sense the dynamics of this model economy is of a stochastic type.

7. Final remarks

In the previous pages we have introduced a definition of nonstandard general equilibrium, together with some of its properties, having in mind the aim of eliminating completely the meta–operator called auctioneer, and of charging directly the individual agents with the task of choosing prices period after period, as it usually happens in the economies of our times. A real advantage of nonstandard equilibrium with respect to walrasian equilibrium is that the nonstandard one is "informatively more efficient", according to Hurwicz (1960), as its working needs a smaller amount of information to be transmitted among agents.

The most general model in §4 mantains the assumption according to which all agents produce only one output and conversely every output is produced by only one agent. There are no serious difficulties in removing the first half of this assumption, while there are some difficulties to supersede the second part, because every agent, in choosing his actual prices, ought to form expectations about prices chosen by other producers of the same goods, and this would complicate someway the picture. But it is to be remembered that very frequently goods are named, that is goods produced by different agents are generally regarded as different by buyers, irrespective of their material characteristics.

A more general model must include, with reference to every agent, a possibility to choose optimal outputs together with optimal prices, namely "Bertrand 'cum' Cournot", may be according to the ideas summarized by Negishi (1982) or by Mas–Colell (1986). To formalize such decisions the conjectured functions $\varphi_j(.)$ become of paramount importance. To this task a new essay will be devoted. We shall be interested also in studying the possibility to obtain some form of paretian efficiency, despite the absence of an auctioneer and the existence of money. For what we saw in §6, money fulfills some some tasks of the auctioneer, of course once every agent agrees to subscribe to the social contract estabilishing a monetary authority endowed with the powers listed in §6. Indeed the social contract is economically well founded because money, using a term introduced long ago by Menger (1871), among all goods is the most "marketable" one, meaning that every good easily exchanges against money. So it seems plausible to insert, in a monetary constitution, the clause that all agents must sell outputs against money, because they safely know that they are able to buy any goods against money, of course when rationing allows for this operation. Some ideas on the subject are contained in Nicola (1990).

Note

My best thanks are due to C.N.R. (Consiglio Nazionale delle Ricerche), Rome, for financial aid in preparing this paper.

References

Benassy, J.P. (1986): *Macroeconomics: an Introduction to the Non–Walrasian Approach*, Orlando, Academic Press, p.45.

Clower, R. W. (1967): A reconsideration of the microfoundations of monetary theory, *Western Economic Journal*, 6, pp.1–9.

Clower, R. W. (1986): Trade specialists and money in an ongoing exchange economy, in R. H. Day, G. Eliasson (eds), *The Dynamics of Market Economies*; Amsterdam, North–Holland, pp.115–129.

Cournot, A. (1838): *Recherches sur les principes matématiques de la théorie des richesses*, Paris, Hachette.

Duffie, D. (1990): Money in general equilibrium theory, in B. M. Friedman, F. H. Hahn, cit., vol.1, pp.81–100.

Edgeworth, F. Y. (1881): *Mathematical Psychics*, London, Kegan Paul.

Feldman, A. M. (1973): Bilateral trading processes, pairwise optimality, and Pareto optimality, *The Review of Economic Studies*, 40, pp.463–473.

Friedman, B. M., F. H. Hahn (eds.) (1990): *Handbook of Monetary Economics*, Amsterdam, North–Holland.

Gale, D. (1963): A note on global instability of competitive equilibrium, *Naval Research Logistics Quarterly*, 10, pp.81–87.

Hahn, F. H. (1982): Stability, in K. J. Arrow, M. D. Intriligator (eds), *Handbook of Mathematical Economics*, Amsterdam, North–Holland, vol.2, pp.745–793.

Hammond, P. J. (1990): The role of information in economics, in *L'Informazione nell'Economia e nel Diritto*, Milan, CARIPLO, pp.177–193.

Hart, O. D. (1982): A model of imperfect competition with keynesian features, *Quarterly Journal of Economics*, 97, pp.109–138.

Hildenbrand, W., A. P. Kirman (1988): *Equilibrium Analysis*, Amsterdam, North–Holland.

Hurwicz, L. (1960): Optimality and information efficiency in resource allocation processes, in K. J. Arrow, S. Karlin, P. Suppes (eds), *Mathematical Methods in the Social Sciences, 1959*, Stanford (CA), Stanford University Press, pp.27–46.

Hurwicz, L. (1986): Incentive aspects of decentralization, in K. J. Arrow, M. D. Intriligator (eds), *Handbook of Mathematical Economics*, Amsterdam, North–Holland, vol.3, pp.1441–1482.

Kirman, A. P. (1989): On the instability of walrasian economics, in M. Galeotti, L. Geronazzo, F. Gori (eds), *Non–Linear Dynamics in Economic and Social Sciences*, Bologna, Pitagora Editrice, pp.85–105.

Mas–Colell, A. (1986): Notes on prices and quantity tâtonnement dynamics, in H. F. Sonnenschein (ed), *Models of Economic Dynamics*, Berlin, Springer–Verlag, pp.49–68.

Menger, C. (1871): *Principi di Economia Politica*, Turin, UTET, 1976 (from German).

Negishi, T. (1961): Monopolistic competition and general equilibrium, *The Review of Economic Studies*, 28, pp.196–201.

Negishi, T. (1982): From Samuelson's stability analysis to non–walrasian economics, in G. R. Feiwel (ed), *Samuelson and Neoclassical Economics*, Boston, Kluwer–Njihoff, pp.119–125.

Nicola, P. C. (1986): Equilibrio interpersonale temporaneo: un modello elementare senza banditore, *Giornale degli Economisti e Annali di Economia*, 45, pp.113–147.

Nicola, P. C. (1989a): Il modello di von Neumann e la teoria del valore, in L. L. Pasinetti (ed), *Aspetti Controversi della Teoria del Valore*, Bologna, il Mulino, pp.219–230.

Nicola, P. C. (1989b): *Una teoria dell'impresa quando i mercati non sono organizzati*, Milan, IDSE (Istituto di Ricerca sulla Dinamica dei Sistemi Economici).

Nicola, P. C. (1990): Edgeworth oppure Walras? Menger è meglio, *Rivista Internazionale di Scienze Sociali*, pp.517–527.

Nikaido, H. (1975): *Monopolistic Competition and Effective Demand*, Princeton, Princeton University Press.

Ostroy, J. M., R. M. Starr (1990): The transactions role of money, in B. M. Friedman, F. H. Hahn, cit., vol.1, pp.3–62.

Samuelson, P. A. (1941–42): The stability of equilibrium, *Econometrica*, 9, pp.97–120, 10, pp.1–25.

Scarf, H. (1960): Some examples of global instability, *International Economic Review*, 1, pp.157–172.

Scarf, H. (1967): The approximation of fixed points of a continuous mapping, *SIAM Journal of Applied Mathematics*, 15, pp.1328–1343.

Silvestre, J. (1985): Voluntary and efficient allocations are walrasian, *Econometrica*, 53, pp.807–816.

Tirole, J. (1988): *The Theory of Industrial Organization*, Cambridge (Mass.), MIT Press.

Walras, L. M. E. (1874–77): *Eléments d'Économie Politique Pure*, Pichon et Durand–Auzias, 1952.

Woodford, M. (1990): The optimum quantity of money, in B. M. Friedman, F. H. Hahn, cit., vol.2, pp.1067–1152.

Real Indeterminacy, Taxes and Outside Money in Incomplete Financial Market Economies: I. The Case of Lump Sum Taxes*

Antonio Villanacci
DIMADEFAS, Università di Firenze
via Lombroso 6-17, 50134 Firenze, ITALY

1. Introduction

The basic model of exchange economies with incomplete financial markets and nominal assets has been thoroughly studied. Cass (1984), Werner (1985), Duffie (1987) and others have proved existence of equilibria. Balasko and Cass (1989) and Geanakoplos and Mas-Colell (1989) have shown that, generically, the equilibrium allocations exhibit a degree of indeterminacy related to the number of states of the world and the number of available financial instruments.

Some work has been also done to analyze the robustness of the indeterminacy result with respect to changes and enrichments in the structural assumptions of the incomplete market model. Cass (1988), Siconolfi (1989) and Siconolfi and Villanacci (1991) have studied economies in which there is no uncertainty about the fundamentals, the so called "sunspot economies". In this model, the equilibrium allocations have, typically, at least one degree of indeterminacy. Pietra (1989) has shown that if assets paying in units of goods are available together with the nominal ones, the indeterminacy result still holds true - even though that is not the case if all assets are "real". The introduction of outside money in the model has also been studied. While there is no place for money with a positive price in the standard version of the complete or incomplete market models, many additional assumptions can be introduced to overcome the well known "hot potato" problem (see, for example, Patinkin (1949)). Magill and Quinzii (1988) have presented a model in which households need to sell

---

*I am greatly indebted to David Cass for many helpful suggestions and discussions. I would like to thank Paolo Siconolfi, Yves Youne's, Michael Mandler, Nancy Brooks, Jean-Marc Tallon, Unal Zenginobuz and Francis Bloch for helpful discussions.

their endowments of goods to get outside money they can buy goods with. In this cash-in-advance framework, there are obviously equilibria with positive price of money, and Magill and Quinzii show that, if inside money is available, their number is generically finite.

The goal of this paper is to study the presence of outside money in a model in which the existence of monetary equilibria is made possible by the requirement imposed on the households to pay taxes using outside money. The standard reference for this idea is Abba Lerner (1947), whose famous quotation is reproduced below.

> "The modern state can make anything it chooses generally acceptable as money and thus establish its value quite apart from any connection, even of the most formal kind, with gold or with backing of any kind. It is true that a simple declaration that such and such is money will not do, even if backed by the most convincing constitutional evidence of the state's absolute sovereignty. But if the state is willing to accept the proposed money in payment of taxes and other obligations to itself the trick is done. Everyone who has obligations to the state will be willing to accept the pieces of paper with which he can settle the obligations, and all other people will be willing to accept these pieces of paper because they know that the taxpayers, etc., will be willing to accept them in turn".

Of course, taxes may be of a different nature: lump sum, proportional to income or a general function of income or prices. In this paper, I present the case of lump sum taxes. Moreover, I assume that financial instruments pay in units of outside money.

In the case in which taxes extract all the money existing in the economy, the main results of the analysis are that, with or without availability of inside money,

(i) an equilibrium exists for any economy, i.e., for any endowment of goods, endowment of outside money and schedule of taxes;

(ii) in an open and dense subset of the space of economies, the equilibrium set of allocations exhibits a degree of real indeterminacy related to the degree of uncertainty - in fact equal to the number of states of the world in period 1.

The basic intuition for result (ii) is given in the next section. If taxes are insufficiently exacting, result (ii) holds in a weaker form - see section 4. In a subsequent paper, I plan to analyze the cases of taxes of a different nature.

Simpler versions of the model presented in this paper can be found in Geanakoplos and Mas-Colell (1989) and Cass (1990). In particular, Cass (among other things) analyzes the leading example in which inside money is available and taxes are state independent.

This paper is organized as follows. In section 2, I describe the notation, the set up of the model and some preliminary results. In section 3, I present the main result of the model. It is necessary to distinguish between the case in which a risk-free asset, or inside money, is not available and the case in which it is available. In section 4, I discuss the results of different assumptions about the relationship between total endowment of money in period zero and aggregate taxes in period one.

2. The Model

There are two periods: period zero (today) and period one (tomorrow). In period zero, there is one state of the world, say state zero; in period one, S states of the world can occur. In state zero, goods, outside money and assets are exchanged. Then, the uncertainty is resolved. Assets pay their yields, goods and outside money are exchanged. Finally taxes are paid using outside money.

Remark 2.1 All the basic notation contained in this section is summarized at the end of the Appendix.

The $S+1$ states of the world (or spots) are labelled by superscript s. There are C physical commodities in each spot, labelled by superscript $c=1,\dots,C$. In total, we have $G = C(S+1)$ goods, described by the pair $(s,c) \in \{0,1,\dots,S\}\times\{1,\dots,C\}$.

Households are labelled by subscript $h = 1,\dots,H$; x_h^{sc}, $(x_h^{sc})_{c=1}^{C} \equiv x_h^s$, $(x_h^s)_{s=0}^{S} \equiv x_h$ are (respectively) good (s,c), all goods in state s, all goods demanded by household h. $(x_h)_{h=1}^{H} \equiv x$ is the demand of goods by all households. $u_h: \mathbb{R}^{G}_{++} \to \mathbb{R}$ is the utility function of household h, $h=1,\ldots,H$. Endowments - e_h^{sc}, e_h^{s}, e_h, e - are defined in a similar way. To start with, prices of goods are expressed in units of account and p^{sc}, p^{s}, p denote, respectively, the prices of good (s,c), of all goods in state s, of all goods.

The notation for outside money and taxes is the following. e_h^{m} is the endowment of outside money owned by household h in state zero; $e_h^{m} \in \mathbb{R}^{I}_{++}$. m_h^{0} is the demand of outside money for storage purposes by household h in state zero; of course, we assume that household cannot issue outside money, i.e., $m_h^{0} \geq 0$. q^{sm} is the price of outside money in state s, $s=0,1,\ldots,S$, and is expressed in units of account; $(q^{sm})_{s=0}^{S} \equiv q^{m}$. t_h^{s} is the tax in units of outside money to be paid by household h in state s; $t_h^{s} \in \mathbb{R}^{I}_{++}$ for $s=1,\ldots,S$. To simplify notation, define $(e_h^{m}, (t_h^{s})_{s=1}^{S}) \equiv t_h$; moreover $(t_h)_{h=1}^{H} \equiv t$.

Remark 2.2 Outside money is different from all the other goods for the following reasons:

(i) it does not enter the utility function;

(ii) it has to be used to pay taxes;

(iii) it can be stored;

(iv) its demand has to be nonnegative.

The notation for the inside financial structure is the following. There are I financial instruments or assets labelled by superscript i; q^{i} is the price of financial instrument i in units of account; $(q^{i})_{i=1}^{I}$ is the price vector; y^{si} is the yield of financial instrument i in state s in units of outside money; $(jy^{si})_{i=1}^{I} \equiv y^{s}$ is the vector of yields in state s by financial instrument i; $[y^{si}]_{s,i} \equiv \overline{Y}$ is the $(S\times I)$ yield matrix; $Y \equiv \begin{bmatrix} -q \\ \overline{Y} \end{bmatrix}$ is the matrix describing the (inside) financial structure; a_h^{i} is the demand of financial instrument i by household h; $(a_h^i)_{i=1}^I = a_h$, $(a_h)_{h=1}^H \equiv a$. To simplify notation, we assume that prices, yields and gradients of utility functions are row vectors, while all the others are column vectors.

Assumption 1. The utility function u_h is C^2, differentiably strictly increasing, differentiably strictly quasi-concave and has indifference surfaces closed in $\mathbf{R}^G_{++}$.

To insure existence, we restrict goods prices to belong to $\mathbf{R}^G_{++}$. We moreover assume that $q^m \in \mathbf{R}^{S+1}_+$.

Assumption 2. Markets are incomplete.

Assumption 3. There are no redundant financial instruments.

Assumption 4. There are no arbitrage possibilities.

Define Q as the set of no arbitrage financial instruments prices.

Assumption 5. $\overline{Y}$ is in general position, i.e., every submatrix of $\overline{Y}$ has full rank.

Assumption 6. Households are sufficiently more numerous than missing financial instruments.

Specific forms of Assumptions 2, 3, 4, 6 consistent with the fact that inside money is or is not available are presented in section 3. Given these assumptions and notation, I can now describe the maximization problem for the households and the market clearing conditions.

Maximization problem for household h

$$\max_{x_h, m_h^0, a_h} \quad u_h(x_h) \qquad \text{s.t.} \tag{P1}$$

$$\begin{aligned} & p^0 x_h^0 + q^{0m} m_h^0 + q a_h = p^0 e_h^0 + q^{0m} e_h^m, \\ & m_h^0 \geq 0, \end{aligned} \tag{P1.1}$$

$$\begin{aligned} & p^s x_h^s + q^{sm} t_h^s = p^s e_h^s + q^{sm} y^s a_h + q^{sm} m_h^0, \\ & s=1,\ldots,S \end{aligned} \tag{P1.2}$$

Market clearing conditions

$$\sum_{h=1}^{H} (x_h - e_h) = 0 \tag{M1.1}$$

$$\sum_{h=1}^{H} a_h = 0, \tag{M1.2}$$

$$\sum_{h=1}^{H} (m_h^0 - e_h^m) \begin{cases} = 0 & \text{if } q^{0m} > 0, \\ \leq 0 & \text{if } q^{0m} = 0, \end{cases} \tag{M1.3}$$

$$\sum_{h=1}^{H} (m_h^0 - t_h^s) \begin{cases} = 0 & \text{if } q^{sm} > 0, \\ \leq 0 & \text{if } q^{sm} = 0, \quad \text{for } s=1,\ldots,S. \end{cases} \tag{M1.4}$$

Defined $X \equiv \mathbf{R}_{++}^{GH}$, an economy is a pair $(e,t) \in X \times \mathbf{R}_{++}^{H(S+1)}$. $(p,q^m,q) \in \mathbf{R}_{++}^{G} \times \mathbf{R}_{+}^{S+1} \times Q$ is an equilibrium price associated to (e,t) iff

(i) household h solves (P1) at (p,q^m,q,e,t), for $h=1,\ldots,H$;

(ii) market clearing conditions are satisfied at the maximizing choices of the households.

The remainder of this section deals with some preliminary problems which have to be solved before stating and proving the results about existence and indeterminacy.

Outside section 4 we adopt the following

Assumption 7. $q^m \in \mathbf{R}^{S+1}_{++}$.

Given this assumption and given the nature of the budget constraints we can normalize good, outside money and financial instrument prices spot by spot using q^{sm} for $s=0,1,\ldots,S$. Therefore, $q^{sm}=1$ for $s=0,1,\ldots,S$ and the household's maximization problem can be rewritten, with some abuse of notation, as

$$\max_{x_h, m_h^0, a_h} \quad u_h(x_h) \quad \text{s.t.} \tag{P2}$$

$$p^0(x_h^0-e_h^0) + (m_h^0-e_h^m) = -q\ a_h, \quad m_h^0 \geq 0, \tag{P2.1}$$

$$p^s(x_h^s-{}_h^s) - (\overset{*}{m}{}_h^0-t_h^s) = y^s\ a_h, \quad s=1,\ldots,S. \tag{P2.2}$$

Remark 2.3 Observe that, because of the adopted normalizations, p and q (besides y) are expressed in units of outside money.

From M1.3, M1.4 and Assumption 7, we have

Fact 2.1 $\sum_{h=1}^{H} (e_h^m - t_h^s) = 0$, for $s=1,\ldots,S$.

The case $\sum_h e_h^m > \sum_h t_h^s$ is consistent with zero price of money in state s and is discussed in section 4. Consistently with Fact 2.1, define

$$t \equiv \{t \in \mathbf{R}^{H(S+1)}_{++} : \sum_{h=1}^{H} (e_h^m - t_h^s) = 0 \text{ for } s=1,\ldots,S\}$$

and observe that the relevant market clearing conditions become

$$\sum_{h=1}^{H} (x_h-e_h) = 0, \tag{M2.1}$$

$$\sum_{h=1}^{H} a_h = 0, \tag{M2.2}$$

$$\sum_{h=1}^{H} (m_h^0 - e_h^m) = 0. \tag{M2.3}$$

Note that if the value of taxes is "too high" with respect to the value of the endowments, some households' budget set may be empty. Each household is able to pay taxes in each state, if she or he is "sufficiently rich", which is the case if

$$p^{s1}e_h^{s1} > t_h^s - e_h^m, \quad \text{for} \quad s=1,\ldots,S \quad \text{and} \quad h=1,\ldots,H.$$

In fact, I am going to restrict the analysis to

$$\Gamma \equiv \{(p,q,e,t) \in \mathbb{R}_{++}^G \times Q \times X \times T\colon p^{s1}e_h^{s1} > t_h^s - e_h^m, \quad \text{for} \quad s=1,\ldots,S \quad \text{and} \quad h=1,\ldots,H\}.$$

Remark 2.4 The conditions defining Γ may eliminate equilibrium prices for "low levels" of p^{s1}. Given that it is still possible to show existence for any economy and indeterminacy for almost all economies, there is no loss of generality in restricting the analysis to Γ. Observe also that other choices of prices to include in the definition of Γ are possible as well.

3. Existence and Indeterminacy

A technical difficulty specific to this model comes from the presence of the nonnegativity constraint on the demand of outside money in the household's maximization problem. This difficulty can be easily avoided analyzing only the case in which a risk-free asset is available, as done by Magill and Quinzii (1988) in their cash-in-advance model. If that asset is not available, things are technically more complicated. A standard use of differential topology techniques requires proving differentiability of the demand function, manifold structure of the equilibrium set and properness of the projection function from that set to the parameter space. (See Balasko (1988), Balasko and Cass (1989) and Balasko, Cass and Siconolfi (1990)). In the present model this approach is prevented by the fact that the Implicit Function Theorem does not suffice to show differentiability of the demand function - see Remark 3.2. The way out adopted in this paper is to follow the general strategy used in Cass, Siconolfi and Villanacci (1991).

First I introduce a set of fictitious economies for which differentiability, manifold structure and properness is obtained. Then a simple relationship between the "true" economy and the above fictitious ones allows me to get the desired nominal indeterminacy result. Unfortunately, existence of equilibria cannot be proved using the differentiable approach (again see Balasko (1988) and others). Following Cass (1990), existence is instead obtained through a simple transformation of the maximization problem for the consumer and of the market clearing conditions, transformation which allows me to use the result in Siconolfi (1989).

Finally, Lemmas 3.6-3.11 and Theorem 3.2 contain the proof of the real indeterminacy result - Cass, Siconolfi and Villanacci (1991) do not analyze this problem.

This section is organized as follows. The case in which the risk-free asset is not available is analyzed first. Theorem 3.1 presents the existence result; then the fictitious economies are introduced and studied in Lemmas 3.1-3.4. Using those Lemmas and the rareness of a border line case - Lemma 3.5 - generic nominal indeterminacy is proved in Proposition 3.1, while real indeterminacy in an open and dense subset of the parameter set is shown in theorem 3.2. Then the case in which inside money is available is discussed. Similar results are proved following closely the proofs used in the first case.

All the non trivial proofs are contained in the Appendix.

3.1 Inside money is not available

Here we assume that inside money, described by the vector $\bar{u} \equiv (-1,1,\ldots,1)^T \in \mathbb{R}^{S+1}$, is not available. In this case, Assumptions 2, 3, 4 and 6 become

Assumption 2'. $S > I+1$.

Assumption 3'. rank $[\bar{u}|Y] = I+1$.

Assumption 4'. $\nexists (m^0, a) \in \mathbb{R}^1_+ \times \mathbb{R}^I$ s.th. $[\tilde{u}|Y] \begin{bmatrix} m^0 \\ a \end{bmatrix} \geq 0$.

Assumption 6'. $H > S-(I+1)$.

Define the set of no-arbitrage financial instrument prices as

$Q \equiv \{q \in \mathbb{R}^I: \nexists\ a \in \mathbb{R}^I \text{ s.th. } Ya \geq 0\}$.

Moreover define $\overline{p}^{\cdot 1} \equiv (p^{s1})_{s\neq 0}$, $p^{-} \equiv (p^{01}, (p^{sc})_{c\neq 1})$ and

$\Delta \equiv \{(\overline{p}^{\cdot 1}, e, t,) \in \mathbb{R}^S_+ + \times X \times T: p^{s1}e^{s1}_h > t^s_h - e^m_h$ for $s=1,\ldots,S$ and $h=1,\ldots,H\}$.

Theorem 3.1 An equilibrium exists for any $(e,t) \in X\times T$.

It is now useful to introduce some notation.

$$\phi \equiv \begin{bmatrix} p^0 & & 0 \\ & p^1 & \\ & & \ddots \\ 0 & & p^S \end{bmatrix} \quad ; \quad \tilde{U} \equiv \begin{bmatrix} -1 & 0 \\ 0 & U_S \end{bmatrix},$$

where U_S is the S-dimensional identity matrix; $m_h \equiv (m^0_h, \ldots, m^0_h) \in \mathbb{R}^{S+1}_+$. Using this notation and the slack variable v_h for the non negativity constraint on the demand of outside money, we can rewrite (P2) as follows

$$\max_{x_h, m^0_h, a_h, v_h} \ u_h(x_h) \quad \text{s.t.} \quad \begin{aligned} \phi(x_h - e_h) - \tilde{U}(m_h - t_h) - Y a_h &= 0, \\ m^0_h - v^2_h &= 0 \end{aligned} \tag{P3}$$

Define $\lambda_h \in \mathbb{R}^{S+1}$ and $\mu_h \in \mathbb{R}^1$ as the Lagrange multipliers associated respectively to the first (S+1) and to the last budget constraints in (P3). Given our assumptions on the utility function, the Kuhn-Tucker Theorem gives the following necessary and sufficient conditions for the solution to (P3):

there exist $(x_h, m^0_h, a_h, v_h) \in X \times \mathbb{R}^1_+ \times \mathbb{R}^I \times \mathbb{R}^1$ and $(\lambda_h, \mu_h) \in \mathbb{R}^{S+1}_{++} \times \mathbb{R}^1_+$ such that

$$Du_h(x_h) - \lambda_h \phi = 0 \tag{3.1}$$

$$\lambda_h Y = 0 \tag{3.2}$$

$$\phi(x_h-e_h)-\tilde{U}(m_h-t_h)-Y\ a_h = 0 \quad (3.3)$$

$$\lambda_h\ \tilde{u}+\mu_h = 0 \quad (3.4)$$

$$-2\mu_h\ v_h = 0 \quad (3.5)$$

$$m_h^0-v_h^2 = 0. \quad (3.6)$$

Using (3.5), (3.6) and the fact that $\mu_h \geq 0$, we have that one of the following conditions holds true:

either $m_h^0 = 0$ and $\mu_h > 0$ (3.5a)

or $m_h^0 > 0$ and $\mu_h = 0$ (3.5b)

or $m_h^0 = 0$ and $\mu_h = 0$. (3.5c)

The equilibrium set is

$E \equiv \{(p,q,e,t) \in \Gamma$: (3.1)-(3.6) and (M2.1)-(M2.3) have a solution}.

Remark 3.1 Since $m_h^0 \geq 0$ for any h, given the equilibrium condition $\sum_{h=1}^{H} m_h^0 = \sum_{h=1}^{H} e_h^m$ and the assumption that $\sum_{h=1}^{H} e_h^m > 0$, in equilibrium there exists at least one household h for whom $m_h^0 > 0$.

Remark 3.2 It is easy to verify that a standard application of the Implicit Function Theorem to the First Order Conditions (3.1)-(3.6) does not allow me to conclude that the demand function is differentiable when $m_h^0 = v_h = 0$ and $\mu_h = 0$.

Let's now introduce the fictitious economies. Consider the two following maximization problems and associated necessary and sufficient conditions with a unique solution (from A.1 and Lagrange Theorem).

$$\max_{x_h, m_h^0, a_h} u_h(x_h) \quad \text{s.t.} \quad \phi(x_h-e_h) - U(m_h-t_h) - Ya_h = 0, \quad (P3)$$

$$\begin{cases} (3,1), \quad (3.3) \\ (3.2') \quad \lambda_h[\tilde{u}|Y] = 0; \end{cases} \quad (FOC)$$

$$\max_{x_h, m_h^0, a_h} \quad u_h(x_h) \quad \text{s.t. } \phi(x_h - e_h) - U(m_h - t_h) - Ya_h = 0, \quad m_h^0 = 0 \tag{P3'}$$

$$\begin{cases} (3.1),\ (3.2),\ (3.3),\ (3.4) \\ (3.6) \quad m_h^0 = 0. \end{cases} \tag{FOC'}$$

Define $(\bar{x}_h, \bar{m}_h^0, \bar{a}_h, \bar{\lambda}_h)$ and $(x_h', m_h^{0'}, a_h', \lambda_h', \mu_h')$ the solution functions respectively to (FOC) and (FOC'). With innocuous abuse of notation define $H \equiv \{1,\ldots,H\}$ and also $\underline{H}$ as the set of all subsets of H. Then for every $H' \subseteq H$, define

$$E^{H'} \equiv \{(p,q,e,t) \in \Gamma: \sum_{h \in H'} (x_h' - e_h,\ m_h^{0'} - e_h^m, a_h') + \sum_{h \in \underline{H} \backslash H'} (\tilde{x}_h - e_h,\ \tilde{m}_h^0 - e_h^m,\ \tilde{a}_h) = 0\}$$

Remark 3.3 For every $(p,q,e,t) \in E$, defined H'' as $\{h \in H: m_h^0 > 0$ and $\mu_h = 0\}$ - the set of "unconstrained" consumers - $(p,q,e,t) \in E^{H \backslash H''}$. Moreover, since from Remark 3.1, there exists at least one household h for whom $m_h^0 > 0$, we have $E \subseteq \bigsqcup_{H' \in \underline{H} \backslash H} E^{H'}$.

Lemma 3.1 For every $H' \subseteq \underline{H}$, $E^{H'}$ is a smooth manifold of dimension equal to $\dim(X \times T) + S$.

Remark 3.4 The dimensional result for $E^{H'}$ confirms the intuition obtained using a "counting-of-unknowns-and-equations" approach. The number of unknown variables (p,q,e,t) is $G+I+\dim(X \times T) + S$. The number of independent equations defining $E^{H'}$ is $(G+I+1)-(S+1)$, i.e., (the number of good, financial instruments and outside money markets which have to clear) minus (the $S+1$ "Walras' laws" corresponding to the equations of the budget constraints of each household). Their difference is $\dim(X \times T) + S$.

Define pr: $\Gamma \to \Delta$, $pr(p,q,e,t) = (\overline{p}^{-1},q,e,t)$ $\pi \equiv pr_{|E}$ and $\pi^{H'} \equiv pr_{|E^{H'}}$ for every $H' \in \underline{H}$.

Lemma 3.2 $\pi^{H'}$ is proper.

Define $\mathfrak{R}^{H'}$ as the set of regular values of $\pi^{H'}$.

Lemma 3.3 $\mathfrak{R}' \equiv \bigcap_{H' \in \underline{H}} \mathfrak{R}_{+}^{H'}$ is open and of full measure in Δ.

Lemma 3.4 For every $(\overline{p}^{-1},e,t) \in \mathfrak{R}'$,

(i) $\#\pi^{-1}(\overline{p}^{-1},e,t)$ is positive and finite and

(ii) for every $(p,q,e,t) \in \pi^{-1}(\overline{p}^{-1},e,t)$ there exists a set H' and an open neighborhood V' of (p,q,e,t) in $\mathfrak{R}$ such that $\pi^{H'}_{|U' \cap E'}$ is a diffeomorphism.

Remark 3.5 Observe that even though $(p,q,e,t) \in E$, it is not necessarily true that $U' \cap E^{H'} \subseteq E$, simply because for some h it could be $m_h^0 < 0$.

Restricting $V' \equiv \pi^{H'}(U' \cap E')$ would not eliminate this problem, because for some $h \in H'$ we may have

$$(p,q,e,t) = \mu_h'(p,q,e,t) = 0 \qquad (3.7)$$

and a small perturbation of $(e,t,\overline{p}^{-1})$ - and therefore of $(p^{\sim},q)$ - may lead to a negative demand for money. The way out is to show that we can find an open and full measure subset of $\mathfrak{R}'$ (and therefore of Δ) in which (3.7) does not hold.

Lemma 3.5 There exists an open and full measure set Δ^* in Δ s.th. if $(e,t,\overline{p}^{-1}) \in \Delta^*$ then for any $(e,t,\overline{p}^{-1},p^{\sim},q) \in \pi^{-1}(e,t,p^{-1})$ there is no h s.th. $\mu_h = m_h^0 = 0$.

Defined $\Delta^{**} \equiv \mathfrak{R}' \cap \Delta^*$, from Lemma 3.4, Remark 3.5 and Lemma 3.5, we have

Proposition 3.1 There exists an open and full measure set Δ^{**} in Δ such that for every $(e,t,\bar{p}^{-1}) \in \Delta^{**}$, there exists an open neighborhood V of $(e,t,\bar{p}^{-1})$ in Δ^{**} for which $\pi^{-1}(V)$ is the finite disjoint union of a family of open subsets W_n of E and $\pi_{|W_n}$ is a diffeomorphism for every W_n.

Proposition 3.1 states that generically in the parameter space the equilibrium set exhibits S degrees of nominal indeterminacy. We are now left with showing that price indeterminacy translates into real - i.e., allocation - indeterminacy, at least in an open and dense subset of $X \times T$.

Theorem 3.2 There exists an open and dense set D^* in $X \times T$ such that if $(e,t) \in D^*$, then the set $X_{(e,t)}$ of equilibrium allocations associated to it contains the image of a smooth S dimensional manifold via a one-to-one C^1 function.

Following Balasko and Cass (1989), we are going to prove this theorem in various steps. Because of the particular features of our model, we have to distinguish the two following cases

Case a. There exists at least one household h such that $[m_h^0 = 0$ and $\mu_h > 0]$.

Case b. For any household h, we have $[m_h^0 > 0$ and $\mu_h = 0]$.

Define $\Gamma^* = \pi^{-1}(\Delta^{**})$,

$\Gamma^a \equiv \{(p,q,e,t) \in \Gamma^*: \exists$ h such that $m_h^0 = 0$ and $\mu_h > 0\}$,

$\Gamma^b \equiv \{p,q,e,t) \in \Gamma^*:$ for any h, $m_h^0 > 0$ and $\mu_h^0 = 0\}$,

$(X \times T)^i \equiv \{(e,t) \in X \times T: \exists (p,q) \in \mathbb{R}^G_{++} \times Q$ such that $(p,q,e,t) \in \Gamma^i\}$ for i = a,b.

Remark 3.6 By definition Γ^i and $(X \times T)^i = a,b$, are open in their ambient space and $\Gamma^* = \Gamma^a \cup \Gamma^b$, $X \times T = (X \times T)^a \cup (X \times T)^b$.

In the following, we are going to prove the conclusion of Theorem 3.2

first in $(X\times T)^{a}$ - see Lemmas 3.6, 3.7 and 3.8 - and then in $(X\times T)^{b}$ - see Lemmas 3.9, 3.10 and 3.11 -. Our proof follows the strategy used in Balasko and Cass (1989), Lemmas 4.4.a, b and c. We distinguish between case a and case b because neither proof of Lemma 3.6 nor 3.9 will apply to both cases. (For a more specific comment, see the end of the proof of Lemma 3.6 in the Appendix).

Let's analyze case a. First of all, we have to "get rid of the inside financial instruments". Observe that if good and outside money markets clear, then financial instrument markets clear, too. Moreover we can rewrite the maximization problem (P3) in a way in which assets do not appear, as follows, dropping h,

$$m^0-v^2 = 0$$

$$\begin{bmatrix} p^0,1 & & & & & \\ & \ddots & & & & \\ & & p^n,1 & & & \\ & & & p^{n+1},1 & & \\ & & & & \ddots & \\ & & & & & p^s,1 \end{bmatrix} \begin{bmatrix} x^0-e^0 \\ m^0-e^0 \\ \vdots \\ x^n-e^n \\ -m^0+t^n \\ \hline x^{n+1}-e^{n+1} \\ -m^0+t^{n+1} \\ \vdots \\ x^s-e^s \\ -m^0+t^s \end{bmatrix} = \begin{bmatrix} -q \\ \vdots \\ y^n \\ \hline y^{n+1} \\ \vdots \\ y^3 \end{bmatrix} a.$$

Therefore, using notation consistent with the above partitions, we get

$$\begin{bmatrix} \tilde{p}^{\alpha} & \\ & \tilde{p}^{\alpha} \end{bmatrix} \begin{bmatrix} \tilde{z}^{\alpha} \\ \tilde{z}^{\beta} \end{bmatrix} = \begin{bmatrix} \tilde{Y}^{\alpha}(q) \\ \tilde{Y}^{\beta} \end{bmatrix} a,$$

$$\tilde{p}^{\alpha}\,\tilde{z}^{\alpha} - \tilde{Y}^{\alpha}(q)\cdot[\tilde{Y}^{\beta}]^{-1}\,\tilde{p}^{\beta}\,\tilde{z}^{\beta} = 0.$$

Defined $n \equiv S-I$ and $\tilde{c}(q) \equiv -\tilde{Y}^{\alpha}(q)\cdot[\tilde{Y}^{\beta}]^{-1} \equiv \begin{bmatrix} \tilde{c}^{01}(q) & \dots & \tilde{c}^{0I}(q) \\ \tilde{c}^{11} & \dots & \tilde{c}^{1I} \\ \dots & \dots & \dots \\ \tilde{c}^{n1} & \dots & \tilde{c}^{nI} \end{bmatrix}$

we have

$$\left[\begin{array}{ccc|ccc} p^0,1 & & & \tilde{c}^{01}(q)\cdot(p^{n+1},1) & \dots & \tilde{c}^{0I}(q)\cdot(p^S,1) \\ & \ddots & & \dots & \dots & \dots \\ & & p^n,1 & \tilde{c}^{n1}\cdot(p^{n+1},1) & \dots & \tilde{c}^{nI}\cdot(p^S,1) \end{array}\right] \tilde{z} = 0,$$

or, shortly, $\tilde{\psi}(p,q)\tilde{z} = 0$.

Therefore the household's problem is

$$\max_{x,m^0} u(x) \quad \text{s.t.} \quad \tilde{\psi}(p,q)\tilde{z} = 0 \text{ and } m^0-v^2 = 0.$$

The associated First Order Conditions are

$$Du(x) - \lambda\, \psi(p,q) = 0 \qquad (3.7)$$

$$\alpha^0(q)\, \lambda^0 + \sum_{s=1}^{n} \alpha^s\, \lambda^s+\mu = 0 \qquad (3.8)$$

$$\tilde{\psi}(p,q)\, \tilde{z} = 0 \qquad (3.9)$$

$$m^0-v^2 = 0 \qquad (3.10)$$

$$\mu\, v = 0 \qquad (3.11)$$

where

$$\psi(p,q) = \left[\begin{array}{ccc|ccc} p^0 & & & \dots & & \dots \\ & \ddots & & & \tilde{c}^{sk}p^{n+k} & \\ & & p^n & \dots & & \dots \end{array}\right],$$

$$\alpha^0(q) \equiv -1 + \sum_{k=1}^{I} \tilde{c}^{0k}(q), \quad \alpha^s \equiv 1 + \sum_{k=1}^{I} \tilde{c}^{sk}, \; s = 1,\dots,n$$

Now define $D_0^{-1}(x_0) \equiv \begin{bmatrix} D_{x^{01}} u_1(x_1) & \dots & D_{x^{n1}} u_1(x_1) \\ \dots & \dots & \dots \\ D_{x^{01}} u_{n+1}(x_{n+1}) & \dots & D_{x^{n1}} u_{n+1}(x_{n+1}) \end{bmatrix}$

$V^a \equiv \{(\bar{p}^{\,1},e,t) \in \Delta^{**}: \exists(p^{\sim},q) \text{ s.th. } (\bar{p}^{\,1},p^{\sim},q,e,t) \in \Gamma^a\}$,

$x_0(p,q,e,t) \equiv (x_h(p,q,e,t))_{h=1}^{n+1}$,

$\tilde{V}^a \equiv \{(\bar{p}^{\,1},e,t) \in V^a: \exists(p,q,e,t) \in \pi^{-1}(\bar{p}^{\,1},e,t) \text{ s.th.}$

$\text{rank } D_0^{-1}x_0(p,q,e,t) = n+1\}$,

$(X\tilde{\times}T)^a \equiv \{(e,t) \in X\times T: \exists\, \bar{p}^{\,1} \in \mathbb{R}^S_{++} \text{ for which } (\bar{p}^{\,1},e,t) \in \tilde{V}^a\}$

$\hat{P}_{(e,t)} \equiv \{(p,q) \in \mathbb{R}^G_{++}\times Q: (p,q,e,t) \in E\}$.

__Lemma 3.6__ $\tilde{V}^a$ is open and dense in V^a.

__Lemma 3.7__ (α) $(X\tilde{\times}T)^a$ is open and dense in $(X\times T)^a$;
(β) if $(e,t) \in (X\tilde{\times}T)^a$, then $\hat{P}_{(e,t)}$ contains a smooth S dimensional submanifold $\hat{P}^{\sim}_{(e,t)}$ such that if $(p,q) \in \hat{P}^{\sim}_{(e,t)}$ then
rank $D_0^{-1}(x_0(p,q,e,t)) = n+1$.

The proof of Lemma 3.2. is a slight modification of Lemma 4.4.b in Balasko and Cass (1989).

__Lemma 3.8__ The set of equilibrium allocations associated to any (e,t) in $(X\tilde{\times}T)^a$ contains the image of a smooth S dimensional manifold via a C^1 one-to-one function.

Now we can analyze case b: (for any h, $m_h^0 > 0$ and $\mu_h = 0$). Being the structure of the proofs very similar to that one of case a, we will be rather sketchy. In case b, we are going to "get rid of __both__ financial instruments __and__ outside money". Observe that if good markets clear, then financial instruments and outside money markets clear. Moreover, we can rewrite the maximization problem (P3) in a way in which both financial instruments and money do not appear as follows, dropping h,

$$\begin{bmatrix} p^0 & & & & & \\ & \ddots & & & & \\ & & p^{n-1} & & & \\ & & & p^n & & \\ & & & & \ddots & \\ & & & & & p^S \end{bmatrix} \begin{bmatrix} z^0 \\ \vdots \\ z^{n-1} \\ \hline z^n \\ \vdots \\ z^S \end{bmatrix} \begin{bmatrix} -e^0 \\ \vdots \\ t^{n-1} \\ \hline t^n \\ \vdots \\ t^S \end{bmatrix} \begin{bmatrix} -1 & -q \\ \vdots & \vdots \\ 1 & y^{n-1} \\ \hline 1 & y^n \\ \vdots & \vdots \\ 1 & y^S \end{bmatrix} \begin{pmatrix} m^0 \\ a \end{pmatrix},$$

i.e., using notation consistent with the above partitions,

$$\begin{bmatrix} p^\alpha & \\ & p^\beta \end{bmatrix} \begin{bmatrix} z^\alpha \\ z^\beta \end{bmatrix} + \begin{bmatrix} Y^\alpha(q) \\ Y^\beta \end{bmatrix} \begin{pmatrix} m^0 \\ a \end{pmatrix}.$$

Therefore the household's maximization problem (P3) can be rewritten as

$$\max_{x,v} u(x) \quad \text{s.t.} \quad \chi(p,q)\, z + \hat{t}(q) = 0$$
$$\beta(P^\beta z^\beta + t^\beta) - v^2 = 0, \tag{P4}$$

where $\chi(p,q) \equiv [p^\alpha | C(q)\, p^\beta]$, $C(q) \equiv -Y^\alpha(q)\cdot[Y^\beta]^{-1}$, $\hat{t}(q) \equiv t^\alpha + C(q)\, t^\beta$, $\beta \equiv$ (first row of $[Y^\beta]^{-1}$).

From the First Order Conditions of (P4), using the fact that $\mu = 0$, we also get

$$Du(x) = (\lambda^0, \ldots, \lambda^{n-1}) \begin{bmatrix} p^0 & & & \vert & c^{01}(q)\cdot p^n & \ldots & c^{0,I+1}(q)\cdot p^S \\ & \ddots & & \vert & \ldots & \ldots & \ldots \\ & & p^{n-1} & \vert & c^{n-1,1}p^n & \ldots & c^{n-1,I+1}p^S \end{bmatrix}.$$

Define

$$\hat{D}_0^{\cdot 1}(x_0) \equiv \begin{bmatrix} D_{x^{01}}\, u_1(x_1) & \dots & D_{x^{n-1,2}} u_1(x_1) \\ \dots & \dots & \dots \\ D_{x^{01}}\, u_n(x_n) & \dots & D_{x^{n-1,1}}\, u_n(x_n) \end{bmatrix}.$$

$V^b \equiv \{(p^{\cdot 1},e,t) \in \Delta^{**}: \exists (p^{\sim},q) \text{ s.th. } (\overline{p}^{\cdot 1},p^{\sim},q,e,t) \in \Gamma^b\}$,

$\hat{x}_0(p,q,e,t) \equiv (x_h(p,q,e,t))_{h=1}^n$,

$\tilde{V}^b \equiv \{(\overline{p}^{\cdot 1},e,t) \in V^b: \exists (p,q,e,t) \in \pi^{-1}(\overline{p}^{\cdot 1},e,t) \text{ s.th. rank } \hat{D}_0^{\cdot 1}(\hat{x}_0(p,q,e,t))$

$(X\tilde{\times}T)^b = \{(e,t) \in X{\times}T: \exists\, \overline{p}^{\cdot 1} \in \mathbb{R}^S_{++} \text{ for which } (\overline{p}^{\cdot 1},e,t) \in \tilde{V}^b\}$.

Following closely the analysis of case a, we get the following corresponding results

Lemma 3.9 $\tilde{V}^b$ is open and dense in V^b.

Lemma 3.10 (α) $(X\tilde{\times}T)^b$ is open and dense in $(X{\times}T)^b)$;
(β) if $(e,t) \in (X\tilde{\times}T)^b$, then $\hat{P}_{(e,t)}$ contains a smooth S dimensional submanifold $\hat{P}^{\wedge}_{(e,t)}$ such that if $(p,q) \in \hat{P}^{\wedge}_{(e,t)}$, then rank $\hat{D}_0^{\cdot 1}(\hat{x}_0(p,q,e,t)) = n$.

Lemma 3.11 The set of equilibrium allocations associated to any (e,t) in $(X\tilde{\times}T)^b$ contains the image of a smooth S dimensional manifold via a C^1 one-to-one function.

3.2 Inside money is available

We assume that inside money $(-q^1,1,\dots,1)$ is available. In fact, because of Assumption 4 and the fact that $\sum_{h=1}^{H} e_h^m > 0$, in equilibrium $q^1 = 1$. Therefore, the financial structure is described by

$$Y = [\tilde{u}|Y^{\backslash 1}], \text{ where } Y^{\backslash 1} \equiv \begin{bmatrix} -q^2 & \cdots & -q^I \\ y^{12} & \cdots & y^{1I} \\ \vdots & & \vdots \\ y^{S2} & \cdots & y^{SI} \end{bmatrix} = \begin{bmatrix} -q^{\backslash 1} \\ y^{1\backslash 1} \\ \vdots \\ y^{S\backslash 1} \end{bmatrix} = \begin{bmatrix} -q^{\backslash 1} \\ \overline{Y}^{\backslash 1} \end{bmatrix}.$$

Assumptions 2, 3, 4 and 6 become

Assumption 2". $S > I$.

Assumption 3". $\text{rank } Y = I$.

Assumption 4". $\nexists\ \alpha \in \mathbb{R}^I$ s.th. $Y\alpha \geq 0$.

Assumption 6". $H > S-I$.

The availability of inside money allows me to get rid of the nonnegativity constraint on the demand of outside money and to rewrite the household's maximization problem as follows

$$\max_{x_h, a_h^1, a_h^{\backslash 1}} u_h(x_h) \quad \text{s.t.} \quad p^0(x_h^0 - e_h^0) + \alpha_h^1 - e_h^m = -q^{\backslash 1} a_h^{\backslash 1}$$
$$p^s(x_h^s - e_h^s) - (a_h^1 - t_h^s) = y^{s\backslash 1} a_h^{\backslash 1}, \; s=1,\ldots,S, \tag{P5}$$

where $\alpha_h^I \equiv m_h^0 + a_h^I$ and $\alpha_h \equiv (\alpha_h^I, a_h^2, \ldots, a_h^I) \equiv (a_h^I, a_h^{\backslash 1})$.

The market clearing conditions are

$$\sum_{h=1}^{H} (x_h - e_h) = 0, \; \sum_{h=1}^{H} a_h^{\backslash 1} = 0, \; \sum_{h=1}^{H} (a_h^1 - e_h^m) = 0.$$

Remark 3.7 Given that households are indifferent between inside and outside money, we can assume that they hold suitable offsetting quantities of inside money. This allows me to rewrite the money market clearing condition as

$$\sum_{h=1}^{H} (\alpha_h^1 - e_h^m) = 0, \text{ with } \alpha_h^1 = m_h^0 + a_h^1.$$

Define the set of no-arbitrage financial instruments prices as

$Q^{\backslash 1} = \{q^{\backslash 1} \in \mathbb{R}^{I-1}: \nexists\, a^{\backslash 1} \in \mathbb{R}^{I-1}$ s.th. $Y^{\backslash 1} a^{\backslash 1} \geq 0\}$ and

$\Gamma^{\backslash 1} \equiv \{(p,q^{\backslash 1},e,t) \in \mathbb{R}^G_{++} \times Q^{\backslash 1} \times X \times T: p^{s1}e_h^{s1} > t_h^s - e_h^m,$ for $s=1,\ldots,S$ and $h=1,\ldots,H\}$.

With some abuse of notation, define the solution to (P5) as

$x_h(p,q,e,t)$, $a_h^{\backslash 1}(p,q,e,t)$, $\alpha_h^1(p,q,e,t)$ and

$$z(p,q,e,t) = \sum_{h=1}^{H} (x_h(p,q,e,t) - e_h),$$

$$a_{\backslash 1}(p,q,e,t) = \sum_{h=1}^{H} a_h^{\backslash 1}(p,q,e,t),$$

$$\xi(p,q,e,t) = \sum_{h=1}^{H} (\alpha_h^1(p,q,e,t) - e_h^m).$$

Therefore the equilibrium set is

$E \equiv \{p,q^{\backslash 1},e,t) \in \Gamma^{\backslash 1}: z(p,q^{\backslash 1},e,t) = 0,\ a^{\backslash 1}(p,q^{\backslash 1},e,t) = 0$ and

$\xi(p,q^{\backslash 1},e,t) = 0\}$.

Using proofs which follow closely those of subsection 3.1, we can show the following results.

Lemma 3.12 E is a smooth manifold of dimension $\dim(X \times T) + S$.

Theorem 3.3 An equilibrium exists for any $(e,t) \in X \times T$.

Theorem 3.4 There exists an open and dense set D in $X \times T$ such that if $(e,t) \in D$, then the set of equilibrium allocations associated to it contains the image of a one-to-one C^1 function with domain an S dimensional smooth manifold.

4. Other Specifications of the Set of Endowments of Outside Money and Taxes

In this section, we analyze the following cases.

Case 1 $\sum_h e_h^m = \sum_h t_h^s$ for some s and $\sum_h e_h^m < \sum_h t_h^s$ for some other s, i.e., taxes may be more exacting than households can afford.

Case 2 $\sum_h e_h^m = \sum_h t\text{-}h^s$ for some s and $\sum_h e_h^m > \sum_h t_h^s$ for some other s, i.e., aggregate endowment of outside money in period zero may be larger than aggregate taxes in some states of in period one.

Case 3 $0 = \sum_{h=1}^{H} e\text{-}h^m = \sum_{h=1}^{H} t_h^s$ for $s=1,\ldots,S$, i.e.,

e_h^m, t_h^s are interpreted as taxes or subsides, so that $t \in \mathbb{R}_h^{H(S+1)}$ and they just redistribute endowments in each state of the world.

Clearly in Case 1 there is no equilibrium because the budget set of some household is empty, no matter which (p,q,q^m) she or he is facing. Therefore, the analysis of this model requires further assumptions. Household may be allowed to use goods (or one specific good, say gold) to pay taxes. Other assumptions about the use of the goods collected by the government have to be made: the government may destroy or redistribute freely or sell the goods. I plan to analyze this problem in a subsequent paper.

In Case 2, the set of possible taxes is

$$T^* \equiv \{t \in \mathbb{R}_{++}^{H(S+1)} : \sum_h e_h^m = \sum_{h=1}^{H} t_h^s \text{ for } s \in S^* \text{ and } \sum_{h=1}^{H} e_h^m > \sum_{h=1}^{H} t_h^s \text{ for } s \notin S^*\},$$

where $S^* \subset \{1,..,S\}$. The proofs presented in section 3 easily apply with minor modifications. Let's briefly state the main results.

(i) The equilibrium set is a smooth manifold of dimension $\dim(X\times T^*)+S$ (once you have normalized the (S^*+1) money prices).

(ii) An equilibrium exists for any $(e,t) \in X\times T^*$.

(iii) In an open and dense subset of $X\grave{a}T^{*}$, the set of equilibrium allocations contains a smooth manifold of dimension equal to $\#S^{*}$.

The reason for which we get a lower degree of real indeterminacy is that if $\sum_h (e_h^m - t_h^s) > 0$ then $q^{sm} = 0$, so that the budget constraint in state s becomes $p^s(x_h^s - e_h^s) = 0$ and the nominal degree of indeterminacy in that state does not translate in real indeterminacy.

The slightly stronger form of result (iii) with respect to Theorem 3.2. is due to the fact that we can normalize good prices for $s \notin S^{*}$.

Observe also that we do not get indeterminacy if $S^{*} = \phi$.

Remark 4.1 The analysis of Case 2 covers the case in which $\sum_h (e_h^m - t_h^s) = 0$ and $q^{sm} = 0$ for some s. This shows that our analysis apply not only to the case $q^m \in \mathbb{R}_{++}^{S+1}$, but to the more general case $q^m \in \mathbb{R}_{+}^{S+1}$.

In Case 3, in equilibrium, there is no demand of outside money. Moreover defined $T^0 \equiv \{t \in \mathbb{R}^{H(S+1)}: 0 = \sum_{h=1}^{H} e_h^m = \sum_{h=1}^{H} t_h^s,$ for $s=1,\ldots S\}$, we have the following results.

(i) The equilibrium set is a smooth manifold of dimension $\dim(X \times T^0) + S+1$;

(ii) An equilibrium exists for any $(e,t) \in X \times T^0$;

(iii) In an open and dense subset of $X \times T^0$ the set of equilibrium allocations contains the image of a smooth $(S+1)$ dimensional manifold via a C^1 one-to-one function.

Appendix

Proof of Theorem 3.1

Define $a_h^0 \equiv m_h^m - e_h^m$, $\dot{a}_h \equiv (a_h^0, a_h)$, $\dot{q} \equiv (q^{0m}, q)$, $\dot{e}_h^{s1} \equiv e_h^{s1} - (t_h^s - e_h^m)/p^{s1}$, $\dot{e}_h^s = (\dot{e}_h^{s1}, e_h^{s2}, \ldots, e_h^{sC})$, $\dot{y}^s = (1, y^s)$ for $s=1,\ldots,S$ and $h=1,\ldots,H$. Then consider the consumer's maximization problem

and the associated market clearing conditions $\sum_{h=1}^{H} (\tilde{x}_h - \tilde{e}_h) = 0$ and $\sum_{h=1}^{H} \tilde{a}_h = 0$.

$$\max_{\tilde{x}_h, b_h} u_h(\tilde{x}_h) \quad \text{s.t.} \quad p^0(\tilde{x}_h^0 - e_h^0) + \tilde{q}\tilde{a}_h = 0$$

$$b_h^0 + e_h^m \geq 0$$

$$p^s(\tilde{x}_h^s - \tilde{e}_h^s) - \tilde{y}^s\tilde{a}_h = 0,$$

The above economy is a particular case of that one studied in Siconolfi (1989) and all the assumptions adopted there are satisfied (while assumption A.3 is trivially satisfied, A.4 is because $e_h^m > 0$ and A.5 because $[\dot{u}|Y]$ has full rank). In Siconolfi (1989), an equilibrium exists for every value of the endowment vector and for every vector of prices normalized spot by spot in period 1. This freedom of choice allows me to choose p^{s1} to guarantee the strict positivity of $\hat{e}_h^{s1}$.

Proof of Lemma 3.1

From the argument used in Balasko and Cass (1988), the derivatives of (FOC) and (FOC') have full rank, therefore, from the Implicit Function Theorem, $(\tilde{x}_h, \tilde{m}_h^0, \tilde{a}_h)$ and $(\tilde{x}_{h'}, m_h^{0'}, a_h')$ are differentiable. Since $H' \neq H$, there exist at least one h solving (P3). Therefore to apply the preimage theorem it suffices to show that rank $D_{e_h}(\tilde{x}_h - e_h, \tilde{m}_h^0, \tilde{a}_h) = G - (S+1) + I + 1$, which follows from the standard argument - see Balasko and Cass (1991).

Proof of Lemma 3.2

Given a compact set C in Δ, we want to show that an arbitrary sequence $\{(p^n, q^n, e^n, t^n)\}_n \subseteq (\pi^{H'})^{-1}(C)$ converges in $(\pi^{H'})^{-1}(C)$, exploiting the fact that $\{\bar{p}^{\cdot 1n}, e^{n,1}n\}_n$ converges in C. Because of the definition of $\pi^{H'}$ we have to verify that sequences of solutions to (FOC'), for $h \epsilon H'$ and to (FOC) (for $h \epsilon H \backslash H'$, converge to limits which are solutions to (FOC') and (FOC) respectively and satisfy the market clearing conditions. Consider first an arbitrary sequence of solutions to (FOC) $(\tilde{x}_h^n, \tilde{m}_h^{0n}, \tilde{a}_h^n, \tilde{\lambda}_h^n)$ and for easy notation drop the "~". From the market clearing conditions, x_h^n is bounded above; since $m_h^0 = 0$, e_h^n belongs to the budget set and therefore, from

Assumption 1, x_h^n is bounded away from zero, we can conclude that $x_h^n \to x_h \in \mathbf{R}_{++}^{G}$.

From (3.1), $\lambda_h^{sn} \to \frac{D_{x^{s1}} u_h(x_h)}{p^{s1}} \equiv \lambda_h^s > 0$ for $s=1,\ldots,S$.

From (3.4), $\lambda_n^{0n} = \sum_{s=1}^{S} \lambda_h^{sn} \to \sum_{s=1}^{S} \lambda_h^s > 0$. From (3.1), $p^n \to p > 0$. From (3.2) and Assumption 5, $q^n \to q \in Q$. With respect to (FOC′), we have that

$\lambda_h^{s'n} \to \frac{D_{x^{1s}} u_h(x_h')}{p^1} > 0$ and - from (3.4) - $\mu_h' \to -\lambda_h \tilde{u}$.

We are now left showing that $(p,q,e,t) \in (\pi^{H'})^{-1}(\bar{p}^1,e,t) \subseteq (\pi^{H'})^{-1}(C)$. This result follows from the continuity of the demand function generated by (FOC) and (FOC′), which is a consequence of Berge's Theorem.

Proof of Lemma 3.3

$\mathfrak{R}'$ has full measure from Sard's Theorem. Moreover, defined $E^{H'}$ the set of critical points of $\pi^{H'}$, $\mathfrak{R}^{H'} = \Delta \backslash \pi^{H'}(E^{H'})$. Since $E^{H'}$ is closed and, from Lemma 3.2, $\pi^{H'}$ is proper, $\mathfrak{R}^{H'}$ and $\mathfrak{R}'$ are open.

Proof of Lemma 3.4

(i) $\pi^{-1}(e,t) \subset \bigsqcup_{H'} (\pi^{H'})^{-1}(e,t)$, from Remark 3.3. Since (e,t) is a regular value of $\pi^{H'}$ for some $H' \subseteq H$ - and $\pi^{H'}$ is proper, $(\pi^{H'})^{-1}(e,t)$ is compact and the result follows - see Balasko 1988, Math 2.6.

(ii) It follows from the Stack of Records Theorem - See Guillemin and Pollak (1974), page 26 - and the facts that (e,t) is a regular value of $\pi^{H'}$, $E^{H'}$ is a smooth mainfold of the same dimension of Δ and $\pi^{H'}$ is proper.

Proof of Lemma 3.5

The proof is an application of the Transversality Theorem - see for example, Guillemin and Pollak, (1974), page 68.

First of all observe that, as a consequence of Fact 2.1 and Assumption 3', if goods markets clear, all markets clear. Without loss of generality, assume that $\mu_{\hat{h}}^{0} = m_{\hat{h}} = 0$. Define

$$F:\ \mathbf{R}_{++}^{GH}\times\mathbf{R}^{IH}\times\mathbf{R}_{++}^{(S+1)H}\times\mathbf{R}^{\#H'}\times\Gamma \to \mathbf{R}^{GH}\times\mathbf{R}^{IH}\times\mathbf{R}^{H}\times\mathbf{R}^{(S+1)H}\times\mathbf{R}^{H'}\times\mathbf{R}^{G}\times\mathbf{R}^{I},$$

$$F((\tilde{x}_h,\tilde{a}_h,\tilde{m}_h^0,\tilde{\lambda}_h)_{h\in H\backslash H'} \equiv \tilde{\alpha},(x_h',a_h',{}_h^{0'},\lambda_h',\mu_h')_{h\in H'} \equiv (\alpha',\alpha_{\hat{h}}),(e_h,t_h)_{h\in H},p,q) =$$

$$= ((\text{FOC})\ \text{for}\ h\in H\backslash H',(\text{FOC}')\ \text{for}\ H\in H',\ \sum_{h\in H'}(x_h'-e_h) + \sum_{h\in H\backslash H'}(\tilde{x}_h-e_h),\mu_{\hat{h}}).$$

Using the fact that the derivatives of (FOC) and (FOC′) with respect to $(\tilde{x}_h,\tilde{a}_h,\tilde{m}_h^0,\tilde{\lambda}_h)$ and $(x_h',a_h',m_h^0,\lambda_h',\mu_h')$, respectively, have full rank and through elementary operations on columns and rows of the derivative of F with respect to $(\tilde{\alpha},\alpha',p,q,t_{\hat{h}},m_{\hat{h}}^0,\mu_{\hat{h}},e_{\hat{h}},\lambda_{\hat{h}})$ is possible to show that rank DF is full. Define $F_{|(e,t,\overline{p}^{\cdot 1})}$ as the function F for given $(e,t,\overline{p}^{\cdot 1})$. Then from the Transversality Theorem, we know that in a full measure subset $\Delta_{\hat{h}}^{H'*}$ of Δ^*, $(F_{|(e,t,\overline{p}^{\cdot 1})})^{-1}(0)$ is empty (it is a "manifold of dimension I-(S+I) < 0"). In other words, for any $(e^*,t^*,\overline{p}^{\cdot 1*})\in\Delta_{\hat{h}}^{H'*}$ there is no $(e^*,t^*,\overline{p}^{\cdot 1*},p^{\sim *},q^*)\in E^{H'}$ s.th. the associated $\mu_{\hat{h}}$ and $m_{\hat{h}}^0$ are both equal to zero. Clearly $\Delta_{\hat{h}}^{H'*}$ is open too.

Consider $\Delta^* \equiv \bigsqcup_{H'\in H\backslash H}\ \bigsqcup_{\hat{h}\in H'} \Delta_{\hat{h}}^{H'*} =$

$= \{(e,t,\overline{p}^{\cdot 1})\in\Delta:$ for any $(e,t,\overline{p}^{\cdot 1},p^{\sim},q)\in \bigsqcup_{H'\in H\backslash H} (\pi^{H'})^{-1}(e,t,\overline{p}^{\cdot 1})$,

there is no h s.th. $\mu_h(e,t,\overline{p}^{\cdot 1},p^{\sim},q) = m_h^0(e,t,\overline{p}^{\cdot 1},p^{\sim},q)^{\sim}=^{\sim}0\}$.

Since $\pi^{-1}(e,t,\overline{p}^{\cdot 1}) \subseteq \bigsqcup_{H'\in H\backslash H} (\pi^{H'})^{-1}(e,t,\overline{p}^{\cdot 1})$, the desired result follows.

Proof of Lemma 3.6

$\tilde{V}^a$ is clearly open. Let's show that it is dense too.

Rewrite (3.7) as

$$Du(x) = (\overline{\lambda}^0, \ldots, \overline{\lambda}^n) =$$

$$\left[\begin{array}{c|cccc} 1,\overline{p}^0 & \tilde{c}^{01}(q)\,\frac{p^{n+1,1}}{p^{01}}\,(1,\overline{p}^{n+1}) & \ldots & \tilde{c}^{0I}(q)\,\frac{p^{S,1}}{p^{01}}\,(1,\overline{p}^{S}) \\ \ddots & \ldots & \ldots & \ldots \\ 1,\overline{p}^n & \tilde{c}^{n1}\,\frac{p^{n+1,1}}{p^{n1}}\,(1,\overline{p}^{n+1}) & \ldots & \tilde{c}^{nI}\,\frac{p^{S,1}}{p^{n1}}\,(1,\overline{p}^{S}) \end{array}\right], \qquad (A.1)$$

where $\overline{\lambda}^s \equiv \lambda^s p^{s1}$ for $s=0,1,\ldots,n$, $\overline{p}^s \equiv (\frac{p^{sc}}{p^{s1}}$ for $s=0,1,\ldots,S$, so that, shortly and with obvious notation, $0 = Du(x) - \overline{\lambda}\;\overline{\Psi}(p,q)$. Observe that

$$D_0^{\cdot 1}\,(x_0(p,q,e,t)) = \begin{bmatrix} (\overline{\lambda}_1^s)_{s=0}^n \\ \vdots \\ (\overline{\lambda}_{n+1}^s)_{s=0}^n \end{bmatrix}_{(n+1)\times(n+1)}.$$

Therefore, we have to show that "det $[\overline{\lambda}_h]_{h=1}^{n+1} \neq 0$" is a dense property. Now, take $(\overline{p}^{\cdot 1'}, e', t') \notin \tilde{V}^a$. We want to show that in any arbitrary neighborhood V' of $(\overline{p}^{\cdot 1'}, e't')$, we can find $(\overline{p}^{\cdot 1}, e, t) \in \tilde{V}^a$.

Take $(p,q) \in \hat{P}_{(e',t')}$ and such that $(\overline{p}^{\cdot 1'}, p^{\sim})$, and $(x_h' = x_h(p,q,e',t'), m_h^{0'} \equiv m_h^0(p,q,e',t'), \lambda_h' \equiv \lambda_h(p,q,e',t'), v' \equiv v(p,q,e',t'))_{h=1}^H$. Then we get

$$\frac{Du_h(x_h')}{D_{x^{01}}u_h(x_h')} - \frac{\overline{\lambda}_h'}{\overline{\lambda}_h^{0'}}\,\overline{\Psi}(p,q) = 0, \quad \text{for } h=1,\ldots,H. \qquad (A.2)$$

Now, keep (p,q) fixed. Consider $(n+1)$ households among which, without loss of generality, $n_1 > 0$ are s.th. $(m_h^0 = 0$ and $\mu_h > 0)$ and n_2 are s.th. $(m_h^0 > 0$ and $\mu_h = 0)$. We want to perturb λ's (and endowments) of those households so that

$$\det [\lambda_h^s]_{\substack{s=0,\dots,n \\ h=1,\dots,n+1}} \equiv \det \Lambda^* \neq 0$$

and (p,q) are equilibrium prices for well chosen (e,t) such that $(\bar{p}^{\cdot 1},e,t) \in V' \cap \tilde{V}^a$.

Consider the equation (3.8) of those households:

$$\alpha^0(q)\ \lambda_1^0 \quad +\dots+\ \alpha^n\ \lambda_1^n + \mu_1 \qquad = 0 \qquad \text{(A.3.1)}$$

$$\dots$$

$$\alpha^0(q)\ \lambda_{n_1}^0 \quad +\dots+ \quad \alpha^n\ \lambda_{n_1}^n + \mu_{n_1} \qquad = 0 \qquad \text{(A.3.}n_1\text{)}$$

$$\alpha^0(q)\ \lambda_{n_1+1} +\dots+ \alpha^n\ \lambda_{n_1+1} \qquad = 0 \qquad \text{(A.3.}n_1\text{+1)}$$

$$\dots$$

$$\alpha^0(q)\lambda_{n+1}^0 \quad +\dots+\ \alpha^n\ \lambda_{n+1}^n \qquad = 0 \qquad \text{(A.3.n+1)}$$

Define Λ_k^s, $s=0,1,\dots,n$, $k=1,\dots,n+1$, as the matrix obtained from Λ^* deleting the s-th column and the k-th row. Now do the following:

1. Perturb λ's in Λ_1^n so that $\det \Lambda_1^n \neq 0$.
2. Adjust $\lambda_2^n,\dots,\lambda_{n}^n,\lambda_{n_1+1}^n,\dots,\lambda_{n+1}^n$ so that equations $(\text{A.3.s})_{s=2}^{n+1}$ are still satisfied.
3. If $\det \Lambda^* \neq 0$, stop; if $\det \Lambda^* = \sum_{s=0}^{n} (-1)^{1+1+s}\lambda_1^s \det \Lambda_1^s = 0$, then perturb λ_1^n; being $\det \Lambda_1^n \neq 0$ (from step 1) and because λ_1^n does not appear in any Λ_1^s, you perturb $\det \Lambda^*$ too, so that you can get it different from zero, as wanted. Again, being det a continuous function, the perturbation can be as small as you want.
4. Adjust μ_1 so that equation (A.3.1) is satisfied.

Perturbations in $(\lambda_h^s)_{s=0}^{n+1}$ imply perturbations in $(\bar{\lambda}_h)_{s=0}^n$ and $\left(\frac{\bar{\lambda}_h^s}{\bar{\lambda}_h^0}\right)_{s=0}^n$.
Through (A.2), they imply perturbations in $\frac{Du_h(x_h')}{D_{x^{01}}u_h(x_h')}$, which, because of the diffeomorphism η: $\mathbf{R}_{++}^{G-1}\times\mathbf{R}^1\to\mathbf{R}^G$, η: $(p,q_h) \to$ (Walrasian demand associated to prices p and income w_h) - see theorem 2.4.1 in Balasko (1988) - imply perturbations in x_h'. Choose x_h so that $\frac{Du_h(x_h)}{D_{x^{01}}u_h(x_h)} = \left(\frac{\bar{\lambda}_h^s}{\bar{\lambda}_h^0}\right)_{s=0}^n \bar{\Psi}(p,q)$, for $h=1,\dots,n+1$, and $x_h=x_h'$ for $h=n+2,\dots,H$. Consistently with the

perturbations of $(\lambda_h)_{n+1}^{n+1}$, take $m_m^0 = m_h^{0'}$, $v_h = v_h'$ for $h=1,\ldots,H$, and $\mu_h=\mu_h'$ for $h\neq 1$. For $h=1$, choose μ_1 consistently with step 4 above. Finally, choose $(\bar{p}^{\cdot 1}, e, t) = (\bar{p}^{\cdot 1'}, (e_h'+x_h-x_h')_{h=1}^{n+1}, (e_h')_{h=n+2)}^{H}, t') \in V' \cap \tilde{V}^a$, so that $(x_h, m_h^0, v_h^0)_{h=1}^{H}$ are the equilibrium choices at (p,q,e,t), by construction.

Observe that we cannot apply this proof to the case in which $\mu_h=0$ for any h, simply because in that case equations (A.3) imply that $(\lambda_h)_{h+1}^{n+1}$ are always linearly dependent vectors.

Proof of Lemma 3.7

Rearrange equation (A.1) as follows

$$\begin{bmatrix} & | & \\ D^{\cdot 1}u_h(x_h) & & D^{\setminus 1}u_h(x_h) \\ & | & \end{bmatrix} = \bar{\lambda}_h \begin{bmatrix} 1 & & & | \; \bar{p}^0 & & | \; \ldots & \ldots \\ & \ddots & & | & \ddots & | \; \tilde{c}^{sk}\dfrac{p^{n+k,1}}{p^{s1}} & (1,\bar{p}^{n+k}) \\ & & 1 & | & \bar{p}^n & | \; \ldots & \ldots \end{bmatrix},$$

where $D^{\cdot 1}u_h(x_h) \equiv (D_{x^{s1}}u_h(x_h))_{s=n}^{n}$ and $D^{\setminus 1}u_h(x_h) \equiv (D_{x^{sc}}u_h(x_h))_{s\neq 0,1,\ldots,n}$.

Therefore,

$$\begin{bmatrix} D^{\cdot 1}u_1(x_1) & | \; D^{\setminus 1}u_1(x_1) \\ \ldots & | \; \ldots \\ D^{\cdot 1}u_{n+1}(x_{n+1}) & | \; D^{\setminus 1}u_{n+1}(x_{n+1}) \end{bmatrix} = \begin{bmatrix} \bar{\lambda}_1 \\ \ldots \\ \bar{\lambda}_{n+1} \end{bmatrix} \begin{bmatrix} & | & | \\ U_{n+1} & \ldots & \ldots \\ & | & | \end{bmatrix}.$$

Multiplying both sides by the full rank matrix $D_0^{\cdot 1} \equiv [D^{\cdot 1}u_h(x_h)]_{h=1}^{n+1} = [\bar{\lambda}_h]_{h=1}^{n+1}$, we get

$$[U_{n+1} | [D_0^{\cdot 1}]^{-1} \; [D^{\setminus 1}u_h(x_h)]_{h=1}^{n+1}] = [U_{n+1} | \ldots | \ldots]. \tag{A.4}$$

We have now to show that

$x_{(e,t)}: \hat{P}^{\sim}{}_{(e,t)} \times \{(e,t)\} \to X$, $x_{(e,t)}: (p,q) \to (x_h(p,q,e,t))_{h=1}^{H}$ is a smooth one-to-one function. $x_{(e,t)}$ is smooth because x_h is smooth for any h. To show that $x_{(e,t)}$ is one-to-one, we have to verify that if $x' \equiv x_{(e,t)}(p',q') = x_{(e,t)}(p,q) \equiv x$, then $(p',q') = (p,q)$. This result comes from the following two facts

(i) using (A.4), $x'=x$ implies that, for some $\gamma \in \mathbb{R}^{I}_{++}$, $p'=\gamma p$ and $q'=q$;

(ii) using the budget constraints, generically in T, $\gamma=1$.

Summary of the Basic Notation

There are

C commodities in each spot, labelled by superscript $c=1,2,\ldots,C$,

S+1 states, labelled by superscript $s=0,1,\ldots,S$,

$C(S+1) \equiv G$ goods, labelled by the pair (sc),

H households, labelled by subscript $h=1,2,\ldots,H$.

I financial instruments labelled by superscript $i=1,\ldots,I$.

x_h^{sc} is the demand of good c in state s by household h;

$$(x_h^{sc})_{c=1}^{C} \equiv x_h^s, \quad (x_h^s)_{s=0}^{S} \equiv x_h, \quad (x_h)_{h=1}^{H} \equiv x.$$

e_h^{sc} is the endowment of good c in state s owned by household h; $(e_h^{sc})_{c=1}^{C} \equiv c_h^s$, $(e_h^s)_{s=0}^{S} \equiv e_h$, $(e_h)_{h=1}^{H} \equiv e$.

p^{sc} is the price of good c in state s;

$$(p^{sc})_{c=1}^{C} \equiv p^s, \quad (p^s)_{s=0}^{S} = p,$$

e_h^m is the endowment of outside money owned by household h in state zero.

$m_h^0 \geq 0$ is the demand of outside money by household h in state zero.

t_h^s is the tax to be paid by household h in state s;

$$t_h \equiv (e_h^m, (t_h^s)_{s=1}^{S}), \quad t \equiv (t_h)_{h=1}^{H}.$$

q^i is the price of financial instrument i;

y^{si} is the yield of financial instrument i in state s;

$$q \equiv (q^i)_{i=1}^{I}, \quad \overline{Y} \equiv [y^{si}]^{s,i}, \quad Y \equiv \begin{bmatrix} -q \\ \overline{Y} \end{bmatrix}.$$

a_h^i is the demand of financial instruments i by household h;

$$a_h \equiv (a_h^i)_{i=1}^{I}, \quad a \equiv (a_h)_{h=1}^{H}.$$

Moreover, $\tilde{u} \equiv (-1,\ldots,1) \in \mathbb{R}^{S+1}$

$$\phi = \begin{bmatrix} p^0 & & & 0 \\ & p^1 & & \\ & & \ddots & \\ 0 & & & p^S \end{bmatrix},$$

$$\tilde{U} \equiv \begin{bmatrix} 1 & 0 \\ 0 & U_S \end{bmatrix},$$

where U_S is the S dimensional identity matrix.

References

Balasko, Y., (1988), Foundations of the Theory of General Equilibrium, Orlando, FL, Academic Press.

Balasko, Y. and Cass, D., (1989), The Structure of Financial Equilibrium with Exogeneous Yields: The Case of Incomplete Markets, Econometrica, 57 (1), pp. 135-162.

Balasko, Y. and Cass, D., (1991), Regular Demand with Several, General Budget Constraints, in Majumdar, M. (ed.), Equilibrium and Dynamics; Essays in Honor of David Gale, MacMillan, London.

Balasko, Y., Cass,D. and Siconolfi, P., (1990), The Structure of Financial Equilibrium with Exogeneous Yields: The Case of Restricted Participation, Journal of Mathematical Economics, 19, pp. 195-216.

Cass, D., (1984), Competitive Equilibrium with Incomplete Financial Markets, CARESS Working Paper, University of Pennsylvania.

Cass, D., (1988), Sunspot and Incomplete Financial Markets: The Leading Example in The Economics of Imperfect Competition and Employment, Joan Robinson and Beyond, ed. by G. Feiwel, London, MacMillan.

Cass, D., (1990), Real Indeterminacy from Imperfect Financial Markets: Two Addenda, CARESS Working Paper, University of Pennsylvania.

Cass, D., Siconolfi, P. and Villanacci, A., (1991) A Note on Generalizing the Model of Competitive Equilibrium with Restricted Participation on Financial Markets, CARESS Working Paper, University of Pennsylvania.

Duffie, D., (1987), Stochastic Equilibria with Incomplete Financial Markets, Journal of Economic Theory, 41, pp. 405-416.

Geanakoplos, J. and Mas-Colell A., (1989), Real Indeterminacy with Financial Assets, Journal of Economic Theory, 47, pp. 22-38.

Guillemin, V. and Pollack, A., (1974) Differential Topology, Englewood Cliffs, Prentice Hall.

Lerner, A.P., (1947), Money as a Creature of the State, Proceedings of the American Economic Association, 37, pp. 312-317.

Magill, M. and Quinzii, (1988), Real Effects of Money in General Equilibrium, MRG Working Paper.

Milnor, J., (1965), Topology from the Differentiable Viewpoint, Charlottesville, University Press of Virginia.

Patinkin, D., (1949), The Indeterminacy of Absolute Prices in Classical Economic Theory, Econometrica, 17, pp. 1-27.

Pietra, T., (1988), Indeterminacy in General Equilibrium Models with Incomplete Financial Markets: Mixed Assets Returns, Preliminary Paper, Rutgers University.

Siconolfi, P., (1986), Equilibrium with Asymmetric Constraints on Portfolio Holdings and Incomplete Financial Markets, CARESS Working Paper, University of Pennsylvania.

Siconolfi, P., (1990), Sunspot Equilibria and Incomplete Financial Markets,

Journal of Mathematical Economics, forthcoming.

Siconolfi, P. and Villanacci, A., (1991), Real Indeterminacy in Incomplete Financial Market Economies without Aggregate Risk, Economic Theory, 1, pp. 265-276.

Starr, R.M., (1974), The Price of Money in a Pure Exchange Monetary Economy with Taxation, Econometrica, 42, pp. 45-54.

Werner, J., (1985), Equilibrium in Economies with Incomplete Financial Markets, Journal of Economic Theory, 36, pp. 110-119.

LIST OF PARTICIPANTS

ABRAHAM Ralph	Dept. of Mathematics, Univ. of California Santa Cruz
ANTOCI Angelo	Dip. di Scienze Economiche, Università di Firenze
ARAUJO Aloisio	I.M.P.A., Rio de Janeiro
AROSIO Alberto	Dip. di Matematica, Università di Parma
BARUCCI Emilio	Università di Firenze
BASOSI Riccardo	Dip. di Chimica, Università di Siena
BASSETTI Antonietta	Dip. Econ. Pol., Università di Modena
BASSO Antonella	Dip. di Matematica. Appl. e Inform., Università di Venezia
BATTINELLI Andrea	Istituto di Matematica, Università di Siena
BELLACICCO Antonio	Università "G. D'Annunzio", Chieti
BELTRAMETTI Luca	Dottorato in Economia, Univ. di Pavia
BERARDI Andrea	Dottorato in Economia, Università di Brescia
BERSANI Alberto	Fac. Economia e Comm. Univ. Tor Vergata (Roma)
BÖHM Volker	Mannheim Universität (Germany)
BORELLI Claudio	Dip. di Economia, Università di Siena
BRONKHORST E.M.	Dept. of Dentistry, Univ. di Nijmegen (Netherland)
BUSSETTO Francesca	Ricercatrice
BUTTI Alessandro	Dottorato in Matematica, Università di Como
CAMINATI Mauro	Dip. di Economia, Università di Siena
CANESTRELLI Elio	Dip. di Matematica Appl. ed Inf., Università di Venezia
COSTA Giacomo	Dipartimento di Economia, Università di Pisa
DAY Richard	Dept. of Economics, Un. of Southern Calif., Los Angeles
DE SANCTIS Angela	Università "G. D'Annunzio", Chieti
DEISSENBERG Christophe	Université du Quebec a Montreal (Canada)
DELLI GATTI Domenico	Dip. di Economica, Università Cattolica - Milano
DRUGEON Jean Pierre	Laboratoire M.A.D., Université of Paris 1 (France)
FERRI Pietro Enrico	Università di Bergamo
FLÅM Sjur	Economics Dept., Bergen Univ. (Norway)
GAERTNER Wulf	Dept. of Economics, University of Osnabrück (Germany)
GALEOTTI Marcello	Istituto di Matematica, Università di Ancona
GALLEGATI Mauro	Ist. di Scienze Economiche, Università di Urbino
GALLIARDI Marco	Università di Siena
GARDINI Laura	Ist. Scienze Economiche, Università di Urbino
GAY Antonio	Dip. Scienze Economiche, Università di Firenze
GERONAZZO Lucio	Dip. Economia Pol., Università di Siena
GIURI Paolo	Università di Siena
GOODMAN Gerald	Dipartimento Statistico, Univ. di Firenze
GORI Franco	DIMADEFAS, Università di Firenze
GOZZI Giancarlo	Dip. di Scienze Economiche, Università di Bologna
GREENBERG Edward	Washington University, Washington (USA)

GUIDI Vinicio	Dip. Scienze Economiche, Università di Firenze
HAXHOLDT Christian	Copenhagen Business School (Copenhagen, Denmark)
INVERNIZZI Sergio	Dip. di Scienze Matematiche, Università di Trieste
JUNGEILGES Jochen	Dept. of Economics, Università di Osnabrück (Germany)
KIRMAN Alan	Dept. of Economics, Ist. Universitario Europeo (Firenze)
LEVATI M. Vittoria	Università di Siena
LONZI Marco	Istituto di Matematica, Università di Siena
LORENZ Hans Walter	Dept. of Economics, Georg-August-Univ., Göttingen (Germany)
MAINO Giuseppe	ENEA, Bologna
MALLOZZI Lina	Dip. di Matematica e Applicazioni, Università di Napoli
MAMMANA Cristiana	Fac. Ingegneria, Università di Ancona
MANCINI Giovanni	Dip. di Matematica, Università di Bologna
MARI Carlo	ENEA, Frascati
MAZZOLENI Piera	Ist. di Matematica, Università di Verona
MEDIO Alfredo	Dip. di Economia, Università di Venezia
MIRA Christian	Ist. National des Sciences Appliquées, Tolosa (France)
MONTRUCCHIO Luigi	Ist. Matematica Finanziaria, Università di Torino
NARDINI Franco	Dip. di Matematica, Università di Bologna
NEGRONI Giorgio	Università di Pavia
NICOLA Pier Carlo	Dip. di Matematica, Università di Milano
PANIZZI Stefano	Dip. di Matematica, Università di Pisa
PEDEMONTE Orietta,	Fac. Architettura, Università di Genova
PEITGEN Heinz-Otto	Inst. Dynamische Systeme, Universität Bremen (Germany)
PERSICO Nicola	Ist. Mat. Fin., Univ. di Torino
PESSA Eliano	Dip. di Matematica "G. Castelnuovo", Roma
PIANIGIANI Giulio	DIMADEFAS, Università di Firenze
PIETRA Tito	Rutgers University N.J. (USA)
POGLIAGHI Laura	Dottorato in Economia, Università di Brescia
POLEMARCHAKIS Heracles	CORE, Université Chatolique de Louvain (Belgium)
RADUNSKAYA Amy	Math. Dept., Stanford University, Palo Alto (USA)
RASORI Andrea	Università di Parma
REICHLIN Pietro	Dip. Scienze Economiche, Università di Roma
RINALDI Franca	Dip. di Matematica. e Inform., Università di Trieste
ROSSET Edi	Dip. di Matematica, Università di Trieste
ROVELLI Bruno	Università Bocconi
SACCO PierLuigi	Dept. of Economics, Ist. Universitario Europeo, Firenze
SAGONTI Emanuela	Dottorato in Economia, Università di Brescia
SALVI Rosanna	Università di Siena
SANDRI Marco	Ist. di Scienze Economiche, Università di Verona
SCALA Claudio	Ist. di Biologia Gen., Università di Siena
SCHICH Sebastian	University of London (England)
SENIGAGLIA Elena	Dip. Matem. ed Inform., Università di Venezia

SPEDICATO Emilio	Università di Bergamo
STEFANI Gianna	Dip. Matematica, Università di Napoli
STEFANINI Luciano	Ist. di Scienze Economiche, Università di Urbino
STENGOS Thanasis	Istituto Universitario Europeo, Firenze
TIEZZI Enzo	OIKOS, Dip. di Chimica, Univ. di Siena
TONDINI Pier Giovanni	Ist. di Scienze Economiche, Università di Verona
TORRIGIANI Marcello	DIMADEFAS, Università di Firenze
TVEDE Mich	Copenhagen Business School (Denmark)
VENTURI Beatrice	Ist. Matematica Finanziaria, Università di Cagliari
VERZELLESI Chiara	Università di Parma
VILLANACCI Antonio	DIMADEFAS, Università di Firenze
VISCOLANI Bruno	Dip. di Mat. Appl. e Inf., Università di Venezia
WEINRICH Gerd	Università "G. D'Annunzio", Pescara
ZAMBRUNO Giovanni	Fac. di Scienze Pol., Università di Milano
ZEZZA Pierluigi	DIMADEFAS, Università di Firenze

Printing: Druckhaus Beltz, Hemsbach
Binding: Buchbinderei Schäffer, Grünstadt